THE MACKENZIE KING RECORD
Volume 1

Karsh, Ottawa
THE RT. HON. W. L. MACKENZIE KING, C.M.G.

THE MACKENZIE KING RECORD

VOLUME 1
1939-1944

J. W. Pickersgill

UNIVERSITY OF TORONTO PRESS

Copyright, Canada, 1960, by
University of Toronto Press
Printed in Canada

To the memory of
ERNEST LAPOINTE
devoted comrade in arms in the longest and closest
partnership in the political life of Canada
and to
LOUIS ST. LAURENT
indispensable colleague and peerless successor of
Mackenzie King
I dedicate this volume as a
tribute of respect and affection

Preface

THIS BOOK is not a biography, though it is an integral part of the biographical project undertaken by the Literary Executors of the late W. L. Mackenzie King shortly after his death in 1950. The task of writing an official biography was then entrusted to the late Professor R. MacGregor Dawson, whose first volume was regrettably not published until after his death in 1958.

When it became evident late in 1957 that Professor Dawson's health was seriously impaired and that he would require assistance if there was to be any prospect of completing the biography, the Literary Executors secured the services of Professor Blair Neatby of the University of British Columbia to collaborate in the preparation of the second volume covering the years from 1923 to 1939. After Professor Dawson's death, Professor Neatby undertook to complete this volume. Early in 1958 I had suggested to my fellow Literary Executors that I would be willing to prepare a rough narrative covering the years from 1939 to 1950 as a foundation for Professor Dawson's third volume. This offer was accepted, and after Professor Dawson's death I was asked by them to complete the volume.

My original design was to prepare a rough narrative from Mackenzie King's diaries and to fill in this narrative later from other sources. I had not proceeded very far before it became clear to me that so much had happened in those war and post-war years that the narrative could be compressed into a single volume only by condensation on such a scale that the result would be as attractive and appetizing as dehydrated food, or by selection of a few high lights to the exclusion of other events which, while less dramatic, were equally important. I did not want to do either and told the Literary Executors I would prefer to do two volumes instead of one.

As the work proceeded I realized more and more that Mackenzie King's own contemporaneous and unrevised record of events would have far greater interest for the public and also far greater historical validity than anything I could write and that I should let him tell the story, adding only what was necessary to make the context clear. Insensibly the character of the book had changed and I found myself presenting Mackenzie King's own record of events.

This book is, then, to be considered not as the third volume of the biography begun by Professor Dawson, but as an independent project in which Mackenzie King substantially speaks for himself. I feel that I too am thus carrying out the wish expressed to Professor Dawson by the Literary Executors "that so far as possible Mr. Mackenzie King might be allowed to tell his own story."[1]

Mackenzie King's diary was kept largely to serve as a record from which he could recount and explain his conduct of public affairs and he had indicated to the Literary Executors that it was to be used for this purpose. I have sought to let his own words recount and explain his conduct and his view of the events of those years. It is my hope that some day it may be possible to publish in several volumes the consecutive day-to-day record of those momentous years. Meanwhile I have tried to select what seemed to Mackenzie King most important, and, as far as possible, to preserve his own sense of relative importance.

Even this task has not been easy. The whole record is so voluminous and most of it is so interesting that the selection of extracts became a major problem. I set certain standards for myself. The first was that my purpose was to present Mackenzie King's public life, not his private life, and references to his private life are therefore confined to extracts from the diary which seemed to have an essential bearing on his public life. The second was that I was seeking to present Mackenzie King, not the history of his times or the views of his contemporaries.

I have rigorously resisted the temptation to include many fascinating extracts reporting the views expressed to Mackenzie King by others where they did not seem to me to bear directly on his own views or actions. On the other hand, I have tried to include, as far as space would allow, all the important extracts giving his own views on the progress of the war and the reactions of the Canadian Government, Parliament, and public to the war and the politics of the period from September 1939 to May 1944, the period covered in this volume.

In quoting from the diary, which was dictated and typewritten and rarely revised, I have not hesitated to correct obvious mistakes in names and in spelling, and even in sense, where it was perfectly clear that what was dictated by Mackenzie King had not been correctly transcribed. The relatively rare extracts from the handwritten diary have not been

---

[1]Preface to R. MacG. Dawson, *William Lyon Mackenzie King: A Political Biography*, I (Toronto, 1958), vii.

changed. Omissions from sentences and paragraphs have been indicated by ellipses. These omissions, apart from rare cases where references are of a character which precludes publication because the persons concerned are still living or because Mackenzie King himself would not have wished them to be published, are of irrelevancies, repetitions, or trivia and have been made almost entirely to save precious space.

While I have used other sources to verify and clarify the record where that seemed necessary and I have occasionally cited these sources, this book is essentially the contemporary record as dictated or, on rare occasions and for short periods, handwritten by Mackenzie King himself. He himself called his diary "the record." Hence my title.

I have tried not to give my picture of Mackenzie King, but his own picture of himself. Because his record of events as they happened seemed to me more revealing than anything else, I have, with one exception, quoted very sparingly from his speeches and correspondence and not at all the views of others about him. No doubt the speeches often disclosed his considered judgment better than his diary, but they are almost all in print in Hansard or elsewhere and I feel the publication of the extracts from the diary will be a greater service to future historians, and to the biographer who will one day have to make a considered judgment of Mackenzie King based on all the available sources.

In order to avoid as far as I could the irritation of footnotes I am indicating here that all quotations in the text, unless otherwise specified, are from the diary. In referring to other persons I have abandoned the conventional distinction between the living and the dead and omitted "Mr." and titles except where they may be needed for identification, though, in the quotations, I have, of course, used whatever form occurred in the diary. The one speech from which I have quoted extensively is the speech in Parliament on September 8, 1939, which summed up so much of Mackenzie King's pre-war attitude that it seemed an essential introduction to his record of the war.

A word about my own connection with Mackenzie King. I have often read that he had picked me out as a promising young man and recruited me for his personal staff. That is not true. I entered the public service by competitive Civil Service examination and became a probationary Third Secretary in the Department of External Affairs on October 14, 1937. Two months later I was seconded to the Prime Minister's office to replace Norman Robertson who was going to Washington to help negotiate the Trade Agreement concluded a year later. At that time Mackenzie King had never met me and he saw me only three times in the next seven months. In the summer of 1938 I began to assist him in the preparation of his speeches, but at no time during the war was I, as has sometimes been said, one of his principal advisers and my direct part in the events recounted in this volume can easily be exaggerated. I was, however, in the Prime Minister's Office throughout the war and until Mackenzie King's retirement and therefore had some familiarity with what was happening.

While I, of course, take full responsibility for everything in the book, I am indebted to my fellow Literary Executors for a most painstaking scrutiny of the whole manuscript and innumerable criticisms and suggestions which have assisted me greatly. Each of them helped in a different way. Mr. Fred McGregor had been a friend of Mackenzie King since 1909 and no living person knows so much about the background. Mr. Norman Robertson, through most of the period covered in the book, was Mackenzie King's principal adviser on External Affairs and, as such, is more familiar with much that it covers than I am. Dr. Kaye Lamb, the head of the Public Archives of Canada, approaching the subject more from the outside, has, I hope, kept me from taking too much for granted. His technical knowledge and vast experience of manuscripts and books have been invaluable.

I am particularly indebted to two of Mackenzie King's colleagues. Rt. Hon. C. D. Howe gave me valuable counsel about the book generally. He also consented to read and criticize several passages relating to events of which he had close personal knowledge. The late Brooke Claxton saw the whole manuscript of this volume and completed his reading only a few days before his death. His suggestions, criticisms, and corrections were as painstaking and thorough as everything else he did in his lifetime. Because of his intimate connection with the events of the period and his prodigious memory he prevented me from making many mistakes. I like to think that this final association in our long and close friendship helped a little to relieve the tedium of the last few months of a life singularly devoted to the service of our country.

To the staff at Laurier House and the Public Archives and especially to Miss Jacqueline Côté I am grateful for constant help in looking up documents from the mass of the Mackenzie King papers.

This is the first book I have published and I am deeply grateful for the understanding help of the University of Toronto Press and particularly of Miss Francess Halpenny.

Finally I express my gratitude to Miss Florence Moore, Miss Shirley Tink, and my wife for the hours they have spent typewriting the manuscript in its several stages. My wife has also contributed her share of criticism.

And I do not forget my debt to the subject of the book from whom I learned much in many years of close association. It is my hope that it adequately portrays his unparalleled service to Canada in the dark days of war and reflects something of my abiding admiration and respect.

J. W. P.

Contents

	PREFACE	vii
I.	Introduction	3
II.	Canada at Britain's Side	11
III.	The British Commonwealth Air Training Plan	40
IV.	The Wartime Election	60
V.	Parliament and the Blitzkrieg	74
VI.	The Linch-Pin	106
VII.	A Winter of Anxiety, 1940–41	145
VIII.	The Hyde Park Declaration	180
IX.	Domestic Interlude	205
X.	The Flight to Britain	236
XI.	Meighen, Lapointe, St. Laurent	268
XII.	The United States in the War	296
XIII.	The Plebiscite	333
XIV.	Cardin and Ralston	365
XV.	A World at War: 1942	408
XVI.	Total War and Party Politics	437
XVII.	A Time of New Beginnings	466
XVIII.	The Canadian Army Goes into Action	494
XIX.	The Quebec Conference, 1943	527
XX.	The Political Watershed, 1943	561
XXI.	General McNaughton's Retirement	604
XXII.	Planning the Post-War Future	630

XXIII. The Meeting of Commonwealth Prime Ministers, 1944	663
APPENDIX	697
INDEX	699

Illustrations

Frontispiece: The Rt. Hon. W. L. Mackenzie King, C.M.G.

Between pages 160 and 161

Mr. King's personal staff for his trip to the United Kingdom, 1941

The Cabinet, 1939

The signing of the British Commonwealth Air Training Agreement, 1939

Air Training Conference, Ottawa, 1939

Mr. King speaking at a meeting in Prince Albert, 1941

The Dominion-Provincial Conference, 1941

Mr. King's trip to the United Kingdom, 1941: his visits to Canadian troops

The funeral procession of Ernest Lapointe, 1941

President Roosevelt's visit to Ottawa, 1943

Mr. King and Mr. Churchill at the Mansion House, 1941

Mr. Churchill in Ottawa, 1941

The Quebec Conference, 1943

Mr. King's address to the Houses of Parliament of the United Kingdom, 1944

The final meeting of the Commonwealth Prime Ministers, 1944

THE MACKENZIE KING RECORD

Volume 1

CHAPTER ONE

Introduction

THIS VOLUME is a record, made largely by Mackenzie King himself, of his leadership of the Government of Canada through more than four and a half years of war, from September 1939 to the end of May 1944. When war broke out in 1939 Mackenzie King was in his sixty-fifth year. He had been Prime Minister of Canada for twelve of the previous eighteen years, and he had been associated with the public service or the public life of Canada for the whole of the twentieth century. His Government had, in 1935, been given the greatest majority any Government had enjoyed in Parliament since Confederation. Despite his age, he was in excellent health and at the very height of his mental and physical powers. To be Prime Minister of Canada was the peak of his ambition and he was absorbed by the demands of his position; he was without hobbies and had virtually no private life.

Because he was unmarried and without close family ties, Mackenzie King confided the day-to-day impressions and secrets that other public men would have given to their wives or intimate friends to what must surely be the most remarkable diary ever kept by a Canadian. This diary is an amazing combination of intimate personal details with the most careful and painstakingly accurate reporting of the events in which he had a part. On the personal side, the diary undoubtedly served the need that most human beings have for sharing their experiences with others; on the public side, it was deliberately designed to provide a faithful record of Mackenzie King's part in public affairs of which he had hoped, one day, to write his own account. Though in his public utterances he tried always to maintain a nineteenth-century decorum, he could and often did express his views, in private conversation and in his diary, without moderation and even with vehemence, and no one had a more acute consciousness of the frailties of others, or a greater readiness in private to point them out.

It is often said that Mackenzie King led a lonely life. This was not entirely true. He did have a very few intimate friends on whom he depended and to whom he gave a life-long devotion which was fully reciprocated. But he undoubtedly felt that close friendship and public life did not mix and he deliberately avoided and even checked the development of intimate personal relations with his political colleagues and other associates in public life. To social life he had a curiously ambivalent attitude. He was a marvellous host and excellent company on a social occasion. He greatly enjoyed dinner parties, dances, the theatre, and, above all, music, particularly Wagner's operas. But every period of social enjoyment seemed to be followed by a period of regret over the time wasted with the vanities of this world in which so much serious effort was required. He was sincerely religious and an almost militant Presbyterian; his beliefs, however, were highly personal and he was convinced that a host of unseen witnesses hovered about him and guided his conduct in emergencies.

He found his principal recreations in two places that were poles apart: he loved the quiet of the countryside at Kingsmere in the Gatineau Hills and he loved the bustle and excitement of New York City. But most of his recreation he found in his work, at which he was as unsystematic as he was assiduous. He had, as all his secretaries learned, a passion for detail and for accuracy, and a fear of making even the most minor error of fact or of form, which resulted in meticulous revising and re-revising of everything he wrote and of everything written for him. This search for perfection meant that speeches and public statements were never completed on time. Deadlines were always being missed and publicity sacrificed, with subsequent regret, in this quest for the perfection never, in his eyes, quite attained. After every speech he always felt and nearly always said: "If only there had been one more day."

Mackenzie King spent most of his working time, during the war and post-war years, in the Library at Laurier House or, when circumstances would permit it, in the Farm House at Kingsmere. He rarely appeared in his offices either at the East Block of the Parliament Buildings or in the House of Commons except to fill in odd hours between meetings or interviews. In his work there were no real priorities, except when there was an emergency or when he decided the moment had come to take action. Then nothing else but the matter at issue had any importance and nobody could move fast enough to please him. Until the moment for action came he was most receptive to suggestions, but once he had begun to act he generally ignored further advice and often sharply resented suggestions.

One of the reasons Mackenzie King worked at Laurier House and avoided his offices was that it gave him greater control of his own time and greater freedom to make his own decisions without undue pressure from others. While he himself did not hesitate to use the telephone, sometimes at wearisome length, to communicate with others, he made it very clear to his staff, to his colleagues, and to others that he should not be disturbed by telephone calls except when something really urgent had to be brought to his attention. As a consequence most of his work outside the Cabinet meetings came to him in the form of memoranda or letters to which he gave written replies. These official communications, together with a vast quantity of private correspondence and a steady stream of telegrams and despatches from the Department of External Affairs, reached such a volume that he could never seem to cope with it from day to day, and, despite periodic efforts to clear up arrears, there was always a backlog which at once oppressed Mackenzie King and unconsciously provided him with an excuse for putting off the beginning of urgent tasks, particularly the preparation of speeches, which he loathed. Throughout his whole career he deplored his misfortune in never finding competent secretaries who could relieve him of this vast load of routine. But the fact was that nothing was routine to which he signed his name, and the simplest letter of congratulation or message of sympathy was revised with the same painstaking care as the most important speech or state paper.

Because he spent so much of his time and did so much of his work at home, the secretaries at Laurier House had a place of critical importance. The key figure in Mackenzie King's staff at Laurier House and, indeed, in his official household was J. E. Handy, now Secretary of the National Capital Commission. He presided over a faithful staff of secretarial assistants of whom those with the longest service and closest relationship to Mackenzie King were Miss L. F. Zavitske, Miss Florence Moore, and Miss Margaret Conniffe. From the beginning of the war to the date of Mackenzie King's retirement, the office at Laurier House was open seven days a week from about nine o'clock in the morning until, usually, about eleven in the evening and a competent secretary was always on hand. Handy, himself, not only worked at all hours of the day and night—the Prime Minister never travelled without him—but he served with unexampled devotion and loyalty. He and his assistants had the difficult task of keeping track of the mass of paper that came to Mackenzie King as Prime Minister or as Secretary of State for External Affairs. They also had the duty of seeing that his decisions and his wishes were communicated to the right person in the Prime Minister's Office, the Privy Council Office, the Department of External Affairs or elsewhere, and that the wires were not crossed. The Department of External Affairs had James Gibson, now Dean of Arts at Carleton

University, as its own representative at Laurier House where he was also keeper of the secret war records and where he performed these and many other duties ably and conscientiously.

Mackenzie King did not differentiate too clearly between the functions of President of the Privy Council, Secretary of State for External Affairs, and Prime Minister, and serious difficulties could have arisen if there had not been harmony between the various officials with whom he dealt directly. When the war started and until his death, the late O. D. Skelton, the Under Secretary of State for External Affairs, was Mackenzie King's closest adviser on all public affairs, domestic as well as external. He also exercised a supervisory eye over the Prime Minister's Office. At that time the Privy Council Office had purely formal functions and there was no secretariat of the Cabinet at all. Arnold Heeney had been appointed Principal Secretary to the Prime Minister in 1938 with the understanding that he would become Clerk of the Privy Council in 1940 and would then be appointed the first Secretary to the Cabinet with the duty of establishing a Cabinet secretariat. When the War Committee was established in 1939, Heeney became its Secretary and attended all its meetings and kept the Minutes. From the date of his appointment in 1940 as Secretary to the Cabinet he also attended Cabinet meetings but no Minutes of these meetings were kept until almost the end of the war. Mackenzie King viewed the development of more formal cabinet organization and records with mixed feelings and occasional resistance, though he did recognize they were essential to the despatch of the tremendous volume of business in wartime. When Norman Robertson succeeded Skelton as Under Secretary of State for External Affairs in 1941, he did not fully occupy the place Skelton had, either in the administrative scheme or in Mackenzie King's confidence, but he very quickly became his most trusted adviser and remained so throughout the rest of the war and afterwards. Walter Turnbull succeeded Arnold Heeney as Principal Secretary to the Prime Minister in 1940 and remained in that office until June 1945 when he became Deputy Postmaster General. Turnbull had charge of the administration of the enlarged wartime office of the Prime Minister and with great patience and conscientiousness he organized or tried to organize Mackenzie King's engagements and other contacts with the public. J. W. Pickersgill was the no. 2 in the Prime Minister's Office after March 1940 but he had, since 1938, had direct contact in his work with the Prime Minister and only a minor share of the ordinary duties of a Private Secretary. Most of his time was spent in assisting Mackenzie King with the preparation of speeches, public statements, and official correspondence. He did not become head of the Prime Minister's Office until June 1945. The diffusion of responsibility among the members of his staff and Mackenzie King's comparative indifference to their respective roles were nicely calculated to cause confusion and misunderstanding, if there had not been unbroken confidence and goodwill in their relations with one another, which happily there always was.

No Prime Minister could have been more jealous of the prerogatives of his office than Mackenzie King, yet, with the exception of one portfolio, he was scrupulously respectful of the ministerial prerogatives of his colleagues. He expected the ministers to direct their own departments and he rarely interfered with their departmental administration, even when he agreed, as he sometimes did, with public criticism of it. The one exception was the Department of Labour, which he had really founded and which he regarded as peculiarly his own. No Minister of Labour, not even Norman Rogers in whom he had exceptional confidence, ever had a free hand, and in every emergency Mackenzie King really became his own Minister of Labour.

He quickly resented any attempt, or appearance of an attempt, by a colleague to speak for the Government, without prior agreement, in any area outside his own department and he himself was careful never to commit the Government to any departure in policy which had not been threshed out thoroughly in the Cabinet. The Cabinet seldom, if ever, reached a conclusion of which he really disapproved, but he often postponed or even abandoned courses he would have liked to take because of the opposition of his colleagues, and only very rarely did he insist on getting his own way when a clear majority of his colleagues dissented. He was wise enough to realize that opposition from his colleagues usually reflected the opposition to be expected from the public, and he did not believe in sailing right into formidable opposition if it could be avoided. Yet, while he did not intimidate his colleagues, he certainly dominated the Cabinet.

Of all his colleagues during the whole period he was Prime Minister, Ernest Lapointe was undoubtedly closest to him. Next only to Skelton's, he relied on Lapointe's judgment in all fields and no one completely took the place of either after 1941. After Lapointe, Norman Rogers, who had been one of his secretaries in the twenties, was closer to him than any other; but in a way Rogers never quite became a colleague rather than a subordinate. For Ian Mackenzie he had a tolerant affection which did not blind him to Mackenzie's more obvious deficiencies. Mackenzie was permitted a degree of personal intimacy which would not have been tolerated in any other colleague after 1941. Until the crisis of 1942,

J. L. Ralston undoubtedly enjoyed a greater measure of Mackenzie King's confidence and esteem than any other colleague, except Lapointe and Rogers, and he never lost his respect even at the height of their differences. Mackenzie King's relations with C. G. Power were close, but mercurial. He felt Power had a political 'flair' which was shared by no other colleague, but he feared what he regarded as Power's recklessness. Until the crisis of 1944, he found a certain comfort and sympathy in his relations with T. A. Crerar who, after Lapointe's death, was his only contemporary in the Cabinet. C. D. Howe he always liked, though he did not entirely understand him. In the later war years and afterwards Mackenzie King came to rely on Howe more than on his other colleagues except Louis St. Laurent, who quickly assumed a larger place in his confidence than any other colleague, though St. Laurent's personal relations with the Prime Minister never had the intimate character of those enjoyed by Lapointe. With J. L. Ilsley there was never any real meeting of minds. Despite this lack of sympathy, no one appreciated better than Mackenzie King the tremendous prestige Ilsley acquired during the war and he accorded him a corresponding respect. Angus Macdonald entered the Government in 1940 almost a favourite and yet two years later there was no colleague he found more unsympathetic. With his other colleagues his relations were much more official than personal though he quite enjoyed J. A. MacKinnon as a companion and he respected and almost feared J. G. Gardiner. One other colleague deserves special mention. For Senator Raoul Dandurand Mackenzie King had an affection almost approaching veneration. Dandurand had been in his first administration and continued to the end of his life to lead in the Senate with intelligence and urbanity. He served Mackenzie King with a combination of independent judgment and unquestioning loyalty which was valuable and valued.

Mackenzie King's tremendous majorities in 1935 and 1940 never tempted him to take the support of Parliament for granted. In the early twenties, when he never had a safe majority, he developed a sensitiveness to Parliament and a respect for parliamentary moods, and the experience of 1942 did not encourage him to depend on the unquestioning votes of those who had been elected to support the Government. Mackenzie King dreaded the opening of a new session and he invariably approached his own speech in the debate on the Address in reply to the Speech from the Throne with something like stage fright. Once the session was launched and he could choose his own time and circumstance for intervening in debates he found Parliament more agreeable. On the increasingly rare occasions during the war when he trusted himself to speak extemporaneously, he was usually pleased and often delighted with the result. But he was always concerned about the record and lived in fear of a verbal slip which might have serious political consequences. Though his other wartime obligations limited his attendance in the House of Commons, and he increasingly shirked the evening sittings whenever he could, he kept a close and constant watch on the debates and habitually gave personal direction to the order of speaking on the Government side.

During the sessions of Parliament, a party caucus was held every second Wednesday and sometimes more frequently. Mackenzie King was a great believer in the value of discussion in the party caucus, though he never permitted the caucus to determine policy. He deliberately encouraged the private members to air their grievances and even to attack the Ministers and, at times, was able in this way to get departmental attitudes and procedures changed without direct intervention on his own part. Essentially, however, the caucus was the place where he explained the whys and wherefores of Government action and policy and suggested the lines on which the Government could be supported most effectively. All those who attended the caucuses seem to have agreed that Mackenzie King's speeches there were among his most effective, and his supporters frequently expressed regret that he did not speak in the same way to the public. He invariably spoke without notes and the only record of these speeches is in the report he dictated for his diary later in the day. One of his wartime colleagues has confirmed the accuracy of these accounts, but he indicated that no report could convey the force and persuasiveness of these speeches.

It has often been said of Mackenzie King that he put party considerations above all others. That he was a partisan is certainly true; but it is also true that, after the general election of 1940, he gave no consideration whatever to the Liberal party organization until late in 1943, by which time the Conservative party had held a national convention where they had chosen a new leader and adopted a new name and a new programme, and the C.C.F. had become, apparently, a serious threat on the national scene. Even then Mackenzie King contented himself with giving the primary impulse to the revival of the party organization and left its development to others, most of whom, like Brooke Claxton, were not then members of the Government.

Mackenzie King undoubtedly loved office and the prestige of office; and it gave him deep satisfaction that the grandson of William Lyon Mackenzie had fulfilled the destiny of his grandfather. But he was not content to enjoy office for its own sake. From the outbreak of the war to its close, he never permitted any other aim to obscure his supreme objective that Canada should make a maximum contribution to the winning of the war. He believed that, to do so, it was essential that the country should not be torn by internal divison or strife, and this it was his constant effort to minimize when it could not be prevented altogether.

Mackenzie King genuinely believed and frequently said that the real secret of political leadership was more in what was prevented than in what was accomplished. Yet his objectives were by no means negative. He always knew the direction in which he wished events to move and the political goals he sought to achieve. He was acutely conscious that political progress was possible only if public support was forthcoming, and he believed that nothing was so likely to set back a good cause as premature action. For him, leadership consisted in having the right objectives, picking the right time to act, and acting decisively and swiftly when that time had come. No one who reads the speech he made to the Liberal convention of 1919 and compares it with the record of his political achievements can doubt that he knew where he was going or that he reached his destination. His progress towards that objective was delayed by the major diversion of the greatest war in history. He led his country successfully through that war with fortitude, with patience, with skill, and at times with audacity, and, at its close, the people of Canada gave him another vote of confidence.

CHAPTER TWO

Canada at Britain's Side

THIS SECOND CHAPTER of Mackenzie King's record deals mainly with the last four months of 1939. During these months, the armed forces of Canada were not involved in actual combat and the Government was chiefly concerned with placing the country on a war footing and making plans for Canadian participation in a conflict of which no one could foresee the shape or forecast the duration.

The decision as to whether Canada would participate in another world war had not been reached easily or quickly. In 1938 and 1939, as war with Nazi Germany seemed to be approaching, the precedent of 1914 was in the minds of many Canadians. In 1914 it had been taken for granted that when the King declared war on Germany, Canada was automatically at war. What the Canadian Government and Parliament had decided was the extent of Canada's participation. No one, in 1939, was quite sure what the juridical situation would be in Canada if the King declared war on the advice of his Ministers in the United Kingdom. From the time of the Chanak incident in 1922, Mackenzie King had contented himself with saying that the decision about war would be made by the Parliament of Canada, but he never specified what Parliament would decide or even how Parliament would decide, and he deliberately discouraged attempts by others to settle these points in advance.

From the time he first became Prime Minister, Mackenzie King had consistently opposed commitments to the League of Nations, to the United Kingdom, to the British Empire or Commonwealth or to any other national or international authority which might involve Canada automatically in war. This was not because he was a pacifist or even an isolationist. There is not the slightest ground for thinking Mackenzie King ever seriously contemplated the possibility that Canada could or would attempt to remain neutral in any major war in which Britain should be engaged. Rather, it flowed naturally from his profound belief in Responsible Government that he instinctively felt any commitment as to the supreme act of a nation should be made by a self-governing people through their own government and Parliament in the light of actual circumstances at the time a specific decision had to be made. As a practical politician he was also acutely aware that no decision to commit Canada to action in advance, in hypothetical circumstances, could be reached unitedly by the Canadian Government or Parliament in the period after he returned to office in 1935.

The best evidence that he was clear in his own mind what the decision would be in a situation in which Britain was involved is to be found in the conduct of Canadian foreign policy for which, after October 1935, Mackenzie King was largely responsible. It was mainly on his initiative that defence expenditures were sharply increased in 1937, even at the cost of some support from his own followers in Parliament. He was clear that the main danger came from Nazi Germany and, after the Imperial Conference of 1937, he visited Germany in order to size up for himself what prospect there was of Hitler's starting another world war. He returned from the visit with three impressions. The first was a feeling that some of the national aspirations of Germany which Hitler had exploited would have to be satisfied or there would be war; the second was that Hitler did not really want to fight Britain and that there was still room for accommodation if British diplomacy was sufficiently skilful and sympathetic; the third was that the military strength of Germany was already so great that Britain and France combined would not be able to match it.

On his way home from Germany, he stopped in Paris to open the Canadian Pavilion at the International Exposition on July 1, 1937. In his speech that day he expressed his own belief that Canada would go to war in defence of freedom, if the Canadian people were convinced that freedom was actually threatened in the world. This speech was intended as a public warning to would-be aggressors; but Mackenzie King was not prepared to have Canada make any specific commitment to stand by Britain and France, or Britain alone, in case of Nazi aggression. He believed that such a commitment would have been regarded by Hitler as provocative and that it might have weakened the chances of the peaceful accommodation he still believed was both possible and desirable. He also believed that the Canadian people would not give united support to such a commitment. For both these reasons, he gave enthusiastic support to Neville Chamberlain at the time of Munich; but his private record leaves no doubt that, if war had come in 1938, he would have recommended Canada's participation.

The direction of his own mind was more clearly revealed in Parliament at the opening of the session in January 1939, when he quoted with approval Sir Wilfrid Laurier's statement that "when Britain is at war, Canada is at war and liable to attack." On March 20, after Hitler had annexed Bohemia and Moravia and established a protectorate over Slovakia, Mackenzie King made a formal statement in Parliament that, in certain circumstances, the Government would recommend action by Canada to resist aggression and he specifically cited the bombing of London from the air as something which Canada would regard as a menace to the freedom of the whole Commonwealth. But Canada did not join in the guarantee given by Britain and France to Poland, and Mackenzie King continued to avoid automatic commitments and to insist that Parliament would make a decision in the light of circumstances if war broke out.

It was, therefore, important that there should be a Parliament in existence to make the decision if a crisis arose. The existing Parliament had been elected in 1935. Mackenzie King wanted to have a general election in the autumn of 1939. But the life of Parliament would not expire until late in 1940 and he dared not ask for a dissolution in the summer of 1939 for fear of war breaking out before a new Parliament could be elected.

After the war had started in Europe, Mackenzie King told Parliament on September 8, 1939, in a speech recommending that Canada should participate in the war, that he had "never doubted that when the fatal moment came, the free spirit of the Canadian people would assert itself in the preservation and defence of freedom, as it did a quarter of a century ago. I have, however, been anxious that when the inevitable hour came, our people should be as one from coast to coast. . . . I have made it, therefore, the supreme endeavour of my leadership of my party, and my leadership of the Government of this country, to let no hasty or premature threat or pronouncement create mistrust and divisions between the different elements that compose the population of our vast Dominion, so that, when the moment of decision came, all should so see the issue itself that our national effort might be marked by unity of purpose, of heart and of endeavour."

He was certainly not exaggerating when he referred to the divisions between the different elements that compose the population. On no other issue was the division so deep as on the question of whether Canada should take part in another war in Europe.

On the side of participation, there was a substantial number, perhaps a majority, of Anglo-Saxon Canadians who felt that Canada should simply follow the lead of Britain. A much smaller, but vocal group, with influential leadership, felt that the best way to defend Canada was in concert with other nations through a system of collective security which would uphold international law and order in the world. A third group, horrified by the crimes of the Nazi dictatorship, was prepared to join in a moral crusade against Hitler. To this third group the few Canadian Communists pretended to belong until Stalin made his pact with Hitler, when they switched over abruptly to opposition to Canadian participation in what, over night, became an Imperialist war. For the Communists the war again became a moral crusade over night when Hitler attacked Russia on June 22, 1941.

Against participation were many of those English-speaking Canadian nationalists who felt Canada had enough to do to look after the building of a new nation in North America and had no real national interest in European wars; they felt that Canada should not be weakened by the sacrifice of another generation of young Canadians in a blood bath in Europe. This same attitude was general among French-speaking Canadians in Quebec and elsewhere in Canada. There were, in addition, the extreme nationalists of Quebec, a relatively small minority actuated mainly by anti-English sentiment, and finally a tiny minority of genuine pacifists with one distinguished spokesman in Parliament.

Mackenzie King's problem as Prime Minister was not just to define his own position; that would have been easy. He had to try to find a common denominator among all these differing and conflicting tendencies in Canadian opinion, and to make sure that the overwhelming majority of Canadians would follow, if their Government felt it necessary to try to lead them into war.

The differences of opinion in the country on participation were not very accurately reflected in Parliament in 1939. The Social Credit group was united in support of the view that Canada should simply follow the lead of Britain. This was also, no doubt, the real attitude of a majority of the Conservative Members, but the position of their party was complicated by the fact that it had changed its leader, and its name and direction, at a national convention in 1938; the new leader, Robert Manion, was seeking to broaden the base of a party which had only one French-speaking Member in the House of Commons and Manion was not prepared to abandon this objective by advocating an automatic participation, in which, moreover, he probably did not himself believe. The position of the tiny C.C.F. group of eight Members was even more complicated. Their leader, J. S. Woodsworth, was a sincere pacifist who had suffered for his convictions in the First World War; he also had an isolationist bias. Their deputy leader, M. J. Coldwell, though his Canadianism was unquestionable, was English-born and sentimentally attached to his native land; he was, too, a supporter of the idea of collective security. The C.C.F. chose to follow Coldwell rather than Woodsworth, and gave their support to Canada's entry into the war, but they tried to reconcile the profound differences in their party by a compromise which called for half-hearted participation in which an expeditionary force would have no place.

There were, however, only 63 Opposition Members: 38 Conservatives, 8 C.C.F., and 17 Social Credit. The Liberal party with 176 Members had an overwhelming majority; but because it included all the French-speaking Members from Quebec except one, it was potentially even more divided on the issue of participation in war than any other party. Mackenzie King was determined, if possible, to avoid any step which would split his party and the country on racial lines; but he realized that the majority of the country would favour participation, as he did himself.

The crisis of 1939 was precipitated by the Russo-German Non-Aggression Pact announced on August 21. The next day the British Parliament was called into session, and on August 23, Mackenzie King announced that the Canadian Parliament would also be summoned at once if the efforts to prevent the outbreak of war should fail. The Nazis attacked Poland just after midnight on the morning of September 1. The Canadian Cabinet met early that morning and, at the conclusion of the meeting, Mackenzie King announced to the press that it was "now apparent that the efforts which have been made to preserve the peace of Europe are likely to prove of no avail. In spite of these efforts hostilities have begun between Germany and Poland which threaten the peace of the world. The Cabinet met at nine o'clock this morning, and in accordance with the intimation given some days ago decided to have Parliament summoned forthwith." After stating that Parliament would meet on September 7, Mackenzie King declared: "In the event of the United Kingdom becoming engaged in war in the effort to resist aggression, the Government of Canada have unanimously decided, as soon as Parliament meets, to seek its authority for effective co-operation by Canada at the side of Britain." He added that meanwhile "necessary measures" would be taken "for the defence of Canada" and that the Government of the United Kingdom would be consulted so that in the light of all the information at its disposal, the Government of Canada would be able to recommend to Parliament the most effective measures "for co-operation and defence." He pointed out that the Government had provided for the immediate issue of a proclamation under the War Measures Act in view of the existence of a state of apprehended war, and had placed the armed forces on active service for the territorial defence of Canada.

When Britain declared war on September 3, Mackenzie King made a broadcast in which he said: "This morning, the King, speaking to his peoples at home and across the seas, appealed to all, to make their own, the cause of freedom, which Britain again has taken up. Canada has already answered that call. On Friday last, the Government, speaking on behalf of the Canadian people, announced that in the event of the United Kingdom becoming engaged in war in the effort to resist aggression, they would, as soon as Parliament meets, seek its authority for effective co-operation by Canada at the side of Britain.

"As you are aware, I have all along felt that the danger of war was such that Parliament should not be dissolved, but be available to consider any emergency that might arise.

"Parliament will meet Thursday next. Between now and then, all necessary measures will be taken for the defence of Canada. Consultations with the United Kingdom will be continued. In the light of all the information at its disposal, the Government will then recommend to Parliament the measures which it believes to be the most effective for co-operation and defence. That Parliament will sanction all necessary measures, I have not the least doubt."

Mackenzie King went on to outline the measures already taken to provide for internal security and the territorial defence of Canada, but he was scrupulous in saying that the manner and extent of Canadian co-operation in the common cause was "something which Parliament itself will decide."

When Parliament met in special war session on September 7, Mackenzie King's concern was to appeal to the House of Commons in such a way as to secure the widest possible approval of Canada's entry into the war. The session itself began like an ordinary session with a Speech from the Throne read by the Governor-General. The first business was the traditional Address in reply to the Speech from the Throne which is moved and seconded by two Members supporting the Government. The next speaker in the debate on the Address is the Leader of the Opposition who often moves an Amendment which is a vote of want of confidence. The Prime Minister is the fourth speaker in the debate and he is followed by the leaders of other parties. The only speakers on this first day were the mover and seconder of the Address. Mackenzie King chose two veterans of the First World War, H. S. Hamilton of Sault Ste Marie, and Joseph Blanchette of Compton, Quebec, to move and second the Address. Manion was the first speaker on September 8 and he offered the full support and co-operation of the official Opposition. Mackenzie King began to speak in the afternoon as soon as Manion had concluded and his speech was broken by the dinner recess. The first half, which was largely an extemporaneous acknowledgment of Manion's speech, was much more impressive than the part which had been prepared and which was delivered in the evening. Any dramatic effect was lost when he concluded by reading a long poem by James Russell Lowell; this the House did not find inspiring.

Mackenzie King began his speech by thanking Manion for the offer of the support and co-operation of the Opposition and recalled that Manion was a veteran of the First World War. He then drew attention to the fact that the mover and seconder were also veterans and that they were "representative of the two great races of which this country is so largely composed." They were also "representative of those two countries, Britain and France, which today have laid their all upon the altar of service and sacrifice in the cause of freedom." He then appealed to the Members to ask themselves where their liberties and freedom came from before they uttered "a word against full participation by this country in the great conflict which is now raging in Europe. Where did we get our constitutional rights and liberties? Where did we get our freedom of religion? We got our many freedoms as an inheritance from those men of Britain and France who never hesitated to lay down their lives for freedom and those of their descent who followed their example on the soil of Canada itself."

He then referred to the plea Manion had made for "toleration and moderation" in judging the opinions of other Canadians, and expressed the hope "that throughout this country our citizens will be as tolerant as they can of differences of view and belief that are honestly held. There may of course be some things said which none of us would tolerate, and none of us will; but I ask, above all else, for a broad toleration. I was glad to hear my hon. friend make that plea, not only on behalf of citizens here in our own country who belong to the two great races, but as well on behalf of those of German descent who also are citizens of our country. May I go a step further . . . and make a plea for toleration on behalf of the German people themselves?

"No more fatal error could be made with respect to the issue at stake in this great conflict than to believe that it is the German people who have plunged Europe into war. Europe has been plunged into war because of a hateful and tyrannical regime which cherishes and is seeking to perpetuate policies which would rob mankind of everything that is dear to the human heart and the human soul. That regime has brought its own people under its iron heel. For the most part, the people of Germany today are slaves, enslaved by a Government, so-called, a dictatorship which holds a rifle at the head of every one of its citizens unless he is prepared to do its bidding. I pity with all my heart the German people in this country and in the old world."

He next said that he had "never dreamed that the day would come when, after spending a lifetime in a continuous effort to promote and to preserve peace and goodwill in international as well as in industrial relations, it should fall to my lot to be the one to lead this Dominion of Canada into a great war; but that responsibility I assume with the sense of being true to the very blood that is in my veins. I assume it in the defence of freedom—the freedom of my fellow countrymen here, the freedom of those whose lives are unprotected in other communities and countries, the freedom of mankind itself."

He then went on to declare the position of the Government in these words: "I shall seek to leave no doubt in the mind of anyone, if there is any doubt existing even now, as to what this Government's policy is. We stand for the defence of Canada; we stand for the co-operation of this country at the side of Great Britain; and if this House will not support us in that policy, it will have to find some other Government to assume the responsibilities of the present. We are committed to that policy, and I believe when it comes to the expression of views of hon. members from every side of this House of Commons we shall find that we have the house very solidly behind us."

He reminded the House that he had announced on September 1, two days before Britain declared war on Germany, that it was the policy of the Government to recommend to Parliament that Canada should support Britain if she went to war. He emphasized the point that the Government had not decided that Canada "would have to go into war willy-nilly." He explained that the Government had "summoned Parliament to express here, as representing the Canadian people, its will and its wish in the matter of this country entering this war voluntarily and of its own decision and right."

With Manion's statement that Canada was one of the prizes Hitler was seeking, Mackenzie King agreed emphatically, saying that "the ambition of this dictator is not Poland" and adding a question and answer he often quoted later in the war: "Where is he creeping to? Into those communities of the north, some of which today say they are going to remain neutral. I tell them if they remain neutral in this struggle, and Britain and France go down, there is not one of them that will bear for long the name that it bears at the present time; not one of them. And if this conqueror by his methods of force, violence and terror, and other ruthless iniquities is able to crush the peoples of Europe, what is going to become of the doctrine of isolation of this North American continent? If Britain goes down, if France goes down, the whole business of isolation will prove to have been a mere myth. There will in time be no liberty. Life will not be worth living. It is for all of us on this continent to do our part to save its privileged position by helping others." Thus, right from the outset, Mackenzie King expressed his belief that it was North American and not just Canadian vital interests which were at issue in the war.

Later in the speech, he made a remarkable and moving reference to J. S. Woodsworth. "I admire him in my heart," he said, "because time and again he has had the courage to say what lay on his conscience, regardless of what the world might think of him. A man of that calibre is an ornament to any Parliament. I do not know what my hon. friend's views will be. He and I have talked over these matters at different times. I know he feels deeply that anything in the nature of war should not be countenanced at all. But I said to him the other day—and I wish to repeat it here: When it comes to a fight between good and evil, when the evil forces of the world are let loose upon mankind, are those of us who believe in the tenets of Christianity, and all that Christianity means and has meant to the homes and lives of men, in the present and through generations in the past—are those of us who have reflected with reverence upon the supreme sacrifice that was made for the well-being of mankind going to allow evil forces to triumph without, if necessary, opposing them by our very lives?"

He recalled to the House that "the sense of impending calamity was not something which was realized all of a sudden. Three years ago the Government indicated its belief in the necessity for preparedness by asking Parliament substantially to increase the amounts required for the defence services of our country. I frankly confess that from that day to this the possibility of a war in which Germany or other nations would be engaged, and which might spread to all parts of the world, has absorbed more of my time and thought than all else combined. Particularly have I been concerned with the position of our own country in the event of Great Britain becoming again engaged in war. I have not concealed my conviction as to what I feared might occur. Time and again when my own followers have been discussing with me many matters of major and minor importance, I have urged upon them the wisdom of keeping constantly in mind the terrible possibility of international conflict, before which all else would soon pale and be forgotten."

He reminded the House of the successive increases in the defence estimates year by year and the resistance the Government had encountered. "Had we gone further," he said, "we would not have received the necessary support to get through our appropriations. We were conscious of the growing threat of war, and basing our policies upon it. Nations have been living under this threat of war year in and year out. The war of nerves, as it has been graphically and appropriately called, has been going on for years. We have been seeking to do our part to put this country's defences in proper shape to meet the fatal moment should it come."

After tracing the course of events leading up to the outbreak of war in Europe, and the action already taken by the Government, he went on: "May I here pause to say this? I have said all along that as regards Canada's entry into war, and obligations ensuing therefrom, no commitments would be made until Parliament met, that Parliament would decide the momentous question of peace and war; whether or not this country is to go into war. Now I wish to make perfectly clear at this moment, that Parliament has been summoned and is here today to decide that question. That question is not decided as yet. The Government have reached their decision upon policy; they have announced their policy, and it is for the hon. members of this house to say whether or not they stand by the Government's policy as it has been announced and as it is being announced today."

He emphasized that "such action as this Government is taking today it is taking in the name of Canada as a nation possessing in its own right all the powers and authority of a nation in the fullest sense. The action we are taking today, and such further action as this Parliament may authorize, are being and will be taken by this country voluntarily, not because of any colonial or inferior status vis-à-vis Great Britain, but because of an equality of status. We are a nation in the fullest sense, a member of the British Commonwealth of Nations, sharing like freedom with Britain herself, a freedom which we believe we must all combine to save." He stated that "the issue being what it is, Britain and France having taken their stand beside Poland to redeem pledges which they made for the purpose of avoiding hostilities and as a means of avoiding further aggression, if Parliament supports the Administration, this country will go into this war to be at the side of Britain, co-operating with her and with France towards those great and imperative ends, and equally to defend its own institutions and liberties." He added that "until this Parliament now assembled is prepared to approve and confirm what has been done under the War Measures Act and what remains to be done under the measures which will be introduced into this House there will be no commitments that will be binding upon this country."

After outlining the various measures the Government proposed to take if Parliament approved, Mackenzie King made it clear that no decision had yet been reached about sending an expeditionary force overseas and he then gave Parliament the pledge which was to become historic: "I wish now to repeat the undertaking I gave in Parliament on behalf of the Government on March 30 last. The present Government believe that conscription of men for overseas service will not be a necessary or an effective step. No such measure will be introduced by the present Administration. We have full faith in the readiness of Canadian men and women to put forth every effort in their power to preserve and defend free institutions, and in particular to resist aggression on the part of a tyrannical regime which aims at the domination of the world by force. The Government, as representing the people of Canada, will use their authority and power to the utmost in promoting the most effective organized effort toward these imperative ends."

Quoting several statements made by Hitler to indicate the scope of his ambitions, Mackenzie King then summed up: "What this world is facing today is deception, terror, violence and force, by a ruthless and tyrannical power which seeks world domination. I say there has not been a time, the period of the last war not excepted, when the countries of the world have faced such a crisis as they face today. I want to ask hon. members and the people of Canada: In what spirit are you going to face this crisis? Are you going to face it believing in the rights of individuals, believing in the sacredness of human personality, believing in the freedom of nations, believing in all the sanctities of human life? I believe you are. I believe that through their representatives in this Parliament the Canadian people will so indicate in no uncertain way."

After the House rose that night (September 8), Mackenzie King realized he had said nothing about the procedure by which Parliament would indicate its decision and at the opening of the sitting next day (September 9) he announced: "The adoption of the Address in reply to the Speech from the Throne will be considered as approving not only the Speech from the Throne but approving the Government's policy which I set out yesterday of immediate participation in the war. If the Address in reply to the Speech from the Throne is approved the Government will therefore immediately take steps for the issue of a formal Proclamation declaring the existence of a state of war between Canada and the German Reich."

The debate on the Address was concluded on September 9. The feature of that day's debate was the powerful speech by Ernest Lapointe, the Minister of Justice and the acknowledged leader of the Liberals of

French Canada, in which he made an eloquent and moving appeal to his compatriots to support active participation by Canada in the war. Mackenzie King described it as "a very noble utterance throughout, very brave and truly patriotic. When he sat down, I clasped his hand with the warmest friendship and agreement in all he had said." That evening an amendment to the Address was moved by one of the Members from Quebec regretting that the Government had not advised "that Canada should refrain from participating in war outside of Canada." At the end of the evening, the amendment was rejected without a recorded vote and the Address was adopted also without a vote. A formal Submission to the King was immediately dispatched by cable to London, and the next morning, Sunday, September 10, exactly one week after the British declaration, the King approved the Canadian declaration of war.

The united support in Parliament for the declaration of war marked a great political triumph for Mackenzie King. But he was not deceived by the apparent unanimity of Parliament. He knew that a large minority of the Canadian people did not really believe that the national security of Canada was at stake and that many of them did not believe Canada was serving her own national interests by participation. He realized that this minority included a high proportion, perhaps even a majority, of French Canadians; that they had accepted the decision to go to war reluctantly, and that they had done so only because of his pledge that the Government of which he was the head would not resort to conscription for overseas service.

Mackenzie King also realized that a substantial minority of the Canadian people, including a majority of the supporters of the Conservative party, had no confidence in his leadership of a wartime government. From the outset he anticipated a campaign for national government of which the real, though unavowed, object would be the replacement of himself by some other prime minister who would be willing to impose conscription regardless of the views of Quebec.

This 'National Government and Conscription' issue, which came up at the outset, remained the central issue of Canadian politics to the very end of the war. At times, it almost disappeared below the surface; at others, it resulted in acute controversy, which, in 1942, and again in November 1944, almost wrecked the Mackenzie King Government. The issue was no mere difference about the best method of prosecuting the war; basically it was a struggle between the two historic races, as it had been in 1917. Every French Canadian remembered the only previous experience of a so-called national government, the Union Government of 1917, which did not have a single French-speaking supporter in the

House of Commons: and for French Canadians 'National Government' and the conscription the Union Government had imposed in 1917 were the symbols of 'English' ascendancy. Most French Canadians feared, and some English Canadians desired, conscription as the sign of the domination of one race by the other.

No one in Canada understood this better than Mackenzie King, the only prominent English-speaking Liberal politician who had stood with Laurier against Union Government and conscription in 1917. He sincerely believed that Canada could not make an effective contribution to the prosecution of the war if the country was torn by controversy over conscription. He was convinced that the only basis for united public support of the war effort was a compromise in which, provided there was no compulsory military service outside Canada, the minority, which did not believe that the war was Canada's war, would accept the will of the majority.

Without the pledge against conscription, Mackenzie King would never have secured the almost unanimous acquiescence of the House of Commons in the declaration of war. And the pledge was received without open protest by the Conservative Opposition in Parliament, which under Manion's leadership was still hoping to secure support in the Province of Quebec.

The agitation for National Government, nevertheless, threatened to begin at once. Arthur Slaght, one of the Liberal members from Ontario who was a close friend of the Premier, Mitchell Hepburn, wanted, in the debate on the Address, to advocate the formation of a National Government. Mackenzie King persuaded him not to speak in the House but to raise the question at the Liberal caucus. Mackenzie King believed that Hepburn, George McCullagh, the publisher of the Toronto *Globe and Mail*, and others in Toronto were behind what he sincerely regarded and almost invariably described in his diary as the first step towards a "fascist" government in Canada. He feared this Toronto combination would be "a difficult lot to fight."

At the Cabinet meeting on September 11, Mackenzie King urged his colleagues "not to countenance a thought of Union Government at present. Gave them my impression of the gang that were trying to get control of Parliament and effect in wartime what in peacetime they were unable to effect; of special privileges they were after."

On the following day (September 12) in the Liberal caucus he asked Arthur Slaght to put the argument in favour of National Government and, in reply, gave his own view that it was better to maintain the ordinary parliamentary system with a responsible Government and an

Opposition with freedom to criticize. The caucus was united in opposing National Government. Mackenzie King also told the caucus there would be no extension of the life of Parliament and warned the Members to prepare for a general election in 1940 at the end of the regular session of Parliament.

The question came up again indirectly that same afternoon (September 12) in the House of Commons. Manion charged there were already signs of patronage and favouritism in the war effort and that the Government was not taking advantage of the co-operation offered by the Opposition. Mackenzie King replied at once and gave his own view of the best way to carry on government in wartime in these words: "Now, as to party politics in relation to government at this time, let me say quite honestly and frankly that there is nothing my soul would loathe so much as an effort on the part of any members of my own party or any members anywhere to seek to make party capital out of a condition such as the world and this country are faced with at the present time. So far as I am concerned I look upon myself today, with all due humility, much more as the leader of all parties in this country united in an effort to do what we can to preserve and defend the liberties of mankind. Personally I believe that we can be most successful in that effort as a Government taking full responsibility but shouldering it fearlessly and courageously, and faced by an Opposition which, as my hon. friend has just said, is as necessary to the full discharge of Parliamentary obligations under the British system as is any other feature of our constitution.

"My hon. friend, as the Leader of the Opposition, holds a position involving a special duty imposed upon him by Parliament. His position is recognized by statute and he is in many particulars in a capacity similar to that of any member of the Government. It is his duty to watch over every act of the Administration to see that it is performed as it should be; more especially is this true at a time such as this. I do feel that what my hon. friend has pointed out as his conception of his duty is what, more than anything else, will help me in my position as leader of the Government to discharge my own obligations in the way in which I should like to see them discharged; the way in which I shall use my utmost endeavours to have them discharged. I wish my hon. friend to be free to criticize, and indeed he will help me if from time to time as matters come to his notice which in his opinion show evidences of party bias, he will be good enough to bring such matters to my attention and accord me an opportunity to discuss them with him."

The special war session of Parliament ended that day, but not before Mackenzie King had undertaken that the existing Parliament would meet again before an election was held.

Even more urgent at this time than the question of National Government was that of strengthening the existing Government and of finding satisfactory incumbents for the two key portfolios in a wartime Government: Finance and National Defence.

Charles Dunning, the Minister of Finance, had been absent from his duties for months because of a prolonged illness. He was not even in Canada when the war broke out, and he clearly could not undertake the burdens of a wartime Minister of Finance. Ian Mackenzie, the Minister of National Defence, though one of the outstanding debaters in Parliament, lacked administrative capacity and other qualities of leadership needed in wartime. Mackenzie King was convinced that he must have a stronger Minister in this Department. The obvious choice for both posts was J. L. Ralston who had been in the Liberal Government before 1930 as Minister of National Defence, and was a leading member of the Opposition from 1930 to 1935. Ralston had retired from public life in 1935 in order to practise law in Montreal. As soon as war broke out Mackenzie King sent for him and on September 5 reminded him of a promise he had made some weeks earlier that he would help in a crisis. He told Ralston he was much concerned about the Defence Department and thought of having Ian Mackenzie made Secretary of State and having Ralston take the Defence portfolio. He also mentioned Finance and, when Ralston expressed a preference for Finance, Mackenzie King at once said he could have whichever portfolio he wished. Before the day was out it was agreed that Ralston should become Minister of Finance. He was sworn in the next day and plunged at once into the work of preparing a special war budget on which J. L. Ilsley, the Minister of National Revenue, who had been Acting Minister of Finance in Dunning's absence, was already engaged.

Since Ralston was not a Member of Parliament, a constituency had to be found for him. He had almost decided to be a candidate in Jacques-Cartier riding at the western end of the island of Montreal when, on October 28, the Member for Prince County, P.E.I., died. Mackenzie King at once suggested to Ralston that he consider that constituency where he would be sure of an acclamation. The esteem in which he held Ralston at this time appears in the entry in his diary which discloses that he told Ralston he would "be glad to see the next Prime Minister representing the constituency that had opened the way for the present Prime Minister to take office and would feel it most appropriate for him to be there." Mackenzie King had represented Prince from the time he became leader of the Liberal party in 1919 until the general election of 1921. He added: "If I were designating tomorrow the man for Prime Minister, I would select Ralston without a moment's hesitation. Years ago, I felt the same way about him. He is the most unselfish man, I think, that I have met, a public spirit equal to Norman Rogers."

According to Mackenzie King's diary, Ralston on September 13 had suggested Norman Rogers for the Defence portfolio. At that time, Rogers was Minister of Labour. They also discussed C. G. Power, then Minister of Pensions and National Health. It took several days to make a decision, particularly as Mackenzie King shrank from the unpleasant task of telling Ian Mackenzie he was going to be replaced. What finally persuaded him that he could delay no longer was a report Mackenzie made as Minister of National Defence to a Cabinet committee on September 15. Mackenzie King described Ian Mackenzie's presentation of the report as "pathetic." On September 19, he determined to make the change, but he had still not decided who was to be the Minister. According to his record, the Defence portfolio was first offered to C. D. Howe, then Minister of Transport, but evidently in a perfunctory way. The real choice lay between Rogers and Power. Power himself, according to Mackenzie King, finally settled the issue by questioning the wisdom of having the Minister of Defence from Quebec, since it might raise the issue of conscription at once. It was then decided to have Mackenzie take Power's portfolio of Pensions and National Health, Power become Postmaster General, Rogers become Minister of Defence, and Norman McLarty, who was Postmaster General, succeed Rogers as Minister of Labour. On September 19 they were sworn in and on the 21st Mackenzie King noted "an immediate relief having Rogers at Defence. We got the first intelligent and clear-cut sort of statement from the Minister of the Department we have had in a year past."

No further changes were made in the ministry in 1939, but a profound change was made in the way the business of the Cabinet was carried out. Shortly after the Canadian declaration of war, C. G. Power had worked out a plan for a number of Cabinet Committees to have supervision of various phases of the war effort. The most important of these Committees was first called the Emergency Council, though the name was later changed to the War Committee of the Cabinet. This Committee was, in fact, though not in name, a War Cabinet. Its first business meeting was held on September 15. The original membership included the Prime Minister, the Minister of Finance, the Minister of National Defence, and other Ministers such as Lapointe (Justice) and Crerar (Mines and Resources) who were designated because of their seniority and experience. The War Committee was also attended by the Under Secretary of State for External Affairs. Arnold Heeney was its Secretary throughout the war and Minutes were kept of its meetings.

Special machinery was also provided for the procurement of munitions and other war supplies. Defence procurement had been a function of the Department of National Defence until early in 1939 when a Defence Purchasing Board was established which was responsible to the Minister of Finance. Mackenzie King did not feel that this Board would be adequate to meet wartime needs. Accordingly, on September 6 he asked Power to prepare a Bill to establish a Department of Supply. The Bill was duly prepared and enacted into law at the special war session of Parliament. Instead, however, of setting up a full-fledged department of government immediately, the Government transformed the Defence Purchasing Board into a War Supply Board with very broad powers, but still responsible to the Minister of Finance. Wallace Campbell of the Ford Motor Company was appointed Chairman of the War Supply Board.

The appointment was not an altogether happy one. Mackenzie King noted on November 15 that "Wallace Campbell, the Chairman of the Supply Board, is an old-fashioned, hard industrialist . . . unsympathetic with Labour organization. While good as an executive, that type is in the industrial world what dictators are in the political world." He asked the Minister of Labour, Norman McLarty, to try to get Campbell to modify his attitude. This was the first hint of a problem that troubled Mackenzie King all through the war. He recognized the need of using leading industrialists and businessmen in mobilizing industry for war, but he felt that some of them, by bringing to the public service from their private business an unfriendly attitude to organized labour, were creating problems for the wartime administration and political difficulties for the Government.

The following day (November 16) Mackenzie King talked with Ralston about Wallace Campbell. He found that "Ralston admired Campbell's ability and driving power but feared he might give the Government embarrassment later on because he had no understanding of Government or Government responsibility to Parliament. Ralston asked to be relieved of responsibility for the War Supply Board." Mackenzie King added: "We both agreed Howe would be the best man to take it on." The ministerial responsibility for the War Supply Board was assumed by C. D. Howe a few days later. His responsibility for defence procurement and industrial mobilization lasted for over seventeen years and was to have tremendous consequences for Canada and the free world in war and afterwards.

Canada had not even declared war when another economic agency which was to have a great influence on the Canadian war effort was set up, on September 3, 1939. The memory of the high prices and inflation of the First World War was still very fresh in many minds in 1939. The Wartime Prices and Trade Board, which was responsible to the Minister of Labour, was established to prevent hoarding and profiteering and conserve civilian supplies. It had a relatively minor role until 1941 when the price ceiling was imposed.

Although no fundamental departures in financial or economic policy were ever taken without Mackenzie King's full concurrence, he did not usually take a very active part in formulating the financial and economic policies of the Government. He had great confidence in Ralston and in Ralston's advisers, particularly W. C. Clark, the Deputy Minister of Finance. When J. L. Ilsley, then Minister of National Revenue, delivered the Budget speech for Ralston, who was not yet in Parliament, on September 12, Mackenzie King called it "as fine a piece of work as he had ever known and marvellously received by the House generally." He showed, however, no appreciation of Ilsley's part in this achievement and evidently had no inkling that, before the war ended, Ilsley's prestige in the Government would be almost as great as his own.

Mackenzie King gave a great deal of personal attention to labour questions, but not so much to agricultural problems, because he did not feel he had the same knowledge of their background. Despite his great love of the countryside, he had had no personal experience of farm life or farm problems. On September 21, the Cabinet considered, for the first time, the problem resulting from British limitations on the entry of apples and several other farm products from Canada. It was agreed that a large expenditure would be necessary to save the apple producers from disaster. To Mackenzie King this looked like the beginning of guaranteeing minimum prices for all agricultural products which he then thought was "wholly wrong excepting in a condition of emergency."

If he left financial and economic problems, except where they directly affected organized labour, largely to his colleagues, he took, from the outset, a direct and continuing interest in the military programme. From the beginning, he insisted on two basic requirements: on the one hand, full Canadian control, and, on the other, the closest integration of the Canadian programme with the United Kingdom programme in every sphere of military activity, including supply. In his own phrase Canada was to fight "at Britain's side."

On September 7, the day Parliament met and the first day Ralston attended a Cabinet meeting, Mackenzie King found his colleagues more favourable to an expeditionary force than he had imagined they would be. He was also surprised to find considerable feeling for conscription or for saying nothing against conscription. Both Lapointe and Mackenzie King said they would have to be outspoken on this point and Mackenzie King indicated the kind of pledge against conscription for overseas he would give.

He told Parliament on September 8 that "the safety of Canada depends upon the adequate safeguarding of our coastal regions and the great avenues of approach to the heart of this country. Foremost among these is the St. Lawrence River and Gulf. At the entrance to the St. Lawrence stands the neighbouring British territory of Newfoundland and Labrador. The integrity of Newfoundland and Labrador is essential to the security of Canada. By contributing as far as we are able to the defence of Newfoundland and the other British and French territories in this Hemisphere, we will not only be defending Canada but we will also be assisting Great Britain and France by enabling them to concentrate their own energies more in that part of the world in which their own immediate security is at stake. The British Government, in reply to the enquiry we have made, have indicated their agreement that this would be an effective and desirable means of co-operation."

He added that "as regards action in other theatres of war and the means and measures that might be taken, certain essential information touching the character of British and Allied action and contemplated plans must be available before any intelligent and definitive decision could be made as to Canadian action even in the immediate future. On this all-important aspect of co-operation in defence, the Canadian Government, like the Governments of other of the Dominions, is in consultation with the British Government. We will continue to consult with the purpose of determining the course of action which may be regarded as most effective.

"The question of an expeditionary force or units for service overseas is particularly one of wide-reaching significance which will require the fullest examination." And he then said: "There are certain measures of economic, naval and air co-operation which are obviously necessary and desirable and which it is possible to undertake without delay. I have already referred to economic measures. The information we have obtained indicates that the most immediate and effective further means of co-operation would be a rapid expansion of air training, and of air and naval facilities, and the dispatch of trained air personnel. These measures we propose to institute immediately."

The military programme was under daily consideration from the time the special war session of Parliament ended on September 12. When, on September 18, the Emergency Council (War Committee) found the cost of the programme proposed would exceed $500,000,000 it was felt this was an expenditure "the country could not begin to afford" and the Cabinet agreed to tell the Chiefs of Staff to work out the best programme they could in terms of a total of $250,000,000. The highlights of the programme announced on September 19 were an expeditionary force of one army division and intensive air training in Canada.

Mackenzie King's own desire would have been to delay the expeditionary force and concentrate on the Navy and the Air Force, and particularly on air training and the production of munitions. But he recognized the tradition of the expeditionary force in the First World War made one in this war politically inevitable.

From the outset, too, he predicted a war of global proportions and terrible ferocity. He was convinced that once the Western powers really became engaged with Germany the war would last a long time and that the outcome was far from certain. On September 17, the word that Russia had joined in the attack on Poland provoked the reflection that he could not see "how Britain and France were to be saved from destruction unless some kind of an Armistice was reached, and a conference held which would give the Germans and the Italians much that they have been demanding." This conviction came out again on November 30, when Mackenzie King was "perfectly horrified to read in tonight's papers of invasion of Finland by Russia. A ghastly bit of ruthless aggression. All part, I believe, of plot between Hitler and Stalin to dominate Europe. I still think both are shaping their plans to converge on British Isles; that England is nearer the point of destruction than she has been at any time. If Germany could wean France away, she would immediately destroy Britain, but the French well know she would return later to possess the rest of Europe. I look to see Japan and Russia come to some understanding and Japan become increasingly assertive in the Orient."

He felt from the beginning that the support of the United States was absolutely vital and believed Canada could help to bring the United States into closer association with Britain and France. He lost no time in embarking on the task of securing this but he realized the task called for tact and understanding.

Early in the afternoon of September 5, Cordell Hull, the Secretary of State of the United States, had telephoned Mackenzie King. President Roosevelt was listening at another telephone on the same line. Hull explained that the President was about to issue the neutrality proclamation required by American law and they wanted to know whether Canada was at war because the United Kingdom was at war. Mackenzie

King explained that Parliament was meeting later in the week to make the decision. Hull replied that the American proclamation would not apply to Canada. Roosevelt then spoke himself and asked Mackenzie King to keep in touch with himself and Hull. In the week between September 3 and September 10 advantage was taken of this technical neutrality to deliver to Canada military aircraft which could not be shipped to Britain or France because of the American Neutrality Law. The delivery of these aircraft continued right up to the moment of the Canadian declaration on September 10. In this friendly and informal fashion, the wartime co-operation between Mackenzie King and Roosevelt, which was so fruitful for the Allied cause, had its beginnings.

At the outbreak of the war Sir Herbert Marler, the Canadian Minister to the United States, was obliged to resign his post because of a grave illness. On September 15 Loring Christie, one of the senior officers in the Department of External Affairs, was appointed in Marler's place. Christie had been Sir Robert Borden's closest adviser during the First World War, and Mackenzie King and O. D. Skelton, the Under Secretary of State for External Affairs, felt that his invaluable experience and his undoubted abilities were needed at Washington. He served there, with great distinction, until the onset of the grave illness which caused his death in 1941.

One of Mackenzie King's preoccupations in the early months of the war was with the proper organization of public information. He was profoundly suspicious of any proposal for a ministry of information and, indeed, of any organized effort to provide so-called public information, but at the same time he realized the need of keeping the public informed, if the war effort and the Government were to receive the necessary public support. This was one problem, however, which he never did solve to his own complete satisfaction. His first attempt was made on September 9 when he saw L. W. Brockington, who was then Chairman of the Canadian Broadcasting Corporation, about becoming head of a Bureau of Information. This appointment was not made because of opposition from his colleagues, but Mackenzie King refused to give up the idea that Brockington was needed in this field and eventually secured his appointment to a position on his own staff which was never too clearly defined. The relationship was not happy, partly because Mackenzie King expected a degree of anonymity from those associated with him which could not reasonably have been expected of Brockington, but neither ever lost his regard or respect for the other.

Mackenzie King was exceedingly anxious himself to be the main source of public information about the war, but he found no other task so agonizing or time consuming as preparing speeches and particularly broadcasts. There is a very revealing and unusual note of self-depreciation in his diary for Sunday, October 1, about "a magnificent broadcast by Winston Churchill on the first month of the war. At its close I cabled him 'Your broadcast magnificent—as perfect in its appeal to the New World as to the Old.' I keep continually reproaching myself at having gone the wrong way about much of my preparation for public life—the time wasted on kinds of research that did not bring me into touch with the great thought of the world instead of with a lot of little things is something to deplore. Also that I have not read more widely and sought to train my memory more. I particularly deplore the time I have wasted in digging up material that should have been worked out for me, and not following more closely from day to day the issues of the day. With the gifts I have inherited, I might easily have been a real force in Parliament, and in the shaping of public opinion in a world crisis such as we are now faced with. The one thing to be sought from now on is to redeem the time that has been lost in that respect."

Over and over again this reflection recurs, particularly when Mackenzie King was with Churchill or listening to his broadcasts. And these occasions were usually followed by another attempt to find someone to do the drudgery and give him freedom to speak more frequently and to better effect.

Early in October Mackenzie King asked Brockington to draft a broadcast for him on the first month of war. Of this draft he wrote: "I confess, while it was well done for the time he had to work upon it, it filled me with dismay, for I saw at once that if I am to do the broadcasting, I shall have to prepare for it very largely myself. I talked with Brockington later and suggested to him the necessity of having the material so recast as to have it reach the man in the blacksmith's shop, with his friends and neighbours; the woman in the kitchen; the labourers coming in from their work on the farm. Nothing else is any good at this time." Those few sentences reveal the impossibility of really effective collaboration between them. Mackenzie King could never bring himself to utter anything with which he did not feel at home. He had to have plenty of time to assimilate what had been prepared for him, and he insisted on painstaking revision which, all too often, stripped what he had to say not only of rhetoric but also of life.

Almost the whole month of October had passed before Mackenzie King finally made his broadcast and, by then, it had grown into two broadcasts, both endlessly revised. October 25 was finally fixed as the date for the first broadcast only because his colleagues felt it should be made before the first of a series of broadcasts on the war by George McCullagh, the publisher of the Toronto *Globe and Mail*; this series achieved a certain brief notoriety because it was terminated by the C.B.C. before all the proposed broadcasts had been delivered. Mackenzie King was still revising the text of this first broadcast on the day it was made and reflected that "this class of work cannot be done hurriedly." It was called "The Issue," and outlined the rise of Hitler, the expansion of Nazi Germany, and Mackenzie King's reaction to both. It included a statement of his own position which was almost a confession:

"If, today, I am prepared to continue to lead a Government charged with the awful responsibility of prosecuting a war, it is because, contrary to every hope and wish I have ever entertained, I have been compelled to believe that only by the destruction of Naziism, and the resistance of ruthless aggression, can the nations of the British Commonwealth hope to continue to enjoy the liberties which are theirs under the British Crown, and the world itself be spared a descent into a new and terrible age of barbarism.

"The growth of my own conviction has, I believe, been more or less paralleled in the minds of most of the men and women of Canada. Today it represents the mind of Canada itself.

"I doubt if two years ago the Canadian people could have been persuaded to participate in another European war. Like Britain, like France, we were determined first to exhaust every possibility of peaceful negotiation in the settlement of international differences. It was not until we beheld every structure of peace destroyed, as quickly as it was erected, that our worst fears became confirmed. We saw forces being loosed upon the world which, if not subdued and conquered overseas, sooner or later would be at our very doors."[1]

The second broadcast, delivered on October 31, was a straightforward statement on "The Organization of Canada's War Effort." Mackenzie King was not fully satisfied with this talk either, and when, on November 12, he listened to another broadcast by Churchill, he found it "an admirable piece of work, leaving with me, as before, regret that I have not, in past years, studied public affairs more closely, concentrating on them and on speaking and writing."

It was not until December 6 that the first compromise on public information was reached with the appointment of Walter Thompson as head of a Bureau of Public Information and L. W. Brockington as Counsellor to the Prime Minister. There were to be many changes before the end of the war and no arrangement ever fully satisfied Mackenzie King.

[1] W. L. Mackenzie King, *Canada at Britain's Side* (Toronto, 1941), p. 39.

Once the special session of Parliament concluded in mid-September, Mackenzie King had no worries about political opposition from the other parties in Parliament. The real opposition was likely to arise from two of the provincial capitals: from Quebec in the form of opposition to effective Canadian participation in the war, and from Toronto, in the form of agitation for a greater effort and, by implication, for conscription. Both types of opposition were not long in appearing, and they were led, ironically enough, by the premiers of the two central provinces who had, so recently, been allied against Mackenzie King and the Liberal Government at Ottawa in what was called the Hepburn-Duplessis Axis.

The opposition of Maurice Duplessis was not unnatural. After a short period as Leader of the Conservative Opposition in the Quebec Legislature, Duplessis had succeeded, after the provincial election of 1935, in uniting the political forces opposed to the provincial Liberal Government in a new party called the Union Nationale and had won an overwhelming victory in the election of August 1936. For Duplessis the Liberals were the hereditary enemy.

The case of Mitchell Hepburn was quite different. Hepburn had begun his political career as a Liberal Member of the House of Commons, first elected in 1926 to support Mackenzie King. In the early thirties, while still in Parliament, he was chosen as leader of the Ontario Liberal party. He continued to sit in the House of Commons until the eve of the provincial election of 1934 in which he won a major victory. Hepburn apparently felt that his support was a large factor in achieving the Liberal sweep in Ontario in the federal election of 1935, and expected to be consulted about the composition of Mackenzie King's Cabinet; indeed he tendered unsolicited advice which was not followed. He and his friends were known to be very resentful of the appointment to the Cabinet in 1935 of C. D. Howe and Norman Rogers whom they regarded as non-professional outsiders. Not long after Duplessis became Premier of Quebec in 1936, he and Hepburn formed a political alliance in opposition to the Government at Ottawa. Hepburn's first public attack was made on both Mackenzie King and Lapointe while they were in London in 1937 for the Coronation and the Imperial Conference. Mackenzie King never found out what prompted this attack, which he had certainly not provoked. In the fall of 1937 and spring of 1938, Hepburn had had a bitter controversy with Mackenzie King over a proposal Hepburn made to export hydro-electric power to the United States. From that time on, relations between them became steadily worse. When a dinner was held in Toronto on August 8, 1939, to celebrate Mackenzie King's twenty years of Liberal leadership, Hepburn not only stayed away but told his Ministers not to attend.

After the outbreak of war, the first opposition came from Quebec. On September 25, Mackenzie King noted in his diary that "the most serious matter that has arisen and it is a very serious one, was the announcement today by Duplessis of a General Election in Quebec a month from today. It is a diabolical act on his part to have made the issue Provincial Autonomy versus Dominion Government, taking advantage of the War Measures Act to have it appear that Ottawa is encroaching on the freedom of individuals in Quebec."

Mackenzie King realized that systematic opposition from a provincial government in Quebec with a fresh mandate from the people would frustrate the effective prosecution of the war. After the Cabinet meeting on that day, he discussed the situation with Lapointe who said he and Power were agreed a victory for Duplessis would be a vote of want of confidence in the Quebec Ministers at Ottawa, that they must go into the fight, and that they would leave the Government if Duplessis won. Mackenzie King agreed they should fight Duplessis, though he did not want them to say they would leave the Cabinet if Duplessis won the election. But Lapointe replied that he and Power believed that the strongest argument against Duplessis would be public knowledge that if he was not defeated the Quebec Ministers would resign from the federal Cabinet and thereby leave the door open to a conscriptionist Government at Ottawa. Although Mackenzie King did not approve, Lapointe, P. J. A. Cardin (the Minister of Public Works), and Power all announced they would resign from the federal Government if Duplessis was successful.

Mackenzie King told his colleagues on September 27 he believed Lapointe, Cardin, and Power could defeat Duplessis. He said the struggle would make their names honoured and memorable for all time, and "would give Lapointe a position even higher, if that is possible, than that held by Laurier in the esteem of Canada."

Early in October, J. W. McConnell of the Montreal *Star* came to see Mackenzie King to offer his help and the help of the *Star* against Duplessis who, he felt, would be beaten. This visit was the beginning of a close friendship which lasted for the rest of Mackenzie King's life.

There was little Mackenzie King himself could do about the Quebec election except await the results. He was overjoyed on October 25 by the tremendous Liberal victory. "The campaign put up by Lapointe, Cardin and Power was really a splendid one," he wrote. "The issue was squarely faced and ably presented by all three. It has given them all, especially Lapointe, an exceedingly high place in public regard." He compared Lapointe with Laurier and said he would have a place second to none as a patriot. Mackenzie King was not exaggerating when he called it a great victory for the Allied cause. "Had the results gone the other way," he added, "Germany would have felt dismemberment of the British Empire had already commenced." On October 25, Mackenzie King and his colleagues had met triumphantly this first political challenge to their wartime administration and the prestige of the Government was correspondingly high.

But there were already the first warning signs of opposition from Hepburn. On September 27, a telegram arrived asking Mackenzie King for an interview for the Lieutenant-Governor (Albert Matthews), Hepburn, and George Drew, the Leader of the provincial Opposition. Mackenzie King reflected that "the fight in Quebec would be that the Federal Government was interfering with autonomy in being too Imperialistic, while the fight in Ontario would be that the Federal Government was not Imperialistic enough and not throwing enough energy into the war effort." He added: "My own opinion is that they will be badly fooled in the end by the strong position which the Government will get, if our people defeat Duplessis."

On October 3, the Cabinet received this bizarre delegation which had been authorized, under the Ontario Resources Act, to offer co-operation to the federal government in prosecuting the war. Under the guise of offering co-operation, Hepburn used this occasion to reverse the attitude of the Government of Ontario to the St. Lawrence Seaway Development by favouring what he had previously opposed. Both Hepburn and Drew stressed the danger of sabotage of power plants in Ontario, and both suggested the Government was slow in placing orders for munitions and supplies and in raising troops. Mackenzie King welcomed the changed attitude of the Ontario Government to the proposed development of the St. Lawrence Waterway and asked Hepburn to have his officials follow the matter up. At the Cabinet meeting later that day, Mackenzie King insisted that the Ontario representations should all be taken at their face value and dealt with seriously. Howe was authorized to take the St. Lawrence development in hand.

It was not until later in the year that Hepburn's hostility became more open. On November 24, Mackenzie King wrote: "During the last two days Hepburn has again been finding fault with our Government, today stating the dollar is in the riding seat at Ottawa, and that the Air Training Scheme would have been far advanced if our Government had not held the matter up some time ago. Both direct lies. Ralston fortunately speaks tonight and will, I think, astonish the public when he lets them see how far we have committed the country financially. Later on I shall make clear the situation as regards Air Training. It is perfectly apparent that Hepburn and Drew . . . and their gang generally in Ontario intend to make matters as difficult for us as possible. Whatever impression they may be able to make in Toronto will not, I think, be shared in other parts of Ontario, and certainly not in other parts of Canada."

Meanwhile, Howe had been working on the St. Lawrence project, and on December 19 had presented a proposal to the Cabinet and been authorized to advise Washington that Canada was ready to begin negotiations. The Quebec Ministers thought the new provincial Government of Quebec would be favourable as the project might mean cheaper power for Quebec. Mackenzie King reflected: "The cost is comparatively light so far as the Federal Treasury is concerned and the project would now serve to give much needed employment at a time when there would be great need of the same, once the war is over. It will probably be all of two years before part of the work would begin. This is a big step and I confess an unexpected step. It shows again another thing about politics; how completely the scene changes, and how conditions help to make some things not only feasible but desirable where they would be neither, if not chosen at the right season."

A good deal of feeling developed in certain quarters late in 1939 about Communist propaganda against the war effort. On November 16, Mackenzie King noted "Lapointe brought in Order-in-Council to suppress subversive activities, particularly Communistic and Nazi activities. I favoured strongly the principle but felt the men who had drafted the Order had gone much too far." Mackenzie King did not object to action against the Communists, but felt the procedures proposed were too arbitrary. This was the beginning of one of the rare differences between the two men. A considerably modified Order was passed a week or two later which completely satisfied neither of them.

During the autumn, the First Division of the Canadian Army had been recruited and had completed its preliminary training. On December 8, Mackenzie King went to the station with Norman Rogers to say goodbye to General McNaughton who was leaving on the first train carrying troops of the First Division on their way to embark for Britain. There were very few at the station as the time and place of departure were secret.

The selection of the commander for the expeditionary force had been regarded by Mackenzie King as one of the gravest responsibilities of the Government. General A. G. L. McNaughton's name was first suggested by Norman Rogers on September 22. McNaughton, then Chairman of the National Research Council, had earlier been Chief of the General Staff. Mackenzie King welcomed the suggestion warmly and Rogers was authorized to approach him. At the Cabinet meeting on October 5, it was decided Mackenzie King should see McNaughton to discuss the appointment. An interview was arranged for October 6, at which Ralston and Rogers were also present. McNaughton made clear at the interview that, in his view, the major effort of the war should be "along the lines of production, and that every effort should be made to arm and equip the troops to spare human lives."

Mackenzie King found the interview "as deeply moving as any I have witnessed in my public life. One felt the enormous responsibilities that were being placed on the individual. There could be no question about McNaughton being the best equipped man for the purpose. I have done my best with my colleagues to remove prejudice which I know there has been against him on account of his tendency to organize matters to the maximum with respect to possible conflict. However, the facts have vindicated the wisdom of his action in this regard. The one thing that I don't like about the associations is the school from which he comes, which was the school of MacBrien, of Bennett, and Herridge." Mackenzie King was alluding to the fact that while R. B. Bennett was Prime Minister, McNaughton—like Sir James MacBrien, Commissioner of the Royal Canadian Mounted Police, and W. D. Herridge, Bennett's brother-in-law and the Canadian Minister to the United States—had all been close to the Prime Minister. He added: "No better evidence could be given of our disinterested action than in giving this command to one who comes more particularly from that particular group. My own association with McNaughton over many years has been friendly, and I have always had a high appreciation of his capacities. I am sure we have made in this, the most important of all choices, the right one."

From the beginning of their wartime relationship there was a bond of sympathy between Mackenzie King and McNaughton which was never broken. On December 7 they had another interview just before McNaughton's departure for Britain, at which the General said "he was 'absolutely content' with everything pertaining to the First Division. The right men had been appointed as officers. He had inspected the different regiments; looked at almost every man. They were in good condition—the medical examination had been very strict because of the many seeking to enlist. They had been well out-fitted. Everything was as complete as it could be, except the equipment which they were to secure in England. He could not wish for a finer body of men. He expressed his strong admiration for Rogers, who, he said, had done excellent work as Minister; had gained the confidence of the Army."

McNaughton expressed concern that more was not being done to mobilize industry. Mackenzie King "thanked him for giving me his views and said I would go into the matter at once. In saying good-bye, he thanked me again for the way in which I had backed him and the sympathy I had shown him in everything, and said that it was what I had said to him that had made him accept the position. I told him he would find me and the Government at his back. I then asked him if he would give a message to the officers and men of the First Division, telling them how greatly I admired their bravery, how much they were in the thoughts of the country, and to emphasize to them the nature of their part in the war as a crusade—defenders of the faith and of civilization against the domination of free countries by barbarism.

"The last word I said to him was to remember that in quietness and confidence was strength, and that God was on his side. We both felt the emotion of the situation. . . . As I talked with McNaughton I felt a little concern about his being able to see this war through without a breakdown. I felt he was too far on in years to be taking on so great a job. Having been through the strain of a previous war he and many others like him might find they had not the endurance that they believed they had. I am even more convinced that the Canadian public would not have listened to anyone else as Commander of the Expeditionary Force."

The First Canadian Division began to arrive in Britain on December 17, the day on which the British Commonwealth Air Training Agreement was signed. It had been arranged that the announcement of the landing would be held for two days and then made in Canada. Winston Churchill beat the gun and on December 18, Mackenzie King recorded his indignation that Churchill should have broadcast the safe arrival of the Canadian troops when the Canadian Government was holding back the announcement for forty-eight hours at the request of the Admiralty, of which Churchill was the head. This was not to be the last occasion during the war when Mackenzie King would express similar indignation over the failure of the British authorities to permit the Canadian Government to make its own announcements and to give the emphasis they wanted to Canada's part in the common effort.

Despite this temporary irritation, Mackenzie King felt that, with the expeditionary force in Britain and the Air Training Plan launched, the foundations of Canada's war effort had been well and truly laid.

CHAPTER THREE

The British Commonwealth Air Training Plan

THE DECISION to go to war was the most important taken by the Mackenzie King Government in 1939, but next to that in importance was the launching of the British Commonwealth Air Training Plan.

After dinner, on September 26, 1939, Mackenzie King was reading official papers and despatches from England, and came upon "a most important one regarding Canada as training ground for airmen on a large scale." He noted that the idea was "to have Canada training ground for Australians, New Zealanders as well as Canadians, and some from the Old Country." This despatch, one of those from Prime Minister to Prime Minister, was the beginning of the British Commonwealth Air Training Plan. The idea of training British pilots in Canada was, however, not new. The peacetime defence estimates for 1939 had included provision for the setting-up of training schools for British pilots to be administered by the Royal Canadian Air Force, although no progress had been made in their establishment when war broke out.

Chamberlain's proposal at once impressed Mackenzie King. No doubt that impression was strengthened by the demonstration of air strength in Hitler's campaign against Poland. Warsaw fell on September 27, and Polish resistance ceased soon afterwards. Not only did Mackenzie King agree with Chamberlain that the most effective military contribution Canada could make was through a great co-operative project to train pilots and air crew for the Commonwealth air forces, but he saw that, with concentration of Canadian energies on air training and air power and therefore less pressure for a larger army, there would also be less risk of agitation for conscription.

When Mackenzie King submitted Chamberlain's proposal for a joint air training plan to the Cabinet on September 28, it was received favourably, though Mackenzie King observed "there was general regret that it had not been made at the outset so that our war effort would have been framed on these lines instead of having to head so strongly into expeditionary forces at the start." The one practical difficulty in accepting was that the Government had already announced a war programme on September 19 which represented all the Ministers believed could be financed or accomplished in the early months of the war. It was nonetheless decided to accept the proposal in principle and Mackenzie King did so in a cable to Chamberlain on September 28.

The British Government thereupon decided to send a special mission headed by Lord Riverdale, an industrialist from Sheffield, to Ottawa to work out the Air Training Plan with the Canadian authorities; missions were also to be sent to Ottawa from Australia and New Zealand.

On October 17, soon after his arrival in Ottawa, Lord Riverdale called on the Prime Minister. In this interview, Riverdale made the mistake of referring to the proposal as "your scheme" and seemed to take it for granted that the Canadian Government would agree, without discussion, to whatever he proposed. Mackenzie King left him in no doubt that it would not be so easy to reach an agreement and "that what we could do in the way of developing the Air Training Scheme would depend, first of all, upon the physical possibilities . . . and secondly, the cost." He added "that it was a pity we had not received the Air Training Scheme at the beginning; before it had come to hand, we had made plans which went as far as we thought it would be possible for us to go." He then told Riverdale "it was very kind of him to speak of the scheme as ours, but it was really theirs, and how far we could go in developing it would depend very largely on what Britain herself would do."

Mackenzie King observed in recording the interview that the British "seemed to envisage most of the pilots coming from Canada. It looked really like a recruiting scheme for airmen from the Dominions." He "was rather amused at the sort of railroading, taking for granted style which Riverdale adopted" and noted that it was "amazing how these people . . . from the Old Country . . . seem to think that all they have to do is to tell us what is to be done. No wonder they get the backs of people up on this side."

During the next fortnight Riverdale was joined by Air Chief Marshal Sir Robert Brooke-Popham as his chief Technical Adviser and by Captain Harold Balfour, the British Under Secretary of State for Air, and there were preliminary discussions with Canadian Ministers and the R.C.A.F. and with officials of the Department of Finance and the War Supply Board. Mackenzie King's first formal meeting with the British Mission took place on October 31; Ralston, Rogers, and Howe were with him. Mackenzie King "opened the conference by reading the first paragraph or two of the British Prime Minister's communication to me making clear that the Air Training Scheme had originated with the British Government; was a War Cabinet proposal, an invitation to our Government to co-operate, and that all we had thus far signified was our acceptance in principle and willingness to co-operate. I said I wished to make this clear so that there would be no misunderstanding as to the extent of our commitment." He then observed to the meeting that the Australian and New Zealand Missions "had not yet arrived, pointing out we were proceeding immediately simply to save time, this being the earliest moment at which the British Mission had found it possible to present its views to our Government."

Mackenzie King next asked Riverdale to set out what his Mission had in mind. Riverdale outlined the scheme in its broad aspects and made a statement of cost. Mackenzie King commented later that "this was blithely set forth as what Canada was expected to do. England was to supply the engines for planes. This Lord Riverdale described as a free contribution from England. He ended up by stating that time was all important, and even more important, were lives." Riverdale then called on Balfour, who "in a light, easy and airy manner spoke about the importance of the matter to the Air Ministry, and of the great expense of the war."

When Balfour finished, Mackenzie King "replied immediately to Riverdale saying that he had spoken of time and lives. I would like him to know we were equally appreciative of both; from the point of view of time, it was unfortunate we had not had this scheme put before us at the outset, before we had worked out what we felt our contribution could be." He noted that the existing programme had been prepared after discussions with the British Government and "now this Air Scheme was being proposed in addition over and above what we thought was the measure of our capacity." He "hoped the spirit of the Canadian people would not be crushed by seeking to place upon them responsibilities and burdens greater than they could assume." Mackenzie King said he would "have the Cabinet made aware of what Lord Riverdale had presented to us," and suggested that the Mission continue its discussions with Ministers and officials.

Mackenzie King noted that he "did not spare Riverdale or the Mission, speaking very plainly. I did so in a kindly courteous way, and without becoming in the least heated or confused, always emphasizing that I thought we would get farther in the end by having no misunderstanding at the beginning." He added, "there was nothing in what either Riverdale or Balfour said which was in the least appreciative of Canada's readiness to co-operate. It was a sort of taken-for-granted attitude that it was our duty and obligation, and that the part of the Mission was only to tell us what we would be expected to do."

He told the meeting that "Riverdale's reference to Britain's free contribution was the wrong way around. It was really Canada that was making the contribution, and that this should be kept in mind." In this connection Mackenzie King reflected: "It will never be known what we have saved this country by making clear that Canada has gone into this war of her own volition to co-operate; also what has been saved the British Empire of possible dismemberment as a consequence of this attitude. We would get nowhere if it were for a moment assumed that as a part of the Empire, it was for the central part to tell the outlying parts what they were to do." He went on to observe that "the worst part of the whole business is that this scheme is, in reality, a recruiting scheme for the British Air Force rather than any genuine attempt for any co-operation."

The next day (November 1) Sir Gerald Campbell, the British High Commissioner, had a talk with O. D. Skelton. According to Mackenzie King's record for that day, Campbell told Skelton that all the members of the British Mission felt blue and depressed. Campbell himself had endeavoured to explain away Riverdale's reference the previous day to a "free gift from Britain" as meaning merely the British contribution to the co-operative effort. Skelton also reported that Campbell had said Mackenzie King's phrase "this is not our war" had been a matter of great surprise, that Campbell understood a reference to this phrase had been included in the report which the Mission had sent to London, and that Campbell added he did not know what they would think of it there, or just what it meant. He had also told Skelton one of the members of the Mission had wondered whether the Prime Minister intended to make a similar statement in the House.

Skelton informed Mackenzie King that he had told Campbell it was not Canada's war in the sense that it did not originate in a German threat to Canada or a Canadian pledge to act in eastern Europe, but this did not mean that Canada had not made Great Britain's and France's cause her own. Skelton had reminded Campbell that every member of the Cabinet had backed Canada's going into the war and would favour carrying it on to the fullest extent possible. As regards any statement in Parliament, Skelton had told Campbell that that might safely be left to the Prime Minister.

Mackenzie King was very irritated when he received word of this conversation. He described Riverdale's approach as "an effort to load the entire scheme on the Dominions" and felt that Riverdale "had given his own hand away when he talked about free gift from Britain to Canada, and that the Mission were trying to extricate themselves from the wrong position they were in by giving a wholly false interpretation to my remark that this was not our war, which was made in reply to Riverdale's statement 'we are making this contribution to you.' I had said in reply that so far as there were contributions, it was the other way, and that what we were doing was for the common cause." He "was particularly incensed" that "this remark had been sent on in a communication to England," and that anyone "had asked whether I would make the same statement in Parliament. In other words, implying that we were a lot of children doing what we were doing because the Mother Country was over and above us all, and that I was playing a double role in taking one attitude in public, and really not trying to help in private."

Mackenzie King thought the matter so important that he decided to talk it over with the Governor-General. He saw Lord Tweedsmuir after dinner the same day (November 1). "I let him read Skelton's statement and outlined the facts to him. He said it was perfectly obvious to him what the remark would signify. Said if Canada had declared war against Russia and Britain had offered to give her war materials, in such a case it would have been our war, and obviously it was not our war in the present situation." Mackenzie King told Tweedsmuir that "he found it imperative to make clear where we stood to avoid mistakes later on. That I particularly resented trying to put me into false position with the British government especially in the light of all I have done and am doing." The Governor-General then told him he had "been writing Chamberlain about different matters, and either offered himself to send a word or agreed to my suggestion—I do not remember which—in reference to this particular incident. He told me he would add a postscript to a letter he had written."

Mackenzie King told "the Governor I thought he ought to have a word with Sir Gerald Campbell. In so doing, I said I spoke to him as the representative of the King in a matter which affected relations between two Governments. That I was astonished at Sir Gerald lending himself to any endeavour to misrepresent a situation or to create a difficulty. That I had invited him to be present at the interview expecting that he would be helpful in the event of any differences arising. The Governor said he could not believe Sir Gerald would be misled in a matter of the kind. That he would surely understand what was meant by the remark, and would not let anything go overseas. I said the message was sent through his office, and that was where it ought to have been stopped. He said he would send for him first thing in the morning and speak frankly to him. I told the Governor I was doing all I could to help matters."

After this troubled beginning, real progress began to be made in the negotiations. By November 14, the terms of an agreement in substantially the form in which it was finally accepted were ready for consideration by the Cabinet. The Air Training Plan provided for the training annually of about twenty thousand pilots, observers, and gunners in some sixty-seven training establishments under the direction of the R.C.A.F. with staffs and teaching personnel from all the partner countries; the main British contribution was to be in aircraft for training purposes. The Cabinet was satisfied with the Plan itself but the financial commitment for Canada was much higher than had originally been thought possible and it decided to make acceptance by Canada conditional on a general financial settlement involving greater British purchases in Canada, particularly for wheat, in order to offset some of the cost. Mackenzie King also decided that before he would sign the Agreement, the British Government must make a public announcement that they considered the Air Training Plan the most effective contribution Canada could make to the prosecution of the war. Chamberlain had made this statement in his original proposal and Mackenzie King wanted to have it published as a counter-argument to the advocates of a larger Canadian army.

After the Cabinet meeting on November 14, Mackenzie King saw Riverdale and Balfour and outlined the position of the Canadian Government. They agreed to cable London and seek approval of these two conditions, so that the Agreement could be initialled on November 16. However, the British Government would not accept the Canadian Government's conditions at that time.

On November 25, Sir Gerald Campbell saw Mackenzie King and explained that the United Kingdom would like to have the air training Agreement initialled at once, subject to later agreement on the terms of any announcement about the importance attached by the British Government to the Canadian participation in the plan, and with an understanding that the Agreement would come into operation only after the comprehensive financial negotiations had been concluded satisfactorily between the two governments. The British were not prepared to make a financial settlement until the arrival in London of Graham Towers, the Governor of the Bank of Canada, who had left for England some time previously but had been delayed en route. Campbell explained that the British Government were most anxious to have an agreement initialled while the Australian and New Zealand Missions were still in

Ottawa where they had been for nearly a fortnight, negotiating mainly with the British Mission. The Australians and New Zealanders had no differences with either the United Kingdom or Canada and they wanted to go home. Campbell argued that if they left before an agreement had been announced it might create an impression that there had been differences of views which were responsible for their departure.

Mackenzie King told Campbell "we were somewhat surprised that more consideration had not been shown Canada by the other Missions"; that "neither Australians nor New Zealanders nor any member of the British Mission that I know of, had asked us whether it would inconvenience us or prove embarrassing to us, if any members of the Mission left before the Agreements were initialled. That I thought Australia and New Zealand would do whatever the British Government wished in the matter of delaying a day or two."

As for difficulties arising if the missions left before the Agreement was initialled, Mackenzie King said "all of that could be avoided by the British Government itself agreeing at once to the conditions set forth, and which had been recommended to them by their own Mission." He added that they "could as well determine the matter at once as some weeks later if they really intended to meet it in the end. If they did not intend to meet the conditions in the end, I did not feel we could defend our position before Parliament and the Canadian people in making vast financial commitments without regard to the means by which they were subsequently to be met. As to Towers, I said I thought it was most unfair for Sir Gerald or members of the British Mission or the British Government to suggest for a moment that the matter could not be settled because of his delay in getting across. That, as a matter of fact, it did not require Towers' presence at all in England to have the matter settled."

Mackenzie King explained to Campbell "that the Cabinet had considered this matter very fully . . . and that it had been there agreed that we would use all expedition in getting messages across, but that we must have direct understanding between the British Government and ourselves on the two conditions mentioned before we could sign any agreement." Mackenzie King could see no difference in principle between signing and initialling and "said we were ready to initial today, tomorrow, or any day, once we received word from the British Government that they were prepared to accept the recommendation of the British Mission as understood many days ago, but that all we asked was to be in the same position as Australia and New Zealand.

"Apparently, from what Fairbairn [J. V. Fairbairn, the head of the Australian Mission, who had recently made a broadcast over the C.B.C.]

had said over the radio, there was a complete understanding between the British Government and the Australian as to what they were agreed to do. I gathered from Sir Gerald himself that there had been no misunderstanding at any time between the New Zealand Government and the British Government as to what their mutual obligations were; that all we wished was to be in the same position as New Zealand and Australia before we initialled any agreement.

"I said to Sir Gerald that we knew in addition that the British Government were prepared to stand behind the New Zealand Government financially to enable them to perform their part, and we understood the same might be the case with regard to the Australian Government. We were not asking the British Government to stand behind us in meeting our part of the undertaking. On the other hand, we felt we could not give that undertaking until we were in a position ourselves to see how we were going to be able to meet it, and that the British Government had known from the beginning that that would not be possible until the terms we had spoken of were met." Mackenzie King made it clear that Campbell "would have to tell his Government, until they were settled, I could not alter the position which our Cabinet had agreed was the only one on which we would be prepared to initial an agreement."

When Campbell objected that the departure of the Australian and New Zealand missions might be misunderstood, Mackenzie King said their departure could be explained not as the result of disagreement, but because they were all so close to agreement.

Two days later, on November 27, Mackenzie King himself drafted a statement to the effect that the Missions had completed their discussions and worked out a basis of agreement which was being referred to their respective governments for decision. He then sent for Riverdale and Balfour and the heads of the Australian and New Zealand missions, who came to his office rather expecting "that we would initial. I said to them it was unfortunate members of the Missions had to leave so suddenly, but they would realize it was not our fault that matters could not be developed further before they were leaving. That we had all done the best we could." He then explained why he could not initial the Agreement. "I think the group present were surprised, but Lord Riverdale admitted quite frankly that what I was saying was reasonable and wondered if something else could not be found which would disclose unanimity on the progress thus far attained." Mackenzie King thereupon produced the statement he had drafted and Riverdale "at once said he thought it covered the ground. Balfour agreed and we had the statement typed and given to the press."

Mackenzie King told the British "quite frankly that, as we had not received the assurances asked for in our message to the British Government, we could not think of initialling the Agreement." He also explained that the Canadian Government wished "to have the question of administration fully understood, and nothing left in a way which would permit of subsequent differences of opinion." He noted: "It was an exhausting interview and I felt very tired."

The following day, November 28, after discussions by the Cabinet, Mackenzie King sent a cable to the British Government making clear again that the Agreement could not be concluded until the general financial settlement was reached and defining more precisely what kind of public statement the Canadian Government wished the British Government to make about the supreme importance of air training in the Canadian war effort. This message indicated that when the questions of administration of the Air Training Plan and of identity and command of formations and units in the field—which were being discussed at this time by Norman Rogers, the Minister of National Defence, and Balfour —and the other two conditions were met, the Agreement would be signed. There was no difficulty in making clear that the R.C.A.F. would administer the Air Training Plan; during the following week agreement was reached on a statement for publication as to the importance attached by the British Government to Canadian participation in the Air Training Plan; after Balfour's return to England and the arrival there of Towers early in December, the comprehensive financial terms were settled.

The final hurdle was the question of the identity and command in the field of Canadian airmen trained under the joint plan. The original proposal of September 26 and the draft Agreement had both made provision for the establishment of separate Canadian squadrons in the field. But it was actually not until December 7 that an attempt was made to define the method of achieving this objective. Rogers and Riverdale discussed the question that day and Rogers then wrote a letter to Riverdale setting out his interpretation of their understanding "that Canadian personnel from the Training Plan will, on request from the Canadian Government, be organized in Royal Canadian Air Force units and formations in the field." In his reply the next day Riverdale gave it as his understanding "that Paragraph 15 of the Agreement implies that requests by the Canadian Government for the incorporation in the Royal Canadian Air Force units in the field of Canadian pupils who have been trained under the Dominion Air Training Scheme will, in all circumstances in which it is feasible, be readily accepted by the Government of the United Kingdom."

Both Rogers and Mackenzie King considered Riverdale's reply was entirely unsatisfactory. Mackenzie King noted on December 9 that the British Air Ministry was "trying to keep Canadian squadrons at its disposal, merged into British forces, creating all the trouble in the air field that was created on land with the army in the last war. This must be avoided at all costs and will be by my standing firm on this matter." On December 10, Mackenzie King reflected in a further comment that it was "really shameful the way in which the British Government in these matters seek to evade and undo and to change the meaning of the most definitely understood obligations."

When the Canadian Government made it clear that Riverdale's reply was not satisfactory, the British Mission put forward a new formula on December 14, under which Canada would have to have Canadian ground crews as well as air crews overseas before squadrons would be identified as Canadian and be placed under Canadian command. While the R.C.A.F. was naturally favourable to this formula as it would mean complete Canadian formations both in the air and on the ground, Mackenzie King pointed out that the Agreement had only to do with pilots, observers, and gunners and did not include ground crews, and that the cost of the plan to Canada had been estimated on the assumption that British ground crews would serve Canadian air crews overseas.

After the British formula was considered by the Cabinet, Mackenzie King had Riverdale, Brooke-Popham, and Sir Gerald Campbell come to his office, where, according to his record, he made clear that "the British had sought to meet our wishes, as they had said, by arranging to have some of our ground men trained in England and to have English trained mechanics come to Canada to take the places of ground mechanics needed for our training scheme so as to permit our men to get into the war. I pointed out, as Power had said, that some people would construe this as meaning that they were giving Englishmen safe positions in Canada and sending our men to the front to be killed. I pointed out the Agreement related only to pupils and we must ask the British Government so to construe it. We asked what the objection was and Riverdale mentioned having to make appropriations in Parliament. My reply was that they were getting Canadian pilots which was what they wanted, and they could offset their expenditure on ground men by our expenditure on ground men required for training schools here. Lord Riverdale said they would have to cable, as it raised a new question. He kept saying that we had got down to the one point."

Before the interview concluded on December 14, Mackenzie King took Riverdale aside and told him "we would have to hold to what had really been understood." When Riverdale suggested a cable from Prime Minister to Prime Minister, Mackenzie King "told him if he got this point settled and got authority to sign that he and I could sign the agreement tomorrow. That it would not need a Prime Minister's message. I said I hoped he might succeed in this." Mackenzie King was "glad I held firm last week, as this question raises an issue even larger than the one we thought was at stake."

The next two days provided a fine example of the way Mackenzie King performed when he was determined to get something settled. In the afternoon of December 15 he had Riverdale meet him in his office with Rogers and Ralston also present. Riverdale meanwhile had himself dictated a statement regarding the disposition of trained Canadian air crews which he thought would be appropriate. They found it acceptable with slight modifications. Riverdale then "dictated another statement in our presence to a stenographer we called in, making the revise exact. Repeatedly he said that he was prepared to sign that statement and kept urging the three of us to accept the statement and me, in particular, to agree to do so. I finally said that I would, to some extent over-ruling Ralston in my efforts to reach a satisfactory settlement. After we had all agreed and had shaken hands on getting matters settled, Lord Riverdale said he would like just to show the statement to his colleagues and would be back very shortly."

Instead of coming back, he "phoned to say that Sir Gerald Campbell and one of his other colleagues thought that, as cables had been sent last night to London after our discussion of yesterday, he should not sign until an answer had come from London." Mackenzie King then urged Riverdale to telephone London, and, after some objections, he agreed to try.

Mackenzie King received word during the evening that the call had been made to London and he might expect a letter very shortly. "I said to myself at once," he noted, "the purpose of the letter meant another objection and delay. I was not surprised, therefore, when a letter came to find that I was right in this." The letter contained a draft of a letter to Rogers in the following terms: 'On the understanding that the numbers to be incorporated at any time would be the subject of agreement between the two Governments, the United Kingdom Government accept in principle as being consonant with the intention of Paragraph 15 of the Memorandum of Agreement that the United Kingdom Government, on the request of the Canadian Government, would agree to the incorporation of Canadian pupils when passing out from the Air Training Scheme into units of the Royal Canadian Air Force in the field. The detailed method by which this will be done will be arranged by an Inter-Governmental Committee for this purpose under Paragraph 15. It would be a condition that the factor governing the numbers of such pupils to be so incorporated at any one time should be the financial contribution which the Canadian Government have already declared themselves ready to make towards the cost of the Training Scheme.'

This draft letter Mackenzie King described as "impossible" and he "immediately sent for Ralston and Howe. Did not like to trouble Rogers to come to the office [Rogers was ill] but read him the letter. We all agreed that what was proposed would not be a satisfactory answer to Rogers' letter and indeed I felt, and the others as well, indignant that the ground should again be shifted. Previous discussion had all been on the feasibility, practicability etc., of having Canadian pilots and airmen work with British service crews. . . . Now the message implied what we have all along thought, that the Air Ministry was trying to exact more in the way of money out of the Government of Canada, or make the position such as to render impossible command by Canadians where service crews were British.

"After discussing the matter with Ralston and Howe, I thought it would be preferable to get our position on record in reply to Lord Riverdale's letter rather than to leave any further possible doubt by further discussions. I accordingly dictated a lengthy letter setting out the whole situation. Ralston made some revisions strengthening the wording. I then sent for Lord Riverdale and he came bringing Sir Robert Brooke-Popham with him. They arrived about 10. I told him in the presence of my colleagues and Sir Robert Brooke-Popham that I was sorry I could not regard his letter as satisfactory. That the last paragraph had raised a new issue altogether, one which seemed to indicate that the Air Ministry attached more importance to money than to human lives. That I was really astonished at the answer. That I had thought it best to answer him by letter myself so that there could be no mistake . . . as to who had been responsible for the fact that we could not sign today, and for further delays.

"In the course of our conversation, I said I thought we had come to the point where I would have to communicate with Mr. Chamberlain direct. Lord Riverdale said he hoped I would do so; that it would be helpful. Lord Riverdale's whole attitude was that he, himself, was quite prepared to sign and thought the afternoon statement satisfactorily covered the situation.

"While I was talking to Lord Riverdale, Ralston and Howe talked to Sir Robert Brooke-Popham. He also joined in the conversation with myself. He interpreted the financial request as being the means of determining the numbers of squadrons which could be designated as R.C.A.F. squadrons. Kept trying to get from Howe and Ralston just how many they would want. Ralston kept coming back to the point of command and the care of our men. That when enlisting large numbers of pilots in Canada, the first thing they would ask would be whether they would be under a Canadian commander. Whether they could look to being in Canadian squadrons rather than in squadrons commanded by British officers. Ralston pointed out quite clearly that, unless there was very clear understanding on these matters on the say Canada should have, there would be a fear among our men that they would be sent into such places as Passchendaele in the last war, and their lives unnecessarily sacrificed. I stated that I would have to give Parliament assurance that we had guarded against this kind of thing. I made clear it was only reasonable that we should ask for this when we were contributing the lives we were.

"At one stage in the conversation, I heard Brooke-Popham say, as the service crews were so much larger than the pilots and air crews, if Canadian squadrons were being serviced by British crews, it would mean that there would be a larger number of 'Englishmen' under the command of Canadians. I said nothing at the time, but made a very careful note of the remark which Ralston and Howe had also noticed and which really, as we said afterwards, let the cat out of the bag. As we had thought, what is really in the minds of the British Air Force is to keep command in their own hands, though they have been obliged to admit, on many occasions, that Canadian pilots have more skill and judgment than their own. In view of this remark, I made up my mind we would have to hold out more strongly than ever against any doubt as to what the position would be once our men were across the seas."

Before the conversation ended, Riverdale said they would have to telephone London again as "the letter he had written had been dictated over the telephone from the Air Ministry." Mackenzie King emphasized the need of haste.

Mackenzie King spent until two o'clock in the morning preparing a cable to Chamberlain and noted: "I was not altogether sorry to have a chance to get the truth of this important situation on record. Chamberlain himself is in France. Were he in England, I am sure a reply would come instantly." In fact no reply came until after the Agreement had been signed and this message did not influence the negotiations.

The next day (December 16) Mackenzie King worked all day both on his broadcast announcement of the Air Training Plan and on getting

Riverdale to sign the Agreement. In his diary he wrote: "I told Skelton early in the morning that I thought I would have it settled before the day was over. He seemed to think I was optimistic, but I felt we must not let the matter drag on." He had no word from Riverdale either in the morning or in the early afternoon; finally Ralston telephoned to find out if any word had come, and to let Mackenzie King know that he was hoping to get away to Montreal around 6.30, but that he would stay longer if necessary. Mackenzie King noted: "No words can describe the way in which he has worked. When I told him that nothing had been received he asked me if there was anything he could do. We discussed whether it would not be better for him or for me to get in touch with Riverdale. We both agreed that it might look like anxiety on our part if I were to 'phone him. That it would be better for him, Ralston, to let Riverdale know that he was anxious to get away this evening, and have a word with him as to whether matters could not be concluded."

Shortly afterwards Mackenzie King had word from Ralston that Campbell and Brooke-Popham were in his office going over a statement together. Mackenzie King told Ralston to let Riverdale know that tomorrow was his birthday and that he "would immensely appreciate it if this matter could be cleared up before this old year of my life was out. That I would like to be able to give to the press some word that I would be broadcasting tomorrow night." Mackenzie King wanted to make the announcement of the signing of the Air Training Agreement before the announcement of the landing of the First Canadian Division in Britain which was to be made on December 19 or 20, and he also felt he would like to have the Agreement signed on his birthday, though this latter consideration was probably not very important.

After Campbell and Brooke-Popham left Ralston, the latter telephoned Mackenzie King to tell him what they had worked out. Campbell and Brooke-Popham were to see Riverdale who was then to call Mackenzie King. When no call came after some time, Mackenzie King telephoned Ralston who agreed to find out from Riverdale if matters could not be settled before Ralston left for Montreal. Ralston was to emphasize to Riverdale the importance of announcing "the Joint Training Agreement before any announcement was made with respect to the troops. Otherwise the value of both announcements would be lost. I said to stress the point that I was sure the British Government would want to have both made as effective as possible, and particularly because of its effect upon the enemy, it would be better to have one announcement follow the other with a couple of days intervening if that was at all possible. That effect would be correspondingly good on the spirits of the

English and the French. To let him know it had ceased to be a technical question, and it was one now in which both Governments were deeply concerned; that he, as head of the Mission, should exercise his own authority."

Ralston gave Riverdale this message and reported to Mackenzie King that Riverdale would come to see him later in the day. Somewhat later, as Riverdale had not been heard from, Ralston telephoned again but could not reach him. Mackenzie King then told Ralston to leave for Montreal and "that I would look after matters myself. He phoned from the airport just before getting on his plane, and I said I would communicate with him in Montreal as to any progress we might make."

By this time Mackenzie King's Principal Secretary, Arnold Heeney, had discovered that Riverdale was dining with Sir Shuldham Redfern, the Secretary to the Governor-General. Though it was then nearly nine o'clock, Mackenzie King was determined to get the matter settled that night. He noted he had made up his mind "that I must use every possible means of getting the Agreement signed before morning," and he accordingly "decided that I would ring up Lord Riverdale at Redfern's, and ask him to see me at once; also that I would ring up the Governor-General and ask him to see me immediately and get the whole situation placed before him as Representative of the King, and as one who could give Chamberlain the true story. I felt, too, that he might be able to assist in bringing the others together." When Riverdale came to the telephone he wished Mackenzie King "a happy birthday. I then told him I was most anxious to see him as soon as possible. He said that he would be along in the morning between 11 and 12. I thanked him for this, but said that that would be too late; that I thought we must get this plan settled tonight. He then said the trouble was he could not get his team together for a time, that they were scattered. Some of them had gone to a game of hockey, others were at dinner, etc. but he would try to get them all together in the morning. I said I was not in the least concerned about the team, that it was he, himself, I wanted to speak to, and hoped that he would not mind my saying I was speaking to him now as Prime Minister of Canada, asking him to come and see me at once in my office on a matter of the greatest importance in connection with the war.

"I spoke about the formula that had been worked out with Ralston. He said he himself thought it ought to be accepted, and that it was all right. I told him he would have to take responsibility if it were not settled, and that I thought consequences were too serious for any time to be lost. Also that I felt it was important that, if further time were lost, the King should know where the responsibility lay, and also Mr. Chamberlain, without any possible misunderstanding. I said I was therefore going down immediately to see the Governor-General, as the King's Representative, and place the whole situation before him. Riverdale then said: 'I will do my best to get the team together.' I said: 'Never mind the team, come yourself,' or words to that effect. He then said that while I was at Government House, he would be on his way to the office."

When Mackenzie King called Government House, he "had quite a time getting anyone to answer the phone. Some boy went and searched for an A.D.C. and word came back that he was having some difficulty finding an A.D.C. and that it was thought that the Governor was in bed. I said I wished to see the Governor whether he was in bed or not. To say that I would be down immediately, and must see him on the most important matter I had ever had occasion to discuss with him." Mackenzie King did not wait to get any message back but telephoned Arnold Heeney to meet him at Government House. When he reached Government House about 10 o'clock, Redfern met him and took him to the Governor-General's bedroom.

"The Governor was propped on his pillows looking pretty frail. He extended greetings on my birthday tomorrow. When I thanked him for the letter which had come by hand in the morning, which I said I was sorry not to have had a chance to reply to through the day, he talked a little of his health and then, finally, I said to him I had come on the most important matter I had ever had occasion to speak to him of."

Mackenzie King told Tweedsmuir what had happened and observed that "at different stages in our talk together, the Governor said it was insanity on the part of these men to delay the matter for a moment. He said: 'You must make him sign at once.' I said that that was my feeling, but how to make Lord Riverdale perform the physical act of signature was another problem. However, I knew that he, himself, was ready enough to sign, and if he, the Governor, was agreeable, I would like to be able to tell Riverdale that it was his, the Governor's view, that he, Riverdale, should sign."

Mackenzie King emphasized that he "was speaking to him as Representative of the King about a matter which affected the King's forces at a time of war; also that I wanted him to be in a position to let Chamberlain know the exact situation and to have his view as to what he thought Chamberlain would wish." Tweedsmuir felt sure Chamberlain would want to have the matter settled at once.

"When I showed him the communication Riverdale had sent me [the draft letter of December 15], he at once said it was outrageous to raise the question of money; that the principle related to the identity and command of all pupils in the field. That that had nothing to do with the question of money. I told him then what Brooke-Popham had said about Canadian air pilots, air crews, being identified as Canadian, while serviced by English crews. That this would mean a Canadian might be commanding a much larger number of Englishmen. The Governor said that was perfectly outrageous. I told him, too, how Brooke-Popham had contended it was essential to have ground crews as well as air crews of the same force. The Governor said that was ridiculous, he personally knew all about these matters, and that there was no reason why Canadian air crews should not be serviced by English ground crews.

"On every point the Governor was 100 per cent with me. He asked me if there was anything he, himself, could do. I said I had debated a good deal in my mind whether I should advise him to do anything or not. I did feel, however, that the situation affected so much the British forces as well as our own that the King and the Prime Minister of England would be alike concerned, that I thought I would not be suggesting anything out of the way if I asked him to send for Brooke-Popham and have a word with him concerning the matter. This was after the Governor had said to me: This is not a technical matter at all. It is a matter of high policy. You must pursue it on that line. I said I thought he could explain this better to Brooke-Popham than perhaps anyone else.

"He then said: 'I will have him come in the morning.' I looked at the Governor and said: 'In the morning? I am afraid that will not do. This matter must be settled tonight!' He then said: 'I will get him at once,' and asked me if I knew where he was. I said: 'No, except I understood he had gone to a hockey match.'

"I said to the Governor: 'Imagine it becoming known that this Agreement had been held up one week over this—it is a clause which should have been settled by the word "yes" on the 8th of December, and now it is to be held over for days longer because men cannot be brought together because they are at dinner parties, or hockey matches, etc.' I then said the matter would have to be settled between Riverdale and myself if the other men could not be reached. I was going to take this line with Riverdale. He said I was entirely right, and asked me if, when I went downstairs, I would ask Redfern to get in touch with Brooke-Popham at once and have him come immediately to Government House. I then thanked the Governor, and left to see Riverdale at the office. By that time it was considerably after 10."

Mackenzie King went from Government House to his office where Riverdale arrived just before 11 o'clock. He told Riverdale he thought they "must settle this matter at once ourselves." Riverdale admitted he

Air Training Plan

felt the statement "prepared by Ralston and himself was quite correct" as a basis for his reply to Rogers. That statement read: "On the understanding that the numbers to be incorporated or organized at any time will be the subject of discussion between the two Governments, the United Kingdom Government accepts in principle as being consonant with the intention of Paragraph 15 of the Memorandum of Agreement, that the United Kingdom Government, on the request of the Canadian government, would arrange that the Canadian pupils, when passing out from the Training Scheme, would be incorporated in or organized as units and formations of the Royal Canadian Air Force in the field. The detailed methods by which this can be done would be arranged by an Inter-Governmental Committee for this purpose under Paragraph 15."

Riverdale confided that "he had a lot of trouble with his own people. I said they would not be held responsible but he would, and he must take responsibility. He said: 'I agree, but it would help me a lot if you could get Ralston to drop the word "the" in front of the word "Canadian." That Brooke-Popham seemed to feel it had a sinister significance. That Canadians could not go unless all of them were in Canadian formations.'"

Mackenzie King pointed out the numbers affected had to be discussed between the two Governments and this "made it quite clear that it was not expected that every individual should go in," but added that he personally "thought whether the 'the' was in or not, the sentence meant exactly the same." However, Mackenzie King would not make the change without consulting Ralston and Riverdale asked him to "try to persuade Ralston to agree to knocking out the 'the.'" Mackenzie King told Riverdale "if he would send for a stenographer, and get under way with signing, I would take up the matter further, but I wanted it understood if the 'the' went out, the Agreement would be signed before midnight. He then said he would agree to that."

Riverdale left the room while Mackenzie King telephoned Ralston, and, after giving him an account of what had happened since he left for Montreal, spoke to him about omitting the word 'the.' Mackenzie King said he "thought it meant the same thing whether it was in or out. He [Ralston] said that he did not wish to hold the matter up, if that was all that was still standing. That he would agree to have it go out, providing I held to the ground that the two things meant the same. I said I would certainly do so. That I thought we need not allow the matter to be delayed further for that one word. I said I would mention to Lord Riverdale that he had left it to me to decide, so that this might carry additional weight with Brooke-Popham. This was agreed between us, and I then had Lord Riverdale return and said Ralston allowed me to decide what should be done, and that, if it would make it satisfactory all round and help him to answer the significant part of Rogers' letter, I would agree to the 'the' being struck out. Lord Riverdale agreed he would sign on that understanding. He had a stenographer come in and dictated the letter to Rogers, on a plain sheet, heading it 'House of Commons,' dating it December 16. I kept stressing my desire to get the whole matter settled before the year was out."

Mackenzie King had Heeney bring in copies of the Agreement for signature, and "sent for Skelton to come up so as to get off his cables to Australia and New Zealand. Lord Riverdale said he would like to have a word with his men before actually signing. I said to him: 'We must take no chances on that.' However we waited for Brooke-Popham. When he did not come, I had them phone Government House where he was with the Governor-General to let him know that Lord Riverdale was waiting for him at the office. As we got on toward midnight, I said we could not wait—must not wait any longer."

They were about to begin the signing of the Agreement when Brooke-Popham arrived. He came into the office as "twelve o'clock was striking. Arnold Heeney was with them, and was the first to shake hands with me and wish me a happy birthday. Lord Riverdale was the next, and Sir Robert Brooke-Popham also extended his wishes. We then had a word as to whether the agreement should be dated the 16th or the 17th. It had been previously agreed that it would be signed on the 16th. Lord Riverdale said for me to fix whatever date I wished. I said as it was now exactly the 17th when we were signing, I would prefer to date the documents exactly on the day on which they were being signed, and would make it the 17th."

Mackenzie King noted that, when Brooke-Popham arrived, "Riverdale said to him: 'the Prime Minister has helped me to reach an agreement. He has agreed to strike out the word 'the.' Brooke-Popham said, 'That is very satisfactory. That makes the Agreement satisfactory as far as I am concerned,' or words to that effect. I said I had done so because Lord Riverdale agreed with me that the meaning was the same whether the 'the' was in or not.

"I should say that I never saw a man look more deflated, in a way, than Sir Robert Brooke-Popham did. He looked indeed as if he had been spanked. His face was very red and his manner very crushed. I think having the Governor-General speak to him was something he had never anticipated, and having been Governor of a Crown Colony himself, he would realize the significance of the word of a Governor in a self-governing Dominion, given in the name of the King."

Mackenzie King added: "I would have stayed with this matter all night to get it settled, if need to do so had arisen."

The final diary entry for the day (December 16) reads: "After all had left the office I phoned Ralston to let him know that the Agreement had been signed. I do not recall ever having heard anyone laugh more heartily. He was really joyous: tremendously relieved. I also phoned Rogers, getting him out of bed, to let him know how matters had been settled, feeling he would sleep all the better for that result. His voice indicated how tired he is but he was pleased to get the final word."

On Sunday, December 17, Mackenzie King spent the entire day working on his broadcast on the Air Training Plan which he delivered that evening. The broadcast referred to the importance attached to the Air Training Plan by the British Government in these words: "The United Kingdom Government has since informed us that, considering present and future requirements, it feels that participation in the Air Training Scheme would provide for more effective assistance towards ultimate victory than any other form of military co-operation which Canada can give. At the same time the United Kingdom Government wishes it to be clearly understood that it would welcome no less heartily the presence of Canadian land forces in the theatre of war at the earliest possible moment." The broadcast continued: "You will recall that, on September 19th, the government announced that a Division was being organized for service overseas, and, as you are aware, no time is being lost in our endeavour to meet the wish of the United Kingdom for the early despatch of an Expeditionary Force."[1]

In fact the expeditionary force had arrived in Britain that very day. At the close of his sixty-fifth birthday that evening, Mackenzie King wrote in his diary: "I felt immensely relieved having both the Agreement concluded, and the broadcast over. It was certainly a memorable birthday. I suppose no more significant Agreement has ever been signed by the Government of Canada, or signature placed in the name of Canada to a definitely defined obligation in human life and in dollars and cents. I could not have put my signature to it, had I not believed, that, in the end, it meant the saving of life and the earlier restoration of peace."

[1] W. L. Mackenzie King, *Canada at Britain's Side* (Toronto, 1941), p. 68.

CHAPTER FOUR

The Wartime Election

AT THE BEGINNING of 1940, with the expeditionary force safely overseas and the Air Training Plan agreed upon, Mackenzie King's most immediate concern was the timing of a general election. Under the constitution an election was required some time in 1940 (the House having been elected in 1935), and he had made it clear at the beginning of the war that he would not consider prolonging the life of Parliament as had been done in the First World War. He was, however, anxious to choose a date for the election which, if possible, would not conflict with an active phase of the war, particularly as he was determined that members of the armed forces should be able to vote wherever they were. The choice of a date had been complicated by the undertaking Mackenzie King had given in reply to Manion on the last day of the special war session on September 12, 1939, that Parliament would meet again before an election. Mackenzie King later described this undertaking as one of the most foolish commitments he had ever made.

At the first Cabinet meeting in the New Year, on January 3, the Ministers decided that the promised session (which was to open on January 25) would be concerned with the war only, and that priority would be given to legislation for the service vote. It was decided also to make no commitment as to the date of the election on the ground of "not knowing what serious developments might emerge."

Though resolved to give priority to the prosecution of the war and the timing of the election in relation to the war, Mackenzie King had two other objectives at this time. He wanted to make progress in establishing Unemployment Insurance and in negotiations for the St. Lawrence Waterway. Progress on the St. Lawrence had become possible when Mitchell Hepburn of Ontario withdrew his objection in November 1939, and the defeat of Duplessis in November 1939 had removed the main obstacle to agreement with the provinces on an amendment to the constitution to bring Unemployment Insurance under federal jurisdiction.

On January 5, Mackenzie King noted in his diary that he believed "we can now get the consent of Ontario, Quebec, New Brunswick and

Alberta. If we do not get the latter I would go ahead notwithstanding. Parliament and the public will appreciate the necessity of having Unemployment Insurance to help to meet the post-war conditions. The contribution will be easily paid during the years of prosperity and it would be two years before benefits can be paid out under the Act. If we succeed in putting through both the Unemployment Insurance and the St. Lawrence Waterway development, it will make a pretty good record for the present administration in this Parliament."

There was in fact no problem about Ontario because, as early as 1938, all the provinces except Alberta, Quebec, and New Brunswick had agreed to a constitutional amendment to establish federal jurisdiction over Unemployment Insurance. On January 8, C. G. Power told Mackenzie King that Adelard Godbout, the Premier of Quebec, was favourable; and Mackenzie King himself secured the concurrence of the Governments of Alberta and New Brunswick. Actually he had more difficulty in getting all his colleagues committed to proceed with Unemployment Insurance. The main objection was from Ralston on the ground of the cost in time of war. "It was," Mackenzie King noted on January 16, "a real fight, but I have the satisfaction of knowing, if the measure is enacted, that it is due to the fact that I have taken a definite stand in Council."

As late as January 15, Mackenzie King told the Governor-General he expected the session of Parliament to continue into May with an election in June. The first suggestion of an earlier date for the election came on January 16 when Mackenzie King had a long interview with Power who strongly favoured "the earliest possible appeal to the country, fearing, as I do, that once fighting begins on a large scale, it may be difficult to bring on the campaign, and there will be a drive for National Government." Later that day the Cabinet discussed the attitude to be taken if the Opposition should prove to be contentious once the session opened. Mackenzie King rejected a suggestion that Manion might be provoked into providing a pretext for dissolution; he insisted the Government must proceed with a sense of "the grave responsibility we were under in having an election at this time; that I was all for doing everything in decency and in order, maintaining a dignified attitude throughout the session." But he would "make clear I would not stand for a battle in Parliament, while lives were being sacrificed at the front; that, if we could not carry on the business of Parliament in an orderly fashion," the Government would call an election in February or March.

In the Cabinet meeting on January 18, Mackenzie King had a long and difficult discussion on the St. Lawrence Waterway with Ralston who objected to diverting funds for this purpose in wartime though he finally admitted he was impressed by the argument about retaining the goodwill of the United States. The Government decided to go ahead.

Just as Mackenzie King was leaving his office after the Cabinet meeting he was told that a Resolution had been passed by the Ontario Legislature by a vote of 44 to 10 condemning the war effort of the federal Government. "When I got into the hall," he noted, "Ralston was going by and had had a word with Skelton, who had told him of the Resolution. I called him back to speak about it. He said to me that perhaps I would now consider not trying to do more to oblige Mr. Hepburn: I would see how little gratitude or co-operation might be expected from that quarter."

For his own part Mackenzie King "felt, first of all, how extraordinary it was that such a Resolution should be passed by a Legislature, but, even more, how extraordinary that any Liberals, worthy of the name, could have supported a resolution of the kind. It shows how completely Hepburn has become a dictator, and how fearful men have become of not bowing to his will and word. I felt no concern about the Resolution, except for the unpleasant kind of campaign which it foreshadows—a campaign in which every effort will be made to make it as personal and contemptible as it is possible for men of Hepburn's and Drew's ilk to make it."

Later that evening Mackenzie King discussed the situation with Lapointe and Norman Rogers. They agreed it would mean an immediate general election. Mackenzie King felt that the Government was "in a very strong position from one end of the country to the other. That Hepburn's action is on all fours with Duplessis'. That he has been living in an atmosphere of groups around him in Toronto; is filled with his own prejudice and hate; and is entirely blind to the sentiment in other parts of Canada. I believe an appeal to the country will bring us back as strong, if not stronger, than we are at present."

He thought "Hepburn's action has given to me and my colleagues and to the party here just what is needed to place beyond question the wisdom of an immediate election and the assurance of a victory for the Government. What really has helped to take an enormous load off my mind is that it justified an immediate appeal, avoiding thereby all the contention of a session known to be immediately preceding an election." An election at once, moreover, would "probably defeat wholly the intent that Drew and Hepburn have very likely had in mind, namely, dissolving the provincial house on an issue of more being done in the war by a Union Government." But "the greatest relief of all is the probability of having the election over before the worst of the fighting begins in Europe. I have dreaded having to choose the moment for the campaign and specially to choose it at a time when human lives are being slaughtered by hundreds of thousands, if not by millions. In this way, we can probably have the election over before the spring campaign in Europe begins. If it does come on, it will give the country all the stronger reason for supporting an Administration that is as united and as powerful as our own. Also it will enable the soldiers' vote to be taken before they go to the front and while most of the men are still in Canada."

On January 22, Mackenzie King discussed a dissolution with the members of the War Committee and found all were agreed on its advisability except "Ralston who seemed to feel the Government should present its case, being a good one, to Parliament and fight it out on the floor of the House." Mackenzie King pointed out the dangers of this course, including the possibility of a dissolution in Ontario and a campaign there for a 'National Government.' He agreed that should a dissolution occur the Government would be charged with running away from criticism, but reminded his colleagues they would be "running into the arms of those who were our masters, not away from them. We were not asking to have our time extended, but were asking to have it ended altogether, if the people had no confidence in us and had more confidence in anyone else."

Mackenzie King was reticent about disclosing his real intentions to the whole Cabinet because he feared a leak to the press. Knowing how bitterly the Conservatives would attack a dissolution without a session, Mackenzie King derived some comfort from reading a statement made at Vancouver by Grattan O'Leary, the editor of the Conservative Ottawa *Journal*, that an immediate election was desirable.

The preparations for the opening of the session were made on the assumption that there would, at least, be legislation to provide for the service vote before dissolution. On the morning of Friday, January 25, the day Parliament met, Mackenzie King was still making final revisions in the Speech from the Throne when the thought came to him that he "ought to bring on the election at once, and that it would be a mistake to keep in the paragraph forecasting the Bill to provide for the soldiers' vote." He consulted Lapointe on the telephone and found him "a little doubtful about taking the passage out, but I told him we could not tell what might develop, and I did not want to have a promise there which was unfulfilled.

"I then said I thought we should not wait till Monday; that we might find some motion would be introduced to the effect that the Government should not go to the country until after certain matters have been investigated. Lapointe said that he was in agreement with whatever I would do. I told him I would like to feel that he also agreed with this step. He said that he did. Asked if we should tell the Cabinet. I was doubtful about that. He was also. He suggested possibility of talking with Ralston who did not like going too soon. I told him this was a matter which I had to decide myself."

Mackenzie King telephoned Lapointe a little later to say he had now definitely made up his mind that it was better to dissolve that day. Lapointe said there would be an uproar and some protest in the House to which Mackenzie King replied that he would then move the adjournment of the House. He did not go to the Cabinet meeting that morning, and it was shortly after noon when he sent word to Lapointe to tell the Cabinet of his decision to have the Governor-General announce in the Speech from the Throne that there would be an immediate dissolution. He then communicated with the Governor-General about the change in the speech. At three o'clock when Parliament assembled, Mackenzie King met Lord Tweedsmuir and found him "immensely pleased that the secret of the dissolution had been so well kept."

The announcement of an immediate election in the Speech from the Throne was "certainly a real surprise to all who were present. My sight was too poor," Mackenzie King wrote, "to see the expressions on the faces of many until I put on my glasses, but it was quite clear that it had taken all present as a complete surprise. I think everyone had been banking on a session, in which everything would be made so difficult that we would have to dissolve and appear to be driven to the country."

In the House of Commons, after its members had returned from hearing the Speech from the Throne in the Senate chamber, Mackenzie King "went through the proceedings as if nothing exceptional were likely to happen, until I came to move the adjournment." He "then asked if I might make a statement in regard to a paragraph from the Speech from the Throne, concerning immediate dissolution." He added that "Manion was particularly bitter and nasty. Complained especially about not having been given a copy of the Speech in advance. I am quite certain that, had he had it an hour before, there would have been a real row either in the Commons or Senate, or both, before we got very far. He could not have been much nastier. The speech he made was clearly from material he intended to use on Monday and gave the best possible evidence of why we should dissolve at once. Up till six, I think the House was too stunned to believe that we really intended to dissolve tonight." As soon as possible after the House adjourned at six o'clock, the members of the Cabinet met. They adopted an Order recommending the dissolution and Mackenzie King took it to Government House himself where it was signed at seven minutes past seven.

A caucus of the Liberal members and Senators was held the day after the dissolution. Mackenzie King "began by telling them that a week or more ago I would have been as surprised as they were, had I dreamt that Parliament would not be in session at this time," and pointed out that, had he not accepted the Ontario Resolution as a challenge, "the epithet 'cowardice,' which was now applied for dissolving Parliament, would have been applied for continuing on under such a censure. I pointed out it was evident from Manion's speech, and what others were saying, just what we might have expected had the session begun with this little campaign started from the outside. That we would have met with some amendments which would have lined up all the Opposition, and, if we had then dissolved, it would have been said we had gone to the country to escape a vote of censure, investigations, criticism, etc. I thought the best evidence that we had taken the right step was that all those who were opposed to us were condemning us for having taken it. If it had served their purpose they would not have been disappointed. It was because their own motives and plans were so completely frustrated that they were as violent as they were."

He next spoke to the caucus "about the lines on which I proposed this campaign should be conducted. I said I would expect every man to be one hundred percent loyal to myself and the ministry. There could be no other than Mackenzie King Liberals as candidates, who would be recognized as such; that if there was any man in the room who did not feel he could be one hundred percent loyal to myself and colleagues, and to our policies, I would ask him to leave at once; that I did not believe there were any such, and, later, I said the evidence of this was that none had left. I went further and I said that they would all be tempted to say that they would pledge themselves to favour National Government; that any who took that step I would not regard as supporters of either myself or the party; that I believed National Government was the first step toward dictatorship—the kind of thing we had in Italy, Germany and Russia. . . . I believed in British institutions, freedom of debate, freedom of discussion, etc., in a government and in opposition, and intended to make the battle of this campaign on those lines."

He went on to compare this election in wartime with Lincoln's election during the American Civil War when "Lincoln had said that now that the elections were over they must try to bind the nation together and forget the difficulties that the election had occasioned. That he he had not planted a single thorn in the breast of anyone through the whole campaign. I told them that I intended to conduct the campaign on those lines. That I did not intend to plant thorns in the breast of anyone. If I could not win without that, I would not win at all. I felt the country would need binding together in the future, and I was not going to do anything to destroy that power."

In concluding, he spoke of maintaining the liberties of the people and defending freedom within Canada as well as the battle for the greater freedom of the world and, finally, drew attention to the great strength of the party in Parliament and the country. He was given "a great ovation."

After the caucus, Mackenzie King received the press and was told that Manion had issued a statement in which he had promised to form a government of all the leading intellects of all parties. Mackenzie King told the reporters "that they had better ask him [Manion] who the best brains were he intended to take in, that the people were entitled to know in advance. That the personnel of my Government was known; it was the present Government that I intended should carry on. I gave them to understand that the election would probably be on the 26th of March; also that I did not intend to leave my post of duty here, even at the risk of suffering politically through not touring around the country; that I had to watch Canada's war effort at headquarters."

The election campaign did not begin at once; but immediate provision was made, under the War Measures Act, to enable the members of the armed forces to vote. Mackenzie King spent several days persuading one or two of his colleagues who wished to retire to remain in the Government, so that an unbroken front would be presented to the country. He decided he would confine his campaigning to broadcasts from Ottawa in February with the possibility of having some meetings in March. He felt that 'National Government' was the only cry of the Opposition with any appeal. On January 27 he noted that "Manion is declaring for a National Government. That bait may catch large numbers." From the outset he decided to stress two notes: "Win the war" and "Preserve Canadian unity."

It was not until February 1 that Mackenzie King began to consider what he should say in his first national broadcast, to take place on the 7th. He was not at all satisfied with what had already been prepared for him and "felt discouraged at the thought of really having again to prepare all these broadcasts myself." He had great difficulty in getting this first broadcast phrased as he wanted it. However, in the end he felt some satisfaction. "One thing I felt particularly pleased about," he wrote, "was that I had been able to speak my mind. To disclose what has been back of my direction of affairs in the last few years and, particularly, to make the stand for national unity, which I feel is the all-important thing. Those who fail to see this, whether it be in the affairs of a party or of a nation, miss the foundation of everything. My whole life has been bound up in this effort." He felt that if the country would stand behind "a war effort which is based on national unity," with "a support that is general from one end of Canada to the other, that, more than all else that has hitherto been accomplished, would establish Canada as a nation, and a powerful nation at that—a nation whose voice will be increasingly heeded by other nations through years to come."

On the morning of February 6, Mackenzie King had barely begun the day's work when he received word from Government House that Lord Tweedsmuir had met with an accident; this turned out to be a stroke from which he did not recover. For the next few days, much of Mackenzie King's time and thought were taken up with Tweedsmuir's illness, death, and funeral, in every aspect of which he took the closest interest which is faithfully recorded in his diary. Tweedsmuir died on Sunday, February 11. Mackenzie King and Lapointe broadcast tributes the same evening and all Liberal political broadcasts were called off for the rest of the week, although Manion refused to agree to a political truce. The first three days of the week were taken up with arrangements for the state funeral and the funeral itself, every detail of which was supervised by Mackenzie King personally.

Immediately after Tweedsmuir's death, Chief Justice Duff was sworn as Administrator and a decision was reached not to recommend a new Governor until after the election. On February 15 Mackenzie King wrote to the King. He "felt I should make quite clear my constitutional right to make an immediate appointment, also on the ground of public policy, which right I am prepared to forego during the period of the election. Also, making clear that it is the Prime Minister who submits names for the King's approval; not the King who submits names to the Prime Minister." This constitutional point is now well established; but in 1940 it was not so clearly understood by the public.

On February 16, Mackenzie King listened to Manion's first broadcast on the election, which he described as "mostly a bitter complaint at my dissolution of Parliament, and doing him and his friends out of opportunity of investigating matters that they were not prepared definitely to specify. . . . He made a plea for a nondescript government, to which he said leaders of both parties would be invited, but he called on the public to condemn the present Government. How any member of a Government that has been condemned by the people could enter a National Government led by himself, is something that apparently he has not foreseen." Mackenzie King did not think it would "affect seriously the position of our party."

After the usual tribulation in preparation, Mackenzie King delivered his second national broadcast on February 21. When it was over he wrote, characteristically: "I think the speech itself was better prepared, but I regret tremendously having omitted a sentence or two."

There were only two days until the third broadcast—this one on 'National Government.' Mackenzie King felt it was a crime to be working on so important a subject under such heavy pressure and added that he would have given anything to have a week to prepare it. The text was being changed right up to the moment of delivery. After it was delivered, his own verdict was that "the broadcast has completely destroyed Manion's appeal on the score of Union Government. The press will see that and will drop the Union Government idea, and will probably become abusive to me personally, and make the attack that I am thinking more of the party than of the State, or something of that kind. What I must bring out is the importance of sharing responsibility in a time of war." He added that "Manion's generalship has been as bad as it can be. He has left the ground of his own party to go on to strange and unknown territory, to form alliances with those who were his political enemies, who will not join with him. Meanwhile, he has really betrayed his friends and his position as Leader of the Opposition. I am sure it means not only a humiliating defeat of his party but the end of his leadership. It is a great relief to have this broadcast over and the Union Government aspect dealt with, and thereby, a real lead given."

The key passage in this broadcast was Mackenzie King's appeal for an unquestioned mandate for his Government. "I am sure," he said, "you will not wish either on the days immediately following the election, or so long as the war continues, to have the Government of this country busy with bickerings and bargainings between opposing groups when its whole effort should be devoted to the prosecution of the war.

"I want to say to you, my fellow-countrymen, very earnestly, that the times through which we are passing are such that no government, except it be a government enjoying the most complete confidence of the people of Canada, can hope to meet the grave needs of the present, and the still graver needs of the future.

"This war demands Canada's utmost effort. Such an effort can be made only by a government which draws its strength from every section of the country and has been given an unquestioned mandate by the people. Can you name any political group or combination of men, other than the present Government, which is likely to enjoy your confidence, or has the remotest chance of being representative of Canadian opinion as a whole? This is the vital question which you, the electors, must continue to ask yourselves between now and the 26th of March. If, in the interval, you have failed to take all these matters into account, it will be too late to retrace your steps once that day has passed."[1] He also stated categorically that if the Liberal party did not win the election they would constitute the Opposition and would not share in a 'National Government.'

Mackenzie King left for Winnipeg and Prince Albert by train on February 25. He enjoyed this interlude very much, particularly his reception at Prince Albert, his own constituency, on February 29. At the end of the day, he wrote: "to bed, greatly refreshed and rejoiced—a perfect day."

The most dramatic incident in the election campaign was the resignation, on March 11, of Harry Nixon from the Government of Ontario in protest against Hepburn's conduct. What particularly pleased Mackenzie King was "the strong exception Nixon takes to Hepburn's alliance with Drew in opposition to the Liberals alike in the federal and provincial House." He felt if there was "any Liberalism left in the Ontario Government" Hepburn would be forced out of the leadership and added: "I do not see how he could dissolve and hope to carry Ministers and Members with him through the campaign which will be directed at the federal Liberal Government. At this stage he could scarcely get Drew to join with him to try a union government experiment in Ontario as I have not the least doubt has been the intention of the two of them right along." Mackenzie King had been expecting ever since the Resolution of the Ontario Legislature that Hepburn and Drew would form a coalition to oppose his Government and possibly try to hold a provincial election before a federal election could be held. He now felt it was really too late for such a development, but was not sure a coalition would not be formed.

The next day (March 12), E. H. Coleman, the Under Secretary of State, and Arnold Heeney came to see Mackenzie King with a verbal message from Albert Matthews, the Lieutenant-Governor of Ontario, who expected a call from Premier Hepburn that afternoon. As soon as he was told why they had come Mackenzie King said

[1]*Mackenzie King to the People of Canada* (Ottawa 1940), pp. 51–2.

to Coleman: "Tell him to act upon the advice of his Prime Minister." Coleman then told him that the first question Matthews "wished to ask was whether he would be justified in asking the Premier, before acting on his advice, whether the views he was presenting to him were those of the entire Cabinet or whether there were differences in the Cabinet concerning the advice he was tendering. I said to tell him that his duty was to accept the advice of the Premier, not to go behind that advice to make enquiries which would suggest that he questioned his honour or loyalty. That, in their relationship, he must accept the Premier all in all or not at all. If he was not willing to accept his advice without question he should dismiss him as being unworthy of enjoying his (the Lt.-Gov.'s) confidence. In that event the Lieutenant-Governor would have to find someone else to act as Premier. Apart from what I was saying to Coleman, I did not think there was any possibility of his being able to do this. Coleman said he felt sure that that was the view I would take, but wished to make doubly certain of it. He said the next point raised by the Lieutenant-Governor was that he thought he might be called upon to form a coalition, the Government to be composed of Hepburn and Drew. That he wondered whether, as the Legislature had prorogued, after supply voted to the present Government, he would be justified in allowing another Government to carry on." Mackenzie King's reply was "that the relations between the Governor and his Prime Minister remained the same. That either he would have to accept his advice all in all or not at all. If a mistake was being made, the remedy lay with the Members of the Legislature or the people. It could not be the Governor's mistake. It would be the Premier's mistake to be remedied by the Members of the Legislature or the people and could not be the Governor's mistake."

No doubt recalling 1926, Mackenzie King pointed out "that dissolution was an all important prerogative of the Sovereign, and that if he, the Sovereign, was obliged to accept the advice of his P.M. on this most important of matters, there were even stronger reasons why he should accept it on lesser matters. To tell Matthews that my view was that he must accept the Premier all in all or not at all, and that I felt he should accept and act upon whatever advice he might tender.

"Before Heeney and Coleman left, I told them that the possibility of formation of coalition government by Hepburn was in no way a surprise to me. It was in no sense of the word a new idea on Hepburn's part. He and Drew have had it in mind right along. Hepburn had it in mind at the time of the last provincial election as was told me by McCullagh of the *Globe* himself in my library. While McCullagh was in

England, Hepburn broke the understanding he had with the *Globe* and with Drew to form a National Government." Mackenzie King said he felt "that Hepburn, in passing the Resolution he did in the Ontario Legislature, was at that time contemplating National Government. Had the Resolution been defeated, he would have there and then joined up with Drew for National Government and gone to the country before our Parliament met. That chance was spoiled by members of his own Government and following voting with him to the extent they did." He believed that "Hepburn and Drew have been watching for a chance ever since to take the step which they were deprived of taking at that time. Their game, from the start, has been to get under way with it before the present [federal] Government appealed to the people. Hepburn will now make an effort to get underway with it before the present elections are over. I am pretty sure that the day will witness an effort on his part to effect this end."

What Mackenzie King expected, did not, in fact, happen. Instead, next day (March 13) he was surprised to read in the morning paper that "Nixon had gone back into Hepburn's Cabinet, but really relieved, as I think it will mean a more decent kind of campaign in the next ten days. Hepburn's colleagues have come to a decision with him, that they are to be free to take their part in the campaign, he to keep quiet, if that is possible."

The following morning (March 14) Mackenzie King arrived in Toronto for a meeting that evening. He received word at the station that Harry Nixon and his wife would be on the platform at the meeting and that Nixon wanted to have the opportunity to speak in order to place his position before the public. Mackenzie King at once agreed and it was decided that the order of speaking would be Norman Rogers first, Lapointe next, then Nixon, and finally Mackenzie King. Sir William Mulock, who was at this time 96, turned up at the meeting at Massey Hall and Mackenzie King insisted that he also be allowed to speak.

The dramatic moment came when Nixon was called on to speak. Mackenzie King "was delighted to see the way the audience received him. His manner, speech and all was really heroic. His presence and what he said, all circumstances considered, reminded me of the types of men that my grandfather must have had around him in the Rebellion days who were prepared to endure all kinds of hardship for the sake of the cause and for personal loyalty. I felt a gratitude for Nixon no words could express. I confess in some measure an equal feeling of contempt for other members of Hepburn's Government who should have been present and were not. They will suffer for it all their lives. Their names in the history of the party and in the country's history will always have a question mark after them. Not a man of them had the courage of his own conviction at a time when it was up to them to show where they stood as Liberals and at a moment when the country itself was at war. One after the other made excuses to avoid embarrassment in their relations with a man who has betrayed his friends, his cause and his country."

Of his own speech, Mackenzie King noted that his "cold fettered him a bit in expression, but that he had got his points across fairly well." Immediately after speaking he went over and shook hands with Mr. and Mrs. Nixon. Of Mrs. Nixon he wrote: "There is a splendid woman. True as steel. She has given him the necessary strength."

The following week Mackenzie King became more discouraged about the campaign as he struggled again with a national broadcast. He was particularly incensed at a public reference by George Drew to Norman Rogers as a "dyspeptic little son of Mars" who had been a "standing joke in every military camp since he blossomed forth as our new war lord last September." This personal attack on Rogers by Drew gave a sharpness to Mackenzie King's last two broadcasts.

His final national broadcast was delivered on March 21. This time he was almost satisfied. "I left the studio," he wrote, "feeling very happy about the broadcast and immensely relieved to have been able to get before the public the facts which I have disclosed. I was particularly happy about its references to the tone of public life and was glad also to get on record my own attitude towards touring the country and the circumstances which had made that impossible in recent years as well as during the campaign itself. I was really afraid in the last two days that this broadcast would not be up to the stamp of the others. It proved to be the best of all."

The following day he recorded his relief and satisfaction that the vote of the armed forces had been completed before any actual fighting had started and that the campaign was nearly over.

Mackenzie King made another broadcast on a group of Ontario stations on Saturday, March 23. He reported that he was so tired he could hardly take in the thoughts he was trying to express, but actually this one, too, was very effective.

The election was on Tuesday, March 26. On Easter Sunday, the 24th, Mackenzie King made an estimate of the outcome of the elections. He felt "the campaign of personal abuse" was going to react against Manion very strongly and that he had made a fatal mistake "when he tried to win a Conservative victory under the subterfuge of National Government." He had heard nothing to "indicate that we were losing any of our own people. From many sources have come evidences of considerable gain. This may mean a sweep. However, experience has taught me not to judge too much by appearances. The soldiers' vote will be against us (though it should not be). On the other hand, it may be offset by a feeling that to change the government in time of war would be a mistake. What will cause us to win in the end will be the record we have made since war commenced, and the conviction which, I believe, the people have that I have around me better colleagues than any group by which Manion could be surrounded, and that the country is safer under my guidance at this critical time than could be possible under his." He thought the majority might be "down to 50, but I would not be surprised with a majority of 70."

During the evening of election day, when it was clear there had been a sweeping victory, Mackenzie King had to give up keeping track of the results to complete a broadcast. Even in his triumph there was the ordeal of preparing a speech, this time of thanks to the people. Late in the evening he spoke to several of his colleagues. He and Lapointe "had a quiet and pleasant talk together. He felt it was a great victory. Had had a rather dirty campaign himself in his own constituency. Was feeling tired. Was characteristically generous in his references to myself. . . . He is a truly noble character. Our names will be linked together in the history of this country. It is a not uncertain example to those who may follow us in the administration of its public affairs."

In view of the violent opposition in a normally Conservative riding, Mackenzie King described the election of Rogers in Kingston as the outstanding victory of the campaign. "We really cleaned up in the province of Quebec," he wrote, "and I thought often of what Sir Wilfrid said to me in this very house, when I told him of my intention to stand by him in North York against conscription—that I would have the province of Quebec for the rest of my life."

It was exactly 2 A.M. when Mackenzie King turned out the lights in his bedroom. "My mind and heart were much at rest at last," he wrote. When all the returns were in, the Mackenzie King Government had 184 supporters out of 245 Members: the greatest majority given to any Canadian Government up to that time.

CHAPTER FIVE

Parliament and the Blitzkrieg

MACKENZIE KING was almost exhausted when the election was over and felt he must have a rest and a change of scene. As the new Parliament elected on March 26, 1940, could not legally meet until the middle of May, he decided once the urgent business had been disposed of and the preparations started for the session, he would make a visit to the United States. Though his first objective was to get a rest, he did hope an opportunity might arise for talks with President Roosevelt and Cordell Hull, the Secretary of State, neither of whom he had seen since the Royal Visit the previous summer.

From the outbreak of hostilities, Mackenzie King was convinced that American assistance would be indispensable to victory, and that no part of the war effort mattered as much as maintaining close and friendly understanding between the Allied powers and the Roosevelt administration. Throughout the rest of 1940, even while Parliament was sitting, he gave much of his personal attention to relations with the United States; these are the subject of the following chapter of this book.

After the election the first matter to which Mackenzie King gave his attention was the appointment of a new Governor-General. His choice, which was approved by the Cabinet on March 28, was the Earl of Athlone, the uncle of the King. Athlone's wife, the Princess Alice, was a grand-daughter of Queen Victoria. Mackenzie King felt "it would be a fine thing for a grandson of William Lyon Mackenzie to appoint the grand-daughter of Queen Victoria—to have her husband as the King's representative in Canada." Before actually making the formal submission to the King, Mackenzie King talked it over further with Lapointe on March 29. Lapointe spoke of the appointment of a Canadian later on. Mackenzie King told him "that had Chief Justice Duff been married, I would have recommended his appointment right now. That, if Lapointe wanted the job when the Athlones had left, he could have it. Clearly, there is no Canadian on the horizon that could fill the position at the moment. As Lapointe said, at this time of war, it would be unwise, and the appointment of the Athlones would be particularly appropriate. It would not be the best moment to change to a Canadian."

Mackenzie King discussed many other governmental matters with Lapointe that evening at Laurier House. He was particularly pleased to find that Lapointe "was in no hurry about going to the Senate. [This appointment had been discussed before the election.] I told him about Ralston as a possible successor to myself, when the time came for me to retire. Lapointe mentioned, however, that Ralston had his heart set on the Supreme Court, and I agreed we should make him Chief Justice when Duff's time to retire comes. Lapointe himself might have pressed for that post had he been other than the unselfish man that he is.

"I stressed the great additional responsibility on our shoulders to maintain standards in all appointments, and to prevent our colleagues, simply because of the numbers supporting us, and the War Measures Act, and the little opposition, doing things that they might feel were all right in themselves, but which might not be justified with the tremendous outlays necessitated by war.

"I told Lapointe we must seek to make the best possible appointments, and get our own younger people and younger members of Parliament to realize that they must begin to consider their future by studying political questions, not wasting their time."

The following day (March 30), Mackenzie King had a long talk with Norman Rogers and urged him to get "additional assistance" in the Department of National Defence. "I favoured keeping the three branches of the Defence Department under one Minister, but matters would have to be so arranged as to relieve him of all detail re air development. He said there were articles in today's Gazette and other papers to the effect there was to be a new Minister there. He asked if that were correct." Mackenzie King replied that he had spoken to no one on the subject, but told him of a conversation he had had with Power "and his desire to be in on some of the war work." He then "asked Rogers exactly how he felt about Power. His suggestion was that Power should be made an Assistant Minister of Defence, to handle the air work and to be able to answer questions in Parliament. I said I would talk with Howe, Ralston and others and have a meeting of the War Cabinet to settle these points before he went to England."

It had been decided before the election that Rogers would go overseas right afterwards and return before Parliament met. They talked about questions that might arise on this visit including "the question of an overseas Minister which I do not favour nor does he. We both think it would be better to have Ministers pay occasional visits. A Minister overseas might create confusion with Headquarters Staff, High Commissioner, etc. I told Rogers what I would prefer would be that he would have suitable representation of his own there, if anything of the kind were needed."

Mackenzie King also talked to Rogers about the Ministers, like himself, "who had a future before them, seeing to it that the Liberal Office was kept on and that the work of Parliament was so organized as to have the younger men realize their responsibilities. I mentioned that I thought Ralston would go to the Supreme Court. Certainly with neither Lapointe nor myself participating in another election they would find the situation very different. They would now have to build up for themselves. Rogers raised the question as to this being my last campaign, but added I could hardly hope for as great a result again. I told him my desire was, if I had the strength, to stay on through the end of the war; to participate in peace negotiations and then to turn over the management of affairs to younger men."

On April 2, before Rogers left Ottawa, the Cabinet gave lengthy consideration to the establishment overseas of an Army Corps of two divisions with ancillary units. Ralston opposed it very strongly on the score of expense but Rogers was equally strongly in favour. Mackenzie King took the position "that the Canadian public would wish to have a Corps, that the pride of the nation would demand that; also, that we owed it to McNaughton and the men who were prepared to give their lives, to let them have, in the way of formation, what they most desired. The people would expect us to be prepared to incur additional expense, if need be, for this national expression."

The decision was left over till the next meeting of the Cabinet: a frequent device of Mackenzie King's when there were strong differences between colleagues. The next day (April 3) the discussion was resumed by the War Committee. The problem was the cost of the ancillary units. Mackenzie King agreed with Ralston that the money would go much further if spent on air or naval services and added: "We could have used our money more effectively if it had all been confined to air and naval services. The national spirit, however, demanded an expeditionary force; would demand it having a full national expression. I stressed the necessity of maintaining the pride and the morale of the little force we have by making them a complete entity. We all agreed that they should be as autonomous as possible." On April 4 an interim measure was approved by which the First Division would form a self-contained Canadian formation along with the other Canadian troops in England.

On April 4 there was a prolonged discussion by the Cabinet of the St. Lawrence Waterway. Ralston still objected to proceeding "on the score that it meant an additional expense to Canada of some sixty million dollars (by 1950), which money, he thought, should go to other purposes at this time. Could not see corresponding advantage, except what would accrue to Ontario for power." Mackenzie King noted that Ralston "does not seem to regard Ontario as part of the Dominion. I pointed out that the goodwill of the United States and the Empire at this time meant more than anything else. To disappoint the President in what he hopes for, above all else, in a Presidential year, might mean the difference between getting essential help or losing it to the Allied Powers at this time." The Cabinet decided that Mackenzie King should discuss the matter with the United States Minister to Canada and to go ahead with a new treaty, if he asked for one. Meanwhile Howe and Cardin (as a senior Minister from Quebec) were to seek the concurrence of Premier Godbout.

On April 5, Mackenzie King talked to Ralston and Howe about proclaiming the Munitions and Supply Act (which had been passed by the special war session of Parliament in September 1939) and setting up the department it authorized. He told them his view "all along had been that the Act should be proclaimed. The question was, what Minister? I thought the Department was a very important one, and was ready to give it to Howe, but Howe did not wish to leave Transport. . . . Howe said he would be prepared to organize the new department as an Acting Minister. . . . I said I would think the matter over further."

The conquest of Denmark and the invasion of Norway on April 9 did not surprise Mackenzie King who was "thankful that our elections were over before this great offensive began." That day he decided on the immediate establishment of the Department of Munitions and Supply. Howe was made Minister rather than Acting Minister, but, for the time being, he remained Minister of Transport as well. Norman Rogers left that day for England.

On April 11, Mackenzie King made final preparations for his visit to the United States. As Lapointe and Crerar, the two senior Ministers, were already away from Ottawa, Ralston was made Acting Prime Minister until such time as Lapointe should return. On the afternoon of April 12, Mackenzie King left Ottawa and did not return until May 1.

When he returned Mackenzie King plunged at once into preparations for the session of Parliament. He was pained, on May 9, to learn that the Chamberlain Government had won a vote of confidence in the House of Commons of the United Kingdom by only 281 to 280, with large numbers abstaining. He anticipated at once that, in Canada, a similar attack would be made on the Prime Minister. "I can see only too well how in this Parliament a dead-set will be quickly made to hold me responsible for everything and to get me out."

That day he told the Cabinet emphatically "that I felt Britain and France were in a very terrible position and that we should do all we possibly could to meet any of their requests." At the end of the day he wrote: "All day I have felt a tremendous sympathy with Chamberlain, who I think has been most unfairly treated. He had to bear the consequences of his predecessors' failure to appreciate the situation in Germany. He, himself, I recall vividly, was one of the first who came out strongly for armament and more armament." On May 10, Mackenzie King fully appreciated "it will not be long before an attack gets worked up against me along lines very similar to that which Chamberlain has had to endure."

While the Cabinet was meeting that morning, he received word that the King had sent for Winston Churchill. Later he listened to Chamberlain's broadcast, announcing his resignation: "The man's voice was full of anguish, but it was the expression of a truly noble and good man. When Chamberlain had concluded I immediately dictated a wire to him, expressing the pride I had in being at his side today as he laid down the burdens of office, and of having been able to assist and to co-operate in giving what assistance I could in the anxious weeks and months and years that had since intervened; that, at this hour, I had the highest admiration and understanding sympathy.

"I also telegraphed Churchill, assuring him of the wholehearted co-operation and support of my colleagues and myself in furthering the war effort of the Commonwealth and wishing him vision and endurance to guide public affairs in this most critical of all hours."

On May 11 Mackenzie King recorded his opinion that Chamberlain would have been a safer guide in the long run than Churchill; this view he modified later, though he never lost his admiration and affection for Chamberlain.

Meanwhile, the official Opposition as well as the Government was preparing for the session to open on May 16. Manion, the Conservative party leader, had been defeated on March 26 and the Conservatives had to choose from their elected Members a House leader to occupy the position of Leader of the Opposition. Hon. R. B. Hanson, of Fredericton, who had been Minister of Trade and Commerce in the last year of the Bennett government, and who had been re-elected in 1940 after an absence from Parliament of five years, was chosen on May 13.

The Blitzkrieg

Mackenzie King at once telephoned to congratulate Hanson who told him he agreed with Mackenzie King's point of view about the House of Commons which, Mackenzie King wrote, "caused me to say a word about believing strongly in an Opposition as against National Government, that, of course, conditions might necessitate that sort of thing at times." Mackenzie King already foresaw another drive for 'National Government,' but a possibility that worried him even more was what he called "an inspired statement" in the afternoon papers of May 17 to the effect that Arthur Meighen, who was leader of the Conservative party in the Senate, was "likely to leave the Senate and come back into the Commons as Leader of the Conservative party, running in one of the by-elections." Mackenzie King believed "the report to be true. With his bitter and sarcastic tongue life will become very difficult for me in the Commons."

The session opened on May 16 and the party leaders spoke in the debate on the Address in reply to the Speech from the Throne on May 20. Mackenzie King always found his speeches on the Address the most difficult of every session. 1940 was no exception. He noted that Hanson took longer and was more critical and less co-operative than he expected, thus obliging him to give a different tone to the opening of his reply.

On this occasion, too, he was preoccupied with arrangements for a separate Minister of National Defence for Air. It was not until the afternoon of May 20 that Power had indicated he was ready to accept the new post and that Power, Rogers, and Ralston had been able to work out a formula agreeable to all three. Mackenzie King had to prepare a suitable announcement during the dinner recess for inclusion in his speech. Power became Minister of National Defence for Air on May 23 as soon as the necessary legislation had been enacted. Mackenzie King felt that the speech as a whole was a good statement of the "government record. In view of the European situation, it did not come an hour too soon." The debate on the Address was concluded that same day.

In his speech to the House of May 20, Mackenzie King had announced the formation of an Army Corps and of other measures to speed up the war effort particularly in the field of production, but he felt sure it would not be enough to forestall a campaign for a more vigorous Canadian response to the shock of the *blitzkrieg* in Europe and he expected this campaign to be focused on a demand for National Government and conscription.

The prospect of such a campaign was heightened on May 22 when Britain, in Mackenzie King's words, "took complete control over the lives and property of the entire population, giving the Minister of Labour the power to tell everyone what they were to do and authority to use any premises for war purposes." Mackenzie King "saw clearly that instant demand would be made for similar so-called national service in Canada. I gather there has already commenced quite a movement against myself as not being active enough; against colleagues as well as myself for being complacent, etc., and some of our own people grumbling along these lines, becoming restive. I told my colleagues we might easily see the party divided into conscriptionists and non-conscriptionists. . . . That I certainly would resign before I would accept any move in the direction of conscription. All this may pile up pretty rapidly." He added: "Yesterday arranged to call a caucus for tomorrow; I shall speak very plainly to the Members there."

At the Liberal caucus on May 23, Mackenzie King lost no time in coming to the point. He told the caucus he had "seen very clearly what is afoot on the part of the Tories; also the Toronto group, Hepburn, etc., to have someone else made leader. To begin an attack on myself as leader with a view to supplanting me and . . . to get a National Government which would bring Tories into the Administration. That that battle was fought at the general elections and I intended to stand by the decision of the people." He next "referred openly to desire to have Meighen brought into the Government. Said I would not countenance anything of the kind in regard to a man who had been responsible for the Wartime Elections Act and for conscription in the last war. Said I had told the people where I stood in my radio speeches in the campaign. . . . That I intended to honour every pledge that was given, not to depart from any one of them."

He went on to "make plain at once just what would happen with respect to change of leadership. In the nature of things, I myself could not hope to carry on many more years. Might, at any time, under strain, feel it better that someone else should take on the leadership. Also that the party itself might feel this would be in its interests. If they would just let me know any such feeling any time, I would be quite ready to step out and help anyone else in the leadership. If, however, I thought desire for change sprang from an effort on the part of some minority to get control, and that division took place in the ranks of the party from anything of the kind, I would like to let them know at once they might expect pretty speedy action on my part. That I was telling them now that they might know consequences in advance; what my method of procedure would be. That it would be well for them all to remember that when I resigned, the Cabinet also resigned. Furthermore it would be my duty to recommend to the Governor-General who should take on the next administration. That some of those who might be wishing to have a different leader might find themselves the most surprised men with respect to the consequences of their action. I mentioned all this because of necessity of maintaining solidarity of the party of which each man was a guardian." He also told them that "before resigning, I would make a statement in Parliament and to the people as to the reasons which had actuated me to take the step I did, and no one need be surprised if they found that statement a pretty telling one."

He reminded the caucus that "already a Toronto group, Hepburn and his Ministers, were beginning the same tactics that they had adopted before the last election. I pointed out how these men had, for years, made our task difficult. That I had taken what they had said quietly to seek to preserve the solidarity of the party. That I did not intend to do so any longer. The people decided as to whom they wanted to manage affairs of this country." Mackenzie King noted that the caucus gave his speech a "magnificent reception."

Although he was opposed to a National Government or any kind of coalition with the Opposition, Mackenzie King felt the need of broadening the base of the Government and of having some leaders in business brought into association with the Government. What he envisaged was a committee to be associated with the War Committee of the Cabinet with Ralston as its Chairman.

At the Cabinet meeting on May 27 one of his colleagues "spoke along lines which indicated we might have to bring in some of the Conservatives, etc., and made references which indicated the possibility of National Government. I said, in that case I would immediately resign from the Premiership; would help in any way I could apart from that. That I did not propose to bring into the Government forces that were going to immediately destroy its effectiveness. There was an instant outcry that I was the only one that could hold even the present Government together. That nothing should be thought of in that way so far as Meighen was concerned. I said I would not object to having Grote Stirling come in from the Opposition if it were likely to prove a help, as a sort of assurance to the Opposition that we were devoting all our time to war conditions." Grote Stirling, whom Mackenzie King liked and respected, was the Member for Yale, B.C.; he had been Minister of National Defence in the closing months of the Bennett administration.

One of the Ministers "suggested what we should have here is more Ministers; possibly four or five to give their whole time to war work. Business men. One name mentioned was Morris Wilson [the President of the Royal Bank of Canada]. I said that I would want to know who these men were and consider how helpful they would likely be. That there was a great danger of having men in the Cabinet who had never been in Parliament; because of their associations, etc. to have them walk out of Council some day—because of some dissatisfaction or worse, have them give the press all kinds of inside information. I thought it would be much better to have these men act as assistants to the War Committee, to be brought into Council at times if so desired."

All this time, of course, the war news was becoming increasingly grave. Later that day (May 27) the Prime Minister and several of the Ministers met with Hanson, Stirling, and Earl Rowe of the Opposition, to give them all the available secret information about the war situation and what was being done to meet it. These three members were chosen because they were Privy Councillors.

The next day, May 28, Mackenzie King told the House of Commons that he had conferred with the Conservative Privy Councillors in the House and proposed, that afternoon, to confer with Senator Meighen and other Conservative Privy Councillors in the Senate, and later with the leaders of the C.C.F. and Social Credit parties. In these conferences full information was given about what was actually happening overseas and about Canada's additional defence effort. Mackenzie King offered to renew these meetings as often as they might be desired and, at the close of the day, he expressed in his diary the hope that these conferences "might help to silence the agitation for National Government."

It was a vain hope. The Conservative Opposition in the House of Commons concentrated its attacks on Mackenzie King's leadership and suggested that Ralston might take his place. On May 29, Mackenzie King told the Cabinet that "the talk of having Ralston become leader was, to my mind, clearly to help destroy confidence in, not only myself, but in the Government in its war effort, with a view to having the situation so developed that, ultimately, a National Government might be brought about in time of war. That the conspiracy was twofold. First, in the direction mentioned. Secondly, to get Arthur Meighen into the Commons."

He then told the Cabinet "what I had said to Ralston before the last elections, that I thought he was the one who ought to take over the leadership of the party. I believed many of the party would prefer him to me. That I might not be the best one to lead in a campaign. At any rate, I had had a long siege, and felt he ought to consider taking the leadership. That he had told me he would not consider anything of the kind. I wanted now, in his presence, to say that I was quite prepared to step out, even today, and recommend to the Administrator [Chief Justice Duff was still Administrator as the new Governor-General had not yet arrived in Canada] the formation of a Government under him, if members of Council believed that that would help in the present situation. Naturally, my first choice of successor would be Lapointe, but I knew he had stayed on only to be at my side and would not take the leadership. My next choice was Ralston, and I wanted him and the Cabinet to know that at once."

He added that he wished "to let them see clearly what the situation would likely be if a change came. I was not sure that Lapointe would stay on under any change. I would like them however to estimate for themselves what the effect of a change would be. I said I would be quite prepared to stay on under Ralston, and accept any post he would like to give me, particularly if he thought well of giving me External Affairs. I would feel happier in devoting my entire time to it. In any event, I could not hope to go on through a period like this indefinitely and they must prepare for possible sudden changes. I then said to them that, at this very moment, I was doing all in my power to assist in bringing the United States and Great Britain together, and while I did not care a bit about myself and the attacks that were being made, . . . that, at this time, it was too critical to allow any longer this underhand treachery to go on and help to unsettle our own loyal followers in the House of Commons, and good honest people in the country. I told them I need not say that I had complete confidence in every colleague, but that was not enough. The people judged by actions and I thought we were getting past the point where silence should be longer maintained. . . . This was a deep-laid plot, which affected the whole power of the Government, and I expected my colleagues to see that it was met in a formidable manner. I could not have spoken more plainly than I did."

On May 30, Mackenzie King was more concerned than ever by the attacks on the Government and particularly by the fear of a concerted press attack in which he expected certain Liberal papers to join. He returned to the question of leadership at the Cabinet meeting on that day saying he thought it was time for his colleagues to speak up. Later that same day Mackenzie King was just about to leave the House of Commons when Earl Rowe began to make a speech, which had been distributed in advance to the press. "When Rowe came to the end of his speech and began saying he had no better friend, etc., an ideal P.M., everywhere recognized as a good P.M. for peace time, etc., our men then began to show how they felt. . . . Gardiner got up to reply. Made a splendid vigorous attack. The Tory party sat like a lot of whipped curs, not a whine out of the lot of them. Our men responded as no party in Parliament has responded in the lifetime in Parliament of the men who were sitting there. It was a tremendous demonstration of the solidarity of the party." Gardiner's speech was really the turning point of the session; from that point on the Liberals began to fight back; and Mackenzie King never ceased to be grateful for Gardiner's decisive speech in that crisis.

At the Cabinet meeting on May 30, Mackenzie King had spoken of "the desirability of forming a Committee on National Security and Defence which would be representative of organized bodies throughout Canada; Chambers of Commerce, Manufacturers, Labour, National Council of Women, etc. who could, above all, study means whereby all military effort could be organized for war purposes and voluntary associations put actively to work in different communities. Something corresponding to the National Patriotic Fund Committee in the last war. That unless we could get this effort organized in the way I proposed I felt the alternative would be conscription, and that would come inevitably because of people wanting to assist but not being organized for the purpose. I would like to have Ralston at the head of any Committee that might be formed for two reasons: (1) because I thought there was a general feeling he had confidence in quarters where I did not have it; (2) that all these questions came down to matters of finance in the end. Better to have the financial end explained to them in the course of discussion than to have the matter come to Ralston to be explained over anew in Council." Mackenzie King suggested that Grote Stirling for the Conservatives and Coldwell and Blackmore for the smaller parties should be members of the Committee, as well as one or two Senators, and that Ralston should choose a number of prominent financiers and businessmen. "My own feeling," he added, "was that an executive of that body could meet with the War Committee of the Cabinet. But I did not propose to bring people into the Government that I did not know for the purpose of trying to please elements that would never be satisfied and were doing what they could in different ways to destroy me and the Government."

He then left his colleagues to discuss the matter themselves. Lapointe told him later that "Ralston and one or two did not take kindly to the larger body but were favourable to a smaller group. When I mentioned to Lapointe the alternatives between organized voluntary effort and conscription ultimately, he thought I was entirely right and said it was a pity we did not have something like the Patriotic Fund at present to absorb the energies of the people."

The Prime Minister referred again to the proposed National Security and Defence Committee at the Cabinet meeting on May 31. He felt the Committee should include business men to satisfy the public that production was being increased as speedily as possible. "I found it impossible," he wrote, "to get the Cabinet to visualize the larger measure. I had made it yesterday as a recommendation to Council. What, however, came out of the discussion were very strong and sensible statements by both Gardiner and Cardin as to the folly of trying to please people that are opposed to us by bringing their friends into the Government."

He added that there was on that day a very different atmosphere in the House of Commons itself and around the corridors. "The feeling even among Tory pressmen and others is that the Tories in the House got their full deserts yesterday and richly deserved what they got. I feel we are losing ground in not getting an organization under way of the kind I have described, but no one seems to find it possible to think of persons capable of fashioning up an organization of the kind or heading it."

The same day (May 31) Mackenzie King learned that the committee charged with putting up the memorial to William Lyon Mackenzie at Queen's Park in Toronto had decided to put the memorial in storage instead of erecting it. They evidently feared criticism of proceeding with a monument to a one-time rebel at this crisis in British fortunes. Mackenzie King was thoroughly disgusted and succeeded in having the decision changed and the memorial completed. This is one of the many examples of the great importance Mackenzie King attached, even at the most critical moments of the war, to matters that others would have considered trivial. A few days later the installation of the memorial was completed without incident.

All through this period, as the situation in France became more serious, Mackenzie King felt there should be greater emphasis on war production. From the very start of the war, indeed, he had stressed the need of increasing production and starting new lines of production particularly of aircraft engines. Just after the dissolution of Parliament in January, he had spoken to the Cabinet (January 29) "of the necessity of Canada getting under way with the manufacture of further arms, rifles, etc. and munitions for our own armies. Not to be counting on what we could buy from England or assuming that these were to be ordered only on British order, that I believed the strongest argument against us in the campaign would be that these orders had been delayed so long. I reminded the Cabinet of my having brought the War Committee together on that very point."

He suggested at that time that Rogers see what "further orders could be placed. Both he and Howe argued that we were turning out rifles and quantities of munitions, etc., that this would be increased, but I could see that their conception of what is needed is not what the public would expect. With Ralston at my elbow, I felt he was watching the treasury very closely. That the last thing the people would forgive would be any shortage at a time of need. I have also stressed the necessity of ship-building time and again, but have met with opposition on that score. That we cannot do more, etc. While I have been the one that has been pressing these matters strongly, and unable to make headway because of the arguments of colleagues, I am the one whom our opponents are blaming as holding back and responsible for not having done more."

Mackenzie King's immediate reaction to the *blitzkrieg* which began on May 10 had been to consider with Ralston and Power and later the whole War Committee whether "in any direction we could not augment and accelerate our war effort." On June 3, he again stressed to the War Committee the need of getting ahead with war production. "It is very distressing to me," he wrote, "to find that Canada is short of planes of certain types, no tanks, etc. and our supply of small arms, ammunition, largely depleted by demands Britain has made upon it, when I begged of War Committee to go ahead with all these things at once at the time McNaughton left for England. Howe and Ralston were strongly opposed to me. Thought I was extreme, foolish in putting forward these demands. Now I imagine I shall have to take all the blame for our not having anticipated the present situation.

"I urged today again the utmost development of planes. Apparently regarding tanks, we can't get from the British the design they want. The British, after giving us one design, had the matter recalled, and have since failed to give another to Washington and here." He added: "They hold back on everything."

On June 6, the Cabinet received a delegation of manufacturers who had come to make representations about what they called misunderstanding in London concerning war production facilities in Canada. Mackenzie King "spoke out from the shoulder" in explaining the true situation and then made the chairman of the delegation, Harold Crabtree, President of the Canadian Manufacturers' Association, take back the word "misunderstanding" and use the word "reason" which was explained in full, and "which comes down to the British seeking to keep the contracts in their own hands to try and buy the goodwill of other nations whose friendship could not be relied upon. Also their [British] mistaken view of the war in which financial and economic control would settle the day rather than the *blitzkrieg*." The delegation was satisfied to have

Vincent Massey, the Canadian High Commissioner in London, take the matter up again with the British authorities.

Mackenzie King added that "we also got them in a tight corner as to having someone to supervise work of production, by telling them to name their man and we would give him the job at once." He noted that "Howe did splendidly in presenting his point of view" and the meeting broke up with the manufacturers applauding.

Mackenzie King made a statement in the House of Commons on June 4 about the emergency action Canada had taken to help Britain in the crisis which had now developed on the beaches of Dunkirk. He had been trying to prepare this statement for several days, but reflected: "There is no cloud without a silver lining. By waiting until today, Churchill's speech explaining the whole situation of the past week or two enabled me to bring Canadian developments into better perspective. [This was Churchill's great 'no surrender' speech.] The statement when I made it in the House was well received, and I think had the effect of allowing the Members and the country to see that, while we were being abused for being slow and indifferent to giving Britain all the assistance we could, we were really making great sacrifices so far as our country is concerned."

The next day (June 5) Mackenzie King spoke at length to the Liberal caucus to prepare the Members "for the possibility of France being unable to withstand the terrific onslaught." He urged the Members to think "only in terms of the utmost war effort that our country could put forward. That that was the obligation which they owed to their own constituencies and their own country because of their return to Parliament at this time."

He dwelt on "the necessity of keeping Canada united and our war effort being based on that; of balancing all matters, going just as far as we could, and not so far as to create a worse situation than the one we were trying to remedy. It was there that I spoke of hoping to be able to see our country go through this war as we had gone through the last general election." He added that "it is not myself that I was thinking of. It was rather the effect on the world situation today; of the confidence that had been born of this in England and in the United States." After referring to his associations with leaders in Britain, he said "that if they got word tomorrow that the Government had changed, that I had gone, that I did not know just what they would feel, in this crisis. That similarly, I did not know what would be thought in the United States. That I had given my life in an effort to try and cultivate good feelings between our country and the States, and the States and Britain, with a view to meeting situations just such as we are now faced with."

In the course of his remarks, Mackenzie King told the caucus that "the one significant word I read in Churchill's speech yesterday was not the rhetorical effect of saying that England would fight on even if she had to fight alone, but the thought of what that really signified. Possibility of England having to carry on this whole fight alone. That that was something they must be prepared to see, and to consider the position of Canada along with the rest of the world in the light of it. To consider, too, what it meant to keep American friendship with other parts of the Empire."

Mackenzie King "got a tremendous reception at the end, and the men were deeply stirred. They were asking me if I could not give that speech to the country. I told them that it was totally unprepared. Just expressed out of appreciation of the world situation."

When Mackenzie King learned in the morning of June 10 that Mussolini was to speak on the radio at one o'clock Ottawa time, he concluded at once that Italy was going to come into the war that day. He telephoned the Leader of the Opposition to tell him he expected Italy to declare war and Hanson offered to second the resolution Mackenzie King proposed to move in Parliament, if Italy acted. He then went to the Cabinet meeting where the Members went over the procedure to be followed in Parliament if there was a declaration of war by Italy.

While the Cabinet was still in session, word came that Italy had indeed declared war. Mackenzie King returned to Laurier House about 1.30 for a hasty lunch and had just gone to his room for a brief rest before going to the House of Commons, when he received word that Grant MacLachlan, Norman Rogers' secretary, wanted to speak to him urgently. Norman Rogers had left for Toronto by air that morning to speak at a luncheon. Mackenzie King was told that the aircraft on which Rogers was travelling had crashed near Newcastle, Ontario, and it was thought all on board had been killed. He noted that when he received the news, his first thoughts were of the telephone conversation he had had with Rogers the previous evening in which Rogers had said he did not want to be away if he should be in Ottawa.

The rest can best be told in Mackenzie King's words: "He [Rogers] asked me if I had been getting bad news today. I told him just what had come from Italy and that I thought the time was getting close when Italy would be in the war, and might be tomorrow. He said he wondered whether, in the circumstances, he should go up to Toronto; that he had an engagement to speak to the combined Empire and Canadian Clubs. I said to him that if he did not go, and nothing happened, such as Italy coming into the war today, the people might become unduly alarmed at the Minister of Defence having to cancel an important engagement. I said I hoped he would be going up by train and take a bit of a rest. He said he would be flying up and would be coming down after the luncheon and would be in the House later in the afternoon. . . . He then said: 'Well, then, the word is *carry on*.' He meant keep right on with the engagement he had made.

"I was thinking these things over when the telephone rang again. It was Chubby Power. I told him I had already got the news. He said Ralston and MacLachlan were with him. He spoke of the terrible loss it was. He then asked me if I would break the news to Mrs. Rogers." Fearing the emotional strain just before he had to speak on the Italian declaration of war, Mackenzie King hesitated, but decided to do so. He went to Rogers' house and was in the midst of telling Mrs. Rogers the news when Ralston arrived.

After they had told Mrs. Rogers of the accident, Mackenzie King "walked into the study where everything was so neatly in order. At his desk, his Bible was lying open. He had been reading it and there was also a manuscript of a neatly written address at one side. I looked at the chapter. It was the 6th chapter of Ephesians. My eyes fell on the words: 'For we wrestle not against flesh and blood, but against principalities, against powers, against the rulers of the darkness of this world, against spiritual wickedness in high places.' And then the following words: 'Stand therefore, having your loins girt about with truth, and having on the breastplate of righteousness.' And, also, the verse that he quoted in the House the last time he spoke: 'Wherefore take unto you the whole armour of God, that ye may be able to withstand in the evil day, and having done all, to stand.' "

Mackenzie King "took the Bible in and read over these little verses to Mrs. Rogers, and told her that that was what he wanted us all to do— to stand fast. She said he had placed the Bible there intending to include that message in his draft for his address in Toronto today.

"It was nearing the time for the opening of the House, so I hurried on, leaving Ralston with Mrs. Rogers. . . . As I drove to the House of Commons, curiously enough, I never thought of doing more than announcing Rogers' death. It never occurred to me that I should follow with some words of appreciation. I was thinking more of the world event—Canada's entry into war against Italy."

As soon as the House opened Mackenzie King made the announcement of Rogers' death and then read what "I had to say about Italy. Hanson was exceedingly nice. The House listened very intently as I spoke and read, only broke in with applause once where I spoke about

Italy's entry increasing our determination to stand at the side of the allies. Hanson's remarks were well applauded where he endeavoured to show the solidarity of the Commons. Coldwell spoke well. . . . The resolution carried without any dissent. . . . When the House adjourned, Hanson, and most of the men from the Conservative Opposition, as well as a number of our men, came over to shake hands and express sympathy. They all knew what close friends Rogers and I were. I felt, too, how deeply moved they were."

Of Norman Rogers, Mackenzie King wrote: "Over the years of our association together, he was unfailing in his loyalty and devotion. He never thought of himself, but always of others—as beautiful a character as I have known. There seemed to be a curious sort of deadness in my mind; nothing seemed, at the moment, to quite break through it. I confess I am terribly worried about the Government. Rogers was the best man I had in the administration, bar none, for this period of war. No loss could possibly be greater to the Ministry. I could not trust myself to write an appreciation."

Mackenzie King did, however, prepare something to broadcast on Italy's entry into the war and he listened to Roosevelt's broadcast from 7.15 to 7.40. He thought Roosevelt "gave a splendid address, promising all the resources of America on the side of the Allies." He felt Roosevelt's speech "surely means that the Neutrality Act will be cancelled, so far as supplying quantities of munitions, etc., to the Allies. I wonder if it is not coming just too late."

There was a meeting of the War Committee that evening until 10.20 P.M. Mackenzie King made his broadcast at 10.30 and then went to see Mrs. Rogers about the arrangements for Rogers' funeral. It had been a terrible day.

The next day (June 11) Mackenzie King gave much of his time and attention to the Rogers family and the arrangements for the funeral. It was held in the Hall of Fame on June 12 and is minutely described by Mackenzie King in his diary. The most moving passage is a reference to Rogers' sons which reads: "Rogers' little boys were there in their grey suits, bare knees, black ties, no hats. The boys were wearing their ordinary suits. It was all an emphasis on reality as against appearance. I had a talk with the little lads, explaining to them about the Hall of Fame, talking of their father, and pointing out to the brothers how, as long as Canadian History continues to be recorded, Rogers' name will have its association with the Houses of Parliament as the first person to be honoured by burial from its Hall of Fame. This truly is as it ought to be."

The Blitzkrieg

The death of Rogers made the reconstruction of the Cabinet imperative. In his diary for June 10, Mackenzie King had written that "the Government will have to be reconstructed somehow. This is going to be a difficult task. I am told the *Globe and Mail* now say that they do not want a Government without me at the head, nor a National Government, but some new men. That, I think, is sound enough, but to find the men is what I will have to do now."

To that task he now gave prolonged attention. On June 11, as a temporary measure, C. G. Power became Acting Minister of National Defence. On June 13, when he received messages from Churchill forecasting the imminent collapse of France, Mackenzie King's immediate reaction was to ask Ralston to take the portfolio of National Defence, telling him he believed it "was absolutely necessary in the situation as it was developing. The only alternative was the agitation to have McNaughton brought back, which would be a mistake, he being needed at the front. If he, Ralston, would take the portfolio at once, that would forestall the fears which would arise, once the real situation becomes publicly known. Ralston said at once that he had feared that might be what was in my mind. . . . He said he was very much wedded to the Department of Finance, liked that work, and felt the other would be a very heavy burden." Mackenzie King replied that he "really felt it was necessary that he should," that it was what their colleagues and the Members would wish and he added "that it was what, I felt, Rogers would have wished."

"Ralston then said something about not shirking any load in a situation such as the present, and said he felt that perhaps he ought to do it, if for no reason other than as a tribute to Rogers and the example that he had set. He said to me he did not want to bargain in any way, but suggested that possibly Ilsley might be considered for Finance, and that he would need an Assistant Minister. . . . He then spoke about the Budget. Said he would like to deliver the Budget. I told him that he would have to do that. My feeling was that I would make it clear he would not take over until he had." Before the House met in the afternoon, Ralston gave his acceptance and Mackenzie King announced it at once, feeling "it imperative to get that announcement made immediately."

In the morning of June 13, Mackenzie King with several colleagues had received a delegation from the Trades and Labour Congress of which Tom Moore was the President. Moore was critical of the attitude to organized labour of the Government and in particular of Howe as Minister of Munitions and Supply. Despite this attitude, Mackenzie King wanted Moore in the Government as Minister of Labour. "We need

Moore to help on the Labour side," he wrote in his diary that night.

That same day, before the House opened, Mackenzie King had the Conservative Privy Councillors in the House of Commons and Senators Meighen and C. C. Ballantyne meet with the War Committee to let them know what was in the messages from Churchill. He told them "that our attitude would be that Canada should stay in the fight so long as England and France, or England itself, continued to oppose Nazi aggression and to fight for freedom. I said I believed that that would be the view of the country as a whole. They all agreed. We talked, too, of our soldiers being in France. I felt sorry for Meighen, as his son is in the Expeditionary Force. I said a word to him at the close, that I was feeling deeply for him. It broke him up visibly for the moment." This is one of Mackenzie King's rare kindly references to Meighen and, perhaps, for that reason deserves to be preserved.

The next day (June 14), at Churchill's suggestion, Mackenzie King appealed to Paul Reynaud, the Premier of France, to continue the fight. (The circumstances surrounding this appeal are related in the next chapter.) Mackenzie King decided to supplement his message by a public appeal to France from his place in Parliament. When he told the Cabinet what he intended to do, "the news," he wrote, "seemed to stun the members who never seem to believe that the things that I am telling them can possibly be true."

In the midst of all the tension, Hanson came to his office that morning "to tell me that he had discovered that Manion has no private means, has saved nothing, and is hard up. He wondered if the Government might not give him some post in connection with the war. . . . I told him I thought it was nice of him to come and speak on Manion's behalf and that I would be quite ready to meet his wishes." A post was subsequently found for Manion which he continued to occupy for the rest of his life.

Most of Saturday, June 15, was taken up with urgent measures required to meet the military and psychological situation likely to result from the imminent fall of France. Yet, in the midst of what seemed like the collapse of the whole free world, Mackenzie King found time to dictate "amongst other things, a communication to the King regarding changes in the Table of Precedence, to bring the Cabinet together ahead of Lieutenant-Governors at federal functions. It seemed to me the limit that, in following the Table of Precedence, a representative of the Lieutenant-Governor of Ontario should be wedged in ahead of Lapointe, Crerar and all of Rogers' colleagues at a service in the halls of Parliament. The function [Rogers' funeral] a federal one in the Capital itself. I told him [the representative] to take a place after the Ministers and resolved there and then to see that the Table was amended immediately." It was.

This incident reflected one side of Mackenzie King's complex character; another was revealed by the final entry in his diary for that day, which reads: "The afternoon paper made mention of the fact that Hepburn's bronchitis has developed into bronchial pneumonia. If this is so, it probably means the end of his earthly life. I don't often wish that a man should pass away but I believe it would be the most fortunate thing that could happen at this time. . . . The sympathy that will be expressed for him will be of a very different character than that expressed for Rogers whom he did all he could to destroy."

Yet there could be no doubt Mackenzie King appreciated as well as anyone, and better than most, what a very critical point in the war had been reached. Sunday, June 16, he spent at Kingsmere and after listening to the radio news, he wrote in his diary: "I felt that the radio was leaving almost too much in the way of hope. With the inside knowledge I had, it was clear that capitulation was all but inevitable." That evening when he heard that Marshal Pétain had succeeded Reynaud as Premier of France he knew it meant the French Government had decided to capitulate and wrote: "My heart is very sad at the loss of France, and above all, at the appalling situation with which the British Isles are faced from now on.

"Today," he added, "I feel there now remains the sword of the spirit with which to fight. It is now left to the British peoples and those of British stock to save the world. They may well become fused into one, if not politically, at least in heart and mind and act, for that purpose. I think now it is clear that my efforts to win the friendship of the United States, to keep the close friendship of the United States to Canada and the British Empire, has been the most needed of all actions in the course of the years that I have had to do with public life." He felt now there was a "real possibility of invasion of our shores, an effort will be made to seize this country as a prize of war. We have, therefore, changed now to the stage where defence of this land becomes our most important duty. It will involve far-reaching measures. We shall have to take them by stages and with care." He reflected that "what is now becoming most apparent of all is that neutrality is the most fatal of all attitudes. In moral issues, neither men nor nations can afford to be neutral except at the risk of the destruction of their moral and physical selves."

That quiet Sunday at Kingsmere was followed by a week of intense activity. On Monday morning, June 17, Ralston telephoned Mackenzie King to say that he and Power had been talking over how to increase the strength of the Defence Department and Power had suggested his becoming an Assistant to Ralston who, in turn, had suggested that Power be Associate Minister or Joint Minister. Power had also suggested taking J. S. Duncan into the Cabinet as Minister for Air. (Duncan of Massey-Harris had recently become Deputy Minister in charge of the Air Training Plan.) "I said," Mackenzie King wrote, "that it would suit me splendidly. I would like to take McConnell of Montreal as Minister of National Security and that would give a business man from both Toronto and Montreal. We could elect Duncan in Kingston. I would take in Moore for Labour. We could elect him in Kitchener. I thought perhaps this should be done today." But it was not that easy.

Later in the morning "Hanson, Leader of the Opposition, came in with Grote Stirling to place before me three matters which they wished me to declare myself on at the opening of the House, otherwise Hanson might find it necessary to make a speech to the nation and an appeal to the people for the requests contained. They both said they wanted to be helpful and not embarrassing, that there was nothing in the proposal which questioned in the least my leadership. Nor had they asked for Union Government, but the taking on of one or two outstanding men that would make the Government more truly national. They wanted to declare that there was a special emergency and that there should be national mobilization of resources, etc. The proposals were as follows:

1. That the Government should declare that a state of national emergency exists in Canada.
2. That the Government propose now to take authority to mobilize all the manpower and all the material resources of this nation for the aid of the Mother Country and for the defence of Canada.
3. That steps should be taken to strengthen the Government by the inclusion of some of the best brains, intelligence and ability in this country, not on the basis of a Union Government, but on the basis of a truly National Government."

Mackenzie King replied that "the thing now was not to alarm the country unduly by talking too soon about 'emergencies.' That the plan now was to steady matters a bit with wider power under the War Measures Act and under the Constitution, providing for a general levy to call out all people we need for national service." He also told them he "had in mind adding to the Ministry."

Hanson and Grote Stirling wanted an answer by three o'clock and Mackenzie King "said that that would not be possible. It would be nearly one before I could reach my colleagues, besides one had nothing official about the situation in France, and, as Churchill was speaking tomorrow,

I thought I should wait until he had spoken and not make a statement in advance pretending to size up the significance of the position as it is now in Europe.

"They asked me, for the sake of the country, would I not feel that I could change my view on conscription. I told them not at all. In the first place I believed it would create a worse situation in Canada than it would remedy. That, if I thought it was necessary, I would just tell my colleagues so, that if other members of the Government thought it was necessary, I would be ready to step out. Hanson said I had some good men in the Government; named Ralston, Howe, Power and Ilsley. He thought Lapointe might be good if he would do more in urging his own people to expect compulsory service. I told him he was quite wrong. That Lapointe was . . . extraordinarily helpful in his experience in every way. I said there were always some men in a Cabinet stronger than others but that the present Cabinet contained a really fine lot of men."

Mackenzie King also told Hanson he would be quite agreeable to taking both Hanson and Stirling into the Cabinet, but he felt it was desirable to have an official Opposition that could be helpful, and they both said "they had not come with that view at all, nor with a view to being critical of my leadership, nor with a desire of having anyone else take hold." Mackenzie King told them "the most I could do would be to give them an answer tomorrow, but that I thought it would be along lines that would be mutually acceptable."

There was strong applause in the House of Commons, that day, when Mackenzie King said that "France dropping out simply meant we would be more determined than ever to do our part. Hanson was quite decent about not pressing me for more today, though he said it was not easy. They had been having caucuses on the matter."

At the War Committee meeting that same evening, Mackenzie King "was somewhat surprised when I heard Power come out strongly demanding that we should have a measure that would enable us to call out every man in Canada for military training for the defence of Canada, in other words to introduce a measure similar to that which England had passed. I found that they had been talking matters over among themselves and that Lapointe was agreeable to this as long as it was for the defence of Canada." Mackenzie King added that he "was surprised to find all going as far as they did, but it was a relief to my mind, in that it amounts to what is right in the matter of mobilization of all resources."

They next discussed the enlargement of the Cabinet. Mackenzie King said he was determined to take in Tom Moore. "Howe was quite strong against him, seemed to think he had been working for short hours in this war period. . . . I told him it was absolutely necessary to have someone who had the complete confidence of Labour, and Moore had it greater than anyone else. We discussed other names. Power was ready to have Duncan become Minister for Air."

The next morning (June 18) Mackenzie King worked on the proposed Mobilization Bill and the explanation of the Bill he intended to give in Parliament. After some changes in the statement had been made by the Cabinet, he read it at the opening of the House. He reported that it was well received. When the statement had been made Mackenzie King asked permission to introduce the Resolution on which it was based. "Got this through without trouble on plea of wishing to introduce the Bill at once. The Bill was not printed at the time I introduced the Resolution. I took full advantage of the intense feeling of the House of Commons for urgent action arising out of the position in which France is and consequent increase of the existing menace to have the House agree to go on with the second and third readings of the Bill the same day. At one moment, it almost looked as though we would cover the three readings in the one afternoon and get the measure through the Senate and assented to at night."

However, a debate did develop and Mackenzie King spoke at some length on the second reading. He had "only half finished my speech when it came to 11. The House gave me the right to go on and when I finished at 11.30, there was strong demand to finish up that same night. I felt, however, that might be crowding Members unduly, having regard to the importance of the measure, and, as Hanson wished to speak again, left it in Committee. . . . The Members seemed very pleased at the outcome of the debate. It looked at one moment as if we might lose several of the French Members but, as Lapointe and I had taken our stand so strongly on no conscription overseas, and were prepared to give further assurances in that direction, we were able to keep the party steady." He concluded the diary for June 18 with these words: "So far as Parliament is concerned, today, I think, will really stand out as one of the most significant in my life in the House of Commons."

There was a caucus the next morning (June 19). Mackenzie King spoke two or three times. He referred to "the pride I felt in the party in standing by the measure the Government had brought down in the way they did. Sought to excuse the one or two Members who had taken exception to certain features. Explained exactly what was meant by mobilization; how it was intended to develop the measure. Referred to different ways in which it will be helpful for home defence.

"Spoke out very plainly about Members indicating Government should go faster and explained how our record had been very rapid. Then took up anew phases of the war. About England being cut out from supplies, ammunition, aircraft, except by Canadian route. Necessity for watching that. Spoke of danger of interned aliens. Also said that Government would not be stampeded in any way. That what we needed was Members to interpret our actions. Spoke of relation with the United States; of their position, of our need of co-operation rather than reliance on them. Touched on registration and other related matters. Got a great reception from the men."

During the afternoon, while the debate continued in the House on the Mobilization Bill, Mackenzie King received a telegram from Premier Godbout of Quebec reporting that the Legislative Assembly of Quebec had rejected, by a vote of 56 to 13, a motion by René Chaloult, an Independent Member, condemning the federal Mobilization Bill. The Liberals had voted solidly against the motion which was supported by Duplessis and the Union Nationale members as well as Chaloult and Camillien Houde. "No one," wrote Mackenzie King, "will ever be able to say what service Lapointe and Cardin and Power have rendered in that Province, and what it has meant to Canada having a Liberal Government in office at this time."

The debate on the Mobilization Bill continued on June 20. In the House of Commons that evening, Mackenzie King was amazed when Hanson suggested that the formation of a National Government should be a condition of passing the Bill. He "felt that by being so precipitate in the matter he [Hanson] had helped me out, as I said most of what I wished to say on National Government without having to prepare for it next week. It was pretty plain talking." In this reply to Hanson, Mackenzie King pointed out that the question of National Government had been submitted to the people in the recent general election and it was rejected by the electorate. What he said about National Government was summarized in the words: "A party which represents in this parliament some 183 members out of a total membership of 245 may pretty well claim to be a National Government in the truest sense of the word." The Hansard record continues: "When the present administration appealed to the people, it did so after the war had been in existence for some time. The policies of the present Administration were known. So also was the personnel of the Administration. All were before the country, and the majority by which the people returned the present Administration indicated pretty clearly that the Government which they wished to have carry on the affairs of the nation during this war was the Government whose policies they supported in the election. More than that, the fact that in that campaign every Member of the Administration from the Atlantic to the Pacific was returned is another evidence of how well satisfied the people were with the Government of the day. . . . I should be glad to hear from my hon. friend the Leader of the Opposition who are the particularly strong men in the group about him whom he feels should be brought into the Administration at the present time. I hope he will not ask me as the leader of the Administration to accept as a colleague any of those in the front benches before me who have said that they thought I was quite unqualified to be the leader of a Government at the present time.

"When I take into the Administration additional gentlemen in order to strengthen it, one of the first qualifications which I shall require of them, as of anyone else, is, loyalty to myself, and not a disposition to stab the leader of the party in his breast when he is trying to serve his country to the best of his ability at a time of war."

After this exchange the Bill passed quickly and, by midnight, had been passed by the Senate. The re-organization of the Cabinet, however, continued to move slowly because of the reluctance of those approached to accept the responsibility of office.

Meanwhile, a relatively minor crisis arose over a request from the British authorities to have the *Emile Bertin*, a French naval vessel carrying $300,000,000 in French gold, detained in Halifax harbour. Mackenzie King did his best to persuade the French Minister to Canada to order the detention of the vessel but he was not willing to have force used for fear it might result in bloodshed and worsen the general French situation. Skelton, the Under Secretary of State for External Affairs, raised the matter again on June 21 and Mackenzie King "gave distinct orders that force was not to be used; to persuade to the limit, to have Britain so advised. Ralston and Gordon of the Bank [Donald Gordon, then Deputy Governor of the Bank of Canada] were most anxious to have force used. Ship kept in by guns from the forts. I pointed out this would create no end of trouble throughout Canada." He was told the British Admiralty had expressed the view Canada should not let the ship go. "I said," he wrote, "we controlled our own country and would not be governed by an Admiralty point of view, but by the position of Canada as a whole. The reaction it would produce among our own people at a time we were applying the Mobilization Act. Also how the Americans would feel in seeing Canada firing on a French ship and what it would lead to in American feeling against entering the war." He added that "with uncertainty of French Government policy at Bordeaux, they may have decided to fight in outlying possessions and want their financial resources to that end. . . . I did not see how we could oppose these orders by force without taking a step that would give rise to all kinds of trouble. I had to decline to see Ralston and the Committee at Laurier House as the Governor-General was arriving at 11.30." [This was the day Athlone first arrived in Ottawa. He was sworn in later that day in the Senate Chamber.] The War Committee finally decided not to use force to detain the ship, which sailed off to Martinique.

On Sunday, June 23, at Kingsmere, Mackenzie King completed a message to be published on St. Jean Baptiste Day "to steady the French Canadian youth" at the moment of the French surrender. He also received the first definite word of the French surrender terms. His diary discloses that he spent much of the day reflecting on the plight of Britain and the prospects of successful resistance. One of these reflections is very characteristic. "I believe," he wrote, "that in the British Isles and throughout the English-speaking world there is perhaps a profounder sense of duty based on religious belief left than is the case with most other parts of the world, and this may save the day in the end. It is clear, however, that certainly the British Empire has come to a moment where its very existence is threatened in the most terrible way."

During that Sunday, he talked at length on the telephone with J. W. McConnell of Montreal about Cabinet changes. McConnell himself had already declined to join the Government because of his age and his health. He was "very strong for the appointment of G. W. Spinney, of the Bank of Montreal. I gather from what he said that [Sir Edward] Beatty equally believes he would be the best appointment that could be made. He is a very honourable man, a Liberal, and in Finance would be a great strength to the Government. McConnell thought Moore would be excellent for labour, and Crabtree for capital, as head of the Manufacturers' Association. Ralston evidently told him of what I had in mind. He also spoke of [Philip] Chester, of Winnipeg, and said that this group ought to silence effectively all opposition."

On June 24 Mackenzie King told his colleagues about his intention to bring in three or four outsiders. He found "when I pictured to them the position, as it has now become, of Europe being an arsenal for Germany, and the possibility of the British Isles being brought to their knees inside of three weeks, and not wishing to have the whole public opinion of Canada levelled at the Liberal Government for refusing to take in leading executives, they all felt, I think, the wisdom of what I was proposing."

In the next fortnight Mackenzie King invited several prominent citizens outside Parliament to accept portfolios, but for one reason or another none of them was willing, apart from Angus L. Macdonald, the Liberal Premier of Nova Scotia. However the rumours of the attempts—and the names mentioned in the press—did a good deal to weaken the agitation for a National Government.

On June 26, Mackenzie King noted in his diary: "Here are five men, all of whom are supposed to be outstanding, to whom I have offered a Cabinet post and not one of them is prepared to run the risk of spoiling their own reputations by taking responsibilities, yet those of us who have assumed this job and are carrying it out are being criticized for not taking these 'best brains' and 'best minds' into the Cabinet." The five men actually invited to join the administration were J. W. McConnell, J. S. Duncan, Tom Moore, G. W. Spinney, and J. M. Macdonnell of Toronto who was offered the new portfolio of National War Services, created to administer the National Resources Mobilization Act.

Mackenzie King then began to consider more conventional ways of reconstructing the Cabinet. Gardiner was to become Minister of the new Department of National War Services and a member of the War Committee, and Angus Macdonald was to become Minister of National Defence for Naval Services.

When, on June 28, Mackenzie King told the Leader of the Opposition confidentially the names of those he had approached, Hanson thought "I had made it impossible to have anything in the nature of a National Government by what I had said the other night of not taking men into the Cabinet who were prepared to stab me in the breast. I asked him if he thought any leader would wish to do anything of the kind."

Mackenzie King also spoke to Hanson about the idea he had conceived a few days earlier of inviting leading members of the Opposition to become members of the War Committee. Hanson asked if he would have Grote Stirling as well. "I said I would be quite agreeable to that. I thought I would have one or two of the other parties represented as well. He then said, for Heaven's sake not to have Social Credit, no one would work with them, that they were against us all. . . . Coldwell, he thought, was at least sensible. I said I might get the two parties to agree to one of their Members coming in. He seemed pleased with the idea. Said he would like to think it over. I said I was trying to meet his point of view, of making it clear that in the war effort we were not trying in any way to monopolize or conceal."

On July 2, this last idea was discussed with the Cabinet. He found Ralston "favourable to taking Hanson and Stirling into the Cabinet. All others were opposed on the score that we would be false to our own following and to the trust reposed in us by the electors, nothing having arisen which would make a Union Government necessary." His colleagues agreed on "inviting Hanson and Stirling into the War Committee of the Cabinet as Associate Members but thought both leaders of other groups should come in as well. It was felt, if this proposal, which would be made to extend over period when Parliament was not sitting, was not acceptable, we had gone as far as we could go."

At the Liberal caucus on July 3 Mackenzie King found the Members "in an entirely different frame of mind than they had been thus far. They all seemed to have come to realize that there is danger to Canada itself in the present situation. Everything was in the nature of the Government doing more and more to mobilize the human and material resources of the country to defend our coasts on the Atlantic and the Pacific; to make co-operative arrangements with the States, etc. etc. The feeling was divided as between whether we should continue to send forces overseas or retain everything for purely local defence." He let the caucus know he had been willing to take a Conservative or two into the Government and noted that "this did not meet with much approval."

On July 5, it was finally decided that Cardin should take the portfolio of Transport in addition to Public Works (C. D. Howe had carried on as Minister of Transport after his appointment in April to Munitions and Supply) and that the other vacancies in the Cabinet should be filled by two Members from Ontario, W. P. Mulock (Postmaster General, vacated by Power) and Colin Gibson (National Revenue, succeeding Ilsley). It was also decided that Angus Macdonald should be a candidate in Kingston which had been Rogers' constituency. The most important of all the decisions and the one taken most reluctantly by Mackenzie King was the appointment of J. L. Ilsley as Minister of Finance. Ralston was sworn as Minister of National Defence on July 5 and Ilsley, Gibson, Mulock, and Cardin were sworn on Monday, July 8; that virtually ended the campaign for a National Government in 1940.

When announcing the changes in the Ministry that afternoon (July 8), Mackenzie King also informed Parliament of the proposal to have representative Members from the Opposition associated with the War Committee of the Cabinet.

Hanson replied on July 11 to the proposal of associate membership in the War Committee and according to Mackenzie King, "he treated the proposal as a trick and not an honest attempt to meet the wishes of the Conservatives in and outside Parliament." Mackenzie King "was too tired to make the most of the case in reply. On the whole, while not covering points to my own satisfaction, did so I think in a manner which pleased fairly well our own following. As a matter of fact, I was immediately relieved when I saw the Tory party and, following them, the other groups were unwilling to accept the invitations. They can say nothing more from now on about every effort not having been made to meet their wishes for inside knowledge with respect to shaping of policy, etc.

"I would never have felt secure with any of them in the Ministry and am immensely relieved to have the whole air cleared of the kind of baiting there has been of the Ministry ever since Parliament opened. I feel now that we have the atmosphere cleared with respect to National Government, etc. and our own position established in a manner which should enable us at least satisfactorily to shut the mouths of those who hereafter in Parliament or through the press may seek to urge further changes in the Administration.

"I confess," he added, "I was surprised at Grote Stirling having apparently shared with Hanson, the views he did. The truth of the matter is that these men cannot get politics out of their minds; are judging others by themselves. Have foolish suspicions; playing party politics for all it is worth. I am, however, immensely relieved in mind that the business has been now threshed through and the case for Responsible Government made out of the lips of the Leader of the Opposition himself."

The next morning (July 12) Mackenzie King read through the previous day's debate and noted that "the attitude of the Opposition had left the Liberal Party wholly and absolutely responsible of itself and dependent on its majority from now on. It means that if our men stay solid, we need be concerned about nothing in the way of continuation of power till 1945 if we so desire." He added that "yesterday's Hansard is an all important historical record."

That evening Angus L. Macdonald arrived in Ottawa, was sworn as Minister for Naval Services, and went to Kingsmere to spend the night with the Prime Minister. At the conclusion of the day's diary Mackenzie King wrote that Macdonald "is ready to accept it [a seat in Kingston] on the understanding it will be for this Parliament only and he can return to Nova Scotia at the next General Election. From this conversation I could see he is quite decided on remaining in the Federal field and will, I feel sure, be a strength and if he holds out, make a real mark there." On this same day Power was sworn as Associate Minister of National Defence (in addition to being Minister for Air) and Gardiner as Minister of National War Services (continuing as Minister of Agriculture).

The rest of the session was an anticlimax. Mackenzie King wrote on July 25 that he was "much relieved this morning to read the Conservative party in Parliament had decided to have Hanson continue as Leader and will defer national convention until the autumn of next year. That would seem to ensure keeping Meighen out of the House of Commons." On July 31, Mackenzie King noted that he felt "the Opposition has been helpful in causing the Government to perhaps determine more quickly and definitely what was to be done in some matters than might otherwise have been the case. On the whole, their attitude has been constructively helpful although there has been more party politics than one would have liked to see at a time like this."

During the month of July Lapointe had been so unwell that he had to leave Ottawa for a rest. On August 2, Mackenzie King "was greatly pleased, on phoning Lapointe tonight, to hear him say that he was quite well again and in the best of shape and will be in Ottawa on Monday. His voice sounded quite cheerful, as though he were really anxious to be back." This news was a tremendous relief. As early as May 11, Mackenzie King had been greatly concerned about Lapointe's failing health and had felt he "would have to count on having less and less support from Lapointe than heretofore which is a serious matter." Then on July 11, Lapointe had come to see him, looking very tired and worn, and told him "he did not want to add to my worries but he had come to tell me that he was afraid that he was suffering a complete nervous breakdown. Thereupon he began to cry like a child. I went over and sat beside him. Said I was not at all surprised that he felt as he did. That I knew what that kind of strain was. He then said he could not sleep and moaned in a way: 'Is this not too bad this had to be?' He said to me in characteristically generous way: 'I hope I am not leaving too much to you and that you will be able to get along without me.' That was when I said to him there was only one thing for him to do. That was for him to go away at once and get a complete rest. . . . We then talked a little together during which time he repeatedly broke down. I did my best to reassure him, saying that in another week, he would feel quite different and at the end of two weeks, would not know himself, but not to bother with the rest of the session. . . . He seemed very grateful and quieted himself and then went out by the side door into the hall, and said he would get straight away."

Mackenzie King felt "quite anxious about him." He observed that he had "failed a good deal. I think he is worrying terribly about the war and the future. It has been a tremendous shock to him. I said to him that naturally the fall of France and the changed conditions would have this effect."

Lapointe's return could not have been more timely because another political crisis had arisen: this time about the national registration undertaken under the Mobilization Act. On Saturday, August 3, Hanson spoke in the House on a matter which had caused Mackenzie King "more concern than anything which has happened thus far. This was a statement made the day before by Camillien Houde, the Mayor of Montreal and a former leader of the provincial Conservative party in Quebec, "defying the Government's registration, and advising people to do the same. The Montreal *Star* had published matter before it could be completely censored, apparently breaking censorship rule." It was suggested that what Hanson had said in Parliament should be kept out of afternoon papers. Mackenzie King said "this was impossible. There would be added to the cry of a free press, the cry of a free Parliament. The whole business is most unpatriotic from the Tory side, and nearly criminal on the part of Mayor Houde."

When Mackenzie King brought the matter before the Cabinet, "all present were virtually agreed that action be taken against Houde, and that immediately. The advisers in the Justice Department suggested Provincial Government taking action. Cardin rightly said, 'Why should we place the burden on the Provincial Government? Why not the Federal Government?' I asked him, in what manner, and he said by the R.C.M.P. He said action should be taken at once. Council then discussed whether Houde should be interned, or dealt with by the courts. It was agreed that, if brought before court, he would be given the opportunity he wanted, namely, speechify, making a display, etc. It was felt if he were interned at once that would deprive him of this opportunity and would be most helpful in the end. It was agreed that the Mounted Police should take this action forthwith. It was thought it had better be taken at night, as there would be no opportunity for photograph displays, etc. I can see, in the whole business, possibility of riots and serious difficulties throughout the Province of Quebec. However, I see no other course. The federal Government cannot afford to have its laws defied by one of Mayor Houde's prominence. I stated in the House that Parliament could count on the law being upheld by the Administration."

On August 5, Mackenzie King was questioned in the House about Mayor Houde by Hanson. He felt the questions "clearly were of a political nature, calculated to make trouble between the Government and the press, also to stir up trouble in Quebec."

During the afternoon, Lapointe returned to Ottawa and as Minister of Justice signed the warrant for Houde's arrest; it was arranged that he would be taken into custody and interned that night. Mackenzie King observed that "Cardin had been timorous in taking this action, largely because of Houde being in his district. On the whole, I think it lends strength to the Government's position to have had Lapointe take the action himself. He had no hesitation about so doing, and our Members report that action of the kind against Houde will be appreciated in the province of Quebec."

Two days later (August 7) the session adjourned on the twenty-first anniversary of Mackenzie King's selection as leader of the Liberal party. When he entered the House of Commons he "was somewhat taken aback, though pleasurably surprised, to see the silver bowl filled with roses on my desk. When prayers were over, Grote Stirling, Acting Leader of the Opposition, came over and congratulated me on the completion of the twenty-first anniversary. Many Members of my own party did the same."

The demonstration in the House and the speeches gratified Mackenzie King. He felt that "some invisible Hand had been getting into shape the event itself to make it a memorable one. To appearances, all was the result of accident. We had hoped to conclude last Saturday, at the latest Tuesday. All unconsciously, those opposed to me politically were helping to make inevitable this memorable demonstration and thereby to attract attention not only of the country but of other countries as well to my twenty-one years of public service at this critical time in the affairs of the world."

CHAPTER SIX

The Linch-Pin*

WHEN Mackenzie King left Ottawa on April 12 for his first wartime visit to the United States, he was simply going away for a rest from the strain of the election campaign. In New York the next morning he received an invitation from President Roosevelt to visit him at Warm Springs, Georgia, later in the month, though even this visit was treated as a holiday to avoid offending neutral sentiment in the United States. He arrived at Warm Springs on April 23, having spent the interval resting at Virginia Beach. On his arrival at 11 o'clock he was taken to the Little White House to meet the President, and except for a short rest in the afternoon, he spent the rest of that day—"as enjoyable a day as any I had had in a long time"—with Roosevelt. The next morning he joined the President about 10:30, they talked for an hour, and the President then drove him down to the Warm Springs pool where "we went in for a swim. We lay in the sun for half an hour first and were in the water for half an hour." After lunch they talked for another couple of hours. Mackenzie King then returned to Atlanta to take the train and, at once, dictated a memorandum of his conversations with the President. He called this "a wholly informal personal visit" in which nothing was discussed in an official way, and noted that "the President spoke without reserve on the different subjects we talked about. Gave me his full confidence." Their talk during the morning of April 23 had been interrupted two or three times by calls from Washington, but Roosevelt had "insisted on my remaining while he was conversing."

Most of their talk was about the war and there was "of course no question about his sympathies. He and everyone around him are all strongly for the Allies.... He was anxious to avoid recognizing a state

---

*"Canada . . . is a magnet exercising a double attraction drawing both Great Britain and the United States towards herself and thus drawing them closer to each other. She is the only surviving bond which stretches from Europe across the Atlantic Ocean. In fact, no state, no country, no band of men can more truly be described as the linch-pin of peace and world progress."—W. S. Churchill, *Saturday Evening Post*, February 15, 1930.

of war between Germany and Norway [the German invasion of Norway and Denmark had begun on April 9] so that he would not have to issue a proclamation of neutrality but would continue to supply Norway with aeroplanes, ammunition, etc." When word came during the morning that both Norway and Denmark were represented at the Supreme Allied Council, and were thus probably formal belligerents, Roosevelt told the State Department "to take another day to find out whether they were official representatives or merely observers. He recalled how he had waited a week and 'phoned me before declaring Canada was at war." Indeed, at every stage in the conversation Roosevelt indicated he was stretching his powers to the limit to help the Allies.

The German occupation of Denmark had raised difficulties about the status of Greenland, where the Aluminum Company of Canada owned cryolite mines which were providing essential supplies. Before Mackenzie King had left Ottawa, the Government had been considering what should be done to provide for the security of these mines. Roosevelt showed Mackenzie King a letter he had received from Cordell Hull indicating that "the Americans were anxious that Canada should not undertake anything in particular. I told the President we had received from the owners of the cryolite mines requests to protect them and had undertaken, in correspondence with Britain, to see that men were supplied who could be of service about the mine in protective ways. That we would expect, however, the British fleet to do what was needed on the Atlantic; also that we had sent up each year a ship to Baffinland which brought supplies to Greenland. That this ship would be taking more in the way of supplies this year than previously." Roosevelt indicated that the Americans would also send a supply ship and that the masters of the two ships should meet before they started out and have an understanding between them as to the best way of proceeding, but that "if a real danger arose, he would have to leave it to the British to deal with submarines, etc. at sea. He thought no effort should be made, either by the United States or Canada, to get possession of Greenland, that whatever was done should be done subject to Greenland managing her own affairs." Mackenzie King discussed the question of Greenland further with Cordell Hull when he visited Washington on his return trip to Canada.

At one stage, Roosevelt told Mackenzie King to tell Norman Rogers that there was some defence equipment belonging to the United States Navy which might be useful on the east coast and in Newfoundland, and that "he could arrange to let us have at a nominal figure. That it was not new. A great deal of it left over from the last war, but quite serviceable enough for the purpose that would be required. . . . That the navy always wanted new things. That he might supply his own people with new material and let us have his old material."

Mackenzie King asked Roosevelt "whether there were difficulties between England and the United States that Canada could be of any assistance" in overcoming, and Roosevelt replied that there had been "a couple of occasions when I thought I would pick up the telephone to speak to you. But those had passed." He did express the wish that the British would act more rapidly to build up their strength.

Roosevelt also "spoke of possibly finding it necessary to send destroyers and cruisers to assist the British" and Mackenzie King "could see he was quite concerned about the inadequacy of the defence of Canada both on the Atlantic and the Pacific" as presenting "a real danger to the United States." During their conversations, Mackenzie King had shown Roosevelt a reference in a speech he had made before the war when introducing Cordell Hull in Toronto in which he had spoken of a moral embargo of aggressor nations and he noted that Roosevelt was greatly interested and had "the moral embargo idea very strongly in mind" in the rest of their talks. Mackenzie King added that he himself believed "this is the method by which America will render its greatest assistance to the Allies particularly if Germany begins bombing unfortified cities in Britain"; he resolved to impress this on Cordell Hull when he saw him in Washington.

He found Roosevelt "was immensely interested in the Canadian elections. Had evidently followed matters very closely and inquired about why there were losses in New Brunswick; how Manion came to be defeated; about Bill Herridge [W. D. Herridge had been Canadian Minister to the United States when Roosevelt became President. In 1940, he had become associated with the Social Credit movement, which had been renamed "New Democracy." He had been an unsuccessful candidate in Saskatchewan in the election]; situation in Alberta." Mackenzie King gave him a general account of the campaign and presented him "with a copy of my radio addresses which he asked me to inscribe to himself."

During their drive on April 24, Mackenzie King asked Roosevelt about his own plans in connection with the presidential election to take place that autumn, but told him "not to think of answering any question if he felt any embarrassment. He was very frank." Roosevelt told him the "man who commanded the greatest respect of the party was Cordell Hull. That Hull, however, was mostly interested only in trade matters and foreign affairs. Had not taken much interest in politics generally and was well advanced in years. Still he thought he was decidedly the best of all." Roosevelt felt that if he could find a young man of the right kind as a candidate for the vice-presidency, whose sympathies with the New Deal were strong, he would like to have Hull become the candidate, and added "that he himself did not wish to run a third term and did not intend to do so. That he could not say definitely that he would not. He would say nothing about it. That that was really his view and intent at the present time."

Mackenzie King said he thought the President was "right in keeping an open mind until the last moment. That I thought it was primarily a matter of his own health and strength. That he would be doing an injustice to himself to take on a third term if he were not equal physically to it. He said to me that he was mentally tired. That if he could get a year off for a rest, it would be quite different. He was sure that he would feel in the best of shape at the end of that time. That he did not think he could go on and take the responsibilities of another term without a period of rest which was not possible when he was in office."

Mackenzie King told Roosevelt he should write "his own memoirs. He said that that is what he would like to do and wanted to do. He told me about having given all his papers and established a library at Hyde Park and put Hopkins in charge. Would have him work out particular subjects that he wished to develop. I said to him: 'Hopkins would probably need a whole staff.' What he wished done was to get the material assembled in this way and then go over it himself in his own language, giving it his own point of view." This, of course, was exactly what Mackenzie King planned to do himself when he retired.

Roosevelt told Mackenzie King "that what he would like to do would be to become a sort of 'Moderator.' He asked me if I did not like that word. I spoke of the Moderator of the Assembly of the Presbyterian Church and said naturally I thought it was a good one. He said it implies more than simply being one who was having to do with the making of a settlement. It was rather the person who would bring others together and reconcile views. I told him I thought he was right in looking on the latter part of his life in that way. That he could not perform a role of the kind as President or head of a political party but, with the experience of his life behind him, he should be able to give worthy service in a large way at a time, for example, of the making of a world peace. I think in this he is very wise. I sought to impress upon him to keep in mind his health and strength."

Mackenzie King was "quite sure" from the way Roosevelt spoke that he was "not trying to conceal his real purpose with regard to a third term. I am sure he is tired and realizes that his energy is not what it was before. He is anxious, however, to make sure that someone will receive the nomination who will be able to carry on his policies." However, he found Roosevelt "better in appearance than I had expected to see him. Not so exhausted. He was much thinner in body. Tells me he has lost ten pounds; also in the face, but not haggard or worn looking, though eyes very tired."

Roosevelt told Mackenzie King that "some little time ago, he was prepared to attempt to form a National Government. I imagine this was at the beginning of the war. That he had sent for the leaders of the Republican party, discussed the matter with them but that they would not play with him. That Knox [W. F. Knox had been Republican candidate for Vice President in 1936; later in 1940 he became Roosevelt's Secretary of the Navy] was inclined to be favourable to the idea but that the others were not. I said to him I thought National Governments were a mistake. That he would be much wiser to hold to his own party. That it only meant a neutralizing of policies to bring opposing forces of the kind together. That . . . I believed there would have been no European war if a National Government had never been formed in England."

Shortly before leaving Warm Springs, Mackenzie King raised the question of the St. Lawrence Waterway. Roosevelt asked how far they had got along in reaching a settlement and Mackenzie King replied "that I would like to say to him quite frankly that so far as we were concerned, except for the interest that we knew he had in the matter and for the promise I had given to have it further discussed if we once reached an agreement with our own provinces concerning it, I would not bring the matter up. That I thought, as a Federal Government, we felt there was not any great demand for the waterways at this time." Mackenzie King had promised Roosevelt in 1938 that as soon as the Governments of Ontario and Quebec withdrew their objections, Canada would resume discussions with the United States, and he now told Roosevelt that since the Premier of Ontario was now favourable to the project he felt it was his duty to agree to go ahead if Roosevelt wished to do so. He added that Ralston did not want to proceed and felt, if they did go ahead, tolls should be charged on all vessels except those of the United States, Britain and Canada.

Mackenzie King found that Roosevelt "was all for paying project by tolls if that were possible. He then said he thought the best thing to do would be to have matters proceeded with up to the point of readiness to make a treaty, but not attempt the treaty itself until after the Presidential election." Roosevelt asked Mackenzie King "to tell Cordell Hull that this was his view. He thought the matter should stand over until after the elections and then, if thought advisable, a treaty concluded and put through at the first session of new Congress."

For Mackenzie King, the suggested postponement to 1941 was a "great relief."

They also discussed a successor as American Minister to Canada for James Cromwell who wanted to retire to become a candidate for the United States Senate. Mackenzie King recommended "someone of a thoughtful type of mind and as good a man as he could get. Just now, with world situation as it was, Ottawa was a very important centre even as between Britain and the United States. That much could be done there by conference in different ways that would be helpful in furthering mutual interests." Roosevelt indicated that the "man he had in mind was Moffat who had been an assistant to Sumner Welles [in the State Department] and was one of the best of the career men."

Before he left Warm Springs, Mackenzie King spoke to Roosevelt "about his paying us a visit in the summer, coming to Ottawa while Lord Athlone and the Princess were there. He said he would be glad, indeed, to consider this and would try to arrange it to come about the end of June."

Mackenzie King "found it exceedingly easy to talk with the President, and those around him tell me that he feels it the same with me. That he has looked forward to my coming as a rest. He certainly gave up all his time to me and took the greater part of both days as a complete holiday for a real chance to share a sense of genuine companionship."

From Warm Springs Mackenzie King went to Williamsburg, Virginia, where he spent two days with Mr. and Mrs. John D. Rockefeller, Jr., which he enjoyed very much. On Saturday, April 27, he travelled to Washington, and he was surprised to find Cordell Hull at the station to meet him. Hull drove Mackenzie King to the Canadian Legation. On the way he expressed regret that the American Minister [James Cromwell] had been in Ottawa for such a short time and said "he had pressed very hard to get someone appointed who would be outstanding." Mackenzie King agreed that Hull "was right in believing the position a necessary and important one in world conditions of real importance to the United States, Great Britain and Canada. There were many matters we could work out at Ottawa which would be helpful all around."

The next day (April 28) Mackenzie King spent some time with

Loring Christie, the Canadian Minister to the United States. One subject they discussed was Greenland and Mackenzie King "was astonished" to find that Christie had been given instructions by the Department of External Affairs "to say that Canada would prepare a defence force for Greenland. I had objected to this to Skelton over the 'phone before leaving [Ottawa] and thought his cable to England did not go that far. Apparently Ralston being concerned about aluminum and Skelton zealous to have Canada rather than England handle Greenland matters on North American basis, had between them gone farther than I think was wise. I thought the position taken by the Americans was wise. Christie agreed that the matter had now been satisfactorily straightened out. Clearly our people had been a little over-zealous in preparing for a little war on Canada's own account."

In the afternoon Mackenzie King called on Mr. and Mrs. Cordell Hull. He found "Mr. Hull was so strongly sympathetic to the Allies and so anxious to do what could be done by the United States that I ventured to recall to his mind his visit to Toronto [just before the war] and what I had said about something in the nature of moral embargo policy. He listened very intently and approvingly to what I said to him. It was stretching a long bow, but I felt the situation was so serious that if I could do anything to help influence American action in the right direction, it was justified and not violating social hospitality. He gave me the freest opening."

Mackenzie King found Cordell Hull greatly concerned "about the danger of Japan fighting for supremacy on the Pacific, if given any excuse to begin a struggle there. He thought that the people did not realize how close to the edge of a precipice we all were, even in America, with possible spread of the war in the Orient," and he felt that "if the British fleet was destroyed in the Atlantic, the United States would be face to face with the problem of defending themselves against world domination by Germany." Mackenzie King observed that Hull did "not take any cocksure attitude so far as the United States are concerned."

The next morning (April 29) Mackenzie King called again on the Secretary of State, this time at his office. Hull told him "how much he and Mrs. Hull had enjoyed my visit yesterday, and then spoke about how serious the situation in Europe was." Mackenzie King "then spoke to him again of an amendment to the Neutrality Act regarding its provisions not applying to a country which had been unwarrantedly invaded," and next "asked him point blank what would be done if Greenland should be invaded." Hull did not think such an invasion probable but said, "if it should come, that would raise ... the question of the application of the Monroe doctrine. He did not say that the Monroe doctrine would apply, but certainly that it would raise that question for consideration." He next spoke to Hull about the St. Lawrence Waterway and repeated the President's view that it would be "better not to have any treaty until about next January, but, in the meantime, to keep working on the basis of a treaty."

Mackenzie King also spoke to Cordell Hull about the presidential election and said "I did not wish to touch on matters outside my own country, but I hoped, nevertheless, for the sake of the world, that he might be the next President. That I felt it was due to his own career." Hull replied that his interest was "primarily in foreign affairs, that he had never wished to be mixed up in domestic problems. . . . He had never given anyone reason to believe that he was anxious for the position of Chief Executive, but thought he had really strengthened his position by having adopted the attitude he had. He said he had never discussed it with the President. Did not know what he had in mind. Said he would like to talk over these matters with him but thought it was just as well not to do so."

Mackenzie King "told him I thought the President was looking to him to succeed. He seemed to be rather pleased at that. Mr. Hull did not at any time say that he would run or that he would not run, but I felt, as we talked, that he probably might have it in his mind, though would make no move for the moment himself. My own guess is that he will be a Democratic candidate and will meet with a good deal of Republican support. . . . I am pretty sure that President Roosevelt will not run and that Mr. Hull will be his own and the convention's choice."

From the State Department Mackenzie King went to call on Henry Morgenthau, the Secretary of the Treasury. The main subject of their discussion was British war purchases in the United States. "Morgenthau spoke very highly of Purvis [Arthur Purvis was a leading industrialist of Montreal who had undertaken responsibility for British purchasing in the United States]. Said they got on with each other perfectly. Sometimes, he said, there were difficulties. Spoke of one he had at the present time which he thought I might be helpful in solving. . . . He said the British were making many purchases from the United States. He found it very hard to get a full statement of what these purchases amounted to in all. . . . He thought results might be serious if they did not get the information." Morgenthau explained that the question was more important than seemed to be realized, because German propaganda was making capital of the quantity of gold the United States was acquiring from the British and the only answer "was the quantities of goods the British were purchasing. He thought it was to Britain's interest as well as that of the United States to have these facts known." Morgenthau told Mackenzie King he thought this "ought to be known direct by Mr. Chamberlain. I said I would see that word got to Mr. Chamberlain very soon."

Mackenzie King lunched at the British Embassy with the Ambassador, Lord Lothian, that day (April 29) and told him about his conversations with the President and Cordell Hull. He mentioned particularly what the President said as to Americans enlisting in the British and Canadian forces "not being obliged to take an oath of allegiance, simply an oath to obey orders." Lothian agreed that it was a mistake to insist on the oath of allegiance, if they could get men from the United States to enlist voluntarily, and said he would cable the British Government that afternoon.

Mackenzie King also told Lothian what Morgenthau had said about getting full information about British purchases and Lothian "said he would try to obtain the data at once." He repeated to Lothian what the President had said about letting Rogers have certain munitions, and what had been said about Greenland by the President and Hull. Lothian raised the question of "the effect of the Statute of Westminster in regard to the present position of Greenland." Lothian evidently felt that since Canada was completely autonomous and an American nation "the Monroe Doctrine would not apply to Greenland vis-à-vis Canada, but that it might vis-à-vis Great Britain. The State Department did not raise the question of the Monroe Doctrine. Had put all their argument on the importance of not giving the Japanese a pretext." Mackenzie King made it clear that what Cordell Hull really feared was that if Britain or Canada occupied Greenland the Japanese might use this action as a precedent for seizing European possessions in Asia.

While at lunch at the British Embassy, Mackenzie King received word that the President, who had now returned from Georgia, would like to see him on his way to the station. When he called at the White House, in company with Loring Christie, Roosevelt said to him: "I did not carry out your advice, Mackenzie, to stay on another day or two, which I would have liked to have done. From the reports received about what was happening, I began to get rather jittery, so could not, of course, enjoy any rest in those circumstances and came back." The President was referring here to the suspicious activities of Italy. He told Mackenzie King what he was trying to do to dissuade Mussolini from going to war and Mackenzie King in turn repeated his suggestion about the possibility of a moral embargo.

At the close of their talk, the President said to Mackenzie King: " 'Well, Mackenzie, if there is more trouble you will not mind if I ring you up.' He turned to Christie and said: 'You will not mind if I go over your head and talk straight across the phone to Mr. King.' Christie said no; on the contrary he would be very much relieved. I said to the President that I would welcome a word from him at any time, to count on me for any help I could be in any way. We then exchanged a word or two about the very happy days we had together at Warm Springs and said goodbye."

Mackenzie King recognized there was no hope at this time of direct American intervention in the war. "The only possibility I see," he wrote on April 29, "is an amendment to the Neutrality Act." He added that "no man ever received a more wholehearted or brotherly welcome than I did from everyone in connection with the Administration with whom I came in contact." Mackenzie King went on to New York on the 29th and returned to Ottawa on May 1.

After the invasion of France and the Low Countries began on May 10, it soon became clear that Britain could not supply the aircraft required for the Commonwealth Air Training Plan and that training could not be speeded up unless aircraft could be secured from the United States.

On May 18, Ralston, Rogers, and Power recommended to Mackenzie King that he should make a direct appeal to the President. Mackenzie King "felt it was going far, yet with the situation so desperate I thought I ought to take this step in a purely personal way, thereby letting him know the British position and our own and the extent to which it was threatened, and threatening also the United States." Loring Christie was away from Washington because of illness, but Mackenzie King learned that Hugh Keenleyside of the Department of External Affairs was leaving for Washington, on another mission. His train was held up so that Mackenzie King could give him a detailed message, rather than telephone direct to the President.

On May 19, Mackenzie King "was pleased tonight to get word of the interview Keenleyside had with the President. While unable to meet the specific request made, which I fully expected he would not be able to meet, he, nevertheless, made suggestions as to means of obtaining some aircraft which I think will be distinctly helpful. Also, a message came from him yesterday agreeing to allow Americans to enlist in Canadian Forces, provided they take the Oath of Obedience rather than of

Allegiance. These two things have been partly accomplished and have been in the main, I think, the outcome of my visit to Washington and the friendship established with the President."

When Keenleyside returned from Washington, Mackenzie King saw him, on May 23, and received a full account of his interview with the President. Keenleyside reported that Roosevelt was greatly concerned over recent developments on the Western Front and expressed the hope that, if the situation deteriorated further, Mr. King could find time to come to see him privately at Hyde Park or in Washington. Keenleyside gathered the impression that Roosevelt was especially concerned about the fate of the British navy in the event of an Allied defeat.

That same day (May 23) the British Government appealed to Mackenzie King to have all available Canadian destroyers sent across the Atlantic to help guard the shores of Britain. The War Committee, after anxious deliberation, decided to let the destroyers go. Mackenzie King's attitude was that if "the Admiralty thought that it would be protecting us more in the end to allow these destroyers to go, well and good." He felt, however, that "we should immediately acquaint the United States with our position." The War Committee agreed that he "should let Roosevelt know the entire situation as a good neighbour. It was due to the United States who stood to suffer if our shores were wholly neglected. It was due to our own people to get from the United States all the help we possibly could."

The following day (May 24), while Mackenzie King was explaining the situation to the Cabinet, he received a telephone call from Cordell Hull in Washington who asked if he "could send someone at once to Washington, someone in whom I had the fullest confidence and could trust in every way, to come and have a talk with him and another person higher up. There were some things that the latter wished me to know. He spoke of the gravity of the situation." Mackenzie King noted that "Mr. Hull used some expression about someone I could trust as implicitly as myself, someone who was discreet, who would not let it be known that he was in Washington or seeing anyone there. I added that he knew, of course, that our Minister was ill, meaning, otherwise, I assumed he would not have wished me to think he was passing over Christie. If either Skelton or Heeney could have been spared, I would have taken either in that order. Everything considered, Keenleyside seemed the best one to send.

"It was quite remarkable that I had got the War Committee to agree last night to let me tell our whole situation to the President and that I had intended to send Keenleyside with that end in view today. As the matter now stands, the invitation comes from the President himself to me to send someone down. I talked later with Keenleyside, and got Rogers and Howe to give him particulars as to our needs."

Keenleyside left by air the same afternoon. "Nothing," wrote Mackenzie King, "could show more clearly the wisdom of my so-called holiday to the States. Imagine being condemned by the public for being there, when the whole purpose was to help the British to keep the bond of friendship strong between England and the United States and Canada and the United States, in this crisis."

On his return from Washington, Keenleyside went to Kingsmere with Skelton on Sunday, May 26, and reported to Mackenzie King that Roosevelt and Hull were "convinced that the French will not be able to hold out. That, any day, their armies will be defeated. That there will be great pressure upon them, by the people, to give up the fight and that the Government would not be able to resist this pressure. This will leave the way open to the Germans attacking Britain speedily and terrifically with superiority in air power of 5 to 1.

"The President and Mr. Hull were doubtful if England would be able to bear up under the attack, and the President has it from what he believes good authority from Germany that Hitler may make an offer of settlement based on turning over of the whole of the colonial Empire; of England giving up all association with Imperial affairs, bargaining only for her own salvation; the price being that, as mentioned, of giving up colonial and Imperial affairs, and the turning over of her fleet as well."

Keenleyside reported that the President wanted Mackenzie King to persuade the Dominions to bring concerted pressure to bear on the United Kingdom not to yield to the making of any soft peace even though it might mean destruction of England comparable to that of Poland, Holland and Belgium and the killing of those who had refused to make the peace, but to have her fleet make its base at different outlying parts away from England and to send the King to Bermuda. The United States would open her ports to the British fleet for repairs. Mackenzie King noted that Roosevelt felt that "in this way a cordon from Greenland to Africa could be thrown around Germany; though it might take a couple of years, Germany would be defeated in the end."

Keenleyside also reported that the United States could not part with any of their aircraft because they had not enough at the present time to meet their own needs, but that the President intended "to have his 'ice patrol' extend to Greenland" and was "prepared to watch our coast and, if a raid made on Greenland, to blow the raider to pieces."

Mackenzie King told Keenleyside to go home and "write the story out before any of us began to talk it over, so that there would be no confusion." He added that "when Keenleyside had concluded his talk with the suggestion that I should seek through Australia, New Zealand and South Africa to bring pressure on the British Government to turn their fleet over to the United States, for a moment it seemed to me that the United States was seeking to save itself at the expense of Britain. That it was an appeal to the selfishness of the Dominions at the expense of the British Isles. Each of them being secure by the arrangement. That the British themselves might have to go down. I instinctively revolted against such a thought. My reaction was that I would rather die than do aught to save ourselves or any part of this continent at the expense of Britain.

"I said at once that if I were to attempt to influence the Dominions in this way, it would immediately be said that I was pro-American. The Tories would be the first to shout it from the house-tops that I was ready to sacrifice the British Isles for a new orientation of world power. I also said at once that I would never try to influence either Australia or South Africa. They were of a different school of thought than Canada and bound to misinterpret or resent our attitude. I said that I would be prepared to pass on the American view to Churchill if that was the desire, but felt whatever I did should be done direct with Churchill and the President and not through others."

During the afternoon of May 26, Mackenzie King "continued to give the matter thought. Decided to sleep on it. Keenleyside returned about 6 o'clock with his material written out. I read it over this evening. It seemed to me that the real intent of the President was not quite clear. One place it said that the President would like Mr. Churchill to know at once, so and so. The conclusion indicated that it was rather that I should get the Dominions to join in presenting the United States view to Mr. Churchill."

Mackenzie King telephoned Cordell Hull the following morning (May 27) and "asked him whether the intention of the message was for me to communicate direct with Mr. Churchill or to get the Dominions together to make the representations referred to. Mr. Hull said it was rather that of giving me the picture as he and the President saw it with a view not to have immediate presentation to Churchill but to having the Dominions, when the time came, tell Britain to stand firm and not part with her fleet or make a soft peace. To see that she was urged to stand firm and take the course suggested by the Dominions.

"When I got this message direct from Mr. Hull, I called in Keenleyside who said that that was quite a different impression than he got from the President. That he felt the President wanted immediate action on my part with Mr. Churchill. I decided there and then to ask him to return to Washington tonight and find out from Mr. Hull and the

President exactly what they wanted." Mackenzie King warned Keenleyside that "the United States might be using Canada to protect themselves in urging a course that would spare them immediate assistance to Britain."

Mackenzie King noted that "Skelton pointed out to me that he thought I should urge strongly on the United States to let Britain have planes at this time as being the one effective means of avoiding the possibility of the next step. I told him by all means to have Keenleyside urge this as my point of view which, of course, was the whole purpose of sending him to Washington in the first instance.

"I put the whole matter of Keenleyside's mission to Skelton who was to give it to him again in these words:

(1) The object the President had in view—was it to have me make known to England the American point of view? If so, for him to tell the President I thought it should be done through the British Embassy at Washington.

(2) If it were desired to have the American point of view made known in a roundabout way through myself—via the Dominions rather than the British Embassy at Washington, I would not think it advisable to try to present any point of view through the three Dominions with a view to influencing Churchill in a manner which might make the greater sacrifice fall on Britain. I doubted the wisdom at any time of my even trying to have dealings with the other Dominions for any purpose. That I would be suspect as pro-American or North American."

Keenleyside returned from Washington on May 29 and reported to Mackenzie King that he had conveyed the view that it would be preferable if Roosevelt approached Churchill direct, but that, if this was not considered feasible, Mackenzie King would be ready to act as an intermediary. He had also renewed the appeal for immediate American aid.

Roosevelt had stated to Keenleyside that the Americans had only 800 military aircraft left in the country and none could be spared. He indicated that he hoped Mackenzie King would act on his own regarding the proposal for the British fleet and present Roosevelt's point of view as though it was representative of Canadian opinion. He felt the case should be put to Churchill at once. If Churchill was not utterly opposed, Canada's initiative would be followed in a few days by a similar argument from the United States.

Mackenzie King spent a good part of May 30 drafting a message to Churchill. "The difficult part," he wrote, "was to try and meet the President's wishes, so far as I could, of having the message appear to be from myself rather than from him, while at the same time taking care to see that it was wholly his point of view that I was putting over and not my own. I wish the message could have gone much sooner. However I believe it will be really deeply appreciated by Churchill, and come at a moment that will be helpful to him and will meet a good response. If it does, it may well be the most significant of any message that has, thus far, crossed the ocean since the beginning of this war. Hitler cannot be defeated nor the British Empire saved without the aid of the United States. Taken in the right way, they are a generous and warm-hearted people and will help. Dealt with in any superior way, every instinct of co-operation will be chilled."

In this message, sent on May 31, Mackenzie King stated the President's views regarding the British fleet in these terms: "The President feels it would be unwise to ignore the grave possibility of the war taking such a turn as would result in France being overrun and Britain so situated that she would not be able to continue to repel mass attacks from the air. As long as there is any possibility of successful defence, the British fleet should be left in action. If the British Isles can withstand the air bombardment, it is possible that a blockade of the Continent and the Mediterranean can be made so effective that Germany and Italy can be defeated. If it became apparent, however, that hope of continued successful resistance was gone, the President fears the United Kingdom in such case might be called on to make a hard choice between a cessation of hostilities based on surrender of the British fleet and parts of the outlying Empire on terms which the Germans might or might not observe, or prolonging the war with a merciless attitude on the part of Germany.

"The United States, cannot, it is considered, give immediate belligerent aid. If, however, Britain and France could hold out for some months, aid could probably then be given. If further resistance by the fleet in British waters became impossible before such aid could be given, the President believes that, having ultimate victory for the allies and the final defeat of the enemy in view, it would be disastrous to surrender the fleet on any terms, that it should be sent to South Africa, Singapore, Australia, the Caribbean, and Canada. He would also deem it wise that, in such a contingency, that vessels that cannot be moved, should be destroyed, especially naval ships under construction, and that the same steps should be taken with regard to merchant marine. It would be equally desirable to save as many merchant craft as could be sailed away.

"Were this course adopted, the United States would assist immediately by opening its ports to the British fleet in so far as this could be done under the most liberal interpretation of international law to permit of repairing, outfitting, and provisioning of the fleet. The United States would do its best to help in the building up of bases at Simonstown, Singapore, Halifax, and elsewhere. It would extend the provisions for the defence of the Western Atlantic, and its fleet would hold the Pacific and especially defend Australia and New Zealand against Japanese or other attacks. As soon thereafter as grounds could be found to justify direct and active American participation (and neither Mr. Roosevelt nor Mr. Hull believes that this would be more than a very few weeks), the United States would participate in a stringent blockade of the Continent of Europe to be enforced by a naval cordon drawn from Greenland to North Africa and by naval units based in the Indian Ocean.

"Both President and Secretary believe that if Germany should threaten any unusual or particularly vicious action against the United Kingdom as punishment for allowing the fleet to escape when further resistance had become useless, public opinion in the United States would demand active intervention. If, for example, the Germans should attempt to starve Great Britain into ordering the fleet to return, the United States would immediately send food ships under naval escort to the British Isles. And interference with such ships would mean instant war."

On June 4, Mackenzie King recorded in his diary that "the greatest feature of the day was, of course, Churchill's speech." This was the speech to the Commons which concluded: 'We shall never surrender, and even if, which I do not for a moment believe, this Island or a large part of it were subjugated and starving, then our Empire beyond the seas, armed and guarded by the British Fleet, would carry on the struggle, until, in God's good time, the New World, with all its power and might, steps forth to the rescue and liberation of the old.' Mackenzie King wrote: "When I saw his concluding words, I recognized at once that the despatch I had sent him had been helpful. When Skelton came over to my office he was filled with delight. Said that Keenleyside had come into his room with his eyes blazing, so pleased to see what he recognized at once as the result of the information we had imparted. I am quite sure Churchill prepared that part of his speech, which was the climax, in the light of what I sent him and that I shall receive an appreciative word of thanks from him which may be helpful in immediate and subsequent developments. As Skelton said, there is good reason for me to be happy at what has been accomplished, both overseas and at home, as a result of direct personal effort in the past fortnight, particularly the past week."

The next day, June 5, while Mackenzie King was at dinner Skelton brought him a message from Churchill which Mackenzie King felt, along with Churchill's speech of the previous day, would help to advance matters with the President. In his message Churchill said: 'We must be careful not to let Americans view too complacently prospect of a British collapse, out of which they would get the British Fleet and the guardianship of the British Empire, minus Great Britain. If United States were in the war and England (were) conquered locally, it would be natural that events should follow the above course. But if America continued neutral, and we were overpowered, I cannot tell what policy might be adopted by a pro-German administration such as would undoubtedly be set up.

'Although the President is our best friend, no practical help has (reached us) from the United States yet. We have not expected them to send military aid, but they have not even sent any worthy contribution in destroyers or planes, or by a visit of a squadron of their Fleet to southern Irish ports. Any pressure which you can apply in this direction would be invaluable.

'We are most deeply grateful to you for all your help and for (the four Canadian) destroyers, which have already gone into action against a U-boat. Kindest regards.'[1]

Mackenzie King sent Keenleyside to Washington on June 6 to deliver this message to Roosevelt. He himself prepared a Memorandum (dated June 6) to be read to the President as an interpretation of Churchill's reference to a pro-German administration; in this memorandum he indicated that the reference had to be read "in the light of the knowledge of Mr. C.'s character, his public utterances and above all his scrupulous regard for strictly constitutional practice and procedure. To Mr. K.'s mind, it means that Mr. C. will never consider any terms of surrender on the part of Britain to the enemy. That he will not so much as discuss them, regardless of what the consequences of continuing the war by England, alone if need be, against the enemy, may be. The only way in which negotiations could ever take place with the enemy on behalf of the United Kingdom, would be by such a division of opinion arising within Britain itself that there would grow up against the Government of the day, a demand for surrender on terms. Mr. C., himself, as a Prime Minister, would never take the responsibility for such a step. If he saw British public opinion ever become so strong that he, Mr. C., felt that he and his Government were in the minority, the only way in which he would bow to the will of the majority would be to go to the King, tender his resignation and ask the King to call on whoever was the leader of the surrender party, to form a Government to negotiate terms of surrender. To Mr. C.'s way of thinking such a Government would be pro-German. It would have the entire responsibility of arranging the

[1] W. S. Churchill, *The Second World War* (Toronto, 1949), II, 145–6.

terms of the surrender. The matter would have past beyond the control of Mr. C. and his Ministers, and as Mr. C. says, he nor anyone could not tell what policy the pro-German Administration—as he calls it—might adopt.

"Mr. K. believes that anyone who knows Mr. C. and understands the British fighting spirit will realize that what Mr. C. has here set forth is a sincere and true statement of what would certainly take place were the point to be reached while Mr. C. is at the head of the Government of the United Kingdom, where any demand for surrender might come from the people of the British Isles as a consequence of fears of total annihilation. He does not believe that this point of view is put forward in any way as either bluff or for the purpose of bargaining but solely to make the position absolutely clear to Mr. R."

Skelton had suggested that Mackenzie King should make his own analysis of the rest of Churchill's message for Roosevelt, but he had rejected the suggestion in a handwritten comment on the memorandum (dated June 7) which reads: "What I have sent is what seems to me essential *at this* stage, if I am to give the President what Mr. C. wishes to have conveyed. I would not be justified in giving any interpretation which Mr. C. would not wish put ON HIS WORDS at THIS STAGE. I am in a sense simply a medium of communication between Mr. R. and Mr. C. to have them clearly understand each others point of view (not my own)."

Keenleyside saw Roosevelt and Hull on June 7 in Washington and, on his return, reported that they did not accept Mackenzie King's interpretation of Churchill's reference to a pro-German Administration and felt that if the telegram really represented Churchill's attitude it was "alarming and distressing." All they wanted, according to the President, was for Churchill to stick to the programme outlined in his speech which Roosevelt described as a marvellous performance worthy of the best traditions of British history. Both Roosevelt and Hull expressed the hope that Mackenzie King would continue the discussions with Churchill not on the basis of "an American plan" but primarily "to save the Empire." Mackenzie King did not, however, send another message to Churchill on this subject until June 16.

Meanwhile, in response to a suggestion from Churchill who had just been to France to see Premier Paul Reynaud, Mackenzie King addressed an appeal to the French Premier on June 14 to urge the French Government to continue their resistance. He read this message in Parliament and indicated he was speaking on behalf of the whole continent of North America. "If I know the heart of the American people as I believe I do," he said, "and as I am certain I know the heart of the Canadian people, I believe I can say to Premier Reynaud, in this hour of the agony of France, that the resources of the whole of the North American continent will be thrown into the struggle for liberty at the side of the European democracies ere this continent will see democracy itself trodden under the iron heel of Nazism."

In his diary he wrote: "I felt it was time that someone spoke in the name of this Continent as a whole to France and I felt sure enough of my ground and what the President had said to me, to be able to express matters in the way I did."

After making his statement in the House of Commons, Mackenzie King sent for Pierrepont Moffat, who had now taken up the post of American Minister to Canada, and read to him what he had said. He wrote later that he could see from the way Moffat's face coloured up, and the care with which he reviewed certain phrases, that he was concerned as to whether the President would approve. Mackenzie King pointed out to him "that I had not gone any length beyond what I was justified in doing in the light of what the President had said at Virginia University. [This was Roosevelt's speech on the entry of Italy into the war in which he referred to Mussolini's stab in the back.] That I had carefully confined my continental reference to material and financial resources and that I had related it to the defeat of democracy itself.

"I then told him I thought I ought to read to him the communications which I had received this morning. I felt that I ought to get the facts before the President. Said I thought of sending Keenleyside but, as he [Moffat] had spoken of having a code himself and the President had told him of our previous conversations, it might be best to let the message go through him."

Mackenzie King then read to Moffat the message he had received from Churchill about his visit to France and asked him to pass on its contents to the President. Moffat "said that he would guarantee that the message would be on the President's desk in the morning. I told him I thought the time had come when Chiefs of Staff, or others, should meet similar officers of the United States defence forces and have a distinct understanding as to what was to be done in the event of attack coming across the ocean. He said the President had already spoken to him about steps of the kind being taken, and they had been in regard to naval matters on the Pacific. He, Moffat, knew about this."[2]

Moffat told Mackenzie King "the President believed there were many

---

[2]These talks about the Pacific had taken place in January 1938. See W. L. Mackenzie King, *Canada at Britain's Side* (Toronto, 1941), p. 167.

things he could do, short of actually declaring war, and was doing all he could up to that point. I told him if in anything I had said, or was saying, he thought I was going too far, not to hesitate to say so to me, that I was not the least sensitive in these matters. I wished him to do anything that would prevent misunderstandings and bring about the most effective co-operation.

"Moffat told me that the President and Mr. Hull had been very disappointed at Churchill's reference to a pro-German Government in Britain, and had come to the conclusion that the message had been prepared before his speech in the House of Commons, which the President had liked very much. I told him I thought that was probably correct. I felt sure, as the President did, that the concluding part of the speech, which the President liked, had been the result of a telegram I had sent. I told him that what I had said [in the telegram] was an expression of what I thought was in the mind of the President himself, but did not make it as coming from him. Moffat indicated that the President should like it as coming from myself. I told him I had tried to get the situation across in the only way I felt I could conscientiously express it."

On Sunday, June 16, when he was sure French resistance would collapse, Mackenzie King "felt very strongly that I should get off to Churchill tonight a communication which would end the kind of bargaining for entry of United States into the war which has been going on. When a communication came from Churchill about 6 giving his own appreciation of the present position, I took advantage of it to write out at once a despatch." In this despatch Mackenzie King "gave it as my opinion that the United States should be afforded opportunity to get bases at Iceland, Greenland, Newfoundland and the West Indies and supply the inadequacy of the defence of our own coasts, etc. The problem over the French fleet, at the moment [the prospect of its surrender], gave a chance to show that the United States' surmises and representations which I sent along some weeks ago, were only too well founded." Mackenzie King also reiterated Roosevelt's grave concern about the British fleet and gave his own opinion that not an hour should be lost in working out plans for the transfer, in the event resistance became impossible, of surviving units of the fleet before there was any possibility of surrender. The telegram envisaged plans made jointly by the United Kingdom, the United States, and Canada for all eventualities.

Churchill replied to this message on June 24 in these words: 'If you will read again my telegram of June 5 you will see that there is no question of trying to make a bargain with the United States about their entry into the war and our despatch of the Fleet across the Atlantic should the Mother Country be defeated. On the contrary, I doubt very much the wisdom of dwelling upon the last contingency at the present time. I have good confidence in our ability to defend this island, and I see no reason to make preparation for or give any countenance to the transfer of the British Fleet. I shall myself never enter into any peace negotiations with Hitler, but obviously I cannot bind a future Government which, if we were deserted by the United States and beaten down here, might very easily be a kind of Quisling affair ready to accept German overlordship and protection. It would be a help if you would impress this danger upon the President, as I have done in my telegrams to him. All good wishes, and we are very glad your grand Canadian Division is with us in our fight for Britain.'[3]

Pierrepont Moffat saw the Prime Minister on June 27 about Mackenzie King's suggestion for meetings between the American and Canadian Chiefs of Staff "with a view to concerting some plans to meet possible contingencies that would affect the security of both countries." Moffat reported that "the President did not feel in a position to give an answer immediately as the message came at the time he was considering the bringing of Knox and Stimson into the Cabinet in June [two prominent Republicans, W. F. Knox and Henry Stimson, had entered Roosevelt's Cabinet as Secretary of the Navy and Secretary of War respectively]," but that he now wanted Moffat to come to Washington on July 1, and in the meantime, "to have a talk with the Ministers of Defence here and ascertain just the particular matters which it would be desired the members of the Defence staffs should discuss."

Mackenzie King arranged to have Moffat see the Defence Ministers, and told him of his message to Churchill of June 16. He explained that he "had communicated with Mr. Churchill entirely on my own, giving it as my own personal opinion that it was desirable to have no misunderstanding between the British and American Governments, on what might become necessary and what it would be best to do in certain contingencies." He also read to Moffat Churchill's reply of "the 24th instant pointing out that Mr. Churchill had evidently felt that it was from his message that I had got the impression that there was an effort of making a bargain with the United States about their entry into the war. I told Moffat that it was, of course, not to anything Churchill had said but rather to certain statements made by others in the United States that I had reference.

"I drew particular attention to the part of Churchill's message

[3] W. S. Churchill, *The Second World War*, II, 227.

which made clear exactly what he meant with reference to binding a future Government, explaining exactly what was signified by the reference to a pro-German Government in one of Churchill's early messages. Mr. Moffat said he saw quite clearly that it was only the constitutional phase that Churchill was trying to make quite clear. He, Moffat, said he, himself, agreed with me that it was wise not to delay taking all possible contingencies into consideration. That he thought the British were unwise in not doing this at once. I told him that I hoped he would impress upon the President exactly what Mr. Churchill felt about the constitutional aspect, his not having the support needed to maintain his attitude of non-surrender against Hitler. I stated, in addition, to Mr. Moffat that I personally felt—and could not say to Mr. Churchill, but which was nevertheless a contingency that had to be faced—that if anything happened to Mr. Churchill himself, no one, of course, could say what some Government in a panic might find it possible to do or might fail to do, and mentioned Churchill was under a terrific strain; that the possibility of his having a haemorrhage of the brain at some stage was not to be overlooked. That for reasons of the kind, it should not be taken for granted that it would be certain, in every contingency, for the British Fleet to be kept out of German hands."

On June 28, the next day, Mackenzie King "was much distressed . . . when Howe told me that he had been talking with Purvis in New York, and Purvis was finding there was increasing feeling in the United States that it was almost wasting material to send much to the United Kingdom; that the feeling had changed greatly in the United States since France had dropped out. This is really appalling and most unfortunate. If the United States does not help Britain, we will have to pray pretty hard for the Lord to hear the prayer that will save the rest of the English-speaking world."

The next day (June 29) Sir Gerald Campbell, the British High Commissioner in Ottawa, came to see Mackenzie King with a request for Canadian support of British efforts in Washington to reach an understanding on finances and purchasing. Mackenzie King promised the support and told Campbell that he "thought it was equally important to get complete understanding with regard to the British Navy, not to be continuing in an uncertain and bargaining way but to leave nothing to chance between the Americans, the British, and ourselves."

Moffat returned from Washington on July 5 and reported to Mackenzie King that satisfactory arrangements had been made for the Canadian Chiefs of Staff to confer privately in Washington with the United States chiefs. If their presence was discovered, it was to be understood that nominally they were in Washington to see Arthur Purvis. Moffat added that there was complete agreement that conversations about working out joint plans were most desirable and necessary.

Moffat also reported that the President and Mr. Hull listened attentively to Moffat's account of Mackenzie King's message to Churchill. At the end of this narration, the President said: "The position at present is that Mr. Churchill has not made any commitments of any kind to us, nor have we to him. We are quite sure, however, that should a critical situation arise affecting future existence of Britain and her Dominions, the action of the British Government would be along lines that would help to secure their future."

On July 13, Loring Christie came to Ottawa to report to Mackenzie King that a close friend of the President had seen him to suggest that Mackenzie King should visit the President at Hyde Park to talk over a common plan of defence for the North American continent, including the Atlantic islands, to be worked out between the two countries, with a view to getting the British Government to join in the plan. Before he left Washington, Christie had been told by Lothian that the British were arranging with the United States to discuss joint plans for the Atlantic and were having certain Americans go to London as a less conspicuous place to meet than Washington.

That same day (July 13) Sir Gerald Campbell advised Mackenzie King that the British Government had been approached informally from Washington about the desire of the United States to secure air facilities in the British West Indies and Newfoundland and asked for the comments of the Canadian Government. Mackenzie King lost no time in expressing the view that it would be highly desirable to have the facilities made available to the United States.

Roosevelt accepted the Democratic nomination as presidential candidate for the third time on July 18, 1940. On the morning of July 19 Mackenzie King read the papers till 9 "particularly enjoying the splendid speech made by Roosevelt to the Chicago Democratic Convention. What he said about staying at Washington throughout the campaign was, I am sure, the result of the talk we had together at Warm Springs and what I told him and showed him of my experience in our campaign. There has been about his renomination the inevitableness of which I spoke as we drove together on the high ridge overlooking the wide plains which surround the Little White House. I feel deeply for him in what will be a great physical strain with the fatigue he, of necessity, experiences but also a great opportunity."

He reflected that Roosevelt's nomination would "probably mean that he will be another war President of the United States" and added: "I was returned as I was because of bringing Canada unitedly into the war. Part of Roosevelt's success will be due to keeping the United States out of the war, even though he may bring his country in later on."

General Crerar, who had just been appointed Chief of the General Staff, had returned from London where he had been posted since 1939. He had been in close touch with General Dill, the Chief of the Imperial General Staff. He reported to the War Committee on July 26 that Dill thought the chances were not nearly 50–50 but 60–40 that Germany would seek to invade Britain within the next six weeks. Crerar added that "if England were beaten down the Navy would immediately come to make its headquarters on the Atlantic coast and we should do all possible from now on to get our harbours, coast defences in such shape as to be of assistance and to be in readiness to co-operate in that possibility. He strongly favoured working out plans with the United States, having this done openly with Britain. I told him I only wished we could get Britain to meet the United States and ourselves on that ground. He seemed to feel much could be done with the knowledge of all parts of the Empire, etc. And with the United States publicly understanding the situation. I told him the latter was not possible until at least after the elections in the United States were over."

At the end of July, Mackenzie King learned from Loring Christie that Roosevelt had become more cheerful about Britain's chances, and on July 30, Mackenzie King was himself "more hopeful about Britain's ability to hold her own against Germany. It may be only the delay in the attack, which will be terrible when it comes. The command of the sea, however, will be the determining factor in saving England, and the ultimate control of the air by Britain."

On August 3, Sir Gerald Campbell informed Mackenzie King that the air facilities the United States desired in Newfoundland and the West Indies were being offered by the United Kingdom and that secret military conversations between the British and the Americans had been arranged in London. The same day he learned from Loring Christie that there were suggestions in Washington of exchanging fifty over-age destroyers for naval and air facilities in Newfoundland and the West Indies. Christie sent word on August 7 that Lothian had twice suggested to him that Mackenzie King should make a public appeal to Roosevelt for the destroyers for Britain. Christie felt this would be a mistake and Mackenzie King noted: "I would not think of so doing. It would help to undo for the future any influence I may have. Such a step would be in the nature of 'coercion.' No wonder some diplomacies fail."

A few days later, Christie informed Mackenzie King that a spokesman of the American advocates of the destroyer deal had given him the impression that no Canadian response to the project had been received. Christie felt that a personal message from Mackenzie King to the President would be advisable. Although he could not understand why there should be any such attitude since he had already made so many appeals, Mackenzie King, nevertheless, on August 12, instructed Christie to see Roosevelt as soon as possible to indicate that the destroyers would be of great and possibly decisive importance and to express the hope that, when discussions for the transfer of the destroyers were undertaken, there would be an opportunity to take up the question of the strengthening of naval defences on this side of the North Atlantic. He was also to indicate that Canada continued to regard the English Channel as the first line of defence for Canada and other democratic peoples. Christie saw the President on August 15 to deliver Mackenzie King's message. Roosevelt told him he had already received assurances from Churchill about the fleet and about bases which he considered satisfactory and that he intended to act in the near future.

The same day (August 15), Sir Gerald Campbell called on Mackenzie King, to give him "very confidential communications regarding arrangements which have been come to at last between Britain and the United States which will ensure Britain getting some of the destroyers at once and the United States the assurance the President has wished that the British fleet will be brought to this side rather than permit it to fall into Germany's hands, should England be crushed. Also an undertaking by Britain to let America have bases in some of the islands of the Atlantic, including the West Indies, Bermuda and Newfoundland. These are the things which I proposed to the [United Kingdom] Government and have been trying to get them to agree to for two, if not three, months past."

Mackenzie King noted that on August 16 "shortly before two o'clock, the 'phone rang, and the girl at the switchboard said it was the President of the United States who wished to speak to me. The President said: 'Hello, is that you, Mackenzie?' . . . I replied: Yes. He then said: 'I am going tomorrow night in my train to Ogdensburg. If you are free, I would like to have you come and have dinner with me there. I would like to talk with you about the matter of the destroyers, and they [the British] are arranging to let us have bases on some of their Atlantic colonial possessions for our naval and air forces. I gave an interview, this morning, to the press in which I said that I was in direct communication with Great Britain with regard to these matters in the Atlantic. That I was taking up with you direct the matter of mutual defence of our coasts on the Atlantic. I thought it was better to keep the two things distinct.' I said to him that was right. He then said: 'I thought it was better to make this announcement at once rather than to provoke a two months' debate in Congress. I have told the press that we will be meeting together. Are you free tomorrow night?' I said: 'Yes.' The President then said: 'I could have my car meet you at Ogdensburg or send it across to the Thousand Islands Bridge for you.' I replied that I would have my own car and would go direct across to Ogdensburg.

"The President then said: 'We can talk over the defence matters between Canada and the United States together. I would like you to stay the night with me in the car and, on Sunday, I am going to a Field Service at 11. It is a religious service, and I think would do both of us good. We could attend it together.' I thanked him and said I would be very pleased to accept the invitation."

Mackenzie King accompanied by Moffat motored to Ogdensburg the next day. Before leaving Ottawa he saw Ralston who gave him a list of military supplies the Canadian forces were trying to procure in the United States and suggested he enlist Roosevelt's support. They reached the President's car at 7 o'clock. Roosevelt was "sitting in a corner in his white suit enjoying soda lemonade" along with H. L. Stimson, the Secretary for War, and one or two of his staff. "The President greeted me with his usual smile and hearty handshake calling me 'Mackenzie' and telling me he had had a very busy day reviewing troops. He looked exceedingly well. Was in a very happy mood." Mackenzie King took an immediate liking to Stimson, and told him "that we were all so pleased in Canada when we saw he had joined the President. The President emphasized that his was not a National Government."

This was the day that Wendell Willkie, the Republican candidate for President, was making his opening speech in the campaign and Roosevelt was anxious to see the text. Mackenzie King "was astonished to see the President eat a huge steak for dinner. Neither Mr. Stimson nor I could have taken one-eighth of it." Before the dinner was over, they had the text of Willkie's speech on typed sheets. The part Roosevelt and Stimson were anxious to see was that on foreign policy. "When it came, the President and Mr. Stimson both said at once that it was all right. Mr. Stimson said it fits into what we are here discussing like a piece in a jig-saw puzzle. We all agreed that it really would help materially to win approval for what we were planning in the way of a Joint Board to work out mutual problems of defence."

During their talk after dinner, Roosevelt and Mackenzie King quickly agreed in principle on the establishment of a joint board composed of an equal number of representatives of both countries to study their common problems of defence and to make recommendations to the two Governments. After that, the President read over all the messages that Churchill had sent to him regarding the destroyers and Atlantic bases. Mackenzie King had received copies of most of them from Churchill. In one message, Churchill had used the expression that the destroyers would be as precious to the British as rubies. When he came to the end of a despatch referring to the role of Canada, the President said: "This is where you come in." Mackenzie King replied "that Churchill had already communicated with me and that I had sent word to him that we were wholly agreeable to the United States being given bases on the islands of the Atlantic and that, as he knew, I had put this forward to Churchill some time ago. As to Newfoundland, I said both the British and our Government would probably have to do with that matter as well as the United States." Mackenzie King added that Power had left for Newfoundland that very day and that Canada was about to spend a million on facilities at Gander airport.

Mackenzie King observed that the President seemed "most anxious to meet the British and to get a *quid pro quo* for giving destroyers without consulting Congress, which public opinion would accept as fair. He said to me that up to the last few days, he had almost despaired of being able to meet the British on this request. That the United States itself had become so alarmed after French collapse, they did not wish to part with any of their own security." Roosevelt's decision not to put the question to Congress was, he told Mackenzie King, based on the advice of Senators and Congressmen who "had said to him: 'For God's sake don't put this question to Congress or you will have a few months' debate on it. Find some other way to deal with the matter!' "

Roosevelt said that only legal technicalities were holding up the transfer of the vessels, and he expected them to be overcome in the following week. He said Mackenzie King "could tell Churchill that that was all that was holding matters up at present. He then went on to say that I could advise him [Churchill] to begin to get the crews across at once unless we had crews ourselves that we could send. He thought it desirable that the men who manned the destroyers should be the ones to remain permanently on them, as crossing the ocean would give them that much in the way of extra experience." Roosevelt also told him of other ships, aircraft, and equipment he planned to make available to Britain.

"As we talked matters over," Mackenzie King continued, "the President made the remark that he did not like having conferences between the two countries on these matters carried on in secret. While that had been necessary to begin with, he felt that way about it. I said I was exactly of his mind. That it was a tremendous relief to have everything worked out in the open, apart from the effect that the Joint Board itself would have. Mr. Stimson spoke about what neutrality had cost the smaller countries. That part of the viciousness of Germany had been taking advantage of their good faith in seeking to preserve their neutrality and attack them unprepared as a consequence. Germany's action in that regard had justified neutral countries taking no chances of that kind of thing repeating itself on this side."

Before the breaking up on Saturday night, Roosevelt and Mackenzie King decided to give the press next day a joint statement they would prepare beforehand, and tentatively discussed the wording of it.

On Sunday morning, Mackenzie King noted, "nothing was said of the previous night's conversations until we were coming back from the Service, when I said to the President I wanted to be sure about one or two things I was free to say to Mr. Churchill." When they got back into the train, Mackenzie King took from his pocket "the paper with a few questions I had noted down in the morning in order to get exact particulars for reply, to be sure I had all of last night's points carefully in mind.

"I then said to the President I disliked taking advantage of all he had done and was doing to proffer a further request, but that I had promised our own boys that I would, if possible, bring to his attention something further in the way of military equipment and supplies that we, in Canada, were most anxious to have. I then gave him the memo Ralston had given to me, adding to it what Angus Macdonald had requested. The President and Mr. Stimson were very nice about the way they received what I gave them and each remarked that they would have a great deal of difficulty. I explained that, as the President was aware, some of our permanent staff had been talking with Mr. Morgenthau. . . . That our men did not wish us to go over Morgenthau's head to the President until we were sure Morgenthau was agreeable to what was being presented. I explained that, by coincidence, word had come on Saturday morning that Morgenthau was quite prepared to have us go ahead. Both Stimson and the President laughed, saying that the difficulty was not with Morgenthau. It was with the defence services." Stimson explained how short the United States was of many of the items on the list and the President promised that he and Mr. Stimson would look over the list carefully together.

Mackenzie King added that while he and Stimson were looking at the list on the sofa, the President began to draft the statement for the press which they were to give jointly. "He did this on a sheet of paper which he took from the basket and with a pencil in his hand. Read aloud the draft he had prepared. It was clearly and concisely worded. Spoke of a Joint Commission. When he had finished the reading of the draft, I asked him whether he thought the word 'Commission' was as good as 'Board' or 'Committee.' Said the word 'Board' had been used the night before in conversation. Mr. Stimson agreed that Board would perhaps be better and the President also did. I pointed out that Commission suggested the necessity of formal appointments by Governments. I then questioned him as to the significance of the use of the word 'Permanent.' He said at once that he attached much importance to it. I said I was not questioning the wisdom of it but was anxious to get what he had in mind." Roosevelt felt the Board should not be designed "to meet alone this particular situation but to help secure the continent for the future," and Mackenzie King concurred. The title agreed on was the Canada–United States Permanent Joint Board on Defence.

When they came to the question of numbers, the President spoke of four or five, at least one to be a layman. Mackenzie King "asked how soon the Board would meet and where. The President added a sentence to say that the Board would meet shortly. I said I thought it might be well to have them meet this coming week and asked if he had any preference as to where they should meet. As he did not express a preference, I suggested it might be well for them to meet in Ottawa." Mackenzie King felt "it would be logical in that we had been working on the problems and the first thing would be for their men to become familiar with what we already knew. Power, for instance, today was in Newfoundland. He would be back and could state the situation as he found it there. The President said that that would be first rate. His idea was after a meeting in Ottawa, they might all wish to go to Newfoundland or to the Maritimes generally with a view to viewing matters concretely.

"The President read the statement a second time. I approved it in its entirety. Mr. Stimson thought it was all right." The statement was then given to the press.

In his diary for Sunday, Mackenzie King added that "on Saturday night, when we were thinking out loud the phraseology of a statement, the President said something about the Western Hemisphere. Mr. Stimson used the word: northern half of the Western Hemisphere. [The scope of the Board was confined to North America.] The President frequently said to me he assumed that, as regards the colonial possessions and Newfoundland, he would take that phase up direct with Churchill. I said that was right, but I thought, as we had undertaken protection of Newfoundland and were spending money there, the British Government would probably want our Government to co-operate in that part.

"During the evening, I had explained that we would not wish to sell or lease any sites in Canada but would be ready to work out matters of facilities. The President said he had mostly in mind the need, if Canada were invaded, for getting troops quickly into Canada. . . . That similarly if the U.S. should engage in a conflict in the South or around the Panama Canal, and had its men concentrated there, that it might help for us to be able to move men immediately through Maine to Portland, for example, which was the terminus of the old Grand Trunk and present Canadian National Railways. He thought we might have to arrange for annual manoeuvres of troops on our respective soils. I agreed that that would be all right.

"Speaking of the sites for bases, he said he would not want the [West Indian] islands even if they were given to him. They were a source of continual local trouble. That as far as seeking to possess them [the islands] was concerned, he was agreeable to have the British have their guns trained on the United States sites to use at any moment if difficulties developed between United States and Britain.

"He had said to Lord Lothian that he did not see why the British had hesitated in the matter of giving these facilities. That as a matter of fact, if war developed with Germany and he felt it necessary to seize them [the islands] to protect the United States, he would do that in any event. That it was much better to have a friendly agreement in advance. I remarked that the British might equally feel the necessity to seize some other islands. I had in mind the Azores and Canary Islands. He spoke of the Azores himself. He said they were causing him anxiety. I told the President about the British deciding to make Freetown on the African Coast a base and that our Halifax guns were going there. He had not known this."

One of the subjects they discussed on Saturday evening was the recent American requirement that Canadians should have passports and visas to visit the United States. "To my surprise," Mackenzie King wrote in his diary entry for Sunday, "the President said that he had been told we wanted them. I said that was the first I had ever heard of it and asked on what grounds. He then said he had been told we were fearful of people leaving Canada because of the Mobilization Act and Registration, and that our people did not want them to get away. I said I had never heard such a thing suggested. I then told him I had prevented our police from adopting a similar measure against the United States, on the score that I did not want to see the significance of our boundary line completely destroyed and its character changed, and hoped later on to be able to get the United States to repeal its regulation.

"When I saw his attitude, I asked if I might communicate with Mr. Hull concerning the matter. The President said: I will take it up myself with the State Department as soon as I get back." Mackenzie King added that "Mr. Stimson had not even heard of the passport requirement. I told him how I, myself, had had to get passport visaed to get over for the afternoon. Mentioned we were losing all the kind of fraternal note that was so desirable between the peoples. He also agreed that it was a mistake. Later at night, when I was saying good-night, I found Mr. Stimson had been talking with Moffat about passports. Moffat said to me I had made a real impression on the President and Mr. Stimson. When Mr. Stimson was saying something about hoping to see me soon again, I said, if they would let me get into the States, I would be glad to come."

Mackenzie King and Moffat left Ogdensburg about one o'clock on Sunday afternoon, August 18, and, on reaching Ottawa, the Prime Minister went at once to Government House to report to the Governor-General. He then went to his office and dictated a long telegram to Churchill reporting fully on his talks with Roosevelt and Stimson.

In his message to Churchill, which gave a very full account of the conversations, Mackenzie King said he had the President's authority to let Churchill know that Roosevelt hoped to arrange, before that week ended, to begin supplying Britain with destroyers brought to Halifax or one or two other Canadian ports by United States seamen to be delivered to the Canadian Navy for transfer to the Royal Navy. Roosevelt had explained that skeleton crews of 70 would be sufficient for taking the destroyers across the Atlantic and that it would be desirable to select crews for the Atlantic crossing who would likely man the destroyers permanently and thus save time in accustoming them to the ships.

He indicated that the President hoped to arrange all this without the necessity of having special authorization from Congress, on the ground that he was obtaining a defence *quid pro quo* in the bases, and that the only impediment in the way of guaranteeing immediate delivery of destroyers was certain legal difficulties which had been raised, which it was hoped to remove by Thursday of that week. He added that some destroyers would then become available immediately, and that the President believed he could keep on delivering them as fast as crews could be supplied. Mackenzie King indicated that the President was also arranging to make available twenty motor torpedo boats, by having them stricken from the United States Navy list as being too small and placing orders for a larger size for the United States, and that he also hoped to let the British have ten flying boats, five of them big navy planes and five big army planes. These would ostensibly be for experimental purposes, in other words, to test out their usefulness in active operations. They were to be flown across the sea under their own power and the President had suggested either that British crews ought to learn how to fly them over or that possibly American civil pilots might be engaged for this purpose. The President also believed that he could let the British have 250,000 rifles, but that it was almost impossible to supply ammunition, and he had been able to secure for them 150 to 200 aircraft, supplied with engines, which had been ordered originally for Sweden.

Mackenzie King referred to the additional large expenditures by Canada for developments in Newfoundland and indicated there would probably be the necessity for co-operation between the three Governments in matters pertaining to that island.

After outlining the agreement for the Permanent Joint Board on Defence and its functions, Mackenzie King observed that the President had suggested that four or five of the fifty destroyers might remain in the Canadian Navy if they were really needed for such purposes as convoying out of Halifax, but Mackenzie King himself wanted Churchill to have the final word as to the disposition of all fifty destroyers.

He informed Churchill that Roosevelt had been quite satisfied with the statement Churchill proposed to make giving the assurance Roosevelt felt he required as to the defence of the Western Hemisphere in order to justify to the public parting with the destroyers and other war materials. Mackenzie King concluded the message by saying he had strongly urged upon the President the need for the utmost expedition in transferring the destroyers and munitions. Mackenzie King was naturally elated by the outcome of his conversations with the President, and he was hurt when the reply from Churchill on August 22 indicated some impatience with Roosevelt's concern for a *quid pro quo* for the destroyers and a querulous attitude to the Permanent Joint Board. Meanwhile, on Monday morning (August 19) he "had a talk with Skelton who said, if I did nothing for the next five years for the country, I should be satisfied with what was now done. Found Ralston in highest possible spirits. Said it had given new life to them all at the Defence Department. Gave him many particulars over the 'phone."

On August 20, Mackenzie King reported to the War Committee about his meeting with Roosevelt, and later had a formal minute concerning the Joint Board adopted by the Cabinet: it thus approved what came to be known as the Ogdensburg Agreement. That same day, he also received Hanson and Stirling, who happened to be in Ottawa. Hanson had requested the interview to ask Mackenzie King about what had taken place at Ogdensburg. Mackenzie King told Hanson he "had meant to give him full particulars. The points he seemed most concerned about were (a) did England know what had been done, and did she approve; (b) were there commitments beneath what appeared in the statement. Was it necessary to bring Parliament together to take any action in connection with the Board. He said rumour was abroad through the city that I intended to summon Parliament. I reminded him of my having told him some time ago of conversations which our Chiefs of Staffs were having with U.S. Chiefs of Staffs. Stirling said that these conversations had been on years ago, while he was in the Defence Department. It is seemingly clear that the Tories wanted to be in on any background of the kind, as indicating they had been alert to needs of joint defence. I explained how matters relating to colonial Empire were separate and distinct. Had been taken up with Britain and told them confidentially of the United States having had representatives in Britain during recent weeks.

"I outlined the President's phone message and gave them a general sketch of what had taken place. Made clear there were no commitments. Pointed out the Board was for purposes of study; that action to be taken on Board matters would have to be by the Executive. That the personnel was being arranged. We would probably parallel the U.S. personnel. Hanson said if there were no Minister, it would not have a political significance. I said it was quite possible a Minister would sit in with Board as, for example, Power, when he returns, would be able to speak of conditions in Newfoundland. I pointed out the Board's functions would include the Pacific as well as the Atlantic. Told them of the President getting a *quid pro quo* and leases for the destroyers, but to keep very confidential the destroyers business till it had been completely arranged. They both seemed quite satisfied with what had been done and, at the close, Hanson remarked that so far as he was concerned, I could feel he was quite satisfied with all that was represented in the statement, its scope being as indicated by myself to him. He also saw no necessity for Parliament meeting to deal with this matter or anything else that had thus far come up."

No time was lost in setting up the Permanent Joint Board on Defence. O. M. Biggar, Q.C., of Ottawa was the first Canadian chairman, and a representative of each of the armed services was included. The Canadian secretary was H. L. Keenleyside of the Department of External Affairs. Mayor Fiorello LaGuardia of New York was the United States chairman.

Before the personnel were announced on August 22, Mackenzie King had a telephone call from Roosevelt about both the personnel and agenda. They decided the first meeting would be in Ottawa on August 26.

In the course of their conversation, Roosevelt told Mackenzie King he thought he had got over the legal difficulty with regard to the destroyers. "He then added that he was getting along very satisfactorily with his negotiations with Mr. Churchill over the air bases. I said how pleased I was to know that, and said to him how splendidly the whole Agreement had been received. The President said it was significant or something to that effect; could not be better. He then said that he understood that our church bells had been ringing in Canada. I said no doubt that was true, but that my own ears had been ringing so much I could hear little else."

Mackenzie King also spoke about the passports. "The President said he had already been taking that up with the Attorney General and the State Department. He thought that the suggestion that we had made (it was really Moffat) of requiring passports but doing away with necessity of any visa, would meet the situation, and that he hoped to be able to work that out. That he was sending two men to discuss passport matters."

On August 26, the Permanent Joint Board had its first meeting in Ottawa. Mackenzie King welcomed the American chairman, Fiorello LaGuardia, and the other American members on their arrival in Ottawa. "A few minutes before," he wrote, "I had received the most alarming message which had thus far come to hand. It disclosed so completely the wisdom of the establishment of the Permanent Joint Board that I read it to those present." This message from the British Admiralty reported that a convoy had been attacked by a U-boat some distance westward of the normal U-boat area and an escorting vessel had been sunk and five ships were missing. The Admiralty thought the U-boat might be on her way to operate off the Canadian coast.

That same day Sir Gerald Campbell, the British High Commissioner, showed Mackenzie King the terms of the proposed lease by the United Kingdom to the United States of the bases in Newfoundland and asked for Canadian concurrence. Mackenzie King showed Campbell the Admiralty message to the Chief of the Naval Staff "about U-boat activity to illustrate how more than ready I was to have this granted without delay, pointing out that our coasts had been left bare of defence to help the British at a critical moment." He told Campbell he had been "surprised at the message from Churchill concerning the island bases, but more particularly that part which referred to the Permanent Joint Board.

I said it showed how much appreciation was given in British quarters to anything that did not suit their particular mood at the moment. That when matters were going badly, Churchill had been ready enough to appeal urgently to the United States for help and to ask my co-operation in getting it. When, however, it looked as if the British might still win because of immediate successes of their air force, they were ready to pull away from United States co-operation."

Later that day (August 26) Mackenzie King talked at some length with LaGuardia. "He grows on one," he wrote. "Has, however, the unfortunate craze for publicity. I had expressed a wish to have no publicity about the meetings of the Board, but it was apparent that he felt that something was necessary for the American press if they were not to be writing all kinds of stories. He told me what he had in mind saying. It really was intended to impress the American people themselves with the common dangers. It was purely voluntary statement on his part for which we could not be held responsible. Did not come from the Board. As such, I agreed to his repeating to the press what he had said to me. This he did later, rather inviting questions so that he could show his skill at parrying replies. It was all, however, to the good, so far as our cause is concerned. I was glad we had so strong and dignified a person as Mowat Biggar as the head of our membership. LaGuardia told me of the President at different times having said to him to go the limit in what he had to say."

Mackenzie King read Churchill's reply to his telegram about the Ogdensburg Agreement to the War Committee on August 27. Ralston, Crerar, and Lapointe "were quite outspoken and indignant." Mackenzie King said he "had thought of ignoring it. They rather felt an answer should be sent which would let Churchill see that his reply had not been appreciated, and make clear how exceptionally wise our action was in the light of the despatch regarding the approach of a U-boat through Newfoundland waters on the day previous." They also noted the contrast between Churchill's messages to the President when he said that the fate of the war might depend on being supplied with destroyers, and the latest one "saying he would rather go without destroyers than to have experts haggle."

The War Committee also discussed the commitment of a million dollars for the airport in Newfoundland and Mackenzie King felt "we should secure at least from Newfoundland ourselves, lease similar at least to that being given the U.S.A." by the United Kingdom.

Henry Morgenthau and his family were visiting Canada at the end of August, and Mackenzie King had entertained them in Ottawa on August

24. In conversation, Morgenthau "repeatedly emphasized his desire to do everything possible to assist the British and this 'for many reasons.' Also said anything he did was the President's doing. That he was carrying out his wishes and would go as far as he could to that end. The trouble was with the services, members of which wished to keep many things to themselves."

Morgenthau hinted that the list of requirements Mackenzie King had given the President at Ogdensburg "had occasioned them both a little concern," because it was "so considerable." Mackenzie King had a meeting later that day with Morgenthau and Howe "and it was agreed that all requisitions, so to speak, should go through Arthur Purvis [who was in charge of British purchasing in the United States] to Morgenthau. That anything said to the President would come in only where absolutely necessary."

On August 30, Mackenzie King went to the Seigniory Club at Montebello, Quebec, to dine with Henry Morgenthau and his family. He had never visited the Club before and was delighted with the old Papineau mansion. After dinner the whole party visited the chapel and the manor house. "I shall always recall," Mackenzie King wrote, "as, in some ways, one of the greatest and most pleasant surprises I have ever had, the charm of that fine old mansion. In itself, it enables one to understand the feeling of the French seigneurs as to their right to control the affairs of the Province, and not to have this control taken from them by Governors and favourites who came out from England. I do not think we have a more interesting old residence or finer in its general appearance than that of the Papineau mansion. Naturally the association of Papineau and Mackenzie was constantly in my thoughts and I confess to a feeling of great pride in what the seigniory itself revealed of the stakes that men were prepared to risk for the political as well as civil freedom to which they were so wholly entitled because of their own part in helping to fashion the liberties of the new world. More than ever, one feels about the Rebellion of 1837–38 that fundamentally its causes were the same as those which brought about the American Revolution."

When Mackenzie King arrived, Morgenthau told him "he had had a telephone message from the President, who knew I was to dine with him that night, in which the President said, first of all, to give me his love and then to let me know that everything had been worked out satisfactorily between Churchill and himself. That 99-year leases for flying and naval bases were to be given free of charge in Newfoundland and Bermuda. On the other islands, leases for the same time were to be given but in exchange for the 50 destroyers. It would be a *quid pro quo*. It was in this way that the President would get over the legal difficulty of not being able to sell destroyers. He had found it possible to exchange one class of war material for something that was even more than its equivalent."

In the course of their conversation Morgenthau again "emphasized his readiness to do everything possible to furnish additional war supplies," but added that "he thought Canada and also Britain should not rely too much on the States for war equipment later on. He believed that we should, for example, begin to manufacture airplane engines ourselves, though it may take a year and nine months to produce them." Mackenzie King reflected that this was what he had wanted done at the outset of the war and added: "We were prevented by British representations in first place and are still yielding to them."

The next day (August 31), Mackenzie King received from Sir Gerald Campbell "the statement that Churchill has communicated to the President and which is to be the basis of an exchange of communications between them regarding the bases. It comes around completely to what I had mentioned in my cable to Churchill and what I thought would be necessary to secure the destroyers without the President going to Congress. Churchill has ingeniously saved his face in previous statements by having part of the bases given free. It is an immense relief to my mind that this has all been so successfully accomplished at last."

On September 3, "the great feature of the day" for Mackenzie King was "the announcement in England and the United States of the acquisition of naval and air sites by the United States and destroyers by Britain." He felt that his political enemies were completely confounded "at a time when events" were "vindicating my whole life's work for better international relations, particularly between the United Kingdom and the United States." This entry in his diary had reference to a disparaging speech made by Hanson in Toronto the previous day. There is no doubt that the Ogdensburg Agreement, the destroyer–bases deal, and the successful air defence during the Battle of Britain all combined to reinforce Mackenzie King's political strength throughout the remainder of 1940.

On September 11, Mackenzie King noted that something seemed to be holding him back from preparing a reply to Churchill's messages before listening to his broadcast on that day. He found this broadcast with its forecast of invasion and tribute to the R.A.F. "intensely moving—an address to the people of the British Isles, informing them of the probable immediate invasion of Britain, and asking them to stand firm, each man in his place. I question if ever in the world's history anything comparable to this speech, in its setting, significance, etc., has taken place. It was heard all over the world. Dealt with the terrible possibilities, and the realization that Britain was the world's citadel of Freedom. I felt strongly that I should send a message to Churchill regarding his broadcast and letting the British people have the assurance of our standing by them at this critical hour."

The message he sent reads: "The people of Canada, in common with those of the other members of the British Commonwealth, listened today with heartfelt concern and deepest admiration to your broadcast addressed more particularly to the people of the British Isles.

"I do not know that I can better express the feelings evoked than to ask you at this time of intense anxiety to give the people of the United Kingdom the assurance that Canada was never more proud of the privilege of having her forces on sea, on land, and in the air so closely associated with those of the United Kingdom and other parts of the Commonwealth in the magnificent stand in the world's citadel of freedom against ruthless aggression and for the preservation of the liberties of men.

"The men and women and the children of Britain may rely on Canada redoubling her efforts to give them all the support in her power in their undaunted and inspiring resistance to the barbarous and inhuman onslaught they are being called upon to endure. They may count on our continuing support to the utmost of our strength. Never were our people more united or more determined."

On September 13 Mackenzie King was delighted to receive a message from Churchill, which gave him "more pleasure than almost anything that has happened at any time. It made so clear my part in bringing together the English-speaking peoples and an appreciation by Churchill of my own efforts in connection with the war; also, the significance of what I have striven to do on this continent." Mackenzie King felt that "Churchill had realized he had not sent the sort of message he should have sent with reference to the Defence Board agreement and the U.K.–U.S. agreement re destroyers and was anxious to make amends in this message, which he certainly did in magnificent fashion. To me, it seems the hand of Providence has been restraining me from sending any message. I would then have thought that the personal message would have been as a consequence of my own. It is now quite clear that what Churchill sent has been independent of any word from me. I feel, with this message coming from him, with the commanding position he holds today, I have now all that I shall ever need in the way of an answer to any attempts at detraction on the part of the Tories. This is a wonderful reply to Hanson and others who were associated with him, e.g., Grattan O'Leary and Maclean's, in their efforts at detraction."

Churchill's message reads: 'I am touched by the personal kindness of your telegram and all our people are cheered and fortified to feel that Canada is with the Mother Country heart and soul.

'The fine Canadian divisions which are standing on guard with us will play a notable part should the enemy succeed in setting foot on our shores.

'I am very glad to have this opportunity of thanking you personally for all you have done for the common cause and especially in promoting a harmony of sentiment throughout the New World. This deep understanding will be a dominant factor in the rescue of Europe from a relapse into the Dark Ages.

'On behalf of the Government and people of the United Kingdom I send you heartfelt thanks for your memorable message.'

CHAPTER SEVEN

A Winter of Anxiety, 1940-41

THE PERIOD which intervened between the conclusion of the destroyer-bases deal in September 1940 and the Nazi attack on Yugoslavia and Greece on April 6, 1941, was one of many anxieties, both external and domestic, for Mackenzie King.

Though he was encouraged by the heroic and successful resistance of the R.A.F. in the Battle of Britain in the autumn of 1940, Mackenzie King continued to expect an even more furious onslaught on Britain in the spring of 1941. He was anxious that Canada should make a maximum contribution to the British resistance and gave first priority to planning the war programme for 1941. In order to ensure co-ordinated planning with the British, Ralston and Howe, the key Ministers of Defence and of Munitions and Supply, visited the United Kingdom at the end of 1940. Next to his concern about the fate of Britain, Mackenzie King's greatest anxiety in this period was to prevent an open breach between Britain and France, which would, he felt, put a terrible strain on Canadian unity. He was very pessimistic about the prospects for the liberation of Europe, though his hope of eventual victory rose after Roosevelt's re-election in November 1940. All through these months and, indeed, right up to the attack on Pearl Harbor, he expected Japan to enter the war on the side of the Axis at any moment; and he was greatly concerned that Canada should provide neither provocation nor excuse for Japanese aggression.

During this period the first session of the wartime Parliament, which had adjourned in August 1940, met to prorogue on November 5; a new session was opened on November 7. This session adjourned at the beginning of December and resumed its sittings on February 17, 1941.

On the domestic front, the most important event of this period was the Dominion-Provincial Conference held on January 14 and 15, 1941, to consider the recommendations of the Royal Commission on Dominion-Provincial Relations for a radical change in fiscal relations between the federal and provincial governments. The Rowell-Sirois Report, as it was popularly called (after the two Chairmen of the Royal Commission), had been published in May 1940, and there was considerable pressure from certain of the provincial governments, notably Manitoba which had urged the appointment of the Commission in 1937, for its immediate implementation. Moreover, the federal Government had an interest in getting the provinces to withdraw from the income tax field so that the income tax on individuals and corporations could be used exclusively by the federal Government in financing the war.

A number of other problems arose in the early months of 1941, the most urgent of which was a growing shortage of the American dollars needed for the purchase of war supplies in the United States; this is the subject of the next chapter. Roosevelt continued to be eager to get a start made on the St. Lawrence Waterway and a good deal of time and attention had to be devoted to negotiations on this subject not only with the United States but also with the Governments of Ontario and Quebec. In the midst of all these anxieties and preoccupations, O. D. Skelton died and Mackenzie King was deprived of his most valued counsellor.

In August, when Parliament adjourned, Mackenzie King badly needed a rest, but during what was left of that month and all of September he was able to spend a good deal of time at Kingsmere, and in mid-October he got away from Ottawa for his only absence between April 1940 and April 1941. He spent October 15 and 16 in Quebec City as the guest of the Governor-General at his quarters in the Citadel. This was his first opportunity really to get to know Lord Athlone and Princess Alice. He found "the Governor very easy to talk with, companionable, with no affectation or side. He knows a good deal about military affairs, is first and foremost a soldier. The Princess is exceptionally clever, very charming; exceedingly intelligent and active. I cannot, however, abide the formal life. . . . One or two days at Government House would exhaust me more than a week of hard work. I feel, too, it is an absurdity for a Prime Minister of a country to have second place in the public eye to any one in official position not belonging to one's own country and in fact appointed by the Government of the country itself."

Mackenzie King went on from Quebec to Halifax to witness the transfer of the American destroyers to the British and Canadian Governments. "Viewing these American ships, still flying the American flag in Canadian waters," he wrote, "and realizing they were warships about to be transferred from a neutral country to one at war, to assist the latter, and this in a harbour at which enemy action might take place at any moment if the enemy might find it possible to make a contact, was a great experience. Nothing more significant has taken place in the present war."

While he was in Halifax, there was a potential crisis over relations with the French. On October 19, Skelton telephoned Mackenzie King from Ottawa, to get his view "as to having our Navy stop French trawlers from leaving St. Pierre and Miquelon" to market fish in the West Indies, with the double object of preventing food getting to France and "also to hold the vessels for British use and the islands of St. Pierre and Miquelon for de Gaulle." Mackenzie King said he "could see no justification for this. We were not at war with France and were not going to precipitate a situation on this side which would make Canada responsible for widening of the breach. I learned from Skelton that Lapointe was strongly of my view. Angus Macdonald not too certain. Thought they would be damned for what they did or did not. Ralston inclined to carry out the will of the British Admiralty and left the matter up to me. I am positive I am right. It proves the wisdom of our maintaining strong the position of a nation making its own decisions and not having decisions made by the British Admiralty through its control of all naval forces."

All through the summer Mackenzie King had insisted on permitting the French Minister, René Ristelhueber, to remain in Canada as the representative of the Vichy regime, despite growing criticism. He was determined to avoid any action which might give Vichy an excuse to declare war. On September 17, he had felt "very anxious concerning possibility of France becoming directly involved in war with Britain. As Power says, he could not imagine our calling Parliament for the purpose of bringing Canada into war against France." For this reason, he had been opposed to the British attack on the French fleet at Dakar. On September 26, when this attack had apparently failed, he felt it was perhaps fortunate "as avoiding more in the way of war, but another gain for Germany and loss of British prestige. Am glad we placed ourselves on record in advance against a move of the kind."

Because of his great anxiety to prevent even a merely formal state of war against France, Mackenzie King was happy to have arrangements made, at the request of the British Government, for Pierre Dupuy, who had served in the Canadian Legation in Paris for many years before the war, to visit Vichy. In due course Dupuy returned to London and on February 13, 1941, Mackenzie King read his confidential report and "found it an exceedingly interesting and able document. Felt very proud that a Canadian could have played so immensely important a part. . . . As

Churchill himself cabled me, Dupuy was the one effective link the British Government had. Dupuy is at present in Vichy again."

Everything Mackenzie King learned in these months about conditions in Europe and the strength of the Germans made him pessimistic about the liberation of Europe. He told his colleagues on November 1, 1940, that he felt it was "very questionable whether Britain can hope to save more than herself and parts of her Empire; finding herself to a large extent isolated in the end except for the friendship that we may have developed further with the United States. It looks to me as though this continent alone were going to be the part of the world to be saved from invasion. . . . That the countries of Europe now over-run by Germany will become free in our day and generation is, I think, very questionable indeed."

But he was overjoyed by Roosevelt's great victory in the presidential election on November 5, and correspondingly more optimistic. "This," he wrote on November 6, "clears both the air and the skies, and makes possible a certainty of assistance to Britain and ourselves which could not possibly have come otherwise, and certainly not without considerable delays. Meanwhile, the British will be given fresh heart, and the enemy will be correspondingly depressed. It means we have the United States with us for the next four years, already committed to give all aid possible to Britain. This should mean, in the end, the certain defeat of Germany and Italy."

On November 6 he telephoned the President at Hyde Park about 10 o'clock in the morning and "asked that my name should be given to him. Received word back he was asleep, but would call me up later. . . . About 2 o'clock received word he was on the 'phone. As soon as I got through I heard his voice say: 'Hello, Mackenzie.' I immediately congratulated him very warmly on the result. Said I was delighted and everyone in Canada was the same. He then said to me: 'I took your advice about not campaigning, but in the last week or two there were some awful things said, and I felt I had to get in and make a few speeches. I said, of course, that was what I hoped and expected he would do in the end, but that I hoped he had saved himself undue fatigue in the campaign. He said he felt tired and needed to take some sleep." After some further conversation, the President said he hoped Mackenzie King would come down and see him before Christmas: that he would like to have some further talks. "I thanked him and told him I would be happy to try to arrange this." He was not able to do so until April 1941. The President also told Mackenzie King "he felt he had been greatly helped by Canada. That there were evidences of Canadian influence strongly in his favour. . . . He repeated that he had been thinking about me, and was very pleased that I had called him up. I told him I was rejoicing quite as much as he."

One reason for Mackenzie King's pessimism about the liberation of Europe was his fear that Japan would come into the war against Britain without involving the United States. He also feared right up until June 1941 that Soviet Russia would join the Axis powers if victory for them seemed in sight. He sought to do what he could diplomatically to discourage Japanese aggression. He had the Japanese Minister, Baron Tomii, to dinner alone on September 7, 1940. During their talk, Tomii asked, at one stage, whether Mackenzie King thought Canada would intervene in troubles (i.e., Japanese attack) in the Malay States or India. Mackenzie King replied that, in 1938, "it would have been difficult to get Canada to go to war over Czechoslovakia. There was no difficulty in having the country go in after the invasion of Poland; that I thought the events since had made British everywhere feel there was an effort to destroy the Empire, and that they would not give up fighting until they felt secure of the future and until the Nazi regime and what it stood for was wiped out. I believed that today we were prepared to fight in any quarter of the globe where the British Empire was threatened.

"I also said I doubted if the United States would intervene for purposes of peace. I thought it was more likely the United States would be fighting for the preservation of democracy and that the fight would be kept up until democracy was saved. It seemed to me that he was feeling the ground as to how free Japan might be in the matter of aggression in the Far East."

When Tomii asked if Mackenzie King did not think that Canada and the United States would be drawn continuously closer together, Mackenzie King replied that he "thought we would on matters of common concern, but I did not think that this would mean any lessening of the tie with Britain, and I thought we all felt it an advantage to be one of the nations of the British Commonwealth—a great safeguard for peace."

On September 26, a letter from T. D. Pattullo, the Liberal Premier of British Columbia, to Mackenzie King questioned the wisdom of calling up Japanese and Chinese Canadians for compulsory military training. Mackenzie King at once told the War Committee he felt it would be unwise to have firearms in the hands of Japanese Canadians, "at a moment when war with Japan was possible." He also expressed concern about the effect on opinion in British Columbia—where the public was more conscious than elsewhere in Canada of the potential threat of Japan and where most Japanese Canadians lived—of calling up either Japanese or Chinese Canadians. It was decided not to proceed. "I really believe," he wrote, "my greatest service is in many unwise steps I prevent."

The next day (September 27) Ribbentrop announced the agreement between Germany, Italy, and Japan, usually called the Triple Axis, which provided that if any country, not at present engaged in hostilities, came into the war against any one of the three, the others would come to its assistance. Mackenzie King felt this pact was clearly "meant to prevent the United States coming to aid Britain once the presidential election is over. Personally I am immensely relieved that the pact has been announced so that all three nations are out in the open in regard to their relations with each other." He felt the formation of this open alliance settled "the question of Anglo-American friendship and alliance. The United States will not allow Japan to get control of Asia and the Pacific. She will go to war first, and I think rightly, if she is to have any life at all. If Hitler succeeded in Europe and Japan in Asia, this continent would be doomed. Between the British Empire and the United States I believe resources are sufficiently great to enable us to have the last word."

On October 8, he felt the situation in the Orient was becoming increasingly serious. The British Government had advised Canada of Britain's "intention to stand by United States if she was attacked by Japan because of United States assistance to Great Britain." They wanted to know Canada's attitude. "Power advocated [at War Committee] our replying we would go to war with Japan because of our obligations of joint defence with United States. Skelton also favoured this view. I took strong exception to it, and majority of others present were with me, particularly Ralston and Lapointe and Crerar. I contended such a statement would be construed as a North American policy rather than a British Empire policy, this at a moment when the United Kingdom was doing everything and the United States assisting only to the extent for which it was being paid. I thought our position would be that we would stand by the side of Britain. What I suggested was that the German-Italian-Japanese alliance should be made the basis of our action, declaring war on Japan if she attacked Britain or attacked the United States because of assistance to Britain."

He added that he regarded "our attitude towards Japan as the most important of all the matters to be considered since war itself began. Just where Canada is going to find herself with Britain's hands as full as she is certain to be, and America watching primarily her own interests, once war with Japan begins, is something that ought to give every one of us the deepest possible concern."

Notwithstanding Mackenzie King's anxiety not to give Japan any pretext for offence, the Government felt that the danger of subversive activities by Japanese Canadians in the event of war was great enough to justify a decision, at the beginning of 1941, to have a compulsory registration of "all persons of the Japanese race in Canada" over sixteen years of age. In order to minimize the effect on the Japanese Government, Mackenzie King saw the Japanese Minister on January 8 and showed him a statement which had been prepared for the press announcing this registration. On the whole, the Minister, he found, approved the statement "in a cordial way though he mentioned what he had heard in British Columbia that the Japanese citizens of Canada would wish to have a chance to be in the fighting forces in order that they might be given full rights of citizenship as had been done with Japanese who served in the last Great War. I told him they were only not being called up for the present as we wished to avoid any situation developing in British Columbia at this time.... As to registration, he did not seem to take any exception, though I was afraid he might think there was discrimination in having only Japanese registered."

At the end of January, the British Government requested Canada to remove contraband cargo from Japanese ships in the Pacific. Mackenzie King told the War Committee on January 28 that he felt "it was inviting far too great a risk, focussing all displeasure of Japan upon Canada, risking the possibility of riots in Vancouver and giving the Japanese, if they decide, an excuse for declaring that we had been guilty of an act of war.... I disliked very much this effort of some parties in the British Government to get us into war at sea. I think that there are some who believe that this might help to bring the United States into the war. It would do quite the opposite. I stood very firm on the ground outlined."

On February 9, Mackenzie King opposed another request from the British Government and "declined to authorize Canadian ships to stop some Russian vessels that were leaving California with vegetable oil which it was thought might substitute for oils that Russia might be sending to Germany. U.S. Government were quite prepared we should take this step but I felt that the situation in the Far East is much too dangerous to have Canada brought into position where we would be held responsible for creating an incident.... It might even suit the slate of the U.S. if a break with the Orient came between Great Britain and Japan rather than the U.S. and Japan. We, however, would certainly never hear the end of it were we responsible." He added: "I had to shoulder this responsibility alone but saw no reason to alter the decision reached by the War Committee re similar request applicable to Japan, some days ago." Two days later the War Committee confirmed Mackenzie King's decision "not to accede to a request from Dominions Office to intercept Japanese ships or Russian ships with a view to bringing them to Vancouver for examination and if need be seizure of contraband cargo."

The question of the interception of Japanese ships arose once more at the War Committee meeting on March 5, after another British request. Mackenzie King "again held out against too quickly deciding to permit action to be taken on the Pacific Ocean, which might make Canada responsible for creating an incident that would have brought the Japanese into the war. The latest British communication changed altogether the original request to have Canada take the initiative in intercepting vessels and [the British] are now only requesting their examination in Canadian ports. I feel that the latter is something we shall have to grant. . . . I told Council tonight that . . . I felt very strongly war was coming between Japan and Britain; that the United States was not likely to go into it immediately. . . . We must be careful to see that Canada is not made the scapegoat for what will involve both Britain and the United States in a war with Japan."

On March 26, Mackenzie King had a long confidential talk with Baron Tomii, the Japanese Minister, who had just been appointed to a new post. He asked Tomii frankly "what he thought Japan was going to do" and Tomii "practically said that if the Germans should invade Britain he thought Japan would seek to extend her territory in the Far East," and added the opinion "that if Britain were to get the worst of it, the United States would not continue the fight. I told him he was mistaken in that; that the United States would certainly see that Hitler was defeated. They realize that the conflict is between democracy and totalitarianism. They do not wish to be a part of a totalitarian world. He told me he thought the future of Japan would go as the future of the present struggle. That if Germany won, Japan would become totalitarian, that if Britain won Japan would become a democratic country. In this I think he is right. I told him that is what the Americans themselves are realizing; that it was to be one kind of world or the other; that I believed they would rather die, as I certainly would, than to be a part of a totalitarian world." Mackenzie King told Tomii he thought Japan "would not try to provoke war with Britain. If she did, she would find the United States with Britain." But despite Tomii's statement that

Japan was not planning to act in a hurry, Mackenzie King continued to believe that country would be in the war at an early date.

While he worried about the war spreading to the Pacific, Mackenzie King did not lose sight of the war against Germany. He had agreed, rather reluctantly, that Ralston and Howe should visit Britain to make sure that the Canadian war programme for 1941 would dovetail with the British. Ralston left Ottawa on November 19, while Parliament was still sitting. Mackenzie King felt that it was adding to his own burden to let Ralston go, and noted in his diary: "He is the most helpful of all the colleagues on the war effort."

Howe left Ottawa on December 4. He was accompanied by three leading business men, Gordon Scott, of Montreal, E. P. Taylor, of Toronto, and W. C. Woodward, of Vancouver, all of whom were then associated with the Department of Munitions and Supply. They were to travel by ship. After seeing Howe off at the railway station, Mackenzie King wrote: "I pray he and Ralston will get through all right and return in safety." The prayer was needed, for on December 14 Mackenzie King had a telephone call from Angus Macdonald who asked if he had had any news of Howe's ship. Mackenzie King said at once "that I prayed that nothing had happened to Howe. He then told me that the ship had been hit, but that they had not received any word as to what more had actually taken place. I was relieved a little to hear that it was off the coast of Scotland, about 200 miles. I said to Macdonald that I thought, in those circumstances, it might well be that his life would be saved; there would at least be a chance of rescue in lifeboats."

They both agreed it would be inadvisable to say anything to anyone about this news until further word came. Mackenzie King recalled that he had spoken to Howe of the risks involved in the journey and that Howe had spoken "of wishing to know the men interested in munition work, supplies, etc. That it would help him in his negotiations. I agreed entirely with that. I also was anxious to have him get the wider acquaintance and secure the added authority which knowing Churchill and association with British Ministers would give him. At this moment of dictation, I am far from despairing for his life though I believe, if spared, it will be as a result of rescue at sea—a perfectly terrible experience." He added that "Ralston and Howe are two most valuable men in our war effort. In some ways, I would have preferred that only one at a time should have been away. There is a certain irony in the situation that Howe, himself, usually prefers to travel by plane and was taking this method to rest."

Just after 7 o'clock that evening (December 14) Mackenzie King was told that the radio news had carried a flash from New York that Howe had been saved. He "immediately rang up Mrs. Howe and gave her this word. It seemed as though she had been sitting at the 'phone so quickly did she answer the call in person. She seemed tremendously relieved. Immediately asked about the other men. I told her I imagined that they would all be safe. That I felt the report must be a correct one. She said that she thought if he [Howe] were saved, it meant that he had some special work to do. I told her that I was sure of that. I did not know what I personally could do without him. Indeed, through the day, I have been turning over in my mind possible men to take his post, but can think of no one available."

Actually the ship had sunk off the coast of Iceland and it was not until December 17, when Ralston telephoned Mackenzie King from London, that he received definite word about Howe's safety. The message Ralston had received from the Admiralty indicated the whole party had been saved and this information was given to their families. It was tragically wrong in the case of Gordon Scott. The news of Scott's drowning came next day from Howe himself and Mackenzie King had to pass it on to Scott's family and friends who were rejoicing at the word he had been saved.

The first steps in planning and organizing the war programme for 1941 were taken before Ralston and Howe left for Britain. At the Cabinet meeting on October 22, consideration was given to undertaking the manufacture of aircraft engines, at a cost of over thirty million dollars. Mackenzie King noted "it would take eighteen months to two years to have a plant constructed and first engine turned out. The expenditure is colossal. Britain would probably go half on capital outlay, but United States, through Morgenthau, has given Howe to understand U.S. may not be able to supply engines later on. Britain has asked earnestly that we should undertake to manufacture some. She may have her factories bombed altogether. It looks as if the war might last for years, the British and Germans both losing steadily their strength and power meanwhile. Unless England secures complete mastery of the air and holds the seas, she cannot hope to save herself, let alone win. Howe admitted that if he had done what I wanted over a year ago, Canada might be on the point of producing aeroplane engines now. I fought for this again, as I did for manufacture of munitions, against both Ralston and Howe from the moment that McNaughton left Canada. Was at it again only a few weeks ago." Mackenzie King added that "there was another vast expenditure to be met—on tanks. The Cabinet all agreed to the large expenditure on manufacture of engines, and we were obliged to accept the outlay on tanks as the War Committee had already authorized expenditure of sufficient money to equip one motorized division.

"View generally seemed to be that Canada's real contribution should be in the air and at sea. Angus Macdonald gave us the alarming news that some 30 or 40 ships had been lost today on convoy off the Irish Coast."

Mackenzie King felt worried about the duration of the war and "whether Canada will be able to maintain the burden she is assuming is questionable. I feel, however, that the time may come when England will have to look to us to supply her needs for war material and that, to save the Empire itself, we must make every possible outlay." At the War Committee meeting the next day (October 23) Mackenzie King expressed concern about the financial control of war expenditures and "took the position that we must be careful to view the war as one likely to last three or four years and not get the country in a position where there will be a financial panic or collapse before the war is over." The following day (October 24) W. C. Clark, the Deputy Minister of Finance, was invited to the War Committee to discuss the financing of the war programme. He was reassuring about the financial capacity of the country. Mackenzie King gathered that "national income will be expanding and enable, in Clark's opinion, further commitments to be met in so far as industrial capacity will permit, without occasioning any financial panic or collapse."

An even more important question politically was discussed at this series of War Committee meetings. Compulsory military training under the National Resources Mobilization Act of 1940 was originally for one month after which the men who had been called up went back home unless they enlisted voluntarily, as some did, for active service. At the War Committee meeting on October 23, there was a preliminary discussion of a proposal to change the compulsory training period from one month to several months with a smaller number of men to be called up in each period. It was agreed that this change was desirable as the training given in one month was almost useless, but no final decision was taken. Mackenzie King supported the proposal because smaller numbers would be involved and more men would be available for war industry. He pointed out, with regard to compulsory training, that he "did not care particularly about present criticism on any course that might have to be changed, but what I felt should be kept in mind was the thing that, in the long run, would prove to be the right thing. I stressed strongly that the thing that was right in itself was bound to be politically the wisest thing."

The following day (October 24) Mackenzie King again referred at the War Committee meeting to compulsory training "as likely to be the subject of main discussion and difference of view in debate, and strongly urged definitely settling policy in advance of the session, the policy being that of giving intensive training to such numbers as may be necessary for national and overseas service, having the remainder drafted into the navy, air force, or, above all else, industry. I also stressed the importance of increasing numbers to be engaged in technical training." The decision was, however, deferred until 1941.

On December 4, 1940, after Ralston and Howe had left for England, the War Committee considered a suggestion emanating from the Canadian Army authorities that to get battle experience Canadian troops should be sent from Britain to Libya, where British troops were fighting the Italians. Mackenzie King strongly opposed the idea partly because he feared that sending Canadian troops to Africa at a time when Britain was assuring the United States they had no need of fighting men might engender annexationist sentiment in Canada. "I strongly stated my view," he wrote, "that we owed it to our men to seek to protect their lives. Other things being equal, the Australians, New Zealanders, South African people were all interested in that zone. Moreover, it was part of the possessions of the British themselves. I thought the logical thing was to have Canadians continue to defend Britain, our position being that we were at the side of Britain, and not to begin to play the role of those who want Empire war. Clearly, the Army people wish this, and Power, I am afraid, has come around to their point of view and has rather sanctioned it with them. He pointed out that our forces were anxious to get into fighting, no matter where it was, and morale was suffering through lack of opportunity." Mackenzie King "insisted on a message being sent to Ralston that no final disposition of troops was to be made until our War Committee had had a chance of getting both sides. Also letting him know, as matters stood, we were opposed to our people being sent to the Suez unless we could be shown that the argument there far outweighed their remaining in Britain."

The military programme for 1941 could not, of course, be settled finally until Ralston and Howe returned from England. Ralston arrived back on January 24. He told Mackenzie King "he felt the situation for Britain was much more terrible than people realized. That he had come back, he would not say anglicized, but filled with more admiration for the people of England than ever, and feeling that everything possible should be done to help win." Ralston reported in detail on the military prospects for 1941 and Mackenzie King "was particularly interested in hearing him say that there had been no thought or desire to have Canadian troops go to Egypt. . . . Also that there was no possibility of any attempt at invasion of Europe this year. Indeed the view Ralston came back with was that invasion of Europe at any time would be impossible until disintegration got under way in Europe. . . .

"Ralston feels," he added, "that additional manpower is greatly needed in Britain despite Churchill's statement from Glasgow." Churchill had visited Glasgow with Harry Hopkins on his return from Scapa Flow in January, where he had said farewell to Lord Halifax, and he had made a speech in which he had indicated that war supplies, not troops, were needed by Britain. This was the prelude to the famous phrase in a broadcast on February 9: "Give us the tools and we will finish the job." Mackenzie King noted that Ralston insisted that more troops were required "because of England parting with such large numbers of men to other areas of conflict, for example, North Africa. . . . He is quite firm on the advisability of a four-months training, of fewer men in preference to the one-month general training. In this, I think, Ralston is right. . . . He also is most anxious for a tank battalion to be across by May; additional troops in the fall, but no thought of a fourth division until 1942."

The day Ralston arrived in Ottawa, Howe, who had travelled with Lord Halifax, the new British Ambassador to the United States, arrived in Washington. When Mackenzie King telephoned Howe on January 25, he noted that his voice sounded strong, clear, and decisive. He felt "both Ralston and Howe could not do other than make a splendid impression in London on the Ministers there. They are gentlemen as well as able business and professional men. Halifax too will see how close members of our Government are to those of the President, and how much of a family we are on this continent."

Howe returned to Ottawa on January 27, and had a long talk with Mackenzie King the same day. Mackenzie King was deeply impressed by what he said. "The story was anything but a bright one. The truth is that among those who are in the best position to judge, there is a strong feeling that it is very doubtful if Britain can win. She may not lose. From what Howe gathers it will take at least five years to defeat Germany." Howe reported that "Churchill and the Government believe that without doubt there will be every attempt to invade England in the spring; that Hitler will not hesitate to sacrifice a million men in the Battle of Britain alone." He found Howe believed "that, without Canada, Britain could not have won. Says Government speaks in the highest terms of Canada's war effort. . . . Spoke of our Army being the best trained and equipped in England." Mackenzie King "felt that Howe had a truer picture of the inside of the situation than Ralston. What he said reminded me of much of the outlook which Rogers had on his return."

After Ralston and Howe got back to Ottawa, the Government settled down to consider the war programme for 1941 in the expectation that Hitler would attempt to invade Britain in the spring of 1941 and that Japan would come into the war at the same time. A meeting of the War Committee to consider the programme was held on January 28.

At that meeting, Ilsley, the Minister of Finance, set a figure of $1,300,000,000 as the limit of what it would be possible for the economy to supply for war purposes in 1941. The cost of the programme proposed by the defence services was somewhat higher. Mackenzie King felt they should accept Ilsley's figure and "thought, within that figure, the Defence Departments themselves should come to an agreement about their respective allotments, each Department should consider particularly what was going to enable us to do the utmost in meeting the situation with which Britain would likely be faced in the next six weeks. I thought Parliament and the country would do everything from the point of view of our readiness to meet, as far as we can, what we now foresee. What might be necessary for a year hence might be important, but not nearly so important as the immediate future. If we got through to the end of this summer, I believed matters would work out all right but what would happen in the interval would decide the issue. All present came around to this point of view."

Agreement was reached on the extension of compulsory military training from one month to four. Gardiner, who, as Minister of National War Services, was responsible for calling up the men, thought the call-up could be so arranged "as to avoid interference with harvesting and seeding time required by farmers' sons. The general feeling was that we should not have any exemption, if that were possible. Ralston expressed the hope that this system might be continued after the war. Lapointe agreed with him. In other words, all seemed to feel that a period of military training for every citizen is a good thing."

The War Committee also discussed the tank brigade and the armoured division. The division had already been agreed to in principle and Mackenzie King noted that "the tank brigade seemed to be a necessary complement to our own Army Corps and the most immediate thing that can be done. While the expenditures involved are very considerable, they seem to be the ones most justified in the light of military needs. It was agreed that I would make public announcements concerning these decisions within the next day or two. I asked that Defence Departments get down in black and white exactly what their programmes were to be for a year so that they could be stated to Parliament in their entirety. Ralston felt that the projects themselves would exceed the Estimates and was very strong against wiping out any of the projects. I could see no reason why they should be wiped out or against making known that some of them could not be completed within the fiscal year. I was, however, against having Parliament vote money for more than it was possible to accomplish in a year's time."

The following day (January 29) at the War Committee meeting, Mackenzie King referred to reports in the press of failures in aircraft production. Howe explained that the failure to meet targets was the result of insufficient time being allowed for planning and development. Mackenzie King noted that "Howe has such complete understanding of the situation that I think he will make a strong and intelligent defence. I felt immensely relieved after hearing his side of the case."

On this occasion Mackenzie King was not too favourable to "further vast developments for four engine bombers to be made in Canada for the British Government on the score that we had already gone to the limit in what we believed it was possible for us to do. However, Howe felt that some of these advanced machines are needed to complete the industry. That we are now over the initial stages and the worst, and should go on to make the programme complete. In these matters, one had to rely upon the Minister's knowledge and advice."

Before the war programme was finally settled, the Dominion-Provincial Conference had been held on January 14 and 15. Mackenzie King feared that Hepburn of Ontario would use the Conference as an excuse for another attack on the federal Government and it was largely to pave the way for the new wartime tax arrangements it considered necessary that the Cabinet finally agreed reluctantly to the request of some provinces to have a Conference at all. At the Cabinet meeting on December 13, nearly all the Ministers had felt the Conference would "amount to nothing. Ilsley said he thought it would last three days, and would like to see the position of each province [on the Sirois Report] properly stated and the whole break up without too great friction." Mackenzie King said that "in the preliminary speech, we would have to construct a mattress that would make it easy for the trapeze performers as they dropped to the ground one by one. I have never believed that the Conference could succeed at this time of war." But he felt that, "were the Government not to make the attempt, it would be blamed for whatever financial disaster will follow, as it certainly will, in the course of the next year or two."

It was in this pessimistic spirit that the Cabinet began, on January 9, 1941, to consider its tactics. Mackenzie King insisted that the approach to the provinces should be conciliatory, not dogmatic or dictatorial or threatening, though he recognized that the federal Government must indicate its willingness to implement the main recommendation of the Sirois Report. He said "they must consider the use that could be made particularly by Hepburn and others, of any opening we might give them for stage play at this time." It had been suggested that a recording of the proceedings should be made for posterity. Mackenzie King was opposed to what he called "dramatizing situations of the kind," and observed in his diary that "dramatization is the curse of our age. . . . I can imagine nothing that would help to destroy more effectively in the public mind, my own position in this whole matter."

The Conference was to open on January 14. The Premiers of all the Provinces were to head their delegations: Hepburn for Ontario; Godbout for Quebec; A. S. Macmillan for Nova Scotia; J. B. McNair for New Brunswick; John Bracken for Manitoba; T. D. Pattullo for British Columbia; Thane Campbell for Prince Edward Island; W. J. Patterson for Saskatchewan; and William Aberhart for Alberta. The attitudes of the various provincial Premiers were well known in advance. Hepburn, Aberhart, and Pattullo were hostile to the Sirois proposals; Bracken, Patterson, Macmillan, and Campbell were favourable, Bracken strongly so; Godbout and McNair were non-committal.

The Sirois Report had recommended a scheme of fiscal readjustments between the federal and the provincial governments which had to be accepted as a whole if their purpose was to be achieved. The proposals for Mackenzie King's opening speech as prepared by the advisers of the Government stressed this point. Mackenzie King refused to take this rigid position and told the Cabinet on January 12 it was "only the conciliatory approach that would get us anywhere in the discussion, and if we take the 'take it or leave it' attitude, that attitude would be blamed for the failure of the Conference." He felt there was nothing "Hepburn and Aberhart would like better than for the Federal Government and myself in particular to take an arbitrary and dictatorial position. Hepburn would run his provincial campaign on the effort of Ottawa to take from Ontario all its powers, privileges, rights, to sacrifice them to Quebec or to the Prairies."

After extensive revisions along conciliatory lines, Mackenzie King read the revised statement to the Cabinet on January 13 where "it was

1. Mr. King's personal staff for his trip to the United Kingdom, 1941. *Front row* (left to right): Norman Robertson, Department of External Affairs; Mr. King; General George Vanier. *Back row*: J. S. Nicol, valet; J. W. Pickersgill; Walter Turnbull, Principal Secretary to the Prime Minister; J. E. Handy.

2. The Cabinet, 1939. *Front row* (left to right): W. D. Euler, Trade and Commerce; T. A. Crerar, Mines and Resources; Raoul Dandurand, leader in the Senate; Mr. King; Ernest Lapointe, Justice; P. J. A. Cardin, Public Works; J. L. Ralston, Finance. *Back row*: J. A. MacKinnon, Minister without Portfolio; J. G. Gardiner, Agriculture; Norman Rogers, National Defence; J. L. Ilsley, National Revenue; Ian Mackenzie, Pensions and National Health; C. G. Power, Postmaster General; J. E. Michaud, Fisheries; C. D. Howe, Transport; Norman McLarty, Labour.

3. The signing of the British Commonwealth Air Training Agreement, early morning, December 17, 1939, from a picture taken with a small camera by Walter Turnbull. *Left to right*: J. B. Abraham, United Kingdom; Lord Riverdale; Arnold Heeney, Principal Secretary to the Prime Minister; Mr. King; O. D. Skelton, Under Secretary of State for External Affairs.

4. Air Training Conference, 1939. First two rows; *front* (left to right): Sir R. Brooke-Popham, U.K.; J. L. Ralston, Minister of Finance, Canada; H. W. L. Saunders, Chief of Air Staff, N.Z.; Senator R. Dandurand, Canada; Rt. Hon. Lord Riverdale, U.K.; Mackenzie King; J. V. Fairbairn, Minister for Air, Australia; E. Lapointe, Minister of Justice, Canada; H. H. Balfour, Under Secretary of State for Air, U.K.; N. M. Rogers, Minister of National Defence, Canada; Air Marshal Sir C. Courtney, U.K. *Second row* (left to right): J. B. Abraham, U.K.; O. D. Skelton, Under Secretary of State for External Affairs, Canada; T. A. Barrow, Air Secretary, N.Z.; Sir Gerald Campbell, High Commissioner for the U.K.; Ian Mackenzie, Minister of Pensions and National Health, Canada; W/C G. Jones, Asst. Chief of Air Staff, Australia; C. D. Howe, Minister of Transport, Canada; W. C. Clark, Deputy Minister of Finance, Canada; Air Vice-Marshal G. M. Croil, Chief of Air Staff, Canada. Arnold Heeney in back row.

5. Mr. King speaking at a meeting in Prince Albert during his tour of Western Canada, 1941. Mr. Diefenbaker is on the far left.

6. The Dominion-Provincial Conference, 1941; Mr. King speaking at the opening plenary session, January 14. Seated around the table are (from Mr. King's left): Adelard Godbout, Quebec; J. B. McNair, New Brunswick; T. D. Pattullo, British Columbia; W. J. Patterson, Saskatchewan; William Aberhart, Alberta; Thane Campbell, P.E.I.; John Bracken, Manitoba; A. S. MacMillan, Nova Scotia; Mitchell Hepburn, Ontario.

7. Mr. King's trip to the United Kingdom, 1941. He addresses soldiers assembled for a track and field meet of the Canadian Army. Behind him is General A. G. L. McNaughton.

8. Mr. King's trip to the United Kingdom, 1941. He inspects a guard of honour provided by Le Régiment de la Chaudière.

9. The funeral procession of Ernest Lapointe, Quebec City, November 29, 1941.

10. President Roosevelt's visit to Ottawa, August 25, 1943. The scene is the main entrance, Centre Block, of the Parliament Buildings. *Left to right*: President Roosevelt, Admiral King, Prime Minister Mackenzie King, Princess Alice.

11. The Lord Mayor of London, Sir George Wilkinson, with Mr. King and Mr. Churchill on the occasion of his luncheon for Mr. King at the Mansion House, September 4, 1941.

12. Mr. Churchill on the steps of the Parliament Buildings in Ottawa after addressing members of both Houses, December 30, 1941.

13. The Quebec Conference, 1943. Behind the three leaders are (from left to right): General H. H. Arnold; Air Chief Marshal Charles F. A. Portal; General Sir Alan F. Brooke; Admiral Ernest King; Field Marshal Sir John Dill; General George C. Marshall; Admiral Sir A. Dudley Pound; Admiral William D. Leahy.

14. Mackenzie King addresses the Houses of Parliament of the United Kingdom, May 11, 1944. Behind him may be seen Rt. Hon. Viscount Cranborne, Secretary of State for Dominion Affairs; Rt. Hon. Viscount Simon, the Lord Chancellor; Mr. Churchill; the Speaker of the House of Commons; Rt. Hon. C. R. Attlee, Lord President of the Council.

15. The Commonwealth Prime Ministers, No. 10 Downing Street, London; final meeting, May 16, 1944. *Left to right*: General J. C. Smuts, South Africa; Mr. King; Mr. Churchill; Mr. John Curtin, Australia; Mr. Peter Fraser, New Zealand.

exceedingly well received. There was entire approval of each section. Nothing more than a suggested change of a word here and there. Lapointe observed there was a vast difference between this statement and the one presented to Council last week." Mackenzie King himself was "a little more hopeful . . . of getting somewhere with the Conference. At all events, I feel sure that we have laid a true foundation on which it will be possible for us or others to continue to build."

Before the proceedings opened on January 14, in the House of Commons Chamber, Mackenzie King "was as pleasant and natural with Hepburn as if we had always been on most cordial and friendly terms. His attitude was, for the most part, quite the same. My own statement, I think, made a good impression. Indeed, I heard no criticism to the contrary, and many were quite complimentary about its balanced effect, moderate approach. This was also favourably commented upon by several of the speakers."

On the other hand, "many spoke of the contrast between Hepburn's attitude and my own, particularly in the manner of speaking. It was thought, too, I think, that Pattullo went much too far in his opposition and Aberhart, while amusing and plausible, was pretty much all humbug." Mackenzie King felt that "Bracken was much too long and, by being as argumentative as he was, helped rather to create the impression that the Conference was being forced more or less at his instance. My own feeling is that there are two influences that are militating strongly against acceptance of the Report. Above all, financial interests having played it up so much through the press, Bank of Canada, etc., and the other: Manitoba has been so insistent on it all." He thought the Manitoba influence was, in fact, too strong in his own office and referred specifically in his diary to Brockington, Heeney, and Pickersgill as all being from Winnipeg.

Mackenzie King himself felt that wartime was "not the time to permanently settle these matters, but I feel equally strongly that not to have held the Conference in advance, to make the situation clear, would have occasioned more trouble in the end. Like all these things, it is not a choice of perfection, but the lesser of two difficult situations." He was, therefore, not at all disturbed when the Conference broke up on January 15 with no agreement on a permanent settlement, but an acknowledgment from all the provincial leaders that the wartime financial needs of the federal Government would have to have priority. He was pleased at the way in which Hepburn had put himself in a bad light. Hepburn went back to Toronto without waiting to attend the dinner given by the federal Government after the Conference adjourned. Of the dinner,

Mackenzie King wrote that he could not "recall any gathering where I ever received a finer ovation, more spontaneous and enthusiastic.... Everyone seemed to have been delighted with the way in which I got through the Conference at the close, and at the avoiding of any rancour throughout."

His judgment of the Conference was that, "while to appearances it has been a failure, in reality it has served the purpose we had had in view, of avoiding attack for not having called the Conference, and particularly what would certainly have followed, invasion of provincial sources of revenue. We have now got the pledge of the Provinces to let us take their revenues if we need them—a tremendous achievement." Indeed, the attitude expressed by the provincial Premiers to the federal powers of wartime taxation emboldened the Government to proceed with the scheme for wartime tax agreements which alone made possible the heavy yet equitable wartime taxation of the Ilsley budgets. Mackenzie King himself felt, on January 15, "immensely relieved that the Conference was out of the way."

If Mackenzie King felt that wartime was not the appropriate time to reach a permanent financial settlement with the Provinces, many Canadians felt that wartime was not the time to develop the St. Lawrence Waterway. In fact, apart from Hepburn and the Ontario Government who had reversed their position when they began, late in 1939, to foresee a power shortage before the end of the war, there was very little pressure in Canada to develop the St. Lawrence. But Roosevelt had had his heart set on the project ever since he had been Governor of New York. By 1941, the United States authorities really feared that a shortage of power might impair the security of the United States and there was a genuine desire on the part of the Roosevelt Administration to get ahead with the St. Lawrence development without delay. Mackenzie King and Roosevelt had agreed at Warm Springs in April 1940 that the negotiations should be taken up actively after the presidential election in November. The Cabinet accordingly made a formal decision, on October 8, to go ahead with the whole project, if an agreement could be reached with the United States and collateral agreements made with Ontario and Quebec.

Mackenzie King took advantage of the presence of Premier Godbout and several of his colleagues in Ottawa for the Dominion-Provincial Conference to discuss the problem, which he knew was embarrassing to Godbout because of the very marked opposition to the Waterway in Montreal and elsewhere in the Province. When the federal Ministers met Godbout and his colleagues on January 17 Mackenzie King said he "would give a good deal" not to have to discuss the question during the war, as he feared it might bring about "a real division" in Parliament and with Quebec, and that if the negotiation was a failure on top of the Dominion-Provincial Conference, there might be a movement to "get another leader." He told the Quebec Ministers that, "but for the war, I did not think either Lapointe or myself would stay in public life at this time. That I doubted if Cardin would." He stated that the only reasons for going ahead were the desire of the Roosevelt Administration to proceed with a project which they claimed was necessary to the long-term defence of the United States, and the importance to the Allies of Roosevelt's goodwill.

Mackenzie King was impressed by Godbout's willingness "even at great risk to his Government, not to stand in the way of anything required for war purposes." There was a good deal of discussion back and forth, over two days, about whether it might be better simply to develop power in the International Rapids and leave the Seaway until some later date. Mackenzie King had a sharp difference with Skelton who did not want the Seaway postponed, but despite Skelton's objection, the Cabinet decided to try to get the Americans to agree to the power development alone, and Mackenzie King insisted there would have to be a written declaration from the American Government that the work was being done in wartime on the initiative of the United States, because he was "afraid that both in the United States and Canada the cry would be raised we are diverting money from making munitions, etc., 'to dig a ditch' if we go ahead with the canalization project at this time." Godbout did not give the final word of his government until January 20, when he telephoned Mackenzie King to say that the Quebec Government "were of the opinion that they would prefer the whole project to be undertaken at once rather than to have only the International Section developed." After meeting with the Cabinet on January 23, Mackenzie King observed "it is now quite clear that as regards both Ontario and Quebec, there is no longer any disagreement between those Governments and ourselves. We have reached the point that I have held out for all along, namely, that of not proceeding with the International Waterway so long as so doing would mean creating an internal problem between Governments, provincial and Dominion, in order to avoid complications of an international character. The next step now is to get proper communications to United States Government and the right replies from that source." On January 29, Mackenzie King gave Moffat, the United States Minister to Canada, a memorandum for the President setting out the Canadian position.

On February 1, he had a telephone call from J. W. McConnell of the Montreal *Star* who read him an article on the St. Lawrence project which he proposed to print or merely to send to Mackenzie King, "setting forth the strongest of reasons why the Waterway should not be proceeded with in this time of war." Mackenzie King told McConnell he "was in touch with the President presenting all the views that he himself had expressed in the article, making clear that the war changed the situation very much and that, if we did anything at all on the St. Lawrence, it would only be done because of reasons of his decided policy, and would be done as something which the public would know the President himself regarded as absolutely necessary in connection with the winning of the war. . . . He [McConnell] asked me the pointed question whether I thought the President wanted to let the power men in the United States see that he had the power to go ahead. I told him I did not think that was the case, but I really felt he regarded additional power as necessary for war purposes. I let McConnell understand that, if I could get the President not to press the matter, I would do my utmost to that end. However, I might find that, if I took too strong a stand, I would be prejudicing the President's assistance to Britain as well as to Canada, and if I had to act in the matter it would be only to prevent this, and that would be made plain in any announcement of what was being done. McConnell agreed that the whole picture might change as a post-war project, but stressed how strong the feeling would be if scientific brains and labour were diverted at this time from war industry to power and seaway developments."

Mackenzie King's fears about the opposition to be expected from Quebec were apparently not warranted. Cardin talked to him about the St. Lawrence development on February 6 and told him "not to be concerned about Quebec. The opponents had gone so far that they were exaggerating the dangers." He gathered from Cardin's words that the Quebec Government "would now be almost disappointed if they did not get a chance to go ahead. I told him of Moffat's coming this afternoon and of representations I had made through him to the President." Mackenzie King observed that "it was a pleasant hour's talk. Cardin was most appreciative of my own attitude towards himself, Quebec and its problems. He referred with justifiable pride to the part he and Lapointe had taken in Quebec's relations to the war and spoke with particular affection and admiration of Godbout and his sincerity and beauty of character."

Later in the day (February 6), Moffat called to tell Mackenzie King "that the President had said he did not wish to see Mr. King embarrassed in dealing with the waterways problem . . . and would be quite content to have the Agreement so drafted as to have the whole question of the deepening of the channel left in a way that would serve to make it a post-war project. When I questioned Mr. Moffat as to whether or not the President would wish to have an Agreement concluded notwithstanding, Mr. Moffat was quite emphatic that that would be necessary, as the President would have to let those interested in the navigation aspect of the problem see that he was not overlooking its importance. . . . The President would be quite satisfied to have the Agreement so drawn as to enable him to get on with the power work in the International Section. . . . The President was quite agreeable to having it made wholly clear that it was the United States that was pressing for the conclusion of an Agreement."

On March 10, Mackenzie King received a draft of the statement Roosevelt proposed to make public on the St. Lawrence, which he considered "the strongest statement that has yet been made by the President as to America's intention with respect to the winning of the war. It looks at the moment as if the St. Lawrence Waterway project, which has been for so long such a nightmare, is now about to prove one of the great achievements of the present Administration. Another international achievement in which the President's name and my own will be linked through the years to come." He added that he took "a little satisfaction to myself in having planned the methods which have brought about an agreement between Ontario and Quebec and the Dominion, and between the United States and Canada. All are now linked in unison in this project, both as respects power and navigation. A false or precipitate step in the procedure might have wrecked the whole transaction."

The actual Agreement with the United States was signed on March 19. Mackenzie King was "very sorry that Skelton had not lived to see this day. He has worked very hard on the St. Lawrence matter; has fathered it all along the way." He felt it was "a mighty lucky thing that I insisted on getting an opinion from the President before we did anything. That opinion, as I had thought it would, has changed the whole aspect of the probable course of debate. We have struck at the right moment, and the wish of the President counts for more than that of any President at any time. The timing in this thing has been perfect, getting the Agreement itself out, just after the Lend-Lease Bill had passed Congress, and the whole continent getting busy with increased industrial activity, shipbuilding, etc."

The death of Skelton, in the very midst of the St. Lawrence negotiations, was an event which had a profound effect on Mackenzie King's life and work. He was in his office in the East Block in the early afternoon of January 28, when Arnold Heeney came in and said he had had "news, very bad news," and then told him that Skelton was dead. Mackenzie King went to see Mrs. Skelton at once and then to the hospital to see Skelton's body. He wrote that Skelton's death "at the wheel of his own car in one of the busiest intersections of the city seems to me to have been a most fitting close to his life and his life's work. He was always very independent, self reliant, liked to direct things himself, and to be in the thick of the tide, to share the life of the active and busy world and of the men on the street."

Later in the day Mackenzie King wrote that while he had realized "instantly all that it [Skelton's death] meant in the way of loss both personally and in connection with my work and to the country at this time . . . that it seemed part of the inevitable something of the discipline which one must not merely face but accept as part of a great purpose. I felt a complete control of my own feelings at the moment and throughout the day. No doubt the feeling that this might happen at any time helped to make the event, when it came, something which had been anticipated. There is no question, however, that so far as I am personally concerned, it is the most serious loss thus far sustained in my public life and work. However, there must be a purpose and, as I see it, it may be meant to cause me to rely more completely on my own judgment in making decisions, and to acquaint myself more meticulously with all that is happening so as to be able to meet each demand as it is occasioned. It is rather strange that in the course of this year, I have lost three men who, spiritually, were in a way closer to myself than any other, Lord Tweedsmuir, Rogers and Skelton. Each of them was a real helper as well as companion in my work. Someone to lean upon as a real support. What I valued most in each case was their sterling rectitude and disinterested purpose. I could count on them all for backing me up in maintaining the right course. No one of the three was strong physically, all had to contend with lessening physical powers but each gained greater strength intellectually. I believe all three are working together today influencing thought and action in this world."

At Skelton's funeral on January 30, Mackenzie King was "deeply impressed with the appearance of Skelton's face in death. It bore a truly noble expression and had the look of a man who could face kings and the world with a sense of being absolutely of the chivalry of God." The following day (January 31) he wrote that both Skelton and Norman Rogers "attempted to do far too much. They took on excess loads. Both had the highest sense of duty, but that does not excuse using judgment in all things. I am positive I would have been in my grave before this, if I had not resolutely gone in for the rest I have, and declined public appearances one after the other, or avoided trying to gain too much in the way of power for myself. On the other hand, I think I have been tremendously at fault in not concentrating more on work and perhaps mastering more myself, and trusting too greatly to the outside aides. I wish, too, I had the unselfishness and selflessness which characterized so strongly both Rogers and Skelton."

On February 6, he wrote in his diary again on this theme: "I can see one of the effects of Skelton's passing will be to make me express my own views much more strongly. Indeed, in that particular, I feel in a way certain relief from pressure that has been constantly exerted to avoid expression particularly in some lines. That, however, I was glad to have him as a guide, but there are times when it was almost too strongly exerted to the extent of unduly influencing Government policy. However, that good far outweighed any effect of limitations in other directions. There was a fine sense of security with Skelton at hand. I shall miss him particularly in not having one, outside the Cabinet, with whom I can talk over matters generally." No one ever completely took Skelton's place, although Norman Robertson who succeeded him as Under Secretary of State for External Affairs quickly gained and retained a greater measure of Mackenzie King's confidence than any other adviser of the closing years of his life.

Politically the winter of 1940–41 was one of the quieter periods of the war years. The agitation for National Government and conscription died down after Parliament adjourned in August and Mackenzie King's prestige was greatly enhanced by the Ogdensburg Agreement and his part in bringing about closer relations between Britain and the United States. Parliament had been adjourned, not prorogued, on August 7, but there did not appear much reason to call it together again later in the year. Indeed when, on October 3, Mackenzie King discussed the question with Hanson, he found him willing to prolong the adjournment until January, 1941, and to allow Mackenzie King to tell the press "that he and I were of the same mind." But, on October 8, Hanson went back on this undertaking and demanded that Parliament meet again on November 5. Mackenzie King, the next day, referred to Hanson's attitude as "annoying and distressing." He noted that the Conservative party was "beginning reorganization in different parts of Canada, and I can imagine will be changing their tactics and become increasingly antagonistic now that the first session of Parliament is over."

As a result of Hanson's insistence, Mackenzie King felt it was the part of wisdom to have Parliament meet on November 5, when the first session of 1940 was prorogued. The new session, which was not to be prorogued until early in 1942, began on November 7. Mackenzie King was resolved to make use of the debate on the Address to bring out the Government's record in prosecuting the war. He decided to devote his own speech on the Address mainly to an outline of his talks on defence with Roosevelt from 1936 up to the Ogdensburg Agreement. On November 9, he "had four or five pages telephoned to Washington to be shown to the President before making the statement itself in Parliament." While he felt sure Roosevelt would approve, he did not wish to take any "chances of embarrassing him in any way." He felt the whole story was "a great vindication of my life's work in . . . relations between Canada and United States and my work and friendships in both countries." On November 11, he was gratified to receive word that the President approved the speech apart from a single phrase which he wished to have altered. The speech itself was delivered on November 12 and was very well received.

While the Opposition was seeking some line of attack on the Government, at this time, Mackenzie King felt that Hanson's leadership was particularly inept. On November 15, he wrote that "Hanson again put his foot in it by reading aloud messages [which had been shown him in his capacity as a Privy Councillor] that would have given the enemy the impression that we had not sufficient shipping, or were sending unseaworthy ships to sea; had something like mutiny on board; giving name of port and of ship and time of sailing. A shocking indifference to war secrecy. I drew attention to the form of his question. He did not take it well in reply. [Arthur] Slaght [the Liberal Member for Parry Sound] then got after him for disclosing war secrets. The upshot was Macdonald, the Minister of Naval Affairs, becoming very alarmed. Wanted press censored re matter. I spoke to Hanson. Got his consent for that. Then came the question of Hansard itself. Got his consent on that provided Slaght's remarks were withdrawn, which went the length of asking that Hanson should be expunged from the Hansard. After six, I had to see Hanson; also the Speaker; Young of the Debates [the Editor of Hansard]; Bell, Hanson's secretary. Telephoned Hanson again, then [Wilfrid] Eggleston, of the Censors [in charge of press censorship], to get the parts expunged which should be expunged, and to prevent the press taking any notice of what had transpired. It was going pretty far with the records of the House but I had to take a chance, and should a question be raised, will get the House to support my action by a vote. This, however, not likely to be necessary."

Apart from Mackenzie King's, the first speech on the record of the Government was one by Ralston on the Army on November 15, and in the week of November 18, the other Ministers gave reviews in the House of the activities of the war departments; Power spoke on November 18 and Angus Macdonald on November 19. Mackenzie King was greatly pleased by the performances of all three Defence Ministers. He described Howe's speech on November 20 as "a perfectly marvellous statement of achievement in work of construction and manufacture of armaments, munitions, and other supplies. Transformation of peacetime economy into a wartime economy—colossal is the only word that would describe the impression left as to the achievement in the time. Exceptionally fine organization for war effort was another outstanding impression. Both Lapointe and I agreed on that. I felt increasingly proud of our war effort once Howe's speech was added to the others. It was exceedingly well arranged, concise, informative, not too long and detailed. I think the stuff is being knocked out of the Opposition. They are being literally overwhelmed with information."

The next day (November 21) Ilsley spoke. Mackenzie King described his speech as "splendid—really a treatise on war finance; principles and policies referring thereto. A year ago, we would not have dreamt that it was possible for the country to even attempt what today it is achieving. Lapointe and I were remarking that since Confederation, there had been no Government comparable to the present in the ability it has demonstrated. The whole war effort has been a magnificent example of constructive co-ordinated effective achievement."

On November 26, a speech on war finance by a Liberal back-bencher from Montreal named Douglas Abbott particularly attracted Mackenzie King who found it "as clear an exposition as I have heard in Parliament of a very difficult subject. I said to Lapointe: 'That man would make a good Minister of Finance. If he can hold his seat, he will have a fine future in public life. He possesses a splendid personality.' "

The debate on the Address went on until December 3. That day Mackenzie King replied to a speech by Hanson. After Mackenzie King concluded, "Roy, the only Member on the Conservative side for Quebec, made an awful speech. Full of effort to create disunion in Quebec. He gave Lapointe a fine opening and he took it well. Made a brief speech which, in what it contained at this time, will be quoted through years to come. In particular its reference to Quebec being solidly British in this war. Each of us got a first-rate reception and it was a fine wind-up to the Debate. All our men stayed solidly with the Government." When the debate concluded, the session was adjourned.

Although this first part of the session had gone well for the Government and the debate on the Address had been disposed of, Mackenzie King began to show signs of depression as the date approached for the resumption of the session in February, 1941. Lapointe, Cardin, and Ralston were all unwell and Mackenzie King particularly missed Lapointe and Ralston from the Cabinet meetings. Moreover the Conservative press was reviving the campaign for a National Government. Mackenzie King himself felt the Ministry needed strengthening, but wrote, on February 6, that he could not "see how the Cabinet can be strengthened without making the whole situation more difficult. . . . Skelton's death removes the one sure support that I had in everything. . . . It remains to be seen what deferred reactions will come from Howe's experience and the heavy load he has carried. Already too much is hanging around his shoulders." On February 11, Power spoke to him "about the need of reorganization of the Cabinet. . . . I told him I had also been considering possibilities . . . but intend, before taking any step, to see that names are publicly canvassed by asking the Opposition and the press to name the super-men that they wish to have taken in, to be sure that they will be prepared to accept, and also that they can be elected, and would be of more service in Parliament than they would in their present positions or in some administrative post. It is in times like this that I miss Skelton very much. It is going to be very difficult carrying on without him, largely because I have no one that was so completely a confidant with whom to exchange views and confidences."

The adjourned session of Parliament resumed on February 17 and Mackenzie King spoke on the first day. "The speech on foreign affairs," he noted, "took an hour and a half. I was quite tired when I stood up but spoke without difficulty to the close. . . . It was an immense relief to me to have this speech on External Affairs out of the way. . . . To have had the whole prepared since Skelton's death and without a chance of talking over matters with him was in the nature of a real achievement. . . . Had I had more time, I would have . . . made a few additional revisions. On the whole, however, the statement . . . I think created a real impression."

The next day (February 18) Mackenzie King had a conference with Hanson and Grote Stirling about a matter he thought had been settled before the adjournment on December 3 when he had met Hanson, Stirling, and Howard Green (the Conservative Member for Vancouver South) in his office with Lapointe, Power, Crerar, and Angus Macdonald, to consider a suggestion made by Hanson for the appointment of a Special Committee on War Expenditures, similar to the Committee on

National Expenditures in the United Kingdom Parliament. The purpose of the Committee was to investigate war expenditures with a view to seeing whether there could be any economies. Though most of his colleagues had not liked the idea in December, Angus Macdonald had backed Mackenzie King "solidly saying we could not consider anything other than accepting the suggestion." Mackenzie King had noted that "Hanson said they appreciated our reasons for not wanting Standing Committees on extent of the forces, amounts of supplies, delivery, etc., because of the British Government not wishing details to be given." A motion providing for the setting-up of the Committee was to be introduced when the session resumed. It had been understood at the meeting in December that the Committee, for security reasons, would sit in camera and that Mackenzie King would explain, in moving the motion, that the British practice was to be followed in Canada.

Mackenzie King showed Hanson and Stirling the proposed motion on February 18, but instead of accepting it they asked for another meeting the next day. When the group met again, John Diefenbaker, the Conservative Member for Lake Centre, was also present and he asked to have the terms of the motion changed so as to enlarge the scope of the inquiry into what Mackenzie King described as "a sort of fishing expedition." They "discussed the pros and cons, going carefully into the British report. We decided, I think wisely, to hold to the text of the British resolution, though, by so doing, Opposition will be able to make it appear that we were limiting enquiry, etc. I feel, however, war responsibility makes this absolutely necessary. Otherwise, we are inviting, first of all, criticism of our policy, which can be discussed at other times, and, secondly, more or less directing the Committee to bring all sorts of things on to the floor of the House, regardless of what thereby might be disclosed to the enemy at a time of war or how injurious exposures of certain kinds might be to our war effort."

This meeting did not settle the matter. On February 24 Mackenzie King and several of his colleagues had another conference with Hanson, Stirling, and Diefenbaker. "I have," he wrote, "been feeling a good deal the strain particularly at the Opposition's attitude in Parliament, starting fresh campaign for Union Government, criticising the Administration as a Party Government; in one word, professing to help, but in the next word, damning everything. Have particularly resented Hanson's method as Leader of the Opposition, of dragging along conferences with a view to pulling out information to use in debate later; asking for memoranda in writing, then making agreements, and subsequently asking for subsequent conferences. When I saw this procedure starting anew, it made me very indignant and I confess I found it difficult to contain my feelings. I spoke out very emphatically to Hanson, in the presence of the others, about the effort of the Opposition to embarrass rather than to help the Government, though professing the latter. I told him of agreements that we had reached which he and Stirling knew were in the public interest and had agreed to, but were now being re-opened because one member of his party wanted to re-open matters. I said I would not take on myself the responsibility of adopting any course which the British Government itself had thought unwise and were not prepared to adopt.

"Hanson made a play of my trying to administer a spanking and talked of withdrawing, but when, in the course of the conference, we had reached again what seemed to be the previous agreement, Diefenbaker told Hanson, in the presence of all, that he would not accept it and he did not think their own party would. In other words, the Leader was put in the position of being powerless either to hold to agreements he had made or to influence the party as he felt it necessary to do in the public interest. What annoyed me most was that the whole matter had been settled before Parliament adjourned in [December] and that I had been doing everything possible to meet the Opposition's view since." Mackenzie King refused to make any change and the Committee was finally established on the basis agreed to in December.

Meanwhile, Mackenzie King had received one proposal for the reconstruction of the Cabinet which he was not prepared to consider. On February 19, Sir Edward Beatty, the President of the Canadian Pacific Railway, came to Ottawa to see Mackenzie King, who soon learned that what he really wanted to talk about was "the advisability of my taking Bennett into the Cabinet." Beatty told him "that in travelling he had found that there was no thought of any change in regard to myself. There was a feeling though that I should strengthen the Government. . . . That Howe had too big a load, had too much to look after, and some of the others were not strong. Ralston, himself, was not too well. That he did not think there was any talk of National Government or changing the present Government but rather the need to get one or two men, who could be a help, into the Government. I pointed out to him how I had tried that a year ago, mentioning to him that I had spoken to Spinney, McConnell, Moore, Jim Macdonnell, etc. Did not find it easy to get men who were suited to public life. I said to him he had better come in himself, half in a joking way and half in earnest. He himself, it seemed to me, shrank away from the thought and accepted the remark much as it was meant.

"He then went on to say that, when Bennett was here last, he had asked Bennett, in Montreal, if he had called on me. Bennett said he had not. That I had not called on him. Beatty said he thought it was not my business to call on him; that he had told Bennett so, and had said to him he should have called on me, and offered his services in any way that would be of help. He went on to say that he had told him, when he had gone to New York to see him before sailing, that he should sit down and write a letter in his own hand to me saying he would welcome a chance to be of any service. . . . He did not know whether I had ever heard from him. I told him I certainly had not. That I was not surprised. . . .

"He said that Bennett was quite changed; that he had become sort of mild-mannered, and thought he was feeling quite different now that the war was on. What he suggested was that I should bring him out and make him Minister of Finance. That the two of us together would make a very strong united front. That the people, through the country generally, he thought, had confidence in Bennett.

"I listened as long as I could, first thinking that I would say nothing more than that I would think the matter over. Finally, I thought I had better say to him frankly that one had to consider, in making changes, whether they were for the better or for the worse. That the main thing in Canada was to keep the country united. While one might not have the best of everything, one had to be careful not to lose the good that one had for some change that would not be as helpful. I asked what I would do with Ilsley. He thought Ilsley could be given another portfolio.

"I said to him I could not imagine Bennett being in the Cabinet one hour without wanting to run the whole thing, and beginning to fight with everyone else. Beatty admitted he had fought with all of his colleagues, and said he had had many fights with him himself. He said he had changed. I said, you cannot change at his age. I said, moreover, the Tory party had kicked him out, when he was ready to run again. He had called the convention hoping he would be offered the leadership again, but they would not have him. That he had left Canada, wiping the dust of his country off his feet. That I had heard him say at the Rideau Club that he would never come back and was going to be buried in England. . . .

"I said to Beatty I would very gladly get out at any time myself and let others take the position I had, if there was the slightest feeling anywhere of desire to change. He told me there was nothing of the kind; that the feeling was quite the other way; that it is recognized I needed some help and stronger men. I said I would like to know who the men were. . . . I said I was quite prepared, if the country wanted, to let anyone else lead, to take any post and help in the war effort. . . . He said something about the next election and the country getting into the hands of a lot of groups. I told him that if he wanted to hand the country over to extremists he better have the two old political parties unite. . . .

"I said to him I was very glad that he had spoken to me as he had. That I recognized, being a friend of Bennett and feeling as he did, he would not have been a true friend of Bennett if he had not put forward Bennett's name in this way, nor would he have been a true friend of mine if he had not spoken to me as he did. I thought his friendship for and association with Bennett gave him a wrong idea as to the welcome Bennett would receive in Canada, coming back at this time. That I certainly knew him well enough to know that he could not be in the Cabinet a day without having some disagreement and wishing to assert himself above everyone else. I told him some evening I would like to have a good talk with him over the whole situation."

The next day (February 20) Mackenzie King spoke to the Cabinet about the personal strain and fatigue he was suffering from, adding "that matters had mounted to such a stage that I felt I was unable to get out from under them without taking a little time off. That I found myself getting over-strung and ready to strike anyone who spoke to me." He then referred to many pressing problems that had to be faced and added that he could see "from this week's discussions in the House, that the Opposition and a portion of the press in the country were again going to urge changes in the Government, strengthening it." He gave as an illustration "the talk that I had with Beatty yesterday and his desire to have Bennett brought back."

On February 22 Mackenzie King noted in his diary that the Opposition were "determined to make the road as bitter as possible, and the large papers are all united in a demand for National Government or what they call further representation in the present Government—a kind of jingo thing that [Howard] Green described as a Victory Cabinet. I see where I shall have to come down to fundamentals of government, first with our own party and then with the Commons and the country, making clear that it is not a choice between perfection and something less, but what is best between the two methods, neither of which are perfect. I intend to hold for Responsible Government against Dictatorship." Two days later (February 24), Lapointe told Mackenzie King he would like to make a speech in the House that afternoon on National Government. "Lapointe," he wrote, "made an excellent speech summing up the whole situation in the words 'not only was I given a mandate to carry on a war government but equally a mandate not to form a National

Government.' Also by asking the question: Why divide the country by professing to unite it?" After several of the Ministers followed Lapointe's lead and took the offensive in debate, the campaign for a stronger Cabinet died down and no changes were made.

Mackenzie King went to Toronto on Saturday, March 8, for one of his occasional visits to his dentist. He found this day a welcome break in his routine. After visiting the dentist, he called on George McCullagh, the publisher of the *Globe and Mail* who was in the General Hospital. Although he did not admire McCullagh, Mackenzie King had a certain liking for him. When McCullagh referred to recent criticism of the Government in the *Globe and Mail*, he "told him I had not come in to discuss the matter at all but wished to see him and express my hope he might get better soon." McCullagh "talked very strongly against Hepburn. Told of how Hepburn had promised, in the presence of his colleagues, to support the Sirois Report. I gathered that he, McCullagh, had promised the Globe's support to him if he supported the Sirois Report. The truth is there are a lot of amateurs alike at Queen's Park and in the Globe office. The latter really want to govern. Think they know as much about the country's needs as the people's representatives."

His next call was on Sir William Mulock and later he went to Divadale, the home of Colonel Flanagan, a millionaire in North Toronto, whom a friend had suggested he visit. He found he had met Flanagan years before and described him as "a warm-hearted, generous soul who has led an interesting life in Texas, South America, and through his business connections and his own discoveries, has come in for great wealth." His next call was on Mr. and Mrs. Leighton McCarthy to discuss the appointment of McCarthy as Canadian Minister to Washington to succeed Loring Christie who was seriously ill—an appointment he had first proposed on February 14.

From the McCarthy's, he was driven by Jack Hammell, the gold mining promoter, to Hammell's house at Oakville. "We had a most interesting conversation on the way out," Mackenzie King wrote, "in the course of which he told me a good deal about his life, having been a prize fighter and explorer in the Northern areas of Canada—ten years without sleeping in a bed, just sleeping on boughs of trees with his wolf dog near him, as a prospector to discover gold, etc." Mackenzie King made this visit as a result of a letter Hammell had written him; he took a great fancy to him and "liked Mrs. Hammell exceedingly, and also the whole atmosphere of the house, grounds and all. It is, of course, a millionaire establishment but there is rest and peace about it, and clearly he is fonder of bits of nature than anything else. . . . When he came to the door to say good-bye he told me to command his services in any way I wished at any time. I really felt I had made a genuine friend."

From Hammell's place, where he had dined, he went to spend the rest of the evening with Joseph Atkinson of the Toronto *Star*. Atkinson told him that Clifford Sifton had been to see him recently to get the support of the *Star* for National Government. "Atkinson," he wrote, "said he believed national sentiment would be better satisfied with National Government or at least with a few outstanding Conservatives, though he could see practical difficulties of effecting anything of the kind. . . . He was glad Lapointe had spoken out as he did. Also Howe and myself. It gave them [the *Star*] a chance to support us against the need of National Government." Atkinson felt the Government was "stronger than it was some weeks ago when the Union Government movement focussed; also that . . . there is no feeling anywhere for anyone supplanting myself. He thinks the country has complete confidence in my part."

The following day (March 9), Mackenzie King noted in his diary that Atkinson had told him "that he knew from his associations with business men in the city that, once the war was over, they would fight as strenuously as ever for retaining their possessions, and he felt sure if I took in the Cabinet any of those who wanted to come in for Union Government reasons, they would be a thorn in my flesh in trying to control financial policies, etc. That he thought all the wealth that was coming from the war should be taxed and returned to the State. I said to him I felt certain that would be kept on. . . . He thought that might be so but he said it was astonishing how very powerful combinations of wealth and business were."

The major event of the 1941 session was the first Ilsley Budget, which was discussed by the Cabinet on March 26. "The choice," Mackenzie King noted, "lay between one kind of Budget which means going into Provinces and taking the bulk of our taxation from income tax, corporation taxes and succession duties—a field which British Columbia, Ontario and Quebec have invaded, going pretty far in this direction, practically monopolizing that field, and offering to give the Provinces back the equivalent of what they had raised this year so as not to rob them of revenues, but to make the burden upon the Provinces impossible should they seek to continue these sources themselves. . . . The other kind of Budget would be one that would increase the sales tax, increase the defence tax, but slightly increase the other taxes."

A question arose at the Cabinet meeting as to whether there should be a conference with the provinces in advance; Mackenzie King "took very strongly the view, as Lapointe also did, that there should be no conference in advance; that we should do what we were going to do in the Budget without a word in advance, as at our last conference we had been told we had the power to do this and should do it, and must exercise that power. The Cabinet became one in that view. There was final agreement on adopting the first plan proposed, the only difference of view being whether it might not be better to impose new taxes on incomes, succession duties and corporation taxes, leaving to provinces themselves to work out their own salvation."

When Ilsley pointed out that it would mean "we could not, next year, get the benefit of the enormously larger taxes there would be growing out of the war profits, we all felt it was better to do the thing that would be the most satisfactory in the long run. What is now being done will last until the year after the war which may mean that, at that time, the provinces will have come to see that the Sirois Report is, after all, what is best for them as well as for us. It is a bold and far-reaching policy but will, I believe, succeed.

"I said to Council I thought with this it would be much as it had been with the St. Lawrence. The exigencies of the war would cause the people to support a far-reaching change of the kind. In all probability, the real conflict would be on when the Budget came down, and the people would be impressed with the need of the course we were adopting, as the only one likely to help us to get what was needed in the way of taxation." Mackenzie King observed that "Clark, the Deputy Minister of Finance, is doing exceedingly good work. His mind is very clear and far-seeing in financial affairs. Ilsley is a lucky man to have so able a group of advisers at his back."

Wheat was also a problem in 1941. On March 11, Mackenzie King referred to a lengthy discussion by the Cabinet on wheat policy, "a problem of very great proportions and significance, involving necessity of cutting down wheat acreage in the West, having farmers adopt alternatives to growing wheat, including summer fallowing, and compensating them for losses to an extent which would keep the income on the prairies up to an amount necessary to avoid the Western situation getting completely out of hand at the time of war." The wheat question was discussed at the Liberal caucus on March 20. Mackenzie King found the Eastern Members were annoyed at what they considered a favoured position for the West. He "asked the Ontario and Quebec men whether they thought we ought to send Western wheat to Japan and Russia to pass on to Germany. There was a general shout 'No.' I then told them that in the last fortnight we had refused to sell twenty-five million bushels to Japan, knowing it would not meet with their approval. I asked whether they did not think the Western farmer needed to be assured something for the sacrifice of his own products in the interests af all. . . . I pointed out that most money being spent on war expenditures was going to Ontario and Quebec. . . . I tried to get them to see the long view and also to be citizens of Canada first."

Organized labour was showing signs of discontent that spring. On March 14, the Cabinet received a delegation of the Trades and Labour Congress which came to protest that some of the Government's announced labour policies were not being carried out. Mackenzie King spoke out very strongly and said "that anyone who did not help to see that our Labour policies were fully carried out would not be aiding Canada's war effort. I made this so strong that later Ralston said he thought I had been giving my colleagues a spanking in public. I had not so intended my words, but had meant them to help my colleagues in dealing with the dollar-a-year men and others who are responsible for the administration of policies. I went pretty far in making clear that some of these men were carrying into their relations with the Government prejudices which they, themselves, had against dealing with unions. I stated in positive terms the Government's determination to see that labour standards were preserved, the right of labour to collective bargaining, etc.

"There were representatives of many trades present and the men gave my words a very warm response. . . . It was abundantly apparent from Moore's words that labour had full confidence in my determination to stand by its position. I felt the time had come when I should speak out very plainly, realizing how important labour is not only in our war effort but also how right it is that they should, as a result of this war, gain a place to which they are more than entitled."

It was during this period that Malcolm MacDonald was appointed High Commissioner for the United Kingdom in Canada. This appointment was welcomed by Mackenzie King who already knew and liked MacDonald. He met him at the train when he arrived on April 3 and took him to lunch at Laurier House. They talked about Mackenzie King's early meetings with Mr. and Mrs. Ramsay MacDonald. "I was able to tell him," he wrote, "I had really met his father and mother when they were on their wedding trip in '96, described the style of hat and dress which his mother was wearing, her complexion, appearance as a young woman, and his father's fine appearance as a young man. Told him of our meeting in the corridor of the University Residence and of having written an article on his father's address before the British Science Association."

He reminded MacDonald that the last words he had spoken to him in London in 1937 were "about advising Chamberlain not to let Britain into war. We both agreed that, if Chamberlain had not succeeded in doing what he had at Munich, that the Empire would never have gone into the war as one, and England would not have been as prepared as it was. Malcolm agreed that history would do justice to Chamberlain's name." From that day on throughout his period of office, Malcolm MacDonald had the closest relationship with Mackenzie King.

Mackenzie King was planning to visit the United States during the Easter recess of Parliament to have a few days' rest before going to Washington to discuss the problem of the shortage of United States dollars for war purchases. He had set April 9 as the date of departure, before the German attack on Yugoslavia and Greece took place on April 6. He received the news of this offensive almost with relief because it indicated that the attempted invasion of Britain had been postponed, if not abandoned. He correctly forecast the early conquest of Yugoslavia and Greece, but the speed of the German advance and the alarm it created led him to postpone his departure until he could be sure of definite arrangements to see President Roosevelt during his visit. He spent the intervening days at Kingsmere instead and, on April 13, he read several articles in which he felt he could "discern clearly the efforts of the Tories to create a sort of fictitious personage out of myself; to create prejudice in ways that may serve to undermine my power and influence as a war-time Premier. Hardly once, from the beginning, have they had any really helpful word to say. I do feel there is need for me to get more before the public and to have some kind of helpful Government publicity in regard to myself."

It was during these days at Kingsmere that he resolved to do something, after the Easter recess, to improve the wartime information services and to try to bring the session to an early close so that he could visit the Western provinces for a series of speeches which would place the Government and the war effort in a better light.

CHAPTER EIGHT

The Hyde Park Declaration

AT THE VERY OUTSET of the war, the federal Government had imposed a rigid system of foreign exchange control in order to conserve the supply of United States dollars and other foreign exchange in the country. But though foreign exchange was so conserved, it became clear, as Canadian war expenditures in the United States began to increase rapidly, that there would be a serious shortage in Canada's supply of American dollars, which would have to be met by some special arrangement with the United States. However, even before the Canadian shortage became serious, the British shortage of American dollars had become acute and, so long as purchases were on a cash basis, there was a real danger this shortage would limit the flow of munitions to Britain. The Canadian Government, the Bank of Canada, and, from time to time, the Prime Minister became almost as closely involved in the British dollar problem as in their own Canadian problem.

The British shortage was brought dramatically to Mackenzie King's notice on July 26, 1940, when J. L. Ilsley, the Minister of Finance, and Graham Towers, the Governor of the Bank of Canada, reported that Sir Frederick Phillips of the British Treasury was in Ottawa, on his way to Washington to discuss the situation with the Secretary of the United States Treasury, Henry Morgenthau. Phillips had stopped in Ottawa to disclose the British problem to the Canadian Government and, among other things, "to see if Canada might not be willing to turn over to the British Government the gold deposits made by the French Government and the Bank of France, in the event of Britain running out of money wherewith to purchase supplies in the U.S. In other words, the British Government would give us an I.O.U. for the gold." This French gold had been deposited in the Bank of Canada for safe-keeping at the beginning of the war and Mackenzie King "took very strongly the position that we were trustees in the matter and could not consider giving any undertaking of the kind."

Three days later (July 29), Mackenzie King had "a call from Sir Frederick Phillips, of the British Treasury, and another who was with him from Washington, who came to speak about the French gold in the Bank of Canada and monies to be deposited here to the credit of the French Government. Graham Towers came first to discuss the matter which would be taken up. I felt that Towers was making rather a plea for me to concede readiness of the Government to let the British have French gold, if the situation got to be very extreme. . . . I made it so plain to Towers that I would not promise anything of the kind that he finally said that I could be sure that Sir Frederick Phillips would not bring up that subject."

Towers indicated that what Phillips "would talk about was the borrowing from the Bank of money paid in on account of planes purchased [by the United Kingdom] from the French Government. I told Towers that I felt very strongly about trust funds, particularly where they involved the honour and credit of Canada, and that I did not expect I would be able to give Sir Frederick any word that would enable him to assure the British Government that their wishes to use French monies in our possession would be granted. . . . I felt that if France became an enemy, the fund should be in the control of the custodian of enemy property to be held until after the war."

In his description of the interview with Phillips, Mackenzie King wrote that "after Sir Frederick had been seated, he opened the conversation in a manner which would assume that I had known all about what he intended to speak on. He began by saying that there were two matters: (1) $400,000,000 of French gold which was in our possession in the Bank of Canada. He was not going to ask us to allow the British to have this gold for war purposes unless as an act of 'generosity and courtesy' on our part, we were prepared to do so. (2) What he really was concerned about was to get the right to borrow from the Bank of Canada what he called 'our American dollars.' He explained that the French had placed orders for aeroplanes in the U.S. with certain contractors. It had been agreed that the British might obtain these planes by placing in the Bank of Canada, American dollars to the credit of the Government of France. The planes would be delivered to them after the monies had been deposited. The contractors, meanwhile, were holding the planes as belonging to the Government of France. What he wanted to know was whether the Canadian Government would not give its consent to the British Government obtaining the American dollars thus deposited to the credit of the French Government, from the Bank of Canada as a loan. . . . I told him that I thought the money was there on trust; that we were trustees, and had no right to allow money to be used for any purpose other than that which might be sanctioned by the French

Government. He said: But these are our American dollars. I told him that I could not see wherein the American dollars belonged to the British after they had paid them over for the planes and deposited them to the credit of France. He then said if we could not agree to this, they would possibly have to forego the purchase of the planes and go without planes. I told him I did not think he had any right to express the matter in that way. That I was astonished, after all Canada had done and was doing to assist Britain in the war, that anyone speaking on behalf of the British Government should seek to place on our shoulders responsibility for the British not being able to get planes in the U.S. just because we were unwilling to allow all the laws of sacred trust to be violated.

"He came back at the matter in two or three ways, speaking of France as an enemy. That these monies were for an enemy, and intimated that England was at war with France. I said that I had not received any intimation to that effect. That, besides, Canada was not at war with France. That I had despatches, which, on the contrary, expressed the hope that anything in the nature of war between France and Britain might be avoided and that the matter should not be allowed to drift in that direction if it were possible to avoid it. . . . He then said he would have to tell his Government what I had said. I said to him I would expect he would; that certainly was what he should do. . . . I felt that while gold meant very much, for a country its integrity and its honour were much more important. That he was asking me in a war which was being waged against evil forces, to do an immoral act as a part of our contribution to the cause. That I did not intend to lend either my name or the name of Canada to anything of the kind."

Mackenzie King added that "When I gave him the answer on two occasions, he sat and looked me steadily in the eye and I looked at him just as steadily for quite a length of time. . . . I confess I felt very indignant and found it rather hard to restrain myself from saying a good deal. I felt it, indeed, a sort of an insult to have a proposal of the kind made to me as the head of the Government." Mackenzie King "felt, as he kept looking at me, that he would have given a good deal to crush me, if he possibly could have. What seemed to surprise him was that when he threatened that he would tell his Government I did not wilt, instead told him it was his duty to tell them, and added that I would be surprised indeed if the British Government would put forward a proposal of the kind . . . that I did not propose to allow my name, or the name of this country, to go down in history as a party to any betrayal of a trust at a time when we were fighting forces of evil. I told him that he could tell the British government that, notwithstanding the reply I was making, and the refusal I was giving to the proposal he had made, we would continue to fight just as zealously for the cause of human freedom and right in which we were participating.

"He and his friend left the office rather silently and I walked to the door of the ante-room with them. Later, I passed them as they were walking back to the hotel from the government grounds. Both of them looked rather stunned and chagrined."

This was Mackenzie King's first personal contact with the British "dollar problem." And despite later overtures from the British, Mackenzie King remained firm in his refusal to have the French gold or French dollars used.

A new aspect of the British dollar problem presented itself to Mackenzie King when the American Secretary of the Treasury, Henry Morgenthau, telephoned him on December 5, 1940. Mackenzie King had already established very friendly relations with Morgenthau when he and his family had visited Canada in August. On this occasion Morgenthau wanted Mackenzie King's advice and help. Sir Walter Layton had come from London to Washington on a purchasing mission at a time when Arthur Purvis, who was in general charge of British purchasing in the United States, was in England. Morgenthau felt Layton's functions were not clearly defined and he obviously did not get on with Layton. He told Mackenzie King "that the sooner Layton got back to England and Purvis returned to Washington, the better it would be. That, at the moment, purchasing for the Empire was held up. That, frankly, he could not do business with Sir Walter Layton. . . . There was really no one, therefore, with whom he was in a position to deal, and that the whole purchasing programme of the Empire was, for the present, at a standstill. That he thought Mr. Churchill ought to know at once, and seek to have Layton return to England at once, and Purvis return to Washington at once. That until this was arranged, matters would continue to be more or less tied up. Morgenthau said he could not say this to Churchill himself but wondered if I could get this word to him. I told him that I would be glad to see that it was communicated at once."

Mackenzie King sent a message to Churchill and, on December 9, received a reply which he telephoned to Morgenthau in Washington, "giving him word that Mr. Purvis will start very shortly and that Layton would be coming home at once; also that Mr. Churchill had arranged, after a good many personal adjustments, that Purvis should be under the [British] Ambassador. That Purvis would be the acknowledged head of all British supplies and technical missions in the United States, whether permanent or temporary. That this unity and focusing would be of the highest advantage. . . .

"Morgenthau said he hoped so, but he was not too sure of the relationship suggested between Purvis and the Ambassador. He could have wished that the former had not been placed under the latter. He was having difficulties in that direction. That since Lothian, the British Ambassador in Washington, had said the British were at the end of their [dollar] resources, he had been having a very difficult time." Morgenthau also told Mackenzie King that he had talked very freely with W. C. Clark, the Deputy Minister of Finance who was in Washington at the time, and hoped Mackenzie King would see Clark on his return to Ottawa to learn "the real position, and that he would like me to know that what he had said to Clark was most important."

Mackenzie King decided to communicate again with Churchill about this subject, and, on December 14, received a reply which he telephoned Morgenthau the same day. "Mr. Morgenthau," he noted, "seemed a little surprised that I had passed on the word about the independence to be given Purvis, but I told him I had taken it on myself to do that, feeling it would be helpful to the situation." Morgenthau repeated again that he had "given Clark a message especially for me. . . . He then spoke of Clark's presence in Washington and said he had been in on most of the discussions with Phillips. [Sir Frederick Phillips was at that time in Washington discussing the problem of paying for British purchases in the United States.] That he, Morgenthau, liked his [Clark's] attitude exceedingly, and that he had been of very great help to them. I mentioned that he was a very fine public servant."

On December 19, Mackenzie King spent an hour or more with Clark, who had just returned from Washington and who gave him a full account of the discussions between Morgenthau and Phillips. "In a word he said that Morgenthau had felt that Phillips of the British Treasury was keeping back some information. The [U.S.] Treasury felt strongly the British were not disclosing their whole hand in the matter of their securities, etc. Also that ground for this had arisen by British saying nothing about the gold holdings which they had in Canada which belonged to the French Government and which Morgenthau felt should have been classed among their assets. Clark was able to get this information privately from Morgenthau and, in conversations with Phillips, persuaded him it was desirable to conceal nothing. He felt Phillips had believed that what the Americans wanted was to have Britain use up her every dollar in payments for munitions, etc., to be left with no reserve when peace might come. That this would put Britain in a very perilous position. She must have some reserve to deal with a situation that might arise then. Morgenthau had made clear to Clark that this was not his motive. It was rather that he might be fully strengthened in what he had in mind when it came to dealing with Congress and getting from that source the help needed for Britain. He had to appear to Congress as being 'hard and tough' in his dealings with Britain to make sure that they would realize her position. He also said that the Treasury of the U.S. knew about the French gold in our Bank here, of Canada holding it in trust, and seemed to take it for granted that we would use that gold for war purposes and regard it as an asset. I told him he might well have said that I had refused to accept that view.

"Clark said that he had declined to include that gold in our assets in the statement which he made, but had attached a small slip making mention of its existence here so that there would be no concealment, should a decision for its use be arrived at later. . . . I told Clark he should let the Americans know the position I had taken next chance that offered. . . .

"Before we had discussed anything, I told him that Morgenthau had said he had given him a special message for me. The special message was to tell Mr. King that he proposed, whatever America did in the way of meeting Britain's needs from now on, should be done outright as a gift. He was not sure whether the President would agree to that. At any rate, it would not do to put forward the idea at the moment, but it was what was at the back of his mind in getting to the bottom of the assets which Britain had and which we have, so that they could honestly state to Congress that Britain was not in a position to incur further obligations for war materials, nor would she be in a position to pay them back."

From what Clark told him, Mackenzie King was convinced "that there is an understanding between Roosevelt and Morgenthau on this point, and that Morgenthau is really representing the President's intention, should he find it possible to carry it out. All this is growing out of the much needed friendly relations between these two peoples." This message from Morgenthau was the first hint of Lend-Lease.

On January 3, 1941, Mackenzie King received an urgent message from the British Government asking the Canadian Government to "extend them a further credit in the New Year to help them with the money required to make purchases in the States until Roosevelt has a chance of dealing with the situation in Congress." Sir Gerald Campbell, the High Commissioner, who brought the message, told Mackenzie King "that the U.S. were sending a cruiser to South Africa to bring British gold from there to the U.S. to set off against American dollars." He felt "it must indeed be humiliating to Britain to have not only to disclose her every asset in this way but to have, in addition to securities being repatriated, this reserve of gold brought from an outlying Dominion to meet her outlays for war purposes."

Mackenzie King explained to Campbell that he "thought Morgenthau was bargaining in the hard way he was in order to be able to state to members of Congress the length to which Britain had gone in paying for needed equipment, etc., and making clear her extreme position. I said I believed he would find later that Morgenthau had more in the way of generosity at heart than others had reason to believe. (I had, of course, in mind the special message Morgenthau had sent to me himself through Clark.) I told Sir Gerald that we would, of course, meet Britain's request which he, himself, had described as what looked like a begging letter, but, in reality, was something needed to meet a very pressing situation. I said, however, I would have to refer it to the financial authorities first."

The outlook improved on January 6 when Roosevelt made the address to both houses of Congress in which he proposed to provide Britain and her allies with ships, aircraft, munitions, and other supplies by the system which came to be called Lend-Lease. To Mackenzie King this speech "was more satisfactory than any I have thus far heard in that it made definite declaration of U.S. intention to produce aeroplanes, ships, munitions and guns for the nations that are fighting the dictators, and to do this without either making a loan or requiring payment, but of planning for re-payment in kind or in commodities later on. I have no doubt that in the end all of that will be wiped out in large measure. It was, too, an open challenge to Hitler and the other dictators to the effect that the U.S. was prepared to stay in the fight until victory was won. Let them see that the U.S. cared nothing about their threats. To me, the most significant of all the phrases was the concluding sentence which ended with the word 'victory.'"

When the President concluded this speech, which was broadcast, Mackenzie King said, as he noted in his diary: "The U.S. is now in the war. That is, she has placed the whole nation definitely behind the forces that are fighting for freedom. What perhaps was as striking as anything was the quite apparent support the President was receiving, as he spoke, from both houses of Congress."

On February 3, Mackenzie King had a long conversation in Ottawa with Arthur Purvis who was on his way to Washington from England.

Purvis told Mackenzie King he felt "very strongly that the English do not understand or appreciate the Americans even yet and that, but for Canada and our interpretation, the two countries would be wide apart." Mackenzie King also gathered from this conversation that "the Americans had been pressing the British to use the French gold here. My opposition to that was known, and seemed, from the way Purvis spoke, to be the one thing that had prevented this step being taken. Morgenthau had wished it to be pressed for but had changed his mind, and they had now concluded that unless the time came when the U.S., Britain and Canada were all agreed it should be seized, and used to meet war expenditures, this step would not be further pressed."

That very day (February 3), Mackenzie King had a letter from President Roosevelt with a hand-written postscript "Do come and see me soon." Mackenzie King felt this was "an invitation I should perhaps heed. I think I know what our talks together mean to him as well as to myself; in this crisis, this may be wholly advisable." It was not until April that he was able to make the visit. By then it was certainly advisable.

When the Lend-Lease Bill was under consideration by Congress it was first contemplated that Canada would also receive Lend-Lease from the United States. Indeed, at the War Committee meeting on February 26, there was some discussion about sending Clark to Washington to protect Canada's interests and to get munitions under the Lend-Lease Bill when it passed. "That," Mackenzie King wrote, "seems to be the most critical thing at the moment." He was overjoyed by the passage of the Lend-Lease Act by the American Congress on March 11, and, the next day, spoke in Parliament of its significance. He "spent the forenoon writing by hand what I wished most to say referring to it as remaining throughout time as one of the milestones of freedom. It points the way to ultimate and certain victory. In what I wrote," he added, "I used certain words and phrases which were taken from the declaration President Roosevelt has made to me, and which will appear in communications regarding the St. Lawrence. It goes further than any declaration he has thus far made in that it indicates that America is in this war until victory is won. It brings back what the President said to me at the start that he had sent word to Mussolini that Italy could not win, and that Germany could not win, and that, if need be, America would see that they did not win."

He concluded this statement to Parliament on March 12 with these words: "The courage, determination and fortitude of the people of Britain in the face of continuous and appalling danger have not only gained the ungrudging admiration of the American people, but they have proved, with inexorable logic, that the strength of Britain is the one great obstacle in the path of the aggressors. The American people know that the magnificent resistance of Britain has made her the main outwork of the defences of the United States. Canada's example, as a nation of the new world, actively participating to the utmost limit in the present struggle, has also had its influence in arousing the people of the United States to their present realization that freedom itself is at stake in this war.

"It in no sense minimizes the magnificent effort of Britain and the nations of the British Commonwealth to say that the aid, the co-operation and the limitless resources of the United States definitely ensure final victory.

"We in Canada may feel more than a little pride in the share we have had in bringing about the closer relationship between the United States and the British Commonwealth. It will, I believe, seal the spiritual union of free peoples everywhere, out of which we may hope to build an enduring new world order."

On March 15, Mackenzie King was astonished to receive a message from Lord Beaverbrook about Lend-Lease in which he said: "Now that the American Government has taken its decision, the grateful recognition of those who benefit by it must be given to your vision in launching the plan. It is proper for us to look forward to a new era of co-operation among the Anglo-Saxon peoples. And for that prospect so full of hope for the world, we must give praise to the leader whose initiative is responsible for such an immense improvement in our conditions."

Of this message, Mackenzie King wrote: "I must say that in the course of my life, nothing has come to me as quite so great a surprise. Naturally, I feel a deep sense of gratitude to Beaverbrook, more particularly as his message comes at a time when so much is being done by the Tory party in Canada, both in Parliament and its press, to belittle my efforts and to detract from the work of the Administration. These records may be invaluable some day as showing how unjust all this criticism is. I did make a great fight to get Britain and the U.S. to co-operate over the leases of bases and did not hesitate to come out with Roosevelt in a joint defence scheme of our coasts before Britain and the U.S. had finally come to agreement themselves. No two men more than Churchill and Beaverbrook know what my efforts have really meant for they were the two who had to be influenced by them to go the length they did in meeting America. The President and Mr. Hull also know what my part in bringing these two peoples together has been. It is deeply gratifying to have the record what it is. Beaverbrook has certainly gone out of his way to show a friendliness and to seek to give due recognition and justice where he has believed it to be due. I am glad I said what I did about Canada's part, in speaking in the House on Roosevelt's signing of the Lend-Lease Bill."

On March 13, the War Committee considered the effect of Lend-Lease on Canada. Clark "gave an exceedingly able and lucid account of the largest problem Canada has ever faced. As matters stand, to do what is expected of us we may have to take something like 65 per cent of the national income to meet war obligations. I believe that is a greater burden than the people of Canada can be led to bear. . . . As matters stand, the Lend-Lease Bill will be used exclusively for Britain. We do not intend to avail ourselves of the Lend-Lease Bill but to allow its advances wholly to Britain. There is, of course, a bigger obligation because of it all than appears on the face of it. I have no doubt the U.S. will wipe off a good part of the obligation especially if Britain loses heavily meanwhile. If, however, she were not brought very close to her knees, the U.S. would undoubtedly keep the obligations arising under the Lend-Lease Bill hanging pretty much over her head to be used to compel open markets or return of materials, etc. It is a terrible position for Britain to be in, bankrupt, insolvent, under obligation to those who were formerly of her own household. Indeed without Canada and the U.S., she would have no chance to exist."

Lend-Lease had solved the British problem but, if anything, it made the problem of Canada's shortage of American dollars even more acute. Mackenzie King went to Washington on April 16 and by this time some solution was imperative. At Roosevelt's invitation he went immediately to the White House. Roosevelt wanted Mackenzie King to wait over and go with him to Warm Springs, or, if that was impossible, to return to see him in Washington after the short rest he had planned at Virginia Beach.

During this visit to the White House the President told Mackenzie King he was moving the American patrols farther and farther out into the Atlantic. He also spoke of the P.B.Y. flying boats he was supplying to Britain. At this point Mackenzie King indicated that "our command was concerned about the possibility of northern Labrador being made a fuelling station—of Germans flying across material and, later, coming in bombers and striking at the Arvida aluminum works, and at Niagara and other vital places." Mackenzie King said "Canada would like to get a few P.B.Y.'s for a few months for patrolling the Labrador area. The President mentioned that his own people thought it was so far north that it was doubtful if there was much danger from that point, but he would like to have his Army and Navy people bring in maps and go over the area with me."

When Roosevelt spoke of Britain getting on much more rapidly with the production of planes, Mackenzie King "spoke of the development of our Air Training Scheme, which was also beginning to make its real contribution. I purposely refrained from discussing financial matters, as I saw how tired he was, and did not wish to introduce this subject until we got away when we could discuss it quietly. I felt it might embarrass the conversation which we would have later, if I appeared to do other than accept his invitation for a bit of a holiday with him."

The next morning (April 17) Mackenzie King called on Cordell Hull. They first discussed the general situation of the war. Hull then told Mackenzie King "quite in strict confidence, that he was having daily confidential talks with the Japanese Ambassador [to the United States], trying to educate him along the line of the wisdom of Japan remaining at peace. . . . What he indicated was that he was working toward an agreement with Japan similar to those that America had with other countries. That he thought the Ambassador himself was ready to sign, but that the Japanese Government did not see things in quite the same way, though he was hoping they might be persuaded." What Hull told him about the Japanese, led Mackenzie King to feel "confirmed in my view that the U.S. did not want to go to war if they can possibly keep out."

He spoke to Hull of "what I regarded as the most serious matter affecting our countries; what he and I were most interested in, namely, preserving normal trade relations between countries." Mackenzie King hoped it might be possible to have "with respect to war materials the components of materials we were producing for Britain, secured from America on the Lend-Lease American basis and that America would place orders with us for things that we could produce. He asked me if the Committees appointed to study these questions were functioning. I told him I doubted it at present. He said he thought they could make studies immediately. I stressed the part relating to the war materials, pointing out that we had neither gold nor American dollars; that, if we became dependent on America for loans and the like, we would have nationalist policies developing after the war."

Hull agreed with Mackenzie King that publicity about Canada in the United States was inadequate. "I told him of my having wanted to avoid any interference when the Lend-Lease Bill was on. Said I had been asking myself whether it might not be well to give a radio broadcast to the U.S. setting forth Canada's position. He said he thought that would be very 'timely' if arranged before some Canadian Club or English-Speaking Union or body of that kind."

Mackenzie King then went to see Henry Morgenthau, the Secretary of the Treasury. It was Morgenthau's twenty-fifth wedding anniversary. After some reference to this occasion, Mackenzie King "spoke about our problem of getting dollars to purchase in the States. He told me about problem with Congress. Said that to get Congress behind him, he had to make clear that Britain was bankrupt. Was having millions brought in to the States, and in that connection had to get gold delivered from South Africa. Mentioned that shipment had come in this morning. He then mentioned that between us, we could reach decisions quickly—if we called a 'spade a spade.' He then said I would not let French gold be used. . . . I then told him about my talk with Phillips, how I had felt offended when he proposed, at the time he did, that we should take that gold and turn it over to the British. I said that I had pointed out that we were administering a public trust; that we were not at war with France. That the gold had been put there by the French Government and the French Bank. That we had kept the French Minister in Canada. That the only relations Britain had with Vichy was through our Chargé d'Affaires."

The conversation then switched to the Canadian financial position and Morgenthau said "he thought our situation was all right till the end of the year. I said: 'Till the end of last year?' He said: 'No, of this year.' I said: 'No, quite the contrary; that we were in a very bad way.'" Mackenzie King then proposed "a sort of barter" of war materials between Canada and the United States. Morgenthau said "he would have anything possible done on this scale to help to get us purchasing power. He asked me if Clark would be prepared to take that up." Both Clark and C. D. Howe were in Washington at the time and Mackenzie King arranged to have Clark see Morgenthau the following morning. Morgenthau "said he would also like to get from us a list of the things that we could manage for them. . . . He spoke of his advising us to have our own industries to produce everything. I told him how we had gone ahead on that scale; that if they began to manufacture here what we were doing, we would be left with our outlays in vain. He said they would pay in dollars for things manufactured by us. I said it would go to purchasing American war material. He said: 'I can do a lot on that line if we can now work out the list of articles that you could manufacture for us. We can place large orders.' He said they were very slow in manufacturing here; it gave one a headache. I spoke about aluminum. Said we could help on that. He said, if we could do anything on aluminum, that would be a tremendous help—aluminum and magnesium. He wondered if we could do any manufacturing in that connection. I told him I did not know. That we would get Howe to deal with that. He then said to me that he and Clark would work out all the arrangements together, and if need be, he would go with me to the President, when I came back on Monday and we could come to a complete agreement on what could be done. He thought this could all be worked out very satisfactorily."

Mackenzie King told Morgenthau "that I had refrained from discussing financial matters with the President until I had talked first with him. Fortunately it was an early morning meeting before he had got worried with the day's work. It being his wedding anniversary he was feeling in pleasant spirits, and with my having had the contact with his family that I had, we got off to a good start together. Indeed, he was particularly nice in the way he responded to my request to talk over matters at all, and, further, in the way in which he expressed his willingness to go as far as he possibly could in the way of getting American dollars. He repeated to me that he could work with Clark, but he found others difficult."

Mackenzie King then went to the Canadian Legation where he saw Clark before lunch, and told him of the conversation with Morgenthau and the appointment for him to see Morgenthau alone at 10 o'clock next morning. Mackenzie King told Clark "Morgenthau was going to leave him to work out matters between now and Monday at which time Morgenthau and I could go with what had been agreed upon to the President, and have matters definitely settled with him. Clark said he had an appointment at 11 with Howe and Harry Hopkins. He wondered whether he should bring Howe with him to Morgenthau. I told him: no, to go himself; that he would perhaps get through in time for a talk with Hopkins later, but to be sure to have Howe here to get together his statement in detail for Morgenthau. Clark said he was tremendously relieved, and he was visibly so."

Mackenzie King then went to luncheon with Sir Gerald Campbell, who had left Ottawa shortly before to become a Minister at the British Embassy in Washington. The new British Ambassador, Lord Halifax, was present and Mackenzie King told Halifax that he "thought a large part of the country was still strongly against being drawn again to any European situation. That the policy of America remained to keep out of war, to defend itself. While the President might be prepared to go pretty far, he had not yet got the country where he could pull it all with him." He added that "Halifax seemed to me to be a little surprised at both these statements, but I felt they were a caution that it was wise to give.

"I also told him before we parted that I could not but wonder what the Nemesis might be some day, in this great country (the U.S.), waxing in wealth as it is, but not prepared to give her blood to help in such a great cause for freedom as the present. That, after all, the Lease-Lend measure was a selfish thing compared to what Greece and Britain were doing. . . . While I believe strongly in keeping English-speaking peoples together, I was stronger than ever for the British connection as far as Canada was concerned."

The following day (April 18) Mackenzie King spent at Virginia Beach. But he was disturbed by the bad news of the campaign in Greece and could not rest. He decided to go back to New York for Saturday, April 19, and to arrange to see the President at Hyde Park on Sunday, April 20, in order to be able to go back to Ottawa on Monday. Before he left Virginia Beach, Mackenzie King spoke on the telephone to Howe in Washington. Howe "said they were making splendid progress; that Morgenthau had said he and I could go to the President on Monday with all the programme of production outlined and get the President's agreement to it. Howe said that, by coming back, I could do more in an hour than could be accomplished in three months. I told him of my seeing the President in Hyde Park and thought I could get his promise there. He said that Morgenthau was going to be at Hyde Park also, he thought. This made me feel that we should be able to settle everything there. I told Howe that he had better stay and, if need be, could go with Morgenthau, though he felt that I was the one to go. I said if it was necessary, I would come back to Washington for that purpose, but I felt that, politically, it would be wise to be back in Canada as soon as possible."

On Sunday morning (April 20) at the Harvard Club in New York, Mackenzie King received Clark "along with E. P. Taylor of the Munitions Dept., a fine looking and really splendid fellow. . . . We had a pleasant talk at breakfast and then . . . we got to work at a long table. Clark produced the draft statement which I had asked him . . . to have prepared as a basis for discussion with the President of what might be given out. We spent two hours going through particulars of the supplies Canada could manufacture for the U.S. Also getting statistics on Canada's financial position vis-à-vis Great Britain and vis-à-vis the U.S. As a result of the discussion I suggested raising the figure of $200 million dollars [for possible United States purchases in Canada] to $300 million dollars.

"At breakfast Clark told me that Morgenthau had said our conversation together had been most helpful. He spoke of my having cleared up to the satisfaction of Morgenthau the position regarding the French gold which we were holding at Ottawa. . . . I immensely enjoyed working with these two men in the Harvard Club, in the quiet of that dignified splendid room."

In the early afternoon Mackenzie King went to Hyde Park. He was met by the President at the front door in his wheel chair. The President extended a warm greeting and then said: "I imagine, Mackenzie, you were a bit concerned about the European situation when you got to Virginia Beach." Mackenzie King replied that he "felt that, with Yugoslavia capitulating and London on fire as she was the day before, that the people of Canada would never understand my being at a seaside enjoying myself, as they would think, for a couple of days." Roosevelt then said: "Your room is all ready for you. It is the King's room in the double sense of the word. You wanted to take a little rest till 4. Suppose we meet at 4. I have some reports to read meanwhile, and we will then go for a drive." Mackenzie King was then taken to "the room that the King occupied during his stay at Hyde Park. The door was opened into the room which I had occupied. . . . What impressed me about the house is the comfort of these old-fashioned houses. The space of the rooms. . . . The day was very warm. Must have been over 80. I got undressed and into bed and went right to sleep."

When Mackenzie King joined him at four o'clock, "the President was at the wheel in his car wearing a white linen shirt, turned down soft collar and no overcoat, no vest and no hat. When I got in beside him, we started off for the little house he had built for himself high up on the hill. He suddenly thought of the Museum which he has just finished and ran the car in beside to let me have a look at the interior. The building is made from the stone of the old stone walls and is most attractive. The interior is really splendid. In the front rooms are hung memorabilia of different kinds, portraits, pictures, etc., models of ships, the Bible which the King presented at the Church, placed in a case for the President, all beautifully arranged—much as at our own Archives. Then there are the stack rooms filled with books and papers—an enormous collection all indexed. The President said to me that the practice was to allow the President to take away all papers and reports at the time of his Presidency. He thought that was quite wrong. That they ought to belong to the public. He was placing all records in this Museum so that they would be available to the public later. Was giving the Museum to the country. . . . He then said he was leaving his own homestead to the country as well. . . . I told him I thought the old house itself was such a fine one and so many of the kind were disappearing there was an additional reason for preserving it for the country. . . . He then told me that the grounds of his estate were not of much value in themselves. There were bits of old pasture. That he did not try to do any farming but was planting large numbers of evergreens. That he hoped to make the place self-sustaining out of selling Christmas trees. . . . He said he had made a thousand dollars out of those cut last year. He would have things arranged so that they would be kept coming on from year to year.

"After conversation had run along on these matters of personal interest for a while, the President then said: As you know, I am having a pretty tough time of it at the present with this defeatist attitude that there is still in the country. The people are so easily swayed by changes; reverses in North Africa; Yugoslav capitulation; situation now in Greece has made everything look very dark for the present. There is only one thing to do and that is to let the people realize that it is only part of a larger plan. That Greece might even be lost and the Battle of the Mediterranean. That there would still remain the Battle of the Atlantic and the Battle of Britain. That these are the battles that will affect the future of the world. . . .

"When we reached the President's cottage at top of the hill, we went through to the front verandah. The day was lovely and warm. The President took off his coat and I did the same. He sat facing the river with one of the verandah posts shading his eyes. I sat to his left on a chair which enabled me to talk direct to him and, at the same time, to get a view of the river. The President then said there were two matters in particular he wanted to talk to me about before Harry Hopkins came.

"He began by speaking of what he was planning in the way of hemisphere defence which would enable him to help Britain. He said convoying would be an act of war. He had, therefore, to avoid that. What he proposed, however, was a patrol and, in some parts, there would be a double patrol. The patrol would cover certain areas and, in connection with the patrol, there would be what was called a sweep . . . the patrol would not keep alongside of [convoys] but would circle around them in a large sweep. This, with a view to detecting submarines or aircraft or a raider. . . .

"If any were seen, immediately the patrol would sound the alarm—would scream out asking what the enemy ship was doing in these waters or areas. The convoy would know what the signal meant and would scatter. If there were British ships nearby, they could come and destroy the raider. He would say nothing about this in the meantime but if an incident took place, would then explain that . . . it was not safe to rely for defence on coast defences—that would be too late—or indeed on naval bases some distance out.... It was necessary, therefore, to have hemisphere defence and the patrols would patrol within the hemisphere area."

Roosevelt referred to having sent troops and planes to Newfoundland and to the establishment of a United States naval establishment at Shelburne, Nova Scotia. Mackenzie King then "spoke to him about letting us have some P.B.Y.'s for Labrador. He said he doubted if it was possible adequately to patrol that Labrador coast, but was sending himself 12 P.B.Y.'s for the coast protection of Labrador and Newfoundland in that area. They would be on hand almost immediately. I mentioned the desire of our men to have some anti-aircraft guns, if possible for Halifax. He said they were the hardest thing to get. I told him of having taken six to Arvida ... the aluminum being of assistance alike to the U.S. and ourselves. He questioned me as to the location of Arvida. Said he thought it was too far inland for anything to be done by planes there. Said they would have to come there from some carrier some distance away. He would advocate returning the anti-aircraft guns to Halifax. He thought Halifax a most important base and said it was unwise to lessen protection there.... I spoke about allowing commercial vessels to come to Halifax. He said that would require an amendment of an Act of Congress and he thought it better not to attempt that. He was anxious not to attempt anything that would make the situation more difficult than it was just at this time.... The President stressed that he did not intend to make any declaration about this widening of the area for the protection of the hemisphere but would let it get out by degrees.

"The President then said the next thing I want to tell you, and I have told it to no one, and am telling it to no one but yourself. Naturally it must be kept most secret. I am in constant touch with Churchill. What I feel very strongly is that we should have a chance to talk together. I have been going over in my mind where would be the best place for us to meet. I had thought of Bermuda, but that, I think, is too far away, and too dangerous. It would have to be some place we could reach in fairly good time and which would be removed from communications. Iceland would be too far for me to go, and Greenland would not do. Newfoundland seemed to me to be the best place."

At this point Harry Hopkins joined them and the President repeated what he had already told Mackenzie King. Roosevelt then said the meeting should be soon and asked Mackenzie King: "How would it be if I accepted your invitation to come to Ottawa, pay the Governor-General a visit at Government House, about the 10th or 15th of May? I could then go ... down to Quebec and over to Rimouski, take a trip to inspect coast defences, the work of our Joint Board. Go down the St. Lawrence and out into the Gulf. I could drop the press on the way and get to this other part by myself. He emphasized how very secret everything would have to be kept and arranged so as not to let anyone surmise what was in mind.

"I said to him I have already extended you the invitation to come to Ottawa—did so at Washington. The Governor-General has done the same. I would like you to come while Parliament is in session. Could you not come and say a few words to Parliament. He said, if it was not too difficult getting in and out, running up too many ramps. I said if it were a fine day we could have the meeting out in front of the buildings, in the open air. The grounds would be crowded as they were at the time of the visit of the King and Queen. He could speak briefly there. He said he would very much like to do that. . . .

"I said, how would it be if the moment I got back to Ottawa, I announced that I had extended the invitation on the part of the Governor-General and myself and that he was accepting it for the early part of May. Had invited him to meet the Members of Parliament. That, of course, everything was contingent on whether he could get away or not. That he had promised to come some time during the year. If he could not make it as early as this particular date, he would come later. Hopkins thought that would be an excellent idea. The President agreed. He said of course something might prevent the other gentleman's coming or his getting away, but that if I got a telegram one morning, to say that he was leaving the next day, or the day after, I would know what it meant."

The three of them later drove to the house of one of the President's relatives for tea. "On the way," Mackenzie King wrote, "we talked a little about some of the defence measures, but more particularly of the talk I had had with Mr. Morgenthau. The President told me that Morgenthau had seen him, after talking with me, and had explained the situation to him. He thought perhaps it might be going a little too far to have something manufactured in Canada for the U.S. to Lease-Lend to England."

Hopkins told Mackenzie King "he had had a very satisfactory and nice talk with Mr. Howe and liked Howe very much. We spoke of different things that could be manufactured in Canada for the U.S.: aluminum, different kinds of ships, gun barrels, explosives, small ammunition, clothing." Mackenzie King explained that the list of supplies Canada could manufacture which Morgenthau had asked for had now been prepared and Hopkins "said he thought it should be arranged that all their orders should be placed through Mr. Howe rather than a lot of contractors coming to Washington lobbying for contracts. I said I believed that would prove to be the best. He said perhaps I would tell Howe to let them know as soon as possible of any factories or other industrial establishments manufacturing for the U.S. and that they would send their men immediately, to view the premises and report upon them prior to the placing of contracts. Either the President or Mr. Hopkins spoke of our doing a good deal in the way of assembling for them.

"It was while we were driving together that I said to the President that, when I talked over the whole matter with Mr. Morgenthau, the latter had said to me he would like me to meet him on Monday, and that we would go together to the President and get his approval of what we had worked out together. That, during the week-end, officials were at work getting things in readiness for us. That I felt a little embarrassed about not carrying out this arrangement with Mr. Morgenthau and had really intended not to discuss it at all with him (the President) until Mr. Morgenthau and I had completed our part. That I wondered whether it would be necessary for me to go back to Washington to see Mr. Morgenthau or whether he would fully understand my having taken up the matter with him, the President.

"The President at once said that he did not think it would be necessary for me to go back. That Morgenthau, as a matter of fact, was nearby, and we could have a word with him when he got back to Hyde Park and straighten out matters here. I said that was splendid; that in the hope or anticipation of some possibility of the kind, I had drafted, before coming, a statement which I thought was of the kind to which Mr. Morgenthau would agree and which would cover the ground pretty well. That perhaps we could use that statement as a basis for further consideration of the matter. The President said that would be first rate. We can take that up after we get back to the house. . . . When the President said he would take up the statement himself I felt an immense relief off my mind, and that the object of the whole mission would thereby be fully achieved."

At tea they talked of the President's ideas for getting people out of cities into the country. Mackenzie King himself "stressed the need of getting rid of cities altogether as largely as possible, with the aid of electric power spreading industry, etc."

It was 8 o'clock when they got back to Hyde Park for dinner. "During the course of conversation at dinner," Mackenzie King noted, "something brought up the fact that my mother was born in New York while her father was in exile. I think the matter came up in reference to some family Bible records. I told the President and Mrs. Roosevelt of the

Bible I have with the registration of my mother's birth and the midwife's earmarks. President Roosevelt paused and seemed deeply interested in that reference."

"As soon as dinner was over," Mackenzie King added, "the President asked me if I had the draft that I had referred to; to come along to his cubby-hole and we could go over it together. We then went into a little study where his table was filled with papers. He sat there in his shirt sleeves and I handed him a copy of the draft. He read it over. Said he thought it was first rate but that there was only one thing he would change." Mackenzie King promptly agreed to this minor change and "pointed out what the whole matter meant as an example of economic co-operation which could be carried on to other fields and made a basic principle in connection with post-war reconstruction. . . . When he had himself approved the draft, I asked him if it would not be well to have a word with Mr. Morgenthau concerning it. He said he would ring him up at once. He got him on the phone. Said: The Prime Minister is here with me. We have been going over the matters we discussed the other day. He has prepared something which covers the ground and he would like to read it to you. I think it is all right. The President then kept his draft and I read from my copy. Morgenthau began by saying he was sorry not to have had the pleasure of seeing me over at his house at tea-time, but hoped I would come at another time.

"I then told him that I had been a little concerned about my undertaking to meet him on Monday morning and to go with him to the President on the matter we had discussed together, but I had felt the President had already been made fully acquainted with what we had said, and that I thought I had in the draft what would be agreeable to him. I had covered the ground which we had gone over between us." Mackenzie King then read the statement and Morgenthau "approved every sentence without exception. Made no suggested change. Said he thought that would cover everything. I said, then there would be no need of my returning to Washington, and he said, not at all, this was all right. So I thanked him and expressed anew my appreciation of the kind way in which he had received me and the generous attitude he had taken in discussing the whole matter."

Copies of the statement were then prepared for the press. As it was practically time for Mackenzie King to leave for the train the President asked him what he intended to say to the press at the station and said he himself would be saying nothing to them until Tuesday when he had his press conference. Mackenzie King said he would say "nothing except that I have been your guest, that any statement that there is to be made will be made by you—anything to be said about matters discussed will be mentioned by you at the press conference on Tuesday.

"The President then said: Why don't you give them this statement yourself when you go to the train? I said I would be delighted to do that, if that were agreeable to him. He said: Certainly. He thought that would be the thing to do, not to lose a minute in giving it out. I said: Could I say this is a statement you and I have agreed upon and just hand it as it was? He said: That was the thing to do." Mackenzie King "then asked the President if he would like to have me initial a copy or would he wish to initial one himself. He said no, you don't need to trouble about that, but let me write on one. He then wrote in pencil, in his own hand, on the original typed copy: 'Done by Mackenzie and F.D.R. at Hyde Park on a grand Sunday, April 20, 1941.'

"Both of us enjoyed so completely the afternoon drive, the talk together and the delightful conversation at the dinner table and felt we were sharing so completely the different matters discussed, the enjoyment of Hyde Park and his own ideals etc. that he really was in the happiest and freest possible moods. I confess that I was never more surprised in my life than when he accepted the statement as a whole without a word, unless it was when he told me to give it out myself to the press when I got to the station. What he wrote on this copy expressed better than anything else possibly could have done, the feeling that must have been in his heart at the time."

Mackenzie King recalled that "at dinner we talked of Canada's war effort and I spoke of how I leaned backwards in trying to prevent American opinion being influenced at the time of the Lease-Lend measure by anything that could be construed by a political party as undue influence on our part. The President and Mr. Hopkins both agreed that Canada was right in that attitude. I said I thought we had suffered in not making our war effort better known and that the time had now come that we should let the people of the United States know more about what we were doing. Both the President and Mr. Hopkins agreed with this. I then said I had thought personally of making a speech somewhere in the States, perhaps before a Canadian Club or the English Speaking Union and outline the highlights of our war effort. That I had spoken to Mr. Hull of this, and he had thought that would be timely. The President then said, I think where that speech ought to be made is before the House of Representatives at Washington, and I would be glad to have you do that. Hopkins agreed. I expressed appreciation of the suggestion. Said that I would undoubtedly attract attention, though I had not had anything of the kind in mind. . . .

"When the President and I were alone in his cubby-hole, I brought up the question of the French gold and of the attitude I had taken, when it was suggested that the gold should be used by the British to make payment for their war supplies. I said I thought perhaps Mr. Morgenthau and others may have felt that in some way there might have been concealment in this matter, or that the British were trying to put on us something that they felt the British should take responsibility for. I said to the President that my first duty in a Government was to see that everything was honourably conducted and that matters in the nature of public trust should be carefully so regarded. The President said he agreed entirely with that. . . . I pointed out, however, that if France got into the war against Britain . . . we would not hesitate to freeze the gold. Then, and if need be, use it against her. This I made plain to Mr. Morgenthau.

"Regarding his visit to Ottawa, the President said that all I need to say to Athlone was that he was coming here only for the day but to make no reference to anything beyond that. After the President had discussed pretty fully the question of arrangement as to meeting place, etc., I said to him, in Hopkins' presence, that that matter is one that I think ought to be thought over very carefully. Remember you two men are the most important and the most needed in this crisis, and it would be an appalling thing if anything should happen to either of you, let alone both. That if the enemy knew you were working together, that certainly would be the one spot they would search out, above all others, and it would be pretty difficult to have you both silent for a time and speculation not take place as to where you were. . . .

"The President's reply to that was that he thought it very important that the two of them should meet and be able to talk over things together. . . . My real feeling was that it was taking too great a risk for anything that could come out of it, but thought it well not to raise that point at that moment; that possibly developments in the Atlantic would, of themselves, settle the matter. Also that Churchill would be pretty certain to view the matter with great caution and might not find it possible to get away. If, however, Churchill felt as the President does, which he may, there might be an advantage in their having a word together which would ensure certain definite combined lines of action. . . . I am sure I was right in not raising an objection at the moment, but will watch carefully to see how things develop meanwhile. I recall what Lord Morley said about not planning too far ahead in politics. That events determine what is possible.

"When the President had signed in his own hand the statement, he gave it to me and I thanked him warmly. Told him how very much I had enjoyed the visit and said good-bye, and expressed the hope that God would bless him and give him strength. He then said: now we will each go our own way for the present; you, to Canada in your car and I, to Washington in mine. We will pass each other on the way. He remained seated in his chair among his papers, looking very happy. I really think the day turned out to be a real rest and enjoyment to him, and that he got a great kick out of our having worked out this Agreement together without any Ministers or advisers or secretaries around, but as something on our own. He feels very strongly, as I do, about this perpetual circumventing of effort by others and the assumption that only those in specialized positions have any brains or judgment. To my mind, there never was stronger evidence of Divine guidance and answer to prayer on that score, more completely evidenced than in this transaction."

Another subject Mackenzie King discussed with the President at Hyde Park was military conversations. He asked "that wherever Canada was concerned, we should be drawn into the conversations, and that, at all events, no commitments should be made before we were fully informed of them. This particularly in the case of Newfoundland. I said our Chiefs of Staff were much concerned about this. That there were conversations between the U.S. and Britain, and between Canada and the U.S. but that where commitments as, for example, re troops, etc. in Newfoundland were concerned, we had assumed large responsibilities there, and we should know fully in advance of any other arrangements proposed between Britain and the U.S. This was said in the presence of Hopkins, and the President replied that he agreed entirely and would emphasize that fact with his military authorities. . . . He said to me that he thought Canada ought to take over Newfoundland . . . that would have to come when the war was over. I told him I agreed; that Newfoundland had not been brought into Confederation because it was a liability but we would have to turn it into an asset."

On his return to Ottawa, when Mackenzie King reported to the War Committee, he found "Howe was overjoyed with what had taken place; shook hands very warmly. Said something about being the greatest negotiator the country had, or something about the world's best negotiator. Could hardly believe so much could have been accomplished in so short a time. Said it had straightened out the most difficult of problems they had had for months."

Mackenzie King also gave one of his rare press conferences at which he "took advantage of the feeling of goodwill on the part of those present to go a little further with the press than I have done formerly. I stressed the intention of changing the attitude of publicity from one of hiding a light under a bushel to one of letting the world know what the people of Canada were doing.

"Also read them secret telegram received from Churchill, some time ago, speaking of his confidence in myself and Canada's war effort in dealing with the question of Imperial Council which some inspired articles have started up again from England. I asked them what possible service I could have rendered in England at this time comparable to that which I had just rendered by being here to discuss with the President the matters which were agreed to between us in getting that agreement. I tried to make clear how little use a Conference in London could be, except for picturesque purposes, compared to each Prime Minister looking after his own Dominion. I gave them a full account of the War Cabinet method of proceeding, and, off the record, told them about the situation in the Near East as I see it. . . . I let out to a greater extent than I have at any previous time, but have come back decided to do more in the way of public contacts and publicity from now on."

The War Committee, on April 23, "discussed matters of command in certain eventualities where U.S. and Canada would be jointly concerned." Mackenzie King could see "a real political danger which may develop out of what is taking place more or less inevitably, and with present enthusiastic approval by Canadians of the aid the U.S. is giving to us and to Britain. Their forces are so much more powerful than our own and so completely needed to protect their own country, as well as ours, because of the gateway which Canada opens to an enemy, that the defence of this continent is bound to be increasingly that of the United States itself. Just what may result from this line it is difficult to say. I, personally, would be strongly opposed to anything like a political union. I would keep the British Commonwealth of Nations as intact as possible. Canada, in time, and sooner than we expected perhaps, would become its centre. It is better to have two peoples and two governments on this continent understanding each other and reciprocating in their relations as an example to the world, than to have anything like continental union."

Mackenzie King reported to the House of Commons on the Hyde Park arrangement on April 28. He was relieved when he "found Hanson was wholly favourable to the Hyde Park Declaration. I was afraid he was going to make an issue of our manufacturing for the States when we should be manufacturing for Britain, not bringing out the point that what was being done for the States was being done for war effort purposes and might be further lease-lent to Britain. He brought up the question of the conference of Premiers. [There was beginning to be talk of an Imperial Conference or a meeting of Commonwealth Prime Ministers in London.] I was too tired to deal with it as I should like to have. Missed a great opening in not referring to the Hyde Park Declaration as against anything I could do in London. Hanson remarked that I was more friendly with the States than with Britain—a poor kind of co-operation in the war effort, when, as he knows, my whole purpose is to bring the countries together as one, without which there can be no salvation for any one of the three."

CHAPTER NINE

Domestic Interlude

THE SESSION of Parliament which had begun on November 7, 1940, adjourned on December 3, and resumed on February 17, 1941, did not adjourn again until June 14, but after his speech on the Hyde Park Declaration on April 28, Mackenzie King did not take a major part in the debates. The first Ilsley Budget was presented the next day (April 29). Earlier in the year, Mackenzie King had taken his full share in the Government's decision to secure a free field for the federal income tax by offering the Wartime Tax Agreements to the Provinces (see chapter 7); otherwise he had little to do with the preparation of the Budget. He wrote in his diary that Ilsley had "really done extraordinarily well in its preparation. It is the largest single transaction ever introduced in the Parliament of Canada. It places a burden that would have been beyond belief on the shoulders of the Canadian people, a year and a half ago. There seemed to be an immediate acceptance of the situation, people realizing that the choice is between present sacrifice or loss of freedom."

During the four months that elapsed between his return from Hyde Park and his departure for London, Mackenzie King's leadership was assailed bitterly on two grounds. His known opposition to the formation of an Empire Council or Cabinet in London was attacked by his opponents as anti-British and pro-American; his continuing opposition to conscription was represented as a lukewarm support for the prosecution of the war. Mackenzie King felt these attacks on his leadership should be met by more positive information about the Canadian war effort and resolved to provide it by better organization of the machinery for public information, as well as by making speeches himself in the United States and by a tour of Western Canada as soon as the session ended. This chapter will be largely concerned with the question of his handling of these attacks.

In addition to the question of an Empire Council, Canada's relations with Japan and France, and, briefly, with Ireland also occupied his attention. There had been a growing hostility to Japan since late in 1940, particularly in British Columbia, where there was strong feeling that Canadian exports of wheat and timber to that country should be stopped. This feeling had been strengthened as a result of a visit by the Japanese Foreign Minister Matsuoka, to Berlin, Rome, and Moscow in the early months of 1941. In order to meet the situation in British Columbia and also to indicate displeasure with the increasingly pro-German attitude of Japan, the Government decided, late in April, to stop exports of wheat and timber to Japan, except where contracts had already been entered into. After this decision was made, Mackenzie King saw the new Japanese Minister to Canada, Yoshizawa, on April 23, to explain "the fears we had concerning trouble arising in B.C." The Minister told him Canada had cut off trade to such an extent that "the Foreign Minister [of Japan] had spoken . . . of doing away with diplomatic relations between Canada and Japan altogether. He pointed out particularly that the U.S. were still shipping wheat and logs and that in Japan . . . some were trying to create the idea that England was seeking to starve Japan or the Japanese. I told him our people had been aroused over the visit of the Foreign Minister Matsuoka to Berlin, Rome, and Moscow. . . . There had been no visit to England. That this all intensified feeling in B.C. We did not wish to let it be given any expression if we could avoid that."

The hostility to Japan in British Columbia was so pronounced that, on April 29, Mackenzie King had the British Columbia Members of all parties meet him in his office in the House of Commons, to tell them of the interview he had had with the Japanese Minister. He explained that the Government was going to permit existing contracts to be carried out in order to avoid too great provocation, and "expressed the hope that, to assist the British Government as well as our own in the present difficult situation, they would not only accept what the Government had done without criticism, but make known to others likely to raise any question the inwardness of the situation."

He found that "with the exception of Howard Green, all present accepted the situation in an understanding way. . . . Howard Green thought it was a sign of weakness to give in at all. I explained that the matter was a *fait accompli*; that the Government would take responsibility for that. All I was asking was an understanding of the Government's action because of the international situation being as critical as it is. Green finally accepted meeting the Japanese on the order placed for wheat, 70,000 tons in all, but said he would have to reserve his right to oppose exportation of any wood."

What Mackenzie King feared was that the Japanese might in retaliation attack the British possessions in the Far East without the United States being involved. He found that "the argument that seemed to weigh most" with the British Columbia Members "was that Britain did not wish us to embarrass the situation with Japan." He concluded the interview by telling the Members that "we must, at all costs, avoid anything which would lead to an additional burden on the shoulders of Britain at this time."

The next day (April 30) Mackenzie King called on the Japanese Minister "on the way home to tell him of my talk with the British Columbia Members yesterday. To let him know they had agreed to co-operate with the Government in doing their utmost to prevent any adverse criticism of the Government's action in allowing the export of the wheat and wood which had been contracted for before the export permits were refused. . . . He then asked me if they [the Japanese] would be free now to make the application anew [for export permits to fill existing contracts]. I said that had been agreed to last week, and that I thought he had understood that that was the Government's decision. . . . He said he would send that word to his Government at once. . . .

"I then said that I hoped he fully understood that, while I felt the United States was anxious to keep out of the war, I also believed that nothing would as quickly bring the States into the war as any attack by Japan on Britain. . . . That while U.S. sentiment might be divided as to active participation in war on the Atlantic, once war started on the Pacific, the story would, I was perfectly sure, be different. Yoshizawa said that he was inclined to agree."

In response to criticism of the continued exports of wheat and timber, Mackenzie King made a statement in the House of Commons on June 11 which he thought would be "helpful in Japan itself and in the relations between Britain and Japan and will clear up the situation so far as Canada is concerned." He felt "the discussion in Parliament was all to the good, as it will let Japan see what my difficulties are likely to be in attempting to continue the trade in wheat or wood. Howard Green of British Columbia [who had criticized the Government in the debate] played a really poor rôle in the whole business . . . though he knows . . . that the British Government are anxious we should take the course we did."

Late in July, after the Japanese had intervened in French Indo-China, where French authority was weak, the Governments of the United States, the United Kingdom, and Canada froze all Japanese assets within their borders. The Japanese Minister called on Mackenzie King on July 26 to protest. Yoshizawa said he had come, on his own account, to "express his keen disappointment at the action which the Canadian Government, in conjunction with the British and the U.S. Governments, had felt it necessary to take, and which had been announced over the radio last night." He felt it "was altogether out of proportion to any step Japan had taken." Mackenzie King replied that "when warships were brought into use and troops were moved, that nothing could be considered as excessive as a means of defence on the part of either Britain or the United States. That Japan had no reason to anticipate any hostile act toward herself on the part of the United States or Great Britain. That we could only construe the use of force by Japan and her occupancy of bases in French Indo-China as a step in the direction of an attack on the interests of both the United States and Great Britain in the Far East. That anything of that kind could not be checked too quickly or effectively."

Yoshizawa contended "there was no difference in what Japan was doing and in what the United States had done in sending troops to Iceland and taking Greenland and Iceland under her protection. I said that, to outward appearances, in the physical movement of men and occupation of bases this might seem to be true, but that there was all the difference in the world, in that it was obvious the United States action was based on self-defence against Germany. . . . Such was not the case with Japan. She had no reason to regard the United States or Britain as an enemy."

Yoshizawa also wanted to find out whether Canada had acted on her own or at the instance of Britain. Mackenzie King "told him that the different governments of the Empire were in constant consultation with each other; that we regarded our position as one of common interest in whatever affected the security of any part, and that, while we had conferred in anticipation of the situation that might arise, our action was taken independently and on our own."

If Mackenzie King was resolved to do everything possible to prevent a break with Japan, he was even more determined to avoid any action which would drive the French Government at Vichy any more completely under German control. There was increasing opposition in Canada to the continued presence in Ottawa of the French Minister, René Ristelhueber, and resentment particularly over Pétain's speech announcing that France intended to collaborate more closely with Germany. Mackenzie King was concerned about this opposition being voiced in Parliament. In order to anticipate it, he had consulted the British Government about whether relations should be continued with Vichy France and whether they continued to attach importance to Pierre Dupuy's visits to Vichy.

(Dupuy, who had been in the Canadian Legation in Paris before the war, was visiting Vichy from time to time.) The British had suggested that Dupuy did not enjoy the use of a cipher and diplomatic bag and that it might be possible to indicate displeasure, and at the same time avoid an actual break, by withdrawing these privileges from the French Minister and from the French consuls in Canada unless the same privileges were given by Vichy to Dupuy.

M. J. Coldwell, the leader of the C.C.F., spoke to Mackenzie King on May 15 about the undesirability of the presence of the French Minister in Canada, and Mackenzie King then decided to try this intermediate course. He was greatly pleased when, in the course of this conversation, Coldwell said to him "that while members of his group might be critical of the Government at times, they had frequently asked themselves who was there in Canada that would fill the position of leader of the Government at this time of war better than myself, or who was there that would be more acceptable to themselves and those whom they represent? There was agreement among them all that I was the only person in whom there was sufficient confidence for that task. If they had to express themselves, it would be in that sense. He thought Douglas [T. C. Douglas, M.P. for Weyburn; from 1944 Premier of Saskatchewan] would be prepared to tell me as much. I thanked Coldwell, and said that what he told me was something I greatly prized and it would be a real help to me in meeting the difficulties and bearing the burdens of the present situation."

The next day (May 16), Mackenzie King sent for Ristelhueber. He found that the French Minister "seemed greatly relieved when I told him that I had just wanted to have a friendly talk with him." As the conversation developed, Mackenzie King told him "that there was certain to be a question raised in Parliament about continuing to recognize the Vichy Government. That the Leader of the Opposition had already spoken to me about it, and that I had asked him to keep the Members quiet for the present. He would see from Hansard that I had avoided any question today. It was certain, however, that a section of the press would demand the severing of diplomatic relations. That everything would, of course, depend on developments.

"After I had got thus far, he said to me that while there was this great world tragedy, there was inside of it a little domestic tragedy as well. That only within the last day or two . . . a young man, Bruce Macdonald [then a civil servant in the Department of Trade and Commerce], had told him that he was in love with his daughter, and that they wanted to be married at once for fear . . . she might have to leave the country before marriage could take place." Ristelhueber said they were waiting till six o'clock that day to get word as to whether they could be married or not. Mackenzie King "told him there was nothing in the world to prevent their marriage that I could see. . . . When I gave this to Ristelhueber, he seemed very pleased and relieved. Kept looking at the clock to make sure he could be back to them by six o'clock. . . . He was quite a different man when he found it was all right for the marriage to take place. He said to me, as he left, well, if I have to go, there will be one member of the family left as a Canadian with you. I will know that I have always had the Prime Minister's friendship and the help of the Prime Minister." The marriage was fixed for May 22 and Mackenzie King attended the wedding reception. In his own words, he "was conspicuously showing my attitude against forces of intolerance that are gaining the upper hand too rapidly."

The very next day (May 23), Mackenzie King saw Ristelhueber to tell him that "the Leader of the Opposition had recently brought up with me the question of our relations with Vichy and, in particular, the continued recognition of the Vichy Government through the maintenance of the French Legation here. That, in the course of conversation, he had asked in particular about the privileges which were enjoyed by the Legation in the way of cipher and diplomatic bag. . . . I had since learned definitely that Mr. Dupuy who had visited France had been allowed neither diplomatic bag nor cipher. . . . That I would be glad if he would ascertain from the Vichy Government whether the Vichy Government was prepared to give to Mr. Dupuy the privileges of diplomatic bag and cipher. That unless they were given, it would not be possible to continue the diplomatic bag and cipher so far as he was concerned."

Ristelhueber saw Mackenzie King again on May 30 to tell him that his Government would not give these privileges to Dupuy. Ristelhueber added "that there was no use of the Government considering it as the German Armistice Commission would not permit it. He used the word 'German' in making the statement. He prefaced what he said by saying that the Government had said they were glad to receive Mr. Dupuy, had appreciated the conversations they had with him, and would be glad to have them continued. Also that they were appreciative of the attitude of the Prime Minister of Canada and of the Government of Canada, but that there was no use considering the cipher and code matter so far as Dupuy was concerned as it would not be allowed. He went on to say that his Government had further intimated if he, Mr. Ristelhueber, were deprived of the cipher and the bag, they did not see wherein there would be any reason for keeping him longer in Canada. The words he used were: 'What good would a Minister be without a cipher and a bag?' . . .

Domestic Interlude 211

I pointed out to him that this was the position in which Dupuy was. . . . I said to Mr. Ristelhueber that it was, of course, none of my business, but if I were a member of the Government of France, with a country as friendly to mine as Canada is to France, I would have felt it was worthwhile keeping a Minister here as long as that was possible, if only to be in a position to deal with any situation that might arise at any moment.

"I felt deeply sorry for him. . . . I said to him that, as far as I was concerned, I trusted him so implicitly that it did not matter to me personally whether he had a cipher or bag or not, but that I could not avoid the question of reciprocal privileges being raised in Parliament, and that he would see for himself that the public would not understand our giving to the Vichy Government privileges to their Minister which they were unwilling to give to ours. He nodded, and said something to the effect that he could understand that, but asked how it was that the question came up at the present time, and said that his Government seemed to think that it was a matter of internal politics, the Conservative party trying to embarrass me. I said to him that, on the contrary, Mr. Hanson had been very decent in coming and speaking to me privately and in preventing his own men from asking questions. . . . That what had brought it up was Pétain's speech that France intended to collaborate further with Germany. . . .

"Then I said to him—speaking between ourselves—we really felt that the French Government was not a free agent, that the Germans were tightening their stranglehold on the country, and that we felt deeply sorry for the people and the Government. It was not the French people or the Government that we were acting against, but simply against this pressure.

"He then said to me—speaking as man to man, quite privately—that he had to admit it was German pressure to which they had to yield, and that he had told me that, in what he had said about not giving the cipher and bag to Dupuy. The Minister himself recalled that if a break came it would be at the instance of France. He was rather thinking aloud as he spoke. I said to him that I would think the situation over; that I would go this far, in trying to keep relations between the two countries, should his Government allow him to remain, as to say that I would be prepared, should the French Government reconsider the situation, and allow Dupuy cipher and bag to immediately see that the same privilege was restored to him. . . .

"I then phoned Robertson [the Under Secretary of State for External Affairs], gave him the substance of the interview, and suggested that, before we took any action, it would be well to communicate with

Churchill to see whether the advantage of having Dupuy still available would outweigh other considerations. A despatch on these lines was drafted and sent off tonight.

"At 8 o'clock, thinking that the Minister might communicate with his Government immediately, I rang him up and said that I would seek to delay as long as I could sending any formal communication to him, and that it might be just as well for him not to say more to his Government at present than that he had made his representations, but that he was awaiting further word. That he had had no final word from the [Canadian] Government. He almost exclaimed: 'Oh, Mr. Prime Minister you are so kind, I cannot thank you enough. I need not say that there has been a definite refusal, but will wait until I hear from you.' I said, 'Yes, that was right.' He seemed most grateful. The [Vichy] Government had evidently made it quite clear to him that he would be recalled if the cipher privileges were taken away." In the event, Ristelhueber remained in Ottawa with cipher and bag privileges though these facilities were withdrawn from French consuls in Canada.

On June 3, Mackenzie King referred in his diary to his fear of "war with France in addition to all the rest, and turning over of French fleet and bases to the Germans. If the war is lost, the fault, above all else, will be the rottenness of some of the political leaders in France and their complete betrayal of the people of their own country. If there ever was a war that illustrated the consequences of evil, this war does."

But Mackenzie King's greatest political anxiety in these months was not because of relations with Japan or even with France; it arose over the question of the formation of an Empire Council or Imperial War Cabinet or some other central institution in London which would require his presence there. Hanson had raised this question in Parliament on April 28, and there was considerable support in the press for some such central organ of Empire.

Mackenzie King's own position had been defined a year before when the question had been raised by Neville Chamberlain late in April 1940. At that time (April 30) he had felt that "with the war spreading in Europe, we may have terrible situations to face in Canada itself and that my first duty is to Canada. That was what Laurier felt when he yielded to the pressure to go abroad; that cost him his political power. [The reference is to the Imperial Conference of 1911; it delayed the election on the reciprocity issue in which the Laurier Government was defeated.] I feel I ought to be in Ottawa and travel through Canada if I travel anywhere. Keep our country united; have its war effort increased." The proposal was forgotten after May 10, 1940, when Churchill succeeded

Chamberlain, but it was revived in the spring of 1941 and Mackenzie King's attitude was unchanged.

His opposition to any kind of Empire Council and his apparent reluctance to visit Britain were pointed to as evidence that he was pro-American and not whole-hearted in his support of Britain. He felt that even R. B. Bennett's peerage would be linked by his opponents with this campaign against him. Churchill had advised Mackenzie King on April 22 that Bennett no longer regarded himself as domiciled or resident in Canada and that he intended to recommend him for a peerage. Mackenzie King wrote in his diary: "It reveals the ambition of the man's life; his own personal glorification and his readiness to use his country to that end, even to the extent of leaving it completely at a time of its greatest need. I shall be amazed if, among the thinking people of Canada, it does not create a revulsion of feeling toward Bennett himself." While he doubted "if there is above a handful of Tories in this country who will welcome the appointment of any Canadian to the House of Lords, and least of all Bennett, at a time like this," he nevertheless expected "we shall hear from him that he has accepted the peerage in order that he can make Canada's voice and influence more strongly heard and felt in the Parliament at Westminster."

But it was the visit to Ottawa of the Australian Prime Minister, Robert Menzies, on his way home from London, that really brought into focus the question of representation of the Dominions in London. Menzies arrived in Ottawa on May 7 and, as Mackenzie King himself observed, "took this city more or less by storm. He is a fine-looking fellow, splendid presence, great vigour, and has a wonderful gift for speaking. He has endless confidence in himself, and does not mind putting himself very much into the limelight. He has qualities not unlike Bennett in his assertive ways, but not nearly so pompous, and much more of a gentleman. Reveals his Scotch Presbyterian origin in his thoughts and views generally. Has many of the qualities of a great leader, but I feel, while his sympathies are broad, he nevertheless is thinking pretty much of Menzies most of the time, and likes very much the environments of high society, palaces, etc., which will cost him, perhaps, dearly in the end."

After talking to Menzies and having him speak to the War Committee, Mackenzie King felt "the one thing that seemed mostly in his mind, and which Churchill evidently had told him to discuss with me, was the desire for a Conference of Prime Ministers—some kind of an Imperial Cabinet. His reasons for it were quite different from those which, I think, would actuate members of the British Government or the *Times*. He was quite outspoken in what he said about it all. What it really amounted to was that there was no British Cabinet, no War Cabinet—that Churchill was the whole show, and that those who were around him were 'yes men' and nothing else. . . . That what happened was, when all were together, Churchill reviewed the war situation, doing so in his eloquent manner. He did all the talking, and no one dared to say no to anything. . . . He stressed that he himself was practically the only one who had ventured to question anything that was done."

Mackenzie King got the clear impression that what was in Menzies' mind was that the Dominions' point of view, when differing from that of the British, should be represented. "It was evident," he wrote, "that Menzies felt strongly about this; that he himself would like to be in such a Cabinet. I sensed the feeling that he would rather be in the War Cabinet in London than Prime Minister of Australia.

"After he had put forward his views, I told him that I agreed very much with what he had said about what Dominion representation amounted to in London; that that was one of the reasons I wanted to avoid being on a War Cabinet; that there had been too much done for the sake of appearances and too little in the way of reality. . . . I pointed out that one had to consider the consequences of Prime Ministers leaving their Dominions, and asked him to imagine what the situation would be if Smuts, Fraser, himself, and myself were all in London with events developing as they are, and being kept there for any time.

"He at once agreed that any meeting of any length of time was unthinkable. He finally came to the point of view that an occasional meeting might serve the purpose. I said the trouble as to that is that, while the occasion lasted, they would appear not to differ with your views, but the moment you had gone, the whole situation would slip back into the position it was before and, in the meantime, you would have incurred the responsibility without power. He admitted that this was true.

"I then said I thought the more effective way was to have individual Ministers go over and take up matters with their opposite numbers. His reply to that was he did not think you could get things done that way. Both Howe and Ralston took exception to that view and said they had been most successful in what they had accomplished."

When Menzies spoke about an Empire Council being needed to decide questions of strategy, Mackenzie King replied that he could not offer advice on strategy without expert assistance. He thought "any Prime Minister, going to England, would have to bring these advisers with him. If they were in England, they would be out of Canada, where they would be most needed. Also, that, even then, I would be separated from my colleagues. I could not say what division might arise in the Cabinet or in the country while I was away."

Domestic Interlude 215

Mackenzie King also referred to Canada's relations with the United States and asked "what service I could render in London comparable to that rendered here in relation with the U.S. I . . . asked him to imagine war breaking out on the Pacific when I was in London, or on the Atlantic with America in the war." Menzies agreed that "no two Dominions had the same problems, and that we in Canada had special problems. He then said that consultation was the thing we should aim at. I agreed as to that, but said I thought we could do that more effectively through the machinery we already have. . . . I said now that he and I had come to know each other, we could combine in a message which would be more effective than anything we could do at a meeting called by Churchill to consider matters there.

"I agreed that the moment might come when some great decisions were to be made, for example, as to peace. . . . I thought we should reserve absences from our own countries for those very special occasions. If we started going back and forth, influence would amount to little at the right time. I think he saw the force of what I said, as I saw the force of what he said. His point of view amounted to the need for a real Cabinet, which he thought the Dominion Prime Ministers could give, and a lack of any confidence in the British Cabinet as constituted."

Mackenzie King found Menzies "a most interesting man. He still has sufficient youth on his side to enable him to get through a great deal, and has real ability. I shall be surprised, however, if he does not find, when he gets back, that he has lost ground and that Labour has been gaining on him. He is too much the dictator to be a persuasive leader of the mass of the people. On the whole, however, I have come to like him very much. . . . I felt I had gained in his confidence and that we would continue as real friends. He has many of Bruce's qualities, but I like him much better than Bruce [an earlier Prime Minister of Australia, now its High Commissioner in London.] There is a certain arrogance, but there is also a very fine nature beneath it all." Mackenzie King predicted at the next Liberal caucus that Menzies would be defeated soon after he returned to Australia, and this actually did occur.

When Mackenzie King bade farewell to Menzies at the station at the end of his visit, Menzies said, in reference to a possible Imperial War Cabinet meeting in London, that "the most he would think of now was a meeting for some special occasion when some practical thing was to be done, but he saw that nothing of a continuous character could be thought of. He emphasized again our having our own problems. . . .

"I told him I believed in doing the things that had results in the end, rather than what might be showing up to appearances in the interval. I also spoke of the big problem of social revolution which is still to be faced in the making of the new order as being the fundamental thing. He said to me: 'Is it not all a matter of Liberal principles?' I said: 'Certainly it was that.' I felt a degree of secret pride in that I had never changed the name of the Liberal party."

The visit of Menzies had two important results. Mackenzie King had gone a long way in discussion with him to kill the idea of an Empire War Cabinet or Council; and Menzies' example had reinforced Mackenzie King's own resolve to travel more and to make a greater effort to secure more publicity and support for his policies.

If the idea of an Imperial War Cabinet was killed, the idea of an Imperial Conference was not. On May 12, Mackenzie King received a telegram from Churchill in which he said a meeting of an Imperial Conference about July or August, for a month or six weeks, would be most desirable, if it could be arranged. Mackenzie King felt "very doubtful if this can be arranged." He also wrote in his diary "that what Churchill is seeking to do is to satisfy public sentiment for the appearances of a complete Empire Advisory Board. I notice he uses the word Conference, not Cabinet. This suggestion has made me more determined than ever to take a Canadian tour in June. I would be better able in that way to size up the position of things in Canada. I can see, however, that I may have to consider also crossing over a little later. In any case, I should welcome the opportunity, but I will not welcome it, and I will not take it, if I risk any possibility of cleavages either in the Cabinet or in the country through an absence which is full of risks and is mostly related to appearances."

It was at this time that L. B. Pearson returned to the Department of External Affairs from his tour of duty as second in command to Vincent Massey in the High Commissioner's Office in London. On May 19, Mackenzie King "had a talk with Pearson, who has just returned from England. Very interesting conversation on the whole situation. He spoke of the amazing calm of the people and their determination. Feels a great concern about what may arise out of Vichy. Thinks Dupuy overoptimistic. Brought his latest report to me. Reported his readiness to begin work at once. . . . Very modest, unassuming. He is going to be valuable to Robertson." This was the real beginning of Pearson's close association with Mackenzie King.

About a month later Mackenzie King was in the midst of preparing two speeches for delivery in the United States when, on June 12, he was upset by a message from Churchill suggesting that he come to England for a meeting in July while Peter Fraser, the Prime Minister of New Zealand, was there and "indicating if I would, he would then cable the other Prime Ministers. The truth is that in the last day or two, Churchill has been pressed in the House to arrange for such a Conference and, to ease his own situation, he is trying to bring it about. Its practical value would, I think, be absolutely nil. Such a meeting would be fairly spectacular and would involve risks wholly unnecessary and most undesirable at the present time." Mackenzie King "could do nothing on either of the speeches until I got a draft of a reply to Churchill well under way."

He was relieved, on June 21, at word from Churchill "that Smuts cannot go to England this summer and that no demands would be made for crossing at least before the winter. Feel it, however, rather unfair. It shows Churchill places the onus on Smuts and myself for not having such a gathering. He may not do so. The latest word is that the statement [to the British House of Commons, about the possibility of a Conference] will be shown in advance." Unfortunately Churchill's statement was not shown to Mackenzie King in advance, and the use made of it by his political opponents was embarrassing throughout his Western tour. On June 24, the day he left Ottawa for the West, Mackenzie King "was much hurt and annoyed today by what Churchill said in the British House as regards myself not being able to attend the Imperial Conference. It was clear he was thinking entirely of himself, of the attacks on his own Administration, seeking to shelter himself by stating with unnecessary abruptness and brevity that neither Smuts nor myself could come to London this summer. He had someone else send the communication saying he had to make the statement in a hurry. . . .

"I admit it was a difficult position but, in view of the very full explanation I had given him and the request made specifically to protect my position and, for the very best of reasons, which he himself acknowledged, I think he should have been a little more considerate. However, it was not unexpected. No doubt the Tory press will begin their attacks on me for not going to London and put it down to some difference re war effort, etc. It might come to result in a pretty serious cleavage. . . . I can only say that I cannot be at two places at once and that Canada is the place that needs me most. The place in which the Empire itself needs me most at this time. I am sure I am right in following my judgment in this matter. Lapointe said in Council this afternoon it was the only thing I could possibly do and all present agreed."

During the course of his visit to the Western provinces Mackenzie King's attitude to a visit to Britain gradually changed, as he came to feel it would enable him to speak with greater authority as wartime leader of the country, though he continued to oppose formal Imperial Conferences or Councils.

One question affecting Britain arose in 1941 on which Mackenzie King did not hesitate to tender decided advice. On May 23, the Irish High Commissioner in Canada, John Hearne, brought him a message from Prime Minister De Valera expressing apprehension that the British intended to impose conscription at an early date in Northern Ireland. De Valera said such action would destroy the friendly feeling and sympathy for Great Britain which existed in Ireland, because the Irish people would feel that it would be an outrage against democracy to force the nationalist population to fight for freedom which they had not themselves been permitted to enjoy. The message pointed out that the Irish Government had done and was doing a great many things to help the British.

Hearne "did not say that Mr. De Valera had asked for any message from me, but took a pad and pencil and asked if I had anything I would wish to say to Mr. De Valera. I said to say that I thanked him for giving me the information which he had, and that I would be glad to have in mind any matter which might be of mutual interest and concern. I then said to Hearne privately that Mr. De Valera had not made any request and I did not wish to make any commitment with respect to what he had said. I thought I could read between the lines of his communication and he, doubtless, would read between the lines of mine."

Mackenzie King felt strongly that the imposition of conscription in Northern Ireland "would have repercussions in Canada which would be unfortunate." The next day (May 24) at Kingsmere, Mackenzie King had a long talk with Malcolm MacDonald, the British High Commissioner, during the course of which they discussed conscription for Northern Ireland. Mackenzie King was "thinking of wiring Churchill myself to speak of the possible effect of this step on American opinion and of its repercussions in Canada." MacDonald thought that would be "most desirable." The next day Mackenzie King carried out this intention, and, on May 27, he observed that "Churchill announced last night that the British Government would not press conscription in Northern Ireland. Resulting trouble would be worse than any good effected. I was delighted at this, and feel sure that my wire arrived just in time, and that it helped toward that end. It may even have been the dust in the balance, though I imagine Churchill would be too wise to have acted differently. I was pleased to see that Parliament had strongly supported his decision. All this should help us in Canada against this issue being raised here.

"Tonight," he added, "I had the Irish Minister, Hearne, come to Laurier House that I might tell him of the wire I had sent to Churchill. I gave him this in strict confidence with permission to let Mr. De Valera know what I had said, but on the understanding that it was to be kept wholly confidential by him. . . . . I had in mind, in telling Hearne what I did, to seek to exert my own influence on De Valera. I pointed out to Hearne that Churchill had taken the stand he did against his own party in order to help Eire. It meant helping De Valera in his difficult position. I wondered whether De Valera himself might not, at the right moment, take a similar action with his own people, were it likely to help the general cause. For example, the moment might come when America would enter the war; if Ireland was unwilling to give Britain the bases, she might allow the Americans to occupy them. But I would go a step further and say that if De Valera was prepared to oppose his people in the common interest, Andrews, the present premier of Northern Ireland, might be persuaded to take a similar stand against his people in seeking to bring about complete self-government in Ireland.

"I said I was not laying down a programme, but was thinking of something that might happen spontaneously; in other words, the whole Irish situation be readjusted while the war was on. A united Ireland with Britain or America getting the use of the bases, and all Ireland helping to defeat Germany. I pointed out that, if this did not happen, it was quite possible Ireland might be out on a limb by itself, after the war was over, without friends either in America or Britain, because of failure to co-operate at the time of need. That this would be unfortunate. I said to him I would be glad if he could get this idea across to De Valera, not as any request from me, but rather as something I would be happy for him to have in his mind."

Meanwhile, the war was going badly. Greece was on the point of surrender and German intervention in Africa threatened Egypt. The question of conscription for overseas service was being raised again and on April 23, Ralston, speaking to the War Committee of the difficulties of recruiting, brought forward, for the first time, the possibility of conscription. As a means of avoiding conscription, Ralston advocated having trainees under the Mobilization Act take over coast guard duties to release volunteers from these duties for service overseas. In doing so, Ralston referred to the division in the country that conscription would create and Mackenzie King said: "it would not only create divisions in the country, but it would in the Government; that there would have to be another Government, if that step were taken; that the people had returned us with the understanding that there would be no conscription for overseas.

"I mentioned that there had been practically no recruiting meetings; that I thought the services of mayors, M.P.'s and others might be enlisted for that purpose, and that a real campaign for recruiting should be started before any thought of anything else. I said this would be the moment to make an appeal, when Greece was surrendering, and the dangers to the rest of the Empire would become more apparent. The truth is the higher wages and the certainty of employment in factories have brought numbers there. This, I pointed out, will be intensified by what is implied in the Hyde Park Declaration. I have felt from the start that Ralston was allowing his men to have us take on more than we really should have in the Army, having regard to what we are doing in the air and the Navy. I am convinced that any compulsion for overseas service would undo a thousand fold the good thus far achieved. After all the unity of the country is the main thing."

Mackenzie King stated his position again to the War Committee on April 30 when he said he "thought we had taken on too much in the way of numbers of men for defence forces, having regard particularly to the need for men for industry; that I felt this war could only be won through weapons and munitions and other equipment and that we could render our greatest service in that line. I thought Ilsley's Budget had placed almost too heavy a burden on the people. It must be remembered that a number of them had never seen Europe and were having a hard struggle here. We would have to be careful not to crush the spirit in any way, or affect the morale. I thought the time had come when we should try to get women into factories and other branches of war service and that this should be coupled with recruiting for men.

"I said quite frankly that I thought the Cabinet should know I would never agree to conscription for overseas. That I would resign, and that I would hand my resignation and that of the Government to the Governor-General, before agreeing to any such policy. I wanted to make the position clear before both Lapointe and Ralston.

"Ralston was equally frank in saying that he believed in conscription. Would like to see it made the rule but recognized that it would only destroy our war effort by spoiling the unity of the country. I felt it desirable to stress very strongly the position so that he might be more positive in his attitude in resisting pressure which might come to him from Defence headquarters."

Agitation for conscription was somewhat unrealistic at a time when the Canadian Army was not in action, though the question of action for the Army was soon to be raised at the War Committee. On May 20 "Ralston brought forward a suggestion from the Defence officials that we should ask the British authorities to have our men put into action somewhere at once—if not in the Middle East, then on raids to France and elsewhere, even if it involved some being killed. This in order to help the recruiting campaign, the idea being that the fact that our men were not in action was causing very few to enlist. Power wanted some battalions raised to be sent at once to Egypt. This over and above what we were already committed for and beyond the numbers which it is alleged we were finding difficulty in raising. The motive of these actions was to have something 'spectacular' which would help the recruiting.

"I said at once that I would not countenance anything of the kind: that it might be my Scotch conscience, or it might be common sense, but I do not feel that any Government has the right to take the lives of any men for spectacular purposes. Moreover, I do not think we should interfere with the disposition of troops, when our policy was that of allowing the High Command to make whatever disposition was thought most effective. I pointed out that Canadian soldiers were doing the highest service in protecting the heart of the Empire and making it possible for Churchill and his Government to carry on with a sense of security for all parts."

The doubts about the success of the recruiting campaign and the growing agitation for conscription continued to haunt Mackenzie King. On June 10, he was suffering from one of his periodic fits of depression about his ability to continue to lead the Government. After the War Committee meeting, he "asked Ralston and Macdonald to wait and have a word with me. When alone, I said to them that I thought one or the other should be prepared to take on the business of government. That I felt things were getting now where it was almost impossible for me to hope to lead the Administration longer. That I thought there was such a difference growing up between the Defence Department and the Civil Government in matters of policy generally that I could not longer hold the two together. That I could see there was a growing pressure for conscription. That I would be pleased to be out of the fight altogether before that battle came; also that I could not countenance the country being committed to projects it was incapable of carrying out, and assume responsibility for anything of the kind. . . . I mentioned to them that I had been leader of the party now for 22 years, and out of the 22, I had yesterday completed 14 years as P.M. That I thought was a pretty good record. I also thought it had given me a certain degree of political wisdom and of judgment but, when I saw that judgment being put to one side and matters pressed from other angles, I could not think of continuing to be put in a false position.

"Immediately each of them began to say I should not speak the way I was, or think of making any decision when tired; to get away from everything for a time. Ralston began to say that, while he felt conscription was inevitable, he did not think it needed to come for a year. Macdonald did not see there was any need of it coming at all. That events within a year would probably change the whole situation. Ralston pointed out how certain communities, particularly Vancouver and others, were deliberately refusing to help in recruiting. Thought Lapointe and Cardin ought to make some speeches in that line. Said he, himself, was in a very difficult position. That they were now citing previous statements against him.

"I mentioned I realized we were all in a difficult position and that was one reason why I was staying on. It was only because I felt if I were to get out it might shake things that I was prepared to stick. Also I felt if I got out and the issue became one of conscription, etc., we would probably have civil war, and they would find Canada's war effort as a whole, which had been so splendid up to the present, would be divided altogether by internal difficulties. We would be playing Germany's game.

"I could see they both realized just where the Government was likely to be if either of them were left to take responsibility of leadership, and Macdonald said I was quite right in not having Canada take on things she could not do. I could see clearly that the mischief is in the Defence Department dealing so exclusively with Government matters. The truth is I was very tired, and have been nearly beside myself today."

It was primarily to offset the agitation for conscription by giving a true picture of the magnitude of Canada's part in the war that Mackenzie King resolved at this time to take positive action to improve the machinery for public information. The War Committee had discussed the subject as early as May 9 and Mackenzie King had complained in his diary at that time that "Gardiner will never get down to having a body that will gather exact information. His work has been largely publicizing. I feel that Department will have to be reorganized or put under some other Minister." From that point on, Mackenzie King began to search for a new Minister of War Services who would concentrate on securing favourable publicity for the war effort.

On May 12, Mackenzie King had made up his mind "that the work of the media of information of Canada's war effort would have to be more effectively co-ordinated, and the whole effort dealt with by some one with imagination, and the work assigned to a separate Ministry." He added that "after trying to get members of Council to make suggestions, with nothing forthcoming, I told them I would take the matter in hand myself."

He felt one important agency of information that should be more effective was the National Film Board. He had John Grierson, the

Government Film Commissioner, to dinner that evening and was much impressed with his "knowledge of the whole work of propaganda, publicity etc., but not particularly taken with his personality. I feel, however, he is the best man available to carry out a really effective programme for films of our war effort, and so have asserted my authority in seeking to get action in this matter."

On May 14 Mackenzie King "let Council understand we were heading for a change" in relation to public information. The day before he had spoken to "Lapointe and Ralston about the possibility of taking Abbott [M.P. for St. Antoine-Westmount, elected in 1940] into the Cabinet and giving him the War Services Department. They both regarded this as a good step. Claxton [M.P. for St. Lawrence-St.George, elected in 1940] is perhaps the abler man as a student and more thorough, but he has not the personality that Abbott has for meeting people in public. Today I talked with Power. He thought the choice lay between Claxton and Abbott. . . . He spoke, too, very highly of Thorson [Member for Selkirk and Chairman of the Select Committee on War Expenditures]. I agree with him on that. Thorson would hardly do for the War Services and he is at present performing a very real job." For nearly a month the three names of Abbott, Claxton, and Thorson were balanced in the Cabinet and in Mackenzie King's mind and Thorson was finally chosen on June 11. On that day Mackenzie King quite suddenly decided to anticipate a question by Dr. Herbert Bruce (Conservative M.P. for High Park, Toronto, and former Lieutenant-Governor of Ontario) about proposed changes in the Ministry by announcing Thorson's appointment before Bruce could ask the question. "When the Orders of the Day were reached Dr. Bruce had not yet come into his seat," he wrote, "so I immediately made a statement to the House. I had not told any of my colleagues whom I had decided upon, except Lapointe whom I met as he went into the House. I think the announcement came as a surprise as Thorson's name had not been prominently mentioned. . . . I had much in mind Thorson's appointment being something that would please those of foreign extraction in the country [Thorson was of Icelandic origin] and, of course, had much in mind his having served himself overseas in the last war and his long term of service in the House of Commons. I had waited till his speech of yesterday [as Chairman of the War Expenditures Committee] was over before seeking to have him sworn in. My mind was made up concerning him after the last conference of the War Committee in my office." Thorson was sworn in as Minister of National War Services on the same day (June 11); as Minister, he was expected to concentrate on public information.

It was primarily to make the war effort better known that Mackenzie King spoke at the Commencement at Princeton University and to the Canadian Society in New York in mid-June. Both speeches were quite successful and probably had more effect in Canada than in the United States. When he returned from New York on June 19, he started to prepare for his Western tour.

The purpose of the tour was to aid recruiting and also, as Mackenzie King put it, to "seek to overcome in the public mind the prejudices which the Tories are seeking to create against me. They are going out of their way to create a wholly erroneous impression as to my personality. It is part of the detraction and belittlement I have had from the beginning of my political career. . . . If I can, I should like to go on this trip, speaking without manuscript. This I should like to do with regard to the radio as well as regards general addresses." The hope of speaking without a manuscript was, in fact, not realized.

Before Mackenzie King's departure for the West, the whole course of the war was changed on June 22 by Hitler's attack on Russia. Mackenzie King was spending that Sunday at Kingsmere, and he took the news very calmly. He listened to Churchill's broadcast, which he described as one of his greatest. Mackenzie King contented himself with a statement to the press expressing very similar sentiments. To him it was an immense relief to have the uncertainty of Russia's "position cleared away and, instead of her continuing collaboration with Germany, having these two great forces in definite opposition one to the other.

"I confess that up to the moment of the announcement of hostilities I had felt that the agreement between Hitler and Stalin was too iron-clad and their purposes too similar to permit of conflict between them. Quite clearly Hitler has been aiming at doing the greatest thing that has ever been done in military history: a line of battle from the White Sea to the Black Sea, in which millions of men will be opposed to each other. Clearly he desires to outdo Napoleon and to have their names brought into comparison; the former suffering defeat in the end and he himself as the victor. I believe this latest venture spells his doom, though it will mean horrible misery and suffering and chaos to millions of innocent peoples in the Asiatic world, and possibly the spread of the war to India, etc. To me, however, it seems almost too good to be true, in that it gives Britain and America further time to prepare for the onslaught against the British Isles and the battle in the Atlantic.

"When one thinks over what Hitler would have gained through an agreement with Russia on any terms, and Russia remaining out of this conflict, with what it now means to have no agreement and actual conflict between them, the net result must appreciably and greatly improve Britain's chances for ultimate victory. Indeed, I feel an immense relief. It should, too, cause sympathizers with Russia and her Communist movement to change their sympathies from hatred of Britain and America to a desire to assist them both. It should lessen Communist activities on this continent."

Mackenzie King left Ottawa for the West on June 24 and when he reached Calgary, which was his first stop, on June 27, he encountered an organized demonstration for conscription and strong criticism because he had not gone to Britain. He decided to refer to both topics on the platform. When he was called upon to speak, "it was obvious there was an organized group to evidence some feeling against the Government, and quite clearly organized for purposes of furthering the movement that is rapidly getting under way in Western Canada for conscription. There is no doubt the Tories are organizing to this end and have the sympathy of the Army in their efforts. Advantage was taken of my presence in Calgary to distribute handbills re conscription, suggesting I should be compelled to answer how there could be total effort without conscription. This gave me a fine chance to deal with conscription four square, which I did."

The meeting was in the grandstand at the Exhibition Grounds and "it was quite clear that at least four-fifths or more of the people in the grandstand were with me, as against the minority who made their presence felt when I made reference to conscription. The others took up the applause when I spoke against it and before the meeting had concluded I think my friends had complete control. It was really a pretty daring procedure." It was also a very trying occasion. In the course of the speech, a lamp exploded which was lighting his notes, and Mackenzie King had to read from then on with the manuscript turned towards the footlights. "I could not see the audience, and was standing in the rain which was wetting the paper as I read. However, I managed to speak with real vigour. . . . No one will ever know what a day of anguish it was at times. It was providential, indeed, that I had decided to speak over the radio from notes rather than trust to speaking extemporaneously. This has made me decide to prepare speeches for all broadcasting on this trip. That will immensely relieve the strain, besides helping for efficient reporting.

"I was more combative than I had expected to be, but that situation was forced by developments of the day. It is clear I have come to the West just at the right moment. The really significant thing of the day was my assertion of Canada's position as a nation at war and the responsibility for representation at Imperial Conferences, etc. being wholly that of the Prime Minister of Canada—something which could not even be shared with the Prime Minister of Great Britain any more than the President of the United States might hope to relieve himself of his responsibility by leaving his country at a time of war, because the Prime Minister of Britain wished him in conference. This is the most difficult position, I think, any public man has ever been placed in at any time: to be obliged, when a war was on, to say that he could not meet the wish of the Prime Minister of England to cross the ocean for purposes of conference with him—his duty being first to his own country, and he, himself, necessarily, the judge at the time of the circumstances which should determine his action. A very difficult position indeed, but one of those places which stand out as significant in the assertion of Canada's position for nationhood."

He met a somewhat similar situation at Vancouver on June 30; "the gathering took place in the large ballroom in the Vancouver Hotel, and the room was filled to capacity, and was as representative a gathering as was ever assembled in the city. Again it was a miracle which led me not to trust to speaking extemporaneously, but to have the material written out for the broadcast. It was a brave and daring stand to take, to face all present and say to them what I knew over 75 per cent were anxious that I should not say. There is no doubt that the feeling for conscription is very strong on this coast. I had to make clear that Canada was not governed by localities, or inclinations of individuals, but by its Parliament. I had the satisfaction of knowing, as I felt would be the case, that before I reached the end the audience would rise to extend prolonged applause. That is exactly what happened. I could almost see the gradual conversion to another point of view as the situation was fully explained."

The rest of the Western tour, which lasted until July 12, was a good deal easier and Mackenzie King's reception became steadily more friendly. On July 3, he felt "perfectly certain that this visit to Western Canada has been the right step to take at this time," but he was coming "increasingly to feel that it would be wise to plan for a trip [to Britain] shortly after I get back to Ottawa, possibly for some time during August."

While he was at Prince Albert, Mackenzie King received, on July 7, a messenger from Angus Macdonald with the secret plans worked out by the United States and British authorities, with suggested amendments by Ministers at Ottawa, to ensure the delivery of American supplies to Britain, with the Americans convoying ships as far as Iceland, and protecting the Western hemisphere by extending their Atlantic patrol to

Iceland. Roosevelt was doing this by Executive Act without any declaration of war. Mackenzie King "read the memo very carefully and approved plan with amendments as suggested. I was immensely relieved when I saw later that the President had sent an official message to Congress advising of his having sent forces to Iceland and of his intention to protect that base." He telegraphed his approval to Macdonald and noted that this was "the most important document I have seen since the beginning of the war. It pleased me that its approval was made in my own constituency of Prince Albert."

In Winnipeg on July 10, Mackenzie King spoke to a joint meeting of the Board of Trade and the Canadian Club. He "could see the audience was in a questioning frame of mind as I began knocking conscription on the head, and referring to my staying in Canada instead of going to England. They were becoming very attentive as I dealt with the world-encircling aspect of the war. Increasingly interested, and I think deeply impressed, with the statement of the war effort, and roused to a pitch of complete sympathy and approval as I concluded on an idealistic note eulogistic of freedom in everything. I was given a tremendous ovation. A second one on leaving the room with other guests at the head table."

Later that day he went to the *Free Press* to call on the Editor, J. W. Dafoe. He had ten minutes with Dafoe and G. V. Ferguson [then associate editor, now editor of the Montreal *Star*]. Dafoe spoke to him about conscription. "Thought we would be wise not to add any more divisions as it would probably necessitate conscription. He thought a referendum in wartime just terrible. He asked me if I did not think matter might be left to Members of Parliament themselves. If they changed their minds for conscription, would not that be sufficient? I would give no undertaking besides saying that I myself would have to hold to the pledged word I had given to the people, and would resign before I would sign any Order-in-Council for conscription. Someone else would have to take on the Government. I also added that I did not think that Canada could be governed by one man, and if Lapointe and I were both to drop out, I feared very much what the consequences might be. Dafoe was afraid that, if things became more critical, the demand for conscription might be so great that not to yield to it would create more division in Canada than to yield. I said for the present I was prepared to keep Parliament to the fore, and would take no action except in accordance with the will of the people's representatives." Dafoe looked to Mackenzie King "a very sick man. He is losing strength rapidly. Has failed much since I last saw him. Most kind and friendly."

Mackenzie King left Winnipeg feeling "more alert in every way . . .

and infinitely more happy than I have felt for a long while past. It is a tremendous relief to know that, at last, it has been possible to visit the Pacific Coast and so many important military, naval, and air force establishments, war industries, between the coast and Ottawa. That chance will perhaps not come again in the course of the war, and indeed, in all probability, will not be necessary. I may make the trip again, if the war does not last too long, as a sort of farewell to the people before retiring from public life. Nothing, I think, would induce me to participate in another campaign. If my life is spared, I should like its concluding years to be devoted to writing and leaving records which might be of value to the country and of service to future generations of Canadians."

Before Mackenzie King left for the West, "Pat" his Irish terrier had become seriously ill. He returned on July 12 to find his dog dying. Pages and pages of his diary for the next few days, all of them handwritten, are taken up with the most minutely detailed account of Pat's last illness, his death in the early morning of July 15, and his burial.

The death of "Pat" not only created a great gap in his lonely private life but made him reflect a good deal about his own future and particularly about how he would spend his time when he retired and what he would do with his property. The day after "Pat" died (July 16) he "got the idea" of making a museum at Moorside, his largest house at Kingsmere, to hold all his papers and records as President Roosevelt had done at Hyde Park. He thought "of tearing down the house there, building one of stone, to house the family portraits, papers, different gifts etc. etc. and to leave all to the nation along with the property. I could, in this way, give back all I have been given, and at the same time retain the association. This, with the pilgrimage which led to it, all told in a volume to be written, would be a gift to the nation worth while. It would be a great interest for the remaining years, and if my life were worthy, it might mean a place of pilgrimage—Laurier House could be given over to International and Industrial Peace—a memorial to Sir Wilfrid as well as myself, possibly with his library replaced there. . . . The whole idea appealed very strongly to me and gave me great vision for my remaining years—if such there are to be. Kingsmere is coming to have its true meaning and its true place in my life."

For the rest of July 1941, Mackenzie King stayed at Kingsmere as much as possible. The Macmillan Company of Canada had arranged to publish a volume of his wartime speeches and he spent some time preparing the manuscript and reading proof.

The most serious worry he had at this time was caused by growing labour unrest, which reached a crisis in a sit-down strike at the plant of the Aluminum Company of Canada at Arvida, Quebec, late in July. On Saturday, July 26, he received at Kingsmere what he described as "a communication from Howe stating that a very critical situation had arisen at Arvida: that the plant had been seized by a group of men led by an enemy alien [this report that the leader was an enemy alien was later found to be incorrect] and was now in the control of 400 men. That several thousands were out of work, and that already some of the furnaces had been checked and metal was cold. That investment of many millions was at stake. That the British as well as ourselves and the United States relied more on this plant for aluminum for aeroplanes than any other concern. That he, Howe, could not get support from his colleagues in having the necessary aid sent to meet the situation. That questions of jurisdiction were being raised which made it impossible for anything to be done. He requested me as Prime Minister to take the matter in hand and tendered his resignation to take effect Monday next as he could not carry the responsibilities without support."

As soon as Mackenzie King received this communication he tried to get Howe on the telephone but could get no answer from his home or office. Though he had arranged to see the Japanese Minister and the British High Commissioner that afternoon, Mackenzie King spent a good deal of the day on the telephone speaking to Lapointe who was in Rivière du Loup; Ralston who was in Amherst, N.S., visiting his mother who was ill; R. E. Powell, the President of the Aluminum Company; Arthur Mathewson, the Provincial Treasurer of Quebec who saw Premier Godbout on his behalf; and Angus Macdonald, who was Acting Minister of National Defence in Ralston's absence from Ottawa. Ralston told Mackenzie King that two companies of troops would be at Arvida early Sunday morning, though he agreed with Mackenzie King that troops should not be used unless this was absolutely necessary.

Mackenzie King formed the impression that the real trouble was that a "smouldering situation" of discontent had "suddenly burst into flame." Subsequent investigation indicated that the main difficulty had been poor relations between management and employees. Lapointe had advised him that the federal Government had no jurisdiction unless there was a request from the Provincial authorities for aid. He learned from Angus Macdonald that he knew about Howe's letter. Macdonald agreed that Howe "must have been overwrought and tired." Macdonald also told him the Company had not asked the Provincial Police to evict the striking men, so Mackenzie King telephoned Powell again and suggested he make the request. Mathewson, who was with Powell, said Godbout felt the Provincial Police could handle the situation, but both he and

Powell felt they should wait until Monday to avoid demonstrations which would have been more likely on Sunday if the eviction took place that day.

Mackenzie King could not reach Howe on Saturday and he spent a good part of Sunday trying to get in touch with him. He "was a little disappointed at Howe not getting in touch with me by phone, which makes me think that he may be feeling that I have not given him time myself for a conference. He did say, on Wednesday or thereabouts, that he would like to have a talk some time, and would come out to Kingsmere for the purpose. . . . He made no specific reference to any trouble. . . . He should at least have communicated with me before writing his letter."

Mackenzie King finally reached Howe on the telephone late Sunday afternoon, and began by telling him "he felt very badly that he had had so much anxiety and trouble these last few days, and said I hoped I had not myself in any way added to it, by not having seen him for a general talk earlier in the week. He at once said, 'not at all,' and began to tell me of the difficulty he had had in getting co-operation in other government departments. I then told him how I had tried to get in touch with him. He said, after he had written the letter, thought it best to take a holiday, and had just got away from everything. I said that perhaps that was the wisest thing to have done.

"He then said, if he could have got the least help from some of his colleagues, at once, he could have saved the whole situation when it was boiling up on Thursday night. That it was due to one man who had come in from the States, spoke different languages, had got into the plant and stirred up the men. That all he needed was a show of force and that the whole trouble could have been saved."

Mackenzie King then told Howe of what he had done, and when he "spoke of having got Powell to speak to the Chief of Police and the Police being ready to evict the men, but that they were to wait until Monday, he told me that the men were now out; that the troops had moved up this morning, and after they had put up a few tents, the whole difficulty was over. . . . However, the leader had escaped. . . . He could, he thought, have captured him at once, and saved the situation. In the meantime, the aluminum had hardened in the pots and several million dollars worth of damage had been done as a consequence.

"I can see his whole action was due to his not having understood this question of jurisdiction; also the keen sense of obligation he is under. He said that, as a Minister of the Crown, he must either have authority and get co-operation, or not continue. I said that that was true, but that we could all co-operate. . . . He then spoke about a thorough investigation, of having the matter gone into in the Courts, if need be, to show up who was responsible. He wanted it made clear to the British Government that it was not his fault that the plant had stopped. That if it came to a question of troops as against aluminum, the British Government would much rather have the aluminum. . . .

"I then told him that, so far as his letter was concerned, he had better consider the part which referred to his resignation as having been dealt with, and have no further reference made to it. He said he wanted a real showdown with his colleagues, to know whether he was going to get the co-operation needed for these situations. That if he could not, he would be of no use to the Government. I told him that I was sure he would get the co-operation, and felt sorry that he had had the heavy strain he has had.

"It was quite clear that he is under a strain. . . . I told him that I would suggest we have a talk together tomorrow at eleven. I would then get the others and we would have the whole thing gone into very fully. That was agreed to and the conversation ended there." Mackenzie King added that "it was quite apparent from the way he spoke that the letter was intended to try to get his own way of dealing with some of these problems than with any real intention of leaving the Government."

July 28 was an exceedingly anxious day for Mackenzie King. During the morning, he had a long interview with Howe, and "found him very upset over lack of co-operation of colleagues. . . . He could get no response to save a situation which he contends will cost many million dollars, but, what is worse, will throw work behind three weeks here, and he says will close aeroplane factories in Britain, through lack of raw material. I tried my best to have him understand the difficulties about using troops in dealing with a provincial and local situation. He said a display of force was necessary, where men were barricading themselves inside a plant carrying on war production, where there was every reason to believe that the trouble was due to sabotage, inspired by enemy agents. He is obviously pretty wrought up and I did all I could to comfort him.

"Later, I spoke of plans for crossing to England. He strongly advised going by bomber from Montreal. . . . Later, he said he thought of going himself, as the situation re supplies was involved in England. I suggested his coming with me. That seemed to please him very much, though he questioned whether it would not be better for me to go alone, rather than having him accompany me. . . . I could see the suggestion was pleasing to him and helped to calm him in the matter of his present feelings."

Most of the time of the Cabinet that day was taken up with the situation at Arvida. Howe "spoke out about the lack of co-operation from his colleagues; that he had tendered his resignation and regarded himself out at the moment, as he could not take responsibility without getting the support needed. He was particularly hard on the Defence Department for having no proper staff and arrangements for communication with Ministers."

Mackenzie King later in the meeting "reduced the discussion to three points: (1) To amend the Defence of Canada Regulations in a way which would enable the Government to get at obvious agitators in plants where war work was being carried out; (2) To have the Mounted Police immediately get information about the men who were responsible for locking themselves in the building and keeping others out, with a view to securing the arrest of any subversive elements, and getting full inquiry into the cause of the trouble. (3) The question of an investigation of the whole matter by a Royal Commission. . . .

"Howe seemed quite reconciled to immediate prosecution as adequate. He seemed most concerned about having to send word to England, which might mean that aeroplane establishments would have to close down for some days, due to lack of aluminum. It will take three weeks to chip out the frozen aluminum from the pots in which the aluminum hardened after midnight on Thursday. In the meantime, we had got together a committee representative of Justice, Defence, Labour, and Munitions to prepare an amendment to the Defence of Canada Regulations, to give power for meeting a similar situation if it should arise in the future."

The next day (July 29), an Order-in-Council was passed giving the Minister of Munitions and Supply power to call out troops to assist the police in the event of sabotage in war production plants. Mackenzie King "insisted on having entire Cabinet present to assent to this Order. I explained the whole situation to them and asked each, individually, of his approval. The Order carried unanimously. I also took up Government's position with respect to collective bargaining, reading from Order-in-Council passed in the spring and giving my view that its principle should apply to Government-controlled plants, as well as to privately owned plants. By being as conciliatory as possible, I managed to keep Cabinet working together, despite the tension. . . . If not for Lapointe, I would have had a particularly difficult time in getting the complete understanding and support for my views, which he so completely shares."

The strike almost caused a misunderstanding with the Government of Quebec because of a reference to it made by Howe which appeared in

Domestic Interlude

the press. On July 31, Godbout telephoned Mackenzie King and "stated that Howe had really done an injustice to his Province and to the Catholic Union, and to the workers, by the statement he had made." Mackenzie King pointed out that he "did not think Howe intended any reflection on the Catholic Union. Where he evidently made a mistake was in saying that the difficulty was due to sabotage by enemy aliens, whereas no enemy alien seems to be in evidence anywhere. The trouble has grown out of grievances. Lapointe phoned me later and I told him that I had agreed with Godbout that the Quebec Government should make its position perfectly clear, regardless of the effect it might have, and that it should not be put in a false position." He added that Godbout was "exceedingly reasonable. My admiration for him grows more and more. He is a thorough Christian gentleman—very thoughtful and careful. I think I shall have to bring him into the Federal Government."

During the war, Mackenzie King and C. D. Howe often differed, and sometimes differed sharply, about the course the Government should follow. This was particularly true in the field of labour relations where their points of view were far from identical. But this was the only occasion where such differences reached a critical point, and there is nothing in Mackenzie King's records then or later to indicate that it left the slightest scar on their personal relations. Moreover, Mackenzie King's conduct over this whole incident shows how indispensable he considered Howe to the wartime Government.

From the moment he returned from the West, Mackenzie King had a visit to Britain constantly in his mind. He mentioned the possibility to Malcolm MacDonald and Lapointe on July 14; and on July 26 told MacDonald he wanted to go on his own and not for any Imperial Conference. After he spoke to Howe of the visit on July 28, he began to make active plans. On August 6, Howe told him a bomber plane was being fitted up for the flight.

Shortly after 6 o'clock that day (August 6), Malcolm MacDonald called to give Mackenzie King a message from Churchill about his proposed meeting with the President of the United States in Newfoundland. Mackenzie King was not surprised to hear they were to meet, but he was amazed that Churchill was bringing the Chiefs of Staff and the Permanent Head of the Foreign Office with him. The message from Churchill expressed the hope that Mackenzie King would approve of the meeting. He did not really approve but, instead, wrote in his diary: "I feel that it is taking a gambler's risk, with large stakes, appalling losses, even to that of an Empire, should some disaster overtake the gamble. To me, it is the apotheosis of the craze for publicity and show.

At the bottom, it is a matter of vanity. There is no need for any meeting of the kind. Everything essential can be done even better by cable communications, supplemented by conferences between officials themselves. Neither the Prime Minister of Britain nor the President of the United States should leave their respective countries at this time. It makes me more satisfied than ever that I have held out against going to England to an Imperial Conference simply for the show that this might create."

Mackenzie King told Malcolm MacDonald he thought "the public in Canada and certainly some of my colleagues and my own officials will think it extraordinary that Churchill should have brought his own staff to negotiate with the United States staff, and ignored Canada altogether. While I had expected a personal visitation between Churchill and Roosevelt I had never thought of their bringing their representatives on Foreign Affairs and Chiefs of Staff, etc. for conference on war plans, leaving Canada completely to one side—simply saying that we would be told what had been done, though having no voice in the arrangements. I said I did not propose to make any difficulties about the matter but that it was on all fours with what has thus far been done between Britain and the States since they have been brought together."

He added that it all bore "out my view that the only real position for Canada to take is that of a nation wholly on her own vis-à-vis both Britain and the United States. That we can never expect to have any recognition . . . in any other way." At the same time he recognized "Britain's problems in not wishing to bring Canada into a conference of the kind, because of being unable also to bring Australia, New Zealand, and South Africa" and "the difficulties of the United States . . . particularly with Mexico and South American republics." He felt it would be useless to make a protest and did not intend to, but did want "to register at this time my own feeling and views in the matter. I have no doubt at all that the Tory press of Canada will now begin to say that neither Churchill nor the President have any confidence in myself, or feel it is necessary to take me into account. That will be the line of attack."

Malcolm MacDonald brought Mackenzie King word on August 12 "that Churchill and the President had met and had agreed on a statement to be given to the press. The British Cabinet had been considering same. I pointed out to Malcolm that here again Canada was being ignored." He read to MacDonald a message he had sent to Menzies earlier in the summer "about means of communication being perfect, and that we had no reason whatever to complain about not being consulted. Here, at once, the very opposite was taking place and over a matter with which we, of all parts of the Empire, were very immediately concerned, as it relates to both military and economic co-operation. I said I personally did not intend to make difficulty, but I could not prevent the effects that this kind of thing might have on others. It was the way in which the British lost their friends, wanting them in foul weather and ignoring them in fair. So long as they got their own way that was all they wanted."

Mackenzie King delayed his departure for England long enough to make sure Churchill would be home from Newfoundland before he arrived. A few days before his departure, Howe telephoned (August 14) to tell him "that Arthur Purvis had been killed in a plane accident that day which had cost the lives of some 20 pilots on board a plane about to start from England. This was bad news indeed. I confess, however, it did not give me the least sense of added danger in the matter of my own crossing. That is all in the hands of Providence. Frankly, I do not feel any concern of life itself though there may be unpleasantness in the travel itself, and a good deal of fatigue in the stay in Britain. I really think I shall enjoy the crossing and the stay, and, I hope and pray, the return."

Mackenzie King telephoned President Roosevelt in Washington on August 17 to congratulate him on the success of the meeting with Churchill. As there had been some suggestion of a visit to Washington before his visit to London, he told Roosevelt that he "thought it best to leave directly for the Old Country, before visiting him at either Washington or Hyde Park. I said now that the conference had taken place, that seemed the wiser course, and he agreed that I should come to see him when I got back. He said he would be either at Hyde Park or Washington and to come any time. I said I thought if I went to Washington first, my opponents might think I was taking my direction from the South, and he would understand my reasons for not wanting my motive misunderstood. He said he quite agreed." On Monday, August 18, Mackenzie King left Ottawa for Montreal to start next morning for Great Britain.

CHAPTER TEN

The Flight to Britain

FOR Mackenzie King, the highlight of the year 1941 was the visit to Britain. He looked forward to it with mixed feelings. He had never flown before. He was concerned about being drawn into controversy with the British Government on the question of Imperial constitutional machinery. He was worried about the reception he would get from the Canadian troops and felt keenly his lack of familiarity with all things military. Above all, he was uncertain about his personal relationship with Churchill. Though they had been acquaintances since the early 1900's and were almost precisely the same age, they had not been friends, and temperamentally seemed poles apart. But he realized, especially after the meeting between Roosevelt and Churchill, how important it was for him to have a closer personal contact with Churchill and how great an effect the visit might have on Canadian public opinion. He also looked forward to seeing the Canadian forces and learning at first hand of their prospects and requirements. He wanted to find out what he could about the general picture of the war and to form his own impression of the British Government.

Mackenzie King crossed the Atlantic in a Liberator bomber in which a small cabin had been improvised, containing a bunk and two reclining chairs. There was a little heat in the cabin, and none elsewhere in the plane. He was accompanied by Norman Robertson (Under Secretary of State for External Affairs), George Vanier (Canadian Minister to France until June 1940, now serving in the Army) and several members of his secretarial staff. His plane left St. Hubert airport outside Montreal (Dorval had not yet been opened) at 11.45 A.M. on August 19, 1941. He described the flight in great detail in his diary, noting that on taking off he felt very little sensation and that there was "nothing in the least unpleasant and did not feel the slightest bit of timidity. Indeed I thoroughly enjoyed the ascent itself and from the moment we began to fly on the level, enjoyed the whole sensation of floating through and above the clouds, getting glimpses of the country below. . . . In the course of travel through the morning I felt no unpleasant sensation, on the contrary, real enjoyment and inspiration. The words that kept coming to my mind were: 'Terrestrial and celestial; seeing a new heaven and a new earth.' " He enjoyed "having Vanier on the opposite side, knowing his sympathy and spiritual perceptions," adding that he did not "get the same companionship out of the intellectual type, with the conventional attitude of some university men whose philosophy is more materialistic."

There was a two-hour stop at Gander where Mackenzie King had a refreshing sleep. The sun was setting as the plane left Gander. During the night he slept pretty steadily. He was enchanted by the cloud formations below him as the sun rose next morning. The first view of Scotland delighted him and, when the plane descended, he was scarcely conscious that it had touched the ground. But though the flight was not really uncomfortable, he developed no enthusiasm for flying, then or later.

Mackenzie King was met by Vincent Massey and, after breakfast, driven to Glasgow where he spent the day and took the night train to London. The first day he was in London, he attended a meeting of the British War Cabinet and had luncheon with the Churchills at Downing Street. He was amazed at Churchill's appearance. "He looked as fresh as could be, and really more youthful than I have seen him on different occasions. He said the trip at sea [for the meeting with Roosevelt] had done him great good."

When the Ministers assembled in the Cabinet room in Downing Street, Churchill welcomed Mackenzie King and spoke enthusiastically of the great part which Canada was taking in the war and "of the unity of Canada, and attributed that to my leadership and long experience in public affairs. . . . He also spoke of my friendship with the President and of what I have done in helping to bring English-speaking peoples together. . . . When he had concluded, I expressed a few words of thanks, saying the purpose of my visit was to find in what way we could make our war effort more effective. That as he knew, Canada was of one mind in its determination to be in the war at the side of Britain till the end, with all the resources, human and material, that we could effectively employ.

"As for troubles, we had not any to speak of with the British Government. That the relations had never been better between the Governments of the two countries. I spoke also of the desire to see something of the situation in Britain, to study the British war effort, and to have the advantage of conferences with himself and his colleagues. Also to see something of our armed forces and, as opportunity offered, to express the admiration of Canada to the British people for their indomitable courage in the manner in which they were defending this citadel of freedom."

Mackenzie King found the manner of discussion in the War Cabinet admirable and formed a very different impression from that given him by Menzies in May. He was fascinated by Churchill's "marvellous way of summing up situations in graphic phrases—a wonderful command of language and knowledge of history which he uses freely, and an ability to keep looking ahead, making decisions in the light of the long run rather than the short one."

When the Cabinet broke up, Churchill took Mackenzie King "downstairs to the basement of the house and showed me the concrete rooms that were constructed there like one large vault. A door on it like the door of a safe. What had been offices of stenographers, but was now the dining room and sitting room. Quite an attractive spot, reinforced with steel beams, concrete, etc."

Before anyone came in to lunch, Churchill spoke to him about a possible Imperial Conference during his visit, saying it was impossible for Smuts to leave South Africa or for Fraser of New Zealand to stay longer in London. He could not say whether Menzies would be coming back or not. Churchill said "he was against any Minister other than the Prime Minister from any of the Dominions attending the War Cabinet. Also if there was one, there have to be four and he did not understand how one Minister could represent them all. I told him that was exactly my view and that I thought he and I were perhaps closer in our views than we imagined. He said he was sure of that.

"I spoke of the impossibility of attending a Conference without bringing Chiefs of Staffs and others with me who were really needed at home. Also that we had our own immediate problems and I did not want situations to get out of hand through any absences. He said that he gathered my political opponents were trying to bull-doze me into coming over and that I was letting them see that I would decide matters myself. I told him he was quite right. That I alone could judge when it was wise to come. I did not wish to see Canada get divided through any absence in London."

At the luncheon table, Churchill said to Mackenzie King "without my having brought up the subject at all, that he saw no need whatever for conscription in Canada. That this was not a war of men but a war of highly specialized machines. . . . I said I was very glad to hear him say what he had and that it relieved my mind greatly."

After luncheon, Mackenzie King and Churchill had a long and interesting talk about the origins of the war and how it might have been prevented. Mackenzie King told Churchill he "thought full justice was not being done Chamberlain . . . that if he had not gone to Munich, the situation might have been much worse. That certainly was so, as far as Canada was concerned; we would never have been able to go to war as a united country. I said I had gone through my Gethsemane knowing that the country ought to go to war and intending to make that my policy, but that I would have lost a good portion of the Cabinet which would have been divided. He asked if I would have lost outright. I said, yes, but that, of course, I could have made up majority from the opposite side, but it would have been a divided Canada. That, as a result of Chamberlain's visit and the deferring of the war for a year, the nation had got a chance to really see the issue and to become convinced that aggression was the aim."

As Mackenzie King was taking his leave, Churchill spoke "about looking forward to my week-end at Chequers. He said . . . he had a broadcast to make that night. Perhaps I could give him a hand in it. . . . As we walked to the door of Downing Street, he spoke of Canadians feeling possibly restive through not being away to fields of action, fighting, but he hoped I would impress upon them that while remaining in this Kent peninsula, guarding its borders as they faced West and South and East, they were maintaining the security of the island. He felt they would be having fighting before the war was over, but his whole point of view was the security which their presence would give to the island in the face of the most terrible danger they had ever encountered."

On Mackenzie King's return to the Dorchester Hotel where he was staying he found Harold Macmillan [the present British Prime Minister, who was then associated with the Ministry of Supply] waiting in his sitting room. When he entered he did not know Macmillan was there and "had to say I remembered him by his looks, but could not place him. When he mentioned his last name, I mentioned the first. We then had a talk together. The call was largely a courtesy one, but to offer any information on Supply matters. I showed him the beginning of the little book [Macmillan's were publishing Mackenzie King's wartime speeches as *Canada at Britain's Side*]. He said he would get in touch with his brother at once concerning it."

That evening, Mackenzie King visited the Ministry of Information where he was received by Brendan Bracken, the Minister, and where he gave a press conference in which he set out his position fully with regard to an Imperial War Cabinet. *The Times* of August 22 reported that: "Mr. Mackenzie King said that they had in existence to-day in actual practice the most perfect continuous conference of Cabinets that any group of nations could possibly have.

"He had been in office for a good many years in Canada, and he had watched carefully the methods of communication between the Canadian Government and the Government of the United Kingdom and the other Dominion Governments. He could not conceive of more effective means of communication than those which existed at present. He was able to receive communications direct from Mr. Churchill and to communicate directly with him. In addition there were communications from the Dominions Office to the Canadian Department of External Affairs. They gave a complete picture of what was taking place in all parts of the world in respect to the war.

"Then they had as their representative in the United Kingdom Mr. Vincent Massey, a former colleague and a very old friend, who knew his (Mr. Mackenzie King's) mind as well as he knew it himself. They understood each other perfectly. Mr. Massey met periodically with the Secretary of State for the Dominions, and was given a personal account of what took place in Cabinet discussions. He was able to express the views of Canada. Further, they had Mr. MacDonald at Ottawa. He kept the Canadian Government fully informed.

"It was important, especially in times of emergency, that decisions should not be those of one man but of a united Cabinet. It might be thought that an Imperial War Cabinet sitting in London would be more effective in reaching the necessary decisions, but he affirmed, from long experience, that the present method was infinitely better.

" 'So far as relations between the two Governments are concerned,' declared Mr. Mackenzie King, 'there never has been a time when they were closer. No single point of difference has arisen since the beginning of the war between us in matters which are essential. In the last War differences did arise continually. The reason for the present position is that before any important step is taken we have been consulted: we have had the opportunity of expressing our views, freely and frankly, and we have considered all aspects of the matter under review. Then a general consensus of opinion is reached. All help in credits, money, and men which we can give we are prepared to give.' "

The Government gave a luncheon for Mackenzie King at the Savoy on August 22. When Churchill came into the dining-room, he at once congratulated Mackenzie King "on what I had said yesterday. Said he was very pleased with what I had said. All the Ministers present spoke in similar terms. . . . Quite clearly what I said was of real help to the Ministers and suited the Government exactly."

At the table, when the conversation had become general, Mackenzie King turned to Churchill and said "I hope you and your Ministers will not expect to have the Prime Ministers of the Dominions leaving their own countries to any more extent than is necessary." He went on to say that he thought "an Imperial Conference at a time of war was an impossible thing. It meant keeping the Prime Ministers here for keeps. That colleagues would have to come along and, in addition, experts, Chiefs of Staffs, etc. . . . that this all meant taking these men away from their own country at a time when they were most needed, whereas by keeping them in their own country, the Prime Minister could consult with his colleagues and, if need be, with M.P.'s and experts and when he gave a decision, he was giving the right one."

When Churchill said he did not suppose the Dominions would wish to have one Minister to represent them all in the War Cabinet, Mackenzie King replied "Most certainly not," and he "stated that it was a mistake to be lumping all the Dominions together and representing a Dominions' point of view as distinguished from the point of view of the Government of the U.K. That we were more in sympathy with the views of the U.K. Government than we were, for example, with the views of Australia. That each had their own problems and had to make their decisions in the light of them. I repeated what I said yesterday about a continuing conference of P.M.'s.

"I said I could perhaps illustrate that best by telling the story that the King had told me about the little Brownies and Cubs and others around his train at night [on the 1939 tour of Canada] saying: 'We want the King,' and his saying: 'You have got him. He is right here. My God, what more do you want.' I said, 'You have already got War Cabinets—five of them. You have got a continuing conference between the lot, what more do you want.' All the Ministers present agreed very strongly, and not only nodded their approval but several of them spoke out emphatically." Mackenzie King returned to this theme a good many times during his visit.

Before they sat down at the table Mackenzie King had asked Anthony Eden [then Foreign Secretary] about the value of continuing Dupuy's visits to Vichy which involved keeping the French Minister to Canada in Ottawa. Eden did not think the visits were of any further service and regarded the Vichy situation as hopeless. But when Mackenzie King spoke to Churchill at the table, Churchill "at once said: by all means, let us keep him. He is of great service. It gives us a point of contact. You are quite at liberty to put it all on to us that I want him to stay. I said: may I make that quite clear? He said, certainly, it was desirable to preserve a contact with France. While Dupuy was over-optimistic and perhaps even deluded himself and others, he nevertheless got impressions and facts which were most helpful. He spoke of Dupuy being in Vichy at the present time. He said: I don't rely on all that he says or is said to him, but it helps me and it is the one contact we have." During the weekend at Chequers Mackenzie King repeated the questions about Dupuy to Churchill and took down the actual words of his reply which were: "I think it is most necessary to keep him, most necessary. By no means let him go."

At the beginning of the Government's luncheon Churchill told Mackenzie King that he would have liked to have Mackenzie King present "at the conference with the President and himself, but that what he really wished it to be was a tête-à-tête where he could get to know the President without any third party. Told him I fully understood the situation and, besides, I could see the embarrassment I would have been to other parts of the Empire. I told him about the talk at Hyde Park and having been the first to whom the President intimated his intentions of trying to see Churchill. When I told him of the Hyde Park conversation, he remarked, 'that was the beginning.' I said 'yes.' Spoke of how Hopkins had learned of it in the President's mind at the time I had, and told him of the intention of the President coming via Ottawa."

Of the meeting with Roosevelt, Churchill said: "We had been writing each other love letters for some time. I wanted to talk with him. It was of the utmost importance that we should talk together. He then went on to say that it is of the utmost importance that we keep very close to the U.S., without the U.S. we cannot win the war. He then said that he would rather have the U.S. make a declaration of war tomorrow, if they had to forego their help in other ways, than to have the declaration delayed and to continue to receive the assistance we were getting. He believed the war would not end till the U.S. was in it. I said to him I thought the President, Stimson, Knox, and Mr. Hull were all anxious to have war declared, feeling it was the quickest way to end everything. That the difficulties were with members of Congress. . . . I said I felt that they should not count too much on the U.S. coming in quickly. That there was a real feeling among the people to stay out of the war altogether."

Churchill also "spoke of the President's great affection for me. Said, in the presence of his colleagues, there was no one who knew the President as well as I did or had the same influence upon America. . . .

"Churchill said he was pleased I had come over immediately for a conference with himself instead of going to Washington, as he had understood from the President I would be doing after his return. I told Churchill that . . . I had told . . . the President that politically it would be a mistake, and that I felt it would not be the right thing to do. Churchill said he was very pleased that I had come direct, and again repeated how glad he was that I was here."

At one stage, he noted "Churchill said he was pleased I had agreed to Bennett going into the Lords. I said I had not any feeling about the matter at all. Told him I had never had any real feeling against Bennett, except for his contemptuous attitude, but that I thought he thoroughly disliked me. Churchill said he had been very unfair to me in connection with Washington. I think by that he meant as to my attitude towards the States as against Britain. He had been quite wrong in that."

Just before the luncheon concluded, Churchill, in proposing Mackenzie King's health, "spoke of the years we had known each other; said that our first talk had been in 1906–7 when he was Under Secretary of State for the Colonies. He said: when most of you fellows were not born; that we had always understood each other. While we might not have seen eye to eye, we had been friends, and that the friendship had grown. He then said that no man in any part of the British Empire had kept his country as united as I had kept Canada. That there was no part of the Empire that was so completely one, and he attributed that to my personal qualities in matters of government. He spoke of Canada's part as having been magnificent and said other things which I do not recall.

"I replied by thanking him warmly, saying that this had been one of the proudest moments of my life to be privileged to hear from his lips, in the presence of his colleagues, the confidence which he had expressed in myself and in my colleagues. That I wanted to say to him that at our Council Table from the beginning of the war, there was one thought that governed all others, which was how we could be of most help to himself and the members of the Government here who were carrying on the great burden of war, and had to perform their work while being bombed from above and shot at from all sides. That we felt they were not fighting their battle only but that of freedom everywhere. That we had, in Canada, never mistaken the issue which was that everything we held sacred on this side of the grave was at stake. I said that I wanted to tell him what his own example and courage had meant to us all, but more than that, his guidance in matters of government. I stressed strongly our sole desire in everything was to give all the help we possibly could and Canada's determination, if the attack should leave these shores and come to ours, to fight to the utmost of our strength and resources. That the Canadians would never give up in a struggle of this kind.

"When I had finished, Churchill was obviously a little moved and turned to me and said: there will be public functions while you are still in England at which a broadcast might be arranged. Would you agree to speak over the radio at a gathering of the kind? I said I would be pleased, in the course of my stay, to do anything that he thought would be helpful. He then turned to the Secretary of State for the Dominions

[Lord Cranborne] and told him to see that something was arranged at once." That was the origin of the Mansion House speech of September 4, which was the high spot of Mackenzie King's visit.

The next day, August 23, Mackenzie King arrived at Chequers just in time for dinner. At dinner, "Churchill talked very freely to me about many topics and also fully with respect to any that I brought up. . . . It is really a great delight to hear him converse. He is quite as eloquent in conversation and speech as in broadcasting. He ranges over such a field of knowledge and interest, always having something enlightening to say. What appeals to me most in him is his instinctive, innate love of truth and right and justice, and his tremendous courage in asserting their claims. Also his great tenderness and gentleness and loveableness in his own home and with his own family. . . . When it was time to go in to dinner, he appeared in the hall above and called down to me and one or two others: 'Now, children, dinner is ready.' He came downstairs and said: 'I suppose it is a long time since you have been addressed that way.' It was characteristic of his whole outlook. At dinner, conversation was very free altogether from any restraint. He was quite clearly enjoying relaxation from his work and entering completely into the spirit of the occasion with a real buoyancy. He really is a big boy at heart, untiring in energy and interest."

After dinner, the whole party looked at some movies and then Churchill went off to work on the broadcast about his meeting with Roosevelt which he was to deliver the next evening. Mackenzie King himself spent an hour in his room making notes of their conversation. They had talked about the employment of the Canadian troops, and Churchill again emphasized the hope "that they would be able to hold out in England . . . he really wanted them for the British Isles. They were protecting the most vital part of all. . . . Referring to saving parts of the world, Churchill said this is the place to save. I spoke to him again about conscription and he repeated that there was no need for conscription in Canada.

"Several times he said: I am so glad you have come over. I told him I had always intended to, and he repeated he thought I had stayed back because they were goading me. . . . He said, if I had been in your place, I would certainly have done the same. I would never go if anybody tried to drive me. I said 'No, that I did not come because I did not want to get into the position that Menzies had got himself into, and of losing the support of the country. That I had to consider . . . the needs of the situation in Canada above all else.' . . .

"He then enlarged on how easy it was to criticize and to want changes —how difficult it was to get ideal men, etc. It was a situation exactly as I see it in Canada. He then said: 'I am a Tory.' I said to him: 'I thought he was rather liberal minded.' He said: 'Certainly, liberal minded, but Tory as regards Crown and Parliament. I must have authority obeyed.' I said to him: 'You are not an autocrat.' He said: 'My God, no, I hate autocracy. I am a servant of the people. There can be no prouder privilege than to be a servant of Parliament. If Parliament says I must do a thing, then I must obey, do the will of Parliament.' I said: 'That was the Liberal side, was the side I attached the utmost importance to.'

"I said to Churchill: 'It is a good thing you were not in the Government before the war, you might have made political enemies.' He said: 'I have many enemies in the Tory party. I am trying to shield them now, many of them from their own mistakes.' I spoke about Baldwin and asked if it would be all right for me to visit him. He said: 'By all means, see him. Never forsake a friend when he is down. His conscience is troubling him. If it were not, I would not be sorry for him. He let things go, too. He might have had me in the Government, I could have helped.' . . .

"He then began to speak quite feelingly to me about himself at the present time, saying: 'I have no ambition beyond getting us through this mess. There is nothing that anyone could give me or that I could wish for. They cannot take away what I have done.' That as soon as the war is over he would get out of public life. I said: 'You should write the story of the war.' He said: 'If I went on after the war what more could be added. What could I wish for.' I said there was a destiny about his life. He had been meant for these times. Speaking of it in a modest way, he said: 'It looks like it, in a way, as though it was meant.'

"I spoke to him about the Japanese. He said: 'I don't believe the Japanese will fight the U.S. and Great Britain.' He then told me what he thought of saying in the broadcast; that if Japan attacks the U.S. she will have to fight Britain. I felt a little concern about this remark. He said that Australia had already approved his saying that, and would I agree. I said I would agree, that is what we would have to do, but I wondered if the U.S. would appreciate this being said. I spoke of it being part of our obligations to defend the U.S. as it was theirs to defend us. He told me that he would confidentially let me read the broadcast which caused me to reserve, till I read it, any remark. I was glad I did reserve it as the language was quite different; was not at all as pointed as what it was in conversation."

Mackenzie King noted later: "Churchill told me on Sunday that he found it difficult to get to sleep the night before thinking of what he had first written about Japan and the war. It was always well when one felt very strongly, when going a certain distance, not to go quite so far but to say something short of the limit. That he, himself, on Sunday, changed the wording of the address so as to leave out the word 'war' altogether and to use instead, 'would find Britain ranged at the side of the U.S.' I told him later that I thought this a great improvement, otherwise headings in the press would all have related to 'War.'"

On Sunday morning, after breakfasting in his room, Mackenzie King "sat before an open fireplace after which I had modelled the one at Laurier House. . . . Churchill sent down his speech to read and also the communication regarding the President's representations to Japan. [The President had seen the Japanese Ambassador to the United States to warn him of the probable consequence of Japanese aggression in Indo-China or Thailand.] In reading the speech noticed Churchill had referred to a bay [in Newfoundland] where the conference [with Roosevelt] was held reminding him of Scotland, also of the coasts of Iceland and Greenland. After Iceland he had said: not Ireland. I thought this reference unwise and thought references to Iceland, Greenland, and Ireland should be left out. To be careful not to antagonize the Irish in the U.S. and in Canada. He agreed I was right and struck it out.

"I was frankly disappointed in the representations that had been made to the Japanese Minister by the President. . . . I continued to tell Churchill and mentioned it again to Mrs. Churchill that while the President, Stimson, Knox, and Hull were all ready and anxious for the U.S. to go into the war, not to believe that that was the wish of the American people. That they were wishing to keep out. That, as regards Japan, I felt they would wish to stay out there as well . . . that Britain would have to do a lot of fighting herself first."

After his reading, Mackenzie King went for a walk and later Lord Cranborne joined him for a long walk. Mackenzie King "explained the whole conscription matter to Cranborne and how fatal it would have been for me to have left to come to England before going through our Canadian West."

At luncheon, Mackenzie King mentioned the verse from the poet Gray on the sovereignty of the conquered air. Churchill "read it aloud and was tremendously taken with it. He kept repeating it over and over again. Told me to use it in my speech at the Mansion House. He thought it a remarkable prophecy. He then began to quote several of Gray's poems which he did exceedingly well. He also quoted many lines from Tennyson's 'Locksley Hall' and the prophecy there of the navies grappling in the blue, but thought Gray's was one of the best of anything he had seen. It really seemed to appeal to him immensely. Speaking of his own speech, he said he had tried to put some art into it." This verse of Gray's was quoted by Mackenzie King in his speech at the Mansion House, which Churchill had told him the previous evening had been arranged for September 4.

At luncheon, "Churchill told Mackenzie King that he had heard from Smuts and that Smuts agreed entirely with me in the line I had taken in my press interview." Churchill's secretary later showed him the telegram in which Smuts said: "I was glad to see Mackenzie King's outspoken condemnation of agitation for Imperial Cabinet. It seems to me unwise, with vast dangers looming in Africa and Pacific, to collect all our Prime Ministers in London. Our Commonwealth system, by its decentralization, is well situated for waging world war, and diffuse leadership in all parts is a blessing rather than handicap. I agree with him that our system of communication leaves little to be desired." Smuts' message was "an immense satisfaction" to Mackenzie King.

At four o'clock in the afternoon Mackenzie King went to bed and rested till seven. He then went out for a walk. Dinner was not until nine o'clock that night as Churchill was broadcasting at 8.30. The guests joined Mrs. Churchill to listen to the broadcast. "There was a profound silence throughout the whole of the speech. When Mr. Churchill coughed, as he did, two or three times, one felt there was a little concern. When the speech was over, no one said a word for some little time. We waited for Mrs. Churchill to speak. There seemed to be unanimity of feeling that it was the best broadcast he had made, and I think it was the feeling of all that the part which related to the Service [a church service on *Prince of Wales* during the meeting in Newfoundland at which Churchill and Roosevelt were present] and the singing of hymns was the most impressive of any."

When Mackenzie King spoke "of the hymns being the most impressive part, Churchill himself said he felt that way. He knew that was the side which would appeal to the people, and America particularly. At the table, he told us that during the Service itself he had felt overcome. He pretended it was the cold he had, but really found it impossible to keep back the tears. Churchill's nature is deeply religious. It would be strange if it were not, with his love of truth, freedom, and justice, and his profound hatred of cruelty, barbarity, and wrong. He quite frankly said there are things beyond which we do not yet begin to understand. I noticed that, in his manuscript, he had changed the word 'One' to 'Him,' in his last revise. . . . At the table, both he and Mrs. Churchill said he would receive numerous letters tomorrow in regard to his cough, sending cures of different kinds. He was very much like a boy out of school when the broadcast was over. A great sense of relief."

Beaverbrook had arrived at Chequers that day and during the evening he asked Mackenzie King "how I gauged public opinion so accurately. How did I get information from Western papers and the like. I told him I did the thing that I thought was right and held to responsible self-government and the supremacy of Parliament in everything. Believed the people understood common sense; also believed in one's integrity to one's word. That I attributed success to these things. I had been close to the people as a source of government, not permitting growth of dictatorship. I told him I had no desire to continue in politics longer than this war and the peace negotiations. He seemed to think that was a good attitude to take, but that I ought to stay and would stay in politics to the end. Spoke about the men in the party as possible successors. Asked particularly about Howe whom he likes very much."

After dinner that evening "Churchill turned on the radio for music, songs, and in the course of the evening began to walk up and down and perform a sort of dance. He turned and said to me: 'could I not do the same,' whereupon I joined him and two of us took each other by the arm and performed a dance together. All present were almost in hysterics with laughter. . . . It was after one before we noticed how the time was passing." For Mackenzie King, "It was really a delight to see him in his own home. I know he was very happy throughout the evening."

Mackenzie King returned to London next morning (August 25) and later that day attended the War Cabinet where there was a good deal of discussion of how to get the United States into the war. "Beaverbrook quite outspoken about the need for some dramatic action being taken which would serve to bring the U.S. immediately into war. He thought they were getting sort of wobbly again. That what was needed was that Churchill himself should go and address Congress. I did not like the idea at all, nor did I think any of the members of the Cabinet did. . . . Much was said about Churchill himself having said: 'Give us the tools and we will finish the job.' That had been responsible for keeping the Americans from coming in, and it was necessary now to look over what had been said, and to alter the position in a way which would make it clear to America that if she did not come in, England herself might not be able to keep up, and that America would be the next loser, that her own future would be at stake.

"There were," he added, "one or two who rather favoured the idea of letting it be known in America that Britain could not meet the situation herself, but the general opinion wisely, I think, was that it would not do to have this impression get abroad, nor would it do for Britain herself to try to induce America to come into the war. Halifax [the British Ambassador to the United States, at home on a visit] said more could be done by Dominion statesmen than by English. A still wiser suggestion was that leading Americans could do most in this way. Beaverbrook seemed to think that Churchill's personality could do more than all else. . . . Churchill felt, and I think wisely, that the best way to have America come into the war was through an attack by Hitler on American ships convoying supplies to Britain. That once an attack came there, the President would be prepared to take action at once without waiting for Congress. That if they waited for Congress, debate might take a very long time.

"I expressed the view that, while the President and the Cabinet were ready to go into the war, it was true the President alone could not bring the nation in. It was to be remembered that his appeals to the people had largely been along lines that what he was doing would help the British, but would also keep America out of the war. That he had a large following for that reason. It was a curious sort of thing, that he should have following of those who wanted to get into the war, and for reasons that I had mentioned, still a larger following of those who would believe he was the one who was finding ways and means of keeping out of it. I said I did not think the British should bank on Americans coming in too quickly. I said that, as regards Japan, they would be prepared to see Britain begin the fighting herself, and it would take some time there before they would come in. I drew attention to the President not having gone far in his words to the Japanese Ambassador; that he had made no mention about peace on the Pacific, and that all that he had said was related to protecting America's interests.

"I thought the best approach was the kind of speech that Churchill had made last night where he pictured the various nations of Europe being drawn into a pit and unable to get out, emphasizing the enlarging power of Hitler and his [Churchill's] inability to meet him at every turn while he was getting stronger himself. In a way, they [the Americans] would have to be frightened into participation."

Mackenzie King noted with particular satisfaction that "after the meeting, Churchill came around to say to me that if I had nothing better to do, he would be pleased if I would come to Chequers for next weekend. He could not have paid me a higher compliment, and it was really touching that he should have done so. He suddenly remembered that I was spending the weekend with the King."

The next meeting of the War Cabinet was on August 28. That same day Menzies resigned as Prime Minister of Australia because of dissension in his Cabinet. He was succeeded by A. W. Fadden, who had been Acting Prime Minister during his long absence in the spring. When the British War Cabinet met, Menzies' resignation had not yet been announced but a report from Australia indicated that Menzies might be coming to London as a Resident Minister from Australia and that there would be no obstacle [from the British] to his attending the War Cabinet. The Australian crisis was naturally discussed, and when Cranborne repeated the report he had got from the press that it was believed in Australia the British Government would accept an Australian Minister other than the Prime Minister as a Member of the War Cabinet, "Churchill at once said this should be denied by the Ministry of Information and the Dominions Office at once. He spoke of the War Cabinet being already too large and of his being condemned for that reason. Anthony Eden turned to me and said: 'where would it lead?' Churchill said the best thing for Menzies to do, if he is bound to come, was to take Bruce's place [Bruce was Australian High Commissioner in London], but he was quite determined not to have any Minister other than the Prime Minister in the Cabinet, and said they would have to take up the matter with other Dominions.

"I interjected that I would give my view at once which was that Canada did not wish a Minister other than the P.M. in the War Cabinet. In the first place, we thought the present arrangement whereby everything was in writing and a matter of record was infinitely preferable to statements made as to what had been understood or agreed upon between parties when, as a matter of fact, their minds may never have met. I pointed out that today I could communicate with Churchill on an important matter, and he with me, and on other general matters through the Dominions Office. Malcolm MacDonald could give us the British atmosphere and sidelights; Massey, the same from London. That I liked to have before me a written document and my Cabinet present, and also advisers there before reaching a decision. Did not think any man should sit in here at Downing Street and give decisions in the name of his part of the Empire. I added that the less it appeared that all matters were being settled by Cabinet sitting at Downing Street, the better it would be for the war effort of the several Dominions. That our people took their stand on the Statute of Westminster. We were a country by ourselves with our own problems, as each part of the Empire was. That it was a mistake to talk of the Dominions' point of view as against the British point of view."

Mackenzie King added that "we had no complaint to make up to the present. That, if difficulties arose on any matter, the Ministers who knew more about it would be over here in short order. If we got into difficulties in government itself I would probably find it necessary to come over and intervene, but apart from this, I thought everything went more smoothly so long as we, as a Cabinet, were asserting our position in communications that were being exchanged, and were of record. It is quite clear they are all considerably perturbed by the latest word that Menzies may resign, be succeeded by some other person, and he, himself, come over as a Minister. Later, Churchill asked me to have my staff keep his office informed as to my movements as it might be necessary for him to consult with me at any moment."

After the meeting of the War Cabinet, Halifax took Mackenzie King aside to say that he thought what Mackenzie King had said was very sensible. Mackenzie King replied that "there was an old school that believed that the Dominions could be kept united by . . . central organization in London. That they were wrong. . . . That the only basis from which to proceed was that laid down by the Statute of Westminster." Halifax said he "was greatly pleased to hear me say this, and that he agreed."

Mackenzie King also had "a little talk with Churchill" after the Cabinet meeting. "Told him about leaving on Saturday. He said he would be disappointed if I could not come to Chequers but if I had to go, he will understand and will arrange everything satisfactorily. . . .

"I spoke to him about how well he looked. I was amazed how he kept up. He told me it was just two years ago that day that, where we were talking in the Cabinet room, Neville Chamberlain had asked him to join the Government. He had not been in the Cabinet on the following day when the decision was reached for Britain to enter the war. . . . He said he had felt well through the past year or two but that one never knew what was ahead or how long the war might last. . . . When he spoke about the future and about his strength in that connection, we were standing in the doorway of the Council Chamber, and he recited lines from 'Lead, Kindly Light' which concluded 'one step enough for me.'"

Most of the next two days was taken up with the final drafting of the Mansion House speech. Just before Mackenzie King delivered the speech at the luncheon on September 4, he attended another meeting of the War Cabinet. He "tossed a note to Churchill to excuse me at 12.30. When he opened it, he made a few remarks to the Cabinet indicating that this was the last day I would be with its members, and repeated much of what he had said at the beginning about the great help which Canada had been to Britain; . . . something about preserving unity in Canada, better than it had been preserved in any part of the Empire, and my long experience in public life, etc. Wished me safe return.

"In reply, I expressed appreciation of the Prime Minister's words. Spoke of having found it profitable as well as a pleasure to be with his colleagues as well as himself in Council. Repeated that relations could not be better than they were between our two governments. Referred once more to importance of Prime Ministers looking after their respective countries." Mackenzie King no doubt made this last observation with greater conviction in the light of Menzies' experience which he felt completely vindicated his position.

Of his speech at the Mansion House, Mackenzie King wrote: "Once I was on my feet, I felt a real security in the matter of speaking, and knew that all was going well. The trip through Western Canada had been a fine preparation. Without doubt, I was conscious, while speaking, that the message was getting across all right, and could see Churchill and others were appreciating sincerely what was being said. I was given a splendid ovation at the close.

"Churchill himself replied, speaking extemporaneously, and paying a tribute which, from him, and having regard to the occasion, was a high honour indeed. He referred to the speech as both memorable and momentous, and to the gathering being the most important of its kind which had been held in the city since the beginning of the war. Referred to what I had said and the manner of saying as helping to reveal what accounted for the 15 years I had held the office of P.M. He was given a great reception when he got up to speak and his words were equally received with rounds of applause.

"Coming out of the luncheon, he told me he was delighted with what I had said, and particularly well pleased with the part that related to America. I said to him I had thought of going a bit further and, like him, had held back. I asked frankly if he thought I had said anything that I should not have said. He replied: On the contrary, I had said exactly the right thing; what was most needed, and what no one excepting myself could have said. He felt certain it would do great good."

Mackenzie King recorded his delight that "in speaking Churchill brought Laurier's name into his remarks. He said to me afterwards that he had spoken ex tempore. Otherwise it might have seemed that matters had been arranged in advance. I was particularly careful not to speak to him or to anyone else of what I was about to say. To take it wholly on my own responsibility as my own conviction and belief."

After the Mansion House speech Mackenzie King spent the afternoon with Herbert Morrison, the Home Secretary, who took him to see some of the devastated areas of London. This visit with Morrison was the origin of the Canadian corps of firefighters. Realizing how desperately trained firemen were needed, Mackenzie King told Morrison he would try to have a corps sent from Canada as soon as possible. That evening Mackenzie King went with Mr. and Mrs. Vincent Massey to visit the Beaver Club, which had been founded by the Masseys as a recreation centre and club for Canadian service men and where Mrs. Massey gave such untiring service herself. He "was very much impressed with the work being carried on there. The best kind of settlement work." Still later that night, in the blackout, he drove with Vincent Massey to see the Air Fighter Command. "Had I not been so tired," he noted, "I would have much enjoyed the sort of romantic experience in moving about halls and tunnels and secret passages through an old country house to the subterranean rooms where young men and women plot on large maps the movements of the different airplanes. . . . Fortunately for all, there was not much in the way of activity but sufficient to disclose how exceedingly interesting and amazingly efficient this whole system of direction of warfare in the air can be."

At the close of the day he wrote: "This day has been a very heavy one, but also one that has relieved my mind beyond all else. I feel the Mansion House speech has been . . . a real triumph. I could now stay on in London for another week with immense satisfaction and pleasure to myself, and to great advantage in the matter of seeing things and meeting people. I feel, however, that the job has been well done."

The following day (September 5) Mackenzie King visited General Montgomery's headquarters at Dover. Montgomery "spoke very highly of McNaughton, but he thought Canadian officers were rather older than they should be, that younger men, about 40, were necessary for the resistance required in the present sort of warfare."

On his return from Dover Mackenzie King went right to Downing Street where he "had a pleasant half hour's talk with the Prime Minister," who "again spoke of my speech of yesterday, saying that he was so grateful for it. . . . He repeated that it could not possibly have been better. That I had said what nobody else could say. He then said he noticed that the 'Times Herald' [an isolationist newspaper in Washington] had come out against me. . . . I said I did not care about the American press; that I had spoken the truth." Churchill "thought that the Americans and the British would have to come more and more together to help to control the world. . . . That he believed the English-speaking democracies must inevitably come more and more into one great organization. He said: 'you and I are helping in laying the foundation for that new order. We will not see it in our lifetime, but it will surely come.'

"We came out of the garden together. He was going to take a sleep. He came to the front door with me. On the way, he said he was so glad we had been in touch with each other. I said I thought the highest compliment paid me had been in extending two invitations to come to Chequers at different weekends, in addition to the one I had spent there. He said he was sorry I had not been able to stay longer and come down. He said if he sent any papers to me marked 'Winch' to know that they were wholly personal, to have my private secretary decode them, and not to let them on to the files." Churchill also told Mackenzie King his visit "had been a great help and success from the point of view of the British Government." There is no question that these many personal contacts with Churchill during the visit established a sympathy between him and Mackenzie King which had not existed before and which continued to the end of Mackenzie King's life.

While he was in Britain, Mackenzie King visited Queen Mary at Badminton on August 27 and spent August 30 and 31 at Balmoral Castle with the King and Queen. Both visits were described in his diary in his usual meticulous detail.

When Mackenzie King arrived at Balmoral, the King was out with a shooting party and he was welcomed by the Queen. The Queen took him "to a little cottage that she had secured over the moors, where, with those who had been out shooting, we would have a picnic lunch. . . . Princesses Elizabeth and Margaret Rose had gone on to arrange the tables . . . the little cottage . . . was only two rooms; one used as a sort of dining room, with a little table in the centre, and an open fireplace opposite the door; the other, a large room, evidently what would be the kitchen with a huge open fireplace with equipment for cooking food. Just before going into the cottage, the Queen presented me to the little Princesses. They were dressed in their little brown coats, and had bare legs. They had arranged the table inside with lettuce leaves for decoration. They were quite pleased with everything they had done to make things look nice. There were no servants. . . .

"The shooting party were late in arriving, and we were getting a little hungry, and the sun bright and clear. After we had sat a little while in the sun, Her Majesty suggested that we go on with our luncheon, each one helping himself. There was cold grouse, a salad, different kinds of sandwiches, bread and butter and cake. Just a simple picnic meal. As we were getting on with the sandwiches, we saw the King and his party coming in the distance. The King greeted me with the words 'Good Morning.' Then asked me how I had enjoyed my 'fly.' I had to think a moment as to what was meant, but Their Majesties then spoke of the trip across. . . . The King then got his own food, and I found myself seated between the King and Queen for the remainder of the picnic. . . . After luncheon, the King and I had a talk of some length and then a walk together."

They drove back to Balmoral about four o'clock and Mackenzie King "had an hour's rest, going sound asleep. I was glad of the rest, as I found the journey rather fatiguing. I was given a cup of tea at 5.30, and at a quarter to six was shown into the King's room upstairs. . . . His Majesty seated himself with his back to the window and gave me a chair opposite himself on the other side of the open fire. We talked for some little time, when the Queen came in to mention that the Cameron Highlanders' band was about to begin the retreat on the front lawn, in front of the Castle. . . . On the way onto the lawn, I met some guests who had arrived: the Moderator of the General Assembly, who is to preach the sermon tomorrow, and the Minister of the Church. . . . The Highlanders, when playing the retreat on the lawn, were a beautiful scene; very picturesque, and the music to my liking, amid the Scottish hills."

After the retreat, Mackenzie King returned to his room and wrote up his diary, noting among other things that "in the drive with the Queen, Her Majesty recalled different incidents of the tour through Canada. Among the first words she said to me, after meeting her in the drawing room, was 'that that tour made us.' I interpreted [the words] as meaning it had helped to make the Empire one, but pointing to herself, she said I mean us, the King and myself. She spoke of it coming just at the right time, particularly for them."

Mackenzie King noted that, at one stage, the King "asked me what had become of the Dunsmuir property [Royal Roads, near Victoria, B.C., now one of the Service Colleges]. I told him of the Government having purchased it and of it being used for naval purposes. I could see that what he had in mind was the possibility of making a sort of Canadian Residence for the King. When we were talking of my visit to Badminton and of the Queen Mother, the King said they feared perhaps she was too old to travel, and asked me whether I thought she might visit her brother, Lord Athlone, in Canada. I at once said that, so far as the country was concerned, they would welcome it very much, that I could assure him the Canadian people would be very honoured to have Queen Mary in Canada. He said the difficulty was the transportation, but he thought one of the large warships might be used to take her across. He said this is entirely between you and me—to say nothing of it."

Shortly before 8.30 the guests assembled in the drawing room. "Their Majesties came in together, addressed a few words to some of their guests, and then all went in to dinner in an informal manner—ladies followed by gentlemen. I was given a seat to the right of the Queen, the Moderator of the General Assembly to the left; the latter was wearing his court dress with lace around one side of the neck, also was in knee breeches. It seemed to me rather nonsensical. . . . The early half of the dinner the Queen talked with me most of the time, rather than with the Moderator. After the ladies withdrew, the King had the Moderator and myself sit on either side of him. He was in kilts wearing the Balmoral tartan. The Queen wore a sort of white lace gown. At the end of the dinner, three pipers marched around the table playing the pipes. . . .

"The King recalled some of the incidents of the Hyde Park visit. Told me of the President, in the course of visit while I was resting, having shown him a map, explaining the different bases and their importance to America. He had cut the map out and allowed the King to keep the bit he had been showing him. He brought it with him to England and, later, saw the Admiralty and explained what Roosevelt had in mind. Not until the meeting of the President with Churchill had the President known that the King had brought the information he had given him to the attention of the Admiralty. . . .

"After leaving the dining room, and coming into the drawing room, tea was served, the Queen pouring it herself, and general conversation for a short time. . . . At eleven o'clock, the King and Queen said goodnight, and I returned and dictated this bit of diary . . . and then to bed. Read the newspapers after going to bed. Felt really sorry for Menzies' downfall, for that is what it amounts to. How true it is that pride comes before a fall. Turned out the lights at midnight."

The next morning (August 31) Mackenzie King walked to church with one of the lady guests. When they reached the Church, Mackenzie King found "about a dozen officers of the Canadian Construction Company were drawn up in formation at the main entrance of the Church. . . . The Royal Family sat in the front row, Princess Elizabeth at the extreme right, almost beneath the marble portrait bust of Queen Victoria. Next to her the Queen and the King and then Princess Margaret Rose. I was in the pew immediately behind." Mackenzie King was impressed by the service which he described minutely. Of the sermon he wrote: "It was a well thought out and well expressed sermon, delivered without notes. The professional dress which the Moderator wore rather irritated me, lace in the sleeves and near the neck and a large ring. I would rather have seen him with simple quiet gown." Mackenzie King "prayed very earnestly that my life might be made a medium through which Divine purpose might fulfil itself in some measure. During the singing of the National Anthem I was immediately behind the King. The thought flashed through my mind that I had been with Their Majesties at a time of great happiness and was now with them at a time of great anxiety, but will be with them again at a time of renewed happiness."

At luncheon Mackenzie King "was seated to the Queen's right, with Princess Elizabeth to my right and Princess Margaret immediately opposite. The latter was quite entertaining in the way she laughed at different subjects that were discussed. . . . She also made her eyes look crossed and tried to amuse others. The Queen told her to stop doing that for fear they might become fixed in that position and the King had also to tell her the same. When I talked to Princess Elizabeth about her broadcast she was very sweet in the way she talked and was very natural in some further conversation we had together."

Mackenzie King took leave of the King and Queen about 5 o'clock. "The Queen walked alone into a small sunken garden filled with most beautiful roses," he wrote, "and the King came with me as I went to say goodbye. They both stood together and talked with me for a short time." Mackenzie King told them "when the war was over we would see them both in Canada again and referred to the Dunsmuir residence. The King mentioned that we had been speaking of it and seemed to think that it would be nice if the Governor-General could have a residence of his own in British Columbia, rather than staying with the Lieutenant-Governor. I said I thought it would make a fine Canadian Residence for the King and Queen themselves, that we would welcome the opportunity of arranging it to serve that purpose. . . . They both spoke anew of what Canada meant in their lives and of the happiness it gave them to think of their welcome there. I said that the heart of all Canada was filled with the deepest affection."

One of the purposes of the visit to Britain was to see the Canadian forces. Mackenzie King spent a good deal of time with General McNaughton and the Army. He visited McNaughton first on August 23, at Aldershot. He found "the drive on the whole was very pleasant though, unfortunately, it began to rain before we reached Aldershot. We were also held up at the railway crossing and apparently had not been given enough time for the trip which unfortunately caused us to arrive, I should think, about a quarter of an hour late. The guard of honour had been standing in the wet. The luncheon was delayed which meant also delay in the afternoon's programme. General McNaughton and the others accepted the situation very nicely, but I could feel that unfortunately I had got off, so to speak, on the wrong foot. After inspecting the guard of honour, I had a short talk with Hugues Lapointe who was out in front. We then adjourned to the cookery school for luncheon."

During the luncheon he talked to McNaughton and Price Montague, the Senior Officer at Canadian Military Headquarters in London, about the relationship between the Army Command and the Defence Department in Ottawa on which there had been some misunderstanding; this they felt had now been cleared up. McNaughton assured him they had nothing whatever to complain of. Mackenzie King spoke to McNaughton also about what he "thought of saying to the men, making clear the Government's position regarding the confidence we had in himself and the freedom to be given the military authorities. He asked me not to do that. To confine what I had to say to a few words about the thoughts that those at home retained for the boys. Many of them were pretty homesick and just something of that kind would be all that was desired. He said that he did not wish to have any one man, and in particular, himself, built up as having too much of control or others being too dependent on him, in case anything should happen to himself and, also, to avoid the additional responsibilities. I felt that the heart of my speech had gone but that, in view of McNaughton's suggestion, there was nothing to do but follow it. I was really so tired by the long trip, and being late, and, as a consequence, the disconcerting effect, and with continual rain, that I found it extremely difficult to keep free from an appalling depression. I would have given anything not to have to speak but, as McNaughton said, it would never do for the Prime Minister to be present on such an occasion and not address some words to the troops."

After the luncheon they drove to the sports field where the grandstand was filled with troops and the sports were already under way. Mackenzie King "was asked to inspect the Guard of Honour and then I was given a seat beside McNaughton, Mrs. McNaughton and some of the Generals. . . . From one part of the grandstand to the right there was considerable booing as I was leaving the stand to go across to inspect the Guard. It was not in any way general, in fact from the left hand side of the stand there was none of it that I noticed. It came from one part on the right hand side, mixed with applause. Quite clearly it had been organized, but I think what occasioned it most was that the teams were in competition, and there was both applause and booing with respect to the different events. It was a little disconcerting and, in my heart, I knew it to be unfair and Tory tactics, but I ignored it altogether.

"Later, when it came to going out to speak to the men, it did not assert itself except in a very limited way. And when I began to address the troops they were perfectly quiet and gave me a splendid hearing.

When I returned to the grandstand was given a fine reception. I felt that what I said was very inadequate. In fact it had begun to pour rain when I started to speak and everything in that particular was as unpropitious as it could possibly be. I made one remark about the spirit of the men which made it clear that they were feeling restraint at not getting to the front. . . . There was one interruption. One man asked me when they were going home. That I ignored."

Mackenzie King found it a "deeply impressive sight to see such numbers of fine young Canadians, all looking strong and vigorous. Some 5000 were present at the sports. The sports themselves however were disappointing because of the weather."

This was Mackenzie King's own impression of the notorious "booing" incident which created quite a stir at home because the Canadian Press despatch describing the incident was featured in many newspapers.

Mackenzie King spent August 26 with the Army. He had a talk with McNaughton who emphasized "that this was a war of production of supplies and that what we should do in Canada is to get a complete survey of our labour and have it proportioned in the way that would be of greatest service. We should not denude our country of its workers."

In conversation about the day's programme, McNaughton told Mackenzie King "for the first time that I would be expected to say a few words to the troops. I felt what was like a dart pass through my bowels. It made me quite sick and faint, and to break out into a cold perspiration. . . . There was nothing, however, to do but face the ordeal. That, however, was the least part of the terror. When I arrived at the First Divisional Headquarters at Marden Park, I was met first by a guard of honour, composed in large part of men from Saskatoon and Prince Albert. After inspecting the guard, I met the officers of the First Division, talked with them individually, and made contacts of a personal character. Was surprised at the numbers with whom I had some intimate association. After this meeting, which was very pleasant, and would have been doubly so had I not been upset by the thought of having to speak, I had luncheon with General Pearkes and the officers. . . . I like General Pearkes very much. He has an extremely pleasant manner, and is, I think, a man of fine ideals, a V.C."

After the luncheon, Mackenzie King drove with Pearkes "to the first town, at which troops had been assembled in the formation of a square. Here, I was really in a condition of agony and fright. I had not expected to see such a formation, and to be put instantly in front of a microphone, without any words of introduction. I had been told by Pearkes, when I spoke of what was expected, that the speech might be half an hour, which nonplussed me altogether. I tried to compromise with five or ten minutes, but really spoke, I believe, for fifteen, but it was really improvising and very difficult. I felt I had made a poor, if not a painful, impression. I then was taken around the four sides of the square, to inspect the front lines of the different units. Was given cheers by the soldiers on leaving the grounds. It all would have been to my liking had I been fully prepared and rested. As it was, it was pretty much the agony of Aldershot all over again.

"To my astonishment, when I thought this was all, I was then told there were three more localities to be visited, where troops would be assembled. Each turned out to be the same size—some 3,000 men at each place, making 12,000 in all. I had again to speak over the microphone. Fortunately, the second time went a little better, but none too well. On the third occasion . . . I found the location for speaking much more pleasant and had the microphone in my hand, finding it comparatively easy to address the assembled group. At the fourth place, where the Toronto Highlanders and Toronto Regiments were located, I again felt I would be confronted with a Toronto atmosphere, and was sensitive thereto but managed, nevertheless, to make fairly appropriate remarks. I much enjoyed inspecting the different units. . . . The men looked in fine condition, though many of them, I felt, were young men who had hardly had much in life of its necessities and but a very few of its comforts.

"I really felt too moved at the thought of all this young life being possibly destroyed to be able to give proper expression to my thoughts. I cannot talk their jargon of war. There is no use attempting it. My words inevitably get into those of thought, and prayer, and Providence, which is not the conventional thing, but the only thing which I feel at heart. I have held to those words, rather than to others. I cannot tell them what we are expecting of them in the way of service. Offering their lives is infinitely greater than anything I myself am called upon to do."

It is obvious from his diary that all day he had been dreading a repetition of the booing for he wrote: "There was nothing today to suggest any ill-will at all. On the contrary, it was quite the opposite. The cheers at the end of the visit to each place were obviously whole-hearted. I could see, in looking at the four sides of the square, that there were no breaks and that all were taking part. . . . I could see that having come over in a bomber . . . had increased the respect of the Forces for myself. It is an obvious sharing of their risks, of danger to life itself in time of war."

He noted that "during the afternoon, I spoke out quite plainly to all the troops about their remaining in Britain. I told them not to let any one say that it was the [Canadian] Government's restraining hand, but that it was the view of the Government of the United Kingdom to have them in this place of vital importance—at the heart of the Empire. I also spoke about the Government's seeking to avoid political patronage and friendship, which were expressions McNaughton used as we were driving together, and told me that he was satisfied that we had followed that policy absolutely, and he was doing the same here. He wanted the men to feel that they can come up from the ranks into any position.

"I tried to say words that would bring to them feelings that they were continually in our thoughts and prayers and that I would be able to carry back messages as to their condition. I complimented them upon their behaviour, appearance, carriage, etc., and friendly relations existing, and also spoke of being able to bring back messages to those at home. Told them I had come particularly to see with my own eyes and to hear with my own ears all I could about their conditions, and I should welcome expressions of view from officers, men, etc. Stressed that Canada's policy was to do the utmost in the winning of the war and that I wanted them to know that the Government was solidly back of the Corps." He added that, "in driving off the grounds, General Pearkes opened the hood at the top of the car and suggested my standing there and waving goodbye. This I did at each of the centres visited."

On August 28, McNaughton drove Mackenzie King from London to his headquarters and they had a pleasant talk on the way during which he got his "first chance to discuss conscription with McNaughton." The subject developed naturally out of McNaughton's emphasis on "the importance, from now on, of planning most carefully as respects disposition of manpower. He keeps emphasizing the need for munitions and materials; says for the first time he is really happy about the supplies coming forward. That he can see now that everything will be along in time that will be needed. He indicated that, for the present, he had the men that he required for the Corps."

Mackenzie King then "said to him that I had not brought up the question of conscription with him as it was a political matter. That I wanted him to know my position, how I felt with respect to it. It was a position held equally by Lapointe. It was that both of us felt that national unity was more important than all else. That we could not consider the present issue apart from the pledges given before the war, at the time of war, and during the general election. That my strength in Canada was the knowledge that people had that I would stand by my word. That if we reached the point where it was felt that conscription was necessary and the majority in Parliament so wished it, that I would resign and leave the leadership to someone who would have to enforce conscription. I would make no complaint, but do what I could to help in other ways. But, believing that conscription would prove disastrous to national unity and the efficiency of our war effort, I could not think of taking any other course.

"McNaughton then spoke about the effect of conscription in the last war, saying that it had not proved to be a help; that men that were conscripted were not of any real service. That it would have been better had there not been conscription at that time. He, himself, was not saying anything pro and con—these were not the words used, but expressed his attitude—as he felt that issue was a political one. He did say, however, that he agreed with me that national unity was more important than all else. He stressed again how important it was to hold to the constitutional position I have held to all along. Said this was necessary in dealing with the Government here." McNaughton left Mackenzie King with "the impression that he had no desire to see conscription introduced, but hoped that everything might be achieved by voluntary effort. He spoke quite clearly about the extra value of voluntary effort."

Mackenzie King told McNaughton he "thought Ralston would like to come over again; might be coming soon. Asked him whether that would be helpful. He said: 'You have asked me a straight question and I will give you a straight answer. I do not think it would.' He then went on to say that Ralston took far too much in the way of details into his own hand. That they all found him rather difficult. That he wanted to do too much, and had got out of his own Ministerial sphere into matters beyond it. I said that was due simply to zeal to accomplish all he could. McNaughton did not dispute that, but it was quite apparent that he would much rather be left on his own here. I said to him I could not guarantee that Ralston would not come, and I would, of course, hold confidential what he had said to me, but that he might wish to come, and I might find it difficult to hold him. I said I thought another reason was that he wanted to make perfectly sure that he understood the Army's position to the full, so as to be able to back it up as much as possible."

On the way to McNaughton's headquarters, Mackenzie King stopped for the formal opening of a road the Army had built, where he cut a ribbon and named it 'Yonge Street.' He had to speak to the sappers in a veritable cloudburst and the whole experience was as dismal as it could have been. When he opened his umbrella he found it in shreds. As the rain poured down, he felt his "whole right leg swell with rheumatism and was afraid I was going to have to go through that agony anew. Fortunately, a little later it passed off with rest. The soldiers gave me a good reception."

This unfortunate beginning cast a pall over the rest of the day. At dinner at the headquarters mess, he was very depressed, could not rouse himself, "and unfortunately did not offer to speak. I really think this was a great mistake and a great disappointment to the men present. It will probably be said, from now on, that the Prime Minister had no word to give to those who invited him to be their guest after coming from Canada to visit the armed forces. It was all part of the result of pressure under which I have been driven, and the inadequate information of what is expected in advance. I had been told I would not be expected to speak at dinner. Had I sensed the thing properly, I would have asked to be allowed to say a word. . . . I knew I could have made a quite effective speech, had I once started to say a word, but I was just in that depressed condition that I was over-sensitive to what I felt might be a critical atmosphere around me. In this, I was clearly wrong. I am sure any words would have been cordially welcomed. When I came back to McNaughton's residence, we talked for a few minutes. Then I went up to my room about a quarter to ten." Mackenzie King left for London immediately after breakfast the next morning.

In summing up his impressions before leaving London on September 5, Mackenzie King wrote: "I feel that, with the Army altogether, I have made a poorer impression than on other sides. First, because of bad weather on different occasions when I have spoken out of doors; and, secondly, the unpreparedness for the different occasions, and great fatigue from so much physical exertion. However I think I have shown a friendliness and a readiness to hear what was to be said, which, in the long run, will do good."

He had another talk with McNaughton that day at his hotel. McNaughton spoke "of the need of having his position more clearly defined by Order-in-Council, to prevent confusion" and "of the desirability of having general lines of policy defined, allowing details to be worked out by himself." Although he "made no reference to Ralston, I could see there was real feeling there. With regard to the desirability of Canadian war materials being given to our own Army first, before being pooled, he regarded our Army as an expression of the life of the nation. It was all right to pool war materials, once our men got their supplies from our own sources, but not until then. Both General McNaughton and Montague were at the station to see me off. I told McNaughton, in Montague's presence, that he could count on my doing all I could to back him up in matters we had discussed together and to get things cleared up as quickly as possible."

Mackenzie King left London on the evening of September 5 and stopped for the night at Ashby Hall, near the R.C.A.F. headquarters at Digby. He spent the following morning visiting a number of Canadian squadrons, and the afternoon travelling by train to Edinburgh and on, by motor, to Glasgow and Prestwick where he spent the night. On Sunday, September 7, he flew back in the Liberator bomber from Prestwick to the new Montreal airport at Dorval. His diary for that day is in his own handwriting. "It was 6 o'clock when I boarded the plane and 6.05 when we took up, first a run up the runway, then the gradual ascent, with the view of the Ayr beneath, till we were lost in the mist of the clouds."

He found the return journey less impressive than the flight to Britain and rather uncomfortable in the last hour before landing. "We landed," he wrote, "at 9.15 Scotch time, 4.15 Canadian time, 15 hours and 10 minutes straight across from Ayr to Montreal without a stop. . . . Lapointe and Howe were at the airport to meet us. They had come by plane from Ottawa. Caught a glimpse of them before landing. It was a happy moment to be on land again. . . . En route Vanier had reminded me that today was a National Day of Prayer. . . . I certainly thanked God with all my heart as we reached the airport safely, and I saw the ground once again solid beneath my feet. Handy [Mackenzie King's confidential secretary] spoke at dinner of how he had thanked God in the same way. He is a noble, true and beautiful soul, a young disciple.

"On landing I shook hands with Lapointe and Howe. . . . Lapointe seemed greatly pleased at the mission, well satisfied. Howe said public feeling in Canada (so far as Opposition went) had changed round completely. That self and party never stood higher. They asked if I would go on by plane to Ottawa but I declined; have no desire to fly for pleasure, or unless absolutely necessary. . . . Was quite touched by the many expressions of evident delight and affection on the part of groups of people, on arrival, at stations en route and at station at Ottawa, people applauding with their hands, one man held up his little child to see me, others telling their children, etc. One could see the delight in their faces, as if one had done some great thing on their behalf. I was greatly impressed at the numbers at the Station, as my movements were all kept as secret as possible. I tried to slip in unnoticed. . . . Drove direct to Kingsmere arriving about 10."

On September 10, Mackenzie King gave the War Committee a detailed account of his visit to the United Kingdom which took three hours.

The subsequent discussion included the subjects brought up by McNaughton with Mackenzie King. "I can see," he noted, "that Ralston is quite antagonistic towards McNaughton on the score that the latter is anxious to get everything into his own hands. Ralston, unfortunately, has the same weakness himself.

"At the close of the discussion, I said I thought it would be better from now on to limit the visits of Ministers to Britain. That I thought it inadvisable to have it appear too much to the public that all matters were being settled in London, rather than that we were managing our own war effort satisfactorily here and were meeting, by the agencies of communication, all that was most essential for conference. I was really trying to persuade Ralston not to go over at present. Suggested it would be better for him and for the Government and our war effort if he took a month off as a complete rest to get in shape for handling of affairs during remaining period of war. He expressed himself as anxious to cross before the bad weather and be back before Parliament assembles rather than going after the first part of the session. I said he must be the judge himself; if he felt it imperative to go I would not stand in his way. It seemed to me, however, that he, on his own account even more than McNaughton, is anxious to get our men into active service beyond the British Isles. . . . Howe said at once that he would forego the trip he had planned. Could manage without going. I mentioned that Lapointe, too, was anxious to go, but said I thought he should stay here."

At that same meeting Mackenzie King "got the Firefighting Corps under way and arrangements made to let Britain have considerable portion of our Catalinas, these matters having been taken up by Morrison and First Sea Lord Pound with me before coming away. Colleagues seemed perfectly satisfied and indeed delighted with the entire proceedings while abroad."

Mackenzie King spoke of his visit to Britain to a joint meeting of the Men's and Women's Canadian Clubs of Ottawa on September 17. He felt this was "a more important speech than that delivered at the Mansion House. Also that it was profounder in its truth and message. What pleased me most about it was that I had succeeded at last in expressing in a way and at a time which could not but attract attention, two or three things that I have felt most deeply, but have never been able to bring before the public or Parliament in a manner which I hoped might be possible. One was the parallel of nationality to industry as respects the supremacy of humanity; the other, the parallel between the issue in the civil war, and the same issue on a world scale today. I really believe this latter thought is, and should prove, as far reaching in bringing up the real significance of the present conflict as anything that has been said concerning it. Also it gives me immense satisfaction to be able, at the end of two years, to show how clearly, at the commencement of the war, I had seen the issue and the probable trend of events. I think the address altogether ought to help to give our people the feeling of fresh confidence in my leadership. I am sure the speech will be greatly appreciated in Britain, and I think it will not be unwelcomed, certainly by the President and the administration, and by most others in the United States."

Senator Raoul Dandurand had come from Montreal to be present at the dinner. Mackenzie King observed that Dandurand "very shrewdly remarked that he thought I was very wise in following up, on this side, the appeal I had made on the other to the U.S. I have said what I believe quite fearlessly and in the belief that the truth of itself easily defends itself, and should be spoken without fear at any time in any place. Curiously enough, I feel about the speech as I have done about the little addition to the Farm. That it is something which has been built up by others. That my prayer to be a medium of expressing the will of God on earth has been answered, and that an inspiration has come to me from those who have gone but continue to work from the Beyond in the saving of men and nations. I feel more and more the truth of the conflict being one between the pagan and the Christian order of things."

The next day, September 18, Mackenzie King called at the American Legation to give the Minister, Pierrepont Moffat, who was leaving for Washington that day, an account of his visit to Britain. Mackenzie King asked Moffat "to tell the President that I found Churchill and other Ministers quite convinced that Britain could not win the war unless the U.S. actively intervened. That Churchill himself had said he would rather lose several months of supplies and have that declaration of war than have the additional supplies without any definite word as to the U.S. coming in. I said that Churchill took this view believing that once in the fight, the U.S. would organize itself as a nation at war, and would vastly increase their supplies. I said that I, myself, had not been too sure that an immediate declaration would be the best thing, largely because I feared Japan might then enter the war, and the U.S. and Britain might find they had too much on their hands. . . . I said I believe that were Russia to go down, particularly in any total way, it would not be long before Japan would come into the conflict. . . .

"Moffat asked me just what I meant by speaking of the U.S. going into the war, whether I meant coming in, in all directions at once, or proceeding as the U.S. was now doing, in undertaking the protection of convoys, etc. I said I did not mean actual physical intervention, but rather something in the nature of a declaration on the President's part, making clear that Germany could not win, and that the U.S. would see that they did not win. That I thought a word of this kind would have its effect in Germany, before things got to the point where life was so wasted that the position of all would become precarious. I stressed with Moffat the feeling one had in Britain, of how small the U.K. was, and how difficult, with Germany's might what it is and will continue to be, for the people to survive the kind of attack which could be made simultaneously in the air, at sea, and on land.

"Moffat spoke very nicely of my speech last night, wholly approvingly, as he had after the dinner itself. I see by the press that he has said publicly that the U.S. will agree with all that I said about deepening interdependence. I think that is the note to make increasingly clear."

CHAPTER ELEVEN

Meighen, Lapointe, St. Laurent

THE FIRST MONTH after Mackenzie King's return from Britain in September was a relatively quiet one. Then, at the beginning of October, he was drawn into the final stages of the discussion on the establishment of the Price Ceiling.

Prices and wages had both begun to rise in 1941 and, with the approach of full employment, there had been growing labour unrest and several strikes of which the one at Arvida had been the most serious. At the outset of the war, the Wartime Prices and Trade Board had been established under the Minister of Labour, to control civilian supplies and prevent profiteering, but without any thought of maintaining a rigid stability of prices. At a later stage, various expedients had been tried to discourage labour unrest by encouraging union recognition and collective bargaining on the one hand, and by reducing undue competition for scarce manpower on the other. For this latter purpose a Labour Supply Board had been established on which the main labour organizations were represented, but it was not very effective.

On August 13, before Mackenzie King's departure for London, there had been some discussion in the Cabinet about the need for more effective control of prices. It was agreed that the Department of Labour was not equipped for this task and no one favoured a new department. "Ilsley himself proposed, as the best solution, the transfer of price fixing, control board, to his department on the score that Finance would be held responsible in the end for inflation." Both Howe and McLarty, the Minister of Labour, were favourable, and Ilsley accordingly became the Minister responsible.

The scheme for a rigid price ceiling was subsequently devised and first considered by the Cabinet on October 3. Mackenzie King had Graham Towers of the Bank of Canada, W. C. Clark of Finance, Hector McKinnon, Chairman of the Wartime Prices and Trade Board, and Norman Robertson sit with the Cabinet during part of the discussion and "present their different points of view. I, myself, took strong issue with the attempt to do everything at once, which is the view that Towers and Clark so strongly hold. They seem to think that we can, at one stroke, legislate to have prices kept where they are and wages, the same. I pointed out that an effort of the kind would probably result in such an upheaval of different classes, groups, that the Government would find itself in an intolerable position. That we would all be made ridiculous in the end by trying to do by Order-in-Council something that the economic forces of the world would defy with impunity. I think I have had some influence in persuading the group and my colleagues in the Cabinet as well, to leave sufficient leeway to enable us to proceed by steps and degrees and to leave sufficient doorways open for necessary revisions as to save the situation."

On October 10, there was another discussion by the Cabinet of "a brief on the subject," after which the same officials were called in with, in addition, Bryce Stewart, Deputy Minister of Labour. Mackenzie King noted that "Bryce Stewart gave a very full explanation of the labour side. All the Cabinet seemed favourable and I held out to the end." When he realized how his colleagues felt, Mackenzie King "indicated how I thought approach should be made as to announcement of policy, making clear it was not intended as a cure-all; that the problem was a most difficult one to deal with. Later appealing to the public to co-operate with the Government to save an appalling situation that might develop, stressing influence of foreign conditions, making very difficult any real solution, and leaving the way open for making clear the methods that would have to be adopted to effect adjustments which time and experience would occasion. Making clear it was only a trial of what seemed the best thing to do." He then arranged to have a "statement for the press prepared . . . setting forth policy." Hector McKinnon was most anxious that the Government, not the Prices Board, should announce the policy and Mackenzie King "agreed with him." He felt McKinnon "has the best political and practical sense of those in the permanent field."

Mackenzie King spent most of the morning of October 14 studying the proposed statement. Much of the discussion at the Cabinet meeting later that day related to methods of fixing agricultural prices which he found "very tedious." He himself at this meeting "strongly advocated" making Donald Gordon, the Deputy Governor of the Bank of Canada, a member of the Wartime Prices and Trade Board.

The next morning (October 15) Mackenzie King met with Tom Moore of the Trades and Labour Congress, A. R. Mosher of the Canadian Congress of Labour, J. B. Ward of the Railway Brotherhoods, and Alfred Charpentier of the Catholic Syndicates "to tell them of what the Government is considering with respect to control of prices and stabilization of wages." He was told that at the recent congresses of all these organizations their members "had expressed an entire lack of confidence in the Government in the matter of its labour policies. They could not understand why we had not enforced our own policies, particularly in the case of the Canadian National Railway employees, and with respect to the enforcement of collective bargaining.

"I had to confess that, as Prime Minister, . . . I shared their impatience about the lack of readiness in carrying out the Government's policies, but hoped that the step we were proposing to take in constituting a National War Labour Board and five regional War Labour Boards might help to overcome that failure." These War Labour Boards were to enforce the policy of wage stabilization which was to go hand in hand with the Price Ceiling. Mackenzie King stressed on this occasion the dangers of inflation and of a collapse in the post-war period if action was not taken to forestall it.

At the outset he found Mosher and Moore "inclined to be combative. Later Moore expressed the willingness of his organization to co-operate in any way; that the men could be brought to co-operate. Charpentier was particularly friendly in that respect. Ward also said his people were anxious to help. Moore was more sceptical as to whether labour could be brought to submit to anything which savoured of compulsory arbitration, but believed if wages could still be obtained by collective bargaining, a general scheme might be worked out." When they complained about being consulted only at the last minute, Mackenzie King explained that it was only in the past few days the new policy had been discussed by the Cabinet and only in the last day or two that it "had been reduced to writing," and that he himself had insisted the labour leaders be consulted before "anyone else." When they objected to the postponement of a meeting of the Labour Supply Board, which had been called for the next day, Mackenzie King agreed the meeting should be held. He felt "the discussion seemed to have effected a measure of confidence and the meeting broke up in a fairly satisfactory way." He later told his colleagues at the Cabinet he "would not become a party to a general policy until all our cards were on the table, and it was definitely understood what the Government's position towards labour would be hereafter. It was folly to attempt any step of the magnitude proposed without having Labour's co-operation."

On October 16, Mackenzie King read to the Cabinet "a statement prepared along the lines I had indicated on our price and wages control policy. Pickersgill had been revising it with [Grant] Dexter [of the Winnipeg *Free Press*]. The Cabinet all thought it was very good. Both

Power and Howe thought I should give it in the form of a broadcast. It was finally decided I would do so on Saturday night. I told the Cabinet very frankly I would sign no Orders-in-Council regarding price or wage control without a distinct understanding that we would see that their provisions were carried out; that I felt . . . we had antagonized labour instead of holding them with the Government as they should be." He "was relieved to hear McLarty say that the Labour Supply Board was getting along fairly well with our proposals. The day was certainly saved by meeting the labour men the day before yesterday." He observed that he did "not know where we would have been if I had not taken in hand the direction of the price control matter, particularly in seeing that it was properly launched."

The Price Ceiling broadcast, which was one of the most effective Mackenzie King ever made, was delivered on the evening of Saturday, October 18. He did not realize immediately how successful it had been. "My voice," he noted, "sounded to me quite tired, but I am told sounded all right over the radio. I got along without any difficulty and apparently gave the right sort of intimate conversational tone to what was said. The radio people thought the speech went very well."

At Ralston's suggestion, Mackenzie King took a hand, on November 7, in securing Donald Gordon as Chairman of the Prices Board, a choice he had been the first to suggest. The establishment of the Price Ceiling was acclaimed by the public, and for the next year price control and wage stabilization were among the least of Mackenzie King's worries.

His great concerns for the rest of 1941 were the weakness of the representation in the Government from Quebec caused by the illness and death of Lapointe and Cardin's continuing ill health, and the threat of another agitation for conscription from a revived Conservative Opposition under new leadership.

R. B. Hanson had attempted to strengthen his own position as Conservative leader by a visit to Britain. On August 11, before Mackenzie King's own intention to go overseas was made public, he had received a letter from Hanson saying "that he would like to go to England in a bomber with two or three of his colleagues. The letter was written with a view to political design and, instead of his trip being intended as helpful, it is obviously meant to be as embarrassing as possible. It gives as a reason for his wanting to go that, as Leader of the Opposition, he has not been able to get information about the war, etc. I felt immediately like saying that I had offered him a position in the War Cabinet, also in weekly conferences, but he had refused both. . . . On second thought, however, I decided to restrict my reply to a word of appreciation of his going to London and offering all facilities possible. Evidently, he has been under the impression that I would not be going. I should not be at all surprised if he announces his own intentions before mine are known, particularly when I write him of what I am planning for the end of the week." When he was at Chequers on August 23, Mackenzie King had told Churchill of Hanson's proposed visit and Churchill had asked: "You would like me to show him every courtesy, to see all that he can? I said: 'Yes, by all means.' He said he would do that."

Hanson actually arrived in Britain after Mackenzie King's return home. Mackenzie King learned, on September 13, "that Hanson had said, on arrival in England, that he had come over as he was unable to get any information from me. Comparing this with the letter written by him, one sees clearly what the plan of political campaign of the Tories is. He will find he will get little thanks in Britain for playing a political game while there." He was annoyed to receive, on September 27, a cable from Hanson "virtually demanding passage back by Clipper. Have had word sent authorizing money to be advanced. Payment to be settled later. I had never assumed Hanson was doing more than asking the good offices of the Government toward having Ferry Company accommodate himself and others, if possible. Characteristically Tory attitude to regard a certain matter as a right, though whole purpose of visit is to condemn government, and not to co-operate."

On the other hand he learned with satisfaction on October 15 that Churchill told Hanson "he and I saw eye to eye in practically everything and that I was one of his oldest and closest friends. He gave Hanson no quarter in the matter of an attack. Apparently, Hanson met with similar rebukes from other Ministers. . . . Hanson appears to have raised a rumpus in London about getting the fares for himself and his colleagues paid to Canada, and got out of paying anything. Apparently, the impression he left in England was none too good in Government circles."

Malcolm MacDonald returned from England the next day (October 16) and told Mackenzie King he had heard "the utmost satisfaction expressed with what I had said and done; that Churchill and all the Ministers were immensely pleased with my speech at the Mansion House." MacDonald also told him "a good deal about Hanson's visit. That Hanson had started in by telling each of them in turn that he and his party had come because they could not get any information from me in Canada. He started to question the Ministers with a view to seeing whether he could not find out something that would reflect on the Government. . . . Churchill had told Hanson and his delegation quite frankly that he saw no need for conscription in Canada. He said to Malcolm: I have been treating your Opposition handsomely, meaning by that that he had them all to Chequers, but indicating he had seen through their motives and had given them nothing other than praise for what Canada was doing."

The adjourned session of Parliament was being resumed on November 3, and Mackenzie King saw Hanson on October 31, to discuss the programme. He thought Hanson looked "very ill. Says to me he was very weak. He might make a speech of an hour on Monday, that was all he wanted to do this session. Doubted if he would do well in speaking. Says the trip in the bomber was quite a tax, particularly coming back, it got cold. Says he has promised his wife never to leave her again. That they mean much to each other. I could hold him down to nothing excepting rambling talk about himself. Said he had not been able to discuss with his colleagues on the bomber what joint report they should make. They had all shot off immediately. Does not care if session does not last beyond a day or two." Hanson made some reference to conscription and Mackenzie King told him it was not advisable to raise the issue at all. "It was playing Hitler's game to divide the country. Our real effort should be along lines of increased production. He said he wanted to tell me that, while in England, he had not opposed the Government, or been critical of us. I might have told him he was a liar, but did not. I really felt as I talked with him that he might not last long."

There was a proposal at this time to open a Canadian Information Office in New York. Mackenzie King had discussed it, on October 9, with Leighton McCarthy, the Canadian Minister to the United States, who opposed the idea and pointed out that within the past few days different editorials had appeared in the *Globe and Mail,* the Montreal *Gazette,* the *Financial Post* and *Maclean's,* "all indicative of a fresh conspiracy." McCarthy added, with Mackenzie King's agreement, "that these papers represent the interests that have been after me from the start, and are the ones pressing for conscription. He thinks they want to begin to get things inserted in the American papers, to be quoted in Canadian papers, to force our hand. I believe he is right. He thinks, too, that the same crowd have in mind getting me out. . . . Once the press fraternity get a hold on things they want to become the Government. McCarthy said he would want to resign his position as Minister rather than take responsibility for the kind of things that might happen through a Canadian bureau in New York." The proposal was dropped at the time.

A delegation from the Canadian Legion had seen the Government on October 21, "to press for total war effort. Really, the aim was one to force the conscription issue. I found it a little difficult to restrain myself from speaking out pretty firmly, as I felt that the veterans' delegation at this time and the presentation of their case as made was, in the main, a matter of politics. . . . When the statement was presented, I simply said that the people and their representatives in Parliament were the ones to decide matters of this kind and I would see they were given that opportunity. I was asked would I accept the views of Parliament. I said I would decide, too, what course might be necessary with respect to giving the people a chance themselves to pronounce on conscription after I saw what Parliament would do. The delegation looked thoroughly squashed, very crestfallen—the last thing they wanted is any voice of the people on this matter, though they professed to represent them."

On the question of leadership, Mackenzie King told the delegation "quite frankly that my conception of leadership was to be saying to those who placed one in that position that I would never yield, come what may, to any force, regardless of what it was—press, veterans, or anything else, which tried to have me act independently of the people from whom I had derived my power and whose confidence I prized more than all else. In the course of the discussion, it became apparent that to some extent we had been talking at cross purposes. The veterans, in urging total war effort, stated that their main concern . . . was for selective conscription within Canada itself; that the conscription for men to serve in the army overseas was only a small part. I told them that I was wholeheartedly for selective conscription in Canada and prepared to press it."

Mackenzie King had a bad cold that day which got steadily worse and he "felt more depressed" at the meeting of the Cabinet "than any I have attended for a long time. With Lapointe and Ralston absent [the former through illness, the latter on a trip overseas], I feel I have, excepting Howe, whose judgment on labour matters is poor, really no one to lean on. . . . The cold, fatigue and exhaustion caused me to feel very much like dropping my position altogether. There is so much continual criticism of the Government in the press, so much perversion of the truth, no real help or appreciation of effort, that one is forced to wonder how long one can hold on." The next day (October 22), he reflected that "this depression always comes on me at the approach of a session or the resumption of Parliament after adjournment. I suppose it is, in part, feeling that one is carrying too much oneself, a feeling tremendously intensified by breakdown of colleagues like Cardin, Lapointe. Absence of men like Ralston and the absence of other strong men at a time when all the vision that is possible is required by the Government."

This state of depression had lasted all through October and was not relieved by a visit Mackenzie King paid to President and Mrs. Roosevelt at Hyde Park on November 1 and 2. When he left Hyde Park for Ottawa, he was "feeling on the whole a little rested for the change of yesterday and today, but nevertheless, very exhausted. Not fair to anyone to be a guest of another in such a condition of fatigue. I was glad, however, that I had availed myself of the President's invitation and that I had the two days with their profitable talks, and talks that might have been made much more so had I been in better shape." This was the least interesting and important of his visits to Roosevelt.

He returned to Ottawa on Monday morning, November 3. Parliament met in the afternoon but adjourned after brief formalities and a review of the international situation by the Prime Minister. It was decided to have a debate on the war effort with statements by the Ministers. But Mackenzie King's main worry was a serious division in the country on the conscription question. At the Liberal caucus on November 5, he "drifted almost unconsciously and precipitately into the question of conscription, and came out very strongly with the statement that no leader had a right to betray the representatives whose support was the basis of his strength, nor had representatives the right to betray the people who had returned them to Parliament. That as regards conscription, it had been clearly stated by all parties in the war election that it would not be employed for overseas service. I said I would never go back on the pledge given the people in that particular. That if I saw the representatives of Parliament were themselves prepared to do that, I would consider whether, before allowing the policy to be changed, I would not have to ask the Governor-General for a General Election, if a plebiscite on the issue did not seem to serve the purpose." He added that he "told them if any of them had a contrary view, I wanted them to speak out. Now was the time to speak on these matters, and maintain the strictest confidence as to what took place within caucus. There was not a single voice raised in objection to anything I said."

He felt he was "very wise in insisting on a caucus at once, and getting our members' minds wholly clear as to my position and that of the party on conscription. There were elements in our own ranks, and even in the Government, that would be prepared to force conscription for overseas, but they will see now that it is hopeless to get the M.P.'s to support a step of the kind, and will be equally afraid to press the matter unduly, lest I bring it squarely before the people which is the last thing any of them want. They will take to cover, I think under the label of compulsory selective national service which, of course, is a principle not only embodied but practically applied under the National Mobilization Act."

Mackenzie King felt that, in his speech in the House that afternoon (November 5), Ralston, who was just back from overseas, "did exceedingly well, having very little time to prepare and also being careful not to go too far in any statement he made. I can see that the Defence Departments intend to make all the use they can of my words re utmost effort, etc., to bring it to bear on the Army's part in the war. Ralston, however, was careful to indicate that a balanced effort was essential. He fortunately stated that there had not, thus far, been time to consider the manpower question in the light of his visit overseas, and this will probably let us get by discussion of that matter until the third Session."

The next day (November 6) Mackenzie King was very anxious about what might be "the possible outcome of the meeting which the Tory party leaders are having in Ottawa tomorrow. Very strong pressure is being put on Meighen to come in to the House of Commons. ... I naturally feel a deep concern, chiefly because my own health and strength is not what it was years ago. I am getting past the time when I can fight in public with a man of Meighen's type who is sarcastic, vitriolic and the meanest type of politician. Even Bennett was better than Meighen as an opponent. Not quite so contemptuous. Bracken's name had been mentioned as a leader. I could wish nothing better, though I would be amazed if Bracken has entertained for a second any offer of leadership from the Tory party. His name undoubtedly has been shoved forward to bring the National Government idea to the fore, which makes clear the Tories are prepared to work under a National Government leader. Hanson, of course, has become wholly impossible. The party organs have denounced him very strongly. ... It may be that with Hanson's health what it is, his determination to quit the leadership, an effort will be made tomorrow to have Meighen take on at once as an assistant to Hanson, pending a choice of the party of a leader at a convention to be fixed at some later time. ...

"Perhaps I should not be too concerned as it is clear the strength of myself and the Liberal party is the thing which is confounding the Tories more than all else. Still to have as leaders of the Opposition in the House of Commons, types of Conservatives I have had to contend with has been a real cross all along the way of my political life. No one will ever know how hard it has been to bear. That and the contemptuous attitude of the Tory press, all of which I have borne pretty much in silence."

Mackenzie King continued to worry about the prospect of having Meighen in the House of Commons again. He heard that at the Conservative meeting on November 7 "it did not take long to dispel any thought of Bracken having to do with their crowd. What appears to have taken place is that it was Meighen's own idea to have Bracken come in as leader, and that he himself would enter the House of Commons at Bracken's side. Bracken refusing to have anything to do with the business, they apparently then began to look around for another nominal head. . . . I have not heard the outcome of today's proceedings, but the evening papers would indicate that men who have come from outside Ottawa have been unwilling to let the little group here dictate the policy of the party as a whole. Apparently, the boost for Meighen is in part to keep Drew out, but there are Western representatives who are for MacPherson" (M. A. MacPherson of Regina, a former Attorney-General of Saskatchewan). That day, George McCullagh, the publisher of the Toronto *Globe and Mail*, told one of the Prime Minister's secretaries, according to Mackenzie King's diary, "that he had come down to support Meighen in order to force the conscription issue, as he was all for conscription. After getting here, he found that the men who were backing Meighen were doing so because of the Government's Price Control policy; that up to the time of my broadcast they had been indifferent about war matters, but after the broadcast felt there was a danger of their way of life being changed and some of their profits limited. They had been prepared to let things run along as they were for the war, but, by old business methods, become millionaires thereafter. Now they were afraid that if they did not get control of government, or of government policy, power would pass out of their hands. McCullagh said he felt rather ashamed of himself trying to support Meighen on grounds of the kind." Mackenzie King told his secretary to "make a note of the conversation as being very significant."

He also recorded his belief that "it would be helping to break up our Dominion to have Meighen become leader of any party or the controller of its policies. With the situation what it is in Canada today, with not a single Conservative in the representation of the Province of Quebec in Parliament, nor, indeed, of any party other than the Liberal party, there would be a solid province—a third of Canada—*en bloc* against the rest of the Dominion, if the other portions tried to force the conscription issue at this time, and make Meighen leader in Dominion affairs. . . . Certainly, the Tory party is at a low ebb today, and deservedly so, with its arrogance, contemptible methods of carrying on political warfare."

November 8 was "one of the most trying days" of Mackenzie King's life, he wrote. "This morning was faced with the probability of having Meighen as principal opponent again in the House of Commons. He . . . will detract from the Government's record, and myself in particular. Every face will be directed against myself, to get me out of the leadership of Parliament and to get a National Government formed. Meighen will be for railway amalgamation, have the C.P.R. and other big interests back of him and Imperialistic jingoes in Canada and Britain alike. He will stop at nothing in seeking to bring conscription into force, will misrepresent willfully, and will have all Canada 'by the ears' in short time. With Quebec hating him, he will hate in return, be arrogant with labour and will seek to stir up the farmers. I can see where all that Lapointe and I have striven hardest to effect will be undone in some degree. But life day by day will be made intolerable by his attacks, misrepresentations and the like."

During the day, Mackenzie King was told that Hanson insisted on resigning the leadership because of ill health and that a majority of the Conservative Executive wanted Meighen to take the leadership at once. He wrote that this word made him "sick at heart. I felt I wanted to give up public life, and avoid the break in my health which I feared might come. The strain is terrible—mental fatigue and physical combined, but depression as well, and feeling of being left alone, old colleagues gone or going, no one to help, and alone at Laurier House . . . no one to talk with." Later in the day Mackenzie King was told Meighen had left for Toronto "saying he would not accept because two or three whose support he needed were against him. . . . When I heard he had gone and that a committee were meeting to see 'where do we go from here' I felt an immense load off my mind."

Still later in the afternoon he got word that "one by one the objectors were weakening and that on Monday three of the committee were going to Toronto to offer him [Meighen] the nomination. The radio tonight said it would be offered to him *unanimously*. There seemed a feeling the Parliamentary party didn't want Drew." During the day Mackenzie King also got word that Lapointe was seriously ill in hospital and he wrote: " with Lapointe gone I have *no one* with whom to counsel as I need to at this time."

The worst of this depression passed and, at the Cabinet meeting on November 10, Mackenzie King spoke "of the action of the Conservatives in choosing Meighen as leader." He told his colleagues his first thought had been that Meighen's entry into Parliament should not be facilitated unless the Conservatives first had a convention to choose him as leader. "But, on second thought, I had concluded that action of the kind would be mistaken; that the better line to take was that the Conservative party's affairs were their own; that, if Hanson resigned, and Meighen was chosen leader to replace him, the Government should not impede his coming into the Commons; that I had to think always of this being a time of war. While I saw Meighen's entry significant of strife, it was not for me to begin the strife by taking any step which could be construed as a desire to maintain government by party lines to the point of keeping out of the Commons the leader of another party, but rather take the line of welcoming a strong Opposition." He noted that "Council agreed with this view. I then pointed out that it was going to be a great burden to me to have to sit opposite Meighen; that I had passed the time when I could stand too much in the way of contention; that, with Lapointe dropping out, I would feel very much alone, as he and I had counselled together for many years . . . that I could only carry on to a certain point; that I would do my best, but had to recognize that, while physically strong, I became mentally very fatigued. They must recognize what that would mean."

On November 12 Mackenzie King "was cheered to receive a letter from the White House in which the President said that 'it is a grand and glorious thing for Canada and the United States to have the team of Mackenzie and Roosevelt at the helm in days like these. Probably both nations could get along without us but I think we may be pardoned for our thoughts, especially in view of the fact that our association so far has brought some proven benefits to both nations.' " "This letter," Mackenzie King wrote, "was an answer to prayer. It certainly gave me reason to feel that I should hold on at all costs."

That afternoon (November 12), he "went into the House for a short time before 6. While sitting there was shown the [Ottawa] *Evening Journal* with an article which stated I had told caucus that I had discussed conscription with Churchill, and he had expressed agreement with my views, etc. I decided this was moment to strike, so I rose at once on a question of privilege. Read the paragraphs. Said I was speaking in the presence of those who were at caucus and denied absolutely that I had ever mentioned Churchill's name in connection with conscription at any caucus at any time, which, of course, is true.

I pointed out that the article had been written to embarrass the Government in its war effort. An apology was due from the British United Press for a communication of the kind in not having spoken first to the Prime Minister about it. I then went on to make clear there would be no conscription for overseas service without the people having a say in the first instance. I made it clear I was for compulsory selective national service so far as the war effort in Canada was concerned, but that as regards conscription for overseas service, that had been settled by the people at the last election which was held during the time of the war.

"I will bet anything that we will find the Tories creeping away from conscription for overseas service, pressing harder than ever for compulsion in our selective service. The one thing they will not wish is a general election or a plebiscite; at this moment, while Meighen is deciding what he is going to do, they will see in it a threat to bring a general election, in all probability before the House re-assembles, on the conscription issue. That of itself will make Meighen think twice. I am convinced that I was directed as to the moment to speak and inspired to say what I did at that time."

The concluding paragraphs of the statement as made in the House read: "I want it to be distinctly understood that so far as the principle of compulsory selective national service is concerned for Canada, in Canada, I stand for that principle. I have never taken any other stand. It is the position that I have held all along. It has been applied in connection with military training and applied in a number of other directions I might mention. How much further it will be applied the House will learn as the Government takes its decisions on that matter.

"But so far as conscription for service overseas is concerned in the armed forces of Canada, that question was submitted to the people of Canada at the last general election, an election which was held in wartime, and in which the leaders of all political parties made their statements to the electorate, and the people of Canada decided against conscription for overseas service. So far as I am concerned, without any consultation of the people on that subject, I do not intend to take the responsibility of supporting any policy of conscription for service overseas."

That evening Mackenzie King noted that he thought "statement of afternoon had real effect. Told Power I thought it would give Meighen cause for reflection. Also his party, where there was intimation of appeal to the people. I had a feeling myself that I wished to register the party's position in Parliament, as I had in the caucus, to prevent wavering on the part of our men and also to make clear our position with respect to compulsory selective national service before anything was said by the Tory party which would have it appear that we were following in their wake in that particular. I felt immensely relieved all evening and in shape for additional work having spoken out as I had. Got to bed before the news broadcast, the first line of which was that Meighen had today accepted the leadership of the Conservative party, as I felt he was sure to do. The announcement caused me less concern in view of the statement made today."

The next morning (November 13) Mackenzie King read in the morning paper "a long manifesto by Meighen, showing with what care he has been proceeding and how the whole business is a carefully planned attack on the Government and myself to get a National Government formed for the issue of conscription, and use the war hysteria to further the ends of financial interests. After breakfast, I made a memo of the arguments against Meighen's manifesto. Debated whether I should speak of the matter before the Houses rises [the session was to adjourn very shortly] or wait for the period in between, or the new [session of] Parliament. I will be governed by circumstance."

At the Cabinet meeting, Mackenzie King "drew attention to Meighen's statement of the morning, and then pointed out that my position now is the same as Sir Wilfrid's was in 1917: that Meighen was no longer for co-operation with Government policy, but opposition to Government policy—opposition first for conscription, National Government, and against our policies generally. It meant the financial forces and the press would rise against us. I wanted to make clear my own position, so that my colleagues would not be embarrassed in any way. I had been careful in my statement yesterday to speak of myself personally, as to continuing at the head of the Government, in the event of the party deciding to support conscription for overseas, so that they would not be embarrassed in choosing another leader at any time. I said I did not want to stay on a moment longer than was desired by the majority of the party."

When one of his colleagues objected that he should not think of retiring, Mackenzie King replied "that I was not talking of retiring— nothing could be further from my thought than that; that I had too much of the spirit of fight in me ever to give up in a contest with the Tories. I thought their policies were wrong and I was prepared to fight for the people to the end. All that I was saying was that my endurance in the matter of fight was necessarily limited, and that they must be prepared to meet the situation should anything occur to me. . . . That while I looked well physically and was well physically, there was this mental and nervous strain which was being increased many fold by the position which I am now in with a man of Meighen's type opposite to me and with the great movement for conscription sweeping the country.... I then said I wanted a caucus for tomorrow, to have the men understand the general position before leaving for their homes."

Following a suggestion that they should fight the conscription issue on the ground that conscription was unnecessary, Mackenzie King agreed "about taking our stand on the merit of the situation, but the question of an election was a matter which should be kept in the background. It was necessary to put the fear of the Lord into the Tories, who did not want to face the people and who knew that the people generally were against conscription for overseas; also, to keep some of our people in line; that so long as our own people stay firm, we could meet any situation.... I did not agree as to attempting any settlement of the conscription question at this session.... It was better it should remain over until the whole matter was carefully weighed."

The Liberal caucus held on November 14 Mackenzie King considered one of the most important of his career. He opened the proceedings "by telling the Members I had brought them together to discuss the situation which had arisen with Meighen's appointment to the leadership of the Conservative party . . . that the whole situation had changed with the manifesto which Meighen has issued, which meant that co-operation with the Government's war effort was no longer the attitude of the Conservative party, but there was now a direct challenge . . . to substitute another Government for the present one . . . that the issue was . . . conscription for overseas service, substitution of National Government, and that both were being used to secure control of the Government by the financial interests which today, for the most part, controlled the press.

"As to our policy, I stated . . . that compulsory selective service is a part of the statutory law—National Resources Mobilization Act, and that it was the Government's intention to extend its application.... The only restriction on total war effort in every respect was that of conscription for overseas service, and that the reason we were opposed to conscription was that, all circumstances considered, it would be playing Hitler's game of creating disunion and would be destroying our total war effort. Historic and other considerations as well as the voice of the people at the elections had to be taken into account. I made clear that the battle would be fought on the floor of the House by the people's representatives. That there would be no question of a general election or a plebiscite, at least, until after Parliament had fully debated the whole question on its merits. . . .

"I then spoke of the situation being exactly 1917 over again. We were confronted by the same leader, being opposed by the same forces. The issue, National Government and conscription—the same motives behind; control of financial interests, the same. The effort would be to destroy me as it had been to destroy Sir Wilfrid. The only difference was that Sir Wilfrid unhappily had been in the minority in race and religion and was handicapped to that extent; that I had a following infinitely larger than the one he had. I pointed out that the effect of introducing conscription in the last war had been to create a wound in the side of Canada which was not yet healed. That we did not want a repetition of this."

Mackenzie King also said "that one advantage I saw in Meighen coming in and directly opposing the Government was that it would give all members of the House a chance to fight in the open for our policies. That I had had to keep quiet. Took everything that was said with a smile as a means of keeping co-operation between all parties in the House, that being the alleged policy of the Tories. That if I started to fight myself, I would be immediately accused of playing party politics, and destroying Canada's war effort by controversy. However, the situation was now changed, and had been changed deliberately by the [Conservative] party to make the session a fighting one, and the members would now be free to express their own views, to enter fully into debate."

After Mackenzie King spoke there was a general discussion. "All, without exception, were agreed that compulsory selective service in Canada was all that was necessary. . . . All seemed to recognize clearly that the main purpose of the Tories was to get rid of myself, and were correspondingly strong in their statements of entire confidence and determination to see that that result was not achieved." In concluding the caucus, Mackenzie King pointed out that "the only thing that could destroy the Liberal party was itself, because a house divided against itself falls. How I had seen Sir Wilfrid's colleagues, one by one, leave him to join forces opposed to him. . . . I wanted them to realize that that was the kind of thing they, themselves, would be up against, and that I had no illusion as to what might take place under emotional stress at a time of war.

"I took care to mention that Meighen had a son in the army, and that factor had to be recognized as perhaps having a bearing upon his actions. I pointed out there were several of my own colleagues and several of the Members who were similarly situated and took a different view as to how Canada could render her best contribution. I mentioned that while Churchill was being cited right and left, no one had apparently thought of quoting from what Churchill himself had said at the Mansion House as to the Canadian national unity under my leadership."

Mackenzie King could not "recall a caucus where I saw the party more expressive of their feelings toward myself and determination to fight for their leader. I saw several of our men, strong men, too filled with emotion to express their feelings. One after the other came up to say it was the best caucus we had had—that the last two caucuses were the best of the party."

Lapointe had not attended the session at all and, all through November, Mackenzie King was greatly concerned about his serious illness. On November 4, he had received a letter from Lapointe "telling me of his condition, and mentioning that in all probability, he will not be able to be present for balance of session. Will be going into the hospital. I 'phoned him and told him to have no concern, that we would manage all right. Possibility of losing him as a desk mate in the House is a grave one indeed." He reflected that "with Cardin really unfit to ever take hold again . . . the fact is that so far as Quebec goes, the whole Province is now without any real federal leadership, and its entire personnel in the Government may have to be changed. Other changes will be essential. The thing now is to get through the remainder of this session, and then tackle the problem of reorganization."

Then on November 8, Mackenzie King had word that Lapointe was seriously ill in hospital in Montreal. He felt virtually certain that he would never be back. On November 11, he "telephoned Lapointe at Notre Dame Hospital tonight. I could tell he was glad to hear from me. Quite evidently has wondered why I have not written or phoned before. His voice seemed to betray a serious condition of health and he himself spoke with considerable alarm about his condition." In his diary Mackenzie King described Lapointe as "the most loyal and truest of colleagues and friends. None has ever been more so to myself. Should he not recover strength enough to help me, at least in Council, I shall be in a desperate plight. The one thing I fear is a sense of obligation too great to carry on longer without a breakdown. This I must avoid at all costs, even that of having someone else take over the Government, though this I shall do only if an extreme situation is reached. So long as my men stand back of me, I will seek not to fail them in any crisis and, most of all, not to fail the country at a time of crisis and war, the worst the world has ever known. I do feel, too, the need for some sympathetic co-operation on the part of at least a few men, even one or two, who have understanding and knowledge of the situation. Crerar comes nearer to having that than anyone else in the Government but he, too, is on in years."

The word Mackenzie King received on November 14 that Lapointe was actually dying was, despite the preparation, nevertheless a shock. He told Lapointe's son-in-law, Roger Ouimet, that he "would get down to Montreal just as soon as possible, and would let him know in the morning what the earliest moment would be. At the time, the House had not concluded its proceedings and I could not say definitely just when I might get away." In his diary he wrote "that no loss could be greater at this time, not to myself only, but to Canada and the British Empire." Ouimet had also spoken about having Hugues Lapointe come home from overseas, and Mackenzie King arranged to have him given leave to return at once.

The House adjourned that day (November 14) until January 1942. The next day Mackenzie King went to Montreal to see Lapointe in the hospital. When he arrived "Ernest sat up to shake hands, and did so again when I was leaving. . . . I tried to take up conversation in a natural way. Spoke of the session. He agreed we had done well in getting through so soon." They discussed bringing Godbout into the Government and Lapointe seemed to feel Godbout should have a provincial election next year and come into the federal House afterwards, but Mackenzie King said "that with Meighen in the House at the next session, we needed an authoritative voice there, and he seemed agreeable to my securing Godbout, if we could."

Mackenzie King urged Lapointe to "take a good long rest," and said he "thought Madame Lapointe was anxious, and it might relieve her anxiety and help him if I could arrange to have Bobby [the familiar name of their son, Hugues] come and see them both. Lapointe said at once: 'on leave for a few days,' and I said, 'yes, I would try to arrange this.' I also said I thought I might make things easier for him, if I indicated a willingness to give up the Presidency of the Council, have him appointed to that position, with a Minister's salary, and free him from the Justice Department and its worries over internment, etc. He thought that might be worth considering."

Mackenzie King also talked to Lapointe about Laurier House and said "he thought the best ultimate disposition was to make it a place for research and studies on international and industrial peace, keeping part of the rooms as they are, not leaving it to any leader. He said that decidedly was the best. I said, in the will, I had made provision for him and a few others to act as trustees to carry on this plan, and had made provision that he and Madame Lapointe were to have Laurier House to live in until the end of their days, if anything happened to me. Lapointe filled up at this, and also, in a kindly way, said: 'you will have many years to live there yet.' I could not but feel, as he spoke, that passing through his mind was the thought that his days might be numbered, and that I had strength for years to come.

"We talked of Meighen, of the contest, of the cleavage his appointment and attitude were creating. He thought it was shameful, but felt Meighen was very vulnerable and would not succeed.

"When I asked about talking over the phone, he said he liked to hear my voice whenever I could telephone. He thanked me warmly for coming down, said it was most kind. I told him I was sorry not to have been able to come earlier, and that I had not written or phoned before, thinking it was best for him to have the entire quiet. I reproached myself, however, for not having done both from day to day. I said I would be in again to see him on Thursday. As I left, he said 'au revoir,' after we had shaken hands, and I called back from the door 'au revoir.' As I look back on the 10 or 15 minutes we had together, I feel that that was quite long enough for his strength. . . . He was very brave. I think, at the back of his mind, is the thought that his condition is very critical. I tried to avoid anything that would make him emotional. For that reason, made but slight reference to what his continued absence might mean to me and all that his life had meant to me."

On his way to the Laurier centenary celebration at St. Lin, on November 19, Mackenzie King went again to see Lapointe in the hospital. Lapointe had just come out of an oxygen tent and was very weak. Mackenzie King told him that "Bobby was on his way out. Was coming by steamer and I could not say just when he would arrive. He then said it was so kind of me to do that for his mother. That she would be glad to see him. I said to him that he might also see him; that he, himself, might revive with the medical aid he was receiving. He said he did not think he could recover. That the doctors had told him of his condition, and that he had had talks with Father Gaudrault who was there with him, and he said, with a little laugh, he is looking after my spiritual condition. I said: 'You need have no concern about the condition of your spirit. No man ever had a purer spirit.' He then said that the thing that made him most sorry to go was to leave us all at the time of so great need, but he added: 'My going will bring the people more than ever to your side.' I said I was quite sure of that, but that I would like him himself to continue at my side."

Lapointe then told Mackenzie King he could see no one to take his place except Godbout at some time in the future. Mackenzie King said he shared "the same view, and would like his permission to tell Godbout that. He said to do so. . . . He then said, would I phone the Cardinal Villeneuve and let him know how ill he, Lapointe, was, and ask him to pray for him. Also to say that he had asked me to thank him for the help which he had given us all in the Government at this time and what that help meant to me. He said that would please him very much. I told him I would do so tonight.

"He then turned to me and said we had been great associates, and reached out his hand toward mine. When he said that, I saw that he was becoming emotionally affected. I said to him no man ever had a truer friend. But for him, I would never have been Prime Minister, nor would I have been able to hold the office, as I had held it through the years. That there was never a deeper love between brothers than existed between us. That we had never had a difference all the years that we had been associated together, in thought and work alike. That I was grateful to him from the bottom of my heart. I then told him that I would be in in the morning to see him before going to St. Lin and would perhaps see him again when I returned. That I would not stay longer tonight. I then leaned over and kissed him on his left cheek. He raised up and kissed me, and we each kissed each other a third time. He then laid his head back on the pillow and closed his eyes and drew his hands up toward his chest. It was a sort of *nunc dimittis*."

The next morning (November 20) Mackenzie King went to see him again. Lapointe "had had a rather restful night and was feeling a little brighter. Asked him if he had much pain. He spoke lightly of the pain. . . . He was as brave as a lion. He said to me: 'I do not know how you keep your head,' and went on to say he thought it was wonderful. I replied that the best one could do was to be as patient as possible. He rose a little on his side and said Pitt was asked one time what qualities go to make a Prime Minister. That some say eloquence, etc., but Pitt said: 'Patience.' I told him that I tried to be patient, and got a little impatient with the press in their misrepresentation of things, and will seek to be increasingly patient. I then said to him recalling our conversation of last night, that I would bring a message from him to the gathering this afternoon and would return after the gathering and tell him about how everything had gone."

Mackenzie King also told Lapointe that he "believed very strongly in personal survival. That I have the strongest reasons for so believing. He then said to me: 'Do you remember the time that our Government was sworn in, and you and I went down to the cemetery to Sir Wilfrid's grave, each of us had a flower, and I turned to you and said: 'Would it not be nice if Sir Wilfrid could see us together here.' He said: 'You turned to me and spoke in a very earnest way, saying: but he does see us. He is right here with us. I am sure of that.' He said: 'You were very emphatic.' "

That day, the centenary of Laurier's birth, Mackenzie King participated in the opening of his birthplace as an historic site. While part of these proceedings was going on, Mackenzie King "had a talk with Godbout in what is the restored kitchen. I told him I wanted him to come to Ottawa, with Lapointe agreeing he was the only one to take his place; that it was very necessary to have him at this time in the light of what we might expect in the coming session. He spoke about his own imperfect knowledge of English. I said that would develop rapidly. That what was needed was someone who could speak with authority of the whole Quebec position. . . . I told him that all of us were agreed upon himself.

"I do not think it is a mere coincidence that this conversation should have taken place in the house in which Sir Wilfrid was born, and on the day which perhaps will be the last in Lapointe's life. It was a handing on of the torch, a continuance of leadership in Quebec and combined leadership with other parts of Canada. French and English, Catholic and Protestant. Later Godbout and I were together when I formally unveiled the tablet on the boulder in front of the house. We were photographed shaking hands over the top of it. It was all impromptu, but the public will see from it the significance of the combined leadership which is likely to follow. Altogether if the whole had been arranged, it could not have been arranged more perfectly."

When he got back to Montreal in the evening Mackenzie King was given a message that Lapointe was probably too weak to see him. He went to the hospital anyway, feeling that "if he was not well, I would not in any way press to go in. On going up to Lapointe's room, I had just a word or two with Madame Lapointe, Odette [Mrs. Roger Ouimet, daughter of Ernest Lapointe] and Hugues' wife. They mentioned that he had been receiving a little oxygen. I said I understood the afternoon had not been a good one, and I would not therefore ask to go to see him but would leave messages with them, just to let him know I had come while he was resting.

"As I was talking, the nurse came into the room and said Mr. Lapointe had heard my voice, and recognized it, and said: 'There is Mr. King' and that he would like to see me. So I went in, just for a few minutes. He was lying on his side, stretched out his hand and shook hands. Thanked me for coming a third time to see him, in so short a time. I told him not to talk, that I had come to tell him about the proceedings at St. Lin. I gave him a short account of how successful they were, but how much we had all missed him. How Fiset [Sir Eugene Fiset, Lieutenant-Governor of Quebec] had read his tribute, and wished me to let him know he was deeply moved by his thought of asking him to read it. Also told him of my having spoken about him, and that I had brought back to him prayers and good wishes of all who were there. I said that he was quite as much in the thought of everyone present as Sir Wilfrid himself whose 100th anniversary of birth we were celebrating.

"I then said to him that I thought I should not keep him as he should rest all he could. He then reached out his hand, and I said to him: 'Ernest, we will see each other again.' He said, with great emphasis, 'there is nothing truer than that.' I then saw that emotion was overtaking him, and I just held his hand quietly till he regained composure; leaned over and kissed him on the cheek. I then quietly withdrew." That was their last meeting, though it was not until the morning of November 26 that Lapointe died.

On receiving word of his death, Mackenzie King gave his personal attention to the funeral arrangements. The funeral was held in Quebec City on Saturday, November 29. Mackenzie King felt that the funeral procession to St. Roch's church was an amazing tribute. "It was snowing as we left the buildings. . . . The streets were lined with people. There were many conveyances with floral tributes. As we went along, and saw the army, navy and air force men lining the streets in places as well as in the march, I turned to Crerar who was just behind me and said: 'Truly Canada has become a nation in the fullest sense. Nothing could have been done in any country in the world more impressively than the arrangements in connection with the funeral.' " Mackenzie King did not think that at "any stage of the visit of the King and Queen to Canada, or at any funeral in Canada heretofore, not excepting Sir Wilfrid's or Sir John Macdonald's, there was a larger number of people gathered in the buildings and on the streets, or more in the way of genuine expression of affection and reverent remembrance. I felt as we walked along how much one owes it to be true to the people."

To the problem of facing Meighen and the campaign for conscription was added the even more urgent problem of finding a successor for Lapointe. Mackenzie King set about the task at once.

In ordinary circumstances, Arthur Cardin would have succeeded to the leadership of the French-speaking Canadians in the federal Cabinet.

He had been fully the equal of Lapointe as a campaigner in Quebec and was probably his superior in many of the political arts. He was a great orator and a highly accomplished parliamentarian. But he was neither known nor appreciated in English-speaking Canada where Lapointe's prestige and influence had been great. And he did not enjoy a close personal relationship with Mackenzie King; indeed, there had been over the years comparatively little sympathy between them. However, these considerations might not have been conclusive if Cardin had been in good health; he was not. On the day of Lapointe's funeral Mackenzie King observed that he was "very frail. Might easily go at any time, though he is fighting bravely." Lapointe was buried in Rivière du Loup, and on the train going there from Quebec, Mackenzie King asked Cardin about a successor for Lapointe. Cardin "agreed as to Godbout, if we could secure him but said almost instantly: 'Why do you not get St. Laurent? He is a distinguished figure; very able lawyer; carries great authority.' " In his diary that day, Mackenzie King wrote: "I feel that he is perhaps the very man most needed, as I must get someone outstanding for the position of Minister of Justice. It is owing to the French, the Bar, the Government, and the country that the Minister of Justice should be a man of exceptional legal attainments. Ralston would be splendid for the office but he is needed where he is."

He tried first to get Godbout. On the day (November 20) he had spoken to Godbout at St. Lin, he found Power was "all for Godbout." Power had told him "he thought I should get a French Minister appointed at once; otherwise they might come to talk of him as the Senior Minister for Quebec; not being French there would be the cry again of the French being ignored." On the return journey from Rivière du Loup to Quebec on November 29 Mackenzie King had "a talk with Godbout about coming into the federal Government at once. Others, including Dandurand, had been talking with him, and he had confirmed himself pretty strongly the point of view which I think he honestly holds that he could be of more service to myself and the Government by keeping the Province itself steady and speaking in its name as the Premier of the Province.

"I pointed out to him some of the features of the situation as it has developed and wherein I felt his presence at Ottawa was imperative with Cardin unable to carry on . . . and Power not a French Canadian. We talked of others. He came back to Brais [Hon. Philippe Brais, then a member of Godbout's Cabinet] as the first choice. When I spoke of St. Laurent, he took quick exception. Later said that perhaps he had spoken too quickly. . . . He admitted he was a man of fine character. He did not think he would be much strength in the Province as a leader in any way. Of course, what I have in mind is the need of some outstanding person as Minister of Justice. I began to feel too tired to attempt to persuade Godbout, in any final way, so told him just to continue to think matters over. I am convinced, however, that he is the only man well enough known, who has sufficient authority to command the respect of his compatriots, and of the country as a whole."

The next morning (November 30), while on the train on the way to Ottawa, Mackenzie King made "a few notes or reasons which came strongly to my mind as to why I should, despite everything else, press Godbout to come to Ottawa and that, immediately." He felt "perfectly sure that if Godbout does not come, the whole situation in Quebec will deteriorate and that will mean a deterioration of Quebec's position in the Dominion, and a deterioration of our war effort." On December 1, he spent a good part of the day writing a letter to Godbout, and then called Godbout on the telephone and read him the letter. Godbout agreed to come to Ottawa on December 4.

Meanwhile, on December 2, Cardinal Villeneuve called on Mackenzie King: "just a friendly call, to express his sympathy in the loss of Lapointe. We had a very nice talk together. He said he thought that our souls were pretty closely in touch with each other, meaning his own, and mine; that we saw things pretty much in the same way." Mackenzie King told the Cardinal "of the difficult position I was in with respect to representation from Quebec, and the need, if the interests of the Province were to be protected, to have strong representation in the federal Government. Told him of my trying Godbout. It was, I think, a bit of a surprise to him but he did not oppose the idea. . . . Altogether it was an extremely friendly and pleasant talk. I felt a real affection for him, and I know he entertains the same toward myself. He showed it quite clearly."

Godbout came to Ottawa on December 4 and talked first with Mackenzie King alone at Laurier House and later at the Prime Minister's office with Dandurand and Cardin present. Mackenzie King observed that: "It was apparent to me as soon as I saw Godbout that he was feeling that he should not leave Quebec. He has two reasons, one that he does not feel his knowledge of English is sufficient for the federal Parliament, and secondly, that leaving Quebec at this time, in all probability, will create a division in his own Cabinet; letting Duplessis get a fresh hold on the Province on non-participation or extreme nationalist lines. He has been talking with some of his friends, and they all clearly have advised him, as I thought they would, very strongly against leaving Quebec. I can appreciate his feelings and reasons. I feel nevertheless that he is missing one of the great chances of his life to render the largest possible service at the most critical of all times in the history of the country and the world, because of the more limited rather than the larger vision. However, I feel I have done what is right in exerting every effort to secure him, and am glad I have on record the situation as I see it.

"The only thing I did not like and which occasioned me disappointment in Godbout was his suggestion made at the beginning of our conversation that I might take Bouchard [Hon. T. D. Bouchard, a senior member of Godbout's Cabinet] into the Government. . . . That one false note changed considerably my own feeling, though I have the highest admiration for Godbout's character and integrity.

"In conversation with Dandurand and Cardin," he noted, "we canvassed different names together. Cardin brought forward that of St. Laurent as the outstanding man from Quebec, likely to be most helpful in the federal arena. They all admitted he would make an exceptionally able Minister of Justice and would be a national figure. Godbout . . . agreed he could command great respect though he might not be a political leader in the Province. Dandurand acquiesced as to his suitability for the position, and there was no other name mentioned which seemed to command equal unanimity. I reminded those present that Power had spoken of St. Laurent as the best man in the Province to run, and that he could easily be elected in Quebec East. They all agreed to this, and that having regard to the fact that the seat had been held by Sir Wilfrid and Lapointe over 40 years together, he would be the most fitting, next to Godbout, of any successor."

That same evening after the Cabinet meeting, Mackenzie King "telephoned Mr. St. Laurent and asked if he could come and see me at Ottawa to discuss one or two important matters. He said he would leave at night and would be here tomorrow at noon." He added: "There is no doubt that St. Laurent's name will command confidence throughout Canada. . . . It is important that Judiciary and the Bar should have every confidence in the one to be appointed. If he accepts, it will relieve me very much of having to choose for that post between colleagues. Ralston would be excellent but to move him from Defence would be misunderstood and interpreted as an effort on my part not to give the support to the army that it should receive."

St. Laurent arrived at Laurier House the next day (December 5). Mackenzie King thanked him for coming so promptly and then said "I assumed he would know what it was I was so anxious to talk to him about. I then said, the question of government was all important at this moment, and the need great for the best men that could be secured. That I was particularly anxious to get someone who would be a worthy successor in Quebec East to Sir Wilfrid Laurier and Lapointe. I believed he was the one to come into the Cabinet as successor to Lapointe as Minister of Justice, and to represent Quebec East."

St. Laurent replied that he was not too sure Quebec East was the kind of constituency where he would make much appeal but added that, "in these times, he realized that every man should be prepared to do what he could to help the country. That he was anxious to do so, but was not sure that he was the right man for the position. There were others who could fill the post." He also referred to his association with "the big interests" and felt "there would be prejudice on that score. He said that perhaps he might say, with due modesty, that his name would command respect among the Bench and Bar in the Provinces, outside of Quebec. I told him I would not except Quebec, that what was needed today was someone in Quebec who would keep the Provinces united, and could speak to the Provinces of the Quebec point of view; interpret the Quebec point of view to the Provinces. That he would be exceptionally good for that purpose. I told him of my talk yesterday with Godbout, of trying to persuade him to come into the Government. . . .

"I told him also of the talks with Dandurand, Cardin, and Godbout together, and of their all agreeing he was the best appointment that could be made from Quebec at this time. He thought Godbout was right in believing he could render a better service in Quebec at this time. It would be a fatal thing if Duplessis ever again got hold of the Government there. Godbout was greatly respected. That he and the Cardinal worked well together, and were both entirely on the right lines in the war. Could do more to influence the people than any others. He said he would like to confer with Godbout; asked particularly about his being favourable to his appointment, and said he would also like to talk with the Cardinal. I told him I felt quite positive the Cardinal would be glad to support him in the office of Minister of Justice. That he was most friendly to me personally and anxious to help. . . .

"Only once in conversation did he refer to desirability of trying to secure someone else than himself. It was clear that what he was contemplating in his mind was a sense of public service. He made it clear that he would not want to stay longer than for the duration of the war, and that his coming would only be for the war service. I said that, of course, could be as he might wish. If he felt he wished to stay on, or return to practice or to take up something else, that could be settled in the light of circumstances. He said that, at 60, to return to practice once it was given up, was not an easy matter, but he did not make any request about a position of any kind."

Mackenzie King noted that, in discussing the winning of the war, St. Laurent indicated "nothing could be done until America moved her armies in. He spoke of the subject of conscription incidentally as likely to arise when the U.S. went into the war; that if they conscripted their men for overseas, it might become necessary to do the same."

On December 9, Mackenzie King "received word over the telephone from St. Laurent that he had seen Godbout and others and that his friends all told him he should accept the appointment, and that he was ready to come to Ottawa at any moment. Stressed the call being what it was in these times and his anxiety to do whatever he could to help. It was arranged he could come on the night train and that I would meet him in the morning."

The next morning before the Cabinet met, Mackenzie King received St. Laurent in his office. He "had just a word or two with him to thank him for having agreed to come into the Ministry. I could see that he was feeling the situation very deeply. He emphasized that other men were giving their lives in the war service, that he could not refuse my request at this time. He did say, too, that he had hoped from what I had said when I told him Churchill thought the war might end suddenly some time next year, that, at most, he would not have to serve more than 2 years. The news today made it look as though it might be several years." Between the invitation to St. Laurent and his acceptance, the Japanese had attacked Pearl Harbor.

When he went into the Cabinet meeting that day Mackenzie King told his colleagues that, after failing with Godbout, he had secured St. Laurent. It gave him "an immense satisfaction to have been able to keep this appointment a secret from the press and the public up to the moment of the appointment itself. I was glad, too, to let the Cabinet see I was now making my own decision on its personnel, and having only such conferences as might obviously seem to be desirable. I have been saved all kinds of pressure by the course taken. I made the appointment over and above all the lower order of political considerations."

St. Laurent was sworn in as Minister of Justice on December 10 and attended his first Cabinet meeting on December 11. Mackenzie King noted that he "took his place in a moment among those present and entered into the debate during the afternoon to good effect. Everyone must have appreciated how invaluable he is as an acquisition to the Government. I think he must have thought Council a little easy going at the outset, but before the afternoon was over, he saw the full significance of the forces that were contending within it. I think it came to him as a good deal of surprise and somewhat painful." The Cabinet into which St. Laurent entered was continuing almost daily to wrestle with the manpower question and the impending crisis over conscription. Neither had been simplified by the entry of the United States into the war.

CHAPTER TWELVE

The United States in the War

MACKENZIE KING had expected war with Japan all through 1941, and his great fear was that Japan and Britain would go to war without the United States being involved. When he returned from Lapointe's funeral on November 30, he was shown a message from Churchill asking for the Canadian opinion "as to movement of British forces in the Far East which might involve hostilities beginning between the British and the Japanese in the first instance." Mackenzie King "took strongly the view that on no account should Britain allow any action to be taken" which might precipitate war with Japan "until the U.S. itself was prepared to begin hostilities. The U.S. have been scrupulously careful to make no commitments. I have said all along that they would be prepared to let Britain begin hostilities but Heaven knows when Congress, if at all, would consent to the U.S. going into the war."

The day being Sunday, he at first decided to put off replying until the next day; but later "both before going to church and afterwards, I felt that the matter was too important to delay till tomorrow and that I should get off a despatch to Churchill tonight so that he would have it in the morning." After sending off the message, he wrote that he believed "there will be war with Japan but I would like to see the United States declare its position unequivocally, or the British stay out regardless of consequences. If they do not, they will be risking the Empire." The following day (December 1) he was "delighted and relieved" to see that the view expressed in a cable Churchill had sent to the President was practically identical with his own. On December 4, Mackenzie King received "a telegram from England which made clear that my message to Churchill had been more than welcome to the Cabinet, and that its contents had been much in mind in the message sent to the President."

All these fears of a war between Japan and Britain in which the United States would not be engaged vanished, of course, on December 7 when Pearl Harbor was attacked.

Mackenzie King had devoted the morning of that Sunday to completing the formalities connected with Canada's declarations of war against

Finland, Hungary, and Roumania which the Cabinet had agreed to on the previous day. He had felt some concern that these declarations had not been approved by Parliament, which had adjourned three weeks earlier. But he convinced himself they were "all part of the same war which began with Germany against Poland. . . . As Roumania, Hungary, and Finland have all been actively engaged in warfare at the side of Germany . . . there would not appear to be any need to summon Parliament to make a formal declaration of war. A state of war exists and the Government's action is a mere recognition of it. Parliament can formally approve, if thought advisable, when it re-assembles. What is important is that all the Dominions should associate themselves simultaneously with Britain in keeping a united front, making their action as immediate and telling as possible. At best, Parliament could be summoned in seven days. To wait that time for the sake of conforming with what, in the circumstances, would be more or less a pure formality, would be foolish."

In the afternoon, Mackenzie King left for Kingsmere and, after a short walk, lay down at 3.30 for an afternoon nap. He had not more than closed his eyes when Norman Robertson called him on the telephone to tell him "there was a rumour that the Japanese had attacked Manila and Hawaii, but only a rumour." He wrote: "It was an immense relief to my mind, however, to know that their attack had been upon the U.S. in the first instance, and that the opening shots were not between Great Britain and Japan. As it was a rumour, I did not get up, but went to sleep, asking for confirmation when it could be given."

He slept till 4.30 when Robertson again called and "said he had had word that the President himself had 'phoned to Lord Halifax, and told him that there had been two attacks by the Japanese, one on Pearl Harbor and the other on Manila. I told Robertson to get War Committee together for 7.00 o'clock—it was then 4.50 P.M. Rested a short time thinking over situation, and then got up, dressed and 'phoned that I was coming into town immediately. . . . Later, after coming into town, I changed this to the entire Cabinet for 7.30. Roosevelt's Cabinet has been called for 8.30 P.M. . . . On the way, thought over question of summoning Parliament. First inclination was the thought that it might be wise to do so. . . . However decided to consider matter further and carefully, and to discuss that phase with Hanson and leaders of other groups.

"Got Hanson on the 'phone about 6.30. He was at Fredericton. Said he would do anything he could; would be here on Tuesday for a conference. It was the earliest he could reach Ottawa. When I spoke of my concern being as to desirability of calling Parliament, his reaction was not to be in haste about that. That papers might demand something for publicity's sake, but he thought it would be better to talk it over with some of my own people and see if there was necessity for it. His tone was distinctly that of not feeling it was necessary.

"I got Blackmore [the leader of the Social Credit group] at Cardston, and had a pleasant talk with him. . . . When I spoke of Parliament re-assembling, he said he did not think it would be necessary to bring members together at this time, specially as we were standing at the side of Britain, and had authority from Parliament to take that attitude. That I could count on any help he could give, but be assured he would approve not having Parliament called.

"Later I got in touch with Coldwell, about 7.15 at Biggar, Sask. He had just heard Japan had declared war. Asked me if it was on the British Commonwealth as well as the U.S. I said I had heard it was Britain as well as the U.S. but had still to receive verification. However, I would take the position that if it were against Britain, we had been authorized by Parliament to stand at the side of Britain in resisting aggression, and that the war being directed against Britain, we would be at her side. He said he would approve that ground and saw no necessity for calling Parliament. I added that the fact that a state of war was existing at the instance of Japan made it desirable for us to have a proclamation issued at once; that we could tie up the Legation here and take other necessary measures.

"I gave Robertson over the 'phone directions to have Order ready to declare a state of war as existing, also the necessary submission to the King, etc. that all might go through tonight. . . . In word from Robertson, he said it was understood Germany and Italy might declare war against the U.S. tonight. This is the most crucial moment of all the world's history, but I believe the result will be, in the end, to shorten the war."

When the Cabinet met Mackenzie King told his colleagues he had been in touch with Hanson, Blackmore, and Coldwell and "that all were agreed that the Government should take immediate action in declaring a state of war to exist between Japan and Canada, the Government basing its action in this matter on the authority of Parliament as given at the commencement of the war when decision was reached that Canada should stand at the side of Britain in resisting aggression." The Cabinet "indicated its approval of proceeding without waiting for any summoning of Parliament." Mackenzie King recalled "that when our troops were landed at Hong Kong, I had given a statement to the press which made clear that we regarded as a part of the defence of Canada and of freedom, any attack which might be made by the Japanese against British territory or forces in the Orient."

He "then took up a draft Order-in-Council which . . . made mention simply of Japan having wantonly and treacherously attacked British territory, and that the U.K. Government had commenced hostilities against Japan, and that the Government of Canada in accordance with decision of Parliament for effective co-operation by Canada at the side of Britain to resist aggression, had associated itself with the U.K. in these hostilities. I pointed out that the draft Order made no reference to Japan's attack upon the U.S. territories and forces, and said I thought it important that a reference should be included for historical reasons; and also for reasons of high policy, that it was well to keep to the fore, because of relation between Britain and the U.S., that the U.S. had been attacked."

There was some difference in the Cabinet about including a reference to the United States and Mackenzie King recorded his surprise "at the length of time it took to settle the question of mention of the U.S." He added that "Ralston, I think it was, suggested that a clause might be inserted that the Japanese attacks constituted a threat to North American security. There was some discussion on that point, and I joined in with those who thought it was better not to bring into this recital a reference to North America as such. I felt a reference of the kind might be mistaken or occasion debate on the question of British Commonwealth of Nations as against North America. It was unnecessary in any event. All agreed. . . .

"Crerar was quite emphatic that it should be clear that we were in the war for Canada's sake, not merely because Britain was at war. I agreed with this and . . . pointed out we had made clear that the threat to freedom in any part was a threat to Canada. That all of this was a part of our interpretation of the defence of Canada as given in Parliament and outside. . . .

"It was exactly 9.15 . . . when I signed the Order-in-Council recommending the submission to the King.

"We then had discussion at some length concerning the measures to be taken at once, and desirability of public intimation being made in one form or another, counselling against any anti-Japanese demonstrations in B.C. and expressing the Government's belief in the loyalty of Japanese nationals and Canadian-born Japanese in B.C. . . .

"After Council had adjourned, and after I had had an interview with the press, the communication came from England . . . stating that the U.K. did not propose to formally declare existence of a state of war until tomorrow. The despatch indicated that they will wait for the action Congress might take. Quite clearly, coming back to the point of view that

I had expressed in my telegram of a week ago, that it was well, if possible, to have the U.S. precede Britain in beginning of hostilities. This communication was a little disconcerting as it gave the appearance of Canada declaring a state of war before either Britain or the U.S. However, as to that, we were simply acting promptly in accordance with the decision of Parliament to be at the side of Britain when she was attacked, against aggression. It was also a clear indication that our action was our own, and not that of any direction from Britain itself. . . .

"It was 10 to 10 . . . when I signed the submission to the King. The External Affairs Department had meanwhile been communicating with Massey to secure the King's approval. We had the Chiefs of Staff in and listened to their representations of what had occurred, and their views on Canada's security. . . . At 11 o'clock, listened to radio news which had the announcement that Canada had declared a state of war to be in existence. This word was also over the U.S. radio. That will be helpful in the light of meeting of Congress tomorrow. . . . It was just 11.30 when I got back to Laurier House and turned out the lights at midnight."

Mackenzie King gave a broadcast on December 8 in which he outlined what had happened and explained that, after consulting the leaders of other parties, the Government had decided it was not necessary to summon Parliament immediately. The following day (December 9) Hanson arrived in Ottawa and Mackenzie King invited him to lunch at Laurier House. Hanson told him again that "he did not think it was necessary to call Parliament for the formalities of approving, unless we had need of some powers which we do not already possess, or had some programme which we thought, in the circumstances, it was necessary to put into operation.

"Hanson then began to speak to me quite openly and to say that he thought it would be absolutely necessary to have a National Government. He thought conscription ought not to be made a political issue. . . . He then went on to say that he thought I was the one to form a National Government and he believed the only person in Canada who could; that he supposed Ralston was a possibility, but he doubted if he could. I said I have told Ralston more than once that any moment he wanted my post he could have it, but I doubted if he desired to do more than do what he could in his present post till the war was over. Hanson then went on to say, I am sure if you would form a Union Government you would go down in history as the greatest Prime Minister Canada had ever had, not excepting anyone. He followed this by saying Meighen feels so strongly on the war that I am sure he would be prepared to take a minor post in the Government. He added, 'I would be willing to come in too, though I am not anxious to take on extra work.' . . .

"Hanson said, at one stage, that with my large following I could do anything I wished. I replied to him that my views of the source of power were very different to those of some other men. I cited Bennett in particular. I said that such success as I had had, I believed, came from the fact that I believed my power came from the people; that it was not something that arose from some 'superman' power which I myself possessed; that I felt I had held that power by being true to the people and to the promises I had given to them. That they trusted me because they knew I would not break faith with respect to their own views and wishes.

"Hanson then said: 'Then you feel that you should not lead?' To which I replied: That is not the case. That I believed the people had a true instinct in most matters of government when left alone. That they were not swayed, as specially favoured individuals were, by personal interest, but rather by a sense of what best served the common good. That they recognized the truth when it was put before them, and that a leader can guide so long as he kept to the right lines. I did not think it was a mark of leadership to try to make the people do what one wanted them to do. . . . I felt very strongly that conscription would divide Canada. Moreover that it was not necessary, that our war effort could be more effective without it. I mentioned what I had said in Parliament about selective service. I was prepared to let others take on the task of leadership if conscription as an issue began to gain ascendancy. He said he had been sorry to hear me say that, but he thought I had spoken very hastily. . . .

"Hanson then asked me if I had completely closed my mind to any other course. I replied that I had an open mind in regard to everything. That I would meet situations as I found it necessary and desirable to meet them, but that I would try to view everything in the light of all circumstances, past, present and future. . . .

"I rather expected him to ask me when the by-elections would be brought on, or to say something about Meighen. The fact that he did not was in itself significant. I felt that there was something at the back of his mind in all that he was saying, which had been part of all that he had talked over with others. While in one sense, therefore, I was surprised later in the afternoon to see the statement he had given to the press concerning the calling together of Parliament, I was not surprised in another sense. It was clear to me also when I read the press statement that it had been talked over and prepared even before he came to Laurier House and no doubt was prepared by Meighen, who, I discovered later, was in the city.

"I noticed Hanson seemed anxious to leave about 2.30 and maybe he was going back to get the statement prepared before he left, later in the afternoon, for the East. He was very pleasant in conversation. We talked at length, mostly of his experiences in crossing the ocean and of his sojourn in London."

In the statement issued that afternoon Hanson said: 'Assuming that there is to be no change in policy with respect to the war, and that the Government is to be carried on as presently constituted and with the same policies, it would not appear to me to be necessary to summon Parliament at this juncture for the purpose of giving Parliamentary sanction to a declaration of war, if such an action be actually required.'

But, he continued, 'If Canada is to make good the oft-repeated assurance that we are engaged in a 'total war' and on a scale commensurate with the implications of that declaration and having regard to recent startling developments, then it is essential that much more be done to put this nation on a total war basis.'

And he concluded: 'Total war may only be waged by the extension without limitation of the principles underlying the National Resources Mobilization Act, and by the immediate repeal of the clause limiting compulsory military service to Canada. The armed forces of Canada, both at home and overseas, including reserves and reinforcements, must be maintained at the highest possible strength consistent with industrial and other requirements.

'In order to accomplish this end, Parliament should be called at once to pass the legislation necessary to amend the National Resources Mobilization Act and to give effect to the new policies which would flow from such legislation.

'It is my view that only a National Government, that is a Government representative of all shades of political opinion, could effectively carry out this program. I made this quite clear to the Prime Minister.

'Canada is surely in an extraordinary position, having regard to the powers conferred on the Government of the United States in the question of compulsory service. That great nation, even before becoming a belligerent, had compulsory national service for the armed forces, and its manpower may be used to defend Canada. On the other hand, Canada has not full national service and her manpower raised by compulsory methods may not be used to defend the United States.'[1]

It was that same afternoon (December 9) that the first of a series of Cabinet meetings was held to consider the war programme for 1942 which had been discussed the week before at the War Committee.

At a War Committee meeting on December 2, when Ralston had first brought forward the army programme, Mackenzie King had asked

[1] Montreal *Gazette*, December 10, 1941.

whether it could be accepted "on the assumption that it would not demand conscription for overseas service. I pointed out that if it did, it was being framed in deliberate opposition to the policy of the Government, and that by agreeing to it, the Government would be virtually committing itself to conscription for overseas service." To this question Ralston replied that "he could not guarantee that conscription might not be necessary. That he always kept himself free to advocate it, if it became necessary, though he would try his utmost to get the men without conscription.

"I told him that, of course, once conscription became necessary, I could no longer lead the Government. He said, of course I would, I would tell the country that I thought it was necessary. I told him that I felt conscription would split the country from coast to coast; create a wound in its side that would never be healed, and that destroying national unity would be upsetting our whole war effort. . . .

"I spoke of there being no representative at the War Committee from Quebec. Mentioned that I had Lapointe's last letter in my pocket saying he was ready to fight very strongly, if conscription became an issue. Also that, on his death-bed, he spoke to me of the injury it would be to the country, and his regret at going and not being here to fight that question. That I had to watch what I knew were the views of large numbers in the minority.

"Angus Macdonald wanted to know why the French should object to conscription. I told him for the same reason that the Dutch, the Irish, the Australians in large numbers objected to it for overseas. That it meant in the case of French Canadians in Canada, in their minds, domination of a conquered people and minority by an Orange Protestant majority. This would never be accomplished without terrific struggle. That more would be lost in the struggle than would be gained in other ways. Lost in actual effort, and lost in value of effort in the eyes of the world. I concluded by saying that a house divided against itself was sure to fall. That would be the fate of the Government or party that tried to enforce conscription for overseas service in this war. Feeling that truth, I would not ever take responsibility for a step of the kind."

The next day (December 3) the proceedings at the War Committee had developed into a debate "carried on quite quietly" between Ralston and Mackenzie King, with much the same arguments repeated on both sides. At the end Mackenzie King had said he "felt the army programme should be kept within limits of what would avoid the necessity of raising" the conscription issue. He had added that "back of all else, I am positive, is the Army's desire to maintain a foremost position, a certain jealousy of the Air Force and Naval Services." Mackenzie King had admitted "the obvious need for Canada to go just as far as she can, short of internal disorder" to support the Army overseas. When Ralston had pointed out the pressure for conscription would grow stronger as men and women had their sons and brothers overseas, Mackenzie King "told him I fully realized that and knew it was the ground on which those who were seeking National Government for their own ends were pushing the conscription issue to the fore. That is the hateful part of it all; the movement has not been worked up by those who have Canada's interests primarily at heart, but by those who wish to keep control of the financial policy."

General Stuart, the Chief of the General Staff, had been at this meeting for a part of the time. Mackenzie King "liked General Stuart's complete frankness and also felt quite impressed by his personality. Indeed I feel every confidence in him. I asked him the straight question as to whether, if this programme were approved, we could count on it being the last demand. . . . Stuart read a paragraph which he had dictated for Ralston, he said, two days ago, which was to the effect that what was being asked, constituted the visible ceiling—supplementing what he had written, he said he felt the Army thus constituted would be a complete organization for fighting purposes." Mackenzie King "asked him directly before he left whether he thought this programme could be carried out on a voluntary basis. That, as he knew, I was anxious to avoid conscription becoming an issue through the country, if that were possible. His reply was that the programme had been worked out so as to fit into the Government policy of voluntary enlistment for overseas. That is what the Staff had aimed at, had worked for, and what he believed could be accomplished in that way. . . .

"I confess these statements from the Chief of Staff . . . impressed me very much and helped to meet the difficulty that has been the only real one which presents itself, namely that of resorting to conscription to get numbers required. I still feel that the same energy, money, and manpower, applied to industry and to other branches, would, in this war, serve a greater purpose, but we have to deal with conditions as they are."

It had then been agreed that the full Cabinet should consider the programme in a series of meetings in the following week. Before these meetings were held the United States was in the war.

Mackenzie King opened the first meeting of the series on December 9, by outlining the proposals of the Army, Navy, and Air Force. Then he had each Minister outline his proposals in greater detail "to indicate what it would require in the way of manpower. Mention was also made of the manpower survey, and how it was proposed to allot different classes and individuals into branches of the war effort in which they were likely to render the greatest service. I then pointed out the discussion would lead inevitably to the question of conscription for overseas service, and that I thought we had better have the views of all honestly and fearlessly given as to consequences of the adoption of such a policy, so that all present would see the picture as clearly as it could be visualized, as to the need, possible effects, etc." He "then took the list of Members of the Cabinet and asked each for his own opinion, in order of their appointment to the Government." He "made a careful summary of all these statements."

In the midst of these proceedings Power received a message giving the details of the losses of the United States Navy and Air Force at Pearl Harbor. Mackenzie King "read the message to my colleagues. When shown to me first by Power I felt it was an appalling blow, one which might well signify a sweep through the British and American possessions in the Orient, like that of Hitler's army through Europe, that it certainly would bring a long extension of the war. Had I not received so many blows myself, from different directions, that I have become almost numb to any impression, I would have been, I think, dumbfounded by this news. I had felt, however, that, as Churchill said, and I have said to others, Japan would not have gone into the war had she not known something of her own strength, and that that should not be discounted.

"I read the communication a second time and said that it raised in my mind at once the question whether or not we should call Parliament together immediately, possibly Monday of next week; that there would be consternation, particularly as it is possible our own coast might be attacked by invaders—which seemed wholly probable. That the public will want to strike out at something, and look for some protection, however unfair their mark might be, and however much in matter of appearances protection might be. That if Parliament was to be called, I thought we should make the announcement almost immediately. . . .

"Before the discussion was over I went to my room, had a cup of tea, glanced at the evening paper and read over the message quietly. While there I was given a copy of the statement that Hanson had given to the press regarding our interview. When I read it over it caused me to feel less inclined to call Parliament. . . . When I returned to the Council table I had the other Ministers continue."

The Cabinet meeting continued until after 7 o'clock and adjourned to resume the next day. When the statements had been made by all the Ministers, Mackenzie King "said very quickly that except at the time we had come into the war itself, I had never felt more proud of my colleagues than I had in the last 24 hours. That I believed each had spoken frankly of what was in his mind, and what lay deepest in his feeling without any reservation, knowing that each was prepared to respect the judgment of the other, that they would not fulfil their duties if they did other than speak out. What had been said at the table might be taken as a miniature cross-section of the attitude of the country. That I felt we were all of one mind in feeling that the unity of the country was an all-important factor in the war effort; that we must weigh very carefully whatever would endanger that unity. It was evident from what had been expressed that that unity would be seriously endangered by conscription. That we must therefore seek to do all we could to accomplish the end we have, short of anything which would make conscription inevitable.

"That . . . we would have to remember that we were dealing today with a condition and not with a theory, and in considering that condition, we would have to take into account past, present and future factors. That it is clear a general election would mean a very serious division in the country and arousing of passion. Doubted if such a thing should be contemplated. Equally a referendum would create divisions. As someone had said, at the end of it, we would be no further along if the referendum went against conscription.

"I would be careful taking any step on our part that would make conscription necessary; that short of that, I thought we should work out a programme going as far as we possibly can to meet what the defence forces regard as essential; that I believed this could be done.

"We had been in difficult places before. I thought there was enough genius and goodwill and ability at the table to work out this problem as well as others, that we had kept ourselves united and the country united for two and a quarter years of war, which was a miracle in itself. Surely we could meet this situation, especially now that Japan was in the war, and in all probability the U.S. would have to take a larger part very soon, probably against Germany and Italy, and our position would be considerably changed. I then suggested we all think the matter over very carefully, and meet again tomorrow at 3."

The Cabinet meeting the next day (December 10) was the first one attended by St. Laurent. They "took up anew the army programme, Ralston presenting it carefully and quietly. I explained the debate we had already had, and the divisions of which it gave evidence. Ralston pressed the matter to the point of saying that, as Minister of Defence, he would have to say on the floor of Parliament that he could not say whether we could get the men for the programme by voluntary enlistment or not. We were, however, determined to get them. If we could not get them voluntarily he, himself, would feel we would have to resort to conscription. . . .

"I took the position that we who were sitting at the table owed it to those from whom we got our power, namely, the people's representatives in Parliament, not to adopt any policy which involved conscription until they, themselves, had approved of our so doing; that it was known to us all present that, at the last caucus, the party had unanimously approved the Government's standing out against conscription, and that the prospect of Meighen's coming into the House had made them the firmer in that stand. I said if, when we met the party, they wished to have the situation altered and support conscription, that would be time enough to face the issue but that we should do nothing in the interval which would make it impossible for us to say that we, ourselves, had not made the issue imperative."

Mackenzie King noted that as the discussion continued it became "somewhat warmer. Power does not agree with Ralston's methods. Thinks if he would call out more men for local defence, he could get all he needed in the way of voluntary enlistment. Ralston sticks to the idea that men are not needed for local defence. I cannot see that, in the light of what may happen on either coast. . . . It is conceivable that if Germany, as she may, gains an increasing control of the sea, now that America will be using the fleet to meet her own situations, that the source of convoys . . . will become the target of Nazi attacks. The Japs, too, will, I believe, make some landing on our coast. What may happen if some bombing planes—as is wholly probable—launched their deadly explosives over New York, and Boston? That is almost as certain now as the bombing of London. Such terrific damage can be done in very few ventures.

"As the discussion became warmer, Cardin, who had been very quiet, spoke out very strongly. Macdonald had been saying he thought the Province of Quebec was mistaken in its view. Also that it might come to see things differently. Cardin told them how the Liberal party had come back with a solid Quebec following after conscription in the last war, and said he believed there would no longer be a Liberal party worthy of the name in Canada if an attempt at conscription were repeated. He did not think one man would be elected in the entire province.

"He very pointedly asked what the policy of the Government was. What was the stand we would take when confronted with a resolution, an amendment moved by Meighen advocating conscription for overseas. That there would have to be solidarity and responsibility; that the Ministers could not take the position that voluntary training was good up to a certain point, and then go for conscription. It had to be, at least, that our policy, we believed, did not require conscription. That if a contrary view was entertained by the Cabinet, he, of course, could easily leave the room by the door, but he felt he should make it clear that, in his opinion, there would not be the following left to carry it out.

"Some mention was made of a referendum and the stand that should be taken on it. I told the Cabinet quite frankly that if there was a referendum, as there might be, I, for one, would speak very strongly against supporting conscription on the ground that it would so divide the country as to make an effective war effort impossible. It would injure the country for years to come.

"I said that I had no misgivings as to what was likely to take place; that perhaps I felt as I did because of having been so much with Sir Wilfrid during the time that his colleagues left him one by one; that I fully expected to pass through a similar Gethsemane, and to see them, one by one, leave me, and that I was quite prepared to endure the experience; that after all, it was nothing to what young men were enduring in enlisting and serving on the field of battle. That I was quite prepared for it, and knew how, under the pressure of excitement of the moment, these matters developed, and how men came to feel, where they had relatives serving and the like.

"Cardin had said that he, if he were alone, was not going to betray all that he and Lapointe had done to try and have the Province of Quebec come into the fight . . . and play their full part. . . .

"I made it absolutely clear that I would not support conscription but would openly oppose it because of the injury it would do to our war effort. I suggested that it might be well to consider how public feeling might change in Canada, if our people began to see their sons slain in Britain and Europe while the Americans were defending their own country at home, after all we had done. That nothing would be the same after this war. No one could say the British Empire itself could be held together, and that, as one who loved the Empire and felt strongly about belonging to it as against belonging to the States, we had to be careful to see that our moves did not lead the people in the latter direction instead of the former now that a hemisphere war was on.

"At a still later stage, I mentioned that it might serve to illustrate what I had in mind if I pointed out to the younger men present what I believe the future might reveal in regard to conscription, as the past had done in reference to myself. I said that my future was in the past. I had nothing to wish for in public life than not to lose the belief that the people had in my integrity. That I had not been in Parliament during the last war in 1917, but had supported Sir Wilfrid in opposing conscription." He then told his colleagues he had urged on Laurier the logical arguments for conscription, "but that I believed Laurier had more knowledge of Canada than any other man, and saw more clearly what would happen. That I believed he was right and that time had shown he was right. Though I was certain of defeat, and it seemed terrible to be ending any prospect of a political career . . . I had as a matter of fact become the choice of the Liberal party at the Convention of 1919 and had been Prime Minister at the time I had in virtue of the fact that the people of Canada themselves believed that Laurier was right, and that I was right in opposing conscription as I did."

Mackenzie King pointed out that he "was simply seeking to allow others to see with respect to a similar condition today what, in the light of history, will probably be the verdict on any repetition of a similar happening, more particularly when we had not only the light of past experience to warn us against it, but until today, the deep resentment felt as a consequence of what had happened." He then "suggested that we might leave the further consideration of the matter over till Monday to give time for further reflection."

He added: "Ralston himself is really the one who has precipitated the whole issue. He has been living close to the matter, and I think has committed himself so strongly to all proposals that he sees no way of modifying any of them. He seems to me to be quite overwrought and is liable to either break or tender his resignation, if he does not get his own way."

That same day (December 10) it was decided to have writs issued for four by-elections on February 9, 1942. It had earlier been decided that a constituency would not be opened for Meighen until he resigned from the Senate, but Mackenzie King did not wish to appear to be keeping him out of the House of Commons. He noted that "the mere mention of writs being issued, I could see, was not without its effect on causing a more careful consideration by everyone of what was involved in letting conscription become an issue. I said that perhaps before Parliament itself had decided the matter, we could get some sidelights on it from the by-elections themselves."

Before the discussion on conscription and the army programme was resumed, Mackenzie King's mind was occupied with possible changes in the Cabinet. He had Tom Moore, the President of the Trades and Labour Congress, come to Laurier House to see him on December 10 and told him "I thought, with the world situation what it had become, it was now imperative he should enter the Government. I reminded him that when we last talked he thought he might come in later. I said I had appreciated that position. Felt that in the interests of unity of the nation, and particularly of labour's interests, he should come into the Cabinet now. That I would back him and support just demands of labour.... Moore then said that he was anxious to help but that he honestly felt still as he did before. That he had no one to keep the organized movement together other than himself.... Labour had got the feeling that the Government was not playing fair with them. He spoke of some of the things we had done as being rather small and unnecessary.... I told him of my effort to get Godbout and his reasons. He pointed out that his situation was the same. He then said: 'Why don't you get Humphrey Mitchell?' I told him Mitchell had been in my mind, but that I thought he, Moore, was the best person that could be secured, and naturally I would prefer him. I agreed that Mitchell would make a good Minister. ... He believed Mitchell would be first rate Minister and would do all he could to support him in every way. He thought if he had some Advisory Committee that could work with him, that could keep the labour situation well in hand."

Mackenzie King told Moore he "would not finally close the matter but would think over what he had said. That I might have even yet to press him again. I also said I would like to be in a position to say that I urged him to come into the Government, that he had declined only for the reason he had mentioned." He observed that "Moore was extremely friendly, not the least critical of myself, but appreciative of my difficulties. Not unfriendly to the Government either. I told him that all the members of the Government would welcome his coming in, and mentioned Howe, in particular, who had told me he would be glad to have him come."

Mackenzie King was particularly receptive to the suggestion of Humphrey Mitchell's name because he knew how highly C. D. Howe regarded Mitchell. A month earlier, on November 7, he had recorded his "surprise and delight" when Howe had suggested Mitchell for the chairmanship of the War Labour Board.

On December 12, Mackenzie King had a long interview with Cardin about a possible change in the Quebec representation in the Cabinet. He also talked to Cardin about Moore and Mitchell and found Cardin would prefer Mitchell "inasmuch as he had been in Parliament and had had administrative experience there, and administrative experience in departmental affairs since." (Humphrey Mitchell had served in Parliament for a year before the 1935 election as a Labour M.P. for Hamilton East; he was not re-elected in 1935, and had been given a position in the Department of Labour; in November 1941 he had become Chairman of the War Labour Board.) "Howe came later, while Cardin was there, and agreed very strongly about Mitchell as preferable to Moore, and the best possible choice in every way." Howe also felt sure Mitchell could be elected in Welland where there was a vacancy. This was not quite as simple as it looked because Miss Helen Kinnear had already been nominated as a Liberal candidate and Mackenzie King, when he saw her on December 18, found her reluctant to withdraw. He never ceased to be grateful to her for yielding in the end to his persuasion.

Later in the day on December 12, Mackenzie King saw Norman McLarty who "took it all in a fine spirit" when Mackenzie King told him he felt "we should appoint a labour man to the post he was holding. Thought of Moore but gave him reasons why Moore would not accept, and said I had thought of Humphrey Mitchell. He and Moore had evidently been talking the matter over in the morning. He said they both agreed Humphrey Mitchell would be the right man. Moore must have brought the matter up himself." As a result of all these discussions it was agreed that Pierre Casgrain, the Secretary of State, should be appointed to the Bench, that McLarty should succeed him as Secretary of State, and that no new Minister should be appointed from Quebec for the time being.

It was not until December 15 that Mackenzie King actually invited Humphrey Mitchell to join the Government. He told Mitchell he "felt the Government was handicapped in not having a 'labour man' distinctly known as such at the Council table. I told him of my approach to Moore some time ago, and recently, and of what had been said by both of us. I then mentioned that Moore himself had, in reply to my question as to whom he would recommend, suggested Mitchell; that I had told him that Mitchell was the one who was also in my mind. I then said my purpose in asking him to come this morning was to invite him to come into the Government to help in this critical situation. That I felt his previous appearance in Parliament would be particularly helpful; also the administrative experience he had since had.

"I wanted someone who could watch labour's interests closely. That I would back him in that regard to the utmost of my strength in everything that was reasonable. Mitchell began by saying that he had never wanted to go into politics; that he had, when he ran in Hamilton, been more or less forced into accepting the nomination. That his ambition was not in public life but that he realized that at a time like the present it was for everyone to do what they could to serve where they could be of most service. He then said that Moore had told him of my talk with himself and had said to him that if he should be sent for, he hoped that he, Mitchell, would not say no. He then said that if I thought he could help, he would be willing to come. I expressed my thanks to him and said

I was sure he would render a very great service, and that clearly it was his duty and his opportunity."

He "stressed to Mitchell the importance of having someone in the Government who knew the labour situation from the inside, and who could see that Orders took account of susceptibilities of Labour. I mentioned Moore's suggestion of an Advisory Board to himself, and said anything that could lend strength to a true representation of Labour I would welcome."

Humphrey Mitchell was sworn in that afternoon, and remained as Minister of Labour until his death. At the same time, Norman McLarty became Secretary of State.

At the Cabinet meeting next day (December 16), Ralston asked whether it was intended "to pursue the disagreeable subject of the previous week" and much the same ground as had been debated at the last meeting was gone over again. Ralston "said he wanted his colleagues to know that, if the subject of conscription came up on the Address [when the new session opened in January 1942] he would have to say that he felt it was necessary to get the men required for overseas. At another stage, he said he was debating whether he should not leave the Government before Parliament met."

Mackenzie King noted that "Power was emphatic in saying that . . . if Ralston would call out a few more men for service in Canada, from the number it would be easy to find the numbers sufficient to make good all wastage and losses overseas. Ralston would not hear of calling out men for service in Canada. I think he is quite wrong in this. There may not be large-scale invasion, but there will be raids, attacks from the air and at sea, sufficiently great to alarm the people. . . . Ralston absolutely declined to consider any reduction in the forces still to be sent overseas. As I pointed out, since the programme was drafted, the position is entirely changed in the light of the defeats the German army has been encountering in Russia and Africa, and the entry of the United States into the war; that the menace to Britain is no longer anything as great as it was when she was dependent for fighting men pretty much on the Commonwealth alone. That makes no difference in Ralston's eyes. . . .

"I suggested, at the end, that perhaps Ralston would let the final decision on Army estimates stand over until we had before us the programmes of other departments: Munitions, Agriculture in particular, and a statement from the Minister of Finance of total expenditure proposed and his ability to raise the revenue necessary to meet it by loan or taxation. Also I thought we should have something before us regarding the manpower situation and concrete proposals with reference thereto."

Mackenzie King added that "it was another trying day in the Cabinet, but I was able to keep calm and, I think, to steady the situation somewhat. Ralston, however, is becoming very rigid and I find it difficult, except because of commitments he has already made to some in the Department, to understand his attitude. It lacks vision and statesmanship altogether. I do not forget that he is thoroughly sincere in believing that the war can only be won across the ocean and that it will be the Army that will be looked to in the end. The mistake he makes is that another division or two from Canada will not compensate for what will be lost in the more effective action in other directions. However, we have reached the end of this year of my life with the Government still intact."

By this time, Mackenzie King was looking for some way of avoiding a showdown in the Cabinet as well as in Parliament and December 16 was the day he first began seriously to think of holding a referendum or plebiscite on the question of conscription; the possibility had, of course, come up indirectly already in Cabinet discussions. After the Cabinet meeting, he drove one of his secretaries "back with me on the way home, and I talked in a general way of what was in my mind. To my surprise, he stated that he believed that, if presented to them in a proper light, Quebec would accept conscription, because of the change that had come about through America removing her restrictions on compulsory service. I said I could not believe that, though I did believe a referendum might be the only way out of the situation. He seemed to think it might be wise to lose no time in holding it, to have it over even before Parliament met.

"I doubt the wisdom of that, though I do think that it might well come as part of Government policy to be set out in the Speech from the Throne. If that is to be done, I shall have to keep this in mind until the very last moment. It would cut the ground out from any amendment to the Address which the Tories might move favouring all-out conscription, for it would be a reference to the people themselves rather than to their representatives."

On December 17 "the significant feature of the day" for Mackenzie King was "that the Manitoba Legislature had passed a resolution to ask the federal Government to introduce conscription for an all-out effort which would involve conscription for overseas. It passed the House unanimously. I am sure it dates back to part of the Meighen plan and relates to his visit with Bracken. However, the minute I saw it I felt I had at last just what I wanted. It gives me the best reasons for an immediate referendum. The framing of the latter is something that will have to be done with care, but I can see wherein, if a referendum is taken before Parliament reassembles, we will be free from all that discussion in the

House. There is no reason also why we should not assert that any programme we are now presenting, we believe will be carried out without the resorting to conscription for overseas in the Army."

He added that "the Government's hand must be free as regards the movements of our troops to the States and along the lines of the coast but, as for overseas, public opinion will have to be very strong. . . . At any rate, it permits a free discussion of the most effective means to be employed by Canada in her war effort, and I am sure that by the time Parliament assembles, there will be a strong feeling of not letting too many men continue to go overseas, especially now that documents are being revealed which point to possible attacks on San Francisco by the Japanese. . . .

"The Manitoba Resolution of the Legislature," he continued, "is on all fours with the Resolution of the Ontario Legislature of a couple of years ago in that, to an extent, it challenges the Government's policy, though not from the same motive or in the same vicious way, but it does open the door to a step which otherwise it might have been more embarrassing to take."

The next day (December 18) Mackenzie King noted that he found his colleagues in the Cabinet "in a fairly quiet frame of mind, somewhat quieted down, and complete French representation: Dandurand, Power, St. Laurent and Cardin" and that he brought up the matter of a referendum, saying, "first, I knew Ralston was anxious about his programme— to place orders as soon as possible in this connection. I saw no reason why they should not be placed at once, leaving the question to be settled later whether the programme was to be carried out in Canada or overseas. Asked Ralston if that would be helpful. He replied: Exceedingly so, and indicated the need for tank brigade material, and said he would bring it up tomorrow at the War Committee. I said to regard that all as settled today.

"I then said I had been giving great thought as to how we could all work out a policy that would keep us all together; that the Resolution passed in Manitoba for conscription had caused me to see that it might not be long before other legislatures might be taking similar steps, and that our hand would be increasingly forced. We might get into Parliament and find the party divided; already, there were some for and some against. . . . The situation might become such that to settle the matter there might have to be a change of Government. One thing I did not want was to see any Government managing Canada's affairs of which Arthur Meighen would be the head, or a member. I said a general election would be impossible in the present situation, but that a referendum might save a controversy, not only in Parliament, but avoid a cleavage in the country. If a referendum were even 50-50, it would be apparent that the policy would not be a safe one to attempt to enforce. The Government would soon see what the complexion of the country was and could govern itself accordingly. I saw no reason why we should not hold to our policy of regarding conscription as unnecessary and inadvisable and to our belief that we could carry through the measures we were proposing without resorting to conscription. On the other hand, that we might reasonably conclude that, with the developments in the war as uncertain as they were, a moment might come when it would be unfortunate were the Government's hands tied. It would be better to trust our Government to administer the country's war effort, knowing our attitude to be what it is, than to let the Government fall into other hands. All I would suggest was consideration of possible agreement on the desirability of not having our hands tied, if the situation became such as to render the step necessary to meet very critical conditions. All this in the light of some legislation being necessary, with the United States in the war, to enable our troops to go to the States, if necessary, and on to our own coasts. [Under the Mobilization Act of 1940 compulsory service was limited to Canada.]

"I found that all present seemed to feel that the way was opening out to a solution, and this the only solution that seemed possible to avoid a split in the Government, which would mean a split in the party and, certainly, a split in the country, with injury to our war effort as a result. . . . I told the Cabinet not to try to discuss the matter, but just to turn over in their minds the wisdom of the course I was suggesting. It was pointed out that Sir Wilfrid had moved an amendment to conscription— the taking of a referendum. . . .

"I felt much relieved that this suggestion met with the general approval it seemed to, and really helped to relieve the terrific tension. It was like a real light at last on the horizon. It holds to my ground that I would not have the Administration enact a measure of the kind without an appeal to the people first. If they turn it down, we know then exactly within what compass the cloth can be cut. Without taking a step of the kind, should the war reach a situation where Canada were invaded, when the invasion might have been saved on the shores of Britain, we would be held responsible by the very ones who will blame us for even considering" conscription now.

In his diary for that day (December 18) Mackenzie King wrote that he felt "anxiety over fate of our men at Hong Kong." On October 2, when the War Committee had considered the British request for two infantry battalions to be sent to Hong Kong, Mackenzie King had agreed most reluctantly, influenced by the urgency of the British request. In agreeing, Mackenzie King "again stressed the importance of care being taken to see that our agreement in that particular did not later afford an argument for conscription." He reflected on December 18 that "those who had been so keen to send our forces overseas realize the kind of reaction likely to follow in the country where losses occur, and the danger draws nearer to our own shores. It was Power himself who was keenest on having the Quebec Regiment go [to Hong Kong], he mentioning at the time that his own son was a member of it. Howe's son is in the Navy in the Far East. Ralston has a son overseas . . . Gardiner also, and one or two Ministers have boys in the Air Force. One can understand their feelings with regard to having others share equally the perils of war. Conscription is sound in principle but has to be related to all factors which are important in their political bearing."

When the question of a referendum was raised in a Cabinet meeting again on December 23, Mackenzie King found both Cardin and Dandurand unfavourable. They feared that the announcement of a referendum would be taken as a sign the Government was considering conscription and that it would lead to a nationalist victory in Quebec. "They and Godbout believed that the entire Province would oppose . . . doubted if even the assurance that the administration would remain in the hands of the present Government would suffice to hold any seats in the province. They were fearful of the results in Quebec and Montreal [by-elections] as it is, and would prefer to have nothing said of any possibility of change of present position till after the by-elections are over."

Mackenzie King "pointed out that debate on the question would certainly arise the minute Parliament met, and Parliament's attitude would affect by-elections. I thought it would be better to have announced a referendum and have it under way so as to remove the subject that far from discussion in by-elections. They, however, felt strongly otherwise. It was clear to me that, all circumstances considered, it would be best to defer final decision till we have a party caucus when Parliament reassembles. Recruiting may keep up meanwhile in which event we might be able to get over the difficulties. I fear, however, that the Army has so forced the hand of the Government in its programme that it has become impossible to avoid the issue." The Cabinet did not discuss the question of conscription and a possible referendum again until the new year.

Mackenzie King observed that "Cardin spoke with great earnestness and revealed clearly how very deep the wound would go in the country's side if there were a majority for conscription even on a plebiscite," and added "the most I urged was a consideration of asking the people to allow the government a free hand, should the necessity demand. I am coming back more strongly to the point of view that conscription will inevitably divide Canada very seriously and do more injury to the war effort than any good that might possibly result therefrom."

In the last week of 1941, Churchill's visit to North America occupied the centre of the stage. Malcolm MacDonald had tea with Mackenzie King at Laurier House on December 22. In the course of their conversation MacDonald asked "if I had had any further word about the arrival of a certain gentleman, and I said nothing further had come, though Howe had announced in Council, four days ago, that his office had received word that Churchill was on his way, and told me on Saturday night, he would be here today." Mackenzie King then expressed "some concern over the meeting between the President and Churchill, with the possibility of not being invited to be present. Not that I personally was anxious to participate. That I saw the difficulty of Canada being represented with other Dominions not equally represented. On the other hand, he knew the tactics my opponents were adopting. They would now seek to have it appear that all that had been said about my being a link between the two amounted in reality to nothing. . . . I said that Churchill must pay us a visit here in Canada."

They were discussing what it might be best to have Churchill do in Ottawa "when the telephone rang . . . the operator said that the President wished to speak to me. In a few minutes, I heard the President's voice saying: 'Hello Mackenzie' and then I replied: 'Hello Mr. President. I am glad to hear your voice again.' He said: 'I am glad indeed to hear yours. You probably know about a certain person who is on his way. He will be arriving in about two hours' time. I will want you here while he is here. I will be having a talk with him tonight, and will let you know just as soon as I can, the exact time to come down.' . . . He then said: 'We will be having an important discussion here. It will be to work out a long-range policy and also a short-range policy as regards the war. It will require very careful thought, and then will probably occasion much discussion. There will have to be a Supreme Council, and I am determined it shall have its headquarters in Washington.' The President followed this remark by saying there will possibly be quite a time over this. I did not say yes or no to what was said in this connection, but asked if I had not better bring one of my Ministers with me, and mentioned Ralston. The President said that will be all right, and then asked if he had to do with naval affairs. I said: 'No, that Macdonald was Minister of Naval Affairs.' The President then said: 'Better have him come also.' The President then said he thought things were going pretty well. I asked him how he was himself and he said he was feeling very well. I said: 'Good-bye, Franklin,' in concluding the conversation."

The next day (December 23) at the Cabinet meeting, Mackenzie King gave his colleagues an "account of the President's talk over the 'phone . . . and of the difficult situations which I thought were likely to arise. Pointed out that it might be necessary for Canada to realize Churchill's difficulties in not showing preference as between Dominions. Also in making allowances for a certain aggressiveness on the part of America and her probable effort at a monopoly of control. Also a certain forgetfulness on the part of Britain and the U.S. combined of Canada's part in the struggle." Despite the extraordinary foresight he showed on this occasion, Mackenzie King himself was often to complain of all these things before the war was over.

Malcolm MacDonald telephoned Mackenzie King on December 24 to say Churchill would be coming to Ottawa and during the afternoon Pierrepont Moffat, the American Minister to Canada, telephoned to say the President would like Mackenzie King to be in Washington by noon on December 26. Moffat indicated the President was "agreeable to my bringing three Defence Ministers with me but did not wish to have military advisers." Mackenzie King told Ralston, who was perturbed, that they would "just have to seek to assist in every way we can, keeping as true a sense of proportion in all things as possible, fighting where something is to be gained, but not wasting energy where it may prove to be useless."

Before Mackenzie King and his colleagues left for Washington a minor crisis blew up which, for a few days, strained relations between Canada and the United States, and created a lasting antipathy between Cordell Hull and Churchill. The crisis was over the French islands of St. Pierre and Miquelon, off the south coast of Newfoundland. These islands had been a source of potential trouble ever since the fall of France. The Governor was known to be anti-British and it was feared that the wireless station was being used to transmit information about convoys in the Gulf of St. Lawrence and off Nova Scotia and Newfoundland. Various proposals had been considered for dealing with this problem including the seizure of the islands by a Free French naval force under Admiral Muselier which was engaged in convoy work in the western Atlantic.

On December 24, Mackenzie King "was shocked" to learn from the radio that Muselier "had taken possession of St. Pierre and Miquelon and [had been] welcomed by the population there. It may prove to be a very critical business and I am terribly annoyed as well as distressed about it. Fortunately, I have fought from the beginning against attempting anything against St. Pierre and Miquelon by force. I have kept up the fight at each meeting of the War Committee and the record is perfectly clear even to the point of Robertson advising de Muselier not to interfere at St. Pierre and Miquelon at this time." He added that "both the British and Americans have blown both hot and cold in the matter, and I have been holding back any action till they agreed upon a course. Only yesterday Robertson had talked with the French Minister and assured him there was no likelihood of any overt act there; that we would confer with him first. When he told me, Robertson said he thought he should go and see the Minister at once. I told him by all means to do so, and to tell him how annoyed I was."

Since October of 1941 the question of St. Pierre and Miquelon had been a cause of particular concern to Mackenzie King and it had reached a critical point at the beginning of December. In his diary on December 1, Mackenzie King had referred to "a lot of time being taken up at the War Committee about these islands." A plan had been devised at that time to send a Canadian official to St. Pierre to censor the wireless messages and, if necessary, to establish control of the wireless by force. Mackenzie King "took strong exception to any action of the kind, pointing out that this was a very critical moment as between Vichy and Britain. That today Pétain was being crowded more than ever by Hitler and was actually meeting with either Hitler or Darlan; that a seizure of a Vichy possession by the Government of Canada was all that was needed to give Darlan an excuse to turn over the French fleet to Germany which is what all who are anxious to save the situation becoming worse, are seeking to avert." He finally said, if the War Committee was "determined to take the view that apparently the majority wished, that I would wish to have the minutes record that I was distinctly opposed, believing that the course was entirely wrong. Once I took this position the others came around to agreeing to have the proposed course submitted to the Governments of the United States and Britain, and awaiting their comments thereon before taking any action."

Mackenzie King had not liked the draft message to Churchill and Cordell Hull which was prepared for him, and, on December 3, had himself prepared a message. In reply to this message, he received conflicting advice from the British, who wanted the Free French to take the islands, and the Americans, who favoured the Canadian proposals. No action was taken, and when Muselier visited Ottawa in mid-December he promised not to act against the islands on his own initiative.

On Christmas day, Mackenzie King learned during the afternoon that "Mr. Hull was very disturbed at what had happened at St. Pierre and Miquelon, and wished Canada to order the Free French forces away and reinstate the Governor. Moffat had come to Robertson who 'phoned me. . . . I advised [Robertson] to have [Malcolm] MacDonald 'phone [Lord] Halifax to see Churchill, and Churchill to see the President to say we would take any action they agreed upon. That what had been done at St. Pierre was by the Free French, not only without instructions on our part but in direct opposition to our policy. This was done."

Mackenzie King left Ottawa for Washington in the midst of this crisis at 5 P.M. on Christmas Day. He was accompanied by the three Ministers of National Defence and Norman Robertson. When his train reached Montreal that evening, Norman Robertson had word from L. B. Pearson of External Affairs in Ottawa that "Moffat had come with another reply which was an ultimatum demanding we should take action immediately. That the situation was critical. He was obviously greatly disturbed. I had Ralston and Angus Macdonald come into my room and talk the matter over. We agreed we could not take action without thereby implying that we had been responsible for what the Free French had done. Also that until the President and Mr. Churchill agreed on the action to be taken, we could not take action without precipitating a new situation for which we would be wholly and solely responsibile. . . .

"I pointed out that Admiral Muselier had been in direct touch with Moffat, and that the best thing to do was to tell the Americans to themselves order the Free French out; that raised the question as to who is in command in that area. This matter, I can see, can only be settled after we reach Washington, but I agree in feeling the same concern that Mr. Hull does. It all bears out the wisdom of the course I pursued in the War Committee, and for which I had to fight in turn different colleagues . . . and absolutely myself refuse to allow any action to be taken. . . . Fortunately I insisted on placing my own views in a telegram alike to Churchill and Hull."

The train was three hours late reaching Washington and Mackenzie King missed a luncheon on the 26th with the President. Shortly after his arrival he went to see Cordell Hull at the State Department. After a brief reference to the Japanese negotiations before the attack on Pearl Harbor, Hull "led gradually into the St. Pierre-Miquelon matter, and spoke of how very serious anything would be which would unsettle the relations between Vichy and the United States, as he had been doing everything in his power to keep the French from turning over the fleet. . . . Also, that all the South American Republics would feel, if force were resorted to in St. Pierre and Miquelon, that all the United States had been saying about not using force was not sincere."

Hull then "suggested that we might appoint a Commission of . . . experts, to look after the wireless, and that Churchill might put out the Free French, restoring the old order. I told him it would not do to have the Governor restored, as he was pro-Axis, and his wife a German. I also mentioned that while we had nothing to do with the matter, Canadian feeling was relieved and pleased with the de Gaulle accomplishment. There was a feeling against me for keeping the French Minister in Ottawa, as leaning too much towards Vichy. We would have to be careful to see that whatever was done would not appear that we were sacrificing the Free French. I said to Mr. Hull I would try to get Mr. Churchill to view the matter in this way. Mr. Hull and I then went over to the White House, where we joined the President and Mr. Churchill in the Oval Room at tea. . . .

"The President was most cordial and friendly in his greeting, as was Churchill. He [Churchill] immediately recalled our tiptoe dance together and spoke in a very friendly way. I felt very happy and much at ease with both Churchill and the President."

After some preliminary talk, "the President opened up the subject of St. Pierre–Miquelon." Roosevelt first asked where Muselier got the ships to attack St. Pierre. Mackenzie King replied that "he had come with ships of his own, and it was his own ships he had used for the purpose. Evidently there had been some thought that in some way the ships had been supplied by Canada or Newfoundland. Both the President and Churchill went over the ground and the situation in Africa and the need to get this incident closed up so as to avoid its developing into a serious question. The President suggested that Canada might appoint a Commission of some kind to look after the supervision of wireless transmission: a representative from Vichy, one from the Free French, and one from Canada: that the Governor might be restored, and the Free French forces withdrawn. Churchill said there must be some compromise settlement and inclined to agree with the President. Churchill admitted that, at one stage, he agreed to de Gaulle taking action but had later taken an opposite stand, as the United States did not wish it. He said he was prepared to take de Gaulle by the back of the neck and tell him he had gone too far and bring him to his senses. He had on more than one occasion behaved in a troublesome way.

"I said to the President it would not do to have the Governor brought back, as he was pro-Axis, and his wife a German. Also, that I thought Mr. Hull had a better idea, which was to let de Gaulle feel that, while he had been precipitate, he had cleared up a certain situation thereby making it possible to have the whole supervision of radio messages properly arranged for. . . . Mr. Hull said he thought he and I were 98 per cent agreed on what should be done. Mr. Roosevelt said he thought it would be best for Mr. Hull and me to work out a suggested arrangement and then it could be considered tomorrow."

Mackenzie King noted that earlier in the conversation Churchill spoke to him "about Dupuy in front of the President. Said he hoped Dupuy would be kept on, as he was the one link he, Churchill, had with France, and he did not wish to let him go. We were right in keeping Ristelhueber at Ottawa. The President agreed with him."

Mackenzie King had a long conversation with Hull next morning (December 27) about St. Pierre and Miquelon. He found that Hull thought Churchill and the President had misunderstood him the previous day. Mackenzie King replied "that he was mistaken in thinking they had not seen his point of view. That Churchill was really going further than he, Mr. Hull, had meant to go by saying that he would take de Gaulle by the neck and give him a real talking to. That he would recall I had pointed out that he, Mr. Hull, had a better plan which was to save de Gaulle's face, telling him that he had helped in a difficult situation re transmission of wireless, but now to get out and save the situation from becoming critical. He had evidently been distressed through the night, thinking of this." Hull then asked Mackenzie King what he thought should be done about St. Pierre–Miquelon. "I said I thought something on the lines of what had been understood between the President, Mr. Churchill, and ourselves. He then said he thought he had better send for the French Minister, Henry-Haye, and propose to him an arrangement to have the wireless supervised by Canada and by perhaps someone associated with their [U.S.] Consul. He spoke about a Commission. I said to him I did not think 'Commission' was the right term; all that was needed were technical experts who would be protected in their duties. He said they had a Consul at St. Pierre; that they might attach an expert to the Consul. I said I thought it would be all to the good to have Americans and Canadians do the supervision of the wireless. He then said that perhaps later they could get another Governor. He was rather for reinstating the present Governor. I said to him at once I thought that would be impossible.

"At that point, the press were waiting for a talk with him. He asked me if I would like to go with him. I said: 'No,' I would wait. When he came back, I said I had been thinking over the Governor part and felt the last state would be worse than the first, if he were allowed to remain. That he, Mr. Hull, must recall that 90 per cent of the vote had been for Free France, and that the Governor had said some word of defiance to the people when he went aboard Muselier's ship; that if he returned as Governor, there would probably be civil strife between him and the people. . . . He asked me if I thought Mr. Churchill would back him up in having de Gaulle withdraw. I said that I was sure he would. He had made that quite clear yesterday, but that it would have to be accompanied by some action such as the removal of the Governor allowing the people to control affairs themselves. I was almost an hour with Mr. Hull.

"When I went into the ante-room, Henry-Haye arrived and I saw him. He introduced himself to me and recalled our meeting at Versailles [Henry-Haye had been Mayor of Versailles before the war, when Mackenzie King had visited France]. He said we must get this difficulty settled about St. Pierre. I said: 'yes,' but avoided any conversation. [Norman Robertson also manoeuvred so as to prevent a photograph being taken of Henry-Haye and Mackenzie King.] I left Mr. Hull with the understanding that he would let me hear from him."

That evening Mackenzie King dined with Mr. and Mrs. Cordell Hull and "all three had an exceedingly pleasant talk together. If I were one of the family, they could not be more intimate or friendly. I was greatly touched to see that he had one of my pictures framed at the side of his bed. He also had the one of Pat and myself in the drawing-room."

At this dinner Hull told Mackenzie King he had learned from Henry-Haye that he had communicated the previous day with Vichy about the necessity for supervision of the wireless at St. Pierre and that Henry-Haye "would advocate that the business should be closed up altogether or, if maintained, should be subjected to supervision by Canadians and some Americans fortifying their Consul General. He, Haye, was favourable to having the Governor removed, and replaced by another, but wanted to have him reinstated for a few days. Hull said that, in view of what I had said, he stressed the fact it would be inadvisable to have him come back at all in case of riots. This Haye was going to put up to Vichy today. He said he told him, Haye, he did not know how England would receive the proposal, or how Canada would likely view it. That he would see what could be done. He regards Haye as having three faces instead of two, thinks he is a mischief maker. He still later told me that the [State] Department was working on some statement to place before Churchill after he had had his rest tonight. I said nothing about the formula not having been submitted to myself. Was just as glad that the matter should be kept between Britain and the U.S. Said to Mr. Hull I supposed further discussions in the matter would be by correspondence." That ended the acute stage of the St. Pierre crisis, and, in fact, nothing was done to expel the Free French forces or change the new régime there.

In Mackenzie King's first conversation with Churchill on the day before (December 26), Churchill had said he would leave for Ottawa on Sunday afternoon. "He asked me if I would go with him. I told him I had my car and would be glad to have him use it. He said they had supplied a car for him and they could be attached together. He said he would stay Monday, Tuesday, returning Wednesday. . . . He said he would make one speech and would like to speak to the Members of Parliament. I said that Parliament was adjourned at present and Members were widely scattered. Would he not like a large audience of say two thousand at the Chateau, with reservations for Members? He said he thought Parliament would be more dignified. I said we could arrange to have the meeting in the House of Commons and the broadcast from there. I would arrange also to have the press generally represented. Churchill spoke about the Press Gallery overhead in the House of Commons. Also, that he liked very much the way things had gone here. He did not wish to be overcrowded at Ottawa, but would leave matters for me to arrange. . . . I then asked him if he would reserve one night for dinner with me—a night for Members of the Cabinet—and a night at Government House. He said he was agreeable to this, but did not want to be crowded. I asked him if I could announce this at Ottawa at once, so that preparations could be got under way. He said yes, but it might be as well not to fix a definite time of arrival until we got nearer to the end of the week.

"The President, before leaving, said he would see me tomorrow. Churchill had appointments with some others . . . and said he would see me tomorrow any time."

In the afternoon of December 27, Mackenzie King and the Defence Ministers went to the White House where they first saw Churchill by himself. The President then came into the room and said: "Mackenzie, won't you introduce your Ministers?" Mackenzie King "presented each in turn. We sat around in a sort of semi-circle." Representatives of other Commonwealth countries were also present. The "conversation was very general. Nothing was said about the unity of command or strategy. . . . In answer to my question as to whether there was more we could do than was being done or done differently, McCarthy [the Canadian Minister to the United States] said: 'more production than men,' which caused Churchill to say: 'I need all the men I can get. I have need of men as well, and men you can let me have, let me have them.' He mentioned the divisions we already had. . . .

"The President looked to me pretty tired and it was clear they were both just filling in time, while behind the scenes the Chiefs of the two Staffs were working together. Churchill is beginning to look rather flabby and tired. I could not help thinking of what a terrible thing it is that the fate of the world should rest so largely in the hands of two men to either of whom anything might happen at any moment."

The next day (December 28) Churchill and Mackenzie King left for Ottawa in adjoining cars on the same train. They dined together and after dinner Mackenzie King talked "about 'my problem' as I called it. I there outlined to him the efforts that were being made to enforce conscription and National Government for the sake of conscription but I felt it would mean splitting the Dominion. He told me that manpower was going to be scarce in Britain owing to numbers in factories. Americans sending over some troops would relieve him somewhat. That manpower was important and any help we could give him in that way would be appreciated. . . . I spoke to him about our present forces and what we had in mind by way of an addition."

Churchill was given a wonderful reception at the station in Ottawa on December 29 and, shortly afterwards, he attended a War Committee meeting at the East Block. Mackenzie King opened the discussion "by enquiring as to the unity of command. He [Churchill] said little beyond that something of the kind had been arranged for the Pacific which would be disclosed later. He then referred to the declaration drafted at Washington, copy of which I had in my pocket and which I read, which he said I had participated in." Mackenzie King noted parenthetically in his record that the extent of his participation was that the British Ambassador had shown him the document and expressed the hope he would accept it as it was, bad grammar and all. Mackenzie King then read the declaration to the meeting and "asked the specific question as to the pledge to give full resources, as to whether that meant conscription or whether it meant that each country would adopt what it believed was its own method to have full war effort. Churchill was quite emphatic that it was for each country to decide for itself, to decide its own method, and that it did not signify any form of procedure to that end."

Churchill "spoke feelingly of Hong Kong, saying that he was not sure at first about sending Canadians on the theory that if the war did not come, they would not be needed, and if it did come, it would be a difficult place to hold. It was thought that the extra Canadian battalions would supply just what was needed for defence." Churchill "stressed strongly his great friendship with the President, and how ready the President was to give things. Said his coming to this side had enabled him to get much more and more favourable results than could have been acquired in any other way. He thinks Harry Hopkins is a wonderful fellow, has a living flame of a soul. Is invaluable. Most helpful. Spoke about the Pacific Coast. Emphasized the need for having troops there in position to fight; thought ships should be carefully watched.

"I spoke specifically about the Atlantic coast and the question of command between the Americans and ourselves in the Newfoundland area. Said quite openly to him the problem we faced was that while we had been in [the war] during two and a quarter years, things would be so arranged that the U.S. and Britain would settle everything between themselves, and that our services, Chiefs of Staff, etc. would not have any say in what was to be done. That in the last war, there had been a Military Mission at Washington. People thought, in Canada, there should be a Military Mission there now, watching Canada's interests. That he would understand our political problem in that regard.

"I got the Chiefs of Staff later to explain the position. He said he thought we should be entitled to have representation there, but expressed the hope that we would take a large view of the relationships of the large countries, to avoid anything in the way of antagonisms."

In the afternoon Churchill was sworn at Government House to the Privy Council of Canada and in the evening there was a large dinner party at Government House. In conversation at the dinner, Churchill told Mackenzie King "he sensed a good deal of feeling that I ought to support conscription or form a National Government to let two or three [Conservatives] have a look in. That he would never press me in any way. That I knew better about my own country than anyone else, but that he had been told by several already that I would be the strongest Prime Minister Canada had, if I would meet my opponents to that extent. . . .

"He asked me whether he could say tomorrow he would welcome another armoured division. I told him we intended he should have it, but I thought that had better be left for us to announce. He might say that some additional help would be welcome.

"I reminded him that Meighen had made a political issue of the question of conscription and had made it more difficult on that account to take in anyone from the Opposition. Also that I had offered them the chance last year, and that there were two other parties to consider. I doubted if they would come in. Also there was no real Cabinet material on the other side. He thought it was mostly because they wanted to be in the picture. I said it was financial interests that wanted control of Cabinet policy. Quite clearly the Conservatives have been urging him to try to persuade me on some of these matters."

The great event of the visit was Churchill's speech in the House of Commons Chamber on December 30 to which members of both Houses of Parliament and representatives of the press across Canada had been specially invited. The seating was similar to that on other occasions when distinguished visitors have addressed the Canadian Parliament. When Churchill entered the House of Commons Chamber with Mackenzie King "there was tremendous applause, all present standing as well as applauding. . . . When the applause ceased, I was about to go forward when the Speaker in a few words called on me to introduce Mr. Churchill. . . . When I went forward to speak, I received a tremendous reception. Indeed in a way quite equal to that which was given Churchill. I was rather embarrassed by it and taken completely by surprise. It was a welcome tribute, and particularly so paid in the presence of Churchill, and is something which was heard over the radio in all parts of the world. It could leave no doubt as to the feeling toward myself.

"I found the reading of my little introduction quite easy, and I think succeeded in giving it the right emphasis. Its sentiments were roundly applauded. When I concluded, I took my seat with Dandurand to my right.

"Churchill was given another great ovation. He made a kindly and, I felt, just the right reference to myself, all circumstances considered, referring to me on the personal side as an old friend, and on the public side, as having been Prime Minister fifteen years out of twenty which helped to bring that fact anew to the public mind."

Mackenzie King felt Churchill's speech "was not as good as the address at Washington. That he showed evidence of fatigue in its delivery and, in part, its matter was less clear-cut than that of some of his other addresses. But it had been prepared with the greatest care so as to say nothing which would possibly offend any party. He had been meticulously careful in that. As we walked down the Hall of Fame together, he said to me: 'What I am going to say will be all right,' and it was. All political aspects had been exceptionally closely watched. At different times, he referred to what a job it was to prepare a speech, this one in particular. He found it hard to get time for it; worked late at night and was at it again in the morning.

"When he had concluded the address and the national anthem was sung, I walked over and shook hands heartily with him. . . . As we stood together shaking hands, there was again very great applause. There was something very spontaneous about the applause with respect to each of us. I felt that the atmosphere had wonderfully cleared, and that his visit had served to put the facts into their right place.

"We left the Commons Chamber together. Went to the Speaker's Apartment. . . . The members of the Conservative party then came in and I shook hands with them all, except Hanson with whom I had shaken hands earlier in the day. Then Glen [the Speaker] and I withdrew and allowed them to have a private conference for about half an hour."

In conversation afterwards Churchill told him the Conservatives "had been feeling that they ought to be in the picture. That they represented a large part of the population. That I had not made a real offer to them about coming into the Government. That all he would say was that as the chance might offer to broaden the base, to do so. When he spoke about my having made no real offer to them, I told him how Hanson had said he had been elected to oppose me, and cited also what Coldwell had said as to his being for Socialism and Blackmore for Social Credit, and all had registered themselves as opposed to coming into the Ministry. Churchill again referred, as he had once or twice, to the difference in men once they got into the Government. Referred to his own case of Chamberlain and himself working together, etc. All that he said was in the best of form and taste and consideration. It was clear he was trying to help the Tories to get some of the recognition they wanted, but realized, as he had told them, that the situation here was very different than in America where the parties were evenly balanced and a coalition needed to carry on the government. That there was nothing of the kind here. I pointed out also to him that in the U.S. . . . Willkie had played a great part. Hanson had done nothing of the kind here, nor had any member of their party come out and said they would support the policies of the Government as Knox and Stimson had. If any of them had done so, I would have been the first to recognize them in the Administration."

During the afternoon "some photos were taken by Karsh of the two of us together, and one or two of Mr. Churchill by himself. . . . He was immensely relieved and pleased with having the speech out of the way, and no further speech to make on this side. I can understand his relief."

Churchill dined at Laurier House with the members of the War Committee on December 30. Mackenzie King felt "the evening went along splendidly. Every one seemed to be in a genuinely happy frame of mind. Conversation was easy and general."

The following day, December 31, Mackenzie King drove with Churchill for an inspection of Uplands Airport. "We had," he noted, "a very nice talk together on the way. He became more confidential; extremely so in fact with regard to the interview with the Conservatives yesterday. The subject came about through a vicious article in the *Citizen* this morning representing that Meighen had not been invited to meet Churchill, being kept out, etc. I told Churchill that it served to illustrate just the kind of thing I was up against with having Meighen as an opponent. As a matter of fact I had learned yesterday, from an authoritative source, that Meighen himself was indisposed, suffering from influenza, but he was . . . at the Albany Club in Toronto, and had sent word to Hanson that he should abstain from being present when Churchill addressed the House, as a protest against the visit being something planned as a glorification of Mackenzie King. Had also sent word as to a resolution which the Conservatives were to draft and give to Churchill. Just what its terms were I do not know. Churchill said he had not received any resolution from them. In speaking of Meighen he said 'yon Cassius hath a lean and hungry look'—which of course is an adequate description of Meighen."

Churchill told him the Conservatives had said that the offer Mackenzie King had made to them "was based on personal allegiance to myself. I said I had made no condition of any kind; that that helped to show how unfair they were. He said that he had told them that that was to be expected of any man who would come into a Government—that loyalty to a leader was a first principle. He did not see how Ministers could stay in a Government who were not prepared to stand up for its head. He asked them whether they would be prepared to come into a National Government now, and they said: 'No.' He asked them whether they would come in on the basis of their representation in the House of Commons. They said no, they would not. That what they would ask would be a representation of their numbers in the country. I told Churchill that all of that had been tested at the election that was held during the war. That the numbers in Parliament represented their following in the country. He said to me further that what they seemed to feel most keenly—to put it in their way—was that this isolationist (meaning me) had come into everything and was getting the credit for everything in connection with the war; whereas they, who for years before had been trying to pledge Canada's part for war, were receiving no place at all.

"I told Churchill there could be nothing further from the truth than this. They had tried to pin the badge of isolationism on me. He could not find in Canada a man who had been stronger for British connection than myself, and for Empire unity, and [I said] that I had taken steps which I thought had led to that unity, that they were the opposite of those which they had been advocating and which would have destroyed unity. I cited complete autonomy of the Dominions, free nations status, and also the establishment of legations and the like. I had been put down as a separatist on these accounts. For a long while their chief cry was that I was pro-American. It was true I had been at Harvard and with the Rockefeller Foundation, and had many friends there. I had always felt that would be helpful and . . . it had proved to be helpful. That when they saw they could no longer take advantage of that attack they were now coming back to this isolationist talk.

"I told him that the Conservative party was more or less bankrupt of men that could help and that Meighen had made the whole business into political warfare, rather than co-operation. That he would see for himself from yesterday's demonstration in the House just where I stood in Parliament and the country. Churchill said he had noticed that—indeed in fact he had spoken of it yesterday once or twice, what a great reception it was. I said that he could be assured that a section of the press who were seeking to get control for purposes of deciding financial policies and the like did not represent the feeling of the country. Their whole effort was a belittlement of myself, that I had purposely refrained from trying to be conspicuous. Felt that with Roosevelt and himself representing the great powers I naturally maintained a sense of proportion in my actions and utterances.

"The Conservatives had asked him about conscription and he had told them that that was a matter for Parliament to decide. This was a domestic matter. It was for our people to decide. He said to me yesterday that he had told them that for a long time to come the question would not be one so much of men as of shipping—how to get across the munitions, arms, etc. and later on men. He had counselled their going softly in regard to some of these matters. . . .

"I said I was so glad he had been here himself to judge just what the forces were that were at work. Last night he said to me that he had told me, and had also said to the Conservatives, that he would not press me for anything unless it was a matter of life and death. That he did not expect it to come to that. That he did not think there would be a successful invasion of Britain. There might even be no invasion, but he kept emphasizing that this war was not like the last. It was a war of machines, of very expensive machines, of strategy, etc., and not numbers of men."

Churchill also told Mackenzie King the Conservatives had said "we could not send our forces into Newfoundland. I said our men were there now. He said only voluntarily. I said: But there had not been need for others; that under the War Measures Act we could quickly extend what we were doing to include those areas. . . . I mentioned to him Power's idea to call up large numbers of men, train them and, out of the number, there would be plenty for voluntary enlistment. He said that he thought that was the right thing and asked me why we did not do it. I said Ralston was opposed, he representing the Defence Department; that the Army was against it. He said: 'Why don't you assert your authority, say that you want it and have it done. I would do that,' he said. It appealed to him very strongly as the right thing. I said I did not like to assert my view against those of the military authorities, not having the technical knowledge, and did not wish to go contrary to military advice. He said, in a case like this, he thought one should use the judgment one had for the whole situation. That that seemed to him the sensible thing to do. I mentioned that I had thought of a referendum, but did not want to create that controversy and, if possible, to avoid it."

As a sort of footnote to his account of the visit Mackenzie King recalled that he had shown Churchill the proclamation putting a price of one thousand pounds on the head of William Lyon Mackenzie in 1837; after reading it Churchill had turned to him and said: "They had a proclamation on my head in South Africa but all they put on it was 25 pounds!" and he had recited the lines from Tennyson "Yet I doubt not thro' the ages one increasing purpose runs, And the thoughts of men are widened with the process of the suns."

Mackenzie King had a few final words with Churchill at the station before his train left. Of the whole visit he wrote: "I feel deeply grateful the visit had gone without incident of any kind that was unpleasant or harmful. I had been with him practically all the time and we have shared most of the hours together and in a very intimate way. I found his nature wonderfully kind, sympathetic and understanding. He is particularly quick to see a political situation."

Later that day, in concluding his diary for the year 1941, Mackenzie King wrote: "So far as Canada is concerned, but for Meighen's entry into the leadership of the Conservative party, and the possibility of his being again in the Commons, I should have little or no concern. I feel a bit worried about the determined attitude of Ralston, who is being backed by Macdonald, and the danger of the two of them being too arbitrary in their stand in support of conscription. . . .

"The demonstration given to myself yesterday by my friends in Parliament will, I believe, have a far-reaching effect. It will let the Cabinet as well as the Tories see where the people are in relation to myself. I shall fight on with a view of the war being won without resort to conscription, without, I hope, a referendum, and without a general election. Possibly a vote in Parliament; letting Parliament decide will settle the matter for some time to come. If Ralston and Macdonald will help, as I believe they will, we shall get through all right. If we master the situation, under God's guidance and help, I believe we shall be able to carry on to the end. Personally, I believe my own strength is greater, despite the additional care, than it was a year ago. Certainly my vision, I think, is clearer and I have less fear and more of faith. . . .

"As I look back on the year and think of Parliament, the readjustment of the Cabinet, the session, the trip to British Columbia, the trip to England, meetings and speeches there, the meeting with the President, and now the grand climax of it all with conferences at Washington, and the visit of Churchill himself to Ottawa, to the House of Commons and to Laurier House, I have a reason to be without fear and to have more of faith. It is a wonderful close to a wonderful year."

CHAPTER THIRTEEN

The Plebiscite

IN 1941, no single question dominated the Canadian political scene; in 1942, the question of conscription for overseas service reached its first crisis, and the Mackenzie King Government almost fell apart before a compromise was finally reached. The crisis was entirely political and psychological. No practical difficulty had been experienced at that time in finding sufficient men to serve in the Canadian forces overseas. The opponents of the Government were, in Mackenzie King's view, seeking to make conscription for overseas service the symbol, in English-speaking Canada, of a total war effort. They were also, in his opinion, making the most of the natural feeling of those with close relatives in the forces that conscription would ensure equality of sacrifice.

Mackenzie King sought to counter this political campaign by a concrete demonstration that Canada was, in fact, making a total war effort. At the same time, he felt that his promise never to use conscription for service overseas would be a serious embarrassment if the needs of the Army overseas for reinforcements could not at some time be met without conscription. He had begun to feel that he and the Government should be freed of this commitment and that this release would require some form of consultation of the people either by a referendum or plebiscite or by a general election. The term "referendum" was first used by Mackenzie King but he later decided that a referendum would be construed as a verdict on conscription itself and that all the Government should ask for was freedom to resort to conscription if necessary; for such a consultation, "plebiscite," he felt, was a more appropriate word. He himself did not believe conscription for overseas service would ever be required.

In his eyes a total effort could be achieved by a combination of compulsory selective service in the Western Hemisphere with voluntary service overseas and drastic mobilization of the financial and economic resources of the country. One of these measures of total war was the so-called "billion dollar gift" to Britain by Canada which had been proposed late in 1941 and actually mentioned to Winston Churchill during his visit to Ottawa at the end of the year. The billion dollar gift was, in fact, an undertaking by the Canadian treasury to pay for a billion dollars worth of British purchases in Canada.

The final decision about the gift was made on January 2, 1942, but Mackenzie King was disappointed that his colleagues generally did not "regard this billion dollar gift as in any way helping to offset the slightest limitation of war effort in any other direction, as, for example, conscripting men for overseas and enlargement of Army to the point which may necessitate this."

The Cabinet resumed on January 5 discussion of the Army programme and the attitude to be taken to the conscription issue in Parliament. Despite some objections, Mackenzie King felt "it was apparent that the Cabinet was largely in favour of granting the extra armoured division overseas provided it would not necessitate conscription. I have felt strongly that Ralston would resign if he did not get the extra armoured division and that Angus Macdonald would follow his example. . . . To lose Ralston and Macdonald at this stage would be to create a panic with respect to Canada's war effort. I believe the whole business can work out if given sufficient time. . . .

"I gave my support to the programme of the extra armoured division, two army tank brigades and extra ancillary troops on the ground that the armoured division did not mean recruiting large numbers of men for a new division. They were already recruited as an infantry division. It meant spending considerable sums on tanks which, however, made an armoured division worth three times an infantry division. . . . The numbers of men for the ancillary troops and reinforcements are not so very large, and, considering that the whole would give an Army overseas, and to that extent strengthen the morale, the pride, and the power of the striking force in Britain, it seemed to me that what was proposed was along the right lines. . . .

"I added that my understanding was that, if the Army were constituted in this way, it would be generally understood that we could not be expected to go on increasing the Army, but would regard this as our contribution in that direction. Ralston would not concede this as a finality, though he said he would hope and expect that such would be the case." Mackenzie King also recalled General Stuart's assurance "that this programme could be carried out without resort to conscription; that I was prepared to go full length short of conscription."

The decision as to the holding of a referendum had been postponed at the last Cabinet meeting on the war programme in the old year. When a referendum now came up for discussion again, Mackenzie King suggested the question might read: "Are you in favour of allowing the Government power of requiring persons to enlist in military, naval or air forces outside of Canada when, in the opinion of the Government, such service may be deemed necessary to the defence of Canada and the efficient prosecution of the war?"

After a good deal of discussion, Mackenzie King asked if his colleagues "could not agree on letting Ralston have his programme on . . . the understanding . . . that we believed conscription was unnecessary; that the programme represented an all-out effort; that we believed this programme could be carried out without resort to conscription." He suggested that, to meet Ralston's position, he should be free to say that "he would reserve his right, if this proved not to be the case, to consider later what further steps might then be necessary." He also "pointed out that any member of the Government could take this stand and preserve his own position. That if conscription became necessary, he could resign, being unwilling to support it; equally if he believed it to be necessary and the Cabinet would not support conscription, he would be free to resign. It would be some time before that question would arise. Meanwhile there might be great change in the world situation." Mackenzie King finally got agreement on that basis, and added they "might have discussed for another week, and I don't think we would have come to a satisfactory conclusion."

But from that day until the session began on January 22, Mackenzie King wavered between the view that the conscription issue should be fought out in Parliament and the alternative that a referendum or plebiscite should be announced either before Parliament met or in the Speech from the Throne.

From the first of the year he had been working on the statement he intended to make in the opening debate in Parliament. On January 6 he told the Cabinet he would like to read a "statement which I believed to be the truth with respect to what is meant by total effort in meeting total war." His colleagues were "under the impression that it was what I intended to say publicly, either over the radio or in Parliament, and members listened more or less breathlessly, as I read the document through. . . .

"I went on to say that, of course, I intended to recast what I had read, but the point I had wished to make clear was that we had, up to the present, been able to accomplish everything without having to contemplate resort to conscription; that this programme did not contemplate resort to conscription, and that we had kept the country united in its war effort up to the present, and that we had no political issue separating the parties until Mr. Meighen himself, as the new leader of the Conservative party, issued a statement in which he made the issue of conscription a political issue which necessarily divided the parties and which made impossible any thought of National Government by the present Administration. He had made clear that the issue between the two parties was that of conscription for overseas service. Very well—Parliament was assembling, and Parliament will have to decide. They would have to decide between King and Meighen and the policies for which they respectively stood."

When he had concluded, "Ralston said at once that I knew that he would be prepared to follow me anywhere and to go any lengths for me, but he hoped I would not make it an obligation for members of the Liberal party never to support conscription. I said I was speaking only of the present and the programme which we were submitting to Parliament. . . . I said I was prepared to be as generous with the party as Sir Wilfrid was and allow each man to have his own views with regard to conscription when it came to stating what might or might not be advisable some time in the future.

"Ralston then . . . said that he was prepared to take his stand against conscription on the score that it would divide the country and might impair our war effort in that way. He added that he had already stated that twice and thought he was the only member of the Cabinet who had said publicly a word to that effect. Macdonald also said he was prepared to oppose conscription on the score that it would divide the country. Neither of them, however, wished to be committed to the Government's not having the power at any time to advocate conscription if they believed the necessity had arisen. . . .

"Ralston did say he hoped he would not have to be put in the position of being a follower of Meighen. . . . Seeing the position as King or Meighen, puts everyone on the spot in regard to their support. I took the view that every member of the Cabinet, except the last two [St. Laurent and Mitchell], came into a Government which was committed to no conscription for overseas."

At this point, a referendum was referred to again and Mackenzie King "said that we would have to wait until we had a talk with members of the party. . . . Cardin seemed to be much impressed by what I had said about Parliament deciding. After Council was over, I had a word quietly with him and he told me that he was going to see if, in some way, he could get the Quebec members to support a referendum. I told him I thought it would be looked upon as an evidence of weakness for any part of the country not to be prepared to have a referendum, and that

The Plebiscite

Quebec might get into quite a wrong position by not agreeing to that step." Meanwhile rumours had begun to appear in the press that the Cabinet was considering a referendum and, on January 9, Premier Hepburn of Ontario stated that a referendum would split Canada from end to end. Mackenzie King observed that Hepburn's statement was "the strongest evidence that the application of conscription itself would have that effect, unless we are to imitate the Prussian totalitarian state at once, and change altogether the democratic basis of government. I pray for power and vision sufficient to be able to express all these matters in a convincing way. I find it so difficult to get what I see so clearly myself, adequately expressed." He was to find this a continuing difficulty as he struggled day after day with his speech for Parliament. That same day (January 9) Howe advised Mackenzie King that the Ontario Ministers had come around to readiness to accept a referendum "though he disliked it." Mackenzie King observed "there remains the difficulty of getting Cardin to take a similar point of view. . . . It may be that Hepburn's opposition to it will help to bring Quebec friends to see that it might be the means of preventing conscription in the end."

On January 15, Mackenzie King discussed the Quebec situation with Cardin and "found that he had considerably modified his views and has come to the conclusion that it is more important that the Liberals should remain in power, and the Government in office, than take the chance of a split, which might lead to a Union Government with the evils attendant thereon. He also feels that Quebec will probably be agreeable to a referendum, particularly as Hepburn and the Tories generally seem so strongly opposed to it. I told him if we had a referendum, I thought it should go in the Speech from the Throne, so as to avoid men committing themselves in the debate on the Address. He agreed that that was right. I said I thought the referendum ought to be to give the Government power to do as it might find necessary with respect to despatch of troops anywhere; that as long as we had the matter in our hands we could control the situation. He seemed agreeable also to this. He did not give his final word."

Mackenzie King observed (January 15) that "very strong war feelings" were "being aroused throughout the country. The conscriptionist gang, through the power of their press and the organization they have effected on the lines of a drive, influence public opinion in all localities, which have a telling effect. I am just as glad Parliament is assembling fairly soon."

On January 18, he "worked out something on the plebiscite which will give the Government a free hand in dealing with developments. I think

I have it framed in a way which every member of Parliament will find it not only possible but necessary to support. . . . At any rate, it is obviously the Government's duty to have itself placed in the position where its hands cannot be tied in virtue of any past commitments."

The next day (January 19), when Mackenzie King read his colleagues a draft of the Speech from the Throne, it at first "seemed to meet with general approval. . . . Then Ralston said that he thought the Tories would not like the paragraphs re referendum; they would construe them as giving the Government a free hand to do anything and would not want to vote for this. He kept arguing for a straight vote on the conscription issue which brought the thing back to where I pointed out I had to disagree. Cardin, on the other hand, evidently moved by Ralston going in one direction, did not think we ought to ask for any release of commitments or say anything about them, nor did he favour going into the Speech at all, but wanted to debate the matter on the floor of Parliament.

"I told him I had, at one time, felt that way. On the other hand, I was anxious to keep our forces united; those of the Government and those of the members of the House." Mackenzie King thought the whole Liberal party could "agree on what I had suggested which would take ammunition from our enemies." He felt he had made an impression on all his colleagues when he pointed out "that I, myself, could not continue at the head of any Government which as much as considered conscription, unless I were released from all commitments in that connection made before the war had reached the proportions it has today."

When he found it was going to be difficult to get any agreement between Cardin and Ralston, Mackenzie King took advantage of an appointment to say that "perhaps they could discuss the matter more freely if I were not present. If they could reach no agreement, I would ask them to come back at half past 8. I got word at nearly 7 that no agreement had been reached, and then asked that they should come back at 8.30." He returned to the Cabinet that evening "quite prepared to drop the referendum matter and have the debate at once in the House, if controversy were to keep up over the referendum matter. To my surprise, I learned . . . they had come pretty well to an agreement and that the matter now was one of phrasing merely. We worked from half past eight till after midnight on discussing the merits of different paragraphs, and the question to be asked in the referendum. . . . Cardin spoke about meeting the members first. I told him I thought we ought to have something definite to tell them. That it would be better to put it in the Speech. He finally acquiesced, indeed, all finally agreed and I got the Cabinet perfectly unanimous. . . . Indeed the best of temper was kept throughout the evening. Ralston wanted me to say that I would, if a referendum carried, immediately amend the National Mobilization Act, giving the Government power to act, but I told him . . . I was not going to make one commitment, in asking to be freed of others. It was nearly one when I got home and after 1.30 when I turned out the lights."

The session of Parliament which had opened on November 7, 1940, was prorogued on January 21, 1942. The new session was to open on January 22. Mackenzie King began to feel, on January 21, that it might be better to take out of the Speech from the Throne to be read at the opening of the new session the reference to the plebiscite and hold the matter "till we had discussed and explained the situation to the Quebec members, in this way consulting them in advance; also that that part of the Speech might be kept as a statement of Government policy to be used as an amendment to any motion for conscription." What prompted this was "St. Laurent telling me he had a 'phone call from Quebec saying they had seen what was suggested in the press, and that if the Government took any plebiscite, they would likely put in an independent candidate against him [in the by-election in Quebec East set for February 9]. Power had also said to me he thought the Conservatives would fight the referendum bitterly and it might be as well to face the conscription issue squarely. I felt, too, that the plebiscite as proposed in the Speech might be taken by anti-conscriptionists as not in accordance with the pledges made at the election, and that it might cause some of the following to feel that they would not be justified in trusting me. . . . To have the whole matter reconsidered, I had the Cabinet meet in my office after prorogation.

"We discussed the whole question from 9 till half past eleven, all agreeing that what was said in the Speech was definitely our policy, the discussion being the wisdom of presenting it to the caucus before putting it in the Speech. . . . However, after going over all arguments again, particularly those that related to procedure in the House itself, it seemed best to let the Speech stand as it was [i.e., with the plebiscite mentioned], the point being that it was a definite statement of Government policy, and any motion in the nature of conscription on the Address would be a negation of that policy and could be voted against by all, whether conscriptionist or anti-conscriptionist." He added that there was "a straight declaration from Cardin that he was prepared loyally to support and to advocate the wisdom of the Government's policy as set out in the Speech. He has played a good part. He is, not excepting myself, in the most difficult position of all." The relevant paragraph in the Speech from the Throne read: 'My Ministers accordingly will seek, from the people, by means of a plebiscite, release from any obligation arising out of any past commitments restricting methods of raising men for military service.'

The new session opened on January 22. As soon as the House rose, there was a Liberal caucus and Mackenzie King lost little time in referring to "what I had said at the last caucus about conscription leading to a demand for National Government so that monied interests might get control of the power of government, that though we were united at the time, some of our men would leave us one by one, and that I was quite prepared with respect to myself, to witness tragedy similar to that which I had seen Sir Wilfrid suffer. I wanted them to know that I was not judging anyone. I believed in the sincerity of the different views expressed. Knew something of human nature and felt they might feel forces around them too great; that I was quite prepared for this, though I hoped it would not be necessary, and trusted we were able and strong enough to find a way to keep our forces united.

"I then spoke of the Government's policy as outlined in the Speech from the Throne. Told them of the struggle we had had in getting a policy on which all could unite, and avoid division in the country that would certainly be playing Hitler's game." He pointed out that, when the pledge not to use conscription for overseas service was given, only a European war was contemplated and added: "Since last we met Japan had come into the war. The United States—right beside us—had come into the war. We were now in a position where our political enemies were taking the ground out from under our feet through our not having power under the Mobilization statute to even move men across the border to the United States or into Newfoundland or to an island on the Pacific, though we had mutual obligations with the States to help to defend each other. . . . I pointed out that now we did not know what course the war might take. For the Government to be in a position where it could not do what it really felt would be necessary to protect Canada in the winning of the war in company with twenty-six other nations working together, was to let the enemy again take the ground from under our feet, and to get, as a Government, into a truly impossible position.

"I then spoke of the position as best illustrated by what was taking place in our by-elections. Said that Mitchell had 'phoned me this morning to say that the Conservative organizer in Welland had telegraphed him that unless he would come out for an out-and-out conscription, he would have to put a candidate against him. I had learned that some of our party in Quebec . . . were thinking they might have to bring out a candidate unless Mr. St. Laurent would come out absolutely against conscription. . . . It represented opposite points of view that existed right in the Cabinet and our own party. . . . I said we had . . . been able to resolve our differences by adopting the policy set out in the Speech from the Throne, which would give us freedom of action, but leave us free to take what course we needed as necessity might dictate.

"I pointed out we would still have to frame our policies in the light of the support we could count on from our party in Parliament. I then spoke of strategy being as necessary in political warfare as in actual warfare, and that we had spent a long time discussing whether we should not first of all discuss our policy in caucus without putting anything in the Speech from the Throne concerning it, but bringing it out in my own speech in the House."

He then drew attention to the danger of an amendment to the Address in favour of all-out conscription being moved by the Opposition and pointed out that, if there were such an amendment, "we could all vote against it on the score that it was a negation of our policy of first consulting the people. That this was a ground on which everyone could stand, whether he favoured conscription immediately or remotely or was against it. I told them that I personally could not—as matters now stood—support conscription for overseas, even if it might mean the saving of our country, in view of the pledge I had given, unless that pledge was removed; as I saw it, unless the people were given a chance to remove the pledge and it were removed, the battle would become one of Mackenzie King vs. Arthur Meighen. . . .

"After stressing that the Government had become united on their policy, I felt if we could unite—if the Members in the House themselves could unite, which would mean the people throughout the country could unite—it was most important we should keep the country united. I left it to others to speak."

After several Members had spoken, Mackenzie King "passed on word to Cardin to speak. He made a splendid speech. Went over the whole ground of our discussions in Council. The length we had gone to help to make things unanimous, of his being prepared to back the Government in its policy in Quebec, and spoke of my having stood by Sir Wilfrid and become leader within two years after conscription had been introduced. . . . He said in this he had followed my vision and words. Told them they could trust me. Altogether he made a passionate appeal—a splendid presentation.

"I followed him, to bring the caucus to a close. . . . I referred to Cardin's health. Thanked God it was restored, and he was able to fight as he was. Told caucus quite frankly that when I knew of Lapointe's illness, how fatal it was, I really felt for a time that I would not be able to carry the load, knowing that Cardin was ill. That by the load, I meant keeping the two parts of Canada together. I told them how Lapointe and I had sat together, as it were, symbolical of the union of the peoples . . . how we had never differed on anything, finding in our common Canadianism higher ground. I could see no one that could take his place, and really wondered what could be done. Miraculously, Cardin had got back his health, and I said I wanted to say a word to him. I then said I would now ask him to take Lapointe's place at my side. That he would have to fill the gap which Lapointe had left as Leader in his Province. (He had been very anxious that I should let others see that I so regarded him and rightly so.)"

Replying to a question as to what would happen if the plebiscite did not carry, Mackenzie King "asked what would likely become of the country if we were to try to force conscription on the people, knowing that the majority was against it. That we would have to enlarge our jails and use our tanks and rifles against our own people instead of against our enemies. We would be playing Hitler's game and dividing the country effectively. I then went on . . . pointing out that . . . we had no right to get into power on one policy and not carry it out. We would be equally wrong if we felt, in the people's own interests, the need of changing the policy and [did] not give them a chance to change it. If they did not change, the responsibility would be theirs. . . .

"I spoke at some length on the effort being a total war effort, but total did not mean 'total' in one direction only. I spoke of what we were doing in the air, at sea, munitions, foodstuffs, finance, and now we were having the whole thing set at nought, identifying conscription for overseas as total war effort."

Mackenzie King, at the end, "had a feeling that all men seemed greatly relieved at our having shown them a way out. Altogether Lapointe's death, Cardin's appeal, and my own position as they see it [are] having a very telling effect. We may even come through the war more united than when we went into it, if such a thing were possible. Perhaps it is too much to hope for, but I nevertheless have faith in the possibility."

On Monday, January 26, Mackenzie King replied to Hanson in the debate on the Address. The speech he delivered had been worked over almost daily for nearly a month. It was, in fact, a treatise on a total war effort. Mackenzie King was greatly pleased by its reception. "If I had seen Hanson's statement in advance," he wrote, "I could hardly have anticipated more clearly his main points throughout. What I had prepared . . . seemed to pretty well cover all of them. I was delighted to find on rising to speak, that I had little or no difficulty in expressing myself; voice clear and not the least bit nervous. No confusion of thought. I spoke offhand for a time and then started the reading. To my great delight, I was able to complete the early part of the speech reviewing the war effort and covering the programme for this year . . . by six o'clock. . . . This was followed without an interruption and with intense interest by the Members throughout. Our men expressed themselves as delighted with the statement made. I must say it read well and was overwhelming in the facts it presented of the extent of our war effort. . . .

"During the speech," he added, "I was warmly applauded in the afternoon while reading the record, etc. The same was true tonight, particularly so in my references to broken pledges, to my own position, etc. Was given another great ovation after concluding. What pleased me most was that for the first time almost in weeks, Ralston seemed to ease up a bit, lose his tenseness. Indeed I had a feeling that he has been warding himself off very strongly against me in anticipation of my possibly saying things in the speech that might not suit his book. However, at six, there was only one sentence which he questioned. . . .

"He remained to talk briefly. He had seen that the reference to increasing the overseas army met with little applause in the House, had met almost with curtness. I took advantage of this to say I thought we should seek, no matter what authority might be granted, to find the men necessary without trying to enforce conscription, not as a commitment in any way, but as something that obviously if we were to hold the House of Commons, we would be obliged to do, and should therefore keep in mind: apply conscription to the Western Hemisphere but seek not to have it necessary to go beyond."

Another long caucus of the Liberal party was held on January 29. At this time, Mackenzie King was greatly concerned about the by-elections which had been called for February 9. A candidate who listed himself an Independent Liberal was opposing St. Laurent in Quebec East on the ground that the Government could not be trusted to prevent conscription; in Welland, the Conservatives, after first agreeing to stay out of the field, had put up a candidate because Humphrey Mitchell would not come out for conscription. There was no Liberal candidate against Meighen in South York, and Mackenzie King refused to believe the C.C.F. candidate had a chance of winning. About the fourth by-election in Montreal St. Mary's he was not worried. Hepburn had just come out in support of Meighen and in opposition to Humphrey Mitchell. Mackenzie King told the caucus that with "four by-elections on, the Government was trying to prosecute the war, but we had a political battle in the House of Commons, and one in the country as well. . . .

"I then said I had taken St. Laurent and Mitchell into the Government as the best men for two exceptional posts during wartime . . . that if we are to lose these two Ministers in a by-election, I would have to ask myself whether it was not my duty to see the Governor-General at once and tell him that he had better send for someone to form an Administration who had the confidence of the electorate. There was great disapproval of this evidenced, to which I replied at once that it was all very well for individual Members to seek to make themselves secure, regardless of the party as a whole, but that I was not going to take the great responsibility I had in connection with the war and be shot at from opposite sides in my own party. I did not intend to be a general going into battle without an army, but what was equally bad, with an army which was divided. They better understand this at once: unless I could get a very solid support I would be obliged to consider very carefully whether I should carry on."

When he spoke the second time, he asked the caucus to consider his own position. "If I was not released from the pledge, I was bound to take the ground of opposing any measure, whether I thought it necessary for the country at this time or not. I would be described as the greatest coward in the country. Equally, if I were to support a measure which ran counter to the pledge, it would be said that I had been guilty of the greatest betrayal in our history."

On January 30, Mackenzie King was encouraged by reading in the press an "amazing statement made by Meighen when speaking in Toronto, which is reported in the Toronto *Star* of January 28: 'If we have to conscript wealth to win the war we will. But people of common sense do not advocate that until the last gasp.' If this statement does not help to destroy his chances, even in his own riding, I do not know what would."

On January 31, Robert Laurier, nephew of Sir Wilfrid and Minister of Mines in Hepburn's Cabinet, came to see Mackenzie King to tell him of his intention to resign from the Ontario Government in protest against Hepburn's support of Meighen. Mackenzie King was quite moved by this visit. "I told him," he wrote, "that his uncle would be very proud of his actions today; that I thought he had shown a fine spirit.... I confess I felt very proud of him and told him so, but it is not an easy situation for him to face. It made me very happy that he had come into the house and had spoken that way and that he had walked out of the door a true Laurier."

Mackenzie King was pleased on February 6 when Laurier had actually resigned, but most of his satisfaction over this incident vanished later when Laurier came to see him on March 19 to tell him his resignation had never been accepted and Hepburn wanted him back. "The whole business of Ontario politics, as exemplified by this episode from beginning to close," Mackenzie King wrote, "is so amateurish and school-boyish that it makes me rather nauseated."

On January 31, Mackenzie King had a difficult interview with Ralston and Angus Macdonald who came to discuss what attitude they were to take on the question of the plebiscite and conscription because "Angus was to speak in Welland, Ralston at caucus and in the House. They wanted to be sure as to how far they could go as members of the Government. I said quite frankly to Ralston that I thought he ought to take the position which he took in Council at the time we agreed to his programme . . . which was that there was no need at the present time for conscription; that if the people would stop their talking about it . . . and get out and do their best to recruit we might get all the men that we required on a voluntary basis. If they could not be obtained in that way, he himself would feel it was his duty to advocate conscription. He said he would not want to go further than that, and made it quite clear that, if the plebiscite carried, he would wish to be free to enforce conscription, if the men could not be obtained voluntarily. To this I said I thought . . . we would have to take the situation, to which an attempted enforcement of conscription would give rise, into account, as well as results which would be obtained from its enforcement. In other words, that the effect of every act would have to be considered in relation to the totality of opinion.

"Macdonald seemed to want to know if this meant if Quebec held out alone—we would not have conscription because one part was holding out? I said I did not mean that at all. I meant that situations would arise in the West, as well as in Quebec and rural parts of Ontario, and elsewhere, all of which would have to be taken into account: men needed for agriculture—demands there might be to keep our men here; also, to save an invasion on the Pacific coast, etc.; that we could not ignore any side of the question.

"Macdonald asked if he could say in Welland that he believed in conscription himself; that, if the plebiscite were to carry, the purpose of it was not to evade a responsibility, but rather to enable the Government to fulfil one. He used the expression that the implication of a plebiscite was to get a free hand, and that he certainly would use a free hand in a way that would serve to help most in Canada's prosecution of its war effort. I said that would be all right, as long as it was made clear that, up to the present, the necessity had not arisen, and it need not arise if there was the right response along voluntary lines. I said we would not enforce conscription simply for the sake of compulsion; that compulsion was a means, not an end."

Mackenzie King observed that "Ralston seemed surprised when I said that I was sure conscription would not carry through the House at the present time. He thinks that it would. In that he is entirely wrong. It would simply split the party in two and make it impossible for any Government to carry on and next to impossible to form any. I told him he would have to keep in mind that there is no alternative but an election."

Mackenzie King added that "Ralston seemed particularly anxious for me to make a statement that I would agree to enforce conscription if the plebiscite carried and we could not get the necessary men without it. I told him I would not, in seeking release from a commitment, make any kind of a commitment. . . . I replied very strongly about taking all factors into account. . . . I want to be able to say that, up to the moment of decision, I have kept my own counsel and made no promise one way or the other."

When "Ralston said he doubted if I realized how strongly the people felt who had sons at the war; how much they resented the attitude of the Government in not saying definitely they were going to act," Mackenzie King "said to him I thought the truth was that he perhaps over-emphasizes the need for conscription at all costs, and that I myself might be over-emphasizing the necessity of unity at all costs, but as for knowing about resentments, etc., the whole thing was centring on me; that I had been used to abuse from the Tories all my life. . . . That I, personally, was looking to the future of Canada as well as to its present."

Mackenzie King reminded Ralston and Macdonald that conscription was "thought of only in reference to England," and he said, "with respect to French Canada, if the situation were reversed and we were in a minority, with France controlling, and we were being asked to send our men to France, there would be a very different attitude. We must take all these facts into consideration. I do not know how far we got, but I think it was far enough to help to meet the present situation."

Mackenzie King continued to worry about the by-elections. He noted on February 2 that "reports keep coming in from C.C.F. and Liberals that Meighen will have a hard fight. That they may beat Meighen. This I do not believe at all. . . . Hepburn's machine will be combined with the Tory machine and will spare . . . nothing to ensure Meighen's return. I confess to being deeply concerned over the effect on Canada as a whole which the present political controversy is having. It is playing havoc with our country's war effort and its unity, just at the moment that our war effort had reached its zenith and was receiving an unbounded praise from Britain. The whole business is as cruel as it can possibly be."

Mackenzie King was also disturbed that his colleagues were not making speeches in the debate in Parliament which would help in the by-elections and he was therefore delighted to learn on February 4 that while he had been out of the House "Ilsley made a splendid speech —much to my surprise, all on the plebiscite." For the next few days the by-elections were naturally uppermost in his mind. On February 6, he had "come more and more to feel that we will carry the two by-elections [Welland and Quebec East] and Meighen the Toronto seat, though I believe the hardest fight will be in Quebec East." He felt it was "really shameful that no Minister, excepting Ilsley, has come forward, since the debate began, with any real desire to present the Government's position in its true light. If Ilsley had not spoken our whole case would have gone by default, though it is as strong and as fine as any administration ever had. The best thing of the day," he added, "is Harry Nixon having come out strongly against Meighen, saying it would be a disaster for him to be re-elected. [Nixon was the member of Hepburn's Government who had resigned in 1940 and been reinstated, had again openly differed with Hepburn and opposed the election of Meighen.] This will help getting out the vote against Meighen in Toronto, and should help in bringing the farmers out in Welland."

February 9 was polling day in the four by-elections and, during the day, Mackenzie King continued to feel "that we shall probably win both Ministerial by-elections, but that Meighen will be elected in York South. I am, however, far from being sure of the result in Quebec East. It may well go against us. Neither am I at all sure of the result in Welland. . . . Howe said they were betting 3 to 2 against Meighen winning in Toronto. That, I think, is sheer nonsense."

When the results began to come in, Mackenzie King "felt tremendously relieved and equally surprised to get this all-round report of Meighen's defeat [by Joseph Noseworthy] and three Liberal victories."

He went to the House of Commons a little after nine o'clock and "was met at the side door by members of our party—cheering and shouting and all wishing to shake hands. They went back to the Chamber and awaited my return there. When I went in I was given a tremendous ovation, which kept up for considerable time and was renewed after the Speaker had mildly called order to enable the debate to proceed. When I sat down, I looked straight across at the Tories—Hanson, Diefenbaker and a few others—as much as to say: 'You have got now pretty well what you deserve.' To our own men in different parts of the House I turned with a pretty happy countenance, and was given a great cheer. When Coldwell came into the House I nodded him congratulations across the floor. He too looked supremely happy. After staying in the House for a short time I returned to my room to complete the statement to the press."

Mackenzie King noted: "I must confess that I was more than surprised at the outcome. It might so readily have gone completely the other way. As it is, nearly every force that was working for disunity and destruction was arrayed as one against me. All my enemies were lined up on different sides. What was an argument for us in Quebec was an argument against us in Ontario, and vice versa. The extremists in Quebec were beaten by faith stronger than prejudice; the same true in Welland. But what we gained at one stroke was the greatest of all—two Ministers chosen from outside the House of Commons—each bringing new and much needed strength to the Ministry (great risk in the case of both). In the case of St. Laurent, worthy successor to Lapointe and Sir Wilfrid. In the case of Mitchell, the best possible man for Minister of Labour; but more than this—Meighen defeated and out of Parliament altogether. Not only Meighen defeated, but the Leader of the Conservative party defeated, and defeated in the strongest riding in Toronto, which means the strongest Tory riding in all of Canada. Defeated while supported by financial interests and the press—everything in the way of organization and campaign power that could be assembled for any man...

"This victory to be achieved at a time of the worst crisis of the war and when feeling was raised to a pitch higher than at any time, and the issue that of conscription. But next to Meighen's defeat, its accomplishment was in large part due to the treacherous action on Hepburn's part going on to his platform, and also trying to organize the defeat of the federal Minister in Welland. There never was such treachery on the part of a Leader of a Government towards another Government supposed to be of the same political stripe." He added: "I felt tonight that public life in

The Plebiscite

Canada had been cleansed, as though we had gone through a storm and got rid of something that was truly vile and bad, and which, had it been successful at this time, might have helped to destroy the effectiveness of our war effort. I felt most grateful to Providence for what Canada had been spared of division and strife."

The next day (February 10) at the Cabinet meeting Mackenzie King found his "colleagues all greatly rejoiced. . . . We all agreed that the campaign had shown what a terrible thing a nation-wide campaign on conscription would be, or what it would mean for any Government to attempt to enforce conscription in violation of any pledge. . . . I told my colleagues that . . . we must find some means of securing men for overseas by voluntary enlistment, no matter what powers we got, unless something wholly unforeseen were to arise."

In the House of Commons that day (February 10) Ralston made what Mackenzie King called a splendid speech, which "disclosed in every line the effect of the discussion in Cabinet. . . . One felt the air had been cleared so that an intelligent view could be taken of the war effort as he presented it. His speech was an admirable bit of work, making clear as he did that he favoured voluntary enlistment for overseas and believed men could be found in sufficient numbers without conscription, if all did their part, and that the plebiscite would not delay in any way the training of numbers of men required, etc. It has helped to clear the air still further and to bring our men again well into line from both extremes."

Ralston stated his own position to the House in these words: 'I have faith in the success of the voluntary method if we all do our part. With the background and traditions which this country possesses, and which it would be folly to ignore, I prefer the voluntary method if it works, and I shall do all I can to make it work. At the same time, we cannot know what is ahead and I feel impelled to say—here I can speak only for myself—that if the voluntary system does not meet the needs of the fateful days before us, then I shall feel it my duty as part of my responsibility to advocate the adoption of the other method.'

Next morning (February 11) when Mackenzie King reached the House of Commons, "St. Laurent was waiting in my office. He seemed greatly pleased with outcome in Quebec. Spoke of campaign being one largely of trust in myself and entirely that of loyalty to Lapointe and myself. He came with me to the party caucus and made a very nice and tactful speech, speaking first in French and later in English. He is a great addition of strength to the Administration. I was immensely struck with his manner in getting in touch with different Members. He gives a fine impression of strength and integrity. Power spoke out of his being the best of candidates. Referred to his uprightness. . . . Concluded by saying that the fight, in the main, was my name and the trust the people had in me. Angus Macdonald said the same of the fight in Welland. Gibson gave a nice account of Humphrey Mitchell. Referred to the part the different Members had taken. Howe, apparently, made a particularly good impression. He, too, spoke nicely at the caucus. I was given a great ovation—standing and cheering. I told the caucus that our total effort had, for the time being at least, put an end to the total war of our enemies."

After thanking those who had participated in the campaign, Mackenzie King spoke of the present position in Parliament. The Conservative opposition had moved an amendment regretting the holding of the plebiscite and calling for total mobilization, and the C.C.F. a sub-amendment calling for the conscription of wealth. Mackenzie King "advised all to vote against the amendments." He also spoke of his trip around the world in 1908: "the strategic places at which he had stopped, and Britain controlling the whole. . . . I pointed out that if these strategic points were taken, the British Empire is gone. No matter whether enemies ever reached this continent on either side we would have, for the remainder of our lives, to consider how we could live in a world where totalitarian states were waiting to fulfil their ambitions of world conquest. . . . I begged them, for God's sake, to stand together and not to let this country get divided."

He drew attention to the fact that the plebiscite "was not conscription or no conscription, but simply a free hand, and . . . to Ralston having said we could raise all the men we needed until March 1943 by voluntary enlistment, if we wished to, and then came out strongly and said conscription might never be necessary. On the other hand, it might, and we could not afford to let our soldiers, whose lives stood between the enemy and our own freedom and our lives, suffer from lack of support and necessary reinforcements, so far as I was concerned. If conscription for manpower became necessary for overseas, I would see to it that it was accompanied by conscription of wealth at the same time; that I did not propose to see human life conscripted and wealth escape. That, if a man gave his life, he gave his all; the millionaires would have to do their share. This met with a great response from the caucus and I was asked . . . later, to enlarge on what I had said." He then pointed out that "we were raising the loan to carry on the war by means of voluntary subscriptions secured through a great drive for the purpose. That corresponded to voluntary enlistment for overseas. If, however, it became necessary to resort to conscription of men for overseas, I, for my part, speaking for myself, would advocate conscription of wealth by taking wealth itself—not having resort to voluntary drives, which would enable men to keep their wealth secure by the State and [be] given rates of interest as well.

"I had in mind Ralston's statement yesterday when he spoke personally and was prepared to resort to conscription if the voluntary system did not supply the men. I made use of parallel words that, although I had not consulted my colleagues, what I intended to stand for was conscription of wealth in the way I had described it. I said, if that view got abroad, I thought we would hear much less about conscription than we have been hearing thus far; that the men who were seeking to save their wealth were the ones who were talking the loudest. . . . I felt, perhaps, that I should have spoken to this effect with my colleagues in advance. On the other hand, I was going no further than Ralston had gone in the House. . . . My own feeling is world conditions will have so changed that the problem will have solved itself without any need for conscription. It was an excellent caucus, and I think it will help us in the votes in the House."

But neither the by-election results nor the general approval of the caucus prevented a split in the Liberal following in the House of Commons. Eleven members from Quebec voted against the Government in the divisions on February 19 at the close of the debate on the Address. Four or five of them had, in fact, been out and out opponents of Canadian participation in the war from the start, but the rest were not. After the vote, Mackenzie King observed that it was "a pity for the Province of Quebec that all the men who voted in this way were from the one province. . . . However, it will let other parts of the Dominion see that it is not all smooth sailing so far as Quebec is concerned. It is the first real break we have had in our ranks since the war started. . . . These men will put Quebec in a false light against the other provinces; Canada in a false light in the U.S. and Britain, and even with the enemy. They also put the Government in a false position as not commanding a solid support when they have no alternative Government to suggest. It discloses the need of forceful leadership in Quebec."

The conscription issue and the by-elections, though constant preoccupations, were not Mackenzie King's only worries in January and February 1942. Before the session opened he had feared that details about the loss of Hong Kong would be received about the time Parliament met. That had happened, and the main business on January 21, before the old session of Parliament had prorogued, was a statement by Ralston on the Hong Kong expedition. Mackenzie King felt it was "a cruel business that this thing should have come to his doorstep, and that it should have been presented to the public at the very threshold of the reassembling of Parliament. It all indicates the mistake it is to try to rush things unduly, also wherein the Defence Departments have taken on more than they had any right to assume."

On the opening day of the new session (January 22) Mackenzie King had agreed at once to a request by Hanson for a Parliamentary Committee to inquire into the Hong Kong expedition. He felt it would really be "a help to us as it will show where the onus really lies, how ready we were to meet a British request, and will put the blame where it ought to be on those responsible for taking some men overseas who should not have gone."

On further consideration, the Government had become doubtful about the wisdom of having an inquiry by Parliamentary Committee and on January 28, Mackenzie King had "had a talk with Coldwell regarding having inquiry re Hong Kong made a judicial inquiry, instead of a Parliamentary inquiry. He saw the force of the argument and agreed. Also, later in the afternoon, saw Blackmore who virtually did the same. Have still to see Hanson." The next day (January 29) he had called on Hanson "and suggested our having Commission of possibly three. Hanson asked me who I had in mind. I said the Chief Justice, possibly someone of the Legion, and some outstanding third person. He said he had something of the kind in mind himself; felt that, with a Committee of Parliament, we had such a majority they could bring in any report they liked. I pointed out that we had to consider the military aspects of the situation; that the inquiry would probably be mostly concerned with communications from England requesting the expedition, the Department of Defence plans with respect to the same." He said to Hanson that a Parliamentary Committee would probably insist on having General Crerar return from [his Army post in] England to give evidence, and that, in a Committee, there was bound to be a "political battle, with scoring on either side, at a time when the press might be announcing the deaths of different men and their relatives suffering anguish. Also, that it must be remembered that Power had a son in the expedition. Ralston had a boy overseas. If they were going to have to attend a Parliamentary inquiry, and be worried with its proceedings, I did not see how they could get on with their work, as the load was becoming unendurable. Hanson said that he felt for both of them and, frankly, would like to help them in any way; that his own position was very difficult—he did not know whether he was Leader or not. He had to communicate with Meighen about everything. He had spoken his own mind on Ralston's report, and then received a communication from Toronto asking [him] to request a Parliamentary inquiry. He said that the only thing that occasioned this was the reference in Ralston's statement to the inadequate training of some of the men, which he thought signified insufficient numbers. . . . He mentioned that he would have to communicate with Meighen."

Mackenzie King had seen Hanson again on February 4; this time Ralston was also present. Hanson had agreed definitely on proceeding by Royal Commission with Chief Justice Duff if he could be secured as Commissioner. "Also Duff to have a free hand in choosing the persons he wished to help him in getting evidence, this instead of a battle between the opposing counsel as though someone was on trial. I took it as understood that Duff would conduct the proceedings as he thought best. Ralston seemed to think that Hanson still was reserving a certain right as to their being held in public, in part, but I think that was out of the question because of publicity being the main objection to a Parliamentary inquiry."

Mackenzie King had then gone to see Chief Justice Duff who "said he would want to talk with his doctor who would probably tell him he was foolish to take on anything of the kind, but if his conscience told him he should, would say it was all right." He had been "immensely relieved" when Duff accepted on February 6. The appointment had not been announced immediately and, on February 12, Hanson had asked to see the Order-in-Council appointing Duff. Mackenzie King let him have a copy of the proposed Order, which had not yet been passed. That day, in the House of Commons, one of the Members had complained of the delay in setting up the inquiry, and Mackenzie King had at once announced the appointment of the Duff Commission. He noted that "Hanson supported what I said, but gave away part of the conversations which were strictly confidential. I was afraid he was communicating with Toronto about the [terms of] reference [of the Royal Commission] intending to run in a political issue on manpower.

"As the matter had been discussed in the House, I wrote Hanson to let me have back the reference as soon as possible. He was out of the House, and I learned later to my surprise that he had been down to the Supreme Court to see the Chief Justice. He had evidently been consulting him about enlarging the reference and getting permission to have counsel for himself. Later, he submitted certain suggestions as to enlargement. . . . I agreed to ring up the Chief Justice and tell him of the suggestions Hanson had made. The Chief Justice agreed there was no need for enlarging the reference as to manpower, but agreed we might meet Hanson on the question of counsel, leaving it to him to appoint what counsel he wished.

"At one time, Hanson wanted to have all the correspondence tabled. I told him it was confidential, and if I was to deal with him in confidence he must not make public what passed between us. . . . I am really deeply concerned about Ralston. He has become obsessed with the Hong Kong matter. Can give thought to nothing else. Looks much older and one can see is suffering intensely and, as Power and I both think, quite unnecessarily."

The news from Hong Kong, and particularly the reports of Japanese treatment of prisoners, aggravated the unrest and hostility towards the Japanese Canadians in British Columbia and the Government decided, in the interests of national security, to move the Japanese Canadians from the coastal area. This decision was prompted both by fear of Japanese raids and by the fear of civil disorder. On February 19 Mackenzie King recorded his own fear that it would be "a very great problem to move the Japanese and particularly to deal with the ones who are naturalized Canadians or Canadian born." Despite that fear, Mackenzie King felt action was essential because "there is every possibility of riots. Once that occurs, there will be repercussions in the Far East against our own prisoners. Public prejudice is so strong in B.C. that it is going to be difficult to control the situation; also moving men to camps at this time of year very difficult indeed. I did my best to get decisions from the Cabinet and matters sufficiently advanced to be prepared for afternoon questions."

Ironically enough, the Government next day (February 20) received a delegation from the Toronto Civil Liberties League, which wished to make representations about the Defence of Canada Regulations. B. K. Sandwell, editor of Toronto *Saturday Night* and a friend and university classmate of Mackenzie King's, headed the delegation, which included J. M. Macdonnell, then a leading business man in Toronto, later a Conservative M.P. and from 1957 to 1959, a Cabinet Minister. Mackenzie King observed that "Sandwell would have had a fine place in Parliament. Has great qualifications. As I looked at Macdonnell I was glad he had not accepted invitation to join Government [in June 1940]; a very rigid, hide-bound type; severe on himself and everyone else. I thought the delegation made out a strong case for need of less rigid interpretation of Defence of Canada Regulations; also for greater justice in manner of trials and of appeals of those interned, and danger of using these Defence Regulations to thwart labour organization, collective bargaining, etc. I let the delegation as well as colleagues see I was strongly in favour of their representations and promised that action would come of them." In fact, certain relaxations in the Regulations were made soon afterwards and, after investigation, many interned persons were released.

That same day (February 20) Mackenzie King had a meeting with Hanson, Stirling, Coldwell, Blackmore and the Defence Ministers and Howe to arrange for a secret session of the House of Commons which the Opposition had demanded. Mackenzie King "spoke of feeling increasingly concerned about telling the House anything in Secret Session that could not be told in open session. We finally got agreement on the understanding that discussion would be confined to general subject of defence of Canada, and considered in a large way, including our contributions to war effort of other countries. That Ministers of Defence would give 'off the record' addresses; that there would then be discussion in the Committee of the Whole, with right of Members to ask questions and make suggestions. Understood discussion would not last longer than the one day—two sittings of the House."

The secret session was held on February 24. Mackenzie King found it "of considerable interest. On the whole, it served a useful purpose of giving something in addition in the way of information to Members, and I think was helpful in bringing home to Ralston and the Defence Departments the necessity of giving more attention to home defence, particularly on the Pacific Coast." The Defence Ministers spoke at length. "The lectures, so to speak, lasted till nine o'clock. Last two hours devoted to usual procedure in Committee of the Whole. An effort was made to string the session over until the next day but I sat on that promptly." Mackenzie King thought the secret session "caused Members generally to feel we could do as well in open session as in secret. There seemed to be a general acceptance of the view that it was well not to unduly arouse the fears of the public by having a further Secret Session."

Meanwhile the Plebiscite Bill had been introduced and Mackenzie King spoke on the second reading on February 25. He "found little difficulty in making a fairly comprehensive, and at the same time, concise and well connected speech. I did not use my notes at all, except for occasional glances, and really enjoyed the opportunity of going ahead and meeting interruptions with the new feeling of stimulus which they so frequently bring. In a way I looked upon the opportunity as one to test my ability to speak without any written manuscript and the greater effectiveness of that method. I could see that the House became increasingly interested as I spoke and, before I had concluded, there seemed to be fairly general acceptance on all parts of what I was saying, and a very marked enthusiasm on the part of my own men." He had "felt a command of the House which I really enjoyed and which gave me confidence. In many ways, though, I miss Lapointe tremendously." On this occasion as on others when he spoke well without a text, he reflected that he "would enjoy Parliament and get much out of public life if I could get rid of the routine preparation."

The next morning (February 26) he felt that discussion of the Bill was "proving to be a sort of educational process. We have kept out of Parliament, and out of the arena of acrimonious conflict both in Parliament and in the country, a discussion of conscription. By the time the plebiscite is taken, the public generally will see the wisdom of giving the Government a free hand, and, by that time, events will have made so obviously clear the way in which the power of compulsory selective service should be exercised that the course to be taken will be fairly, if not wholly, obvious, and national support secured for it." While this hope was to prove too optimistic for the full duration of the war, it was a not entirely inaccurate forecast of the outcome of the conscription crisis of 1942.

Later in the debate on the Bill that day (February 26) Hanson quoted passages from Bruce Hutchison's book, *The Unknown Country*, "to make a kind of personal attack on myself, to take away some of the support that had been given me of late by my own followers in the House. He tried to twist words that Dafoe meant to apply to Prime Ministers generally, as being necessarily to some degree egotistic and autocrats to hold their own with Cabinets, and used them as though they were applied to myself in particular by Bruce Hutchison.

"I paid no attention to this, but he went on to quote what Hutchison said about my reading the Bible, having faith in prayer, and believing in immortal life. He made the astonishing statement that he himself used to read the Bible, but had no time for it now. Personally, I felt proud to have this declaration made in Parliament of foundation of my beliefs. I have always hoped that the day might come when, in the Canadian Parliament, I might stand for the kind of thing that Gladstone stood for in the public life of England in the matter of political action being based on religious convictions, and the latter known and boldly stated."

The second reading of the Plebiscite Bill was concluded that day; the committee stage and third reading took until March 4. Meanwhile General McNaughton had come home on leave in early February and

Mackenzie King had had several opportunities for discussion with him. When he had met McNaughton at the station on February 4, Mackenzie King had observed that he was "very friendly and will be most helpful. He may even enable us to get over the conscription difficulty. I think he, himself, would like to avoid the use of conscription for overseas." They had had a long talk on February 5, during which McNaughton had told Mackenzie King that "he would never have taken the present post he has but for the confidence he had in me. . . .

"I said I felt that, without wishing to indicate any final judgment in the matter, it seemed to me we ought to regard the complete Army, as now constituted, as representing Canada's contribution so far as the armed forces were concerned, having, of course, in mind the reinforcements necessary. The General agreed with this."

When they had talked about the relations between McNaughton and Ralston, McNaughton "said he had found a happier relation and better feeling all around in the Department than he had noticed before. He believed General Stuart's appointment [as Chief of the General Staff, where he succeeded Crerar late in 1941] had helped to this end. I told him we all found Stuart very satisfactory to work with."

Mackenzie King had felt that McNaughton "agreed with me entirely about the necessity of keeping the country united—that was basic. That to risk division was to risk the whole effectiveness of our effort. As far as I could see from our conversation, and I tried to touch all the points that had been subjects of controversy, we were really at one in all our views, including the advisability of having men from here to supply the Army overseas from volunteers rather than from conscription, and the desirability of getting along without the latter."

In summing up their talk, Mackenzie King had observed that "the General . . . seemed to be entirely satisfied with the way things had gone, are at present, and were going. Agreed that we had done marvellously in every way, and was resentful of the political discussion which had grown up, though he wisely said he would keep out of that despite every effort they would make to draw him in."

At a dinner Ralston had given for McNaughton on February 9, Mackenzie King had spoken of the place McNaughton "had made for himself and for Canada in Britain, and the confidence he enjoyed on all sides with his men, officers, British Government and Canadian Government; of the load he is carrying in having three sons in the war; absent from Canada three Christmases; need for rest, etc. Told of his having the entire confidence of the Government and of the people of Canada." In replying, McNaughton "spoke of the feeling that he had the entire confidence of the Government; that we had given him everything he had asked for; had not made a single appointment for political reasons; had left the Army to make its own appointments." Mackenzie King had felt McNaughton's speech was "all that could possibly have been wished for, either by the Government or the Defence Department. It has been a splendid thing, his being here at this time. It has had a good effect on Ralston; brought them closer together, and I think satisfied Ralston's mind as to nothing more being required than keeping the Army at the size now provided for and seeing that new reinforcements were provided."

Two days later (February 11) General and Mrs. McNaughton had dined at Laurier House. After dinner, McNaughton had told Mackenzie King "that he was deploring the fuss that had been stirred up in Canada over conscription; that, of course, he had to keep out of it altogether, but that the matter should not have arisen at all. He said, as a matter of fact, if your Government had sent word to me overseas that they were contemplating conscription, I would have asked, for God's sake, not to do anything of the kind."

On March 6, McNaughton gave the War Committee "an excellent review of all phases of his relations and that of the Army overseas with the Government. Nothing could have been more satisfactory. McNaughton concluded his remarks by saying he and his fellow officers had complete confidence in the Government and in the support we had given them, and which he knew would be given. . . . He stressed the readiness to have Ottawa determine the policy fully but urged the desirability of leaving to himself and his organization the actual working out of details. Ralston and he have had a good deal of discussion in this matter. . . . I think he and McNaughton have been able to reconcile their differences. It is clear that each of them has been greatly exercised over the possibility of not having the final say. However, McNaughton said, in Ralston's presence, that he thought they had worked out everything satisfactorily between them." At this meeting, "McNaughton stressed the importance of the Canadian Army remaining intact in Britain to hold the heart of Britain, and to be ready when the time came to invade the Continent."

On March 17, General McNaughton in a private talk with Mackenzie King told him that "he had reached a complete understanding with Colonel Ralston about the freedom he was to have in the matter of carrying out policy. He said that he had had to talk very plainly to Ralston, even to say to him that he would not continue to hold his present position unless he had the full authority he felt he should have in the matter of executing plans, once policy was settled by the Government. It was plain that the difference between them dated back to the time when Ralston was previously Minister of Defence. McNaughton said, at that time, he had his resignation written out and would have handed it in, had the election not come in 1930 and changed the situation. . . .

"I told him I thought Ralston was over-conscientious and in some ways supersensitive; that his purpose was the highest. I agreed he had the fault of keeping too much in his own hand. I said to the General that, too, is what your friends told me is your failing. . . . I said to him that Ralston had quite frankly said to me he would be entirely willing to have any other arrangements made if I had so desired; that all he wished was to make the best contribution he could to the war effort.

"I then said to the General, speaking quite confidentially and intimately between ourselves, that I would like to know your own mind as respects some of the things that have been suggested, for example, I have been asked by different persons if I would not consider bringing you back to Canada instead of having you continue in command of the Army overseas. I have replied that I felt a step of the kind at the present juncture might only serve to break your heart, as I thought you had before you the formation of an Army, complete in all respects, and would wish to command it in action. The General said that was entirely right. He thought his place was in the Old Country with the forces there. He only hoped he had not delayed too long in getting back. . . .

"I said I thought that his relations with the British High Command were of a character which no one else could hope to share. He agreed with this and spoke of his close association with Brooke [Sir Alan Brooke, Chief of the Imperial General Staff] and thought that in every way he should be in England. . . . He said, of course, the time may come when I will have to come back anyway. The reference in this connection was the impairment of health and years. He followed it by saying that he had had a closer call than he was prepared to confess at the time he was laid up some months ago. . . .

"I asked him quite frankly about my understanding of his future needs for men, saying I would like to be clear in my own mind in dealing with the situations that would arise in Canada itself, with respect to the sending of more men overseas, and asked him if I was right in understanding that he did not intend to ask for, and did not wish, a larger Army than that for which provision has been made, except, of course, the necessary reinforcements. He told me that that was entirely right, and went on to say that he and his fellow officers at Headquarters had never really urged or wanted conscription. What they were interested in was selective service—getting into the Army the men best qualified, and getting into industry the men that could serve there. He continued to stress the need for more in the way of war equipment. He then said I have never asked or wanted conscription. As a matter of fact, conscription, today, would be an embarrassment indeed. I cannot see how for eight months hence we can deal with more men. . . .

"I went on to say that I was most anxious to avoid any divisions in Canada and that, if a cleavage over conscription could be avoided, I was anxious to avoid it. The General instantly agreed that preservation of unity in Canada was all-important—that it should be kept constantly in mind.

"He then said to me: I have been telling everyone who has spoken to me about it, and many have, that I think the plebiscite is entirely the right thing for you to do; that, if we ceased to take account of moral values, we might as well give up the cause we are fighting for; that nothing could be more harmful than for a Government to ignore its pledges.

"He said: 'I did not think that there should have been a promise made of *No Conscription* at the start, but having been given, it should be kept and honoured in the way you have done.' I said some might not agree about not giving the promise, but I thought without it Canada would never have come into the war as she did, and that Quebec would never have made the contribution to the unity of Canadian effort that she did after the war commenced, and that weighing in the balance all things together it will be found that the highest interest had been served by the course taken. He said that might be the case.

"I asked again if he was entirely satisfied with everything, and he said he was. . . . The General thanked me repeatedly for the understanding way in which I had approached his problem and the support I had given him, and repeated that, as he had taken the command, having confidence in myself, he was holding it because of that confidence. . . . Our conversation lasted an hour, and was most satisfactory and cordial."

The next day, when Mackenzie King called on McNaughton to say goodbye, he repeated the substance of what he had said the day before. "As I talked with the General," he noted, "I thought he was looking much older. I feel he has aged quite a bit, and indeed I would not be surprised if he would find that his strength may become increasingly less equal to the great task he has."

The representation of the Province of Quebec in the Cabinet, weakened by Lapointe's death, was further weakened in March by the death of Senator Dandurand. On March 11, Mackenzie King, while at breakfast, learned that Dandurand was ill. He went at once to the Chateau Laurier where he "found Senator Dandurand looking quite white." The doctor was trying to get a private room in a hospital, "but he pleaded in vain for a room at the Civic Hospital and also at the General Hospital. . . . I said I would go to the Hospital myself and secure a room while they got the ambulance." Mackenzie King got a room personally and when Dandurand arrived "had a little talk with the Senator."

In the afternoon, he visited Dandurand and they "had a pleasant talk together." He then went off to look at the X-ray plates and when he returned "told him that after seeing his insides and what a splendid sight they had been that I was prouder of him than ever; he was great fighting material and that I thought he would get along all right. He laughed with me and spoke of the possibility of his being back in the Senate next Tuesday night, and felt relieved from the pain. . . . I did not say good-bye to him but only au revoir."

While he was at dinner, Mackenzie King received word that the Senator was dying and by the time he reached the hospital Dandurand was dead. He felt "it was a marvellous way for a man's life to end. To have lived to be over 80, still leading the Upper Chamber as Government Leader; making a speech of an hour on international relations; active, keen, useful to the very end. Dandurand's passing leaves me as the only member of the original Cabinet I formed in 1921. It leaves me fifth from the top of P.C.'s in Canada. I feel particularly concerned about the province of Quebec. In Lapointe's and Dandurand's passing it has lost two of the best friends—if not the two best friends—next to Laurier, which the Province has had and this at a time when leadership is more needed than ever. It is going to be difficult to find a leader for Quebec. Cardin has not the strength to last."

He was further disturbed by a difference between Cardin and Godbout about political organization in the province which he tried to settle by having them meet him on March 13. He felt the situation in Quebec was "appallingly difficult. No longer any of the real leaders left. . . . I had Godbout to lunch and we had a pleasant talk together. I stressed to him the importance of the Government receiving all help possible in the plebiscite campaign. He agreed as to its real significance to the Province."

When Mackenzie King was in Montreal on March 14 to attend Dandurand's funeral, he was "rather touched that Chubby Power came to the car" to accompany him to the funeral. He was reminded that "Dandurand had been with me on the car the last time I went to

Montreal, which was to Lapointe's funeral. The thought just flashed across my mind how Power's coming aboard was not without significance in this connection. . . . I pray, however, that he will be spared, for he is very helpful and able."

His concern about the situation in Quebec was even greater on March 19 when he found Power was worried about "the position of himself and St. Laurent and Cardin; that if the plebiscite is defeated in Quebec, it will be very embarrassing as it will appear they do not represent the Province. I told him we would cross bridges when we came to them, but to remember that the plebiscite was not a general election and could only rightly be considered as a test of popular feeling. He told me that there was a very strong not only anti-British but anti-participation feeling in Quebec. That he no longer felt he had influence there because his name was English. I pointed out to him the inconsistency of that remark in that he had said that my name counted for everything, and that the whole campaign would have to be run in not risking my going out of office."

J. S. Woodsworth, the C.C.F. leader, also died at this time. On March 23, Mackenzie King referred to the many tributes in the House of Commons "all praising Woodsworth's sincerity and evidencing the very real regard in which he was held. His real purpose seems to have come out more strongly of late. His voice, when pitched high, as it usually was in the House, served to discount much of what he said, and to create a wrong impression as to his attitude which seemed to be one of fault-finding and scolding more than of constructive persuasion. His life, however, was clearly one of fine Christian public service, and he has left a real impression on the country."

Mackenzie King had a talk on March 24 with D. C. Abbott (then a private member from Montreal), who urged him to broadcast on the plebiscite before Easter "as he says nothing will rally Quebec except a positive statement from myself that I am anxious they should support the plebiscite." He made his first broadcast on the plebiscite on April 7 and was far from satisfied with the result. He was also greatly worried about the reaction in Quebec, where it was increasingly clear that no one wished to support the plebiscite. Mackenzie King even had difficulty in getting Cardin to broadcast. He himself made a second broadcast on April 24 which was much better than the first and was directed mainly to Quebec. He was disappointed that, apart from Philippe Brais, the Quebec Government was not active in the campaign and thought "Godbout and his other colleagues have made a mistake in not coming out and making clear what the issue is. I must confess I have never myself been able to express to the people the real object I have had in the plebiscite, namely, that of being able to discuss the question of conscription on the merits without fear of motives being misunderstood."

A friend, he noted, thought it had been a mistake to say in his second broadcast that "if I did not believe that, as head of the Government, I continued to enjoy the confidence of the people who, time and again, have returned me to office, I would not wish to remain in office an hour longer."[1] Mackenzie King "could see at once that this was what the [Ottawa] *Citizen* and other papers would jump on. I had taken this thought out of the first broadcast and should, perhaps, have kept it out of the second. My feeling, however, was that, at this stage, it was necessary to strike the enemy (this time the NO's) in the most vital spot, and to bring all the force I could bring to bear on the people at the present time. I think it will be seen on the whole that it was wise tactics. It will help to bring some of the clergy and others in Quebec, who have looked only at the one aspect, to see the wisdom of continuing their support."

The next day (April 25) he "was not surprised to see that the *Citizen* had featured resignation possibility in its headlines, giving the wrong slant. I felt however that the Tories will have their minds pretty well made up to vote 'yes.' Should any change to 'no' it will help to distribute the 'no's' more generally in the other provinces, and thereby not make Quebec quite so conspicuous." He considered it had "been the most difficult campaign for speaking I have ever known. The reason, I suppose, is that the appeal has to be made to all political parties and every word said will serve pretty much to operate a double-edged sword."

Later that day, Hanson "wired that my speech was being considered as [asking for] a vote of confidence in the Government by my saying that I would take the affirmative vote as confidence in the Government." This telegram referred to the one sentence quoted above. Mackenzie King prepared a reply and arranged to have the reply broadcast over the radio. In it he indicated that an affirmative vote in the plebiscite would not be regarded as a vote of confidence in the Government but merely as an assurance that they had freedom of action regarding the conditions of military service. He wrote: "It distresses me to have said anything that was capable of being so misinterpreted. I feel sure had I not been so tired I would have watched this end of it." The correction may have been unfortunate; Cardin later maintained that if he had stuck to his statement and made no correction there might have been many more affirmative votes in Quebec.

The vote on the plebiscite was held on April 27. Mackenzie King's "own guess as to the result of the plebiscite is that the affirmative vote

[1] W. L. Mackenzie King, *Canada and the Fight for Freedom* (Toronto, 1944), p. 146.

should be about seventy per cent over the Dominion as a whole. If it is that, it will be good indeed. . . . Quebec, I feel, might give thirty per cent for the affirmative. It might even reach thirty-five." He added that "some of the Tories will immediately be after declaration of conscription for overseas. My belief is that we shall never have to resort to conscription for overseas. . . . All we shall have to be sure of is reinforcements of the Army at present in Britain. If there is any pressure on the part of our men to enforce conscription, just for the sake of conscription, I will fight that position to the end. Quebec and the country will see that I have kept my promise about not being a member of the Government which sends men overseas under conscription. The only exception I will make in that will be that our own men need additional numbers which could not be obtained voluntarily, but I do not think this will be the case."

When the votes began to come in, the "returns from Quebec were quite depressing. I found it difficult to shape up anything for the press that would help to save the feelings of the Quebec people. . . . By midnight, I had begun to make the different revises and shortly after got a copy to the Press Gallery of what, I thought, seemed on the whole a pretty satisfactory statement. It made clear that the plebiscite had given the Government and Parliament a free hand and that the will of the people would prevail. I cannot say I felt any real elation over the result, though an amazingly large affirmative vote made clear the people had trust in myself and the Government to see that their rights would be wholly protected. A table showing the returns by constituencies made it perfectly apparent to me that the governing factor was the racial and, possibly, race and religion combined, the French Catholic minority feeling it would be at the mercy of [the] English Protestant majority. I felt very strongly that to keep Canada united, we would have to do all in our power [to keep] from reaching the point where necessity for conscription for overseas would arise.

"As I looked at the returns, I thought of Durham's report on the state of Quebec when he arrived there after the rebellion 1837–38, and said he found two nations warring in the bosom of a single state. That would be the case in Canada, as applied to Canada as a whole, unless the whole question of conscription from now on is approached with the utmost care. The returns show clearly the wisdom of not attempting any conscription through coercion and in violation of pledges. Whatever is done now will be done with the will of the majority, expressed in advance, and if proceedings are taken in the right way, will be gradually acquiesced in by those in the minority."

CHAPTER FOURTEEN

Cardin and Ralston

WHEN the Cabinet met on the morning after the plebiscite (April 28), Mackenzie King "said to the Ministers that the Government appeared to be safe." Nothing could have been further from the truth. In reality both the Cabinet and the Liberal membership in Parliament were split three ways. Most of the Quebec Members and Cardin in the Cabinet wanted no action taken as a result of the plebiscite which would bring conscription any closer. A number of Members from other provinces and several Ministers, with Ralston and Angus Macdonald in the forefront, really wanted immediate conscription or, if not that, at least a firm pledge that conscription would be used at once if voluntary recruiting failed. A third group of Members wanted to do whatever was necessary to ensure a maximum war effort; most of them felt that only a Government headed by Mackenzie King could ensure this, and, accordingly, they were ready to follow wherever Mackenzie King might lead.

At this first Cabinet meeting, Mackenzie King expressed the view that the first step should be to extend the area for compulsory service to take in the Western Hemisphere; Canada would continue to rely on voluntary service for the forces overseas. He found that Ralston disagreed with his view that there should be a gradual approach. Ralston said he had expected Mackenzie King to feel the result of the plebiscite "was a great victory, the greatest the Government had had—a verdict to go ahead, and a mandate to go ahead now for all we were worth, etc. He thought that there should be no two or three steps in reaching an objective, but that we should regard the affirmative vote as a demand to remove the clause in the Mobilization Act which restricted its provisions to Canada and then be prepared to send any of our men anywhere. Angus Macdonald did not go so far. He thought that we should remove the restriction in the Act, but make it clear we did not intend conscription beyond the islands, etc. around about or beyond this hemisphere.

"St. Laurent took the view very strongly that I had made the two statements that the Government should be free, but that, in everything it did, it should submit matters first to Parliament, and Parliament pass upon it." Mackenzie King said his understanding was "that Parliament would have to pass on every step we took which involved more in the way of conscription. Ralston replied that Parliament might not be sitting and that we might want to act very soon. I said Parliament could be kept in continuous session and could be brought together in seven days." Mackenzie King "saw we were back to where we were at the time we made the original decision to hold the plebiscite, and thought it inadvisable to press the matter further" that day.

It was not merely in the Cabinet that Mackenzie King found differences as to the meaning of the plebiscite. On April 29, he observed the Members in caucus were "all very sensitive at the moment, particularly Quebec Members. They seem to be in a quandary as to whether to sympathize with me in disappointment over Quebec, or to congratulate me on the country's confidence, etc. Quebec Members who supported the Government feel that I have been let down by the Province generally through the action of the others. They also feel very keenly that they themselves have been put into a very disadvantageous position in their own Province, and that, for the moment, the rebels are on top. I am seeking to have them see that it is the final stage, and not the first, that counts in matters of the kind."

On May 1, Mackenzie King was told that the Ontario Ministers had met the day before and had agreed to try and have the Members from Ontario generally support all-out conscription at once. He then spoke to each of the Ontario Ministers and had a particularly sharp exchange with C. D. Howe. Later he wondered "whether I made a mistake in speaking so sharply to the Ontario Ministers. I have never dealt with my colleagues in that manner before." The next day (May 2) he received a letter from Howe "bearing evidences of annoyance. Felt I should not allow that feeling to last, so rang him up on the 'phone to explain reasons for my feeling as I do."

Mackenzie King decided, on May 1, that "the thing to do is to get the same freedom from legislation as we have had from the pledge, stating the Government's policy to be only the extension of application of conscription for the present . . . to the Western Hemisphere . . . making some pledge which would bring us back to Parliament before we actually enforce conscription. In that event I can always have my colleagues understand that they will have to find another leader if there is an attempt to bring conscription into force where that is not necessary."

Accordingly he told the Cabinet on May 5 that he felt the Government should ask Parliament to remove the restrictive clause entirely from the Mobilization Act, and announce that conscripted men would be liable to serve anywhere in the northern half of the Western Hemisphere; later, if conscription was required for reinforcements overseas, the Government would "go to Parliament, give the reasons therefor, and ask for an expression of confidence before putting conscription for overseas into effect." Ralston "took exception to going to Parliament a second time, regarding that as tying our hands, and spoke of the possibility of a situation being desperate and [our] needing to put conscription in force in a hurry. The debate might last a long time. . . . Angus Macdonald supported Ralston."

This was the beginning of a debate between Mackenzie King and Ralston which was not settled until the middle of July. As Mackenzie King put it, the only difference was "whether, in stating the Government's policy, I should say that we would, when we felt it necessary to enact conscription, do so by Order-in-Council and then come to Parliament for approval, or whether we should advise Parliament of our intention to proclaim conscription for overseas for certain reasons, and then make that a question of confidence."

Mackenzie King favoured the second position. He reported that at the Cabinet meeting of May 5 "Ralston and Macdonald argued strongly against what I had proposed. Ralston, at once, said he did not think he could support that, and Macdonald said we would have to go to Parliament each time we wished to have a battalion go overseas. Macdonald has become very aggressive and more or less unpleasant in his attitude. Ralston, very set and determined." Mackenzie King was "a little afraid that Ralston will hold out to the end and tender his resignation, though I believe that if I hold firmly to the ground of trusting Parliament as well as the Government, which is what I have asked the people to do, he will see that, in resigning, he would be showing a lack of confidence in Parliament which would not be a very good ground for resignation."

He noted that he intended "to stand firm, be the consequences what they may, on having Parliament approve the decision of the Government to apply conscription for overseas before . . . any Order-in-Council for the purpose comes into effect." Mackenzie King thought if they made no hasty decision but "let the matter be dealt with by stages, we would find the problem will solve itself. . . . I counselled strongly against doing anything that would make more marked the cleavage between Quebec and the rest of the Dominion, that our effort should rather be to allow as much in the way of process of healing to take place as we could."

There was a long Cabinet meeting on May 6 which "went over much the same ground as yesterday." When Mackenzie King "mentioned that unless there would still be opportunity for Parliament to have its say before conscription was finally resorted to, there would be undoubtedly pressure from the Defence Department to have it introduced at once," Ralston "took offence at this remark and said that he thought that that was at the back of my mind; that I would be feeling he would be bringing pressure at the back of Cabinet to enforce conscription. . . . He said he had come to Council in the morning feeling that he might have to break with his colleagues in the matter of not agreeing to a second discussion on the plebiscite; that he was prepared to do all he could to avoid conscription coming any sooner than was necessary and, I understood him to say, he was prepared to have the Cabinet agree among themselves that Parliament could be consulted in the manner he had described, but he did not think anything should be said about it in advance. . . . I told Ralston he was quite mistaken in thinking anyone would question his action; that he himself had spoken about the staff taking that attitude. Angus Macdonald then followed by saying he himself could not agree to a second discussion. . . .

"I said they were both too good patriots to precipitate a crisis in the country such as their withdrawal from the Government would involve. Our business was to keep the Government united and to meet one step at a time. Cardin had also joined in to say he really doubted whether he should stay after he had lost the confidence of Quebec. It would give him a certain amount of satisfaction to get out simply to let them see what the result of their action had brought about. He was anxious to avoid taking any step at once, even of repealing Section 3 [the Section of the Mobilization Act restricting compulsory service to Canada]. . . . St. Laurent was very strong about my being obliged to keep my word as to advising Parliament before a decision was made." No conclusion was reached and the discussion was put over to the next day.

When the Cabinet met on May 7, Mackenzie King "began by saying I thought we ought to bring in an amendment to the Mobilization Act at once. I hoped it might be possible to agree in time to place notice on the Order Paper today." He recalled that he had already told Parliament "that, when we made the decision, we would come to Parliament, present the views of the Administration, and would let Parliament discuss the matter on its merits."

This statement started the debate all over again and Mackenzie King "pointed out that I had used the words 'our responsibility to Parliament' [in a speech on the plebiscite] and that we would have to decide how we would exercise that responsibility in the light of circumstances as they might exist at the time the decision was made. If, for example, there were a holocaust and need for immediate action, and Parliament were not sitting, it might be necessary to take a decision and go to

Parliament to have it confirmed, but that if Parliament were sitting, I thought we would wish to present the matter at once and ask for a vote of confidence in the Administration. I said I would not care to seek to administer conscription unless by a vote of confidence by Parliament in the first instance."

Mackenzie King thought his colleagues were with him, "excepting Ralston and Macdonald, feeling that we should go to Parliament before passing an Order that would apply conscription." But a new difficulty appeared when Cardin "held strongly for not repealing Section 3 at present. The rest of the Cabinet, however, all felt that if we did not take some immediate steps to make sure that we have complete freedom of action in the Cabinet, the Government's position would be attacked and begin to deteriorate. It would all be put down to finding it expedient to keep Quebec, etc., and we might lose ground that we never could recover."

After two hours of discussion Mackenzie King decided they should adjourn until the next day. When the Cabinet met on May 8 he "opened the proceedings by saying I had come to the conclusion we must today give notice of the Bill re Mobilization Act. . . . I then spoke at some length of the points on which I thought we had reached agreement. Mentioned that I had done my best to reconcile the opposing views." However the same debate was revived again and Mackenzie King finally said "my position would be that we would make no commitment either for or against going to Parliament first or later, and would decide it in the light of circumstances at the time; that would be part of our decision and that was what I meant by responsibility to Parliament."

Mackenzie King noted that "Cardin spoke at length about thinking he had better not stay on. He felt we should let the Act remain for some time and repeal when it became necessary. He did not think, in view of all he had said, that he could keep up his place in public life and support the measure. I said that, in the years I had been at the Council table, there was no colleague who had resigned and I thought we would get through without any resignations. He and I would talk over the situation together. It did not arise, at any rate, at this time. Everyone should wait and see what would be done and what was to be said on the second reading, and wait until the time came later for any action that would have to be taken. I finally said to Council I thought I would have to ask them to agree to let me initial the Bill as passed by the Cabinet." The Bill, to be known as Bill 80 from its number on the order paper of the House of Commons, simply repealed Section 3 of the National Resources Mobilization Act which restricted compulsory service to Canada.

As he initialled the Bill to amend the Mobilization Act, Mackenzie King said he "thought we had taken the right steps up to the present and had taken the right step now on this Bill. Except for the tenacity with which Ralston and Macdonald fought, even to the time of my initialling the Bill as approved by Council, I had Cabinet solidly with me." In this he was mistaken; he did not, in fact, have them all solidly behind him.

When Cardin came to see him the next afternoon (May 9), Mackenzie King observed that he had a letter in his overcoat pocket which he put into his coat pocket when he came in. He "knew this was his resignation." Cardin "opened up the subject by saying that he felt he had lost his influence in Quebec by the way the Province had voted, but that he felt that the step which the Government had taken yesterday left him in a position where the people would turn on him if he stayed in the Government. That he could not see what change there had been in conditions that made this step necessary, and that if the Government had been able to wait a couple of months before altering Section 3, we might have been able to show a change of conditions which would make the step necessary, and he might have been able to get others to line up with him"; he did not think that possible immediately. Mackenzie King "sought to explain to him that, while we were anxious to get rid of Section 3 as a contradiction to the fact we were making a total war effort, and to bring legislation into line with the real purpose of the plebiscite, that our policy was not changed, and would remain that of trying to get men by voluntary effort, etc.

"He went over a good deal of what had been said in Council. Took strongest exception to the fact that colleagues were unwilling to state definitely that they would come to Parliament before applying conscription for overseas. He subsequently read me a letter which he had written tendering his resignation and saying that, in taking a private Member's seat, he would do what he could to keep calmness and moderation on the part of Members and to explain the position generally. I told him that I would not accept his resignation at present. . . . I sought to have him make no decision until we got into the second reading of the Bill, but he thought that [any delay] would put him into [a] position as though he had been forced into Opposition. . . .

"I said to him that the most serious part of his resignation, particularly if it were accompanied by Members from Quebec in solid block refusing to support the Government's amendment, was that it might compel me to resign and have someone else take charge of the Government. I then read to him what I had said in a radio broadcast that if I lost [the] confidence of those who had returned me at different times, I would not wish to stay in office a minute. . . . Cardin said that I must not resign on any account. I told him I would have to consider the matter very carefully. I advised him to let all the French following from Quebec know that was a real possibility."

Mackenzie King reminded Cardin that he had been very concerned about his illness and absence from Ottawa, and "hoped he would keep that in mind in connection with what might help me at this time. He spoke very feelingly of the gratitude which he had for what I had done in that connection, and especially in his illness. . . . I mentioned to him he was the oldest colleague, and the only one that had tendered [a] resignation. I confess I cannot find fault with his attitude generally. It has been forced on him by the attitude of other colleagues, and the blame of the present situation lies on the shoulders of the Toronto men who forced the issue of conscription as they did. . . . I said I would keep the letter—it was dated today—until we had had a further talk and asked him to say nothing about it. That I would not accept it at present."

Later that Saturday (May 9) Mackenzie King reflected that this was "quite the greatest crisis that has faced not only the party but the country. It will now be said that I am responsible for the whole situation, and there is not likely to be much mercy shown from either one side or the other. However, I feel I have done what has been right at each step, and I believe this will be proven beyond all doubt before the war is over. It may help in the end to let the country see whether I am needed at the head of affairs at this time, or whether anyone else can do better."

A rumour of Cardin's resignation spread over the weekend and Mackenzie King spent much of Sunday preparing a reply to Cardin's letter and a statement for Parliament. He did not see Cardin again, but on Monday morning, May 11, sent the letter accepting the resignation, and completed the statements he proposed to make in the House on first reading of the Bill. He then told his colleagues about Cardin's resignation, and gave his own interpretation of Cardin's reasons, concluding that "what caused Cardin to feel he could not possibly remain . . . was the effort to have the Cabinet decide that it would enact conscription by Order-in-Council first, and go to Parliament after, instead of going to Parliament, stating we intended to enact the Order, and asking for a vote of confidence before so doing in order that an action so all-important might have the backing of Parliament. He felt it was useless to try to resist further what seemed to be a determination to have conscription at any price, when he knew his own Province and many parts of the Dominion would not agree to it being so forced, and that any attempt at its enforcement would be disastrous."

After referring to his efforts to dissuade Cardin and reading the exchange of letters Mackenzie King "said I wished to speak to the Cabinet very solemnly, to tell them that in Cardin's opinion, we would lose practically all the Members from Quebec; that we now had only one French Minister from Quebec, with Dandurand and Lapointe both dead and Cardin gone. . . . St. Laurent [was the] only one from Quebec, and he quite new, and in the House only since [the] by-election. . . . I added it was obviously clear that the Government could not carry on without Ministers from a Province which represented one third of the population. . . . That I did not think any Government could enforce conscription in Canada in the light of what the plebiscite revealed to be the feeling of the entire French Canadian population, including those in other provinces than Quebec . . . unless the House of Commons were united in backing a step of the kind. I said I thought I had to make it perfectly clear that I doubted if any Government that attempted anything of the kind could carry it out, and that the responsibility would be very heavy upon whatever Administration attempted it.

"Everyone listened in perfect silence. I gave them to understand I myself would not head an Administration charged with such a task. Our real problem today was not to allow a civil war to develop in Canada at a time we were seeking to fight an international war. . . . I then said we ought to be conciliatory with our French friends and seek to meet the situation in other than a coercive way."

Mackenzie King then read the statement he had prepared for the House on the plebiscite, which was agreed to, with a slight verbal change suggested by Ralston. He also read the statement he had prepared to explain the introduction of Bill 80. "It too was received without a word of objection excepting at the end where I had used the word 'discussing' the matter, Macdonald thought I should have said more than discussion and something that denoted action. Someone suggested the words 'deal with.' I accepted them at once, and made the change, but that was all." He felt that "it must have been difficult for Ralston and Macdonald to see the situation so clearly outlined, as I have wished it to be from the start, and have to accept the wording, knowing that the entire Council were with me in the statement. However, I think Cardin's resignation, and the whole picture as it is now foreseen, has had a sobering effect on those who feel that, as an Executive, they can ignore Parliament."

When Mackenzie King reached the House "the galleries were filled; Members were very expectant. . . . On motions, I announced Cardin's resignation. Read the correspondence which was followed very closely by the House. Hanson made an unfortunate remark when it was concluded, wanting to know when the next resignation would be made. There was immediate dissent in the House which made the rest of my course easy. I then read the statement on the plebiscite." This statement merely announced the vote and stated the plebiscite was not a vote of confidence in the Government or a mandate for conscription but merely a popular verdict giving the Government and Parliament freedom to decide the question on its merits. Mackenzie King "waited till the Speaker called 'introduction of bills,' and then introduced the amendment to the Mobilization Act." He read the explanation, which indicated that Section 3 was being repealed to remove any legal restriction on the freedom of the Government but made it clear that the Government did not intend to send conscripted men overseas at that time. He felt that "I may find later there is something in the statements that has not been what I would have wished, but I am inclined to think that, for once, I have been able to get everything over without much, if any, in the way of error."

That evening Mackenzie King went to the Chateau Laurier Hotel and "had a very pleasant half hour with Cardin. We talked over the situation, not disagreeing in any way. He spoke particularly of his own province not supporting as they should have the YES vote, thereby weakening his power in the Cabinet. He thought they had seen, the day after, that they had made a mistake. He felt if the Government had been ready to wait a little time before taking any action, they would have come around, but I explained that meantime the Government would have been getting into a very compromising position; other provinces would have said we were seeking to compromise on account of Quebec. He agreed that this was right. He said he did not think some of his colleagues had appreciated the great fight he and Lapointe had made first at the time of the declaration of war. Next, in the fight against Duplessis, and then finally the fight that he had made at this time on the plebiscite. I agreed with him on that. . . .

"He believes Quebec men have all still their confidence in me and will support me on everything except this Bill. He says that he, himself, will do his utmost to keep the Liberal party together, and not let the French Members become a wing of the Nationalist movement in Quebec. We discussed his seating and I left it to him to choose where he wished to sit. Told him he might be back again some day. To keep that in mind. I added that I would feel very sorry about his going were it not that I felt the condition of his health was such that with responsibilities of two departments [Cardin was Minister of Public Works and of Transport], he could not possibly hold out long without a complete rest. He said he had no doubt that that would be the view of his doctors."

At the caucus on May 12, Mackenzie King "could see from the looks on faces of many of the French Canadian Members that they were deeply concerned and seemed to be facing a discouraging situation." He appealed for understanding and asked Members "not to accentuate differences," and then expressed the view "that had we not taken the course we did to avoid an open split in the House of Commons on conscription in the debate on the Address, instead of our party being together today, and having three or four months' time to meet the situation, we should have been faced with a battle in the House of Commons from its very opening and up to the present on conscription versus no-conscription for overseas, which would have split our party, divided other parties, and made for chaos in the House of Commons and in the country, while we were in the midst of this world war; that, in all probability, we would have lost at least one of our by-elections, if not both, and Meighen might have been in the House today." He explained "why the Bill was introduced at this time. To have delayed longer would have made an agitation through the country that we were bowing to Quebec and not getting a free hand when we had asked the country in the plebiscite to give us a free hand."

When he was asked if the Government would undertake to advise Parliament before putting conscription into force, Mackenzie King "pointed out that I did not wish to get rid of one commitment in order to make another. It was impossible to say what conditions might be when it became necessary to introduce conscription, and if, and when, it should become necessary, I thought it better not to give our opponents the weapons to use that we were still being limited in our power to take a certain step. I emphasized, however, that I thought they knew my attitude well enough toward Parliament to realize the position I would take, and I thought that, by the time any action became necessary, all would fully understand the situation and matters would be made so clear by events that the question of a second debate might not arise at all; that, as long as I was the head of the Government, I was not likely to take any action myself without appreciation of the conditions.

"I was asked by one of the Members if it would make any difference if they did not support the Government on this particular amendment, though strongly with us on everything else. I replied to that, that it would make a considerable difference in my power to take a course that I thought might be most in the interests of all. I felt Cardin had left the Government mainly because he felt he had not the confidence of the Quebec Members. . . . I said it was the same with myself. If I could not keep the following I had in Parliament and their trust in me to do the right thing, my influence in the Administration and in the country would be that much less important. I would have to consider very carefully whether I should seek to carry on when I had not the support I needed in an all-important matter. They would have to consider the alternative of someone other than myself taking charge.

"I sought to make it clear that the purpose of the Bill was the same as the purpose of the plebiscite, to remove restrictions in the eyes of other countries, and especially in the eyes of the United States."

He addressed himself "to the two groups that seemed to be forming in opposition to each other over the plebiscite. First, to those who felt they must hasten on with conscription, I said they must realize what the real situation was with which the country was faced. I then repeated what I said in Council about conditions in Canada as a whole resembling those in Quebec at the time of Lord Durham in his report. I said we will easily come to have two nations warring in the bosom of a single State while [a] world war was on. . . . I then said I would now wish to speak to others who were seeking to prevent the Government getting at once the full powers it should have . . . a course which might prejudice the lives of those who already had volunteered to serve overseas; who stood between the enemy and his powers of destruction and ourselves in seeking to preserve our lives and the country itself from destruction. . . . I then spoke of there being no longer any such thing as overseas. Modern inventions had made it possible for submarines to cross the oceans, operate in our waters, and return for refuelling. . . . I drew from my pocket a brown envelope with red seals and said that they would be surprised to learn that therein was the word that an enemy submarine had torpedoed a ship in the waters of the St. Lawrence, west of Gaspé, and that this morning the survivors were being landed on the shores of the river in the province of Quebec. I said I hoped they would not imagine this was an isolated happening. . . . I said I thought, in view of this, the men who had stood by the Government should now feel they had a complete answer to others who have been opposing and who have been saying there is no danger to Canada, Mr. King was exaggerating. . . .

"I concluded what I had to say by mentioning that a couple of weeks would probably pass before the Bill would be taken up again, and that I hoped none would commit themselves until we saw how matters would develop."

Mackenzie King himself felt he "had made a mess of my presentation of material," but "throughout the afternoon, it became apparent from what Members were saying that the meeting . . . had lifted the depression under which many of the Members were and they began to see daylight ahead." He noted that "Paul Martin [Liberal M.P. for Essex East] told me he had felt much relieved by what I had said at the caucus in the morning. He had been disappointed at . . . my not being able to give an assurance that there would be a chance for debate on the decision to extend conscription for overseas, should that become necessary. I explained the inside of the situation to Martin, the governing reasons in this matter.... He thought if we could go the length suggested ... we would be able to keep most of our own Quebec following.... Martin told me that ... I only needed to assert myself and the country would follow me. He felt I should know this, as I might get discouraged at times."

After the deaths of Lapointe and Dandurand, there had been no French-speaking Member from Quebec in the War Committee and, on May 13, Mackenzie King told St. Laurent he wanted him to be a Member "to have Quebec represented." He had spoken to Ralston, who "wholly agreed."

That same day he had a meeting with Ralston, St. Laurent, and the Chiefs of Staff and told them what he had learned in Washington at Easter about the military plans of the allies. (The visit to Washington is described in the next chapter.) He then said to the Chiefs of Staff that he "had a further reason for wishing the interview and that was to discuss with them the situation that had arisen out of the plebiscite, and what it signified. I said that, in my opinion, it was like an X-ray plate of a condition in the country which could not be ignored. That some people interpreted the vote as one favouring conscription. I, myself, believed if the vote had been on conscription that conscription would have been defeated. If it had been for conscription, I, myself, would have voted against conscription. Be that as it may, it was clear that one third of the population of Canada were not even prepared to trust the Government on the possibility of having conscription introduced. That an entire province was solidly against it. That they had to consider not only the danger of ever reaching the point where conscription became necessary, but also the all-important question of how it was to be administered, and consequences of attempting to enforce it. I did not believe conscription could be enforced against Quebec without great resistance and riots. Recalled the difficulty Borden had, even after he had Union Government....

"I said I wanted to let them know now that I, myself, felt that no Government could enforce conscription that had not the House of Commons well behind it.... I then said to Stuart he would recall the talks we had in [the] War Committee when I had questioned him specifically about the programme for the coming year, and he had given me assurance he did not think conscription would be necessary to carry out the programme we had subsequently agreed to. Stuart said he remembered it quite well, and did not now believe conscription would be necessary for that programme. He thought we would be able to get the men we needed by voluntary methods. I said that they must all make greater efforts than ever to ensure that conscription will not have to be resorted to. . . . Stuart said that he thought the only thing that might necessitate conscription would be some terrible fighting where large numbers of lives were lost. I drew their attention to the fact that the plan of campaign as outlined in communications I had read did not contemplate an offensive until the spring of 1943. . . .

"What I wanted to impress upon them was not to take the vote of the plebiscite as a vote on conscription, but to know that the Government had a real political problem in [a] large sense in the maintenance of national unity, and work must be directed toward that end. Stuart and others then told me that they were wholly conscious of this and were doing all they could in that direction." Mackenzie King said he wanted "now to make perfectly plain the situation as I saw it." He noted that "the interview lasted for considerably over an hour and was in the best of feeling throughout. I made plain that, as a Government, we were trying to help the Chiefs of Staff all we could, and we wanted them to help us with our problems."

He "felt it immensely helpful having St. Laurent there. He is so sensible, so straight, and so exceedingly able. St. Laurent is a complete match for Ralston on the legal side, and speaks out with a vigour for Quebec that none of the Quebec Ministers seemed able to do through sensitiveness of their position and being in the minority. St. Laurent does not suffer in any way in that particular."

Mackenzie King expected that Power would agree with him completely about the situation in Quebec, and when he told Power in conversation on May 21 that he felt strongly conscription could not be applied without a vote of confidence in advance, "to my surprise, he took the view that would mean a second debate, that he did not think Ralston or Macdonald would agree to it, and that he himself did not feel he would. In fact, he thought he would have to consider carefully his own position, if the Quebec Members went against it, and resign, being without any support in the Province and his own constituency having voted against him in the plebiscite."

Mackenzie King observed that "this attitude of the three Defence Ministers worked out in combination is the most trying and difficult one to face. It makes my position extremely difficult. Even if it leads to resignation, I certainly would feel bound to accept that course rather than attempt to reverse the whole of my life's attitude towards relations of the Executive to Parliament."

Before the debate began on Bill 80, another Liberal caucus was held on May 27. Mackenzie King repeated much of what he had said a week earlier, but was evidently in much better form. In the course of his speech he "spoke of those who were trying to make themselves secure in their constituencies, saying they would support the party otherwise, and I told them I did not intend to be made a convenience . . . and that they had better gather the full import of those words. If they were not prepared to trust the Government, and could not trust me, the sooner they let me know this the better. I concluded what I had to say, after indicating it would be some time before conscription would be needed at all, by drawing attention to a remark made by [Ernest] Bertrand [later a Minister], from Montreal, that there were some who wanted conscription immediately whether it was necessary or not, and there were others who would not have conscription even if it was necessary to save the country. Both were the wrong attitudes and the only right attitude was to have no conscription unless it was necessary, and, if it was necessary, then to have it. I said that would be the position I would take in Parliament." At the end, Mackenzie King "said that when it came to the time it was necessary to have conscription introduced, so far as I was concerned, I thought they knew what I felt about the relations of the Executive to Parliament and that I, for one, would never think of attempting to have conscription enforced without the support of Parliament. I got a tremendous reception and . . . I think it has created a real impression, but I am not at all sure that we are by any means out of the woods."

Angus Macdonald wrote to Mackenzie King on May 28 taking exception to what he had said at the caucus about going back to Parliament before resorting to conscription and suggesting it did not accord with what had been decided in the Cabinet. Mackenzie King was not able to discuss the letter with Macdonald, who was absent from Ottawa, until June 3. He then told Macdonald "I thought he had forgotten the talk he and Ralston had with me in my library at the time of the plebiscite when they were urging that if the vote were in the affirmative, we should follow it by some action, and that that action would be only to enlarge the area of Section 3 to include [the] Western Hemisphere, Newfoundland, Labrador, etc. . . . That that was why, when I spoke in the House, I had said that before conscription for overseas was finally adopted, we would come to Parliament and discuss it on its merits. . . . We were now taking both steps as one."

Mackenzie King went on to say that the understanding reached in the Cabinet "had reference to what I should say on the introduction of the amendment. That I had held strictly to what had been agreed there. I was now doing my utmost to have it made quite plain that the present debate would be the only one on conscription. That I thought if he had followed exactly what I had said in caucus, he would see that I had not gone further than make clear that responsibility to Parliament would have to be my guide, and that I shall have to construe it [that responsibility] as I saw it just like everyone else; that I had made no commitment on the part of the Government."

Mackenzie King found Macdonald's "mind was so much occupied with the naval situation on the coast [on June 3–4 the Japanese had attacked Dutch Harbor in the Aleutians] that he had already begun to think of the debate in terms of it. He said he thought it would make matters much easier for me in regard to getting an immediate decision, and one decision to suffice. I told him I thought it would also make it much easier for others to see how unwise it would be to attempt to apply conscription for overseas immediately, and make clear, as I had said, that events of the war would show it would, before the time came to apply conscription for overseas, be made apparent that we needed all the men we could get to protect our own country. I felt we had gone much too far in the numbers we had already sent out. That is going to be the reaction, I am sure." Mackenzie King felt "the people of Canada and especially of British Columbia will be in a state of consternation over the Japanese being able to establish bases in Alaska which will enable them to attack our country and to prepare for its invasion."

At the War Committee meeting on June 4, Mackenzie King "could see quite a change in the attitude of Macdonald, Power and Ralston. The latter spoke about flying out to British Columbia to meet General Stuart and make perfectly sure that everything is in good shape. He felt Stuart was satisfied in his own mind that this was the case but he, Ralston, did not know whether Stuart had grounds for that belief and thought of trying to make doubly sure. My advice to him was not to go; that it might create a sensation in the country and that it would look as though the Government was a bit panicky.... It is Ralston's failing," he added, "wanting to run everything himself. I know how strongly McNaughton resented it and I am afraid he will get into difficulty with Stuart and others if he takes that particular role."

When Ralston raised the question of sending more troops to British Columbia, Mackenzie King said he "felt we should get more men out there if there was any way of having this done. Ralston said he did not want to take away too many men from Eastern Canada. I said I also agreed with that.... Power and Macdonald were quite quiet. Said nothing as I spoke, but I think they have come to realize there will be an attack against both the Navy and the Air Force for letting everything go off their coasts—in doing so little to defend our coasts and looking only to the European scene." There is no question that the increasing prospect of a Japanese attack on the west coast did weaken the pressure for sending conscripted men overseas.

Mackenzie King worked for weeks on his speech on the second reading of Bill 80. On June 9, the night before the debate opened, "there remained still a few of the most important parts to be inserted. Concrete statement regarding policy—no extreme view to be permitted to prevail—not necessarily conscription but conscription if necessary. Much of what I had to say on national unity; what had to be said on the glory of Canada's overseas war effort being all voluntary. A word to the Members about their relations to their constituency. How they should proceed and one or two other final touches. These were all very important bits."

He had decided that his first speech should be "altogether devoid of anything provocative—persuasive statement, and if the Opposition made the debate provocative, then I could, in reply, meet the situation more effectively. This meant sacrificing much material that I, myself, would have liked to have included as to conscription having been raised for political motives. I felt clearly in my own mind, however, that I should not give the wrong lead at the moment, but seek to have reason rather than feeling or passion prevail at any stage of the debate, if that were possible." During the afternoon of June 9, he decided to say nothing at all about going back to Parliament for a vote of confidence, and to hold "all of this in reserve myself for what may be necessary to get a vote of confidence when the time comes. I felt an immense relief once this had cleared up in my own mind."

After he had spoken in the House on June 10, Mackenzie King wrote: "I felt as I read my speech that the early part of it was well worked out, very logical, very clear, and that it completely knocked out any argument that could be raised on anything that could be said about the plebiscite being a mandate, etc. As I reached the end, however, of the first part I felt that the speech was too long. I also, for a moment, thought that some bits of it were missing and was considerably perturbed and felt that I did not give to the further reading quite the same careful expression that I had to the first. Also I was conscious of the last part being too long, and felt that the Members were having difficulty in holding the intense interest which had been in evidence through the first hour.

"What, however, distressed me most while reading, was Ralston at my side making notes, while I was speaking. I felt he was distinctly critical of what I was saying and resented what I was saying about absence of need for conscription at the present time. When I was finished he did not say a single word to me, but sat there with his lips tightly together as though he was storing up something of which he did not wish to speak at the moment. He has worked himself so completely for conscription being the only thing, and regarding the plebiscite as a mandate that I think he has come to feel that the Government's policy should be immediate action, whether anything was necessary or not."

Mackenzie King noted in his diary that day that he had "not been conscious of any time in Parliament when I have felt everyone more or less in a tense and critical mood, and deeply concerned themselves and inclined for these reasons to be silent rather than expressive in regard to their feelings." Like the public, he realized that this was one debate of which no one could predict the outcome and that the life of the Government depended upon his leadership.

The next morning (June 11) Mackenzie King "was too tired physically and mentally to really feel the same relief that I otherwise would have felt about having the speech over, and having on record what it contained. However what affected me most has been Ralston's attitude showing quite clearly that he was not pleased with what I had said. During the day, however, I found that Ralston's attitude of mind was not shared by others. I was particularly interested to hear that Ilsley had said he thought it was the best speech I had ever made; that it made the whole position perfectly clear."

Cardin spoke on June 11 and made what Mackenzie King described as "an impassioned speech and most effective. Was vigorously applauded by most of the men on our side, here and there from others as well. I, myself, sought to lead the applause where he referred to his own and Lapointe's part in campaigns; what was owing of consideration to the Province of Quebec, etc. However, I was surprised that he directed his attacks so completely on myself and that he went the length of speaking of the Province of Quebec as being betrayed. I shall be able to reply effectively to that, for the Speech from the Throne [in which the plebiscite was announced] makes clear that he, himself, agreed to the policy set forth there. . . . Cardin was unfair in this. He was also most unfair in trying to have the House believe that the Government would keep Orders in a secret drawer and try surreptitiously to get conscription under way without anyone being able to make a protest. He knows perfectly well what my own attitude and position and intention is. I was very glad that he and some others in the debate stressed the necessity of Parliament not being ignored before any final step was taken."

Mackenzie King felt Cardin's speech "let Ralston, Macdonald and a few others see just in what position they had placed the whole party; the extent to which they were causing my attitude to be wholly misrepresented and misunderstood. The truth is that unless we can get through without ever having to have conscription for overseas service, the C.C.F.'s who will now vote against us and the Quebec Liberals will make an alliance which will cause them to have the control of power in the next Administration. They will get all the forces that are opposed to conscription on their side without losing any of the radical forces that would welcome conscription as, for example, the working classes in the cities and towns. It will be an ill day for Canada if the country comes to be ruled by that particular combination. That is why I have always believed in the Liberal party as against extremes of Toryism and immature Radicalism."

At the Cabinet meeting next day (June 12) Mackenzie King "said I thought we should at once consider very carefully the position as it is in the House of Commons, and Cardin's speech. That I had been disappointed in his speaking of Quebec having been betrayed; that he knew better than that. He knew I had done everything possible to safeguard Quebec's position and to avoid internal differences." Mackenzie King was resentful of Cardin's suggestion that the Government might act "clandestinely" with respect to conscription. He "pointed out he [Cardin] had emphasized the fact that parents might find their sons in Britain before they knew anything about the Order-in-Council having been put into effect. I said this might begin to bring about trouble in the matter of men being called up under the Mobilization Act. It was raising the same kind of fear that led to resistance . . . to conscription in the last war. I drew attention of Council to the fact that the Government's policies had been settled in the Speech from the Throne, and that Cardin had been in the Cabinet and agreed to the wording of the Speech which expressed distinctly the words that the Government believed it should have a free hand in time of war, which was the whole policy underlining the amendment. . . . I then said the Cabinet would see the position the party was being placed in because of our not agreeing to come back to Parliament. That it was apparent we were going to lose both the C.C.F. and Social Credit party and, from Quebec and Ontario, some of our own following. I then said I thought it was absolutely necessary that when the time came, if it did come, to put conscription into force, Parliament's approval should be given. That we had lost considerable support already through not making perfectly clear as to how this would be done. . . . I said I wished Ralston himself, when he spoke, would make clear that the Government had no intention of proceeding in any clandestine way. That there would be the fullest publicity before any step was taken. . . . I then said that I thought I had more than met the difficulty which had been mentioned in Council as to not standing for a second debate . . . what I thought was absolutely essential was to recognize the responsibility to Parliament in taking a step, even one that we had been authorized to take, through enabling legislation, at the moment we were proposing to take action. . . .

"Immediately Ralston spoke of this being all right once the Order was signed and before actually putting it into force, but to ask the Parliament's sanction before would be to provoke a second debate, etc. I said that that part could be easily regulated. That I would fix a time for the House. That what I would do would be to tell the House [that] the Government had decided to take this step. Give them the reasons and then say that I had allowed [the House] a day or two—at the most— to express its approval or disapproval of the Government's action. If they approved, well and good. If they did not approve, then the Ministry would resign, and a Ministry would have to be found who could carry on and take responsibility for all that would happen in the war for not taking the step. Angus Macdonald then threw back his head, as he had done previously, and said 'oh no, it could not be done that way . . . the Order should be signed first or it would be all over again' and Ralston continued to urge the point in the same way. . . .

"When I saw we were back where we were at the time of the introduction of the amendment, I thought I should at once make very clear my position, so I said, very quietly, that I thought I should say to the members of the Cabinet, so that there could be no question when the time came, if it did come, when a concrete position might present itself, as to how I would view my responsibility, that I would not embarrass any of my colleagues in the matter of any differences there might be, if I found that such arose; knowing what I felt, feeling as I do about my responsibility to Parliament, I would just go down to the Governor-General and ask him to accept my resignation as the head of the Administration and to call on one of my colleagues to take the position I was now filling.

"I said to them I would like you to consider the position exactly as I see it now. We are sitting here. The House is in session, will be in session again this afternoon in an hour or two. Does anyone suppose that if that action [conscription for overseas] had to be taken today, with the knowledge of what is owing to Members in the House of Commons, that I could sign an Order to put conscription into force and go an hour later and tell the House that this had been done, and ask for confidence in my action? Would I not be told at once that if I expected the confidence of the House they had a right equally to have expected mine? That I should have come and told them of the decision and asked for approval first; that I would have got it, I assume, practically unanimously, if the need were apparent, as I believe it would have to be before the step were taken. I said I would never do that. . . .

"There was complete silence in the Cabinet. . . . I could see that all my colleagues excepting Ralston and Macdonald were solidly with me. . . . I felt an immense relief and an immense feeling of calm once I had made this final statement and my position wholly clear. I know I am right, and, what is more, every member of the Government, who has any regard for government, knows I am right. I felt that I had gone to the extreme limit with both Ralston and Macdonald and all they represent. . . . From now on I feel that the course ahead is clear. If it is agreed that Parliament will approve the Government's action before any action is taken I will, d.v., stay on and do my best. . . . I shall never be at the head of a Government that will enforce conscription without having Parliament share that responsibility to the full with me."

Late that afternoon Ralston came to see Mackenzie King in his office in the House of Commons. Mackenzie King "was not surprised, after I had asked him to sit in the big chair just opposite me, when he said: 'Mr. King, I think I will have to resign. I do not see any other course. You and I do not see eye to eye; have not for some little time and I think the thing to do is to get out at once.' I said to him: 'Why do you say that, Ralston? You know there is no need for any step of the kind. There is no member of the Government whose services I have appreciated more than yours and whose wishes I have sought to do more to meet. I have gone the length of allowing myself and the party to be put in a wholly false position on this question of our responsibility to Parliament just because I knew what your problem was and wished to go the full length I possibly could to help to realize the confidence I had in you.' He then said this coming back to Parliament a second time was something he could not agree to. That he felt the people wanted action and that he interpreted the plebiscite differently than I did. Regarded it as a mandate and that they wanted to go ahead. That he had received a letter from a constituent in Charlottetown who said to him he hoped the Government now meant business and would go on. He thought all my action was directed towards pacifying the French. . . .

It would mean the whole business over again, and having the country run by Quebec, to have another debate.

"I told him he was quite wrong in this. That time was a great healer of differences; also I was a great believer in events determining situations. He said that he knew that I was and it was remarkable how well I had succeeded and the degree of success that had followed my method of procedure.

"I told him that if we were to take a step of the kind that I would be myself forced to ask the Governor General to find someone else to carry on the Administration. He said 'not at all,' that I should not have to do that; that he thought he could do best by getting out and speaking in different parts. Thought he ought to go to Quebec and other provinces and persuade them of the need of the situation, etc. I said that was not where his strength lay. It was in carrying on the Administration at this time and doing all possible to keep the country united.

"I then asked him if others were influencing him in any way to try and get me out of the Government, inasmuch as they thought I stood in the way of conscription? He said at once that was the last thing he had in mind. He added that he had not spoken to anyone in the Government about coming to me now. That he had felt I had stated very plainly to the Cabinet what my position was, which was right. I remarked I felt I owed that to my colleagues. That he felt was true, but it made clear the difference between us which he indicated could not be reconciled. I said I did not mean anyone in the Government, but meant others outside. He asked who. I spoke of men of means, some of the press, who are anxious for titles. They were all ambitious in that way. He assured me that nothing of the kind had occurred. I think he is right in that."

Mackenzie King then spoke of the possibility of Ralston taking his place, and Ralston "said it was the last thing in the world he would ever wish to do and indicated nothing would induce him to do it. I believe this is correct." Mackenzie King felt that "the truth is he just wants to have his own way and is prepared to sacrifice me or the party to have it; justifying no doubt his conscience in that this is a war where men are being slain and that conscription is necessary for victory. He does not see the political aspect, using that word in its best sense, at all."

After they had gone again over the point at issue, Mackenzie King "spoke about the need for both of us doing everything possible to keep the country on an even keel. That we must consider the interests of the country and the war before everything else. He then spoke of my speech in the House and said it had all gone in the direction of trying to please Quebec and as away from conscription. That the people had given me great confidence and he thought I should express appreciation of it and readiness to go ahead.

"I replied that it was no appeasement. It was to gain understanding. That my aim in the speech, as in everything else, had been to work for unity and to preserve unity to prevent prejudices, breaches widening, etc. That he must realize that that must be the supreme duty of the Prime Minister. I pointed out that we had been very positive about what we would do if the need arose. He seems to feel that I should not have said anything about 'if.' . . . We went over the same ground two or three times. . . . I told him I did not think it was well to attempt to reach any decision on a matter of this kind when we were both at the end of a long day and it would be much better to let the whole matter stand until we saw whether, if the occasion ever did arise, the decision was going to make any difference in the course to be taken. I intimated to him, at one stage, I was not restricting him in any way in what he wished to say.

"Finally, before leaving, he said he wished I would think over carefully again the point of having approval immediately after signing. I told him that I would continue to consider the matter right along, through the future, as I had right along in the past. Would do everything I could to meet the situation, to avoid any breach, but I did not say 'yes or no' as to what the decision would be. I took that as being settled; and it seemed to me that the last remark was implying that he was laying the ground for action later on, rather than for immediate action. I can scarcely believe that he will resign when it comes to the time, on the particular ground on which he is urging his resignation. It would never stand in the light of day. I feel, however, that he is putting all possible pressure on me, knowing I regard his services of great value and that the country does, too."

Mackenzie King went on to observe again that Ralston was a man "who likes to have his own way" and that he had given him more cause for concern "than all the other problems put together." He added that "Cardin, too, has revealed a streak that I may have had reason to be suspicious of, but have not allowed myself to believe. After all, I kept him in the Ministry against the wishes of several of my colleagues, and at the cost of considerable weakness to the Government, throughout the whole period of his illness. I really saved his life by so doing, and he knows that. To have made his whole attack on me, and to have talked about my betraying Quebec, when he knows, and has said so often, that he sees my position has been made impossible by one or two of my colleagues, reveals that his nature and his purpose is something very different than I believed it could be. It is perfectly clear that he is seeking to build himself up as a political force and is ready to do so along demagogic lines. However, I shall wait and see how all this turns out."

That same day (June 12) Mackenzie King saw an article in the Ottawa *Journal* "to the effect that our Government might be sustained only by Conservative votes. That has caused me to consider carefully what course I should, from now on, pursue. I will never stay in office an hour by any Tory support. I can see where the Tories would like nothing better. They would feel it was helping to pave the way for National Government and to give them added support. However, I have said, in one of my radio addresses, that if I lost the support of those who have given me their confidence I would not wish to be in office a day. If I do not get the majority of our own people, I would certainly ask the Governor to call on someone else to form a Ministry. I am wondering whether I should not make this fact known before the vote comes; whether I should make it known in the House, in speaking, or to our party in caucus. I do not like to have any talk of resignation getting abroad. That would be fatal, and yet, not to let the Members know what to expect, might also be a mistake. . . . If they knew I was ready to go out, they would change their tone."

When Ralston asked to see him again on June 15, Mackenzie King decided he would do his best to persuade him to postpone his resignation "until after the debate, but would accept the resignation rather than yield to his request that an Order-in-Council should be signed before obtaining a confidence vote from the Commons. I sent for St. Laurent and told him of my talk on Friday with Ralston, and of word received for an interview. He seemed greatly surprised. Said that a question of the kind would cause the Canadian people to think that there was need for immediate conscription, and that such would be very harmful. . . . He did not believe Ralston really would carry out such an intention."

When Ralston arrived "he came back to the old ground and said there was a very narrow division between us. It was just a matter of getting the approval of Parliament before rather than immediately after signing of the Order-in-Council. I repeated that that was the difference between really taking Parliament into our confidence and meriting their approval, and, on the other hand, appearing to distrust Parliament and causing its Members to feel they had been affronted. I pointed out how all the debate was making clear that our real difficulty today was that of appearing to ignore Parliament. That, as he knew, I had risked the whole party's position in not saying at once we would get the approval of Parliament before taking the final step. He admitted that that was so, but said he could not see how, having the power, we should not exercise it and not go back to have our actions approved until we had taken the step. There was nothing further that was particularly new or which differed from what was said the other day. . . .

"He then talked a bit about the preparation of his own speech, wondering how he could say what he felt without running counter to the position I had taken. I replied there was no need for a commitment at this stage beyond general terms of responsibility to Parliament, as it might have to be exercised in circumstances that were as yet wholly unforeseen and unknown. That events might settle all matters before that stage was reached. He then said to me he was going to Montreal. If I received a letter from him the next day or two, that I would understand why it was written. I said at once that I hoped he would not feel [it] necessary to write any letter. . . . That I wished he would wait until the debate was over."

When Howe spoke in the debate on Bill 80 on June 16, Mackenzie King felt "nothing could possibly have been better. . . . The greater part of the speech was perfectly straightforward. He came out in splendid fashion about misrepresentation of our war effort in the States being due to what was said by a section of the Tory press, etc. The greater part of his speech was on what Canada was doing in war supplies to all parts of the world, and what was needed for our Army, Navy, Air Force, etc., showing that unless we were to sacrifice the greater service we were really rendering through a balanced effort, we would have to stop drawing on further men for overseas. He also stressed the need of what was required for the defence of our own country. He delivered the speech very well, in considerable part ex tempore. I was delighted with him. No colleague could have given his leader better support."

Mackenzie King spent part of that afternoon (June 16) with J. W. Dafoe of the Winnipeg *Free Press* who "spoke most appreciatively of what I had done; of the course pursued which he said he thought had been entirely the right one. In the course of our talk, he told me that he thought he ought to let me know that there had been a well-organized movement between Toronto and Montreal and other parts to definitely get into power a Government that would control post-war policy. The Government to be one that would get rid of any French influence in the Cabinet, and he added, also Catholic. To try to put French Canada out of the picture of Canada altogether, the idea being that after the war immigration should be encouraged from Britain in large numbers. That the French would be opposed to immigration. British immigration should flood the country after the war. French Catholics would be opposed to this, and of course the movement [intended] getting me out of office along with Ministers from Quebec.

"Dafoe said he and the *Free Press* had been asked to become a party to this movement. He supposed it was because of the lurid past of Dafoe and the Siftons. That he had written a letter which he thought would be of historic value and would make real reading some day when it was published. I did not press him for any details but it was clear that he meant he had denounced the whole business most emphatically and exposed the wrong of it. He went on to speak of how wrong anything of the kind was and how completely mistaken.

"I told him of the present situation and spoke particularly about feeling that I should ask the House for a vote of confidence before signing any Order-in-Council to send men overseas, allowing a couple of days for debate. He told me that he, himself, fully approved of that course. . . . I let him know that the only difference in the Cabinet was over that one point of signing before or after asking Parliament for a vote. He said that was purely a technical point, and did not think it gave grounds for any difference with anyone in the Cabinet. In other words, he was agreeing that, as Prime Minister, I should adopt that course if I so desired."

That evening (June 16) St. Laurent spoke in the House on Bill 80. Mackenzie King considered "the speech he made was from every point of view, a great achievement. It was well thought out; well delivered, and exceedingly well received. Just the very thing that was most needed at this time. St. Laurent has been in the most difficult of all positions, coming into Parliament at a time of crisis and encountering, at the very outset, the most difficult problem that has faced Canada since Confederation. He has come into the House of Commons almost unknown in political life, though as one foremost in his own profession; came in with followers from the Province who do not know him and very few of whom he himself knows. He has chivalrously championed the most difficult of all positions, holding completely the larger vision, and appreciating to the full all that is required of courage and sound judgment to meet it. Following on top of Cardin's resignation, his task was doubly difficult, but he has rendered a service to the Government, to his Province, and to the country which is beyond words.

"Members of the House," he added, "were immensely taken by his eloquence, and above all by the nobility of character that shone through it. He gave new life and leadership to his compatriots from Quebec, and they felt, I know, the force of both. He was given a great reception at the end of his speech. . . . I waited till the applause was about to die down, then rose from my seat and walked over to his desk. He rose and we shook hands together. I thanked him most warmly. It was a symbolic meeting. I had found a colleague from Quebec who was a worthy successor of Lapointe and Sir Wilfrid. That, I think, was apparent to the House. . . . It was a real triumph, and I doubt if any maiden speech in Parliament—for such it was—has equalled it in importance or effect."

Mackenzie King spent most of his time in the House during the debate on Bill 80. On June 18, he referred to a speech by "[Ernest] Bertrand of Montreal, first of Quebec Members to be outstandingly in favour of the Bill. I thought he made a first rate argument and I formed a high opinion of his ability and manner of speaking. Indeed, many of the Members have been a surprise in the talent they have shown. I was sorry not to have heard [Joseph] Jean, who has two sons in the Army, but who is opposing the Bill. He has done so in a very nice way. No better example could be cited of the reason why every consideration should be shown to French Members. I have had both of these men in my thoughts tonight for Cabinet preferment. My feeling is the fact that because either one or the other has not been able to support the Government on the Bill should not make any difference when it is agreed that Members generally will support the Government in the final action." Bertrand and Jean did in fact both become Ministers.

On June 21, Mackenzie King received the news that the wireless station at Estevan Point on Vancouver Island had been shelled by the Japanese the previous night. He felt this Japanese attack on Canadian territory would have an "effect upon Canadian feeling with regard to conscripting men to be sent overseas to Europe which is, of course, all that the conscriptionists are really concerned about, and to win their point regardless of the effect on Canada itself."

Angus Macdonald spoke in the debate on June 22. Mackenzie King noted that "he kept within the strict letter of not disagreeing with the Cabinet policy generally, but certainly departed from the spirit of the Cabinet and its general view as to not seeking to enforce conscription until absolutely necessary. . . . I could not take exception to the speech as worded. It was deliberately intended to offset the impression of other colleagues who have spoken thus far."

Mackenzie King felt that Ralston, who spoke on June 23, "made an exceptionally able speech." He noted that "Ralston did not hesitate to rather emphasize the differences with some of his colleagues. He made an excellent all-out effort speech but, I think, identified the whole of it much too closely with the Army overseas, not sufficiently with the Army that we might require in Canada as well as overseas. I felt, too, that he was seeking to make it difficult for me to say anything about coming back to Parliament for a vote of confidence. He made no reference to the responsibility to Parliament end of things, and in one place, he said something to the effect that 'I [Ralston] intended to act' putting himself, as I saw it, in a position where [if] in any way he might encounter opposition in the Cabinet to making an immediate decision, he might resign on the score that he was being delayed, but to the public leaving rather the impression that he, himself, would have the say, once the power was given by Parliament to the Government, and that it would not be the Cabinet that would decide. This one part of the speech I felt had been thought out with a good deal of care and design, and from the manner of its delivery, I felt it was very significant. That we would have to study that aspect of it with care. It made me feel, [he] not having said anything to me in advance of this part, that he had been doing so with design. However, it gave me just what I need to justify me in making clear my position as Prime Minister in relation to asking Parliament for a vote of confidence in the Administration."

That same evening (June 23) Ilsley brought down his Budget, which Mackenzie King felt "was a remarkably fine and able statement, and a splendid budget from the point of view of making it apparent that no one was to make money out of this war. Those that could afford should pay with taxation to the extent of making them change their standard of living. I was interested in watching the C.C.F.'s [The C.C.F. had moved an amendment to Bill 80 advocating conscription of wealth.] It certainly came as a surprise to them. Arguments re amending Mobilization Act Amendment will lose force now."

Mackenzie King was absent in Washington for the next two days. He spent June 25 at the White House where Churchill was also staying. The war was going very badly everywhere at this time. The British had just lost Tobruk in Libya. In his diary, Mackenzie King noted that "Churchill at luncheon and elsewhere spoke of criticism in British Parliament of himself over Tobruk. . . . He was sure those who had taken the step would be sorry, and before any time was over would ask him not to press for a vote. He intended, however, to bait them on and to make them vote. He said Parliamentary government could not be carried on by mere debate, letting people say what they liked, but it was also by decision and registering of where they stand. He intended to force a vote to show what support he had. He said, at a time of war, no Government could carry on without Parliament at its back." This statement greatly impressed Mackenzie King who naturally related it to his own position regarding a vote of confidence on conscription.

The next day (June 26), back in Ottawa, Mackenzie King spoke to Ralston about his speech which he described as "a wonderful speech. That he must have put infinite work on it. That he had not left any dust on the floor in making a case for total effort. That the only part I was inclined to take exception to was reference to his saying that he would see that conscription was carried out without any delay; leaving rather the impression that it was the military authorities and not the Cabinet which would settle that question. He said to me that he thought he had been careful to say that he was speaking only for himself. I said that I thought he did say this, but the impression left was that he himself rather than the Cabinet would settle the matter. He said of course he did not mean that."

On July 7, Mackenzie King "sent word in the morning that I wished to have a full Cabinet, this being the day on which I was to wind up the debate. When I seated myself at the table, found every chair filled. . . . I spoke to the Cabinet quite quietly but pretty much in the following words: I felt that I should tell members of Council exactly what I intend to do at this time. If when the vote is taken tonight, there is not a majority of our own party over all the three parties opposite, I intend to ask immediately for the adjournment of the House and go at once to the Governor-General and tender him my resignation. I will not try to carry on a Government in time of war by those on whose loyal support I cannot count. . . .

"I said Members of Council might be free to tell Members of the party what my intention was. I did not intend to mention it in the debate, but I wanted the party to know exactly what was in my mind. I said I would discuss with the Governor-General the question of a dissolution or sending for some other member of the Government to form an Administration. That I would advise against a dissolution. I thought that it would be wrong to have the country drawn into a state of turmoil at this time. That I had substituted the plebiscite for a referendum to avoid political controversy, and would not do anything to arouse controversy if that could be avoided. I then said some member of the Cabinet will have to take my place in the Ministry.

"Also said that I intended in what I had to say tonight . . . to be very positive about not permitting any second debate on conscription, but that, once Cabinet decided for conscription, should that become necessary, I felt that it would be necessary for me to be assured of the confidence of Parliament before attempting to enforce the decision, and that I would so indicate to Parliament. I said that I had been subjected to a great deal of criticism. Had taken a stand of avoiding conscription, if that was at all possible. As it might be felt that I was, therefore, not the one to be entrusted with its enforcement . . . I would need to have the expression of confidence. Moreover, I did not think members of the Opposition or anyone in the House should be allowed to get away with mere discussion but should be obliged to vote, and by their vote let the country see where they were standing. Whether they were helping the Government or withholding their help to the Government at this time when there was need for Government support in the Commons."

He then referred to what Churchill had said in Washington and "made clear I would not allow more than two or three days at most for debate [on the vote of confidence if the Government decided conscription was necessary].Would apply the closure if need be. I felt the need to tell the country of this attitude now so that Members would not feel I was trying to spring a surprise, or that decision for a confidence vote had grown out of some last minute discussion in the Cabinet. I made a clear demarcation between a second debate on conscription and a vote of confidence or non-confidence in a Ministry headed by myself for enforcing conscription.

"There was dead silence all the time I was speaking, and when I had finished, for some moments after. Ralston then spoke about going to Parliament a second time, and of a vote being taken after the signing of an Order rather than before. I pointed out that that would be a strange way to treat Parliament; to show no confidence in what Parliament was likely to do before asking their confidence was a poor way to get an expression of it. That I felt by telling Parliament of the decision in advance of signing the Order, we would get a very good vote. . . .

"I stated I thought once the Bill had carried, was law, that the press —even the Quebec press—would begin to assert . . . that the people ought to accept it. Certainly when it came to seeing who is to administer the law, and confidence was asked, Quebec would support me rather than risk a change. This gave a chance for the party to reunite, and also to continue the work of administration during the war. . . . Ilsley was rather helpful as feeling the need of Parliament back of the Government with all he has to get through in his legislation. Macdonald was less assertive though obviously still of his old views. . . .

"The discussion ran on until about 2 [P.M.]. I was feeling pretty tired and was feeling the strain considerably, so said that I thought perhaps Members of Council might like to discuss the matter further by themselves, and stood up and moved towards the Council Chamber door. They all said: by no means to leave; for us to remain together. I said I thought they would be freer to consider the full situation by themselves. I then left. At first, they were going to come out at the same time, but finally remained behind, and they continued talking over matters until almost 3. Did not seek to ascertain what had been said, but learned that Ilsley had spoken about feeling the need of Parliament at his back, and that nothing definite had been concluded."

Mackenzie King's speech in the House did not come until the evening (July 7) and he worked on it all afternoon. When he got to the House of Commons at about a quarter past 8, Ralston was in the anteroom of his office. "I told him to come in. When he came in, he said he felt he had no alternative but to tender his resignation. . . . Was sorry to have to take the step but he could not do otherwise. I pointed out to him there was no difference between us excepting one of procedure on a small technical point. He said, 'No, it was one of principle, of not having any delays but needing action.' I said to him to wait till he heard what I had to say in the evening in the debate before writing his letter. I thought he would find we were not very far apart, and had so worded what I was going to say as to leave little or no margin between us, and to speak only for myself on the one point which was needed in order to get the confidence that would be required to carry on. I was really trying to make the situation workable should conscription become necessary. As Coldwell was speaking, and his time nearly up, and I was to follow, I said I would have to hurry back into the House so he returned to his room."

When he went into the House, Mackenzie King found there were still one or two more speakers and he returned to his office for a short rest. While he was resting, his secretary brought in a letter from Ralston. He "opened it and glanced at it quickly, and saw it was his resignation. Noticed that he spoke about approval of decision. Felt I had all I needed in that to show the line of demarcation between us. It left him without any real ground for him to stand on for resigning. To resign would mean he was not trusting Parliament at a time when, above all others, he needed the help of Parliament. Felt he could not afford to go out on those lines, though, knowing his tenacity, I felt that he might hold tight to his resignation, particularly as I can see that, through [my] opposing his views, he was becoming somewhat antagonistic toward myself. He came into the House while Joseph Harris, M.P. for Danforth, was speaking. I said to him he and I would talk this whole matter over later, to say nothing to anyone in the meantime.

"When I began to speak, I had his letter in my folder, opened, on top of my manuscript. I put it back into the folder but it came out in part while I was drawing out my manuscript. Was rather amused that in speaking, the resignation was actually in the House on my desk, in front of me. It was the thing that might well have embarrassed anyone whose mind was not definitely set, regardless of consequences, knowing that one was absolutely in the right. I took care to speak slowly and distinctly and with the right emphasis.

"The galleries were crowded. The House was extremely attentive and tense. Members loudly applauded my references to the extremists who were unwilling to defend their own families or Canada. Our Members, too, appreciated the reference to the stages at which there had been no need for conscription, making clear it had all been political agitation.

"I was a little surprised that there was not some applause when I made it clear I was coming back for a vote of confidence. However it had been known pretty generally throughout the House that there was a difference in the Cabinet on this point. Some of them could not see clearly the difference between coming back to Parliament and asking for a vote of confidence. Many Members, not being certain how the matter might be received by others, refrained from showing their approval though I know that to most on our side, this aspect was welcome. I also know that it made the difference of from 5 to 6 votes, and might have made a difference of 10 on the division.

"I was given a good reception by our men when I concluded. I felt no concern in speaking and really felt fresh when I had finished. Ralston did not applaud. Sat quite quietly. Later in the evening, he turned to me and said that I would have made a good lawyer the way I had handled the whole business, particularly the responsibility to Parliament. That eased my mind very much as I felt it might be a sign of his letting me know later he would be prepared to withdraw his resignation. Before he left the House, he told me not to feel he could make any change in his attitude. I told him to take a good rest, and we would talk the matter over in the afternoon tomorrow."

While preparing his speech, Mackenzie King had "thought of dealing with the question of some Members not having confidence in me as one who should be at the head of a Government that had to enforce conscription, and had written out something about Diefenbaker's attitude. . . . However, I did not, owing to pressure at the end, get that part into my speech. I did make a general reference to the attitude of some of the Opposition and their supporting press. Hanson interrupted me to ask me to name any single member of their party who had said any such thing. I replied that the member two seats behind him was one, without mentioning Diefenbaker's name. Diefenbaker then got up and said if I meant him, I was quite in the wrong. I told him I did mean him, and that I had intended to speak of him, but thought it was best not to bring any names into what I was saying. . . . They all began to challenge me to put the statement on record at once or withdraw. I told them I would give the statement tomorrow."

While the Opposition continued to demand a withdrawal, one of Mackenzie King's secretaries who was in the gallery sent him the Hansard with the passage marked [July 7, 1942, pp. 4009–10]. Mackenzie King noted, "it came just in time for me to quote. I was absolutely right in what I had said, and the House applauded very loudly. There was great applause from the House. Diefenbaker tried to make out I had taken the wrong inference, but his words were there quite clearly. If the whole proceedings had been planned, it could not have been better. Came in absolutely at the right place. . . . I felt a real delight as I watched the incident develop."

When the vote on Bill 80 was taken, the majority was 104 and Mackenzie King calculated that this was a majority of 30 of his own supporters. "It was clear we had not to rely upon any of the Opposition to give us the majority necessary to sustain the Government." He added that "an amusing incident followed the division." What happened was that the House went into Committee, the Deputy Speaker took the Chair, and the Prime Minister at once moved that the Committee rise and report progress, a motion which is not debatable. Before the motion was put, as Mackenzie King related it, "Hanson tried to get in some words for the press which would give them a lead. Referring to my remarks, he said the Government had looped the loop three times. He was called to order and was clearly out of order as the motion before the House was not debatable." Hanson appealed the ruling of the Chair and a division was taken on which the vote was 137 to 44. "The effect of the division was to let the entire party vote as one in opposing the appeal from the Chair," Mackenzie King wrote, and added: "It was a great thing on the same evening to get a chance for our own men to show that they were with the Government on everything else and had no ill will toward myself."

The following morning (July 8) Mackenzie King was awakened by word that Ralston was on the telephone. "When I took the 'phone at the bedside and answered," he wrote, "he said he had been uncertain as to what he should do as respects attending the meeting of the War Committee at 11.30; having tendered his resignation he was not sure whether he should attend. . . . He said there were several important matters that affected the Service and, perhaps for that reason, he should come, but would like to be sure, if he did, it would not prejudice in any way the position he had taken in the letter. I said to him that certainly, by all means, to come; that there would not be any prejudicing of his position in any way. I had not accepted his resignation and he was, therefore, still in his responsible position as Minister; that he and I would have a talk together during the afternoon. I hoped he would think nothing further of the matter until then. That I was sure we would be able to work out the situation ourselves. He then said he would come."

Before seeing Ralston that afternoon, Mackenzie King told St. Laurent "of Ralston's resignation and of the talk we had had together and read over to him the letter which Ralston had written. He said it had not come to him altogether as a surprise. . . . He thought, if Ralston left, no matter what might be done, it would clearly make a division which would necessitate a general election, which would be very serious at this time. It might come at a moment of terrible crisis. I said I would not take the responsibility of advising an election under any circumstances. St. Laurent pointed out that, regardless of how I might seek to avoid it, the situation would be such as to make it inevitable. He thought this should be made clear to Ralston and have him realize he could not escape being responsible for precipitating a situation of the kind. . . . I then spoke to St. Laurent about the procedure which he thought it would be wise to follow. . . . He thought the thing that would weigh strongest with Ralston was his action in precipitating an election. He said he surely must see he has a real responsibility to avoid consequences of the kind. . . . I thought St. Laurent was right in advising me to see Ralston alone. I felt all along I should carefully avoid letting it be known that any resignation had been so much as thought of by any one."

Mackenzie King then saw Ralston and told him "it was out of the question altogether for me to think of accepting his resignation; that he knew as well as I did that the country, and indeed our whole war effort, required his continuance in office in his present position and, above all, the avoidance of any break; that, if it went out to the public that there was a difference between the Minister of Defence and the Prime Minister, which was responsible for the resignation of the former, it would create a situation that would be very serious indeed, and one which certainly would not be justified on any grounds of existing difference between us.

After all, the matter was merely a question of procedure, and a technical matter. It was not one which affected action in any way.

"He came back, however, that it was a matter of principle. We went a little over the ground we had discussed before, and I pointed out that the rest of the Cabinet, with the exception possibly of Macdonald, did not share his view, and I did not think he had distinguished sufficiently between going back to Parliament either on the question of conscription or approval of the decision, and my asking for a vote of confidence because of the reasons such as Diefenbaker had given, that of having no confidence in myself to enforce conscription for overseas even if the decision were arrived at to that end.

"Ralston then began to speak as though his attitude had grown out of what I had said last night, whereas his letter had been written before I spoke." After a good deal of discussion about the exact meaning of what he had said the previous evening, Mackenzie King "then sought to explain to Ralston that the course I was taking was really to help him in the event of conscription becoming necessary; that he would find that the Quebec Members would be prepared to reunite in a matter of confidence. I believed they would take the view that, as the matter had become law and the Government had reached a decision, it was well then to fall in line and express confidence in the Government rather than continue to oppose us, and that enforcement of conscription would in all probability come along without incident of any importance, particularly as events will show at the time that the Government had been right. . . .

"I then said to Ralston I did not want to have to bring different influences to work on him. He and I should be able to settle the matter satisfactorily. I did not want to go to the Governor-General and have him cable the King and the King request Ralston to stay. Churchill to do the same, etc. I stressed again what an election would mean; how inevitable it would be, if the thing had got more divided; of my determination not to advise it under any consideration. That would have to fall to the lot of someone else. That no matter what I might do I was sure that the step was inevitable, if he persisted in his attitude.

"I spoke to Ralston of his needing more help in his own Department. He said to me that he thought he had suggested before quite sincerely and would again that I should become Minister of Defence myself to take charge over all the others. I laughed at the idea and said it was impossible to even consider it; that I had not, as he knew, any military training and would not even understand how properly to express the different relationships."

Mackenzie King "said quite frankly what I would like, above everything else, would be to have someone else take the office of Prime Minister. Let me continue as Minister of External Affairs and give to the Prime Minister all the help I could. If anyone could be found who would take my position, I would ask that this be arranged at once. Ralston then said there was no one else that could. I said, equally, there was no one else for his position at the present time. We must both realize that our personalities were of importance only as they affected the war effort and that we must think of that to the exclusion of everything else.

"I said to Ralston that what I would like would be for him to ask to have his letter withdrawn. If he did not wish that, I would write him a letter myself, if that is what he wished, to have the position on record. I thought matters could stand in that way until some occasion arose, should it ever happen, that there was a real difference on any fundamental matter between us.

"I should have mentioned before that, in asking him about the fundamental difference of attitude, he said I was too conciliatory; that I kept on seeking to conciliate and that I thought too much about the unity of Canada. He did not think, with the vote we had in the plebiscite, and the vote we got last night in the House, that we should consider any further those who took a different view. He himself felt we should go straight ahead and ignore any opinion other than that of the majority. I pointed out to him in reply that there necessarily were the military and civil points of view; that a government could only be carried on by composing differences and that time was required; that we were dealing with great forces which, by taking only one point of view, could not be controlled, but which, through combined effort, could be.

"As we got near the end of the conversation the two real points that I think have been in Ralston's mind right along, and that were governing his present action, came out. The first was, as he had mentioned to me before, that the people he keeps meeting, particularly those who, like himself, have a son overseas, keep asking why the best of our men should be sent overseas and the slackers allowed to remain? They feel impatient about this and want to see these other men incur some dangers, etc.

"My reply to that was that, as he knew, those types of men were not likely to be of much real service overseas; that all slackers were as liable to conscription as anyone else; that the thing I thought should be done to men of that type was to give them, if they were not to be of real help to our volunteer force, stations at some outpost where they would have to endure hardships like everyone and where they might be of some real service. . . .

"The other point, and I believe the real one right along, was when he said that he himself, as I knew, was very stubborn, etc. He had come in to do a piece of work; had given up his practice, etc. and that he had a certain pride which he must preserve. I was struck by the use of the word 'pride.' He had taken a certain position that we must go ahead and he did not see how he could yield to any other position."

Mackenzie King asked what he "could do that would help the situation. He said to me that it was not, of course, for him to suggest but, if I could write him a letter which would make it clear he was free to take whatever course he liked, that he would be pleased if I could say something along that line. . . . To this I replied I had already made clear I did not think there was any issue between us which should cause any resignation; that if, for example, when the time came, if it did come, when conscription would have to be applied, and I should refuse to act on his recommendation, which he would regard as imperative, that then there would be real ground for his resignation, but I did not think anything of the kind was likely to arise.

"I believed he felt, as I did, that if we could get the men without conscription it would be better. Equally, I felt that if that could not be achieved and it was clear that the other course was necessary, I would have to take my responsibility of either being willing to remain in the Government to enforce conscription or resign. Not that I would dislike the business of enforcing conscription; that was nothing as compared to bringing the country into war. . . .

"I said to Ralston that he would admit I had never at any time blocked him in any of the recommendations that he had made. I had supported him in getting the Army to the size it is. I had tried to uphold him in every way. He admitted that that was true. I said he need not feel there was a danger that I had in mind any thought of shirking any responsibility. . . . I thought we could trust each other to work together in the national interest and in the interest of the cause of the war itself. I said I would be glad to go over carefully what I had said, and write him a letter, which I would show him before sending it to him, to make sure that it was on the right lines."

Mackenzie King concluded by noting that he "told Ralston just to continue on and to think of nothing further. He spoke about wanting to get this thing off his mind. I told him I was equally anxious to try and get things settled tomorrow."

It was not until after the House rose the next evening (July 9) that Mackenzie King saw Ralston and showed him the draft letter he had prepared. "When he had finished the reading," Mackenzie King noted, "he said that we were both tired and perhaps it would be better to wait until the morning as he would like to read it over further. . . . I said I felt that was what would be advisable."

They had some discussion about the significance of asking for a vote of confidence and Mackenzie King referred to "Churchill's attitude in respect to the last motion as being one primarily of confidence in himself, and the effect upon the war effort of confidence in the Prime Minister being undermined. All Ralston would say is he thought it would be just the other way, by signing first, expression of confidence would be all the greater.

"It was clear that he was simply trying to find some way of still preventing that step. He then went on to say that there might be a difference of opinion at the time of signing, and that it would be better for him to get out now than at that time. I said if there was a real issue, that would be a different thing but to get out on a matter of procedure would be a great mistake. I did not think he would find that any difference would arise that would create an issue, once it was apparent that it was necessary to resort to conscription. That I did not think he would find me difficult in a situation of the kind. That I realized the decision would have to be, in the main, the decision of the military advisers, and the country, knowing how strongly I had sought to avoid conscription, would have all the more faith in the need for it and be the better prepared to support it, if, on top of that, I were to tell the House it was necessary."

They discussed the possibility of delays and Mackenzie King pointed out "that Parliament would have dealt with the matter long before" the necessary action could be taken to get the troops ready to go overseas.

"He then said to me: women sometimes had an intuitive sense, and their feeling would be: why these continuous delays. Why not let us get on, etc. That in an instant gave me another impression of a force at work I had not thought of, and also what may be in Ralston's mind. He may really be wishing to get out of office altogether and to find some excuse that would leave him in a position before the public for taking a high stand, etc. in so doing.

"There is no doubt that the strain is telling on him. . . . I am perfectly sure that Mrs. Ralston is doing all in her power to have him quit before he breaks down, and that in all probability she is pressing him very hard to take advantage of this occasion. She has never wanted him to be in public life.

"Finally before he left, he said to me: would I say publicly I would not allow any length of time for debate, what time would I be prepared to allow? I said: 'Most certainly.' Even in the course of the present debate, if I were asked, I would say that, at most, two days should be given, and I would say there ought not to be an hour of discussion. I would certainly say at once that the time would be definitely limited so that the public would know there would be no further controversy; no unnecessary discussion."

When they resumed their discussions on July 10, it was largely on the points made by Mackenzie King in his draft letter to Ralston. Mackenzie King asked him to give back the letter so it could be modified to meet Ralston's objections. When Ralston handed back the draft letter "he said when I sent the answer not to ask him to read it over with a view to making any suggested change. That he was very tired and would like to rest and think about it over the weekend before replying. He did say that when he wrote a reply, he would have to say in it he might take a certain course later on in certain circumstances.

"He spoke then again of the possible opposition there might be to him in Council when, on the advice of his military authorities, he were to recommend conscription. It was that delay which I think he has been thinking about more than any other, and the fear that he would not be able to make out his case.... I have thought all along that that was where the real danger would come. It was for that reason I felt it advisable, in advance, to make known my intention of seeking a vote of confidence. Also I know that, unless this were known to the authorities, conscription would be immediately introduced just to satisfy them regardless of the effect on possible consequences in the country....

"Ralston looked an ashen grey in colour and his face terribly set with lower jaw protruding as though he was going through a terrific strain. I think he has felt that I would yield and that my position is perhaps stronger than he had realized. He used the expression I was a very careful letter-writer when saying he would like to have till Monday to write out what he had to say. I told him by all means not to try to do anything till he got wholly rested. We talked pleasantly of other matters. I then came back to Laurier House and began to write out what I wished to say."

It took several more days to get the letters redrafted to the satisfaction of both, but the immediate crisis was over.

Mackenzie King moved third reading of Bill 80 on July 23. During the debate he "kept holding back my speech so as to have as many as possible precede.... When Hanson concluded, I started at once. To my surprise I spoke for nearly two hours. Did so with only a few notes. I felt I was on a higher pitch at the beginning than I wished to be, and there were moments when I felt I was not expressing myself as clearly as I should have liked, or following too logically what I wished to say. However, the speech seemed to hold the rapt attention of our own men who applauded.

"I was quite surprised later in the evening to find that what I had said had really made an impression upon the Members on our side, both French and English, who seemed to be greatly pleased. It was a fighting speech. There were one or two references to the Tories I might have left out but they came on the spur of the moment in answer to interruptions. Otherwise they would not have been included.

"I felt a little embarrassed all the time of speaking with Ralston at my side following closely what I was saying, and knowing what his objections were to any promise to go to Parliament, and Macdonald also present and watching closely, but when it was over, I was relieved to find Ralston raising no objections and asking how I managed to get the material together for the speech in the time I did. He has been terribly worried about the Hong Kong inquiry and his mind was full of anxiety on that score. We had been expecting that debate to come on at any moment." The vote on third reading was 141 to 45, but only two French-speaking Liberal private Members from Quebec voted for the Bill.

The next morning he wrote: "I felt an immense relief at the debate being over, and the Bill through the Commons. I do not recall before having seen Members come to me literally with tears in their eyes and shaking in what they were saying, but this was true of several of the Quebec men who felt badly at having had to vote against me. . . . I was really surprised at how deep the feeling was, and expressions of evident loyalty. I have always recognized the difficult position in which the Members have been placed, and I think they have seen that I, too, have had trying experiences through it all. I am sure, however, that the right course has been taken, and that indeed I have been given both guidance and strength." Throughout the day, he was greatly surprised to discover that his speech the evening before seemed to have made a real impression. Several Members "said to me that my speech had helped to make the situation easy for them and others. It had helped to save the whole situation."

Meanwhile, Mackenzie King and Ralston were drawn closer together again by a common concern over the Hong Kong inquiry. Mackenzie King had received Chief Justice Duff's Report on June 4, "accompanied by a personal note saying that the Report gave a clean bill of health. . . . Its wording really made me rejoice. It contains a first-rate crack at Drew [George Drew had been counsel for the Leader of the Opposition], the implication being that once there was possibility of fighting due to change of Government in Japan, the Government should have reconsidered the force. The one single shortcoming was lack of initiative and speed in getting off a half a dozen vehicles on one ship. . . . The point on which the Opposition had hoped to make so much capital, namely few untrained men, reason being lack of sufficient manpower, is cleared up splendidly, the Report showing that there was nothing to that whatever. . . . There could not have been a finer vindication of the Government's whole attitude in undertaking the expedition and the manner in which it was handled. I phoned Ralston after reading the Report and told him of its contents. I could feel the joy in his heart and sense of relief which, in his case, I know, is particularly great."

The Government had no further concern about the Hong Kong inquiry until the evening of July 13, when Mackenzie King "read a letter received during the day from Colonel Drew of Toronto, regarding the Hong Kong inquiry, a perfectly appalling communication attacking the Chief Justice, insinuating he had used part of the evidence and concealed other parts in order to make a finding which was not in accordance with the facts. . . . I have never read a more extreme or dangerous type of letter. At the close it mentioned that copies had been sent to Hanson, Coldwell, and Blackmore."

The next day (July 14) in the Cabinet meeting, Mackenzie King informed his colleagues of Drew's letter. There was considerable consternation, and it was decided to consult George Campbell, K.C., of Montreal, who had been Government Counsel, "as to course which should be taken. I felt strongly that the letter should be suppressed if that were possible, and certainly not made public." At the opening of the House that day, Coldwell asked for the tabling of Drew's letter. "I had in mind," Mackenzie King wrote, "not taking any responsibility for its tabling and also in mind what the Council's view seemed to be [that] we should not seek to refuse to table it if requested. I therefore said if Coldwell would take responsibility for its being tabled, it would be tabled tomorrow. He did, and there the matter ended for the moment."

Later in the day (July 14) Mackenzie King went to see the Chief Justice, who "was, as I anticipated he would be, greatly annoyed at Drew's behaviour. Spoke of it as the worst he had ever known, and of the whole procedure as being a plot in Toronto to try and oust me. . . . He thought that the letter should not be tabled on any account as it purported to divulge information that was wholly secret. . . . I arranged to have Ralston and St. Laurent see the Chief Justice tonight and Campbell to come from Montreal to have a talk with the two Ministers."

The next day (July 15) after the War Committee meeting, Mackenzie

King saw George Campbell, K.C., of Montreal, who gave him a written opinion that the letter should not be tabled on the ground that it purported to publish secret information communicated to the Commission by the United Kingdom Government on the understanding that it would be kept secret. Later in the day Mackenzie King saw Coldwell and Hanson. He reported that Hanson "told me privately that he was opposed to what Drew had been doing and would say nothing against the Chief Justice. That he was not for discussing the Hong Kong report at any length. He told me he had tried arguing a case with one arm tied, but never had tried to do it with two arms tied." Mackenzie King reminded Hanson that George Campbell was President of a Conservative Association in Montreal, and had been appointed as Counsel for the Government in order to be sure that the matter would be above any party consideration. He added that "it was apparent to all present . . . that he [Drew] was simply out to make all the political capital he could; that any step that was taken was certain to result in a flare-up in the press, especially as he, Drew, had communicated his letter to the press." In the light of the legal opinion, Mackenzie King refused to table the letter.

On July 17, Mackenzie King expressed the view that the Conservatives expected "to make the Hong Kong inquiry the path by which they will keep on demanding further facts, and the evidence as a means of arousing public sentiment against the Government. It is a cynical business at a time when the country should be united in the face of war. We have beaten them pretty well on the conscription campaign, and they are now trying another trap along with it. I told my colleagues that I understood that weekend articles were likely to appear indicating a difference of view in our Cabinet, all of which was part of the same campaign."

That day Mackenzie King "received another letter from Drew at noon . . . to give additional material for others in debate. Hanson asked if I intended to table it. I said no, for the same reason I had declined to table the other letter."

The debate in the House on the Hong Kong inquiry began on July 27. "Shortly before noon," Mackenzie King wrote, "there was quite a scene when I began taking Diefenbaker, of Lake Centre, and Hanson, to task over some of the insinuations they were trying to make, and the effort to prevent me from speaking. I referred to the tactics as being typically Tory and that they were actions of a mob. Diefenbaker had sought to have it appear I was responsible for some references to my grandfather, in his struggle for freedom, in some book of instructions for the training camps. . . . The whole thing was more of an emotional outburst. . . . I think the incident rather pleased our men, but after lunch Hanson brought the matter up as a question of privilege. I quickly withdrew the remark about the 'mob' and agreed to have the whole incident expunged from Hansard. I was not in any way ashamed of it, but realized that, as Prime Minister, I should not have used that particular expression.

"Throughout the day," he added, "it was difficult to restrain one's self from taking exception to what different speakers were saying in their references to the Drew letter, the report of the Chief Justice, etc. I did break in a couple of times, and would have done so at greater length and oftener, but for being anxious not to be drawn into a position where ground might be given for my being expected to table either the evidence or the Drew letter by making references to them. I felt that, on the whole, the debate went remarkably well, so far as our side was concerned, and that the Opposition were getting the worst of their tactics."

Mackenzie King was delighted by the vote of confidence (130-34) on Hong Kong on July 28. "Tonight," he wrote, "I had as fine a tribute paid to me as has been given to any Prime Minister at any time. I took it in this personal way because I know that it was meant as such, and the victory for the Government was as complete a victory as any party has had at any time. To appreciate it to the full, one has to go back to the beginning of this Parliament and more especially to the beginning of the present session. At the opening of the session, we were threatened, as a party, to become hopelessly divided and Parliament to become a battleground between conscriptionists and anti-conscriptionists, with a similar battle being waged throughout the country at large. It could only have ended in one way, and that would have been a break-up of the party, and our war effort would have suffered tremendously, and conscription been brought in despite all pledges and in violation of all pledges at the expense of my own leadership and that of some of the members of the Government. Something like a National Government [would have been] brought into being which could only have functioned in a way that would have made bad situations worse.

"Instead of that, during the session, the people themselves have relieved the Government of its pledges. There has been the fullest possible discussion in Parliament of the whole conscription issue. The Government has now full power to use conscription for overseas if necessary. In the meantime, the political aspect of the agitation has been fully exposed. Fears have been allayed, and estrangements have been lessened. . . . On top of all this, the men who felt it necessary for political reasons to vote against the Government on Bill 80 returned en masse tonight to vote confidence in the Government in voting down an amendmet which related to matters of the Department of Defence, and to give

Ralston all possible support and an ovation as well. All along, I have had to save him from himself, and the party from disruption because of him at the cost of great anxiety and strain to myself. If the party had known that I had, at this time, the tender of his resignation in my hands, and that not withdrawn, I doubt if one of the number who voted against us on Bill 80 would have been present to lend their support to the Government tonight, to say nothing of several others from other provinces as well. As it was, men came back from all parts of the Dominion to register their votes in support of the administration. . . .

"The Hong Kong business," he continued, "has been the most distressing thing next to conscription of the whole situation. The two have been so interwoven that each made the other a more difficult subject to deal with. To have got the vote we did on conscription, and the vote we did on a non-confidence motion re Hong Kong was certainly a triumph. I confess I felt a sense of inner rejoicing and would have rejoiced outwardly as well, had I not been so greatly fatigued. . . . I think this vote will help to settle forever the question of Meighen's return to public life. I imagine MacPherson, of Regina [M. A. MacPherson had been Attorney-General of Saskatchewan, 1929–34, and a candidate for the leadership at the National Conservative Convention in 1938] will be the choice, and an effort will be made so to arrange matters as to have him take on the leadership at the next session of Parliament."

Mackenzie King was very happy at the caucus on July 29. He "told caucus I had called them together to express my thanks for the support Members had given the Administration last night, mentioning it as one of the greatest tributes ever paid to a Prime Minister or to a Ministry. . . . I expressed what it meant to have a vote of confidence at this time. I told them of the anxiety I had had in deciding on different courses and . . . that the darkest hours are still to come . . . the most terrible time of all when our own men will begin to cross to the continent and large numbers be slain. I asked them to see where the Administration would be; where all would be if, when that time comes, it could be said that the Government had not taken all the power to itself that it needed to help to do our full part. No caucus has pleased me more. What pleased me most is that many of the men have been saying that I was right again. That I have been right. That I have led them right. I spoke highly of Ralston; his devotion, his zeal, etc. He made a short speech in which he spoke particularly of myself and the burdens I had and the patience, etc., saying that he pictured the possibility of struggle for the next four years."

The session adjourned on August 1. The first conscription crisis was over.

CHAPTER FIFTEEN

A World at War: 1942

DESPITE his preoccupation in 1942 with the struggle for survival of his Government at home, Mackenzie King never lost sight of the struggle for the survival of the free world. He realized that Canada could not have a major share in the direction of a global war, and he never attempted to claim a greater voice or influence than he believed the relative strength of Canada would sustain. But he never hesitated to express his own views when he felt Canadian interests were at stake, or when he feared a major error in world strategy was likely to be made.

The tide of Japanese conquest in Southeast Asia created great alarm in London and Washington about the security of India. Mackenzie King felt the Indians could not be expected to resist Japanese aggression unless they were assured of self-government. Ever since his visit to India in 1908 he had been sympathetic to the Indian cause; for him the aspirations of the Congress party were as valid as his grandfather's struggle for Responsible Government in Canada, and in 1942 he expressed these views to Churchill. On March 15, 1942, in the midst of the discussions preceding the plebiscite on conscription, he went even further and sent a message to Nehru through the Chinese Government "letting him know of the part Mackenzie had taken in the struggle for Responsible Government in Canada, and of my readiness, as his grandson, to do all in my power, and have Canada do all in her power, towards seeing that any undertaking given by Britain to India would be fully implemented. I said that India would be able to count on Canada doing all in her power towards obtaining immediate self-government for India at any conferences that might be held in the matter." A few days later (March 21) Mackenzie King told Malcolm MacDonald he felt "there was a real danger of India being lost to Britain" and also informed him of his messages to Churchill and Nehru.

He spoke to MacDonald, too, about the lack of recognition by the British Government of Canada's position in the combined war effort, and contrasted "the readiness of the United States to grant us representation on Boards, while Britain hesitated, the reason being that if Canada is represented they would have to give a place to all the other Dominions as well." When Herbert Evatt, the Australian Minister of External Affairs, visited Ottawa in April 1942 following a visit in the United States, Mackenzie King found they had very similar views that there was "too great centralization of power in London; too great monopoly of control of strategy and all else from there. Even in Canada with our strong assertion of our own position, we have, I think, taken risks greater than we should have ever permitted ourselves to do. This is particularly true of both Halifax and cities on the Western Coast."

Evatt brought an invitation to Mackenzie King from Roosevelt to the next meeting in Washington of the Pacific Council, composed of representatives of all the nations at war with Japan. When he accepted, Roosevelt asked him to come direct to the White House for "a quiet evening together." Mackenzie King felt "the political significance of staying the night with the President at this time is very great both in Britain and in other parts of the Empire as well as our own, and with other countries. Just now it is particularly necessary when there is a tendency to recognize only Churchill and the President, and to crowd both Canada and myself off the map."

Mackenzie King arrived in Washington on April 15 and went immediately to the White House. When he was shown into the President's office, "the President was sitting working in his shirt sleeves, white shirt, no vest or coat. Gave me a very warm welcome. Laughed a little about his attire. Spoke to me about the plebiscite which I told him I thought would be all right [it was to be held on April 27]. He thought the tactics I had adopted were good. He then said a word or two about the Pacific Council and we went in together into the Cabinet room."

In the evening Mackenzie King dined with the President and they talked for about three hours after dinner, covering almost every aspect of the war. The most important of all the subjects they talked about was the mission of General Marshall and Harry Hopkins to Britain to discuss an early offensive against the Continent, which Roosevelt strongly favoured. He told Mackenzie King he had got word that night that "agreement had been come to between the British and Americans to begin the offensive against the Germans very soon." Mackenzie King "found it a little difficult to get in much of a word as the President kept pressing the importance of this offensive, and seemed to be much relieved that the word of agreement had come to him that night. However, I did get a chance, when he had concluded, to begin and press my point of view anew which I did much in these words: I said I thought we all agreed with the importance of offensive tactics, but nothing required more care in the matter of exact knowledge of the situation in so far as it could be obtained, for example, the relative number of men likely to be engaged on both sides, particularly the method of transportation, the shipping available and the exact time." He pointed out how few troops there were in Britain and added "that if armies got across to Europe and were massacred there, there would be no saving Britain from the armies that would cross over to occupy the island." He told Roosevelt that McNaughton "seemed to feel that they should be prepared for an offensive in the autumn but did not think of anything before.

"As I kept pressing my points home to him," he noted, "the President finally said that, of course, we will, too, carefully consider the exact time to cross, but he thought by keeping up the agitation for immediate offensive and causing the Germans to expect it at any moment, might cause them to draw off some of their forces from Russia, relieve the pressure against Russia in that way, and it might even be that, as a consequence, the offensive need not come off for some time. I added that we would have to be sure of reinforcements."

Mackenzie King also told the President that the Commonwealth Air Training Plan would expire in March 1943, and that the Canadian Government felt it might be a good time to include the United States in a conference on air training programmes. "The President at once said that he thought that was a good idea, and I then suggested possibly South Africa in addition to Australia and New Zealand. The President then spoke of some other countries of the United Nations who were training pilots on this continent. He referred to Norway, the Netherlands and China. He made notes on the cover of a brown envelope, and said he would take up the matter in the morning." The following morning the air training conference was duly agreed to; British concurrence was secured and an announcement was made while Mackenzie King was still in Washington.

During a talk with Roosevelt on the same morning (April 16) Mackenzie King told the President he thought Canada should have a place on the Munitions Assignment Board which had been set up in Washington by the United States and the United Kingdom to allocate munitions to the various Allied forces. "The President," he noted, "said that he agreed with my point of view that Britain and the U.S. and Canada were the big producers. That the other people were always asking and receiving, and that Canada ought to be represented on a Board which would have Britain and the U.S. on it. He said Harry Hopkins would be here next week, and that he would tell him that matters should be arranged in this way."

Mackenzie King enjoyed this visit to the White House. He liked to be alone with Roosevelt, who obviously found it agreeable to have someone to talk to who was sympathetic, knowledgeable, and somewhat detached from the American scene. "What I noticed all through," Mackenzie King wrote, "was how much my own method of proceeding resembles his in some particulars. The need to get away from people, to get quiet and to turn to the country, etc. He said he would be planting trees during the next few days."

Shortly after Mackenzie King's return from Washington, the First Sea Lord of the Admiralty, Sir Dudley Pound, visited Ottawa. In the course of a talk with him on April 24, Mackenzie King "mentioned being concerned about an offensive being commenced too soon; that I thought the Americans did not realize how little Britain had in the way of divisions in Britain, and how difficult it would be to land troops in Europe, and also how few were the numbers that they, the Americans, would be able to land overseas. Pound told me that Marshall had, he thought, felt that all his troops were being sent to Australia, New Zealand, and the Far East, and that he might not have men in Europe unless he made some move at once toward an early offensive there. He came with plans worked out, but found that the British already had anticipated all that he had in mind, but were able to show that much more in the way of preparation was still needed. He [Pound] spoke as though there could not be any thought of an offensive until the fall. There might be raids, etc., in the interval. In his opinion, too much care could not be taken." Mackenzie King felt "considerably relieved."

The Air Training Conference proposed by Roosevelt and Mackenzie King in April was held in Ottawa late in May. It included the representatives of all governments whose airmen were being trained in Canada as well as representatives of the United States. The only aspect of this Conference which directly concerned Mackenzie King was a suggestion that it might be formally opened by the Governor-General. The proposal had been mentioned to Athlone who was quite put out when in the event he was not invited. Mackenzie King went to see him on May 26 and Athlone asked him "if I did not agree about the importance of the Governor being identified with a meeting of the kind. I told him no, that I did not, and said I thought I could convince him that I was right." Mackenzie King then pointed out that the other Governments were all represented by diplomats stationed in Ottawa and not even by members of their Governments and that "for the Governor-General to have appeared at the Conference, with no one on a Ministerial level but our own Ministers, was not emphasizing, but was minimizing the dignity of his office.

"I then told him, however, that the real reason was that, while the United States were prepared to discuss with Canadians matters of mutual interest in this connection, there was a bitter feud on between the British and the Americans at present over 50,000 planes that had been promised to them and which the Americans wanted to keep for their own people. . . . If Lord Athlone had appeared as Governor-General and Commander of the Forces to open the Conference, the impression would have been created in the United States that it was Great Britain's move, using Canada as her instrument, and that would have in Montana, Kentucky, and other Middle States, and elsewhere, created an entirely erroneous impression, and caused great embarrassment to those who were working on these problems at Washington. We knew that, while Americans would work with us, they would not work with the British on many things, and we had to keep this in mind. I explained that the Cabinet had considered this aspect when I was not present and had agreed that, on this score, it would be a mistake to have the Governor-General come.

"I went on to tell him there had not been any real precedent; that, at Imperial Conferences, the King had never appeared, they having been opened by the Prime Minister; but that the strongest precedent was the meeting of the Allied Nations, where every country was represented: when they met in London in June and again in September, they were welcomed by Churchill, the Prime Minister, at the first Conference, and [at] the second, which was after the Churchill-Roosevelt meeting, they were met and addressed by Eden. The King did not figure at these gatherings. . . . The Governor-General was very nice about it all and was much interested in what I told him. . . .

"I went on to speak about how difficult it was to get the British to allow us to have Canadian squadrons in England. When we wanted to get a thing done, we did it through the Americans. We had had, for example, with the Munitions Board, more trouble with the British than we had had with the Americans. . . . Power was fighting for the right to have Canadian squadrons instead of having Canadians . . . part of the Royal Air Force. . . . I spoke of Churchill making no mention whatever of the Dominions. . . . I asked him how he could expect us to get French Canadians to enlist on the score that it was Canada's battle that was being fought and not some Empire affair."

On May 8 Mackenzie King read in the newspaper that the Japanese Minister, Yoshizawa, had left Ottawa, and "felt a great pain in my heart that I should have let him and his wife go without a word." When he mentioned this to an official in External Affairs, he was told that, according to protocol, there was no need of his saying good-bye. Mackenzie King replied: "I was not interested in protocol, was thinking of my heart and what was right to do. . . . Must remember that when all this war is over, we may wish to bind together the different countries and Yoshizawa might be helpful in that way, if his faith in me were not destroyed. Besides, I did not want him and his wife to go away with a pain in their hearts which I could have spared them. . . . Luckily, they were to stay over in Montreal for some time."

He then arranged to speak to Yoshizawa and his wife on the telephone, and kept one of his secretaries "in the room while I talked, so that he could hear what I was saying. I said to Yoshizawa that I had been sorry not to have known about arrangements of his departure or that he was leaving. I had meant to come over and say good-bye to him and his wife. I wanted him to know that, during all the time he had been here as Minister, in his relations with me I felt he had been wholly honourable, also that our personal relations had been very pleasant. . . . Yoshizawa spoke very feelingly, saying he thanked me very much for this word of good-bye; that the friendly relations which we had shared and my friendship while they were here would be among the memories he would cherish through all his life; that he had valued my friendship and thanked me particularly for saying what I had about his honourable conduct—that he was very grateful for that."

In the middle of June 1942, Mackenzie King first learned about the research into the atomic bomb. On June 15, he "had an interview with Malcolm MacDonald and two scientists from England" about "the acquisition of some property in Canada, so as to prevent competition in price on a mineral much needed in connection with the manufacture of explosives. I was given a very interesting account of the particular mineral and its latent possibilities, but [they] made clear it was desirable that the British and American Governments should work together in their research upon it, and seek, if possible, to outdistance the Germans who have already secured some of it from the Belgian Congo though this supply may have been lost in a ship that was sunk.

"The whole business was very secret but it was represented that it was quite possible that it might, within a very short time, lead to a development that whichever country possessed this mineral in time would unquestionably win the war with its power of destruction . . . being so great. I agreed to have the matter discussed with Howe and with C. J. Mackenzie of our Research Department. The latter already has some knowledge of what is being done in research lines in this matter.

"They met during the afternoon, and at 6.15 I met Howe and Malcolm MacDonald in my office. They told me there had been complete agreement among them as to desirability of Government not only controlling, but owning, the particular mineral deposit in question, and I was asked if I would authorize the Government getting the majority of shares from the owner. Howe thought there would be no trouble in securing this so that the Government might prevent others entering the field or sending up the price. I agreed to this step being taken at once so long as Americans were advised in advance of the intention. Also that we were taking the step we were to meet the wishes of the British Government. Both MacDonald and Howe thought it inadvisable to have anything said to any other members of the Government or anyone else. . . . I had no doubt in my own mind about the wisdom of authorizing the Government purchase of the properties in existing circumstances. It was pointed out that even if the war should end soon, it was important to keep anything of the kind away from the enemy in a post-war period."

Churchill made his second visit to Washington in late June of 1942. On June 23, Mackenzie King "received word that the President wished to speak to me." After the usual preliminaries, Roosevelt said: "Winston and I are sitting together here. We want you to come down to Washington for a meeting of the Pacific Council on Thursday. If you could be here at 11.00 in the morning, I would like you to come direct to the White House. Then to be present at meeting of Pacific War Council. After luncheon, we could have a talk, and there might also be a meeting between Winston and the Dominions. . . . The President . . . asked me if I could do that. I said: Yes, I would be glad so to arrange."

Mackenzie King arrived in Washington on June 25, and went at once to the White House; he was taken to "a Conference room where I met different representatives of the British Dominions. After we were assembled, Mr. Churchill came in. I was near the door, and was the first to be greeted by him. . . . When we were all seated, Churchill, who looked remarkably fresh, almost like a cherub, scarcely a line in his face, and completely rested, though up to one or two the night before, began to review the whole situation."

In his diary, Mackenzie King gives a very full account of this review. He noted that "Churchill reserved to the last part of his talk, the reference to the European front; here he spoke very positively. He said, using the expression 'By God,' nothing would ever induce him to have an attack made upon Europe without sufficient strength and being positively certain that they could win." He stressed the desirability of keeping the Germans believing that an attack was going to be made "to throw off as many of their men as possible from Russia, and [of having] commando expeditions, making attacks here and there, but he did not think that they could afford to contemplate the invasion of the continent before the spring of 1943, despite the number of troops that the Americans might be able to send across. . . .

"When he had concluded this part of his address, he stopped and asked if there were any matters that others wished to speak of, and turned to me. I said that the last subject he had dealt with was one about which we were the most concerned. That we felt very strongly he was right in what he said about the necessity of overwhelming forces, and not taking unnecessary risks."

The meeting of the Pacific War Council was held immediately afterwards in the United States Cabinet room. "On the way down," Mackenzie King noted, "Churchill took me by the arm and told me confidentially that he was leaving in the afternoon. I told him about our situation here; my majority of what should be 180 might drop to 30 or thereabouts. He did not like that. I said it was inevitable with the conscription issue coming to the fore as it was; that I thought we would get through all right in the end."

The President presided at the Pacific War Council and spoke first of the foothold which the Japanese had recently obtained in the Aleutian Islands. Roosevelt "asked me whether the people in British Columbia had become alarmed. I said I thought they were, but that they realized they were in good company. He said that so far as Japanese attack in the Pacific was concerned, referring particularly to the Aleutians, that it should be regarded as coming third in priorities, with the situation now developing in Egypt and the Russian front." At this time the British were being driven back through Libya towards Egypt and the German advance into Russia was still in progress.

After the meeting of the Pacific Council there was a luncheon at which Cordell Hull was also present. At the luncheon, Churchill was seated to the President's right and Mackenzie King to his left. They talked of the situation on the Pacific Coast. Roosevelt "thought the Japanese were foolish in thinking we would be much affected by these attacks they were making on the Pacific Coast. That it was not likely to alarm the people unduly but rather to strengthen their feeling of resistance. It was clear that he, himself, did not contemplate much in the way of an attack on our Pacific Coast, but felt that the possession of the bases at Kiska and elsewhere was to help to meet the situation that might develop between Japan and Russia. The President mentioned he would like to come to McGill for the degree they had offered him, and then for a day and night in Ottawa, and up to Georgian Bay for a couple of days, probably with Leighton McCarthy, but doubted if he would be able to get away, as something always kept him back.

"We talked quite a little of the Budget which seemed to be a matter of real interest to nearly all present. (Ilsley had delivered his Budget on June 23.) The President was particularly interested in the step of our taking a hundred per cent on excess profits, giving back twenty per cent after the war, and the adoption of the policy of compulsory saving. I mentioned to him that few persons even of the greatest wealth would be able to have an income of more than $37,000. He said that his own suggestion had, in that way, gone by the board for the present.

"I had a most interesting talk with Harry Hopkins who said that the United States was planning to put 480,000 troops into Britain before the spring of next year. . . . He said he agreed with the view that there should be a preponderance of power before the attack was made on Europe. That it was well meantime to keep up the view that a sudden attack might be made at any time. I felt immensely relieved to gather that, at last, agreement seemed to have been reached not to attempt any invasion of Europe this year.

"After luncheon," he added, "I had a word with Hopkins about Canada being given representation on the Assignment Board. He said he had written McCarthy about this [McCarthy being Canadian Minister in Washington], but his letter clearly showed he had not understood our position or wanted to understand it. He took it as related to Canada's needs instead of to her rights as a producer. The United States and Great Britain wish to keep all assignment work in their own hands. In other words, they get entire credit for distribution of many supplies which we produce." At this luncheon, Sumner Welles was present and he spoke to Mackenzie King about another difficult diplomatic situation, advising him to maintain diplomatic relations with France "despite anything Laval might say or do."

After the luncheon, "the President and Mr. Churchill hurried away, saying good-bye to the guests at the foot of the elevator leading to the upstairs hall. The President spoke about our meeting again soon at Hyde Park or elsewhere." Mackenzie King returned at once to Ottawa, and to the debate on Bill 80 and the Ministerial crisis.

In August, units of the Canadian Army took part in the raid on Dieppe. On August 19—the day of Dieppe—General Stuart, the Chief of the General Staff, who was just back from Britain, told the War Committee "the raid on Dieppe had been carefully planned, worked out, practised over at the Isle of Wight for a month past." While the Cabinet was meeting "the first authentic word came of its extent and probable extent of our losses. It was that casualties were heavy. Number of Canadians taken prisoners, but also many killed and wounded. One felt inclined to question the wisdom of the raid."

Mackenzie King's misgivings about Dieppe were not dispelled later. On August 21, when he read accounts of the raid, he was "still not too sure of the wisdom of what was attempted. It goes back, I feel, above all to the time when it was felt it was necessary to have the Canadians do something for a variety of reasons. I still have a feeling that the part of wisdom would have been to conserve that especially trained life for the decisive moment. It may, in the long run, prove to be for the best but such is war. It makes me sad at heart."

On September 19 when he read the official account of the Dieppe raid, he wrote in the same mood of regret: "Somehow I cannot help feeling that it would have been better had all forces been kept intact, until the moment when it was absolutely advisable to attempt invasion. I question if the information gained could begin to equal the heavy losses. Moreover the enemy themselves are able effectively to represent the whole episode as a gain for themselves between the numbers taken prisoners and those who have been killed. It is a very serious blow to the Canadian forces. My intuition and belief expressed at the War Cabinet some months ago was, I believe, sound."

On September 21, an unusual problem arose. A message came from General McNaughton, who had just been at Chequers with Churchill, seeking Mackenzie King's views about his going on a mission to Moscow to discuss a proposed military campaign in northern Europe, a campaign of which the British Chiefs of Staff did not approve. Mackenzie King's immediate reaction was that Churchill "was making a mistake in not agreeing with his own advisers and that he should not be allowed to draw McNaughton into a situation that might prove a disastrous one—moreover a situation which would involve a complete change of plans for our Army."

Mackenzie King telephoned Ralston and "told him I had no difficulty in making up my mind as to what should be done. That I felt the Prime Minister was exhibiting a weakness of his own which was to take great chances himself against the advice of his own advisers, but I did not think we should sanction what was proposed or even have McNaughton go to Moscow. That in relations with Moscow, their own advisers should take matters in hand. It is clear from McNaughton's message that he does not wish to undertake the task of either going to Moscow or what is proposed. He feels our people would be inevitably drawn into the venture, if he were to go to Moscow. I could see from what Ralston said that he shared the same view."

Mackenzie King told Ralston he "ought to communicate with McNaughton and indicate that the more natural course would be for a mission of the kind to be headed by one of the Chiefs of Staff of Britain." He noted that "Ralston himself was inclined to think the mission was largely for public consumption, largely to help to keep Stalin in a proper mood. That a British mission had gone. Willkie was there. Now here comes another General, an entirely new person. I told him I thought there had been too much done for the sake of appearances, and not enough looking at the realities, that both the Germans and the Russians were given to the latter, while too often those of us who were opposed had believed we could get along by substitutes, façades and parades here and there; that I felt we would be drawn into a difficult situation, if once McNaughton went at the head of a mission."

It was Mackenzie King's fear that if this venture was "opposed, it would be said that, but for the opposition, the plan would have succeeded. If accepted, and the plan was a disaster, it would be said that the Government should have, with the knowledge of McNaughton's report, opposed it strenuously. I myself, am prepared to stand by my impressions and convictions regardless of all else."

Mackenzie King saw Ralston and Stuart, the Chief of the General Staff, on September 22 and they worked out a message to McNaughton in which they indicated "(first) the natural course would be to have one of the British Chiefs of Staff head any mission; (second) the danger, notwithstanding all that might be said as to no commitments so far as Canada was concerned, of being drawn into the venture because of McNaughton's going, through having consented to his preparing a plan. General Stuart used the expression that we had been sucked into the present position. The (third) was the embarrassment which heading a mission might occasion McNaughton in his relations with the Chiefs of Staff in Britain in the present and in the future, and the (fourth): the kind of comment to which his heading a mission would give rise in Britain, in Canada and in the United States. He would be discussed at once in terms of a Generalissimo for a second front."

In their discussion Mackenzie King also mentioned his feeling that "it might well be a sort of crucifixion of McNaughton himself to be confronted with Stalin, and made responsible for either bowing to pressure from Stalin on the one hand, or incurring his disfavour by opposing some wish of his.

"Personally," he added, "I feel very strongly that Churchill has had this venture in mind for a year or more. He spoke to me in England about the possibility of rolling down the map from the North. He spoke again in the same terms at our Council table in December. . . . The appalling part of the Churchill proposal is that it completely alters all that has, thus far, been planned for our Army, and involves changes in methods of fighting, etc. I cannot bring myself to think of even the possibility of the venture without seeing how appalling its possibilities are."

That afternoon Mackenzie King received a message from Churchill through Malcolm MacDonald requesting that McNaughton be allowed to go to Moscow. He decided not to reply until after discussion by the War Committee the next day. He felt it was "by far the most difficult decision that has thus far had to be made. I am afraid that Churchill's great weakness is that he has his own plan of campaign; has the idea of a Marlborough in his mind. Is more of a Commander in Chief than a Prime Minister and will not accept the advice of his own advisers. There is a certain pride of authorship in a campaign which carries some men away. I am afraid that, in this, his mind being set in certain directions, it may be difficult for him to change."

Mackenzie King feared that "not to meet his wishes outright might seem to be refusing to take a step essential at the moment of 'the winning of the war.' On the other hand, to agree to the step, in the light of what had been sent in communications by McNaughton, and particularly by what is in his appreciation, is to be accused of having not had the courage to oppose a course of action which was filled with obvious dangers for our Commander and a course that might lead to certain disaster with respect to our own troops. I had firmly resolved, regardless of what Churchill might feel, to make clear that I do not think that McNaughton should be singled out for the mission he has asked him to undertake. It has been pretty much my lot throughout my public life to have to oppose courses proposed, and save men from their own mistakes. I cannot but feel that in this particular matter, Churchill is determined to adopt a course which has been in his own mind for a long time past. . . . However, I think Churchill knows me well enough not to misunderstand my motive and to appreciate my giving him the soundest advice I can in the most fearless way."

The War Committee considered the messages from McNaughton and Churchill on September 23. Mackenzie King found the Ministers "were all very strongly against the whole project as being almost fantastic in its hazards and against McNaughton going to Moscow because of the false position in which it would place him, and also what it would involve in the way of commitments in advance on what might be decided upon. McNaughton has made clear it would certainly involve commitments, notwithstanding what Churchill had said as to no commitments."

Mackenzie King himself stressed strongly "the necessity of having Roosevelt made aware of the whole project, and approve of McNaughton going to Russia. It was clear from McNaughton's wire that the British Government were trying to keep the matter one between Russia, Britain and Canada. We pointed out that it was a major feature of the war strategy, and that the President would certainly feel he should have been made aware of it in advance."

Mackenzie King reflected that "one could get no better example of the wisdom of not having a War Cabinet in London with only a Prime Minister on it, who would be without the views of his colleagues in giving a decision and would be certain to encounter their opposition if he proceeded without consulting them."

When a reply had finally been sent to Churchill, Mackenzie King felt "immensely relieved at having made clear we did not think it was wise for McNaughton to go, and particularly having expressed the view that a mission should be headed by British officials with American representation as well, if McNaughton were to go." The next day (September 25) an answer came from Churchill. Mackenzie King noted that Churchill's wire expressed disappointment over the reply and attempted to meet the arguments of the Canadian Government, but "added that if we, after considering these representations, still held to our own view, he would have someone else go." The War Committee stuck to its original decision.

The following day (September 26) Clement Attlee, then Deputy Prime Minister of the United Kingdom, was in Ottawa. He dined alone at Laurier House with Mackenzie King who "explained to him fully our concern with respect to the communication sent Churchill. He thought Churchill would be very understanding about it." This was much the reaction expressed to Ralston when he was in England in October: Churchill told him that once he realized McNaughton was against the project, he himself "thought no more of it." The whole project was indeed then dropped. Ralston added that Churchill "did not seem put out at the attitude we had taken."

On this visit in September, Attlee made a very favourable impression on Mackenzie King, who wrote of him: "Attlee himself is so modest and anything but commanding in appearance that one wonders at his remarkable achievements and the position he has come to occupy. The secret of it is, however, as he himself said to me as we talked together, that he had never really sought any of the positions that he has come to fill. They were all the outcome of a natural desire to serve his fellow-men. The fact of his being Secretary of Toynbee Hall to me was the greatest of all bonds between us. Gave the key to the purpose of his life."

Another disagreement with Churchill developed over the shackling of prisoners of war. When the news had first come of the shackling by the Germans of the prisoners taken at Dieppe, Mackenzie King had agreed with Churchill's view that retaliation was inevitable, but he was not long in having second thoughts. At the War Committee meeting on October 10, "all present were unanimous in the view that we should not seek to compete with the Germans in their brutalities; also that we should ask Britain to seek mediation of protecting power and Red Cross to end what had taken place. We agreed not to attempt any three to one fettering as an unwise policy of retaliation and one which the Allies were certain to get the worse of in the end." After the meeting, a message was sent to Churchill advising him of the feeling of the Canadian Government. Mackenzie King told the Cabinet "we were no good to Churchill, or anyone else, unless we gave him our own honest opinion; that I was sure our view on this matter was a sound one."

Meanwhile there was trouble with the prisoners who had already been shackled in Canada. On October 12, Power and Angus Macdonald discussed with Mackenzie King the difficulties with the German prisoners at Bowmanville who had created a disturbance. They "all agreed it would be inadvisable to attempt to hand-cuff large numbers. To begin with we had not the hand-cuffs. Also agreed that Churchill was wrong in trying the reprisal business."

Ralston, who was in Britain, was advised of these views. When he returned to Canada he reported that Churchill was disappointed because Canada would not agree to his proposal to increase the manacling of prisoners. "At War Cabinet, this afternoon" (October 21), Mackenzie King noted, "I took the view that we should notify the British Government we did not intend to keep on with the manacling, and that unless the Protecting Power had been successful in arranging intervention, we would not continue it at the end of another week. Ralston said he was not in favour of manacling but that, as Churchill was very much concerned about our keeping on, he did not think we should stop at once." The next day (October 22) Mackenzie King was upset by "the publication, by *Time*, of a communication regarding the difficulties at Bowmanville in shackling prisoners. A very sensational statement appeared, which may do great harm. Gives Hitler just the kind of ammunition he wants. All goes to show the folly of shackling prisoners at the outset and the wisdom of our decision not to attempt it on more than the present scale." The following day he received from Vincent Massey, the High Commissioner in Great Britain, who was alarmed by the implications of the policy, "a statement of reasons why we should begin immediately to end policy of shackling prisoners." Mackenzie King directed that a despatch, much in the terms suggested by Massey, should be sent to the British Government. "Churchill," he wrote, "will not like this, but he is wrong in the point of view he is taking in this matter." Nevertheless, though the Canadian Government wanted to end shackling, they hesitated to act without British concurrence.

On November 7, Mackenzie King talked with Malcolm MacDonald, who had returned from England the day before, "on the question of the shackling of prisoners. . . . Churchill had said to him, in the first conversation after his arrival, that he was afraid Canada was going to let them down on the shackling business. He had not said this in any unkind way but a mere statement of fact. MacDonald had said to him that far from letting him down, we had felt that the policy had been thrust upon us. It was against our judgment. We had made our protest and had continued to back him. He thought that was quite the opposite of letting him down. . . . MacDonald mentioned that Massey had been greatly concerned about the whole business."

It was not until a month later that the shackling was finally settled. When Mackenzie King learned on December 7 that Churchill was going to make a statement in the British House of Commons and there was uncertainty as to how it might be phrased, he decided not to "wait for the announcement to come from Britiain, when we were again not consulted, but to issue orders tonight on our own that it was our intention to immediately unshackle German prisoners in Canada. We were going to give this to the press at midnight. Meanwhile . . . orders to prison camps were being prepared in the Department of Defence." Before the statement was issued, Churchill called Mackenzie King over the transatlantic telephone about the shackling and told him they had word that "the Swiss Government wanted till the 12th to arrange matters and he hoped I would be agreeable to allow matters to stand until then. I said at once that would be quite all right. He went on to say that the matter was being solved in accordance with my wishes, but the Swiss Government wanted time. I said we attached importance to being able to make the announcement simultaneously with the announcement in Britain. . . . It was a great relief to me to get this final word and it was very fortunate that word came before we had said anything to the press." The shackling was finally stopped in Canada on December 10.

While this difference over the shackling of prisoners was taking place Ralston and Howe had both been in England. They returned on October 21. From their reports Mackenzie King confirmed his impression that the Canadian Army would not likely be in action in 1942. He noted "it is now clear that no question of conscription will come up before another session, and may not come up at all." At this time the invasion of North Africa was being planned, and while he was in England Ralston heard that rumours were rife that the reason the Canadians would not be taking part in this North African expedition was "because the Government did not wish the Canadian Army broken up. He had run this rumour to earth. Found out from [General] Brooke they had not been asked to take any part because Britain wanted to keep them in the British Isles themselves. Ralston made it clear we were agreeable to have them go wherever they might be needed, subject of course to the approval of the Government of any particular project proposed."

The Allied landing in North Africa raised, in an acute form, the question of relations with the French Government at Vichy. This question had been increasingly troublesome all through 1942, and was, of course, not just a question of foreign policy, but one with strong domestic implications as well. The conscriptionists tended to identify the Free French and General de Gaulle with themselves and the Government at Vichy with the isolationists in Quebec, who, in many instances, expressed strong sympathy for Pétain. On the question of relations with France, as on the conscription question, Mackenzie King found himself in the middle, suspect from both sides.

In December 1941, he had refused to give any encouragement to the Free French to seize the islands of St. Pierre and Miquelon: but, when the seizure took place he had passively but stubbornly objected to any proposal to restore the status quo ante. During 1942, the agitation over the seizure of St. Pierre gradually petered out and the Free French remained in control. On February 6, Mackenzie King had told René Ristelhueber, the French Minister, "that Canada was not responsible for St. Pierre and Miquelon or any of the incidents there," and that "there were some things one could do no good by injecting oneself into. I thought this was one. That I had enough to worry about without taking on unnecessary troubles." At the same time he told Ristelhueber that Canada intended to continue diplomatic relations with the French Government. But when Laval took office in Vichy in April, the question of continuing relations was once more considered. This event had just taken place when Mackenzie King discussed the question of France with Sumner Welles in Washington and Welles had said "he thought the best course would be for us not to change the French Minister until we saw how matters developed." Notwithstanding this talk, Mackenzie King had found feeling so strong against Laval when he returned to Ottawa that he had sent for Ristelhueber and spoken to him about resigning and staying in Canada.

"I said to him I wanted to speak personally and not officially," he wrote, "and then told him it looked as though we might have to sever diplomatic relations with Vichy. I said to him I did not know whether he might perhaps be considering the possibility of resigning himself; that I wanted to say to him that if he did he would be most welcome." Ristelhueber thanked him but explained why he did not feel he could resign. Mackenzie King added that Ristelhueber "was not surprised that I have had to consider his return, but hoped, even yet, that it might be possible for Canada to continue our relations with France until we saw how matters might develop."

After consultation with the British Government and a talk in Ottawa, on May 9, with Pierre Dupuy, the Canadian diplomat who visited Vichy from time to time, Mackenzie King had concluded it was not desirable to sever relations completely and the Government had compromised by having the French consulates in Canada closed. Mackenzie King had been greatly impressed by what Dupuy was accomplishing in France and there were discussions, which came to nothing, about strengthening the Canadian mission to Vichy. The Allied landing in North Africa on November 8, however, made the continuation of diplomatic relations impossible.

Indeed, the attitude of the Government at Vichy to the Allied invasion made immediate action essential. On Sunday, November 8, Norman Robertson suggested to Mackenzie King that it might be advisable to issue some statement which would clear up the confusion, and referred to "the statement Mr. Hull had made at a press conference this morning, showing wherein the State Department has been fully justified in its attitude in retaining diplomatic relations with Vichy [so far]. . . . I said to him at once that I thought we should issue a statement and base it upon the one made by Mr. Hull. That our reasons for retaining diplomatic relations were identical with those of the United States, only in addition that Mr. Churchill had wished us to keep Dupuy as the only window that he had open on France." Robertson accordingly had a statement prepared along these lines. Mackenzie King "was exceedingly pleased with the way in which it was worded. Made just a suggestion or two in the way of slight change. It was so well worded that I did not even request him to read it a second time. Said to issue the statement at once to the press, and send copies to Great Britain and the United States." Robertson also recommended that Canada suggest to the British and American Governments that all three countries agree on "a policy of non-recognition of the Government at Vichy, asserting that they were not a legal Government." The fear was that the Government at Vichy might make a declaration of war on Canada; if Canada had already declared that the Vichy Government had no legal existence, such a declaration would have no validity. Mackenzie King had not himself thought of the "possibility of the French declaring war against Canada, and the advantage it would be to have this doctrine of non-recognition stated before any such declaration might be made by France, and the importance of it psychologically." The suggestion appealed to him immediately and he authorized that messages be sent to London and to the Canadian Minister in Washington, with instructions to McCarthy to see Cordell Hull to urge this course.

The messages were sent off that night and about noon the next day (November 9) Robertson telephoned Mackenzie King to tell him he thought "McCarthy did not understand the situation very well. Was not too sympathetic to the idea that he should suggest to the Secretary of State, Mr. Hull, that the non-recognition policy was one which it would be advisable for the United States, Great Britain and ourselves to agree upon and to become the policy of the United Nations." Mackenzie King himself telephoned McCarthy and said he would like to speak direct to the President if Cordell Hull did not object. Later he had word from McCarthy that Hull "would, in fact, welcome my having a talk with the President. As to the point about legal government, he said Mr. Hull used the expression that that was a metaphysical point but was prepared to give it further consideration. I debated on 'phoning the President immediately. Thought it best to wait to see if some word might come from Dominions Office. Finally a telegram arrived in which it was pointed out that the United Kingdom, not having diplomatic relations with France, could not take the initiative in stating a position; suggesting that perhaps reference to there being no independent existence so far as the Vichy Government was concerned might be enough for our purpose at present. However, I felt we should press our point and rang up the President, having the private number at the White House, a little after 6. Word came back immediately that the President was engaged at that moment but would call me up about 7.15.

"At 7.15, the President called and told me he had been with his doctor fixing up some trouble with his nose at the time I had 'phoned, then went on to say he hoped I would be sure and come down and pay him a visit, and that he had written me a letter which I would receive. I then told him that we were considering our position vis-à-vis France and wanted to be perfectly sure that the line we were proposing to take would accord with the views of the United States. That there was one aspect of the matter that I wanted to bring particularly to his attention. He then asked me if I had seen the statement that he had issued about an hour before.... He then read to me the statement that he had given out, he said, just an hour before. I said that I thought the statement was all right, but that there was a point that I wished to make very clear. I thought he would quickly see it and he might feel it advisable further to consider.

"I then pointed out that we were proposing to take the view that, as the men at Vichy had ordered resistance to the American forces in their attempt to help to liberate France, and had done this after the President's message to France was known, it was clear that they in no way represented the people of France and could not be described as a legal or constitutional Government in any sense representing the French people. That, in other words, by this very fact, they had made it clear that they did not represent the French people. In other words, they had really committed suicide.

"The President replied, showing he clearly understood the point: 'In other words, they ain't.' I said that was it exactly. I then read him the passage from our despatch which referred to psychological significance making it clear that were they to declare war against the States or ourselves, it would be psychologically helpful both in France and outside to have it known in advance that they were not regarded as the legal Government of France but were just a German puppet government. The President said he thought that was all right and that he would have a word with Cordell about it in the morning, and would phone me again. I then said we would have to give out our statement tonight; that if he saw no objection, I would like to issue it along the lines I had expressed to him. He replied that his statement was practically along the same lines, and that certainly it would be all right for us to issue the statement I was proposing to issue. I had, previous to my conversation with the President, written on a sheet of paper what I thought of saying. This I read over to the President and later it was made with the exception of changing the words 'United States forces' to 'United Nations forces.'"

After the telephone conversation Mackenzie King had the statement prepared on the lines of what he had read to Roosevelt; this he proposed to give verbally to Ristelhueber who was to see him later in the day. He then called a Cabinet meeting and secured approval of the statement. He next saw Ristelhueber in his office, and "shook him by the hand saying I was always glad to see him, but that unhappily there was much of suddenness associated with our meeting. He greeted me very warmly and said Mr. Robertson had told him what to expect. That naturally he felt very sad. . . .

"I then read him very slowly and carefully the statement without handing him a copy. He then spoke of the statement which I had issued last night and said he hoped that it might have helped to prevent any further action at this time. I said to him he would see, however, that once orders had been issued by Vichy to resist the armed forces of the United Nations that were seeking to relieve France, that no other course was open than to view the act of the men of Vichy as that of a puppet government of Germany, and their acts as not representing the people of France. Mr. Ristelhueber then spoke of the terrible pressure they were under, and said I would notice there had not been much in the way of resistance, and he had hoped that my statement would perhaps carry things along for a time sufficient to show that there was not going to be real resistance. . . . He then, by way of explanation of what had been said and done by Vichy, put his hands around his throat and said that that represented the position in which the Government were. He believed they were doing their best to hold things until relief came, but the pressure was greater and greater on them. I said that only bore out what I had said to him in a statement that the Government had become a puppet government and was not a legal or constitutional government in any sense representing the people of France. . . .

"He finally asked me what he should say to his Government. I said to him the Government did not exist as far as we were concerned, but I recognized he would have to consider his own position in reporting. That perhaps I had better let him have a copy of the statement which I had read to him so that he would know exactly the terms of our conversation together. I then gave him a carbon copy of what I had read, again explaining the full import of it to him.

"As he was leaving my office, he asked whether he would send this message in cypher. Robertson was present in the outer room and heard this remark. As reference was made, in what I had read to him, to no further cypher messages, Robertson suggested it might be sent 'en clair.' I said the [French] Government would probably get it from the radio; that I had already let the radio know of the [Canadian] Government's view and decision. Robertson stressed the advisability of sending the message 'en clair' in either English or French. I then walked with him [Ristelhueber] to the head of the stairs by the elevator and shook his hands again saying that I hoped God would bless and protect both him, his wife and family."

On November 11, Mackenzie King had a talk with Ristelhueber who "was quite concerned as to just what he should do. . . . He had had no word of any kind from his Government. He did not seek to conceal his rejoicing at the thought of a French Government being established in Africa which would be allied with the other forces. He agreed we had taken quite the right course the other night. All day yesterday and this morning, I have been rejoicing over the manner in which we permitted Vichy to become separated from Canada without severing any relations ourselves with the French people, or taking any diplomatic act in the conventional diplomatic manner, but simply taking the position that the Government at Vichy had ended as a French Government and was really a puppet government of Germany.

"Hitler's communication to Pétain giving his reasons for breaking the armistice and virtually taking possession of the Government at Vichy itself makes it clear that the designation of a puppet government is the appropriate one for the Government that may remain at Vichy. Never was a course of procedure more justified by the outcome of events than the one we have taken in holding the French Minister here to the last moment. Canada held out to the last minute in demonstrating its fidelity to the French people. To have delayed a day longer, even a few hours longer, would have been a fatal mistake. . . . Hitler's action today and Pétain's vain protest was a fine vindication of our course."

Before the year ended there was another dramatic change in the complex French situation. Between half past nine and ten on Christmas eve, Mackenzie King heard the report that Darlan had been assassinated. He "could not help but feel that everything considered, it was all for the best for the Allied cause. The Vichy French and the Free French would never unite around Darlan. His last utterances and his death might help to bring them together. It will also remove a great embarrassment between the French and the Americans and the British in regard to any agreements that might have been made with Darlan. He has certainly done his utmost to oppose the Germans since going to Africa. One hesitates to say whether that has not been his aim from the outset.

However, it does seem to me that History will say that his services to the Allies at the end did not make up for his behaviour in the previous period."

On Christmas Day, Mackenzie King went to see Ristelhueber at the French Legation. He reported that Ristelhueber "was quite touched by my coming in to see him. . . . He brought in Mrs. Ristelhueber, also Denise, her husband and their little baby—a young Canadian. We had a short talk together. Poor Mr. Ristelhueber and his wife both looked very worn and very sad."

Mackenzie King made another visit to Washington at Roosevelt's invitation before the end of 1942. This visit was one of the most pleasant and relaxing he had with Roosevelt at any time during the war. He arrived at the White House for the weekend on Friday, December 4, in the morning, and was received at once by Roosevelt who "was sitting up in bed wearing a grey sweater." Mackenzie King began by congratulating the President "on the achievements of North Africa" and they had a long general conversation about the progress of the war and their difficulties at home.

When Roosevelt had to go to his press conference, Mackenzie King walked across to the State Department for a talk and lunch with Cordell Hull whom he found rather disgruntled, and particularly unhappy about his relations with Sumner Welles and with the British. He returned to the White House for tea alone with the President and once more the talk ranged far and wide. In the evening he went with the President and Mr. and Mrs. Harry Hopkins to dine with the Crown Princess of Norway at a country house where she was living just outside Washington. Mackenzie King enjoyed the evening very much. The next day (December 5) he lunched again alone with Roosevelt at the White House. Much of their talk was about the future of European colonies in Asia and self-government in India. During their talk at luncheon the President told Mackenzie King about the origin of the phrase: 'United Nations.'

"He said he and Winston had been discussing together [December 1941] what name they would give to the countries that were fighting for freedom. They worked over the thing until pretty late. At night had worked out a phrase about countries that were determined to stop aggression or opposed to aggression—something like that. Countries united in opposing aggression. The President said he then went to bed, and later began to go over in his mind certain phrases with the word 'united' in it. He thought of the word 'nations.' He said he could hardly wait till the morning to tell Winston of it. Finally when morning came, he did not wait for breakfast but got his man to take him in his chair to Winston's room and knocked at the door. Winston called out to come in but that he was taking a bath. He said he walked out of the bath in a few minutes and had not a stripe on him. The President said: Winston—pointing at him—I have it: the United Nations. Churchill at once said that was the title to call them. I said to the President: properly baptized at the same time. The President mentioned it was like adopting the idea of Seeley's Expansion of England. This was the expansion of the United States. The United States had grown into the United Nations, etc. (The pride of authorship is one of the strongest of the temptations of most men—natural enough.)

"At the end of the luncheon the President said he would like to discuss tonight the question of disarmament, and bringing Stalin into the picture. He said that was very necessary. . . . He said Russia was going to be very powerful. The thing to do now was to get plans definitely made for disarmament. He said: 'We will take a quiet little evening.' He said he had to work this afternoon. Would I drop in and have tea with him, and later we could have dinner. There was no one else here but Harry Hopkins, his wife and himself. We would have some moving pictures after."

Mackenzie King noted that one of the subjects Roosevelt mentioned at lunch was Newfoundland and that he had "said to the President: 'You said to me, some time ago, that Canada ought to possess Newfoundland.' He said that is my view. You might be able to make something out of Newfoundland. He then went on to speak of the island as suitable for raising sheep and mentioned about the soil possibly serving for an industry of the kind."

Roosevelt also said at lunch that "he had told Churchill how embarrassing it was for him to receive communications as he did in large numbers from Australia asking that the United States should take Australia into its orbit. Never again would they have anything to do with England. He said the feeling in Australia is very bitter against Britain and he doubts if the feeling can ever be overcome. As I dictate, I confess I feel we must be careful in Canada not pressing things too far in our manpower policy, etc., or we will set up in the Dominion a similar reaction."

At dinner Mr. and Mrs. Harry Hopkins were also present. After dinner, they looked at movies. Mackenzie King found it "a real recreation and most pleasant. As it was getting on toward 10, I asked the President if he did not think we should retire and let him rest. He said: 'Oh, no, we want to have a good talk now about another matter.' He had said earlier in the day: 'I want to speak particularly about Stalin tonight.' When we returned to the chart room, the President sat on the sofa and told me to come and sit beside him there, to get his good ear, the right ear. . . . Harry Hopkins later came in and sat down for a few minutes and then retired. The President then started in at once on what he has in mind as a post-war programme." Mackenzie King noted that "in rough outline, what the President said was as follows: We talk of the four freedoms. Two of them we cannot do much about. Freedom of religion is something that the people have to work out for themselves. The State cannot improve anything. Then freedom of speech: that too is something that will take care of itself. . . .

"We come to the other two which are freedom from fear and freedom from want. Of the two, the first is necessarily the most important as the second depends on it. As respects freedom from fear, that can only be brought about when we put an end to arming nations against each other. What should be done was to have, first of all, the big policeman who would be the four powers: Britain, the United States, Russia and China." He felt Germany should be deprived "of all right to make planes, tanks, guns, etc., but not take away any of her territories nor prevent her development in any way. For police purposes, the four powers would have to have the control of the air. Take, for example, the British before the war were spending so much on armies of no use against Germany. They would save all that they have formerly been spending in the way of protection. They would be getting protection from international police. They should, therefore, pay a tax for the upkeep of the force and make contribution of money to that end. It would be a mere fraction, not a tenth of what they otherwise would be spending. . . .

"From this, the President went on to say what he thought would be best to do with Germany. He did not think she should be dismembered in any way but that the old States of Germany should be restored. . . .

"I said to him I thought, in any peace settlement, if it could be arranged to compel representative institutions, that would be most desirable; not allow any decision affecting the people at large to take place without agreement through their representatives or otherwise. I pointed out how Hitler had closed up the different state parliaments and then ultimately the Reichstag. That if the people's representatives had had a vote on war, war would never have taken place.

"The President then said that he thought the plebiscite (he pronounced it 'eet') could be made effective means, and suggested this as to bringing together of different states, etc., or moving about populations and the like requiring something like two thirds votes. Plebiscite to be taken periodically—not the first year, but the next, etc. He dwelt at considerable length on the merit of the plebiscite. I said he would see how effective this had been in Canada re giving Government powers.... As I listened to the President speak, I felt that our own plebiscite was going to stand out in history as a pretty far-reaching instrument of a democratic Government....

"The President then said: to effect all this, I, of course, would have to get Stalin to agree. He ought to be consulted. I said: 'Certainly.' I then asked him whether he thought Stalin would agree. He said that he believed he would. That he thought Molotov was an imperialist but he believed Stalin was less and less on those lines. I asked if he thought he was interested in post-war problems. He said: certainly, and the reason he gave was that Stalin had sent word to him that he hoped no final settlement would be made with regard to North Africa without his knowledge and consultation with him. He was clear that he expected to be consulted. I said 'Certainly.' ... He said that it was clear that the United States, Britain, China could not defeat Russia. I do not know whether or not he meant as related to Russia's ultimate aims. The thing to do was to get them all working on the same lines.

"He then came to what he said was confidential and added: 'for God's sake, don't give me away.' Then went on to say: 'it seems to me I ought to have some meeting arranged between Winston, Stalin and myself. I doubt if Winston and Stalin together could have their minds meet over some of these post-war questions. I could perhaps act as a medium between them, in helping to bring them together. It seems to me that where there are two great powers that come near each other but never quite combine, there is always a bit of a barrier in between them. I could perhaps help to get views reconciled.'

"I said to the President, the difficulty of course was the time and place of meeting. He said he thought this all ought to be done very soon. It was quite possible Germany might crumple up at any moment. ... We should be prepared with our post-war plans in advance; if we are not, we will have difficulty in getting the war to end speedily and getting agreement on the steps to be taken. I said the real difficulty was the problem of the leaders leaving their countries at the present time. I asked if he had in mind having Stalin come to Washington. He said: no, but they ought to meet at some secret place. He had in mind Iceland, but obviously that was not a good place at this season. He said they might have to wait until spring. I replied: In the spring a large offensive will be coming off, and that might be a very difficult time. No matter which way the subject was looked at, there were these obvious difficulties. The President then said he had thought of Nome, Alaska. I said that was better. That Stalin would not have difficulty in coming that way. He said to me: Churchill could come back via Canada; could stop somewhere in the North. I said Russian planes were already coming to Edmonton. They could take off from there to Nome. I said I suppposed it was impossible to have anyone to represent him in any way. He said it would have to be kept absolutely secret; he would have to be personally there. . . .

"I then said to him: you feel pretty confident of peace with Germany. He replied: yes, and I then went on to ask whether Chiang-Kai-Shek should be in any conference. The President's reply was that he thought what should be done was to defeat Germany first; demand unconditional surrender, and then for the three powers—Britain, United States, and Russia—to turn to Japan and say: now we demand the same of you. If you want to save human life, you must surrender unconditionally at once. If not, the three of us will bring all our forces to bear, and will fight till we destroy you. Russia would then be persuaded to attack Japan. It would not take a year to bring about her defeat. He was not sure that the Japanese would accept any unconditional surrender, and would probably seek to fight on. . . . If the Japanese did not accept unconditional surrender, then they should be bombed till they were brought to their knees. At present, Russia too busy to attack Japan, and Japan too busy to attack Russia.

"In the course of conversation, I drew the President's attention to the significance of the Rush-Bagot Agreement, in dealing with small powers like Belgium and a large power on the other side, and also the International Joint Commission. I thought that might be made the basis of international police to enforce the decisions of the International Joint Commission."

After concluding the outline of the evening's conversation, Mackenzie King also noted that "at dinner, we had quite a talk about Beveridge's report [Sir William Beveridge's Report to the United Kingdom Government on Social Security]. The President said the Beveridge report has made a real impression in this country. The thought of insurance from the cradle to the grave. That seems to be a line that will appeal. You and I should take that up strongly. It will help each of us politically as well as being on the right lines in the way of reform. From this remark, I seemed to feel that the President has in mind a fourth term and that he feels it will come as a result of winning the war, and the social programme to be launched. I remarked we had most of this programme already between the federal government and the provinces. The President remarked, not as to burial. This is the worst racket we have in this country. He did not think the country will stand for socialism. I added that it was all important to stress Government in Industry as well as in the State; get away from any one party to Industry. . . . Outlined thoughts of four parties to industry. This aspect the President had not been thinking of so much. I spoke of my *Industry and Humanity*. Of the fears outlined there re unemployment, etc., and the President said he would look up that again and thanked me for drawing his attention to it. He added we should stress this programme in both our countries."

Mackenzie King added: "When I came back to my room, it was just a minute or two of eleven o'clock. It must have been just five to eleven as I left the President. Sat down at my desk and wrote by hand the main points of the conversation with the President as I had it fresh in my mind. As the President had said, he wanted to make it all so simple that the programme could be easily understood. What impressed me particularly was his desire that we should both work together on the lines of social reform in which we had always been deeply interested. I felt in listening to the President that he was naturally anxious to be responsible for planning the new order. . . .

"I feel happy that in my *Industry and Humanity*, written after the last war, there will be found pretty much the whole programme that now is being suggested for post-war purposes. The parallel of the Beveridge Report will be found in my scheme of social insurance and all the question of fear, etc., set forth quite elaborately. I believe that book could, at this moment, be made the basis of the whole social programme. Also matters of arbitration and the like. How I wish I had more of youth and less of the fatigue of years on my side! I must try to get in shape for this post-war work. That has been my real purpose in life. I felt a relief from the mere thought of dealing with social questions and reform, instead of these problems of war and destruction. I felt tremendously pleased. It may be that when the war is over, new force and energy will come toward the furtherance of these larger social aims."

On Sunday (December 6), Mackenzie King lunched with the President and Mrs. Roosevelt who had arrived from New York that morning. After luncheon, when the guests were saying good-bye, Mackenzie King said he "should perhaps be saying good-bye as well, as I knew she would be very busy. She then said she understood I was not going today. 'The President told me you are not leaving until tomorrow night'. Mentioned that she had invited Mr. and Mrs. Morgenthau to come to dinner. I said I had been present for a good part of the week, and felt that I should not take up more of the President's time. Mrs. Roosevelt said he enjoys a talk, and it was a good chance to rest. Perhaps I should have stayed but, as all arrangements were made, I felt I should be back in Ottawa on account of the pressure of work, and had decided it was better not to wait over."

After lunch, Harry Hopkins "came in to have a little talk. Asked me if there was anything in my mind I would like to speak about. He then said to me that the President and I should keep in close touch with each other. He felt that I could be of very great help just now in the problems that are coming up relating to post-war. . . . He spoke of really needing someone with whom the President could talk, to whom he could telephone if necessary. That he and I understood each other so well, that I should not fail to see him frequently. I said I felt the President was so busy, I did not like taking up his time. He said: 'Come as often as you can. He always likes to see and talk with you.' I told him to let me have word any time that he, himself, might see a chance to do anything that would be helpful; not to hesitate to call on me. He said, as he was leaving, he hoped some time he might get up to Ottawa to see us. I said for him to bring his wife along. We would welcome them both and would see to a special invitation being sent."

When Mackenzie King saw the President again in the afternoon, he said: " 'Why, Mackenzie, I thought you were staying over until tomorrow night.' . . . He spoke of having enjoyed the talks we had had. I told him I had immensely profited by them; also had enjoyed the rest."

Roosevelt "then spoke of the position in the Mediterranean, from now on. The President said he had, this afternoon, sent word to the Chiefs of Staff in Washington and also to the Joint Staffs in England to ask exactly what they had thus far decided about the next moves, and what were the points they were still debating. He said, when you think it took from January till June before we settled on Africa and definite plans for the campaign, you see it is time we got the next step settled or next move determined. . . .

"He asked me if our men were getting more anxious to go. I said they had always been anxious but that McNaughton and the High Command generally had felt it was better to keep a strong hitting force pointed at Germany from the north. He said he felt that very strongly. It would be a great mistake to do anything which would take away the German armies that are now concentrated in occupied France and in the north—anything which would make them less fearful of an enemy invasion. He thought what the Canadians had done at Dieppe was a very necessary part of the campaign. It made clear how terribly dangerous the whole business of invasion across the Channel was. . . .

"He then spoke of the mission he had given Governor Lehman to arrange for relief of the European countries. Said . . . he hoped he might be spared to see the day when some of the Prussian Generals—Hitler and others would all be out of the way by then—would be getting down on their knees before Lehman, who was a Jew, and begging of him for a morsel of bread. He said he had told Nelson Rockefeller about that the other night—a fine young fellow. Nelson had replied that far from being unchristian, it was in complete accord with the Christian doctrine. I added the word that it certainly was in accord with Christian teachings as to man's salvation in the end, and teaching to the effect that any injustice that one had done in this world would have to be undone through forgiveness in the next.

"I then spoke of the time and said: 'Good-bye.' Referred to my embarrassment at addressing him as 'Franklin' when we were together and often by letter. He replied . . . that apart from anything else, I was older than he was. I spoke of our long friendship. . . . He then turned to me and said he wanted to congratulate me very strongly on the splendid way in which I had managed everything in Canada and extended best of wishes. I said I might be out of everything in a short time, one never knew. The President replied: far from that, you will be busier than ever, or words to that effect. He told me to take good care of myself, and I gave him similar advice."

Despite his close friendship with Roosevelt, Mackenzie King was never without suspicions of the ultimate designs of the Americans. On December 30, at the last meeting of the War Committee in 1942, he took strong exception to a proposed joint study of territory opened up by the Alaska Highway. He referred to "the efforts that would be made by the Americans to control developments in our country after the war, and to bring Canada out of the orbit of the British Commonwealth of Nations into their own orbit. I am strongly opposed to anything of the kind. I want to see Canada continue to develop as a nation to be, in time, as our country certainly will, the greatest of nations of the British Commonwealth."

CHAPTER SIXTEEN

Total War and Party Politics

THE FIRST CONSCRIPTION CRISIS ended on August 1, 1942, with the adjournment of the session of Parliament. In opposing the demand for conscription for overseas service, Mackenzie King had pointed out again and again during the session that it was not necessary to a total war effort to have military conscription for such service. However, to offset the pressure of the conscription campaign, the Government had gone further in the direction of a total effort than might have been feasible politically in a calmer atmosphere.

The maintenance of a rigid price ceiling accompanied by almost equally rigid stabilization of wages, for instance, was something the United States was never able to achieve. Under the Selective Service Regulations brought into force in March 1942, compulsion in the use of manpower had been extended far beyond military service. Moreover, the period of compulsory military training, originally one month, had been extended to four months in 1941, and before the first period of four months expired, it was decided to keep all conscripted men in the army for the duration of the war. From this pool of conscripted men, and from those about to be called up, came a steady stream of volunteers who kept up the strength of the armed forces—at times to the detriment of equally essential civilian service in the production of munitions and supplies. Finally, the budget of 1942 had come reasonably close to conscription of wealth.

Throughout the latter half of 1942, there was repeated evidence that the burden of war was becoming irksome to one section after another of the public. During the session that ended in August, there had been an incipient rebellion of the Liberal Members from Saskatchewan over the ceiling on the price of wheat to the farmers. At the last Liberal caucus, there had been loud outcries about the weight of taxation. The growing restiveness was no doubt partly the result of the continued inaction of the Canadian Army, interrupted only by the raid on Dieppe.

Mackenzie King found that the agitation for overseas conscription virtually ceased after Bill 80 passed. During the remaining months of 1942, he had, however, to cope with several major problems arising out of the total war effort. He was also considerably distracted by political developments.

On August 5, he made one of his periodic visits to Toronto to see his dentist and call on old friends. He had luncheon with Sir William Mulock, who gave him "an affectionate greeting and began speaking about my work and plans." Mackenzie King told him "that I did not think I would take part in another campaign. That I wanted to devote the latter part of my life, if possible, to writing and reviewing some of the political experiences. . . . I did not think I had the physical strength for more campaigns. He said something about my finding that the people would not let me out. That I might have to stay."

Mulock also said he proposed to remember Mackenzie King in his will, and added that "he was speaking of the matter now, as I had been speaking of my plans for the future, and he thought he would like to let me know. . . . What he said to me was a real surprise, showing great, deep affection. I told him I could think of no honour greater than to have such an expression of confidence and affection from him. That he had known me longer than any other person and more intimately in my public life and work." Mackenzie King observed that "Sir William will be 99 in January" and that he was wholly unimpaired in his faculties and wonderfully alert. On this, as on many other occasions during the war years, Mackenzie King derived great encouragement from these occasional visits to Mulock.

After his return from Toronto, Mackenzie King spent a few quiet days at Kingsmere. On August 7, the twenty-third anniversary of his selection as leader of the Liberal party, he wrote: "I would like to round out a quarter of a century and to lead my party if I had the strength for it, as long as Sir John had led his from the days of Confederation. I could not hope to equal the number of years he was in office, as Prime Minister, nor could I hope to equal the years that Sir Wilfrid led his party though, if spared till early September, I shall have been Prime Minister for a longer period. I would like to have to do with the Peace Conference at the end of this war and, if it is God's will, to devote some years to taking part in the shaping of the new order, once freed from the strain of leadership in Parliament in that period."

Early in August, Mackenzie King tried to help Ralston get the assistance in the Department of National Defence they had both agreed he needed. Ralston wanted Victor Sifton of the Winnipeg *Free Press* to become Deputy Minister. On August 6, Mackenzie King had "a very frank talk with Sifton" with Ralston present. He asked Sifton "if he differed in any way in policy with Ralston. He said quite frankly that he did. He thought the Army was too large and that we were undertaking too much. He did not like the idea of being Deputy, unless he could do everything that the Minister wished. I said that I thought Ralston himself felt that the Army was too large, and that his hands were being forced by others. . . . That if he were there he might help to steady the situation in that particular. That Ralston was in a very difficult position. . . . He made no definite promise. He agreed to talk matters over with Ralston at night. I doubt if he will accept. He had written positively that he would not, but the talk will do some good, and can do no harm."

Though Mackenzie King blamed the conscriptionists mainly for obscuring the magnitude of the Canadian war effort, he also felt the Government was not itself getting the facts before the public, through the existing Bureau of Public Information in the Department of National War Services. He had accordingly arranged to have Charles Vining, a recognized authority on public relations, prepare a report; it recommended a Wartime Information Board which would be largely autonomous. Mackenzie King gave the Cabinet an outline of Vining's report on August 11, and "stressed the importance of clearing up the war information business. I said I thought we should secure Vining for the purpose." He then had Vining come in to explain the report and noted that "Vining gave a splendid review. . . . I know it impressed all the members with the extent to which both the Government and the country were suffering through not having proper publicity. The necessity for a proper organization was made abundantly clear and all members, I think, felt that Vining was the man for the job."

After the Cabinet meeting, Mackenzie King invited Vining to become Chairman of the new Board, and told him "the Cabinet felt this was the most important service in connection with Canada's war effort, next to the operations in the field of battle, and indeed it was not without its effect upon this." Vining agreed, reluctantly, to accept and as Vice-Chairman suggested Hon. Philippe Brais, who was Government Leader in the Legislative Council of Quebec, and, as such, a member of Godbout's Government. On August 22, Mackenzie King got Brais' consent to act if Godbout was willing to release him from the Quebec Cabinet. Mackenzie King noted that he appeared "to be a fine type of personality and may yet become a federal Minister." From the outset the Wartime Information Board was scrupulous in keeping its activities objective and in avoiding any propaganda for the Government, and its very objectivity undoubtedly made it an invaluable means of helping to secure public acceptance of the manifold restrictions of the later war years.

The need for better public information was nicely illustrated at this time by a visit Mackenzie King had on September 5 from C. A. Bowman, the Editor of the Ottawa *Citizen*, who had just returned from England after a two months' visit. The *Citizen* had been very unfriendly to the Government for some time and, on this visit, Bowman "made a remarkable confession to me, very frank and with no comment—simply said he wanted to see me to tell me that Canada's war effort was magnificent—so regarded everywhere in England, but not known in Canada."

At the end of January 1943, Vining had to give up the chairmanship of the Board because of ill health; and on his recommendation N. A. M. MacKenzie, then President of the University of New Brunswick, was appointed Chairman. The day-to-day direction of the Board was carried on by A. Davidson Dunton, its general manager.

The Steelworkers Organizing Committee was very active in 1942 and, in late August, began to threaten a strike unless its current wage demands were met. The Ministers directly responsible for the maintenance of controls on prices and wages felt these demands threatened to destroy the whole stabilization policy. At the Cabinet on August 26, Mackenzie King read a letter he had received from the leader of the Steelworkers Organizing Committee, Charles Millard, and found all his colleagues were "against any yielding to him. I confess his attitude of publicity, giving letters to press in advance, so belligerent, . . . changed my mind about seeking to meet him, though I feel the steel industry should be put on a national basis and inequalities speedily adjusted. . . . I feel, as I write, I should send Millard a further letter placing him and his position in their true light."

The next day (August 27) Mackenzie King's decision was strengthened by a feeling that the C.C.F. were playing politics in combination with Millard and he was convinced he "should expose his [Millard's] tactics and their significance in his own words. His position is so vulnerable that he may think twice before having the different steel mills close down, but I doubt it. However the case against him will be largely made before he acts, if does." He accordingly wrote a long letter to Millard; this was reported in the press, and on August 29, he complained that the "papers, as usual, have given wrong emphasis to my letter to Millard, calling it an appeal not to strike. It was a solemn warning, making clear to Millard the position in which he was placing, had placed and would place himself in light of his own expressed views of effect of a strike at this time."

On August 30, Mackenzie King had Humphrey Mitchell, the Minister of Labour, invite Millard to Ottawa, "which opens a door, or keeps it open and if he will see to some sort of inquiry, will save the situation. I told him today, if Millard ordered a strike without meeting him, the law should be set in motion against him—for direct defiance of the law—knowing what the injury would be." The strike was averted at this time, by the establishment of a Commission to investigate and prepare a report. On September 3 Mackenzie King noted: "Much 'phoning re Steel dispute. . . . Mitchell spoke about a Commission of three. I agreed—am anxious to avert strike and have men get justice. I feel I have saved a situation that might have been very critical, first by being firm with the men, next going farther with colleagues, including Mitchell, than they had wished or intended to go in meeting the steel workers—the furnaces have been banked at Algoma for some days. Once out—a long time to start up again." He added, characteristically, "What we prevent even more than what we do is what counts most in the long run." But prevention in this case proved to be only postponement, and the problem had to be faced again by the Government early in 1943.

Millard and the Steelworkers Committee were not the only ones who were putting pressure on the price ceiling at this time. On September 22, Mackenzie King had a "conversation with Ilsley about the debate which is going on in the press between Gardiner [the Minister of Agriculture] and [Donald] Gordon [the Chairman of the Wartime Prices and Trade Board] over the price of beef and cattle." Gardiner felt the price ceiling on beef was keeping the selling price of cattle too low. Mackenzie King " 'phoned Gardiner to issue no further statements," and arranged to have the matter discussed by the Cabinet on September 24; at its meeting he made it "clear at the outset, that I did not think either Gardiner or Gordon should have begun a controversy in the press. Further that the Government's policy must be carried out, which I supplemented by stating policy to be that set forth in my address on the cost of living, stabilization of prices and wages. Gardiner presented his arguments. Ilsley the arguments of the Prices and Trade Board. I was afraid the discussion was going to be very heated, but managed to keep it from so developing. Gardiner stated the prices of cattle had not been fixed on level agreed to. Ilsley said this was a statement of fact which, if correct, he would see was properly met."

Mackenzie King "was immensely relieved when the session ended amicably." He noted that Ilsley was "showing signs of strain and little wonder. He . . . says he cannot possibly do his work if there is to be endless controversy between him and Gardiner. I pointed out that Gardiner was right in taking exception to the controversy between

Gordon and himself in the press. The whole business is making clear how almost impossible it is to attempt regulation on the scale this war is rendering necessary. I said that the whole policy of control of prices, etc., as now carried out, was the antithesis of what Gardiner, Ilsley and I believed in as a wise permanent policy, that it was all based on nationalism; that internationalism and freer trade were the only basis on which permanent peace could be secured, but that the war rendered necessary our present policy."

As the conscription crisis receded, Mackenzie King decided he should fill the vacancies in the Cabinet's representation from the Province of Quebec caused by Casgrain's appointment to the Bench, Cardin's resignation, and Dandurand's death. After considering many possibilities, he had come by September 23 to the conclusion "that the best thing would be to give [Thomas] Vien a seat in the Senate and run [Major-General L. R.] LaFlèche in his constituency—Outremont," and also to appoint Ernest Bertrand and Alphonse Fournier from the House of Commons. This was the solution eventually reached on October 6, not without a great deal of further discussion and many alternative proposals.

During the course of considering these changes in the Cabinet, Mackenzie King made this odd entry in his diary on September 25: "I confess I would, if the men were available, welcome bringing into the Government one or two prominent Conservatives—I mean available in the sense of being men who would be helpful in the war effort. Meighen obviously could not and would not work with our Government. His bitterness toward myself is already apparent in the statement he has issued in respect to the convention being held in Winnipeg. [A Conservative convention had been called to choose a new party leader.] Not one of the number has either supported us or given us a chance to either bring them into the Government or send them on a mission as Roosevelt has Willkie. We have, of course, confidence in Manion. I would be ready to send him anywhere."

Mackenzie King saw General LaFlèche, who was at this time one of the Deputy Ministers of National War Services, on October 5 to discuss his entry into politics and the House. He told him that "during the last year I had thought frequently of him and of the possible service he could render, . . . and felt he could be helpful in bringing about greater goodwill between the provinces. I then said that I did not know what his politics were but, of course, in discussing the matter of Government with anyone I would expect that they would be prepared fully to support the Ministry in all its policies. . . . He asked me if I would like to know his politics. I said I would be interested if he cared to tell me. He then said that he had always voted Liberal all his life. That his father was a Liberal." When Mackenzie King "asked about his views on conscription he said the word had no terrors for him; that he thought it was easy to persuade the people that there was nothing to be afraid of in it. He agreed, however, that as a result of the way conscription had been introduced in the last war, and, he added,—you know I was through all that and saw what it was like—that it had left a bad record in Canada. He felt conscription should not be resorted to unless there was absolute need for it for reinforcements. . . . I asked him about the Army and said I was sure the Army would not need to be increased beyond its present size, to which he replied: I hope not. . . . That he knew the difficulties were increasing now in connection with the National Selective Service and he felt that we could not possibly consider doing more." They then discussed portfolios and finally settled on National War Services. Mackenzie King "went on to say that I thought more could be made of that Department than had been made of it. That my idea was to have it a Department which would bring all voluntary organizations together and give them proper direction in war effort. I thought he could be helpful in that way. . . . I wanted the Minister to help to mould public opinion. He said he saw the force of that."

Later that day (October 5) Mackenzie King saw Ernest Bertrand and told him "that I understood he had learned what was going on by way of trying to get a seat for LaFlèche. . . . That I understood he was ready, if need be, to go to the Senate or take a seat in the Government or do whatever was desired of him. He said . . . that this was a time of war and he was ready to do whatever he was asked. That his constituency was next to Vien's and he would be prepared to have LaFlèche run there if it was desired. I told him that I was going to speak to him about coming into the Government, but wished, in doing so, to have it understood it might only be for a limited time and that it might mean his going to the Senate or receiving some other appointment later. He said he was quite pleased to do whatever I wished. I then said to him . . . that I would like him to take Fisheries. He rather laughed at this and said the last thing he had expected to be was Minister of Fisheries, but that he would do his best."

On October 6, Mackenzie King saw Alphonse Fournier and told him "he was anxious to bring in one of those who had supported the Government on all votes on Bill 80 [Ernest Bertrand]; and one from those who had not found that possible [Fournier], but was prepared to support the Government on its policies from now on, and, should conscription be found necessary, prepared to support conscription; and a third one [La

Flèche], outside of Parliament, who could help to reconcile the factions in Quebec." He then told Fournier about approaching Bertrand and LaFlèche and added that he would also like him to join the Government. Fournier "listened very attentively to all that I said, and then said to me: Mr. King, you will remember I told you long ago that I was prepared to follow you in whatever step you might feel was necessary with regard to conscription. That has been my position ever since, and I have so stated it to others. I said I hoped there would be no need for conscription but if there was, I would expect him, if he came into the Government, to support that policy. He said he would be quite prepared to do so." Fournier became Minister of Public Works, a portfolio which had been held by J. E. Michaud as Acting Minister after Cardin's resignation, and Bertrand succeeded J. E. Michaud, who became Minister of Transport, as Minister of Fisheries.

In order to have the War Services portfolio available for LaFlèche, Mackenzie King recommended the appointment of Thorson, who held it, as President of the Exchequer Court. General LaFlèche was to stand for election to the House in Outremont, the constituency Vien had represented. This by-election, along with two others, was held on November 30. The three new Ministers had been sworn in on October 6, and General LaFlèche won his seat in the by-election.

In the latter part of 1942, Mackenzie King found time to make speeches in Toronto and Montreal and to the Pilgrims in New York. The most remarkable of these was a speech to the American Federation of Labor at Toronto on October 9, in which he forecast the post-war programme of the Government for full employment and social security. For once, Mackenzie King was genuinely satisfied with his speech. When he saw Sir William Mulock later, he found the old gentleman "was delighted with every word of it. Thought it a memorable speech, very far-reaching, and added the applause sounded as though it would go on all day. It was really a great tribute."

While he was in Toronto, Mackenzie King saw Joseph Atkinson, the publisher of the Toronto *Star*. Atkinson told him "he thought that the Tories, who had been pressing for total war . . . were beginning to feel that they had had enough of total war, and were beginning to wish they had not said quite so much about it." Mackenzie King found "Atkinson was very pleased with my address. Thought it one of the best I have ever made. . . . Atkinson said he hoped above everything else that I would continue as Prime Minister after the war, to get some of the things done that he felt I alone would be able to get done. The kind of things that I had been speaking of in my address. He did not want to see reaction get control. I said I had doubted much my own strength to continue on, and if I really expressed my personal desire, it would be, if a chance afforded, to quit at once. Both he and Hindmarsh said there was no one else who could take hold. They asked about Ilsley as a possible successor. I told them I thought the ablest man in the Government was St. Laurent. He would be my choice in a moment were he not of the minority in both race and religion. I could not choose as between other members of the Government."

Mackenzie King also spoke on October 16 at a large dinner in Montreal in support of the Victory Loan. When he came to report it, he felt he had given the right view of the war; that there was "more truth in it than has been given by many speakers. . . . Coming out frankly showing wherein the tide has not yet turned, and the forces that are at work behind and beneath the front of battle. I think I have gone further than either Churchill or the President in giving the people a true picture of the appalling danger of the present world menace."

On the train going to Montreal, Mackenzie King had another evidence of the pinch of total war. He encountered Robert Laurier, the Minister of Mines in Hepburn's Government, who spoke to him "about the Government's decision to close the gold mines [to obtain men for war industries]. Mentioned, and I think rightly, that there should have been some consultation with the Department of Mines in Ontario." Mackenzie King had already foreseen the possibility of such complaints a month earlier when the need for manpower had come up for discussion and observed that he could now "see we are going to have endless trouble with the Selective Service people and Wartime Prices and Trade Board, and the powers which they have through their exercising them without sufficient conference. This has been a bolt right into the camp of the forces that have been shouting loudest for a total war effort. They are now beginning to shout about being hurt themselves. A total war effort in their minds means an effort to save their gold, and not help to win the war by allowing their men to work on materials needed for war purposes."

Indeed, by far the most serious problem which arose late in 1942 was the crisis over the administration of National Selective Service, which had been organized in March 1942 to allocate scarce manpower to essential services. On September 23 the War Committee had given detailed consideration to proposals from Elliott M. Little, the Director of National Selective Service, and counter-proposals from Donald Gordon, the Chairman of the Wartime Prices and Trade Board, on the most effective way to use the scarce manpower in the war effort. At the meeting,

Gordon and Little were present, as well as General Stuart, the Chief of the General Staff, and General Letson, the Adjutant-General. Little read a statement setting out the powers he thought National Selective Service should have to meet the essential demands for manpower. The regulation of employment proposed was so detailed and so extensive that the Cabinet did not believe it could be enforced. Mackenzie King found his statement "an amazing one, setting forth, in my opinion, a condition of things which, if followed, would create chaos in the country." He noted that "Ilsley reacted very strongly" and when he raised the question of expenditures involved, Ilsley "said it was not the money but the impossibility of having a democracy submit to the things that were suggested. ... The Government would have to become a complete dictatorship and not even allow delegations to be heard if it was to carry out what was suggested.

"It was then proposed by Ilsley that Gordon should be allowed to read his statement." Gordon's approach was to take means to meet obvious needs for manpower rather than attempt to regulate the whole field of employment. Mackenzie King thought "Gordon made a first-rate and very sensible presentation. Equally strong for the utmost effort. At the end of the discussion, I drew Council's attention to the difficulty we had had in dealing with 20,000 Japanese and removing them within a certain time, etc. I stressed how impossible it would be to move whole communities that had been built up around certain industries and which meant practically closing up community after community in different parts of Canada. Cited what would result from the complete closing of the gold mines which was one of the industries mentioned which would have to be closed up. I pointed out the effect of that would be to bring the large daily papers into stronger antagonism than ever against the administration. The *Globe and Mail* was owned by Wright and gold-mining interests. ... That, ... combined with what would naturally be felt by the people, was apt to create a revolt.

"I said I thought the only sensible course was one of gradualness, not in any sense of being dilatory or slow, but of meeting each situation in a way which would enable it to develop rather than obstruct from the start. Pointed out, for example, the wisdom of calling in the different people affected, and asking their co-operation, having them feel that they were patriots in assisting the Government to achieve what it was aiming at. I pointed out there were certain evils which publicity would cure more effectively than force. That any procedure which involved filling the jails with people would not succeed in the end. On the other hand, public opinion would be brought to bear on any class of meanness or shirking when it came to getting the numbers that we wish to secure."

No decision about ways of allocating manpower was reached at that time and had in fact to be postponed because of a visit Humphrey Mitchell made to the United Kingdom. Mitchell was Minister of Labour and National Selective Service was one of the responsibilities of his Department. On his return, Mitchell dined with Mackenzie King on November 16. Mackenzie King found Mitchell "rather evasive in replying to my questions about Little beyond saying that Little had drawn up what he called a 'charter' which set out what he thought was necessary for the Department of Selective Service, which he felt went far beyond any powers that should be given to anyone other than a responsible Minister. Little had asked on Saturday if he could meet me as soon as Mitchell returned. He had suggested Sunday. I told him that would be impossible but said I would see him and Mitchell some time Monday. Early this morning, I sent word to Mitchell to come to dinner and to Little to come to Laurier House after.

"Little greeted Mitchell in a friendly way. The three of us had a short talk together, and then Little finally said that he had come to speak of the situation in the Department. That he felt he had not received the support in his work that he should have received. That there was obstruction and unwillingness of others to co-operate and particularly lack of co-operation on the part of the Minister. He then looked directly at Mitchell and drew from his pocket a letter which he handed to Mitchell saying that that was his resignation. He then handed me a copy of the letter which had been written during the afternoon.

"It complained of the way Mitchell had received his so-called charter in the morning; of Mitchell not having discussed the situation with him, as he should have done. He then said to me that he felt he had not the backing of the Minister or his co-operation, but rather that the Minister was making things difficult for him and that he would like to have his resignation accepted at once.

"Mitchell had not seen the letter of resignation until that moment. He stopped to read it through. Mitchell then expressed surprise and said he thought it was a very uncalled-for communication. Was unnecessarily sharp and unfair. That all this had come as a surprise to him. That he had never had any differences with Little; that he could not understand the procedure. He explained he had only got home at noon on Sunday." Mackenzie King then expressed regret that Little had tendered his resignation before they had a chance to discuss matters, and hoped he would not press it. Little "then drew from his pocket another communication which he said set forth the minimum of what he regarded as necessary in the way of authority to whomever was to control the selective service. He said that represented his minimum, or rather what he had intended as his minimum before he had resigned. That he would only agree to that minimum now on the condition that he had nothing further to do with Mitchell as Minister. That he felt the Minister had continually ignored him and he had no confidence in him as one who would cooperate in work."

After going through the memorandum, Mackenzie King "remarked that it meant creating a sort of second department," but said he "could see the possibility of something being worked out on those lines, but would wish to consider that matter with my colleagues."

After they had discussed the situation in the Department of Labour for about an hour, "Little asked me if I could not accept his resignation at once. I told him I thought it was unreasonable to suggest that. That it was not for me to decline or to accept his resignation. That was for the Minister, and [I] said that I hoped he would let that matter stand until I had had a chance to consider the situation with my colleagues, . . . and see if we could not work out a way that would be satisfactory. He asked me if that could be done by Wednesday afternoon. I told him I thought we should at least have the week to see what could be done. It involved much in the way of consideration of other Ministers whose time, like my own, was necessarily taken up in part with some most pressing matters. He did not decline this but, as he was leaving, he said he hoped the matter could be settled by Wednesday afternoon. As he was going out, I spoke to him in a kindly way about appreciating difficulties, etc., but said I hoped we would find a way whereby he could be kept on. He made it clear this could not be done as long as Mitchell was the Minister. When I returned to talk to Mitchell, he spoke of Little being very narrow, not having background nor adequate experience. Apt to act impulsively, to go too far, etc. . . . Mitchell did not stay long after the talk."

The next day (November 17) Mackenzie King had Mitchell tell the War Committee "what had taken place since his return." Mackenzie King then read Little's letter of resignation. "Mitchell read one which he had prepared in reply accepting his resignation. A much too long communication. If two such communications were published, as is quite possible, they will make more difficulty for the Government than anything which has happened since the conscription issue. Indeed the effect may be even more disastrous as the whole business will be made one of attack upon the Government for being unwilling to enforce not only conscription but National Selective Service. I told Mitchell by no means to give the letter to Little but to wait until we had discussed the matter further tomorrow. In the meantime, I would like to talk with MacNamara and Bryce Stewart" (respectively the Associate Deputy and Deputy Minister of Labour at the time).

Mackenzie King found "on the whole Ministers are inclined to share Mitchell's views and certainly from some of the representations made by Little, it would appear that he, himself, has not gone out of his way to try and get certain things done as well as he might have done. I really feel that these men are finding the tasks they have assumed too vast for their accomplishment. We have been building up a huge bureaucracy to cope for the first time with the most difficult of all problems, an interference with individual liberty at a time of war."

That evening Mackenzie King was very pessimistic about this aspect of the war effort. He could not "see how we are going to get through this matter without a real break, and that in relation to the most difficult of all situations with which the Government could be faced at a time of war. The whole business will play into the hands of the Tory party just at the time that we have by-elections in three constituencies and just before the Conservative Convention in Winnipeg. It is just the very kind of thing which more than all else the Tories will wish to have, and which a man like Meighen will be able to play up to a point which may even lead to his being again selected as the Leader of the Conservative party, though I can hardly believe that a younger man will not be chosen. It would even give Hepburn a chance to start out afresh. I and not Mitchell or any other member of the Government will be blamed for the whole business. However, in these things which lie so largely beyond one's control, one can only await the outcome, doing the best one can meanwhile."

On November 18, Mackenzie King had a talk with Bryce Stewart, the Deputy Minister of Labour, who was giving up that post shortly to return to his regular employment in New York. Stewart thought "that Little is unequal to the task. There had been more publicity than performance so far as he is concerned. The Minister has given him plenty of powers but that he is unequal to seeing them properly exercised. That what he wants is complete power himself, rather than power under a Minister." Mackenzie King asked Stewart "to have Mitchell modify the letter that he was proposing to send Little in reply to his. Keep it to a dignified statement of facts."

Later he saw MacNamara and noted: "I like him very much: his quiet confidence, his clear vision and sensible way of speaking. He was quite emphatic that Little had built up a big place for himself. Had a band of pressmen around him. Says that he has been employing these men. They had not been appointed to the staff and that he, MacNamara, had often difficulties with the Civil Service Commission in getting authority to take them on and give them back pay. He says . . . that Little wanted to get everything in his own hands, to be a sort of czar." MacNamara also told Mackenzie King that "if, as Deputy Minister, he had full responsibility, he could have Selective Service work proceed wholly satisfactorily. Had no doubt about that. . . . He said, speaking frankly, he had supposed I was agreeable to having him appointed Deputy when Stewart left. I told him that certainly that was in my mind, but I wanted to be sure as to whether, as Deputy, he felt he would be able to handle the entire work and particularly have the Selective Service work carried out properly. He said he had no hesitation in saying that that task could be performed."

During the day Mackenzie King wrote: "I fully expect before the day is over, we shall have a first-class explosion—the worst that could have happened at this time. The fact that Little was not prepared to wait even over Sunday in making his demands to the Minister and writing out his resignation on Monday before seeing the Minister and myself, causes me to feel that he may be operating with forces that are anxious to precipitate a sensational political situation. It is just one more big storm that we will have to go through which, I believe, we will, in the end, weather all right. It all goes back to conscription and National Government campaign."

Later the War Committee "discussed the situation that had arisen between Humphrey Mitchell and Little. Mitchell and I gave those present an account of what had taken place. Mitchell read a letter that he had re-drafted after my talks with MacNamara and Bryce Stewart, making it much shorter and holding to statement of facts. . . . All were agreed that his [Little's] actions made clear his determination to get out. They make equally clear how . . . little sense of responsibility he owes to the Government of the country that he has been serving at the time of war. . . . It was apparent that Little's letter in part had been intended to stir up feeling against the Government no less than against Mitchell. It was quite apparent from his wording it was not written only in relation to Mitchell." Mackenzie King felt "that it is all related to the Winnipeg convention, and giving to the Tories just the material they will want. First of all, to justify bringing together all classes for the Winnipeg convention—the kind of call that Meighen sent out and the material for the next session." The War Committee decided that "Little's resignation would be accepted at once; that I would see him first and draw his attention to the objectionable clauses and ask if that was the particular letter which, in the light of reflection, he would wish to be the one finally presented."

When Mackenzie King saw Little he "said to him he perhaps would be aware matters had reached a final stage. That he had spoken to me about wishing to have everything closed by Wednesday night. That, as he had made it a condition he would not serve under Mitchell under any circumstances, he would realize there was no alternative for me other than to accept his resignation. He said he admitted that that was quite true, and that he had intended it should be. That he had taken the course he did toward that end. He realized I had my responsibility to a colleague and could not be expected to take a stand against a colleague as contrasted with one who was in a different position.

"I told him that I believed if there had been a chance for discussing matters at all, everything could have been satisfactorily adjusted. As he knew, I was open-minded about what additional powers should be given. He then said he would not have written a letter as he did but for the way Mitchell had behaved. . . . I then said to him, now that matters were being terminated, as he had said to me that the letter had been written under these provocative circumstances, I would like to ask him whether this was the letter he would wish to have permanently on the records as that containing his resignation, or whether he might wish to have it relate only to facts. I said, for example, that the last paragraph . . . certainly would be construed by a large section of the public as having a motive quite different to that which he, Little, was alleging was the real cause of his resignation. I also spoke of the third clause of the letter and said I had mentioned it to him when we were talking and he had agreed that he was not complaining about myself or the Government. I said certainly that clause could be taken as a reflection on the entire Administration. . . .

"I spoke about the reference to party politics and asked him if there had been any interference for political reasons. He said there was nothing except fuss there had been over the Unemployment Insurance Commission [Little had wished to bring it under his control as Director of National Selective Service, and had been opposed by the Commission]. Little went on to explain "what he meant by 'political reasons' by asking why the Commission had to continue as a Commission instead of being totally absorbed by Selective Service. . . . In reply to my question as to whether he would wish the letter to go as it was or not, Little said that he would be prepared to reconsider it before final action was taken. He left the office with this promise."

Mackenzie King then made arrangements for Little to see Mitchell "between 8 and half past," a time selected by Little. Mitchell telephoned about 9 to say that Little had not yet called him. Mackenzie King "then called Little myself. Told him that Mitchell was waiting, and asked when he intended to see him. He said he would see him right away; that he had been doing as he had promised, seeing his staff, telling them he had resigned and to stay on. I then informed Mitchell that he would see him at once. A little later, I learned from Mitchell he had just 'phoned him, and Mitchell had asked whether it was the letter as originally written he wished to have stand. Mitchell had said good-bye to him, and that was all there was to that. Mitchell told me that when he first called, Little's letter had already been in the hands of the press for some time."

At the end of his entry in the diary for November 18, Mackenzie King confessed he "felt much disturbed over this episode of Mitchell and Little for I see in it a prolonged political struggle; continuation of the National Government issue. Certainly Mitchell's absence has helped to lend to the Winnipeg convention all that they may need for their purposes, to make their gathering just what Meighen would wish above all it should be. However, they will not, I believe, succeed in the end."

Arthur MacNamara succeeded Little as Director and, in fact, the resignation of Little was quickly forgotten, though an effort was made to turn the manpower problem into a political issue. On November 18, Mackenzie King noted that John Bracken, the Premier of Manitoba, was attacking the Government's handling of the manpower problem. "It will," he wrote, "be the conscription issue over again but directed at the National Selective Service." He felt that the statement from Bracken made it quite apparent he was "in touch with Meighen and others probably in relation to forthcoming Winnipeg convention. I don't think, however, anyone will think of him as a leader in federal politics. . . . What he probably is seeking is a chance to enter National Government if that should ever be formed." Before a month had passed Mackenzie King changed his mind about this judgment that Bracken would not become the leader of the Conservative party.

After Little's resignation, there was a redoubled attack on Humphrey Mitchell from Conservative sources as well as from sections of organized labour and from the press. Mackenzie King himself from time to time throughout 1942 had recorded growing doubts about Mitchell's adequacy for the post in the face of the hostility of organized labour. His diary shows that during his visit to Washington in early December, he had practically made up his mind he would have to replace Humphrey Mitchell as Minister of Labour. After his return, he spoke, on December 8, to Power about the possibility of his taking on the post of Minister of Labour and Selective Service, and to his surprise found Power's initial reaction not unfavourable, though he pointed out some serious objections. He then told Ralston of his interview with Power and "said to him I had in mind possibilities of his [Ralston's] taking on the position of Minister of War, appointing a separate Minister for the Army, and his exercising authority over all three war departments, being their representative in the War Cabinet, thereby ceasing to be an advocate of the Army only, but occupying the role of judge, which was the one that all of us in the War Committee should take. Ralston said he feared it would be impossible for one to control Ministers under him." Mackenzie King told Ralston he "had been thinking of making Abbott Minister for the Army. He, Ralston, would still, of course, have his interest in the Army. He admitted the Army was very close to his heart. He had fought so many battles for them that he felt he would like to see them through.

"I said it would be recognized that he had the Army at heart, but everyone would feel he was seeking to be impartial between the three forces. He admitted we needed someone to co-ordinate the work of the three. . . . I said I had thought of making Macdonald Minister for Air [and of] moving Mitchell to the Navy, he having been at sea. That idea seemed to appeal to him. He agreed that Mitchell had got in quite wrong with labour and would be a target at the next session. . . . He asked if he could talk the matter over with Angus Macdonald, and I said by all means to do so."

When Mackenzie King talked to Power again on December 11, he found Power felt it would "be a mistake politically to appear to be yielding to labour and letting down a colleague who was universally praised when he came into office and who has suffered because of the difficult role he has had to fulfil. . . . He said he would go to labour if I said so, but I told him there would be no sense in making changes which were not agreed upon by all of us immediately concerned." In the event Mackenzie King decided to ride out the storm over Mitchell and it gradually subsided.

Great political changes took place in the closing months of 1942. There was a marked rise in the support for the C.C.F. in the country and a developing alliance between that party and a section of the trade union movement which gave Mackenzie King some concern. But his main interest was in developments in Ontario and in the leadership of the Conservative party.

On October 21, Hepburn resigned as Premier of Ontario and was succeeded by Gordon Conant; Hepburn remained Provincial Treasurer. The news reached Mackenzie King at a War Committee meeting and some of his colleagues suggested that Hepburn was preparing to attend the forthcoming Conservative convention in Winnipeg which, Mackenzie King noted, "is to be open to all comers who are not satisfied with the present Government." He added that he had been told "that the convention promises to be a much divided affair. Younger men are determined to have a new leader who will help to bring the party into power after the war when the present Administration goes to the country. The general thought is that MacPherson, of Regina, may be chosen. On the other hand, what Meighen has in mind is to have the convention declare for National Government with different persons agreeing to support Bracken as leader. Bracken would be a fool to allow himself to be used for such a purpose. Meighen is blinded with his feelings of bitterness and determination to have his own way on National Government, as representative of the big interests. It may well be," he added, "that Drew, Hepburn, and one or two others will gang up with him for some such result. If they do, they will have to wait some time for their leader to get a seat in the House. I should rather imagine they will choose MacPherson somehow and let him go about the country a bit instead of getting him into Parliament and destroying his chances of leadership by a failure there before the present Parliament is over."

Mackenzie King's "own feeling about Hepburn" was "that something personal has occasioned his resignation. . . . I cannot imagine his real reason for resigning being other than something personal to himself, . . . though it is quite conceivable that his friends . . . have promised to spend any sum in an effort to defeat me, and they may feel that they can find means of securing him the leadership or, at all events, a lieutenancy in the National Government that is to be."

Whatever the reason, Mackenzie King was delighted. On October 22, he wrote: "There is nothing truer than that, for the most part, we seal our own fate. I have had to endure a lot of very insulting and even vicious things at the hands of three men in particular: Meighen, Bennett, and Hepburn. The careers of all three have been ended by their own hatefulness, which has reacted upon them in their own followings." He added that "Hepburn, after having continued in the office in defiance of rules made for preservation of popular rights, is discovering that his own powers and his power politically were rapidly diminishing. Ambition, combined with venom, has helped to bring about his destruction. . . . Hepburn will find, once he is no longer Premier and ceases to be a Minister of the Crown, that few will be left to do him honour or to honour his name."

Mackenzie King telephoned Conant, the new Premier of Ontario, and congratulated him. They had a very friendly conversation. He noted that he felt "much relieved to have a man of Conant's ability and experience at the head of affairs in Ontario. I wish he were not so reactionary. I think he starts with a handicap, taking over at Hepburn's instance. What he should do is call a convention and ask his own party to confirm him

Total War and Party Politics 455

in the leadership of the Government. Personally, I would have liked to have seen Nixon chosen leader. He could have carried the Province as the leader of the Liberal party. I rather doubt if Conant can do that. He is too much of the Hepburn type in his belief in force and in his irreconcilable attitude toward those who do not share his views. . . . However, one step at a time. Hepburn is now out of the premiership for all time. He will be out of public life for all time very shortly. That will make an immense difference in the feeling of all our Liberals, both provincially and federally. It gives me fresh heart and hope. . . .

"I was right in my surmise that the cause of Hepburn's resignation was a personal one. His expressions and intention to get out of public office altogether, cease to be even a private member, made that wholly apparent. It is clear he had been planning to get out for some months past, and has finally acted in an impetuous, impulsive way, as he has done in everything else."

Two days after Hepburn's resignation (October 24), John Hackett, a prominent Conservative from Montreal, and R. A. Bell, Hanson's secretary, came to see Mackenzie King "with a letter to ask for reduced rates for those attending the Winnipeg convention. . . . I suggested giving them the same rates as those in existence when the C.C.F. held their convention." He told Hackett that "as the convention was open to all who wished to further Canada's war effort, I was thinking of going myself. He said I would be very welcome. He did not think Hepburn was likely to be present or that he would have a look-in if he did."

On October 26, Robert Laurier came to see Mackenzie King ostensibly to seek his advice as to whether he should stay in the Ontario Government. Mackenzie King told him there should be a Liberal convention in the Province to choose a new leader and that he "believed if the convention chose the right leader, an immediate appeal to the people, if possible, while the Conservatives were worrying about their convention in Winnipeg, might lead to a return of the Liberals. I asked him if he thought anything would induce Harry Nixon to join the C.C.F. if he were ignored. He said: 'No.' He was sure Harry would not. He was a sound man who thought out the problem before speaking."

Mackenzie King added that Laurier "then went on to say that Conant had said to him if he were in Ottawa at the end of the week, he would be glad if he would have a word with some of the powers that be, and then indicated myself, and to ask if I would not appoint Harry Nixon to the Senate. That was the real purpose of Robert's visit, as Council was meeting tomorrow. He wanted to know what he could say to Conant. When I heard this, I thought it was infernal cheek. Conant who has opposed us bitterly, to ask, as a first request, that we should help him out of his difficulty by side-tracking the one man who is really entitled to the leadership and who has adopted the sound course."

Mackenzie King was "particularly careful in what I said in reply," and he told Laurier "to do anything of the kind would be looked upon as a bargain, and as a part of some pre-arranged plan. That were I to appoint Harry Nixon now to the Senate, it would be said at once that his resignation had been made for that purpose, and that there was collusion between us. I pointed out that already the papers had an item to the effect that Nixon was to receive his reward in that way. I said I would not be making appointments to the Senate for some time. . . . Robert said he agreed entirely with me; that the appointment would be misconstrued."

During the day, Mackenzie King telephoned four of the Ontario Ministers and suggested to them that "the thing to do was to have constituencies pass a resolution asking immediately for a convention to determine, first of all, the question of leader, although that need not be mentioned in the calling of a convention. I pointed out this would put no onus on any federal Minister or Member or any Ontario Member, but would bring the initiative from the right source, namely, the constituents to whom the Member was responsible. If these resolutions could be passed from day to day all over the province, a convention could soon be brought into being." Although the Ministers did their part, this advice was not heeded except in a few constituencies, and no convention was held in Ontario for some time.

About a month later, on November 30, three federal by-elections were held. LaFlèche won in Outremont by a substantial majority, but the results in the other two—Saguenay and Winnipeg North Centre—were not favourable to the Government. Neither could they give much real comfort to the Conservatives. Mackenzie King noted that the victor in Saguenay was "Dorion, Tory organizer, and branded as an Independent," and the Winnipeg constituency was, as he feared it would be, won by the C.C.F. candidate, Stanley Knowles.

On the day of the by-elections, it looked to Mackenzie King "as though Bracken intends to seek the Tory nomination on the score that it would really be an all-out National Government convention. In this he will be Meighen's puppet. I doubt if MacPherson will run because of ill health. I don't care who gets the convention as long as it is not either Meighen or Drew. . . . I should not, however, be surprised if Meighen forces himself ahead, and had the convention so manipulated as to carry it. We shall have a hard time with the Selective Service issue made the question of conscription and National Government over again."

On December 9, Mackenzie King was greatly relieved to learn "that Meighen had definitely resigned the leadership of the Conservative party. I do not much care who is selected now, though I shall be sorry if it were Drew. . . . It looks to me as if the choice lay between Bracken and MacPherson. I should think that MacPherson would win. Bracken should be refused admission to the Tory party and thrown out of the party of which he is now the leader. He owes his long tenure of office to the Liberals, who have supported him, and the Progressives. He owes nothing to the Tories. He has made a fool suggestion that the party should be called Progressive-Conservatives. This, after being a leader of the Liberal-Progressive party.

"What a hopeless position the Conservative party is in," he reflected, "when at each convention it seeks a change of name, and this is more or less the case at general elections as well. It were as though the name of the party itself had become distasteful to its own members. To think of Manion, a Liberal, being the leader and changing the name to the National Government party; and now Bracken, a professed Liberal, suggesting the name be changed to Progressive-Conservative party. Certainly, one's enemies will have been well confounded in the pass to which the Conservative party has now come. Meighen sees himself as an actor passing from the stage. It has been a very poor role that he has played in the public life of Canada. It fills me with amazement to see one person after another declaring that he wishes to be considered in the running for leadership: Harry Stevens, Diefenbaker, Howard Green, MacPherson have also declared themselves. Bracken, to the extent of being willing, if the platform is satisfactory to him—an extraordinary position for a man who is leader of a provincial government composed mostly of Liberals. . . . Clearly Bracken is simply Meighen's puppet. There may be a dark horse, but I have not heard Sidney Smith's name mentioned. The party would be wise if they took a young man. Denton Massey would be a good possibility, though it would take some time for him to acquire political knowledge and skill. Were I wishing to see the Conservative party thrown into utter confusion and the worst possible choice made, and the one that would give me the least possible trouble, I would hope that Bracken might be chosen."

The next evening (December 10) Mackenzie King recorded his opinion that Meighen's speech at the Winnipeg convention was "exceedingly poor, less acrimonious than usual, and with a note of disappointment and sadness at the end. That he should have spent the greater part of his speech attacking the C.B.C. and the denial of the right of broadcasting for political appeal, seemed to me an exceedingly weak close to his public career. Like Bennett, he is responsible for his own defeat. He himself, personally, is more responsible for his political career being now at an end than all other forces combined. Both have been far too bitter and contemptuous and autocratic. Of the two, Meighen was the worst."

Grattan O'Leary of the Ottawa *Journal* reported the Winnipeg convention for that newspaper and Mackenzie King found his "article on Bracken's behaviour . . . amazing. It describes the conceit in a man demanding that the party should change its name for one that he would give it; next, that he would be sure of being elected on the first round of votes, etc. I felt, in reading the proceedings, that unless the members of the Conservative party had lost the last remnant of pride which they have in the party's existence, Bracken would not get his name into nomination. Before hearing what had been done, I believed in this so strongly that I put Bracken out of the running altogether and thought that those nominated would be: MacPherson, Smith of Manitoba, Green, Diefenbaker, and Stevens. The chance of success being in that order. I had concluded that Drew would not have his name put forward. However, I was amazed when I learned that Bracken had been nominated. . . . I went to bed immensely relieved with what had taken place. It matters little to me which of the number is now chosen. I can think of no unpleasantness comparable to that which would have resulted if either Meighen or Drew had been selected. I have reason indeed to be grateful for having been spared to see my political opponents so completely confounded, and especially those who were markedly political enemies."

He felt "wholly vindicated in my stand re conscription, seeing that the word has been carefully kept out of any declaration of policy. . . . Moreover, little has been said about an all-out effort. It is pretty plain that the convention has realized that the people of Canada feel that the Government's record in that particular is an exceptionally good one."

Mackenzie King on December 11 "was sorry to see that Green had collapsed on getting up to speak. He is perhaps the most sincere of all the candidates in his zeal in certain directions. My feeling is the contest will be between MacPherson and Bracken. I shall be surprised if MacPherson does not win. I would think Stevens would be at the bottom of the poll. Diefenbaker and Green a good deal behind the other two. . . . I have been interested in seeing how careful the different speakers have been in not going out of their way to say unkind things. . . . Everything considered, they have been, for a Tory gathering, remarkably careful in that particular, which shows that I have the confidence and regard of the country; and also, possibly, my years and very long tenure of public office may be counting for something."

Total War and Party Politics 459

That afternoon (December 11) before lying down for a rest, Mackenzie King "felt so sure the Conservatives would not go back on one of their own, i.e., the bona fide Conservatives, for leader, that I drafted a wire to have in readiness to send MacPherson in the event of his being chosen. When I came up from my rest, I was amazed to receive a memo giving the first returns of the ballot, in which Bracken was leading MacPherson by almost double the number of votes. I thought carefully over whether or not I should congratulate Bracken. . . . I feel that he has betrayed the Liberals as well as others of Liberal views who have given him the support which has kept him in power for so many years. Save for posing as a Liberal, he would never have been able even to form a coalition with a Tory in it. Now he has been prepared to deliver that entire following over to a political party whose policies he himself has fought bitterly throughout the past. One might say even up to the hour. But he and Meighen began to intrigue between them to have him take over the leadership from Meighen himself. From the outset, I suspected a design in the open-door policy of the convention. . . . My own view is that oil and water cannot mix, and that the convention has only succeeded in making confusion worse confounded for the Conservatives. Their action in taking Bracken, his platform, and the name of the party, are all evidence that they have recognized that, as a party, the Conservative party is dead. They are now seeking to effect its resurrection by a false leader, who has given them his support.

"I did not send any telegram, but drafted a message to the press, saying I would reserve what I had to say until Bracken was in the House. I did say that, knowing something of the responsibility of leaders and their followers, at times like the present, he was to be congratulated on the support he had received from the members of the party he was to lead. That made it clear I was not congratulating him myself or on behalf of our party. I shall write him privately, saying I was surprised at his running at all, and equally at his appointment, but will refer to the friendship of past years and express pleasure in the thought that we will be able to work together in the House of Commons in a manner which will maintain the best traditions of British parliamentary government. I can see the note he is sounding is the *omnium gatherum*. He has made, I am sure, a terrible mistake. The Tory party, as a party, has made an even worse mistake. Apart from all else, Bracken's age means that in a short time the party will have to choose another leader." His diary entry for December 11 concluded with these words: "Bracken's appointment makes it easier. He, at least, will not be in the House of Commons of the mean and nasty type as were the other leaders I have had to face, and some I might have had to face. . . . To have life reasonably tolerable in the House of Commons means in itself much in the way of possible prolongation."

Later that day, at the funeral of an old friend, Mackenzie King met Manion. They "had a very pleasant talk together as we drove from the house to the church, and from the church to the cemetery, and I took him back to his office. He said the greatest mistake he has made was ever leaving the Liberal party, but that they had used him at the time of the 1917 elections and Meighen had gotten him into his Government, and he found it difficult to break away."

On December 21, Mackenzie King listened to a broadcast by Bracken who "was very moderate in tone, . . . rather pathetic in some of his . . . personal references and, in that regard, over conceited. The substance part of the speech will read well. . . . Altogether, however, I fear that the speech will be anything but pleasing to the Conservatives. I am afraid Bracken has got himself into a terrible mess. After listening to his address, I dictated a letter to him. I had meant to send it ere this."

Mackenzie King experienced a great deal of frustration in the latter part of 1942 over his determination to place restrictions on the supply of alcoholic beverages as part of the total war effort. He had first raised the question with his colleagues on August 11 and found little enthusiasm. The subject was raised again on September 12 by a delegation from the United Church. Mackenzie King "was deeply impressed by and wholly in agreement with all representations made by this delegation. Ended up by telling them that if they would send me a memorandum of what they had said, I would use the material for a broadcast. I have been feeling for a long time I should speak on the need for temperance in connection with our war effort." On September 14, Mackenzie King had "told Cabinet I thought we should press on in the matter of curtailing the liquor traffic."

It was not, however, until mid-November that Mackenzie King himself began to work actively on the problem. At the Cabinet meeting on November 12, he "was very disappointed, disheartened, and discouraged to find that, after having the Department of War Services work for nearly two months on this matter, . . . nearly nothing came before the Cabinet excepting what I, myself, had suggested." He "spoke out rather indignantly to the Cabinet about this way of dealing with matters and allowing time to run on indefinitely. I said I thought the policy should be to not allow any more revenue from sales of liquor, of beer, spirits, and wines, than what there had been in the year at the commencement of the war. This was in accordance with our policy of not allowing profiteering as a result of the war." He suggested that liquor advertising should not be more than a fixed proportion of the total advertising in any paper. He "had in mind the wiping out of publications which owe their existence to liquor advertising. LaFlèche had suggested a reduction in spirits to 75 per cent, wines 80 per cent and beer 85 per cent. . . . Ilsley spoke of our having to give subsidies to provinces to make up their losses. I said if necessary we should do that, and let the people see they would have to pay extra taxes because of attitude of provinces that would not fall in line. . . . Ilsley also spoke of it requiring conference with the provinces. . . . It was a very disheartening business and took a good deal out of me."

On November 19, Mackenzie King "despaired of getting ahead with the Temperance business. It seems to be impossible to get anyone, Minister or public servant, who will really grapple with the question and get the data that one needs to get, in even discussing the matter in the Cabinet. However, this afternoon, I did take up the matter and pressed it very hard. I agreed it would be unwise to make the broadcast or take any step until by-elections in Montreal and Winnipeg were out of the way. Also I realized I could not possibly get material together in time. . . . I got the Cabinet to agree to what had been recommended by LaFlèche. . . . Also I pressed for the dilution of spirits, and asked if they would be ready to take that step as well. Further we should arrange for an early closing of places selling liquor, and that something should be done about advertising. In the meanwhile, Ilsley is to see what is necessary to discuss with the provincial legislatures.

"When the question of dilution of beer was opened, I pointed out that nowhere do men love beer and drink more than in England, and the British Government had made important dilution there. I felt very weary and tired in discussing the matter and told colleagues I thought the time had come when we should cease to be a Government of which it could be said we had no policy on matters of this kind which affected the great body, and that this was a measure which was absolutely necessitated by the war, apart from anything else. I get no help from anyone. . . . Listened to arguments about the uproar that will be raised, ignoring altogether that this is due simply to special interests and people who are no less selfish in their habits, forgetting that nations as such are made up of decent honest people who only want what is right carried out."

No further developments occurred until December 10, when the Cabinet spent most of the afternoon on the liquor question, Mackenzie

King "fighting for a reduction in quantities of spirits, wine and beer released; also for dilution of strength, and limiting hours of sale. Got Council to agree on reduction in quantities: spirits by 30 per cent . . . wine by 20 per cent, and beer by 10 per cent. Also agreement to reduction in strength of spirits sold and taking fortification out of the wine. Most of the Cabinet felt that to dilute beer would be a mistake. The general feeling was that beer drinking was particularly among industrial workers . . . and that it would be a mistake to go too far in the matter of beer." The reduction in hours and banning of advertising were objected to by some of the Quebec Ministers and it was decided to discuss that question further with the Premier of Quebec. Mackenzie King found it "a very trying and fatiguing business, but . . . got agreement on a definite policy being announced next Friday and said I would give a radio broadcast that night."

On December 12, Mackenzie King received "a telegram from [Dr. John] Coburn of Toronto [a United Church Minister who had been on the delegation in September] complaining of the delays in having any policy announced or any address given." He telephoned Coburn and "had a very satisfactory talk. He spoke particularly of the need to stop liquor advertising, mentioned he had been backing me up very strongly before his colleagues. Was anxious to help me as well as the cause. I read in the morning *Citizen*, Charlie Bishop's article referring to myself in which he spoke of my strong will and determination to control the Government. This and the public liking in the Prime Minister a man who had the strength to assert his own will. The article of Bishop and Dr. Coburn's telegram made me decide absolutely I would insist on liquor advertising being completely stopped, despite all opposition in the Cabinet."

Accordingly Mackenzie King asked the Cabinet on December 14 "to meet my wishes in the matter of completely prohibiting liquor advertising throughout the whole time of the duration of the war. . . . When I saw there was to be another round of discussion in the matter from the Quebec point of view, I said quite openly that the one attack that was made against the Administration was that I was in the hands of Quebec, depending on my majority there. That the hardest attacks I had to endure from my own following and other parts were that I had stood firm in the matter of not permitting conscription to be introduced before it was necessary. That I intended to maintain that stand because it was right and necessary, but that I would never allow it to be said that I was in any way controlled by Quebec or any other province. I pointed out that as regards liquor advertising, that was not an invasion of any rights of the Province of Quebec. That rather Quebec was invading other provinces through permitting advertising in Montreal to be distributed through Ontario, when Ontario had abolished liquor advertising. I made it perfectly clear I would not go back from that position and said I could see from the attitude of the other members of Council that practically all the Cabinet believed I was right. This was agreed to and I said that was settled.

"I then raised the question about the eight-hour period for sales. I said Ilsley had written me a letter about it being preferable to make an appeal to the provinces instead of trying to use our over-riding jurisdiction to compel them to fall in line. Ilsley had made it quite clear we had no machinery for enforcing a regulation of the kind, and might find ourselves in a position where some of the provinces could defy us. I said I was quite open-minded in the matter. In fact, had come to the conclusion it would be preferable to make a public appeal to them, and if it were not accepted, I then later would take action. All Council agreed to this.

"I then tried to get the Cabinet to agree to beer being reduced by 20 per cent instead of 10 per cent, but there was opposition to this. As I had gained in other points, I did not like to press this one too strongly.... I should have held to my guns, but I realized that members had gone pretty far in meeting me on the other points, and were fearful. Moreover I was counting upon reducing the output of beer by the diversion of men from breweries to war industry, and also new regulations as to pooling of sale, etc. I thought this would make a compensation for not going farther.... It was a great relief to my mind to get the programme through as well as I did."

On December 15, before the Orders-in-Council were passed, Mackenzie King "made another try at reducing somewhat the strength of beer but the argument was that the Government would get little thanks from the temperance people for a nominal reduction and no end of grousing from miners and others on the score of the King Government having supplied them with sloppy beer, with obviously no advantage in the matter of consumption and ... I thought it well not to press the matter. I do feel, however, the brewers are getting off far too easily and they should be called upon to make a much better sacrifice. However, they will suffer most through the cutting off of advertising." He "was immensely relieved to get the matter through without any further real discussion. I know that if I had not taken this whole matter in hand myself, it would not be through tonight, and I doubt if anything would have been done before Parliament met, if indeed at that time.... I am glad to have it as something accomplished before this year of my life is out." He felt "the measures agreed upon will be a birthday gift worthwhile to the nation itself." The broadcast announcing the new regulations was delivered on December 16. The federal regulations were effective at once and obliged the provincial governments to institute rationing to conserve the limited supplies.

The year did not end without another difficult step in maintaining the total war effort. On December 18, the Cabinet had to decide whether to start rationing butter. Gardiner was in Western Canada and he telephoned to object "very strongly." He "thought when Bracken entered the House, with his understanding of the farming situation, there would be more difficulty in defending some of our policies. We had [Donald] Gordon and [Gordon] Taggart [a former Minister of Agriculture in Saskatchewan who was one of the Administrators in the Wartime Prices and Trade Board] come to the Cabinet to explain the reason why the change should go into effect at once and not stand over until Monday. It appeared that already word has gone out to have things in readiness for announcement on Sunday night so that, before shops open on Monday, rationing can be put into force. If left over for a week, even for one day, shops will still be open and there will be a panic in the way of a rush in some quarters. I was astonished to find in Toronto many families are without butter at all and many incidents were occurring there and elsewhere. All Cabinet decided we would have to stand by what had been done. I 'phoned Gardiner at Regina tonight. He was very outspoken about the whole matter. Said he will have to consider whether he can stay in the Government where one man can decide what is to be done and over-ride the policies of the Department of Agriculture. He had reference, of course, to Gordon. Ilsley said his life has become intolerable with these continuous fights with Gardiner. It all comes down again to too large an army. They have been buying up most of the butter."

Despite all his other preoccupations, Mackenzie King found time, during 1942, to give some thought to the development of the National Capital. On January 15, he had spoken to Cardin, who was then Minister of Public Works, "about the Government acquiring land in Hull, putting up buildings there . . . as a means of improving that area and helping to bring it ultimately into an Ottawa district." After the ceremony at the War Memorial on November 11, Mackenzie King told the Cabinet "that the real memorial should be to make the City of Ottawa and Hull into a district, and the Ottawa river flowing in between." He was glad "to hear Fournier say that Public Works are now planning for one of the new buildings to be put on the other side of the river. I advised clearing up old space and not using parks for the purpose." These were the first steps leading to the establishment of the Government Printing Bureau in Hull, though the first idea was to move the National Film Board there.

At the close of the year, Mackenzie King took a good deal of satisfaction out of what had been achieved in 1942. On December 31, he wrote in his diary: "While our problems are great and will be greater still, there is not the appalling anxiety which there was this time a year ago. Most significant of all, I think, has been the way in which the wisdom of our policies has not only been confirmed by the progress of events, but that our enemies have been so completely confounded. When I think of Meighen seeking to usurp his way into Parliament a year ago, and of his being now completely defeated, and out of public life, and the Conservative party with a new name and a new leader, and Hepburn out of the premiership in Ontario, Bennett safely out of the country altogether, and Manion anxious to help all he can, I have indeed reason to be thankful for some of the changes that have come in the course of the year."

CHAPTER SEVENTEEN

A Time of New Beginnings

WHEN THE YEAR 1943 opened Mackenzie King believed the conscription issue had been settled; he was convinced the war would ultimately be won; and he began to look ahead to the future with some confidence. The newly named Progressive Conservative party under John Bracken's leadership he did not consider a serious threat; he was much more disturbed by the rising strength of the C.C.F. which, he felt, must be countered by increased emphasis on the post-war policy of the Liberal Government. There was no period in the war when the war itself seemed so remote from Canada as the first six months of 1943: the fear of defeat had passed and the Canadian Army was not yet engaged in actual hostilities. With the reduced sense of urgency came labour unrest and a general weariness with war and its restrictions, which was reflected in August in the substantial vote received by the C.C.F. in the provincial election in Ontario and in a marked deterioration in the fortunes of the federal Liberal party.

A sense of urgency began to return with the landing of the Canadian troops in Italy in July, and the first meeting of Roosevelt and Churchill at Quebec brought the war closer to Canadians. Active steps were taken in September to revive the Liberal party machinery and prepare a post-war programme. By the end of the year, there were signs of a revival of the prestige of the Government and of a greater popular acceptance of the burdens of war.

The first serious problem the Government faced in 1943 was the threat of a steel strike which had been postponed in 1942 by the appointment of an investigating Commission. The majority report of this Commission simply recommended that the existing Wage Stabilization Order should be upheld; a minority report made by King Gordon, at that time a prominent member of the C.C.F. party who had been an unsuccessful candidate for Parliament, recommended the adjustment of sub-standard wages. Most of the Ministers felt that any departure from the letter of the Wage Stabilization Order would undermine the price ceiling, and some also felt it would create unrest among the farmers.

A Time of New Beginnings

Once the Commission made its report, there was immediate danger of a strike. At the Cabinet meeting on January 12, Mackenzie King found most of his colleagues did not want to make any concessions. "Personally," he wrote, "my sympathies are wholly with the men. I think their wages are too low, and that some way should have been found to avoid a strike. . . . There may be a background of justice in the letter of the law, findings of original Board, etc., and no doubt a strike is aimed at the stabilization of wages policy of the Government, but some means should have been found to avoid this difficulty and would, I believe, have been, had the War Committee members of the Cabinet and the Minister of Labour been more sympathetic with the human rights of labour." Mackenzie King "felt very strongly that the majority report [of the investigating Commission] had been based on a far too narrow and legalistic interpretation of Order," and "saw no reason why Commission as a whole should not have given the broad interpretation which King Gordon gave to the reference. I felt a strong case had been made out for increasing wages of the sub-standard employees, but not a case for those receiving higher rates."

On January 14, he cited "to the Cabinet, some pages of King Gordon's report, showing wherein as regards the sub-standard workers the case had certainly been made out." He "was really amazed and distressed at the attitude of most of my colleagues. . . . I was left alone to debate the side of the workers, other members keeping silent, with the exception of Angus Macdonald, who did come out and say he thought there was a real case for the men in the sub-standard group. He realized what the conditions were in which they were living in Sydney."

Mackenzie King recommended that the Cabinet "invite committees of both employers and employees to come at once and meet the entire Cabinet. . . . This was finally agreed upon. Ralston whispered to me to have meeting as soon as possible—that time was everything." Mackenzie King felt that most of his colleagues had "a closed mind to anything excepting that . . . any compromise would mean the destruction of the policy of Wage Stabilization and Price Ceiling." When one of the Ministers spoke of King Gordon's report being "a politician's and the features which it mentioned being all intended for political ends, I said it was exactly the kind of report which I myself would have made, and had made repeatedly when I was Deputy Minister of Labour."

Mackenzie King found on January 16 that no one in the Cabinet "seemed to have any real suggestion" as to how to deal with the situation, and he told his colleagues he "thought the matter should be referred to the National War Labour Board, the Board given power to make adjustments of lower rates, and Mitchell relieved from the position of Chairman of the Board while the inquiry was on. [As Minister of Labour, Humphrey Mitchell was Chairman of the National War Labour Board as originally constituted.] That men should return to work in the first instance. I spoke of a liberal and not a legalistic interpretation being given to the Orders-in-Council. . . . It seemed to me that in framing the reference in the original Order, legal hands had sought so to frame both that they would be sort of iron-clad with no room for argument one way or the other, affording little if anything in the way of leeway. Ilsley was very insistent that the Government should not indicate that the wages were in any way sub-normal, and very strong on not permitting any change. He was also against having the industry regarded as a national industry saying it would mean change of wages all through the country. What these men did not seem to see was that unless some leeway was afforded, this strike situation will go from bad to worse and will end up with the Government having to yield much more and possibility of its price ceiling and wage stabilization policy being broken, and the war effort very seriously impaired."

Mackenzie King added that, before the Cabinet met, he had nearly an hour's talk with Howe, who, in the course of it, "said he saw no reason why the industry should not be regarded as a national industry, and also said that if the dispute were referred to the National War Labour Board, he thought I ought to say to Mitchell there was no reason why there should not be a levelling up of the lowest wage groups in other industries as well as in the steel. I think he had in mind the coal mines. This coming from him in his quiet way seemed to me to indicate that the employers themselves felt that there was need to make some concession."

The Ministers were to meet the representatives of the Steelworkers immediately after this meeting on January 16. It was understood that two representatives of Philip Murray, the President of the United Steelworkers in the United States, would also be present. Meanwhile unauthorized strikes had started both at Sydney and at Sault Ste. Marie. At the time fixed for the meeting, the representatives of the two steel companies turned up; "Mosher alone of the labour men had turned up, but had no authority to act. Murray's men from Washington were here but as the entire delegation had not arrived, they did not wish to meet the Government without a chance of conference with their men in the first instance." Though some of the Ministers wanted to call the whole conference off it was finally agreed to meet on Monday, January 18. Mackenzie King, that day, first had a talk with his colleagues and, at the outset, Howe handed him "a memo indicating the length he and Mitchell agreed I might be justified in going. It declared the steel industry a national industry. Made provision for further revision before National Labour Board. This seemed to me to signify that Howe realized some concessions had to be made. It eased my mind a bit to have this concession come from that source. It made it easier for me to gain its acceptance by all my colleagues. This I did in a very few words before employers and men came in."

When the meeting opened, Mackenzie King said that he "felt nothing was to be gained by recriminations with regard to the past. That we were faced with a very serious situation, and that I proposed not to raise any question about the men being out on strike without authorization from their own organization." He stated that the purpose of the meeting "was to see if all present could not find the means of getting men back to work immediately, and steel which was sorely needed, produced. I then said that I intended to read to them some very secret communications. I would ask that this information should be regarded as strictly secret. That as far as anything else that might take place in the conference, I had no desire to impose any note of secrecy. . . .

"I then read to them the naval signals giving the communication from the Chiefs of Staffs which was to be made to the President and myself, setting forth the effect of the U-boat menace, certainty that if it were not overcome it might not be possible for the allies—for the British and U.S.—to continue to prosecute the war. That while it could not be said the war could be won by sufficent escorts, it certainly could be lost without them. . . . I made it clear that the communication had no reference to the strike. It had been received before it had taken place.

"I then summarized another confidential report, showing that the British had had to reduce the number of divisions of their army, the air force to give up some of its men and priorities, and the navy to make other sacrifices, but all with a view to increasing the numbers of men to be made available for the construction of escort vessels and merchant marine ships." He also "gave them particulars of the losses of ships" in recent convoys.

"I then said I was giving this to everyone that they might recognize responsibility placed upon them to do all that was possible to bring the strike to a speedy close. This applied equally to employers and employees, to every member of the Government and myself. This must be kept uppermost.

"I then read a telegram from St. Catharines workers urging acceptance of the minority report and Mitchell's resignation. Said that if I believed this strike had any reference to forcing Mitchell's resignation, I would not have called the conference nor would I continue it for an hour. I said I thought Mitchell had been very unfairly treated. No Minister had ever received more general commendation than he at the time of his coming into the Government. I had asked Moore to become Minister. Moore had urged Mitchell. That a man's character did not change in a day. His life had been identified with labour. That he was no more representative in the Cabinet of labour and responsible exclusively to them than the Minister of Finance was to bankers and brokers and financiers, or the Minister of Justice to the lawyers; if any of the latter asked me to change the Minister, I would tell them they had better mind their own business. I pointed out Mitchell's responsibility, like every Minister's, was part of a collective responsibility which all were responsible to Parliament for as representing the people. That when the House of Commons carried a resolution demanding the resignation of a Minister, there would be time to consider whether action should be taken upon it or the Government itself resign and ask someone else to carry on business of the Government at a time of war.

"I then read a communication that had come from Tim Buck [who was leader of the Labour Progressive (Communist) party] in which it was stated that the strike was the result of labour policy of the Government. I made it clear that the Government's labour policy, price ceiling and wage stabilization policy had been accepted by the people, by Parliament, and that the Government was standing by it in the interests of the country, and no class more than labour. I then said if the strike related in particular to a challenging of that policy, there would be no further negotiation with anyone in the room. I then sought to explain the significance of the Government's policy by the charts which showed what the increase in the cost of living had been as compared with what it was over a similar period in the last war, and pointed out that any attempt to endanger that policy would only result in agitation in the country during the war which would make the role of every worker more difficult, and after the war render largely worthless any savings which men may have had meanwhile. I then suggested that we should hear from the parties to the dispute and since the strike had taken place in Sydney and Algoma, we might hear from their representatives.

"Mosher and Millard were among the first to speak as well as representatives of Sydney and Algoma Steel Works. The leaders at once stated that the strike was not directed against Mr. Mitchell and repudiated completely the telegram from the Communist Labour Conference, signed by Tim Buck, saying that they were in no way responsible to that organization or its views. Stress was laid on the legalistic interpretation of the Order-in-Council, and the fact that matters affecting the cost of living had not been admitted for consideration by the Board.

"When the employers spoke, they stressed the fact that they had no differences with their labour. That they were in a position of not getting any profit, and their attitude seemed to be that if the Government would help both of them, the situation might be met."

The meeting adjourned for lunch and during the afternoon, at a further meeting of the Cabinet, Mackenzie King suggested to his colleagues that Mitchell might be replaced as Chairman of the National War Labour Board by Mr. Justice C. P. McTague of Toronto.

The next morning (January 19) there was further discussion of the steel strike in the Cabinet, and Mackenzie King told his colleagues he "thought it was up to the Cabinet or the Board to find a way or make it. The situation could not be allowed to run on indefinitely. I again said to the Cabinet it was my duty to place once more before them the situation in the Atlantic with regard to the U-boats, and read part of the despatches anew. . . .

"I then said I wanted them to consider where we would be when Parliament met next week, if the strike was still on. We would be faced at once with an amendment to the Speech from the Throne which would throw into the arena the whole question of conditions in the steel areas," and that "once actual living conditions began to be exposed, the Government would find itself terribly on the defensive. We would get no sympathy from anyone opposite, and a number of our own men would be considering their futures in relation to social security. I asked them to think of the position of the Government itself. I said in the end we would have to make concessions and had better make them at once. . . . What was it proposed to do next if we got no settlement now? . . . I then pointed out how impossible it would be to compel men to work. Prisons and soldiers would accomplish little.

"I asked the Cabinet to concentrate on that side. This led to Mitchell coming out with a statement that he thought 55 cents, including cost of living bonus, might be given as a minimum wage. This as distinguished from a basic rate. Howe agreed with this at once, again making it apparent to me that Howe is the one who is really determining how far others should go, and using Mitchell toward that end. Mitchell is far too much in Howe's pocket. However, the minute I heard this suggestion made, I felt I had secured what was needed to put the Government in a position which it could defend. I said to my colleagues the important thing was that, if the men did not accept what we proposed, that we at least would have made a proposal which we could stand on. That I thought the advantage of the proposal made was that everyone could understand it—55 cents as a minimum wage, and we would have the public behind us and could keep the public in line on that basis. Immediately it was said that if we did this for men striking, we would then be met with similar demands by coal miners. . . .

"I again stressed the meeting of one situation at a time, and above all the wisdom of having a clear case which all could understand when we were discussing it. . . . I watched till a moment came when I thought I could close the discussion on the lines of the 55 cents minimum wage and what we had proposed yesterday regarding war industry and new board." It was also agreed to try to get McTague to be Chairman of the War Labour Board.

When the meeting with the representatives of management and workers was resumed Mackenzie King "stated what we felt we would be prepared to do if the men were immediately returned to work. . . . On the whole, it seemed to me that once I made the statement, there was relief with regard to the situation. The one question that came up was whether we could not allow the new Board to review the situation from the point of view of the cost of living. In other words, to take what we were proposing and to allow the Board to re-examine whether with conditions what they are in the two localities, the basic rate as then raised might not still be further raised. However as this touched the wage structure generally, it was felt by the members of Council we could not go that far. I myself would have been wholly prepared to, particularly as the men in the industries are frozen in their employment. They cannot get employment in another industry. It, therefore, is only right we should be perfectly sure that their living conditions are adequately met. It may yet come about that something of this sort will have to be agreed to."

Mackenzie King noted that he felt that if that point had been agreed to at that moment the strike "would have been settled there and then. However, when this was declined the representatives of the men of Algoma Steel made an impassioned speech about not being able to accept. . . . The representatives of Sydney made another impassioned speech indicating they could not expect their men to accept this. . . . The American representatives kept very quiet. Millard then summed up the situation in what I thought was a very fair way. He made it clear that the real thing which should be considered, namely, was the cost of living, and in relation to conditions at the two works.

"Mr. Cross [of Dosco] and Sir James Dunn [of Algoma Steel] spoke for the employers. Their attitude was rather that they had no difference with their employees; also that they would be embarrassed having to meet extra demands. They rather put it up to the Government to help both of them. . . .

"I then once again reminded all present about what I had said at the beginning of my remarks. Made clear that the Government had gone a long way in meeting the men before they returned to work. Also in trying to give to the leaders something sufficient to enable them to get the men back. That we had our responsibility to Parliament, and through Parliament, to the people, and had gone just as far as we believed circumstances would permit. That I hoped they might find it possible to accept the Government's terms, but to please realize that it would not be possible for the Government to go further. We would have to consider what course should be taken if the matter were not settled forthwith.

"Millard and others thanked me publicly for the patience that I had shown through the whole hearing. There was not an unpleasant word spoken, excepting by the two local leaders who evidently felt they ought to say something of the kind so as to tell their men when they got back what they had said. As we broke up, Millard and several of the workers shook hands with me in a very pleasant way. Everything considered, the conference I think was as good as we could hope for."

Mackenzie King "felt we had now a position which we could defend in Parliament and which would win for us the support of public opinion. Anything less, I believe, would have put us in the wrong before an impartial public opinion." He noted that "Millard was quite frank about saying that his difficulty was to be sure that the men would accept any suggestion from him to return to work after the long delay there had been in discussion. He wanted me to know that if he had to say anything publicly about the settlement, it would not be in any way against me personally, but just regarding the Government's attitude. I told him I thought he had handled his case very well. This seemed to please him very much. As a matter of fact, I was most agreeably surprised and pleased with the way he and the American representatives acted throughout." Immediately after this meeting a statement of the Government's offer was given to the press.

On January 22, Mackenzie King received from Millard "a very courteous letter with an enclosure agreeing with the Government's decision in principle, but suggesting clarification of clauses. The clarification suggested sought to enlarge the significance of the settlement beyond the companies concerned." When Mackenzie King told the

Cabinet of Millard's letter he found "an obvious change in attitude of some, particularly Howe. . . . They have all begun to see how very serious the situation is, and that the Government cannot simply dictate and use the big stick but must be conciliatory." A statement was worked out during the day, agreed to by the Cabinet in the afternoon, and given to MacNamara to discuss with Millard and his two American associates. The terms of the statement "were not wholly acceptable to them. Some further modifications desired re letting National Labour Board consider representations re cost of living." Therefore, "to save time and help bring matters to a conclusion," Mackenzie King went personally to the office of the Minister of Labour and helped to work out "a final draft which MacNamara felt would be accepted. He had allowed the men to leave. 'Phoned them the final draft which they said they would accept. I then signed the letter enclosing the draft. Except by taking the matter in hand myself, I doubt if this could have been settled at this time. St. Laurent was particularly helpful. Mitchell was wholly in agreement with the last revision."

Mackenzie King again noted, on January 25, his feeling "that the strike would not have been settled but for my taking the matter in hand as I did, and the confidence which the men had in me. That is a fine tribute to have come after some forty years of identification with labour problems."

Meanwhile, Mackenzie King had asked Judge McTague to become Chairman of the National War Labour Board. He met McTague and Humphrey Mitchell on the morning of February 2, when "McTague outlined the changes which he thought should be made in the War Labour Board to make its proceedings successful. I liked exceedingly his whole attitude toward the problems of labour. As he said to me over the 'phone, our minds run on parallel lines on that subject. He wanted to have proceedings in the open, himself and two others to constitute the Board and the present Board, more or less of partisans, to be an Advisory Committee. He desired to build up a sort of labour jurisprudence. . . . I agreed to McTague's suggestions at once, Mitchell also agreeing." Later that day, to the Cabinet, Mackenzie King outlined the discussions he had had with McTague and Mitchell. "Ilsley once again put forward the doctrine that even if there were injustice in the wage stabilization policy, we would have to continue injustice if the policy itself were to be maintained. I said quite openly that such a basis could not be supported in public. I went on to show that he was taking much too rigid an interpretation of what was involved in the relations between wage stabilization and price ceiling." The Cabinet eventually approved the suggestions for the new Board. "Fortunately Howe came in on his return from Boston in time to give complete approval to what McTague had suggested. He has come to see the need for a man like McTague and the wisdom of his attitude. I strongly advocated making all war industries, national industries. The Government has completely agreed to this." As it turned out, the new National War Labour Board did succeed in making minor wage adjustments without destroying the stabilization policy or the price ceiling.

In the new and more agreeable political atmosphere of 1943, Mackenzie King first began to consider the possibility of continuing in public life after the war. George Graham who had contested the Liberal leadership in 1919 and later served in his Government died on January 2. His death brought Mackenzie King third from the top of the list of Canadian Privy Councillors. On January 3, he wrote, "extraordinarily significant is the fact that, of the two preceding, Sir William Mulock was the one who was responsible for my coming into the public service and Aylesworth the one who nominated me as leader of the party. . . . If I should outlive Mulock and Aylesworth and still be in office, I will be, with the exception of Sir John Macdonald, the only Privy Councillor who has been at the head of the list of the P.C.'s of Canada while still holding the office of Prime Minister. When one thinks of what I have had to endure in the way of detraction from the very beginning of my public life, it would certainly appear that there are forces at work much more real and enduring than those which appear on the surface."

On January 4 he "was very much hurt" on reading an article in *Harper's Magazine* by Professor E. K. Brown who had spent six months on his secretarial staff earlier in the war. What Brown had sought to do was to give an objective portrait of Mackenzie King. But the Prime Minister felt it was unfair and held him up to ridicule. Brown, he wrote, "was trying to show that the public had one point of view whereas, in reality, if they knew me, they would find I was quite different. In seeking to make his contrast, he fell into the error of painting one side solely as it is represented by Tory propaganda. He even went the length of speaking of my being disliked in all the English provinces." Mackenzie King never ceased to resent this article of Brown's. On January 7 he noted: "I have been thinking a good deal in the last forty-eight hours about the future. In part perhaps as a result of the effect of Brown's article and the sort of talk to which it will give rise." He added that, on the way to George Graham's funeral, Ian Mackenzie had told him that what he believed "the party would like and would be best for the country would be for me to lead the party through another general election. To make the post-war programme of social reform, and the peace conference, the main subject of appeal. That it would be a natural rounding out of my life-work. . . . I agreed with him that nothing could more completely please me if I had the physical strength and endurance; that I was not anxious to stay on were I to become, in any way, impaired in health or lose mental vigour."

The next day (January 8) Mackenzie King heard that Bracken's main reason for taking the Conservative leadership was the hope of becoming Prime Minister of Canada, and that he had been "asked by Meighen if he knew what was being offered. That it was the premiership of Canada. . . . I would be surprised if he would be able to hold the different people together till the time of an election or if he would be able to realize his ambition even if he and several Conservatives were elected. The chances were there would be four parties, not one of which would be able to command a majority in the House. The party with which others would be least apt to ally themselves would be the Conservative party."

At this time Mackenzie King had more or less set August 7, 1944, the twenty-fifth anniversary of his leadership, as the date for his retirement, but he was already hoping to have a part in shaping post-war policy. On January 10, he read a speech by Sir William Beveridge referring to "Lloyd George, the leader of the last war, having been responsible for old age pensions; Churchill, leader of the present war, having been responsible for introducing unemployment insurance, and added that Churchill might round out his career by getting through health insurance or the entire social security programme. That programme I made very much my own from the days I was Deputy Minister of Labour. It is all set out in my *Industry and Humanity*. I should be happy indeed if I could round out my career with legislation in the nature of social security." To the Cabinet, on January 12, he pointed out the need for social security legislation at the forthcoming session of Parliament or, if not legislation, consideration of a future programme. At this same meeting, he "pressed strongly for the appointment of parliamentary under-secretaries, or assistants to Ministers from among M.P.'s. The necessity of bringing younger men to the understanding of problems and particularly having a group of Assistant Ministers who would be thinking in terms of post-war aspect of the situation, while Ministers themselves were giving most attention to the winning of the war."

There was the same emphasis on the post-war programme and social security in the drafting of the Speech from the Throne. Mackenzie King noted on January 24: "I had, this morning, worked out a good part of the speech on social insurance speaking of the need of a charter for social insurance in Canada. Made use of my *Industry and Humanity*. Indeed was impressed to see how completely the whole outline was to be found there. It looks as though I am to have the privilege of completing the circle of federal social security measures which, with the exception of the Annuities Bill, I was responsible for beginning. . . . It should really help to mark an epoch in development of Liberal policy in Canada."

Mackenzie King had the draft speech considered by the Cabinet on January 26, and "got through without question the statement of a national plan of social insurance to be charter of social security for the whole of Canada. A magnificent declaration . . . of Liberal policy than which nothing could be better."

As the session approached Mackenzie King was interested in knowing who would actually lead the Opposition in the House of Commons. Bracken, the leader of the national party, had as yet no seat in the House. On January 19 he had arrived in Ottawa and called on Mackenzie King, who had found him "very easy and pleasant to talk with. He looked to be considerably older and strained. I said to him that I thought he was a pretty courageous man to take this job on at his years. I also said I thought he had a pretty difficult reactionary wing to deal with. He said he had never taken a party part in politics. That he was just interested in the public service. He would not be afraid of the extreme wing in his party, as he had laid down his own conditions there. Said he was no debater and speaker, and would find the House of Commons difficult. I told him anything I could do to help him in any way would be very gladly done. He and I could talk all matters over in the frankest way. I asked him when he was coming into the House. He said he did not think much of the offer I had made. [Mackenzie King had offered to call a by-election in Selkirk, Manitoba, which was vacant as a result of the appointment of J. T. Thorson to the Exchequer Court.] I said it was the only thing we had to offer. . . . His whole attitude was completely friendly and rather provoked sympathy. I agree that he will find the whole situation for a time very trying. I told him that I had really expected that when he came to Ottawa it would be with us rather than to be with others."

Mackenzie King heard on January 26 that Hanson had had a heart attack and "rang him up at the Chateau before leaving the office, and went over to see him. I confess he looked to me as though he might pass away at any moment. We had quite a long and pleasant talk together. . . . When I asked him about the session, he told me that he did not feel equal to continuing the leadership of his party [in the House]. That he really had never wanted it. That he was pressed into it at the start. . . . That he had told the party over and over again he did not want to stay. Was only doing so because there was no one else. . . . He did not know when Bracken would take over."

Hanson then said he expected a new House leader would be chosen and they had some talk about Meighen's defeat in South York the year before, during which Mackenzie King told Hanson "that it was Mitchell Hepburn who had defeated Meighen." Hanson mentioned as possible successors to himself, Graydon, Green, and Diefenbaker. Mackenzie King observed: "I would myself prefer their appointment in the order mentioned. The Tories seldom choose a decent man. They are likely to take Diefenbaker as being the most bitter in his attacks. On the other hand, Bracken's coming in may make a difference, and Graydon may be chosen."

The next day (January 27) Mackenzie King heard "over the radio that Hanson had definitely retired from the leadership of the party and that Graydon had been appointed to succeed him. I felt greatly relieved and pleased at this word. Tried to get Graydon by 'phone but could not reach him. I could not but think of how completely my political enemies had been confounded as a result of the policy determined upon, shortly before this time a year ago, and how completely that policy had been vindicated and how different the situation on the eve of this session to that on the eve of the last." He recalled "the defeat of Arthur Meighen who had left the Senate to usurp the leadership of the Conservative party with a view of destroying myself and others in the Government at Ottawa. Have seen his retirement from public life. Seen Hepburn resign leadership of party in Ontario and help to defeat Meighen in Toronto. Have come now to where the Leader of the Opposition, Hanson, another of the old guard, has retired. A temporary leader appointed and a new leader of the Conservative party chosen from outside the party altogether—one who had not yet found a seat in the House of Commons. There never was a more complete confounding of the politics of one's enemies than is exhibited by this debacle of the old Tory party which has tried to cover up its disasters by giving itself a new name. In one round, while they have been talking of my not being a leader, I have succeeded, after defeating Bennett as the leader of the Conservative party, his successor Manion as the next leader, Manion's successor Meighen as the next leader, and now witnessing the fourth leader, in the last few years, without a seat in the House."

A Time of New Beginnings

The session of Parliament opened on January 28, and the next day Walter Harris and Maurice Hallé, both in uniform, made "splendid speeches" in moving and seconding the Address in reply to the Speech from the Throne. Mackenzie King "felt proud to see these two men in uniform from different provinces standing together as a symbol of the unity of our country in its fight for freedom." On the following Monday Mackenzie King spoke extemporaneously on the Address. There never was an opening which he took more calmly.

He found the atmosphere in the House in the opening days very tranquil. He was relieved but a little saddened by a speech by Cardin on February 9, which, he wrote, "made clear he had lost ground. It gave evidence of a man who had become soured. Also who . . . went out of his way to misinterpret intention of the Government regarding Orders-in-Council calling out men under the Mobilization Act for outlying parts of the country. He was trying to square himself for what he said last session but was clearly creating prejudice. Without realizing it, he destroyed the whole isolationist position by saying that the dear Chinese were fighting for Canada . . . that but for the Russians, we in Canada would be signing a peace not of our own making, thereby making perfectly clear that unless the enemy is destroyed overseas, our position is gone. Yet he closed by making an appeal which in tone related to colonial days. . . . He did not rouse any of his own following. Got very little applause. I felt sorry for him. It was like witnessing a spent force."

His reaction was very different to a speech made the same day by Brooke Claxton, who, he thought, did "remarkably well. Had practical suggestions to make whereby the business of the House could be more realistic in relation to concrete problems. The speech gave evidence of lots of study; careful preparation and his style of speaking has greatly improved. I felt satisfied I would not make a mistake if I appointed him my Assistant as President of Council." The actual appointment was not made until May 6. Mackenzie King told Claxton his appointment was "due to his own industry" and the fact "that he worked well with officers around my own department. Told him to master all that related to Boards and Committees coming under President of Council and to be prepared to make statements in the House on them. He was most appreciative."

On February 18, Cardin moved a vote of want of confidence calling for the suspension of call-ups for military service, and Power suggested that the best way to meet it was for Mackenzie King to speak at once, because "my name was stronger in Quebec than any other force, and . . . if I could deal with the amendment and tell our men that I wanted to know where they stood, I would rally the Quebec members better in that way than they could be rallied by anything the other Ministers might say. I agreed to do what was wished."

The next day (February 19) Mackenzie King noted that "after Pouliot had spoken in the debate, I rose immediately to answer Cardin's speech and to expose the significance of the amendment. I spoke practically without any reference to the notes that I had. Found it very easy to present what I had to say and made quite a strong appeal. In the course of what I was saying, I was roundly applauded by our own men and indeed from different sides of the House. When I got through, I got a tremendous ovation and notes began coming in from different Members, very strong in their approval of what I had said.

"I was delighted to find that our own French-Canadian following were pleased with the line I had taken. It really came down to a matter whether Cardin's leadership in Quebec was to be recognized above that of my leadership in the Dominion. Cardin's amendment was really an easy one to deal with. I think what I said was a bit devastating with respect to it. The course taken bore out what I have been feeling so strongly of late that I have been ruining my real capacity to speak and to impress the House by using manuscript, which would keep the record foolproof at the same time leaving to posterity a record that could be defended through time, rather than convincing one's contemporaries and gaining the enthusiasm of one's contemporaries in support of Government's policies through expounding them in a manner which would make a popular appeal."

He added that "the House was alive with recognition. It was interesting to see how quickly the whole Parliament Buildings became alive over the speeches that had been made, and then men began talking of it as the best speech I had ever made, etc. It cost me less in effort and preparation than any speech delivered since I have been leader of the party."

Cardin's motion was defeated on February 23 by a vote of 195 to 15. "The effect," Mackenzie King wrote, "has been to destroy Cardin's influence both in the House and in the Province of Quebec and worse, to destroy it throughout the rest of Canada. . . . He cannot form any party of his own after this. All his own fault. He should never have moved a want of confidence motion. He showed wrong feeling and spirit in so doing. Cardin was followed by [J. S.] Roy who brought in an amendment in regard to Dr. Shields of Toronto and his propaganda. [Shields was a fundamentalist Baptist preacher in Toronto whose attacks on Catholics and French Canadians from the pulpit were greatly resented in Quebec.] It threatened to be very embarrassing to the Quebec members. I had to do the best I could in thinking up a few things to say. The Speaker had said it was in order. I took the line that there was a time and place for everything, and that to begin the debate on race and religious prejudices was the worst thing that could be done in the House at this time of war. . . . The effect was to end the debate and happily to get a vote which left the Government with a better majority than ever— 194 to 8."

Mackenzie King did not find the new Progressive Conservative Opposition very formidable. On February 12, he told Graydon "I thought Conservatives had made a mistake in not appointing him at once the leader of the party. That I believed he would yet come to be the leader. He said the public wanted someone with experience. I reminded him that I came into the premiership without much experience save that gained in Laurier's Administration, defeating Meighen who had been at the head of a war administration. I said I thought his party had succeeded in making two parties: the progressives and the continuing conservatives. He spoke to me about my own public life as he saw it. That I have never said anything unkind about anyone. Also never had attacked anyone, and only when some unfair advantage was taken of me, gave back something of what the occasion seemed to merit. I told him I had never cared for personalities in public life, and saw no necessity for them. Believed apart from this, men went further who were conciliatory and most interested in the subject itself. I said I believed he would have a long and useful career. He had shown real ability in his position as leader and that I hoped, some years hence, he would remember what I was now saying to him."

Mackenzie King noted on February 17 that "very shortly after the opening of this session, a gentleman . . . who is a great friend of John Bracken's, came to me to say that he thought Bracken and I ought to try to get together. That he knew positively that Bracken would be prepared to work with me, and that he felt we were the only two men who could carry on the government of the country in the next few years. This man told me that he had talked matters over with Bracken though he was not coming from him to me direct. I simply said that Bracken and I had always been friends and that time alone would indicate what the developments might be. Bracken was now the leader of the Conservative party which I thought he would find it difficult to lead. I want to make this of record as being of interest, particularly as Bracken expects to keep out of Parliament until the election comes on. He will get pretty tired of that before another year rolls by."

On March 5, Mackenzie King "had Graydon and his wife to dinner" at Laurier House. They "had an exceedingly pleasant evening. A delightful talk at the table after which I showed them over the house, and we then had a very pleasant talk in the library. . . . Mrs. Graydon said her father would be tremendously proud to see her motoring with me in the P.M.'s car, as we drove along. She has been brought up a very strong Liberal. Is, herself, a charming person. Graydon is equally pleasant and charming. To my mind, he is the right man to lead the Conservative party. Would be the best choice, 100 per cent better than Bracken. . . .

"Both he and his wife said that I could not begin to know what a happiness it had been to them. I assured them it was an equal happiness to me, as it certainly was."

On March 16, Mackenzie King had Stuart Garson, "the leader of the Liberal party in Manitoba, to dinner." He "was very favourably impressed with Garson and confess felt more impressed with Bracken's character as disclosed by Garson who knows him intimately. The situation as recounted by Garson, of experiences of Bracken's Government when in minority, very similar to some I had in similar circumstances."

At the Liberal caucus on March 24, Mackenzie King "spoke for about half an hour very emphatically on the questions of elections and social security matters. . . . I said that this week would witness the third anniversary of the greatest Liberal victory in the history of the party; that, for the life of me, I could not see why, with the largest majority any Government had had at its back, anyone should be thinking in terms of an election this year, while the war was on; that I would not say there would be no election, because one never knew what developments might come, but, so far as I was concerned, there were only two things that would cause me to ask for a dissolution: one was that if differences should develop in our own ranks which would make it difficult to carry on government; and the other, if the Opposition parties, combined possibly with some of our own party, would make matters so difficult that the Government could not carry on its war efforts satisfactorily. As an alternative to dissolution, I might take the step of resignation myself, leaving it to someone else to take the responsibility of leadership, giving them what assistance I might. That we had come dangerously near one or other of those courses last year, and I hoped nothing of the kind would arise again. I said that opponents claim my main interest was in keeping the party in power—in other words, keeping myself in office, and that, if they only knew the truth, I was very far from desiring continuing in office, except from the imperative duty of so doing. I looked upon the party not as an end in itself, but as a means to an end. I did not want to keep the party in office unless I thought it was the best instrument for carrying on government . . . all I wanted from now on was to see the war won and, until that happened, everything else was wholly secondary. I said if the war was not won, none of us would be returned at an election. If it [the war] should result in a stalemate, the present Government will certainly not be returned. If we have a victory, I thought that was the time to speak of an election. The Government that could carry through a war to a successful victory would stand a good chance of gaining the confidence of the people over experimenters and different groups. I made it clear that victory was the only thing that counted and that what all of us should do was to work as never before toward that end.

"Speaking of social security, I said I would never allow an appeal to the people on social security measures at a time of war with a view to bribing them to support the Government because of what it would pay out of the public treasury. They must realize the real nature of what was involved in a social security programme. It was social revolution. . . . That this could not be done in a day, but would take years. . . . It was wrong to think of increased outlays on anything that could be avoided until victory was won. Important, however, to keep everything in readiness for the peace." Mackenzie King was told after the caucus that it was one of the best the party had had.

The magnitude of the financial outlays for war gave Mackenzie King a good deal of concern early in 1943. He had not been impressed, at the outset, by Ilsley's proposal for Mutual Aid (the Canadian equivalent of American Lend-Lease) which was first discussed at the War Committee on January 13. He expressed the view that Canada was taking on "more than the nation was capable of carrying and told him [Ilsley] I thought his measure would meet much more opposition in Parliament than he believed." When the Cabinet considered the Mutual Aid proposal again on January 22, "all members of the Cabinet approved this measure as a very important one. Neither Ilsley nor Ralston were present but both had advocated it before. Indeed it was Ilsley's measure. I was surprised at the unanimity, and doubly so at the favourable attitude of the Quebec Members in the light of the opposition there was last year."

The War Appropriation Bill was discussed in Cabinet on February 19, when "Ilsley made it clear he would not allow expenditures beyond $5½ billions. The Defence Departments had cut down their expenditures, but were reserving the right to say that they might run beyond the figures given." Mackenzie King took the position "that Parliament would not support the Government in larger expenditures. Indeed I felt we would have tremendous difficulty as it is." He added he was "not sorry that Ilsley, on the one hand, has found that he has let the defence forces go too far, nor, on the other, that they themselves have seen they have gone too far. It has at least put a stop to attempts at going further for a while. I have done my utmost to meet requests of the defence forces which should be met. Now all have seen that we have gone the limit. I have been prepared to support matters as far as we can; doing all we possibly can to make our effort a total one."

At the War Committee meeting on February 24 "there was a very tense discussion between Ilsley and the Ministers of Defence. All see now that they have got into a well-nigh impossible position. Ilsley has allowed expenditures by leaps and bounds on the theory that his Department could provide the finances up to any figure to meet a total war effort. He has now to provide for five and a half billion dollars. Ministers' estimates would run him past that considerably and Ministers of Defence refuse to cut down. In some directions saying their commitments will not permit of this. . . . He finally said that he would not, no matter what happened, agree to expenditures above the total figure. I backed Ilsley strongly and said I felt sure the House of Commons would be behind him rather than the Defence Ministers. We were going to have very great difficulty in defending amounts called for. The hardest thing to defend will be the billion dollar expenditure for materials for United Nations [Mutual Aid] when there is not enough money to provide for our own forces first. . . . Between the demand now for men as well as for money, we have reached a ceiling that pretty well settles the question of any attempt at any further conscripting of men for overseas service. That issue has been silenced by holding the fort for a year. . . .

"It was really in some ways the most trying of any of the situations I have seen in the Cabinet. I sometimes wonder whether Ilsley may not break entirely with what he has undertaken. He told me later that he has never known a time when everyone seemed so bitter against everyone else." Mackenzie King "thought it best to hold over, for this week, any statement by Ilsley in Parliament. He was anxious to debate the War Appropriation measure at once. I told him and the Cabinet I thought he should get down the Budget first."

At the Cabinet meeting on February 26 the Budget was discussed, and Mackenzie King felt that the Budget resolutions amounted "pretty nearly to a revolution in the order of things as they have been in the past." This was the Budget which raised taxation to the wartime peak. When the Budget was presented to the House on March 2, Mackenzie King noted that "Ilsley was in remarkably good form. . . . He was very much in earnest in parts of the delivery. Seemed to be greatly pleased and, naturally so, when it was over. I shook his hand and congratulated him warmly at the conclusion of his speech. On the whole, the House accepted the Budget remarkably well. I doubt if any number really understood what it meant, particularly the portion relating to income."

His own assessment of the great burden on the Canadian people made Mackenzie King all the more grateful for a message from Churchill he received in reply to one he had sent him about a recent illness. Churchill sent "to all members of the Parliament of Canada my heartfelt thanks. I recall with gratitude the warmth of the reception which you all gave me when I visited Canada in December 1941. In the darkest days Canada, under your leadership, remained confident and true. Now the days are brighter and when victory is won, you will be able to look back with just pride upon a record surpassed by none."

One subject which gave Mackenzie King no satisfaction was the continuing opposition to the Wartime Alcoholic Beverages Order of December 1942 and the pressure for relaxing it. On January 15, Premier Godbout had come to see him about the effect on the Quebec weekly papers of the loss of liquor advertising and urged that it be permitted with "the firm using its name for furthering war effort purposes. I said that the matter would have to be dealt with by the Cabinet, and I thought probably by a Committee of the Commons. That the brewers had opened up the battle themselves, and had put me and the Government in the position where we were being asked, at their instance, to withdraw or alter our policy. They had taken this course. They had only themselves to thank if they had made it impossible for the Government to alter it." Mackenzie King told Godbout "frankly it was an outrage to think that the Government and its policies would have to be governed by a press that would only express its views as the liquor interests might dictate."

Later in January, Premier Conant of Ontario arranged a meeting of representatives from all the provinces who saw the Cabinet on January 28 to discuss losses of provincial revenue resulting from the restrictions on the supply of alcoholic beverages. Mackenzie King reported that "most of the Premiers took no exception to the principle but wanted to be compensated for their losses."

At the Cabinet meeting on February 2, some of the Ministers supported the representations of "provincial Ministers as to allowing the brewers to sell an additional amount of beer to prevent their year's balance running out before the close of the year," and the need of enabling "working-men to get beer and keep them contented in industry." This was the same meeting that had been considering the new terms of the War Labour Board and Mackenzie King told his colleagues "this Council makes me laugh; opposing labour in its efforts to have just treatment, and in the next breath, pleading for the rights of the poor working-man to have his beer. . . . I got the overwhelming support of Council against making any concession to the brewers."

Notwithstanding this decision, Mackenzie King did later agree to some concessions. On February 19, the Alcoholic Beverages Order was amended to permit public relations advertising by brewers and distillers. This did not satisfy those who wished the Order more drastically amended. The Cabinet, on February 23, discussed the "question of allowing a larger sale of beer because of supply for year being so short, owing to large sales at Christmas and hoarding. Practically the whole Cabinet urged that I should agree to a larger distribution. Argument put forth that working-men were wearing buttons 'no beer—no bonds.' I said the way to deal with that matter was to have the police prosecute those who were responsible as interfering with the war effort. Was told the police were already being instructed to look into that. Ilsley was very strong for need not to interfere with Victory Loan sale. Howe spoke of possibility of men refusing work in war industries. It was apparent that the sales have been arranged so as to embarrass things as much as possible in some of the provinces. I was told all would be quite smooth and satisfactory once this larger allowance was permitted. I held out positively against any change that would increase the amount." When Colin Gibson showed Mackenzie King a pile of protests he had, the Prime Minister said he would agree to a further change to increase the quantity of beer available for sale if Howe made the request. The matter was held over for further consideration later in the week. Meanwhile he had telephoned two leading members of the temperance organizations, to indicate that it might be necessary to make some concessions to the pressure. He noted that "they saw the reasonableness of my attitude and agreed to it. It was an immense relief to me to have this assurance from them."

When the subject was raised again at the Cabinet meeting on February 26, Mackenzie King told "Council I had given the matter much thought and was prepared to sign the Order-in-Council as drafted but would not agree to any change which would permit of a larger consumption of beer than that provided for [in this Amendment]. I then came out with the announcement of my intention, if there was any trouble, to advocate the nationalizing of the whole brewing business. I said we could do all this under the War Measures Act; if beer were needed for the troops, we could supply it in that way; if needed to avoid riots, we could supply it, and would have control of revenues to be derived from these sales." There was some further discussion but Mackenzie King made his position "so strong and plain that no member of Council said anything further. I signed the Order [increasing the supply of beer for 1943 to allow for accumulation before rationing was started by the provinces] and that was all there was to it." Later that day he told one of the provincial Ministers from Quebec "that even for Godbout, I could not undertake to go further than I had."

On March 2, Mackenzie King was "much hurt to read statement made by Rev. John Coburn, to the Ministerial Association, telling of private conversation with myself re abstinence during war period and particularly reference to Winston Churchill. A perfectly shocking breach of confidence. Specially in the light of my request to him in a recent letter to say nothing of the matter at any public gathering. At noon received wire from Coburn saying that statement was breach of confidence done by reporter against instructions. That does not undo the mischief and harm. To begin with, the statement as referred to by the press carries a wholly erroneous inference; seemed to indicate that I had been other than abstemious all my life. However these are the thorns in the crown which a man wears while he is in public life."

The next day (March 3) "when the House opened Dr. Bruce of Toronto started to try to put on Hansard the press item relating to what Coburn had said to the Ministerial Association in London. I saw at once what [he] had in mind which was to get this on Hansard and give publicity by provoking a reply which would lead to further discussion. When I saw what he was seeking to do, I rose to my feet at once and prevented his getting the item on Hansard. I did so, in no uncertain terms, saying that I did not propose to allow him to advertise himself by what he was seeking to do. The House was with me. They all thoroughly dislike him and supported the Speaker in not letting him proceed." Mackenzie King added that the question of restricting alcoholic beverages was "the most difficult I have had to deal with, both in the Cabinet as well as outside, this year." And the trouble was not over.

The newspapers on March 10 "contained another speech by Coburn in which he disclosed what I had said privately about the people serving cocktails. It just served to revive the whole business that I thought had been settled about private conversations, and one more thorn to bear at the time when one is overworked and overtired." He telephoned Coburn and asked him to "say nothing more about any talks with myself, which he promised to do."

The next day (March 12) Mackenzie King and several of his colleagues received Premier Conant and two of his colleagues who came "to tell of their difficulties in administering the rationing of beer. They brought with them pictures of line-ups at shops, and told of the great difficulties they were having. It all came down, in the end, to an appeal to let the rationing process begin from the 1st of January and not be dated back [to December 16]. They are prepared to compel the sale of beer per bottles and on the basis of having a ration card. I pointed out that the purpose of our policy was to restrict the sale of beverages, and outlined the very easy way, the extremely generous way in which the brewers had been treated. I told them I was prepared to nationalize the whole brewing business. . . . I felt some case was made out with regard to the over-selling during the three months after my speech and before rationing, but gave them no promise."

On March 18, Mackenzie King "spent the forenoon trying to draft a message to the Ontario Premier, Conant, regarding the request of his Government to have local regulations re sale of beer relaxed. Brought the matter up in Council. Said I disliked having to bring up the subject again. I read Conant's letter and said I proposed, unless colleagues took an opposite view, to point out the Government's policy was to curtail the sale of alcoholic beverages; that less cut had been made in sales of beer than with wines or spirits, and give other reasons why request for larger sales should not be permitted." Though there was a good deal of dissent, Mackenzie King "finally told the Cabinet I would send the answer I had suggested and went on with other business." The next day (March 19), Mackenzie King completed his letter to Conant "refusing extension of any increased allowance of beer. Glad to get this out of the way today. The Ontario Government shows surplus of over ten millions and budgeting for another ten millions, some seven million actual revenue from liquor."

At the Liberal caucus on March 24, Mackenzie King referred to "all the fuss" over beer and pointed out that the Canadian restrictions were much smaller than the British and that "we had not lessened the strength; all we had done was to take 10 per cent off an amount which had increased 60 per cent since the war. I did not see how we could have done less and done anything at all.

"I then told caucus that I had become so accustomed to detraction and vilification and the like throughout my many years of public life, that anything of the kind did not affect me in the least; that I would not be found yielding to pressure of the kind. . . . It was much wiser to hold to the position we had taken than to count on ever satisfying the liquor interests. I said what was important was that the people should know whether we were a Government controlled by these interests or not." That was the end of the matter for several months.

On March 26, Mackenzie King went to Montreal to attend the funeral of Sir Edward Beatty, for many years President of the Canadian Pacific Railway. He recalled that the last time he had talked to Beatty "he had come to Ottawa . . . to speak to me about taking Bennett into the Cabinet." He felt there were "many parallels in Beatty's life and my own. It seemed in a way to possess me pretty strongly today. The fact that neither of us have been married but have lived our lives in our work— one in industry and the commercial; the other in the political. Both interested, at heart, in matters of social well-being, public service in different forms. I wish I had made my life as broad as his in its different interests, but perhaps in the wider interests of politics it has, in the end, had this larger significance. We have both, I think, cared but little for what is known as social life and have retained a sense of perspective, a certain humility, and have not been carried away into self-assertion, but owe what we have had in the way of position and the like to character based on the early training we have had, and religious conviction and faith."

Though the conscription issue was no longer active, there were other manpower problems to face in 1943. In the War Committee meeting on April 14, there was "a very trying discussion on the question of manpower. Howe had put in an extremely strong letter stating he could not continue to take responsibility for the Department of Munitions and Supply if he could not get men for coal mines, basic industry of lumbering, etc. Ralston was just as determined in the opposite direction that there should be no further sheltering of men in other industries. . . . The question came down to a matter of a few thousand coal miners and metal miners. . . . To save a very difficult scene, I suggested we meet again on Friday with the Minister of Labour and Deputy Minister present."

There was another very heated discussion over the question at the War Committee meeting on April 16. "Ralston is determined not to allow any man to be exempt from calling up but [is] giving way on their periodical recalling so far as miners are concerned. Howe equally strong on insisting that no more coal miners should be called up. Also workers in basic metal industries. Mitchell and MacNamara were present and they, too, joined with Howe and the rest of the Cabinet against Ralston, all feeling that we were threatened with a serious coal shortage next winter. . . . I think Ralston is extremely difficult to deal with on these matters, unyielding; will have to climb down by degrees. Howe again threatened he would not stay in the Government to take the responsibility for the situation he saw ahead unless given immediate relief. Mitchell and MacNamara seemed to feel they could work out the necessary adjustments."

The dispute was not finally settled that day and came up again before the War Committee on May 5, when the discussion was "almost exclusively on the need for miners for coal. Ralston is extraordinarily obdurate in this matter. I feel too that both Power and Macdonald support Ralston too strongly. I feel we are sending far too many men overseas, and that we have not sufficiently guarded the home needs which will prove to be the basis of war needs. One had to fight almost singlehanded when it comes to trying to control this situation. Some progress was made in helping to keep miners at work in the mines and to get them back out of industry, and to prevent their going from now on into the armed services, but I feel we should have gone much further."

The discussion was resumed by the Cabinet on May 11 when Mackenzie King "read Howe's letter to Cabinet re coal miners. I intend to have a show of hands at the meeting of Council later in the week so that each individual would have to take his responsibility for or against getting men into the coal mines at all costs. There has been far too much chattering back and forth and seeking to make me responsible for the decision.

"I outlined an Order-in-Council the Selective Service had prepared. Read their request for further consideration before it was passed. Council agreed to this. . . . I then gave Cabinet fully to understand that it would be on the shoulders of all, and the majority would decide. I think this will leave the Defence Ministers pretty much alone in their efforts to keep drawing men in the army and other services when they are more needed for basic industries than anything else.

"I told Council of my own view which was that the whole war effort was dependent on the success of the basic industries, . . . and that we must, at all costs, avoid fuel famine in Canada. . . . I think what was said today will cause others to settle up difficulties meanwhile."

On May 14, "the morning was spent in discussing mostly the shortage of coal problem. . . . The Defence Department as well as the officials had taken advantage of the warning I gave last night that I would demand a show of hands, if necessary today, on determining our policy. They had gone a long way in making concessions above what they intended originally to make. On the other hand, Howe made it abundantly plain the situation we were facing was much graver than, up to the present, we had had reason to believe. When the whole Cabinet were present, I had MacNamara, of the Labour Department, and Henry Borden, of Howe's Department, come in and sit with us. I took up the draft Order-in-Council which had been prepared as a result of what was settled at the last meeting."

In the course of the discussion, Mackenzie King recalled the coal famine in western Canada on which he had reported in 1906. He felt this reminder "helped all members to realize how terrible was the situation with which Canada would be faced if we did not meet the fuel shortage in time. It helped me to get through the Order in the end. I kept waiting till I saw the whole Cabinet practically united. . . . I got the Order through with the support of all present, excepting Ralston, who said he would still have to differ from the rest of the Cabinet. However I had been successful in preventing any acrimonious discussion and getting the Order through without a show of hands which I really think was a triumph, all considered."

Throughout the early months of 1943, Mackenzie King was frequently concerned with the plight of the Liberal party provincially in Ontario. During February there were rumours of an election and also of a convention to choose a new leader. On February 23, Mackenzie King had a talk with Arthur Roebuck, a Liberal M.P. from Toronto, who "made it clear that he was going to seek the leadership of the province. Seemed to feel he would be able to win and said there would be utmost co-operation with Ottawa if he did. He thought Harry Nixon was too weak. I told him I had a high regard for Nixon and felt that what was really necessary was for the two of them to work together in a campaign. He was prepared to offer Nixon anything he wanted in the Government, if he won."

On March 27 Harry Nixon came to see Mackenzie King about the forthcoming Liberal provincial convention. Nixon thought the contest would be between himself and Roebuck with Conant coming third. Mackenzie King told Nixon he would have to maintain neutrality as all were friends, "and I would naturally wish to continue to share the confidence of each. He said at once that, of course, that was what he would himself expect. He did not ask me in any way to support him by speaking to others, but said he was anxious to get my opinion on one or two things. What he was particularly anxious about was whether an election should come immediately after the convention. I told him, without any hesitation, the sooner he brought the election, the better. On no account to be led to extend the life of the Legislature another year. I said I had reason to feel that the Government would be quite safe in appealing to the people before mid-summer as anyone could see that the length of the fight in Africa, submarine menace, etc., rendered extremely unlikely any probability of invasion of Europe until later at least in the year."

Mackenzie King advised Nixon "to devote a good deal of time to the preparation of his address for the convention, to make clear that the people were sick of personalities, and wanted government based on principles and policies. To lay great emphasis on the rights of the people as the source of all government, constitutional issue; not to try to imitate anyone else but to be himself. . . .

"He had heard that he himself was not colourful enough as a leader.

I said that had been said of me more than of anyone. I had managed to get the largest majority of any leader for the reasons I had mentioned to him. I told him not to make specific promises but to hold to generalities. To make clear the war must be won first; that everything would have to be shaped in the light of events but to promise honest government and hold to his interest in the people. He, himself, is looking very much better. Says it is a tremendous relief to be rid of the incessant wrangles they have had in the Cabinet. He said on no account would he let Hepburn participate in his campaign or give him any support. I think he is the man who deserves to be chosen."

Premier Conant also came to see Mackenzie King who told him "I thought it unwise for me to take any part in the convention and proceedings, or to indicate any preferences; that all were friends of mine. He agreed that that was the only course for me to take. It was really pathetic his appeal for understanding and sympathy, having regard specially for the way he joined in with Hepburn against myself."

The Ontario Liberal convention was held at the end of April. Mackenzie King noted in his diary for April 30 that "the event of the day—one of real significance in the history of the Liberal party and to me personally—was the Liberal convention in Ontario which opened yesterday. Hepburn was said to be in the city [Toronto] but to have been 'gotten out'—or away. His resignation as leader of the party was handed in to the convention by Harry Johnston, the Secretary; he sent no word or letter—no acknowledgment to the party of any kind for their support of him—in all his shortcomings—Conant who had accepted the premiership 'at his hands' and has held office arbitrarily ever since, had a nervous collapse during the early morning and was taken to the Toronto General Hospital—withdrew his candidature—evidently saw quite clearly he had no chance for the leadership and would be defeated on the balloting so he, too, was not present at the convention."

Mackenzie King was greatly pleased by the news that Nixon had won the leadership by a wide margin on the first ballot. "The whole affair," he wrote, "is a remarkable evidence of the moral forces that work in the unseen realm, and of the vindication of right in the end. It has taken a long time to get Hepburn and his gang out of the control of the party's affairs, but they have each in turn killed themselves, beginning with Hepburn himself. Nixon, the man who has been most outspoken in his support of myself, . . . is now the leader by an overwhelming majority."

He added that "it was a King-Hepburn battle so far as the province generally was concerned, with a complete routing of all the Hepburn forces, and he and his right and left bowers left wounded and bleeding on the field—no one prepared to lend them succour of any kind. . . . It is a great triumph—a wonderful expression of loyalty. It reveals the extent to which, despite 'everything,' I have been able to keep the party together, in provincial as well as federal politics and this by 'non-resistance,' by refusing to enter a quarrel and through allowing my enemies to confound and destroy themselves. Again I say it is the evidence of a moral order that controls in the end."

The change in the Liberal leadership in Toronto encouraged Mackenzie King further to think of staying on in public life. While he was in Toronto on April 19, he had dined with Joseph Atkinson of the *Star*. At dinner, Atkinson "spoke again of his first meeting with me at my father's office in Berlin [Kitchener] when he had come as a reporter to report the Assizes and I had driven him out to Woodside. He prefaced what he had to say by mentioning that all of his family had had to struggle for their livelihood. None of them had had the advantages of special education or association with the learned professions. . . . He then said when I came into your home at Woodside, I saw the fire in the library, the books, pictures and all, it was to me as though I had seen for the first time what I had read of in books as the ideal of the life in country homes in the Old Land. It spoke to me of all that I had most liked to read about. He went on to tell me of the indelible impression the visit had left."

When Mackenzie King expressed doubt "about contesting another election, he told me he did not think I should feel that way. I did not need to take much part. My name had already been built up as something people believed in and would cling to and all I would need to do would be sufficiently to identify myself with continuance of measures I had championed throughout my life. He was quite strong on that. He then went on to say that he personally knew what my motives and what my aims had been, and how absolutely unfair the criticisms toward myself were. . . . He doubts if the war will end before the fall of next year. It may be longer still. He would like to see a general election next year so as not to run into the last hour. I told him the election would depend on the position with regard to the war."

On the whole these early months of 1943 were the easiest period of the whole war for Mackenzie King, and they gave him renewed confidence to face the future and a growing resolve to go through another election.

CHAPTER EIGHTEEN

The Canadian Army Goes into Action

THOUGH the domestic political front was relatively free from anxiety for Mackenzie King in the early months of 1943, he was continuously concerned about the military outlook, and particularly about the prospect of the whole Canadian Army or a part of it going into action. The possible use of two Canadian divisions in an attack on Italy was first broached at the beginning of February, but it was not until the end of April that a decision was reached, and not until July that the Canadians landed in Sicily. Meanwhile, Mackenzie King visited Washington while Churchill was there in May, and had several conversations with Churchill and Roosevelt looking far beyond the immediate campaigns of 1943. Almost in spite of the wishes of the Canadian Government, a Canadian brigade was included in the American expedition against Kiska in the Aleutian Islands.

General Stuart, the Chief of the General Staff, returned from conferences in England at the beginning of March, and on March 4, in Ralston's presence, gave Mackenzie King "a full account of his interviews with McNaughton and our own headquarters staff and the British staff, giving exact information as to what had been decided at the Casablanca Conference between Roosevelt and Churchill and the programme for the present year—the plan for the invasion of Europe." Stuart reminded them that there had been discussions of the employment of Canadian troops in the Mediterranean area, and that two expeditions (one to the Canaries and one to Sardinia) had been tentatively agreed upon between McNaughton and the British staff with the concurrence of the Canadian War Committee, but that, when Churchill returned from Casablanca, the plan was changed and McNaughton was told that the Canadian Army was to be kept intact for an invasion of the Continent somewhere on the French coast in September.

Stuart also reported that, apart from a few specialized troops and reinforcements, no additional men would be required, and that "the one and only problem of meeting McNaughton's wishes is that of shipping. The difficulty there will continue to be for a long time to get across those that we are already in a position to send."

Stuart was, however, worried about keeping the troops out of action so long with a possible deterioration of their morale. Mackenzie King insisted they should stress "that it is Churchill's and Brooke's action—the action of the British Government as part of the High Command—that keeps our men in England, and is keeping the two Corps intact. As far as our Government is concerned, all know that we [are] ready to have men serve wherever they can do so most effectively, and would have had some of our men in North Africa, if we had had our way and had not been over-ruled."

Although the plan then was to begin the invasion across the Channel in September, Mackenzie King "had a feeling that what was proposed looked to me as if the real invasion would not take place this year, but would come in 1944. That I felt a shortage of shipping and U-boat menace being what they were, I did not see how they could be sure of keeping armies supplied with food, munitions, etc., where everything of the kind had to be brought across water and landed, until at least the sea routes were comparatively secure."

At the War Committee on March 11, Mackenzie King asked Stuart specifically whether the estimates of men required for the Army included reinforcements and was "given the assurance that they did." With that assurance, it seemed to him "quite clear that we shall now be able to get through this year without having to apply conscription for overseas service. It is equally clear, however, that when the battle does come in which our forces will be engaged, a page of our history, which however glorious it may be termed, can hardly fail, because of the concentration of forces in numbers and time, to constitute a Gethsemane as well [*sic*]." He added the reflection that in order to secure the air superiority and control of the sea required to ensure success of the invasion, "the delay of an additional year would be more than worth all that otherwise might be involved."

Four days later on March 15, a message was received from Churchill "stating that the Casablanca plans provided for the bombing of Germany prior to and preparatory to all else. That there were quantities of American planes in Britain. Americans were wishing to get their ground crews over and man these planes themselves. There was so little in the way of shipping that to serve that end, it would be necessary for Canada to give up the shipping space which has been allotted to us, and on which we had been counting, for the next few months." Churchill asked Mackenzie King to agree to this change in the allotment of shipping space.

Mackenzie King "felt it would be a great disappointment to Ralston but it really was a relief to my mind. I have been afraid of a second Dieppe. By that I mean anxiety to do something to keep up the morale, but something which, if attempted in the way of an invasion, would be suicide unless there was absolute certainty of troops being supported as they would have to be by men, munitions, etc., from across the water." The next day he talked to Ralston who "was quite put out about Churchill's wire; had a feeling we should oppose it, not agree to it." Mackenzie King could see the force of Ralston's arguments, but "told him that, on the other side, there was, of course, this to be remembered: that if it should ever happen that, through a refusal of Churchill's request, it were known that we had held back the going of American air crews intended for immediate fighting, insisted upon our own men going first, after we had been in the war the length of time we had, there would be strong resentment if, as might happen, great losses should be suffered by our men through their being taken into action on the Continent before every possible and necessary preparation had been made."

Mackenzie King noted that Ralston realized that to agree would mean "numbers of troops will be kept in Canada through summer, with continual demands that they should be employed in industry or farming. Also fears our troops in England will be very restless, hard to sustain their morale, and also the Canadian public will think our troops are being deliberately withheld from active service. I suggested to Ralston that before making any reply to Churchill, he should communicate with McNaughton asking his opinion on the wire from Churchill to me. This was agreed to."

Before considering Churchill's request the War Committee on March 17 was briefed by Admiral Noble of the British Admiralty on the shipping situation and the submarine menace. Mackenzie King asked him how early an invasion could come. Noble "said that he did not see how it could very well come before the month of September and that it might well go over until 1944." When Noble left the meeting, Ralston read the reply he had received from McNaughton, which indicated "that Churchill's wire was the result of the decision of the combined Chiefs of Staff. . . . McNaughton ended by saying there was nothing we could do but to make the best of it." Mackenzie King felt that it looked "as though some factors had been overlooked at and after the Casablanca Conference which were really vital. I personally have felt very strongly that we must be perfectly sure of getting rid of the submarine menace before attempting invasion. Not to be absolutely sure of that would mean that our armies would simply be landed on European soil and massacred between the devil (Germany) and the deep blue sea. The armies will want action speedily but I believe it would be wise to wait another year unless, in the meantime, more can be accomplished at sea than seems probable at the moment. . . . It may well be that in meeting Churchill's wire, we will be saving the lives of many of our men."

The War Committee decided to accede to Churchill's request but asked that Canada "should have the benefit of two additional ships which will be crossing very soon." At the same time Mackenzie King agreed "to having it suggested that the original plan of having some of our men go to Africa should be reconsidered." [This evidently refers to proposals for action against the Canaries or Sardinia.] Mackenzie King noted that he "would not have approved the draft message to Churchill except that I felt it was just as well to have it clearly of record that I was not, and the Canadian Government were not, seeking to hold our men in Britain, if they could be more usefully employed elsewhere."

On March 20, Ralston asked Mackenzie King to see him and General Stuart about a telegram Stuart had received from McNaughton, disclosing that McNaughton had not been consulted about the transfer of shipping space to the American air force, apparently because of the illness of Sir Alan Brooke. In the message McNaughton set out his view as to "the lines on which Canadian forces should be made available and decision reached upon their service." His first point was that forces were "to be used where and when they can make the best contribution; (2) Recognizes that the strategical situation can only be focused by the Chiefs of Staff Committee; (3) That the proposal for use of Canadian forces should initiate with that Committee; and (4) On receipt of the proposals, McNaughton should examine them objectively and report with recommendations. He concluded by saying that he did not recommend pressing for employment of forces merely to satisfy desire for activity or for representation in particular theatres."

Mackenzie King "was so well satisfied with his statement of the true position that, without referring to the first part, I said at once 'that seems to me to be all right.'" He could see, however, "that both Ralston and Stuart had something else in mind and were obviously anxious to get off some message to McNaughton. Stuart outlined the position as he saw it, which was that the morale of the troops really necessitated their being brought into action some time soon; that if there was to be no invasion of Europe this year, it would be impossible to hold their morale;

that they had gone over to fight, and some of them will have been there for four years. Stuart also said he thought men needed battle experience, some active fighting before going into a large and important engagement. . . . He said that McNaughton had become too far removed from the troops; that Crerar was nearer to them and understood them better. He was positive Crerar and the others would wish to have some action very soon in North Africa or elsewhere. . . .

"Ralston took the same view but on a somewhat different ground. His thought was of the political repercussions in Canada of our men being kept out of action so long. He feels that they do not yet believe in England that it is not due to some action on the part of the Government, and he fears that that view will grow; also that it would be very difficult to keep large numbers of troops in Canada without having a demand made that they should go back into industry. He is anxious to get reinforcements over."

Ralston and Stuart had drafted a telegram which they wanted Mackenzie King to send to Churchill to seek his view "as to the possibility of Canadian troops being employed in North Africa." Mackenzie King was quite disturbed by this suggestion which, he felt, "goes the whole length of placing me in the position, as head of the Canadian Government, of settling the strategy so far as Canadian troops are concerned and virtually asking approval of this from the Prime Minister of Britain" and said he would wait to see what reply Churchill would send to his previous telegram before sending another message.

Mackenzie King noted that he then gave Ralston and Stuart his own frank appraisal "that the submarine menace had upset all the plans, had become much greater than was anticipated. That it was now apparent that unless it could be overcome it would be suicidal to attempt an invasion. That it would take several months, and probably the greater part of a year, to overtake the submarine menace, if, indeed, it could be effected in that time. Large quantities of aircraft were necessary and long-range aircraft had still to be manufactured, and numbers of escort ships. . . . Landing craft were also needed. That since landing in Africa, Americans had found they had much to learn. Also progress much slower than anticipated and the whole plan at Casablanca set back because of difficulties there. . . . That all these things pointed to the terrible dangers of trying to invade Europe before adequate preparation. I said nothing more hideous could be contemplated than the cutting of the life-line between this continent and Europe, yet this was possible unless an umbrella of aircraft could shelter convoys all the way across the Atlantic. Airfields would have to be built in Labrador, Greenland, Iceland, and

Britain, which would ensure the necessary bases for the continued successful operation of aircraft." He added that he "felt perfectly sure that . . . there would be no invasion until next year. Stuart and Ralston then said that they had both come to that conclusion themselves."

Later in the day, when looking over the proposed message, Mackenzie King felt Ralston was "seeking to have the whole ground shifted, and use me, as Prime Minister, to put forward the point of view of the Defence Department which controls the Army, as being that of the Government. I intend to make very clear that the Defence Department can make its own representations to McNaughton, but that I will not let my name or office be used to further their point of view as against McNaughton's, nor the civil government in Canada to interfere with the Chiefs of Staff Committee in London in the decisions upon strategy. . . . I shall insist on keeping the plane between Prime Minister and Prime Minister and the President above all departmental levels. Also avoid being rushed into premature decisions. I shall decline absolutely to raise any question with Churchill which does not necessarily arise out of communications which came from him or which may be necessitated by something newly initiated here. My mind keeps going back to McNaughton's words to me that he did not intend to allow life to be unnecessarily sacrificed.

"I said to both Ralston and Stuart," he noted, "that Germany, Russia, Japan—these countries had their millions. We had our thousands. We could not afford to let the number relatively so small be sacrificed at all in order to satisfy current clamour. . . . Much better to wait with the certainty of winning growing greater day by day, than to lose once and for all time, by premature action."

The next day (March 21) Mackenzie King received Churchill's reply to his first message. The ships for immediate transport were made available to Canada and "he made the significant statement . . . that the postponement of the balance until early in the July-September quarter will not affect the availability of the Canadian Army for whatever operations are undertaken this year." Mackenzie King felt that statement meant that major operations across the Channel were "not to be expected in 1943. They will probably come in 1944. Regarding North Africa, Churchill states that only one more division is to go from Britain, and it is already committed and under special training. Plans, therefore, too far advanced to permit of Canadian divisions being sent, and no further divisions likely to be required. That, too, is satisfactory so far as the conservation of our men is concerned. Churchill's last word is that he appreciates the anxiety of our fine troops to take an active part in operations and is keeping this very much in mind." Mackenzie King observed that "the record, therefore, shows that we have been urging the employment of our troops, and that it is quite clear that the Chiefs of Staff Committee in England and the Prime Minister feel that they should be kept where they are.

"The situation," he reflected, "now shows how exceedingly wise it was not to go in for conscription for overseas in Canada. I think it makes obviously clear that nothing of the kind will be required. Indeed the whole mischievous situation is that already we have far too many men overseas than we should be keeping there—many should be in employment here. Ralston and Stuart are really embarrassed by having got the numbers up to the point they have for training in this country. I think from now on we should view that aspect in a more realistic fashion. At any rate, it is a great relief to know that we had gone literally to the limit, and were being told by Britain herself that, without additional men, the Canadian Army strength is now available for all that is required of them this year." He did not think "on this subject, any further communication to Churchill is necessary."

That same day Mackenzie King also noted that he "felt more convinced than ever that my duty was to back up McNaughton rather than Ralston. Back of all else, there is a feeling between them which I think warps Ralston's judgment a bit; also the Army has got to such proportions that it is again being affected by domestic political situations arising out of its numbers which may not best serve the interests of all in the end. I made up my mind to hold firmly to my own judgment."

Mackenzie King's conviction that there would be no invasion of France in 1943 was confirmed by Anthony Eden when he visited Ottawa at the end of March. At the War Committee meeting on March 31, he "made clear to Eden that we were prepared to have our armed forces employed wherever Chiefs of Staff Committee felt they could be most serviceable—that we were not directly or indirectly holding them to Britain. In fact, told him of desire of Defence Department here—Crerar, with consent of McNaughton, to have division and a half, or two divisions, go to North Africa, and it was a disappointment to them when this was cancelled [evidently a reference to the proposed expedition to the Canaries]. Eden made it clear . . . that he felt McNaughton and the British would wish to keep the Canadian Army intact for a final blow. Ralston went out full length in stating his feeling of the need, because of morale and battle training, of our men getting experience and of his feeling that they should get into action somewhere. He went so far that I felt it necessary to say that Ralston's words were, of course, to be construed in the light of none of us wishing any action to be taken that might prove to be disastrous or suicidal, simply for the sake of action. Everything would have to be most carefully prepared prior to attempted invasion." Eden told Mackenzie King later "that he was sure they all felt very strongly on how completely fatal it would be to try an invasion too soon."

It was not until almost the end of April that the project of sending Canadian troops to North Africa to take part in the invasion of Italy was proposed by the United Kingdom Chiefs of Staff Committee. Mackenzie King told Ralston at the War Committee meeting on April 28 he felt this was "really a decision made because of representations since made by the Defence Department. He agreed with this, and said the mention of the British Prime Minister having agreed [in the message from the United Kingdom Chiefs of Staff sent through McNaughton], indicated that it was related to our representations. He added he was 100 per cent behind the decision. That it would give battle experience without which it was questionable whether the morale of the Army could be maintained. All members present approved of the communication Ralston was sending, giving final approval to McNaughton."

At this time, the War Committee had no definite information about the revised plans for operations in the Mediterranean and it was more or less accidentally that Mackenzie King learned that information was coming from Washington to the Chief of the General Staff through military channels which was not being shown to the Minister of National Defence or the Prime Minister. At the War Committee meeting on May 14 he "spoke out very strongly against some of the officials of the Defence Department not forwarding to me, as Prime Minister, important documents which came from our military staff at Washington, in particular the one containing [General Maurice] Pope's appreciation of the strategic outline of the war strategy of the present year. Also that copies had not been given to Minister of Defence or to the War Committee. I said that no document in the public service should be concealed from the Prime Minister. It was the duty of Ministers of the Crown, Deputy Ministers, and others not to withhold documents but to see that any document the contents of which were likely to be of importance to the Prime Minister, should be brought immediately to his consideration. . . . I made it clear that the Prime Minister in the last analysis was responsible for every act of government and that no official could regard communications as coming to himself as distinguished from the Ministers, unless they were distinctly marked 'Personal.' "

He added that "one communication had come from Washington speaking of a particular operation in the present war, as being the

'Husky' operation—a term that has been used by the military authorities for some time past." 'Husky' was the code name for the planned attack on Sicily. He noted that "neither Colonel Ralston, Power, Macdonald or myself had ever known of such an operation by name until the telegram mentioning it had come last night. We were all agreed that this was simply absurd. I pointed out the position I would be in in visiting Washington and meeting with Mr. Churchill and the President and their reference to any operation of the kind, and to my having to inquire what the particular operation meant. I spoke of the whole position as humiliating. I made it clear that a direction was to go from the War Committee to the Chiefs of Staff and stated . . . that I was to have for my personal possession, these different communications, that I might be in a position at any time to take full responsibility for what I had done, and to defend the position in the light of information given to me. . . . I stated I wanted all communications of importance given me immediately, and it would be my discretion entirely as to how I would use them; how far I would impart information they contained to others.

"Power said that he had told the Chiefs of Staff that the roof would be raised when I saw communications were being withheld. The Defence Ministers felt as indignant as I did about the whole business."

Mackenzie King's outburst occurred just before he was leaving for Washington to confer with Roosevelt and Churchill at the White House. Churchill had actually arrived in Washington on May 11 and the next day Mackenzie King had a telegram from him suggesting they meet in Washington the following week, using the Pacific Council as a pretext. On May 14, he received an invitation from the President "to come direct to the White House. He would be glad to see and talk with me again, and that the meeting of the Pacific Council would be on Thursday." Mackenzie King arrived in Washington on May 18.

During his conversation with Churchill on May 18 they discussed the military action proposed for 1943. Churchill told him he felt the thing to do was to get Italy out of the war, and to start this operation from Sicily and Sardinia. In speaking of invasion across the Channel, Churchill "said he did not want to see the beaches of Europe covered with slain bodies of Canadians and Americans. That there might easily be many Dieppes in a few days." Churchill then said: "One of your divisions is going now to take part in the attack from the South. You have a number of your officers getting training in North Africa. I said to him that it looked as though McNaughton had been anxious to keep his Army together. On the other hand I thought the Chiefs of Staff had felt the men needed battle training and that they should take

The Army in Action

part in the campaign in other parts. He said that it might be that Germany would show signs of crumbling up toward the end of the summer. If she did, they should be ready to make an attack from Britain, but he felt it was better to wait . . . than to take a venture in which there might be no chance of succeeding. . . . I said I was glad to hear him say he would not take unwarranted risks of invasion from Britain. That I thought that was sound. He stressed this again very strongly saying that there was no doubt in his mind. The enemy might be very strong there and losses might be very great."

Churchill then suggested that Mackenzie King should see Lord Cherwell in the morning to be informed of certain very secret developments. The following morning (May 19) Lord Cherwell told Mackenzie King "about certain experiments that had been made and that I had learned confidentially about from Malcolm MacDonald, some little time ago." These were the atomic energy experiments. He noted "that both the British and the Americans have been experimenting on similar lines. The latter have made contacts with Canada for some of the raw material and power needed, and are now unwilling to let the British know what they have done. This is because the Army has got hold of the matter. It has been removed from the realm of the scientists into the hands of the Army. They are as difficult about it in their relation with Britain as Stalin had been in telling of what was being done in Russia."

During his first talk with Churchill, Mackenzie King arranged that Ralston and the Canadian Chiefs of Staff should come to Washington to confer with the British Chiefs of Staff and also to attend a Commonwealth meeting at the White House on May 20 at which Churchill gave one of his appreciations of the war. At the conclusion of Churchill's speech, Mackenzie King expressed thanks on behalf of all and, at Ralston's request, he stressed again "Canada's attitude toward the use of her forces. I said I would like to take advantage of the presence of the Chiefs of Staff, and Mr. Churchill, to make it quite clear once more that we recognized that strategy had to be left in the hands of the British and American Combined Chiefs of Staff, with Churchill and the President giving the ultimate decisions. That we wanted it known that we were prepared to have our men serve wherever they could be most helpful in the winning of the war. That we were quite prepared to have them fight as one great Army. We were equally prepared to have the forces divided up. To be used in the different parts of the world where they could be of most service.

"Churchill replied that the Canadian Army had rendered a great service. They had guarded the heart of Britain. They had been her only protection at a time when she had little else in the way of protection. That he appreciated our readiness to have our forces employed wherever they could best serve; that they were proceeding on that basis subject, of course, to securing in advance our approval of whatever might be proposed."

Before Mackenzie King left Washington, Churchill told him "there will be no invasion of Europe this year from Britain. I tell you that. As you know, some of your men [one division and one tank brigade] will be in action in the Mediterranean. They will be in the forefront of the battle. It will probably be some weeks yet."

After Mackenzie King got back from Washington, he compared notes with General Stuart. Stuart made it clear that it was understood that, after the Canadian troops had gained battle experience in Italy, they would be brought back to Britain, "to impart," in Mackenzie King's words, "to the other divisions in England, the experience they had gained in actual battle." Mackenzie King noted that Stuart's statement of the plans generally "was exactly in accord with what I had gathered from other sources. This operation was the one to be known as 'Husky.' He, General Stuart, had told no one of the details, etc., except Colonel Ralston and myself." Mackenzie King told Stuart "that Churchill had told me emphatically there would be no invasion of Europe from Britain this year. That it would come next year. He had also told me that our men would be in the front of the battle for the island of Sicily. I do not recall whether he (Churchill) said they would be brought back to England after some of the fighting. My recollection is that he did."

Mackenzie King's talks in Washington had, of course, ranged far beyond the plans for the Italian campaign and the employment of Canadian troops. As soon as he had reached the White House on May 18 he was shown into Mr. Churchill's suite, where Churchill received him, lying in bed. After greeting him, Churchill began to talk to him of the speech he was to make the next day to the Congress. He "was very worried lest he might say anything that would be embarrassing. . . . He indicated that he had not completed his speech and would be taking a little sleep before dinner, which I took, of course, to mean that he would not wish the conversation to take up too long."

After some discussion of the progress of the war and the plans for the Italian campaign, Churchill said something about a conference of Commonwealth Prime Ministers in London. Mackenzie King suggested they could discuss that after Churchill's speech had been delivered and then said to him: "Would I be impertinent, having in mind he had shown me his speech in advance in England when I was his guest at Chequers, to think that he might like to have me look over what he proposed to say—not to consider this a request but a readiness to do this if he so desired. He at once thanked me, and said he would be glad if I would. I said I could read it over while he was taking his rest and would leave word with his Secretary." Mackenzie King noted that, as he was taking leave, Churchill said "he and I had had a dance together in London on one occasion. He asked me what the occasion was. I told him it was after his broadcast. Perhaps we might have another one tomorrow night."

Mackenzie King went through Churchill's speech very carefully. He noticed "that like his other speeches, it referred only to 'we' as meaning Britain and the U.S. forces. It seemed to me that this reference first came in relation to the air forces that had worked together in Africa; that our people would be much hurt, and I felt also that Australia and New Zealand and South Africa as well as the Indians would have a right to feel hurt, if no reference was made to all of us. I told Rowan [Churchill's Private Secretary] that I thought it ought to include some reference there to make clear that when he spoke of 'we,' he was referring to all the forces of the different Dominions as well as the British Isles. To remember he was very near Canada speaking on this continent, and that our people would be sensitive to having no reference made to that part. After all, the Air Force had been doing a good deal of bombing over Germany and had helped materially in the African campaign. . . . I said I thought it would be well to have this included in the speech and indicated where I thought the reference should come." Mackenzie King pointed out that one other phrase was very ambiguous and suggested how it should be changed.

The next day (May 19), at noon, Churchill was to speak to the Congress. The President's party and Churchill's party assembled in the White House for the drive to the Capitol. While they were conversing, the Duke and Duchess of Windsor came in with Mrs. Roosevelt. "The Duke," Mackenzie King wrote, "saw me standing there and immediately came over and shook hands very warmly. Brought the Duchess over to shake hands. . . . He seemed to me to have regained some of his old charm. He could not have been pleasanter than he was.

"When Mr. Churchill came down, he talked a bit about feeling like Carton before he was executed. Seemed anxious to get off to Congress. As he went to his car, he sent his aide back for me to accompany him. I sat to his left in the car. . . . Churchill . . . found it difficult waiting while the party were lining up in the cars behind. He turned to me and said he had gone over his address and made considerable changes in it." Later during the delivery of the speech Mackenzie King noticed Churchill "brought in a very kind reference to myself, but I did not see that he brought in the Dominions in relation to the war effort in quite the way that I had hoped he would. It is still the combination between Britain and the United States."

Mackenzie King sat in the Executive box. He was at one corner with the Duke of Windsor at the opposite corner. "It did seem to me a strange thing," he wrote, "[that] I should find myself in that relationship vis-à-vis the Duke, former King of England, and each of us, guests of the President of the United States, and that I should have been the one to drive to the Capitol with the Prime Minister of Britain at this time of war when he was about to address both Houses."

When Churchill concluded his speech there was a luncheon given by Congressman Sol Bloom and Senator Tom Connally which Mackenzie King greatly enjoyed. "After the luncheon," he noted, "members of the Senate and Representatives of the foreign committee came into the room, and Mr. Churchill was subjected to a quiz. This was as interesting an hour as I have had at any time." Churchill asked Mackenzie King to drive back with him to the White House "and kept giving the V-sign to the crowds on the way. He repeated to me that he thought his coming at this time had helped. . . . I told him I was very sure that what he had said to Congress would be most helpful. Thanked him for his personal reference. . . . After reaching the White House, Churchill and I went in to see the President in his office. He . . . gave me a warm welcome. Said that Congress had given me a good hand. He had heard the proceedings over the radio. He told Churchill he was pleased with what he had said."

Though for Mackenzie King this was a memorable experience, he did not forget that the change he had suggested in Churchill's speech had not been made. Back in Ottawa, on May 26, when he was reporting to the War Committee on his visit to Washington, "I said quite frankly to my colleagues I thought we would make a great mistake if we allowed further expenditures on war effort for overseas to embarrass the country in dealing with its domestic problems, for example, fuel and other matters of the kind. It was perfectly clear to me that, so far as Britain and the United States were concerned, there was little thought of giving credit except in very general terms to what was being done by Canada. Would receive little recognition. Churchill in all these statements was clearly determined not to make special mention of the

Dominions when referring to efforts in which the British and U.S. were engaged. Equally determined, if possible, to effect, and in so far as possible, centralize the direction of Empire affairs."

This last observation had reference to the talks he had in Washington with Churchill about an Imperial Conference or a meeting of Prime Ministers in London. The subject had first been broached earlier in a cable from Churchill which Mackenzie King had received on April 4, suggesting "that some time this year we should have an Imperial Conference in order to show the whole world the strength and union of what we should call in the future the British Commonwealth and Empire. Let me know what you think." At that time Mackenzie King had written: "My first feeling was one of appreciation of Churchill's feeling I was of assistance to him, and of a readiness to do anything that would be of help to him, even to crossing the Atlantic for consultation with him. I doubt, however, the wisdom of any Imperial Conference and, certainly, can think of nothing that would create more confusion than any Conference that might be called upon to decide the question between Commonwealth and Empire. It looked to me as if Churchill, knowing that the possibility of invasion of Europe is unlikely this year, is seeking to find something in the way of Empire display to draw attention from the absence of invasion by creating a different kind of interest in an opposite direction. I shall take time to send the needed reply."

Before he had got around to replying, Mackenzie King had received a further message on April 13 stating that Churchill "had come to the conclusion it was necessary to have a conference of Prime Ministers. In the telegram, he gives an outline of what he proposes to send to each of the Prime Ministers of the Dominions. It is to be a conference dealing with negotiations that will take place at the time of the peace, and related to postwar organization. Fortunately I had not yet sent off the telegram which I had meant to send to his first message. It is perhaps as well that I did not because I would have taken, in what I was saying, strong exception to an Imperial Conference and given reasons therefor. I had intended, however, to say that I thought a conference of Premiers on the very matters to which Churchill has referred, might be a good thing. Now I can reply without taking any exception to his proposal, and will offer to endeavour to suit the convenience of others in the matter of time."

When Churchill brought the subject up again at Washington, on May 18, he referred to Mackenzie King's preference for "a Conference of British Prime Ministers to an Imperial Conference. He did not quite see what the difference would be, but was interested in what I had mentioned. I said to him . . . I would not worry him with discussion of that today."

They did not return to the subject until two days later (May 20) during a long conversation alone at the White House, when Churchill opened the subject by saying to Mackenzie King: "You must come over for the meeting of Prime Ministers when it is held. I know it will be difficult in some ways but you must come." Churchill advised him to travel by ship. Mackenzie King replied that he was "not concerned about the means of crossing. That I would personally prefer to go by bomber. . . . What I really had most in mind was the political danger that might arise out of the Prime Ministers of different parts being absent from their own country while the war was still on, especially as all was going so well now. That I would not like to see anything happen to myself or others similar to what happened to Menzies who had, when he got back, found he had lost support in his own country through being overseas. I said to Churchill: 'You know, the minute I cross to England, immediately there is a cry raised that I have gone into the imperialist camp, and a nationalist sentiment begins to develop at home: Not in the province of Quebec only, but in the West and in other parts of Canada. What people are really afraid of is the imperialist idea as against the complete independence of the parts.'

"Churchill turned at once and said: 'You are the outstanding imperialist today. Not only do you stand out in history as the great unifier of your country, but you will be judged by the war effort of your country at this time, and there has been nothing finer in the whole war; what Canada has done under your direction has not been surpassed, and you will be identified for all time with that part. Also you have been a great mediator as between different countries.' He made some reference to the States and Britain and also different parts of the Empire. It was with this view of things that he used the term 'imperialist,' meaning more, I think, taking the world outlook than any identification with a centralized form of government as against a decentralized. He kept repeating the outstanding position which I now had as a unifier and mediator. Those were the words that he kept repeating.

"I spoke then about the dangers of these other countries feeling that the different parts of the Empire were, so to speak, ganging up against them. He then spoke very passionately about the finest thing that the world had was this congeries of states and peoples, all brought together as one. That he wanted to see that grow as one and develop, and that no peoples could take exception to our keeping our own community as one before the world.

"He then said to me that he was interested in the idea of the Conference of Prime Ministers as against an Imperial Conference. I said to him that the Conference to my mind, especially as he used the word in connection with the British Commonwealth and Empire, implied a discussion of constitutional questions which I felt would, at a time of war, be perilous. He said: 'Oh, no, I had nothing of that kind in mind.' I added that a conference meant bringing staffs of experts and the like, and I felt further that it would raise questions that would be embarrassing."

As an example Mackenzie King mentioned the question of representation of India and then finally said to Churchill: "You know that all I wish to do at this time is to be as helpful as possible in any way, and there is nothing that I am not prepared to do which will help toward that end. If I can help to keep all parts united, I shall not consider the possible consequences from any other point of view. So far as inconvenience, physical dangers or the like are concerned, that does not matter in the least. That with others doing what they were, and men sacrificing their lives, I would not stop to consider anything other than what would be most helpful, and for him to count on that at all times. That I really wanted to have him feel that I wanted to be a help to him with his tremendous load. I could see he was feeling very deeply all that he was saying, and that there was almost an emotional moment as the two of us parted at the door."

The subject of the Prime Ministers' meeting came up again when Mackenzie King said good-bye to Churchill on May 21. It was just before lunch and Mackenzie King went right to Churchill's room, where "Churchill sent word to come right in. As I came in he appeared in his white linen under-garments; little shirt without sleeves and little shorts to his knees, otherwise quite bare excepting for a pair of slippers. He really was quite a picture, but looked like a boy—cheeks quite pink and very fresh. . . .

"I said I had just come to say good-bye, and have one word. He then began to talk about the Conference, and . . . said: 'You must come over. We could not have a meeting without you, and what I feel is you have the strongest position of any man outside of the United States, with the United States. They all trust and believe in you here and you are the strongest man for this country. There is every reason why you should hold the same position within the Empire. It must be recognized that you have that position both in the Empire and here. As I see it and as I said in talking with the President and you together, I would be glad— in any Western Hemisphere Council—to have Britain's interests entrusted to Canada as a member of the North American Council. I would be glad to have you take on all our interests in America. We would be in the Council of Europe and of Asia, and certainly you could look after this hemisphere.'

"I did not say much in reply beyond intimating that that was something that would have to be carefully thought out and considered. I did not give it either approval or disapproval. I had in mind, of course, my own feeling that it would not do for Canada to assume to act for Britain. It is the old question of what was up at the time of the last war when Borden was prepared to have his Minister to Washington reside at the British Legation.

"I repeated to Churchill that my concern was, in regard to the meeting in London, that of questions arising which it would be difficult to settle. The importance of the Prime Ministers watching their own countries, etc. I said to him, however, you can be sure that I am only anxious to help and will try and fit in with whatever is best." In the event, the Quebec Conference in August drove the meeting of Commonwealth Prime Ministers out of the picture for 1943.

Mackenzie King spent a good deal of time with both Churchill and Roosevelt during his stay at the White House. He dined with both of them and with several other guests on the day Churchill spoke to the Congress. There was nothing very notable in the conversation until the other guests left and Mackenzie King was alone with the President. Roosevelt then outlined some of his ideas about peace-making and post-war international organization. Roosevelt felt there would have to be a Supreme Council representing all the United Nations, and he stressed particularly the need of "someone who could fill the position of Moderator—someone who would keep his eye on the different countries to see that they were complying with the agreements made in connection with the peace, for example, limitation of armaments. . . .

"It would be the Moderator's duty possibly to warn in advance and, if necessary, to have the Council meet to take such action as might be necessary. He said, of course, the difficulty would be to find the man for that position. He would have to be someone who would have the confidence of all the nations. Smuts would be an ideal man for that position, but when the time came, he would be too old. The President then said, referring to himself, I could myself fill that position. I would have the confidence of the countries. I have forgotten just what reason he gave for doubting whether he could take it on. It may have had reference to his being required for further services in the office he is now holding."

After the meeting of the Pacific Council the next morning, Mackenzie

King had lunch with Roosevelt, Churchill, and Harry Hopkins. Hopkins left right after lunch and the other three talked for some time. Roosevelt referred again to his idea of a world "Moderator," and after again dismissing Smuts because of his age, Roosevelt said to Churchill "Mackenzie would be accepted by the entire world. All countries have confidence in him. I simply laughed and said it was very nice of him to speak in that way but he must not be extravagant in what he was saying or words to that effect.

"Churchill then said: 'Is it not a fact that we three men who are at this table now, have had more experience in government than any other men in the world today.' The President said he agreed in that. I said there is no doubt in my mind that, but for you two men, the free countries of the world would have lost their freedom and these other powers would be in control. Churchill said: 'there was nothing truer than that.' The President, too, agreed that if they had not combined, and each played the part they had—combined together the strength that now exists—the whole situation would have been different. They then returned to my years in public life and the part I had taken. . . . Churchill said: . . . 'I remember in 1905, you were a Deputy Minister in Sir Wilfrid Laurier's Administration, and your coming to talk with me about some legislation. We put through some Act for you.' I replied that was an amendment to legislation to prevent fraud, and explained that in 1905, I conducted a special investigation into fraudulent practices which had been carried on in England to induce men to come to Canada as strike breakers. That Lloyd George had put the thing through. Churchill added, 'Then you became Minister of Labour.' I said I had been in Laurier's Cabinet from 1909 to '11. Churchill said 'That makes nearly twenty years of office.' He said: 'You have been dealing with public affairs since 1900—over 40 years. Referring to my years of leadership of the party and being in Parliament that time, he said: 'You have had much more of continuous office that I have had.' . . .

"They then, however, came back to the position that I held as between Britain and the United States; I understood both of them, and had their confidence as no other man. Roosevelt referred to our association going back to Harvard days, and Churchill to the beginning of 1900, and spoke of that period of time during which I had known each of them. The President then repeated what he had said about my holding a position which any country would recognize, and they both remarked that it was true that the three of us . . . at that table at that time had a place in government and experience that no other three men in the world had today."

They also discussed the question of raising the Canadian Legation in Washington to an Embassy. Roosevelt pointed out that the Latin American countries had all done so and that "Canada was the only country on the continent that had not an Embassy. I said that I had not favoured an Embassy up to the present out of sense of proportion. . . . Felt that we should take matters a step at a time, and added that I was thinking of having the Legation changed into an Embassy. I asked Churchill what he thought about it, how they would feel in England if that were done. Churchill's reply was that he thought Canada should be as strong in every way as she could be. That she should have as strong a position on this continent as she could possibly have. That he favoured her being given all the recognition possible and making her position felt. He said he did not know how the Foreign Office would view the matter. I pointed out it was for us to make our own decision. He agreed entirely with that."

When the President referred to the need of the consent of the King of England to the change, "Churchill at once said: 'No, he is the King of Canada just as much as he is the King of England. Canada has complete control of her own affairs. Mackenzie has just as much say in regard to what Canada is to do as I have in regard to Britain,' or words to that effect. I said we have a perfect equality of status, not stature but status, in all that pertains to our domestic and external affairs. Something was said about foreign policy. Churchill said that it was not an easy matter to reconcile all views but that we [members of Commonwealth], of course, would keep each other informed but that we [Canada] decided our own."

Churchill added that "Canada should be just as strong an American Western Hemisphere country as she could be. Equally she should hold as strong a place as she could within the British Empire. That that was all to the good for both. He went on to say that Canada could not be too strong as a North American country. He hoped that there would always be the closest relationship between different parts of the Empire. A great thing had been built up—this collection of peoples united as they were with common aims. That so far as this continent was concerned, he would be glad to see Canada represent more and more the British in relation to the United States. He then spoke out quite strongly about Canada and her exceptional position in interpreting the two countries to each other.

"Both he and the President made some reference to my own part in that connection. This then led Churchill to speak quite passionately and strongly to the President, using the words: 'I am saying this in the presence of Canada's Prime Minister, deliberately to you, Mr. President. I beg of you not to keep aloof from the European situation, once this war is over, or in arranging for a final settlement of the war. And once the war is over, there will have to be a Council of Europe, a Council of Asia, and a Council of the Americas. Over all will be a World Council in which there will be a final appeal. You, Mr. President, should be on all three Councils. We should be perhaps on all three Councils, though I should be glad to have Canada represent the British as well as their own interests on the Council of the Americas.'

"The President indicated that he was not too sure how far America should go in being on a European Council. This caused Churchill to say quite earnestly: 'You are needed there as much as ever in your own interest. We have had two wars into which you have been drawn, and which are costing America a lot. Neither of them originated here. They both originated in Europe, and they will arise there again unless some of these countries can be kept in proper control by the rest of the world.' "

Mackenzie King noted that, later in the conversation, "Churchill continued his plea with the President not to let America become isolated from Europe. That he wanted to see the strongest friendly relations between the British Empire and the U.S. That there could not be too much friendship between them. Equally he wanted to have the President realize that different parts of the Empire could meet together and discuss matters of common concern to them without, in any way, being assumed to be taking a stand against the United States or any other countries. What he clearly had in mind at the time was the meeting of Prime Ministers in England or Imperial Conference to which he is attaching much importance as evidencing the unity of the Empire."

Roosevelt had told Mackenzie King in an earlier conversation that he had sent a message to Moscow that he "wanted to see Stalin himself; he was a little concerned as to how he could tell Winston." At Mackenzie King's farewell talk with the President on May 21, Roosevelt returned to his message and to his concern about Churchill's reaction. "Mackenzie, I want to tell you what was in my letter to Stalin. I have told him—and here he was repeating what he had told me the night before last. I feel that he and I ought to meet and have a talk together, but I feel embarrassed as to how Winston might feel. What I should say to him. I have a hunch that Stalin does not want to see the two of us together, at least at the outset, and that he would like to talk with me alone but just how to say that to Winston, I am not sure.

I replied that I thought Winston would thoroughly understand. That he, Winston, had been in Russia and has seen Stalin there. They had talked together alone, and particularly if he, the President, were going to see Stalin where he had indicated (he had told me this before), Winston would see that it would seem perfectly reasonable for him, the President, to see Stalin at that place by himself. He told me that what he had in mind was seeing him in Alaska, possibly at Nome. . . . Behring Sea was exactly the same distance from Washington as it was from Moscow. Stalin could make the journey easily in two days each way.

"He then said to me: what I was going to propose, Mackenzie, is that I come to Ottawa and spend a day with you there, and that we then go on together to see the Alcan Highway. He repeated the word 'Alcan.' I said I hope he will use the words 'Alaska Highway'—nobody likes 'Alcan.' I said in Parliament I never used the name but have emphasized the other." Roosevelt continued: "After we had gone over the Highway, I could go on to Alaska and you could take another route. He thought the time might be August. I said I would be delighted to go with him as suggested. Was particularly anxious to have him in Ottawa to speak on Parliament Hill. . . . I said: 'You would have a tremendous demonstration on Parliament Hill.' People would come from B.C. and the Maritime Provinces, from all over in fact, to express their feeling toward him.

"He then said: If, by any chance, something should prevent Stalin making the trip, what I would like to do is to come to Ottawa just the same though perhaps this might be in July. I would have my revenue cutter on the Great Lakes. We could get aboard there and take a trip through the Great Lakes up to the Georgian Bay, and have a week's rest and fishing together there. He asked me about fishing, I said I did not know just what it was like in the Georgian Bay, but I would have inquiries made in the meantime. He said: you and I could have just a quiet time and rest there. I told him that idea also was excellent. He then said to keep this in mind but very secret."

Mackenzie King told Roosevelt that "Winston was anxious to have me come to London, to a Conference possibly of Prime Ministers, and that I felt I should do that when the time came. The difficulty was for Smuts and Curtin, and all of us, to get over at the same time. There were matters between different parts of the Empire which he felt we should discuss. That I thought the interpretative side of my work could be helpful at such a time. The President agreed with this."

On his way back to Ottawa, Mackenzie King spent Saturday and Sunday in New York and on Sunday (May 23) went by subway to

Coney Island. "The whole trip," he wrote, "was full of interest, first of all seeing the kinds of people aboard the train; mostly all foreign descent, many Jews, the sort of literature being distributed, etc., and an even greater contrast of peoples and garbs at Coney Island itself. Different money-making booths, people basking on the beaches, some even in boats. After a walk of a mile or two, delightful in fresh air of the sea and bright warm sun, we had for lunch fish food at the one important Hotel: the Half Moon."

At a meeting of the War Committee on May 26, Mackenzie King was informed of the proposal to have a "contingent of Canadians join with the Americans in an attack on . . . the Aleutians." Mackenzie King's impression was that General Stuart, while in Washington, "had brought up the possibility first of all with one of the American officers, and that the American soldiers had discussed the matter between themselves, and finally a request had come to Canada from one of the American officers for our co-operation in the attack. Stuart seemed to feel that this was advisable in order to have Canadian troops gain battle experience. He further felt that the forces which have been raised under the National Mobilization Act were really first class men, and good fighting material, and it would help to remove prejudice against them, were they to take part in what was obviously the defence of Canada against the Japanese. Personally I think the Minister of Defence should have been the one to be taking, if anything of the kind were contemplated, the initial step in discussion with the War Committee of the Cabinet."

Mackenzie King's initial irritation that this Canadian participation in the expedition had been suggested to the Americans by the military authorities coloured his whole subsequent attitude to the Kiska expedition. The following day (May 27), at the War Committee meeting, it became clear that the Permanent Joint Board on Defence had also considered the proposed expedition. Mackenzie King "took the position very strongly that the Joint Defence Board had no right to take any step which entered the field of strategy and operations. That the Americans were to report to their Government on matters of defence, and Canadians to our Government but it was for the Governments to consider their recommendations, and to decide on operations, etc. . . . Next, I objected strongly to our Chiefs of Staff and others of the High Command in Canada negotiating with corresponding numbers in the U.S. before the Minister had a full knowledge of what was proposed, the War Committee included, and, most of all, myself as the Prime Minister.

"It was fully apparent," he added, "that Stuart had gone ahead with his own officers and Pearkes, on the Pacific Coast, and that he, Pearkes, had gone further with his corresponding number in the States, in agreeing to a course of action which would involve our troops being engaged actively with U.S. troops against the Aleutian Islands. I did not object to the project as such, but pointed out that the procedure was entirely wrong; that the Government would be in an indefensible position if it were allowed to go further without being wholly regularized." Nevertheless the Cabinet agreed "to have a token force assist in driving the Japanese out of" the Aleutian Islands.

Mackenzie King himself "pointed out that action against the Japanese in the Northeast Pacific would psychologically have a good effect in the United States, in Australia, and in Canada as helping to balance the actions of Americans and Australians combined in the South West Pacific." He "asked pointedly the question whether the planned action would make it any more difficult for us to obtain reinforcements for overseas. Stuart's reply was that it would not make any difference whatever. He spoke of the advantage of battle training, etc. It was finally agreed that the communication would have to come from either the President to myself, or Stimson to Ralston, to get matters on Ministerial level and out simply of the military level; indeed this whole thing has worked from the bottom up instead of from the top down." Mackenzie King noted that "Ralston had been very deeply annoyed at Stuart proceeding without giving him his confidence."

The following day (May 28) Ralston came to see Mackenzie King "quite upset from the fact that the press had just sent him word that some of our men were on the way to Attu in connection with combined operations with American forces. He had pointed out that Pearkes had been giving orders. He told me that the men were already on their way. He decided that he would have to have a very straight talk with Stuart, tonight, and take strong exception. It was indeed an alarming moment in that it indicated that the Army are going ahead with operations without the Cabinet having even sanctioned them."

It subsequently turned out that the only men that had been sent forward were eight officers who were to go as observers, and that the plan of operations had not yet been decided upon. It was agreed that no men should go forward other than the officers who had gone until the whole matter of participation had been settled by the War Committee. Mackenzie King noted that "Ralston had made no statement to the press, but we concluded it would be as well to inform the press that eight officers had proceeded as observers. That when the matter comes up on Monday [in the House of Commons], to treat it all as part of the joint efforts of our own and American forces in carrying out joint protection of the Pacific Coast. It has been a lesson I think for all concerned. . . . The wisdom of my judgment in insisting on seeing all communications at once, and responsible Ministers ditto, has been more than clear."

Mackenzie King did not get over his annoyance quickly. "I feel incensed," he wrote on May 30, "that our forces should have been drawn into this business, without knowledge on the part of or request from the Joint Chiefs of Staff at Washington. I would have insisted on a cancellation of the whole thing, were it not that . . . to have cut it off would have raised a serious situation re relation to U.S. and Canadian armies on the Pacific, and probably involved Stuart's resignation. As it is, the whole business has been caught just in time. . . . In the circumstances we have done, I think, the best we can, and taken the only course that would not have made the situation worse. Had it all been a part of the recent Conference at Washington, nothing could have been better—as it is, it must continue to be a part of the joint arrangements on the Pacific Coast for mutual benefit." On that rather sour note, the planning phase of the 1943 military operations ended.

The public, of course, knew nothing of the decision to have the Canadian Army share in the attack on Sicily or of the impending expedition to the Aleutian Islands. Despite the very large part Canadian sailors and airmen were taking in actual combat in 1943, the sense of remoteness of the war from Canada remained strong until the landing in Sicily early in July.

On the other hand, there was a good deal of interest in Canada's relations with the Allies at this time. Madame Chiang Kai-Shek, who had come to North America to enlist support for China, made a visit to Ottawa and addressed both Houses of Parliament in June; the magnificent and increasingly successful Russian resistance to the Nazis had excited widespread admiration and support, particularly in Toronto where Mackenzie King participated in a Canadian-Soviet friendship rally; the formation in North Africa of the French Committee of National Liberation under the joint chairmanship of Generals de Gaulle and Giraud and the emergence of a separate French Army had been welcomed in Canada; an unfortunate statement by J. H. Clark, the Speaker of the Ontario Legislature, forecasting eventual political union of Canada with the United States had, when it was reported in the press, aroused latent feeling for the British connection; and the apparently subordinate role of Canada in the higher direction of the war excited some national resentment which was not entirely appeased by Mackenzie King's visit to Washington when Churchill was there in May.

Mackenzie King was particularly concerned to offset the impression created by Speaker Clark's forecast of political union. It was drawn forcibly to his notice by Sir William Mulock, then 99, with whom he lunched in Toronto on June 21. Mulock said "he felt, everything considered, Canada would be better off as a part of the British Empire than she would as a part of the U.S. In other words, that nothing could be better than our present position being part of a large company of free nations, perfectly free in the management of our own affairs. . . . I told him I agreed entirely with that view. . . . I thought I would come out publicly and make some statement of the kind."

The very next evening (June 22) in Ottawa, Mackenzie King took advantage of a dinner of the Empire Parliamentary Association in honour of a delegation of British M.P.'s to speak "about the importance of maintaining the British Empire and having it develop along lines it has thus far developed and the mistake it would be to have any political annexation with the U.S. It would mean loss to the finest thing North America has to give, namely, association of the two nations at peace through machinery devised for the settlement of international differences."

While the British M.P.'s were still in Ottawa a delegation of United States Congressmen and Senators also visited Canada. Mackenzie King spoke to a dinner for both the British and the American delegations on June 28 "about the fears of the British lest we should become particularly attracted by the U.S. and the fears of the U.S. of different nations of the British Commonwealth ganging up against them in dealing with peace and postwar matters. We were a nation on our own with our own views, etc. Also that our relations with the States made this continent a pattern for world organization. Made clear in the presence of both groups Canada's intention to follow her own policies; co-operation alike vis-à-vis Britain and U.S. . . . I pointed out that our mission was to help to diffuse through the world the relationship that has developed between the different parts of the English-speaking world."

He did not, however, permit these manifestations of attachment to the British connection to overshadow Canada's position as a nation in her own right. On July 1, he made a statement in Parliament on Canada's status as a world power and then asked "that the House should join in singing 'O Canada.' It was apparent as I read the statement that the Opposition did not like at all its references to Canada's progress at a time of war, and some of the Tories actually showed irritation at my reference to there being more harmony in Canada today than at any time since the outbreak of war. Tommy Church [member for Toronto Broadview] disclosed the Tory mentality by asking later why we had sung

'O Canada.' I replied that if he did not know, I was sorry for him. Both he and Hanson suggested singing 'God Save the King' at once, but there was no response, feeling that this was one day on which our own national anthem should suffice." He added that "the country comes secondary to monarchy in the Tory mind. Happily we have on the throne in Britain at the moment, a King and Queen for whom we can earnestly pray and joyfully sing. Were they of a different character, I do not know what would happen to the institution of monarchy."

No doubt Mackenzie King had in mind a conversation he had had a few days before (June 25) with Sir Percy Harris, a British Liberal M.P., who had told him that some of the Conservatives felt he might have inspired Speaker Clark's statement and that they kept saying Mackenzie King was "responsible for not having allowed our men to go into action and for keeping them so long in England. This notwithstanding all that Churchill has said and what has been repeatedly stated by Ralston and others, and all of us in public, both in Britain and in Canada." Mackenzie King told Harris the Conservative attitude was easily explained; that "Hanson had said to me that he and Meighen would come into the Cabinet taking any positions I would offer them. That I would be even greater than Sir John Macdonald if I formed a War Cabinet. They would have the press and all support me. What they cannot get over is the way I have defeated all their machinations, those of Meighen, Hepburn, Bennett, et al."

Shortly afterwards there was a debate in the House on the Estimates of the Department of External Affairs. Mackenzie King noted July 9 that "the Tory party are again talking Empire, single foreign policy—an Imperial Cabinet and Imperial Council. Single aviation policy, etc. Yet they are taking the attitude as well that Canada should be more represented on committees in the U.S., not have an inferiority complex, etc. A most contradictory attitude. I asked Claxton to speak and present our point of view and he did so at night very well."

Mackenzie King saw political danger and a threat to national unity in another quarter when he learned that the Canadian Navy would not accept French-speaking recruits who were unable to speak English, and that it had been suggested such prospective recruits might be allowed to enlist with the Free French. At the War Committee on June 18, "in the presence of the Ministers and the Chiefs of Staff," he wrote, "I stated this was an indefensible procedure, and could not be, for one moment, regarded or tolerated as an expression of Government policy." When it was explained that signals were given in English, which it was essential should be understood by all personnel, Mackenzie King replied that schools for the purpose should be provided, and added that he "could not imagine any subject that would raise such a furore throughout Canada and be less defensible, should it be known that, when Parliament was appropriating millions of dollars for the three armed services, French Canadians who formed one third of the population of the country were being virtually excluded or ostracized from one of the services. I asked all present to imagine what would be said when it was placed within the power of anyone to represent that not only was this the case, but that those who were practising it were seeking two things in addition, to have the Canadian Navy so closely intertwined with the British Navy as to become virtually a part of it, and, on the other hand, were supporting a policy that many men who were precluded from enlisting in the Navy, should be conscripted for service overseas. I did not spare the expression of my indignation and said I wished to have the minutes record the fact that any practice of the kind was opposite to the policy of the Government, and should not be countenanced for a moment longer."

All through the period from his return from Washington until the landing in Sicily, Mackenzie King felt and expressed a good deal of concern about the seeming indifference of the country to the gravity of the war. On June 4, he said good-bye to Walter Harris and Hugues Lapointe who were going back overseas and "told both of them how proud I was of them. Both spoke in very kindly, indeed affectionate terms. My heart aches to see these young men leaving to participate in the terrible situation which lies ahead." On June 18, the War Committee was given the estimate of probable casualties for the next sixteen months. The estimate was 115,000 and Mackenzie King wrote "no word I have thus far heard caused me a greater pain in my heart than the thought all of this implied in the lives of the men serving in the Army, and to our young country."

The feeling of remoteness began to disappear and indifferences vanished once the Canadian troops landed in Sicily, though the first successes created false hopes of an early end to the war. On July 7, when the invasion was imminent, Ralston told Mackenzie King the proposed communiqué announcing the landing referred only to the forces of the United States and the United Kingdom. Ralston felt keenly that the Canadian participation should be mentioned and Mackenzie King told him to "get off word to the authorities accordingly to see if this could not be arranged." The next day (July 8) Mackenzie King received a message from Vincent Massey, the Canadian High Commissioner in London, which "indicated that for reasons of security, the British were not sure that anything could be said about the participation of the Canadians. This made Ralston and myself . . . feel quite indignant. We immediately planned to send wires to Massey and also to Washington to say that we thought the proclamation should contain mention of Canadians participating." They also decided to have L. B. Pearson, who was Chargé d'Affaires in Washington in the absence of Leighton McCarthy, "get in touch immediately with the authorities of the U.S. and explain our indignation at the wire from Britain and get their co-operation in having mention made in any proclamation and also the P.M. given a chance to make a statement." Norman Robertson suggested that Mackenzie King "telephone either to the President or to Harry Hopkins and ask that Pearson get a chance to have an interview with them. I telephoned at once. Got the White House in a few minutes and almost immediately Harry Hopkins. The girl on the phone first mentioned that the President was at dinner and Hopkins with him; would I wish to interrupt or would I wait until after dinner. I said I wanted to speak to Hopkins at once and within a minute or two, he was at the phone."

He told Hopkins he "was very anxious to get a message to the President and wondered if the President would be willing to see Pearson during the evening. Hopkins said at once he was sure the President would. That he would 'phone Pearson and ask him to stand by and would 'phone him as soon as the President could see him." Very soon afterwards "word came that Pearson had had a very pleasant twenty-minute talk with the President and Hopkins together. The President had agreed with all of the points raised and said mention should be made of Canada's participation; also that I should make a statement at the same time. He would see that all of the points mentioned were met.

"I could not help remarking . . . how different the attitude of the Americans was from the British. Was it any wonder that our people began to like the Americans; were antagonized at the English, and were beginning to be more and more friendly with the Americans? There could be no more striking example than this, that, after our men had been defending Britain for nearly four years, we were told by the British authorities that, for reasons of security, no mention can even be made of Canada's participation when a division and more are actually within a day of risking their lives off the shores of Sicily in an engagement with the enemy in the waters of the Mediterranean."

The following day (July 9) Mackenzie King was busy in the House all day with the debate on the Estimates of the External Affairs Department. "Up to the very moment of adjournment," he noted in his diary, "I was hoping that some word would come which would let me give to the House either the communiqué only announcing the launching of the invasion, or my statement as well. Through the day, cables and telephone messages had gone back and forth between Massey and ourselves and the Defence Department trying to get from the British Government the right to have the announcement made in terms of Canada's forces as well as those of Britain and the U.S. The word came that for security reasons, etc. this would not be done. We had, however, the promise of the President that it would be done, and I felt that that would work out. However there seemed to be further complications through the day in that it was reported that Eisenhower was objecting to bringing in a reference to Canada."

When Mackenzie King went to his office in the Parliament Buildings after the House had risen, he found all his staff looking "quite upset. Ralston came in also in an inquiring and anxious frame of mind." The word that had been received "seemed to indicate that the promise of the President had not been carried out and that Eisenhower had found it necessary not to include mention of Canadian troops. . . . The situation looked pretty desperate as it was certain that the press in the morning would have the full story, and that, in all possibility, it might contain some reference to Canadians, and I would be left in the position of having, as Prime Minister, said nothing about our forces. Curiously enough, I did not feel any deep concern, but believed all would yet work out. Ralston was very much worried, indeed so much so that I felt sorry for him."

The reason given for not referring to the Canadians was military security. Mackenzie King "accepted the position, feeling that if the security reasons were as mentioned, there was nothing to do but submit." He was urged by Ralston and others to explain the situation confidentially to the press. He refused, saying "there was only one thing to do, to adhere to the undertakings. I said I would get home so that the press could not reach me." When one of his secretaries in the Parliament Buildings said that some flash had come to Montreal to indicate that the invasion had started and he was being questioned, Mackenzie King told him "to hold firm and say nothing but to close the office up and get away." He arranged to have Arnold Heeney give him any word which might come and "it was understood that if only the communiqué came, it would be given at once, and I wrote out by hand what should be said by the Prime Minister here. On the other hand, if the chance came to have my statement, it was all ready for the press, to be given to them at night. I also asked that arrangements be made to have me go on the radio at eight o'clock in the morning."

Mackenzie King left for Laurier House shortly before midnight. Just after he arrived there, Arnold Heeney telephoned "to say that release had come for the communiqué. I said then to see that it was given immediately to the press." Shortly afterwards Heeney telephoned again "to say that a flash had come from Washington beginning with the words 'British—United States—Canadian forces have launched an attack on Sicily.' As this had come from Washington, it was clear that the world would know at once that Canadian forces were engaged. I said to Arnold to have my statement given at once to the press, and to arrange for my going on the air in the morning at eight o'clock." As soon as that had been arranged, Mackenzie King "phoned to Ralston who had got the word meanwhile and was greatly relieved. The amazing part of this whole business is that, notwithstanding Canada has defended Britain for three to four years past, all that this has cost the Government and our men in the way of disappointment, the British Government—who were left with the final say—were making it impossible for any reference to be made to Canada's part."

Mackenzie King added that if he "had not 'phoned to the President direct and got his undertaking, Canada's name would not have appeared and apparently the wires show that every effort was made to block the President's assurance after it was given. However, it was carried out and we owe to the U.S. that mention is made of Canadians as well as U.S. and British forces being in the attack for the liberation of Europe. The irony of the situation was that in the debate through the day, the Tories were taking the attitude that there should be only one policy—an Empire policy—that we should take the word of Britain. In other words, whatever Britain might do would be right. They went out in the open to say that when Britain was at war, Canada was at war.

"I could think of nothing that would so incense the people of Canada as this, were the facts known. What would have been felt by the troops and by the Canadian people, if no mention had been made of Canada's part, I cannot say. . . . Were it not for my friendship with the President, and the position of confidence I have established with him, and my sense of freedom to appeal to him at a moment of crisis to get justice for our Canadian troops, no mention would have been made of our part in this momentous episode."

He reflected that "if the day ever comes that the people of Canada should incline in some political affiliation to the United States rather than to Britain, it will be that the British Government itself and their officials will be responsible for it. On the other hand, if the Empire is held together, it will be to men like myself who are being represented as separatists, etc., that this would be due."

The incident did not end there. When the sitting of the House of Commons opened on July 14, there were some questions by Hanson "about the officer-in-charge of our forces in Sicily. The Government began to be attacked on not giving out information. Hanson used remarks such as: 'I hope we may not be left out of this show altogether.' Knowing what I had been through, and not wanting to have this experience again, feeling that it was necessary to say something to the country about the difficult position in which we were placed in making announcements where the matter was one of combined operations, etc., I felt it desirable to follow up Ralston with a statement making clear that I did not intend, if possible, to allow the services of our troops to be sidetracked or ignored. I thought it, therefore, desirable to tell the House something of the experience I had had on Friday night that they might see for themselves just how embarrassing situations could be. I felt when I had concluded it was one of the most significant statements I had made and I really marvelled at having been able to make it in the form I did on top of all the fatigue of continuous sittings during the last few days."

The next day (July 15) in the House of Commons, Coldwell "brought up again question of why we had to get our news from England regarding Canadian forces, referring to the fact that Canadian newspapermen were prevented from using information that our first divisions had landed in Sicily; asking why announcements respecting operations of Canadian forces were made from London and Washington; whether those should not be made from Canada." Mackenzie King wrote that: "Continuing to feel strongly on the whole situation and knowing what the feeling was on the part of the press and the country in this matter, and what it is certain to be, unless situations like those of Friday last can be prevented from arising again, I took up the matter myself and enlarged upon what I had said yesterday, going the length of making it clear that I had had to 'phone Roosevelt to get the authority needed to make the announcement I did. I felt in my heart it was due to the President to let the country know that he had played as fairly and squarely as he did. I did feel that the situation needed to be exposed more than it had been thus far. It was really unbelievable that with all Canada has done in this war for Britain, that our position should have been so completely and deliberately overlooked by the British—not only overlooked, but specific reference made to their own forces and none to ours; completely leaving us out of the picture. I felt when I had finished speaking that what I had said would not be pleasing when read in Britain but I felt nevertheless it was necessary to save worse situations later on. What I said was received by applause from all sides of the House." The following day (July 16) Mackenzie King noted he had "a fine letter from Grattan O'Leary [of the Ottawa *Journal*] yesterday congratulating me on the stand I had taken. I thanked him over the 'phone today."

This whole incident almost provoked a quarrel with Churchill. On Sunday evening, July 18, Malcolm MacDonald brought Mackenzie King "a telegram from Churchill stating he had seen the text of my statement in the House and asking [MacDonald] for suggestion re reply [to an anticipated question in the British House of Commons]. Indicated he could not accept situation. The telegram at first appeared to me to be somewhat insolent. I told MacDonald if Churchill made any difficulty in his reply to me, and controversy arose in the country, I would regard the situation as paralleling Hepburn's action in criticizing the Government's effort, seek a dissolution, and go to the country. That I felt Canada was solidly behind me in the position I had taken in standing up for Canadian forces. I let him see how indignant I felt and the degree to which Britain was taking credit exclusively to America and herself, and deliberately leaving Canadians out of the picture after they have given last three years to safeguarding Britain, and the Government subject to criticism for holding them back from action in active theatres."

The next day (July 19) Mackenzie King discussed with Malcolm MacDonald what kind of reply he should make to Churchill's message. He noted that "MacDonald wished me to outline a draft of what I thought of saying to Churchill, and offered to look it over and revise it in a way that he thought might be helpful. I told him quite bluntly that I would not make any draft; that I thought Churchill ought to prepare his own statement. I had said all I wished to say, on Hansard. I was not there in a position to make any defence of myself. Whereupon Malcolm offered to draft out something which he would show to me later as something that might be said."

When MacDonald returned with the draft, Mackenzie King "thought the statement prepared for Churchill to make in the House had been well drafted. When it was suggested to me that it should go from me, I, at first, strongly opposed the idea. Later on, Malcolm pointed out that anything I would send, Churchill would be more likely to act upon than something he knew had come from MacDonald. I decided I would let the message go as from myself."

In his subsequent statement to the House, Churchill indicated that the request for specific reference to the presence of Canadian troops had been agreed to at once by General Eisenhower, but that the word of his acquiescence had reached Ottawa more quickly from Washington than from London. He concluded by saying he had had a very agreeable interchange of telegrams with Mr. Mackenzie King and "the misunderstanding, for which nobody is to blame, can now be regarded as cleared away."

On July 20, Mackenzie King noted that "Churchill, this morning, made a statement in the British House in answer to question re recognition of Canadian troops. While it will serve to avoid fresh difficulties arising, it is not a fair statement. Indeed it makes the issue quite other than the one which in fact it is. However, with war on, it is perhaps as well to let the matter lie where it is."

CHAPTER NINETEEN

The Quebec Conference, 1943

AT THE VERY TIME (July 19) Mackenzie King was discussing with Malcolm MacDonald the message to Churchill about the landing of the Canadian troops in Sicily, he had on his desk, unanswered, a cable from Churchill stating that he and Roosevelt would like to have a meeting in the near future and suggesting that it be held at Quebec. While Malcolm MacDonald and Norman Robertson were still with him at Laurier House, he read them "the paragraph from Churchill's wire about meeting Churchill and Roosevelt at Quebec. I had prepared an answer to send, cordially approving the idea. I asked Robertson what he thought of it. He said immediately he thought my own position would have to be very carefully considered." Malcolm MacDonald "felt it would be embarrassing for me to raise the question in my position, and . . . said it would be better for him to do it . . . and make it quite clear that it would be a mistake to have the meeting at Quebec unless I were more than in the position merely of host to Churchill and Roosevelt in the eyes of the people. . . .

"I, myself, felt that to try to get Churchill and Roosevelt to agree to this would be more than could be expected of them. They would wish to take the position that jointly they have supreme direction of the war. I have conceded them that position. I feel, however, that should I be host at Quebec and meet them both on arrival, and be with them all the time they were there, the Conference would be regarded as between the three, as in fact it would be, in large part, without having the question raised too acutely or defended too sharply.

"Churchill mentioned he and I could discuss other matters also. It made it imperative I should show ready acquiescence in the suggestion. I drafted a reply but, in the light of what was said by Robertson and MacDonald, added a paragraph to the effect that the position of Prime Minister of Canada would necessarily have to be considered when the meeting was on Canadian soil. However, before sending this to MacDonald to transmit to Churchill, I decided to strike it out as sounding a note that might be resented by Churchill on the morning that he was about to reply to a question being asked him in the British House regarding recognition of Canadian forces. I, therefore, let my answer go in the most cordial wording possible, without reserve."

The next day (July 20) Mackenzie King made sure "that Malcolm MacDonald sent a message to Churchill about making position of the Canadian Prime Minister at any conference at Quebec what it should be and preventing me from being put in a false position before the Canadian people. My own feeling is that Churchill and Roosevelt being at Quebec, and myself acting as host, will be quite sufficient to make clear that all three are in conference together and will not only satisfy but will please the Canadian feeling, and really be very helpful to me personally." On July 23, he received a message from Churchill which "made quite clear Churchill saw the need of Conference appearing to be an Anglo-American-Canadian conference."

The proposed meeting at Quebec cut across the plans Roosevelt had discussed in May with Mackenzie King for a visit to Canada which would culminate in a meeting with Stalin in Alaska. Roosevelt still wanted to make the fishing trip to Georgian Bay he had suggested at that time, and to visit Ottawa. On July 22, Mackenzie King told the Governor-General of the possibility of the President "being here early in August. His Excellency at once said that they would postpone, if need be for a week or so, their planned visit to Prince Rupert and the North. I then told him of the communication from Churchill regarding possibility of Churchill and Roosevelt meeting at Quebec. He was struck by the idea. When I spoke of the Citadel, he said that, of course, he would place it at the Government's disposal, and added that he would arrange to have some of his staff go down."

Mackenzie King reflected on July 23 that it was "indeed a big venture. When I become host to the P.M. of Great Britain and President of the U.S. at a conference with them both at Quebec in the old capital of Canada, it will be a pretty good answer to the Tory campaign of 'our leaders, Churchill and the President.' [Mackenzie King was referring to a leaflet issued by Knox Church in Winnipeg describing Churchill and Roosevelt as 'our leaders' and also to sponsored advertisements for Victory Loans with similar pictures and designations.] Indeed, I doubt if there will have been a comparable event in Canadian history. It will serve to link the whole past and present of Canada into the world history of today."

The following day (July 24) Leighton McCarthy came to Ottawa with several messages from Roosevelt including word that the fishing trip "was likely to be a matter of a week at Manitoulin Island and that the President appeared anxious to have it of a character that would give him complete freedom with his own party. Would be glad to have McCarthy or myself come for a day, but evidently wished to keep week more or less free for discussion by themselves. I told McCarthy that was a great relief to my mind. Personally I was not anxious to go on the trip at all, especially as other matters had come up which would make it, along with what I had said in the House, inadvisable that I should be too much with the President at this time."

McCarthy "thought the President would be prepared to come to Ottawa on his way back from Manitoulin but, even there, he might be pressed for time." He also brought a message from the President setting out the difficulty of including the Canadian Chiefs of Staff in the Quebec Conference without creating difficulties with the other Allied nations. Later that day (July 24), Mackenzie King told Ralston he "thought the only thing to do was to take the position that, as host at Quebec, I would not permit anything that would embarrass other United Nations but would expect both the President and Churchill to realize what our situation was and play fair. I said I felt sure we could work out what would be quite satisfactory in the end. I told him I thought it would be best for me to stay at the Chateau. . . . To be crowded into the Citadel with Churchill and the President, and possibly their wives, and to have to act as immediate host there, would be intolerable. . . . Ralston agreed this might be best, and also agreed with me that we should take a broad attitude and trust to the right thing being done. I let him know that the President had been doubtful if he would come to Canada at all, if arrangements were such as would embarrass him with other countries. I said to Ralston the important thing was to have the meeting held at Quebec. That, of itself, would cause all else to work out satisfactorily."

Of Mackenzie King's attitude to the Conference, Churchill wrote at a later date: 'It was Roosevelt who suggested that Quebec should be the scene. . . . The President, while gladly accepting Canadian hospitality, did not feel it possible that Canada should be formally a member of the Conference, as he apprehended similar demands by Brazil and other American partners in the United Nations. We also had to think of the claims of Australia and the other Dominions. This delicate question was solved and surmounted by the broadminded outlook of the Canadian Prime Minister and Government. I for my part was determined that we and the United States should have the Conference to ourselves, in view of all the vital business we had in common. A triple meeting of the heads of the three major powers was a main object of the future; now it must be for Britain and the United States alone.'[1]

[1] W. S. Churchill, *The Second World War*, vol. V (Toronto, 1951), pp. 66–7.

Mackenzie King's diary for July 26 shows that he plunged into the detailed planning of the Quebec Conference at once, and he gave it almost daily attention until the Conference opened. He was worried about how he could be in Quebec to meet Churchill and, at the same time, give Roosevelt a proper reception in Ottawa. On July 27, he telephoned Roosevelt to discuss some of the arrangements. In the course of their conversation, Roosevelt suggested it might be better if he left the Ottawa visit over until after the meeting at Quebec. Mackenzie King agreed and told Roosevelt "the real question in regard to the Ottawa visit is the demonstration I want to have staged on Parliament Hill. That means that I must have freedom to give publicity to the visit some days in advance, especially if I am to have Members of Parliament here."

Mackenzie King also told Roosevelt not to be concerned about the problem of Canadian participation in the Conference; that he, as host, would "watch carefully any situations. The President then said that would be first rate. You can be host to us and your Chiefs of Staff hosts to the other Chiefs of Staff."

On the afternoon of July 30, the Governor-General came out to Kingsmere, as he quite often did, sometimes with Princess Alice and sometimes alone. He had tea with Mackenzie King who noted that they had "toast and some fresh strawberry jam and cake and tea. The Governor thoroughly enjoyed the jam, took no less than three helpings. Before starting off, in an embarrassed sort of way, he asked me if I had any little cottage I could let him and Princess Alice have for a few days. That they would like to get away by themselves quietly before going out to the West. . . . He said they would be glad to come out by themselves and just look after themselves. After canvassing different situations, the Governor asked about the little farm house here. I at once said: 'Of course, they would be most welcome here, and it would be an honour to the little house to have them stay.' He said, in a quite simple way, it is strange, he said; we have wanted to be in that little house. We have such a liking for this little house and would be so glad to be here for a day or two. . . . Finally it was arranged that if I go down to Quebec on Monday week, they will come out and stay here before going to Quebec themselves. . . . I was really touched by the almost child-like delight. The Governor repeatedly said how much this little place appealed to them; the air and the beauty. The peace of it all. I can understand exactly what they want. It is to be away from everybody and everything for a little time.

"As I dictate, there comes to my mind the changes which are wrought by the whirligig of time. Little could my grandfather have seen when he was in prison and in exile, or my father and mother when they were making their sacrifices for the children's education, that some day one of their name would be entertaining the President of the U.S. and the Prime Minister of Britain at the Citadel of Quebec (where my father's father's remains lie) at a time of world war, and that, in the same week, the granddaughter of Queen Victoria would be finding her moment of rest and quiet and peace in the home of one of their own."

On August 1, Mackenzie King received word that Roosevelt had arrived at Little Current on Manitoulin Island and that the fishing was good. The next day he learned with satisfaction that "the Commanding Officer has given me his quarters in the Citadel grounds. Apparently there is further accommodation there, good cook, everything separate and plenty of room for members of my secretarial staff." As a consequence, Mackenzie King gave up the idea of staying at the Chateau Frontenac. The arrangement was very satisfactory. He was in the same building with Roosevelt and Churchill who occupied the Governor-General's quarters at the Citadel, but in his own separate apartment.

The actual Conference at Quebec between Roosevelt and Churchill and the British and American Chiefs of Staff began on August 17 and concluded on August 24, but Churchill arrived in Halifax on August 9 and in Quebec on August 10 where he spent a day before going on with his daughter Mary to visit Niagara Falls and Hyde Park. Mrs. Churchill remained in Quebec where Churchill returned on August 15. Mackenzie King was in Quebec continuously from August 9 to August 24 and he returned there again for a meeting on August 31 of the War Committee at which Churchill reported on the results of the Conference. During the Conference, Roosevelt, Churchill, and Mackenzie King and their own immediate staffs were in the Citadel; but the whole of the Chateau Frontenac Hotel was taken over for the military staffs.

On August 4, there was a message from Churchill suggesting a formal British-Canadian Conference on the day following his arrival. Mackenzie King felt Churchill was "asserting the position at once that, while at the Citadel, he would be, as it were, on his own soil, and that our relations with him will be those of Canadians in conference at London. I shall have throughout to maintain with care and due deference our own position as a country in no way subordinate to Britain—in any aspect of its domestic or external affairs. A very difficult position for me."

Mackenzie King left for Quebec on Sunday, August 8. In the afternoon of that day, Sir John Anderson, who was Lord President of the Council in the United Kingdom Government, had tea at Kingsmere and talked with Mackenzie King "for an hour during which time he gave me a most interesting account of the development of the *U.* [Uranium] and *H.W.* [Heavy Water] developments describing the processes. I was astonished to hear him say it would probably be two years before the present experiments would reach the stage where they could be practically applied. They will give control of the world to whatever country obtains them first. He explained that the Americans had an enormous plant for development purposes, covering many acres of ground. There had been great difficulty getting agreement between the Americans and the British on the development, each apparently wishing to go along lines of their own. President Conant, of Harvard, had explained to Anderson that as enormous expenditures had to be made secretly for the purpose, Americans had to do the development on their own as there still persisted the old myth that where they worked anything jointly with the British, the British got ahead. It was not true but nevertheless a myth which would be effective in post-war times, once the Government had to publicize or tell what had been done. . . . He mentioned that leading scientists in Britain and America had been working on this for a long time. The root secret of it all was some atomic power. As he developed the matter scientifically, my own mind made a parallel between power of the mind that comes from tapping deeper sources of energy as explained by William James.

"Anderson said he had reached an agreement which he thought the President and Churchill would both sign. It made Canada also a party to the development. Much of the *U.* and *H.W.* are in our country. He had explained to the Americans that Britain cared nothing about the post-war profit-making industries of the matter, but was concerned for war purposes. They knew that both Germany and Russia were working on the same thing. Germany had made certain developments in Norway, near Oslo, which the British had destroyed once; they had restored it, and the British had destroyed it again. He thought Russia with its enormous scientific development along mechanical lines might perfect the discovery first of all which would be a terrific thing for that country, should such be the case. He, himself, said that, while the war might be over before the development came, it would be a terrific factor in the post-war world as giving an absolute control to whatever country possessed the secret. At the same time, if anyone of the competing nations came first, they would be sure of immediate victory, so powerful was the destruction this discovery was capable of effecting."

Mackenzie King arrived at Quebec in the afternoon of August 9. About 6 p.m. he received word that Churchill had landed at Halifax and that Roosevelt proposed to announce Churchill's arrival at his Press

Conference in Washington the next afternoon. Mackenzie King felt "it would never do to have the landing of the British Prime Minister in Canada given out by the head of a foreign country, and nothing said in advance by the Prime Minister of the country to which he had come, and in which he was a guest. I felt I had only to speak to the President to get this cleared up quite satisfactorily." He accordingly telephoned Roosevelt who told him "he had had a wonderful trip and was feeling fine. He liked that part of the country [Manitoulin] very much. . . . He said: 'You did not come; you were not as fond of fishing as I am.' I replied that I had a good deal to do here looking after arrangements. The President then said to me: 'Have you had any word about the arrival?' I replied: 'Yes, that our friend has arrived safely.' " Mackenzie King then suggested that he send Roosevelt "a message to say that our friend has arrived safely. That I have met him and that we are together at the Citadel. That I understood he was having a conference tomorrow. That he might give that word to the conference that he had heard from me to this effect. He said: 'I will give that out at the press conference.' I then said: 'I thought that I should give out the word of his arrival in Canada about the same time or better still, a little before.' He, the President, could then say he had received the word from me of Churchill's arrival, and that we were both together at the Citadel. He replied: 'Yes, he would make that statement in that way.' Agreed that I should give the announcement first." They had some discussion of Churchill's plans to go to Niagara Falls and Hyde Park and the time of Roosevelt's arrival at Quebec, and agreed to make plans for Roosevelt's visit to Ottawa after Roosevelt reached Quebec.

The next day (August 10), Ralston arrived in Quebec from England and at once had a long talk with Mackenzie King in which he said "the Americans were pressing very hard for the invasion of Europe from the North this year. He, Ralston, agrees that is impossible. He agrees it would be Dieppe all over again. . . . The big question that has to be settled when Churchill comes is whether the Allies will go on invading Europe from the South. The Americans wish to stop when Sicily is completely occupied. They will then favour getting ready from the North." Mackenzie King found Ralston was "all for another division going to Sicily and into Italy."

After this talk, Ralston and Mackenzie King "went together to the Chateau where we had a meeting of the War Committee. All members were present excepting Angus Macdonald who was with Churchill. I outlined to them all what had taken place from the time of Churchill's first wire; then drew attention to the different matters likely to come up for discussion. Asked them to be prepared to discuss matters with Churchill tomorrow."

After lunch on August 10, Mackenzie King went to the railway station at Charny to meet Churchill. "As Churchill stepped off the platform of the last car," he wrote, "I greeted him very warmly and then Mrs. Churchill and Mary. Introduced them to the Lieutenant-Governor and to Premier Godbout. Churchill wished to walk along the road a short way so as to greet the people assembled on either side. They were mostly young persons but they applauded enthusiastically. He and I drove later by the Plains of Abraham, past Wolfe's monument, and then into the Citadel grounds. Churchill kept commenting on the beauty of the country and magnificent expanse of the river. . . As we passed Wolfe's monument, he asked me if that was where he was slain. Mentioned that his home was in Westerham, and remarked on his having shown me a monument [of Wolfe] there."

Almost the first thing Churchill said during the drive to the Citadel was: "I hope you won't want us to hurry away. I would like to make a good stay." He at that time was thinking of staying on in Quebec after the meeting with Roosevelt and said that from Quebec "he could readily keep in touch with the President, and go back and forth, if need be." He added that he and Mackenzie King "would carry on the war from this side. When Churchill spoke of the stay, I said I was glad to hear him speak of not hurrying away. That the country would welcome his having a complete change here. That I had been hoping he might plan to stay a while. He rather indicated that the Citadel was where he would make his Headquarters.

"He then said to me: 'I would like to go up to Toronto and drive through the streets there, as I have done in London.' He said 'You and I will go together, if that would be agreeable to you.' I spoke of the pleasure that would be. I suggested to him that it might be well to do the same in Montreal. He said: 'I would be glad to do that; anything that you suggest.' At a later stage, I said to him I thought it might be pleasant were he to take a journey across Canada; go out to the Rocky Mountains. He said: 'Yes, I remember Lake Louise, and what a lovely place it was.' He thought it would be very pleasant for Mrs. Churchill and his daughter. He kept explaining what a great joy it was to them to see Canada.

"As we went along, he brought up different matters in a quiet way. He said: 'We have got them beaten, but it may take some time.' I asked him how long. He said: 'One, possibly two years. On the other hand, no one knows what might happen in Germany. It might be six months, but there is also Japan.'

"In speaking about not hurrying back, Churchill said: 'Much more can be done by giving time for things to develop. I can do more with the President by not pressing too hard at once. He is a fine fellow. Very strong in his views, but he comes around.' I said I understood his difficulty would be to persuade the President not to be too quick about fighting from the North instead of from the South. He replied: 'Yes.' That there would have to be much careful work done there. That the trouble was the Americans did not realize how long it took to accomplish some things. He felt it would be very hard to get into Germany. He was entirely for going on with the war in Italy. . . . He said that our men had done well in Sicily. Remarked upon them being the hinge, with the Americans to one side, and the British on the other."

During their drive, Churchill also spoke about the recognition of the French National Committee which he hoped to persuade the President to agree to. The question of who should be recognized as representing France in the Free World had been a source of potential division ever since the fall of France. After the assassination of Darlan on Christmas eve of 1942, General Giraud had been recognized by the United States as the French Commander in North Africa and for a while there was some danger that Giraud would be the representative of French authority for the United States Government while de Gaulle would represent France to the British. Fortunately this danger seemed to have been averted by the formation at the beginning of June 1943 of the French Committee of National Liberation. This union of all the forces of French resistance outside France was particularly welcome to the Canadian Government and, when General Giraud came to the United States in July to arrange for supplies for the French forces, he was invited to visit Ottawa.

An effort had been made to symbolize the new French unity at the dinner given to Giraud by the Government on July 15, by including as guests both Bonneau, who represented the Free French in Canada, and Ristelhueber, the former (Vichy) Minister. On this occasion, Mackenzie King made what he regarded as "one of the best speeches I have made at any time. I had prayed very earnestly before getting up to speak that I might have help and [I] know that the prayer was answered. The whole gathering rose to their feet and cheered me when I concluded. Many spoke afterwards of what the speech meant. This was all the more remarkable in that my guest did not understand English and I had a difficult time during dinner to keep my thoughts concentrated.

"General Giraud made, I am told, an exceptionally fine speech. I could follow it slightly but St. Laurent told me, after dinner, it was one of the most moving speeches he had listened to in all his life. It was a direct statement by an honest man speaking fearlessly and simply in regard to a great episode in history. He brought us all very close to the very heart of the war. He appealed to me as a very great patriot. He speaks without notes and, as he told me, without preparation, just saying what he feels and believes."

From the time of Giraud's visit, the Canadian Government was anxious to recognize the French National Committee as the official representatives of the French people but they had not yet acted. Churchill now said in Quebec that he was glad Canada "had held back" as he felt "it was better for us all to act together." Later in the day (August 10) they again discussed "the question of recognition of the French National Committee, Churchill emphasizing how very warmly the President felt against de Gaulle. Said that he, himself, thoroughly disliked de Gaulle, though he had many manly qualities. . . . He enlarged repeatedly on de Gaulle's mischief-making and the concern he had caused in different countries. He thought the bringing of Giraud to America perhaps had been a mistake. It had enabled de Gaulle to make headway in his absence, but all that was said by way of having me understand the President's feeling, and the importance of our not issuing a statement of our own on recognition until he and the President had discussed the matter. It would be helpful to him in getting the President's consent to have it said that we, in Canada, were most anxious to have the French Committee recognized. At another time he said to me he thought it would be a splendid thing to have the recognition given by the two of them from Quebec. I agreed that that would be a good stroke. I, however, suggested that consideration ought to be given to having simultaneous declaration rather than a joint declaration." That in the end was what happened but it was only agreed on at the very close of the Quebec Conference.

When Churchill and Mackenzie King reached the Citadel from the station, Sir John Anderson was already there to see Churchill. Mackenzie King told Churchill "that Sir John had been out to Kingsmere on Sunday. He asked me if he was pleased with the arrangements he had made in regard to the [atomic] project. I said I thought he was. Churchill said it was too important a matter to let others get ahead of the rest of us on it. There had been some effort, he thought, on the part of the Americans to get ahead of the British." After dinner that same evening, Churchill discussed the atomic project, which had the code name "tube alloys," with Mackenzie King and secured his agreement to the suggestion Churchill planned to make to President Roosevelt that C. D. Howe be made a member of a combined policy committee of the United States, the United Kingdom, and Canada.

Mackenzie King dined with Mr. and Mrs. Churchill and their daughter, Mary. When Churchill came in to dinner, he handed Mackenzie King "a pink coloured communication which he said to Mrs. Churchill and myself had just come to him from Stalin. The communication from Stalin contained congratulations upon the success in Sicily. It also stated that he was sorry not to have been able to answer previous communications for some time as he had been at the front with his armies. It went on to say that he felt it would be well to have a meeting with the President and himself in the near future. Churchill remarked that Stalin had been very indifferent and was rude; as he had not answered some of his communications, he, Churchill, had stopped writing him for a time, and he thought the obvious silence would let him see he would have to fall in line. . . . He said that he would send him a nice message today from Quebec which would cheer things up and restore relations between them."

During dinner they discussed "the announcement of the invasion of Sicily. Among other things, I mentioned that I had communicated with the President because Eisenhower had to do with the military operations, and I wanted an assurance from the highest quarter that . . . we were at liberty to make a statement." Mackenzie King added that he could get no such assurance from the British who "had simply passed on a word of our desire to Eisenhower, but that we had never got a communication back from the British Government, and that we were not to make an announcement for another twenty-four hours. . . . I told him of our hearing the American War Office announcement about our troops, and that I then felt free to make the announcement I did. . . . Having received the direct assurance of the President, I felt safe when I learned that the War Office had mentioned Canadians, and let my statement go."

He told Churchill that what was particularly irritating was the fact that Massey had been informed that the President had given this assurance, and that, although the British authorities knew this, he later received word "we would be assisting the enemy if we made mention of Canadian troops participating. Also that we had never got from the British Government any word back that Eisenhower had either agreed or not agreed, and received also no authority at the time from Britain which we had received from the United States. . . . Everything was said in a quiet, pleasant way, making clear the situation. I mentioned to him that I had had some messages from Attlee, that I thought he [Churchill] must be perhaps away in North Africa. Churchill told Mackenzie King several times during this conversation that whenever he was "deeply concerned over a matter not to hesitate to ring him up, if need be; say I was worried over a situation, and he would do all he could."

Mackenzie King felt that "the evening conversation made clear to me Churchill's desire to clear up any possible misunderstanding, and to get complete agreement between us. I got a good chance both at dinner and after to speak of my problem which is Canada's problem—namely the need of our having the Canadian people feel that we were really having a voice in all matters pertaining to the war. I explained that I fully understood the necessity of safeguarding the position of other United Nations and other Dominions, but pointed out that there were two lines of pressure which were very great and which he would understand. One was the Opposition in Parliament which was continually drawing attention to Canada not being represented on this or that Committee.... In other words whether I was letting Canada's position go by default, so that when it came to the time for peace, we would have no real voice. The other pressure was that from my colleagues in the Cabinet and from members of the Permanent Staff, External Affairs, etc., who were always at me to be asserting more strongly Canada's position, not allow anything to pass without taking it up immediately.... I sought to make clear, at all times, the sense of proportion which we had sought to keep and the avoidance of embarrassment."

On August 9, the Government had lost four by-elections and on the way to the Citadel from the station, Churchill told Mackenzie King he hoped "the by-elections are not causing you worry. I said I had expected to lose all. That our price control policy with the freezing of wages made it very difficult to keep labour against parties that were promising all kinds of things. Also we had no organization. Had been giving our time to the war effort. He said: 'My experience is that by-elections don't mean anything when you come to place a really large issue before the people.' ... At another time he referred to the by-elections as a fire started on ice. That it blazed up very much at the beginning, but did not necessarily spread ... went out after awhile."

Mackenzie King referred to Smuts' success in the recent South African election and Churchill "said that it was really wonderful. He is coming to England in September and turned to me, and said: 'Are you coming? Will you come?' I said: 'Yes, I was prepared to.' He then said: 'If you and he are there together, it does not much matter about the others.'"

The next morning (August 11), Mackenzie King called for Churchill shortly after 11 to go to the meeting with the Canadian War Committee at the Chateau Frontenac. At the meeting, at which Sir John Anderson was also present, Mackenzie King "explained that we fully understood the position as to Churchill and the President being the directing heads [of the war]. The Conference at Quebec was between themselves and between the Chiefs of Staff of the two countries, but also we realized the position of the other Dominions and United Nations, and that they would recognize how the Canadian people would feel as to the necessity of Canada sharing in all matters pertaining to the war as largely as possible. This more particularly as we had been a couple of years in the war before the U.S. . . .

"We then went through the various topics, most of which had to do with difficult questions that had come up, and which had resulted in misunderstanding. The first item was the position of the Canadian troops. Ralston dealt with this in a very frank way. Then there came the question of the recognition of the French National Committee."

Mackenzie King himself brought up "the question of post-war civil aviation planning [on which Canada had taken the position that there should not be a concerted or unified Commonwealth plan]. Churchill was quite outspoken on this, saying he had taken the whole matter in hand himself. They must have a preliminary conference in Britain with the other Dominions. If we could not see our way to attend, they would have to proceed without us. He was quite strong on his views there. I explained that our view was based on the larger conception of the working out of the whole post-war relations. That if the U.S. got the opinion—to use their own expression—that we of the British Empire were ganging up against them, they would immediately take a similar attitude toward the British Empire and it would become a test of strength. That by having proceedings begun, as we were accustomed to, in all the matters that we were taking up, by sharing to a large extent information in confidence from the beginning, a spirit of co-operation would be developed in the long run. I pointed out that we in Canada might wish to take a North American point of view on some things rather than the British Empire point of view. That with four thousand miles of boundary between us, planes going back and forth, Russia our nearest neighbour on the north, U.S. relations with Russia, etc., the whole problem here was a continental trans-oceanic problem in a very different way than it was in so far as Britain was concerned. I pointed out that naturally we would wish to co-operate as completely as possible with Britain. That we were at the mercy of the U.S. without being part of a larger combination, but what we were really thinking of was how question of co-operation could be best worked out.

"Crerar made an important contribution when he said it was not so much the question of the Governments, as the opposition that would be aroused in the press of the U.S. once they got the idea that an Empire policy was being developed versus a U.S. policy. He said the whole isolationist group would start their fight against Britain. I followed this up by saying I agreed with all that Crerar had said, except I would not limit political opinion in the U.S. to isolationist policy; that private air lines were the most powerful of the private interests in the U.S. and their lobbyists the most powerful. They would control the U.S. press generally and very soon the whole U.S. press would be combatting Britain in a way which the Government of the U.S. itself would have to bow to.

"Churchill was quick to see that this was a new point of view. He turned to Sir John Anderson and said 'you had better take a note of this and explain this all to our colleagues when you go back to England. I had thought it was only a North American point of view that you were concerned about.' It was quite clear that what we had said had made a real impression on him, and was something the significance of which had not entered his mind before.

"I spoke about the use of the term Anglo-American, and the omission of Canadians. Churchill explained his difficulty, which we all said we understood. . . . At the end of the meeting, I said that . . . perhaps Mr. Churchill might think from the number of issues we had raised that we had only grievances to speak of, forgetting that the whole war effort was being carried on in complete harmony and co-operation. Churchill was quick to say that he thought that everything which had been brought up was quite correct. He was so glad he himself was here to discuss the matters. Said the whole discussion had been most helpful, so much so that he hoped we would regard the meeting as a mere adjournment, and that we would have another conference next week. He then spoke about the announcement [about what had taken place at the meeting] to be given out, and, when he began to discuss it, he said perhaps we had better draft the notice at once. He then took his pencil and made a draft which I handed to Heeney. The meeting lasted until nearly two o'clock."

Mackenzie King noted that "Churchill was obviously greatly pleased with the meeting, as indeed were all the members of the War Committee of the Cabinet. He and I drove back together from the Hotel to the Citadel, where he had invited a number of persons to lunch. We had kept them waiting for an hour."

In the afternoon Mackenzie King took Churchill to call on the

Lieutenant-Governor of Quebec. After leaving Government House they drove to the Legislative Buildings, and there "were met at the door by Godbout who led us . . . into the Cabinet Council where his colleagues were seated on either side of a long table. He introduced them all in turn to Mr. Churchill. Godbout then sat at the head of the table with Churchill on his right and myself to his left. . . . To help along conversation at the beginning, I spoke to Mr. Churchill of the [Quebec] Government having been very helpful to our Government in our war effort. They had many problems here but dealt with them in a co-operative way. . . .

"On the way, I had suggested to Churchill to say a few words in French. He, himself, said he would like to say a word or two to the Quebec Cabinet. He began speaking in French, rather slowly but choosing his words carefully. He became quite emotional toward the end as he referred to Quebec and the historic significance of the meeting here, and what it might mean to the world to have decisions made in this old city which would help to relieve the situation in France. He spoke about his great desire to see France restored, given a worthy role and place in the world. . . . There was quite a silence after he had completed speaking. I, myself, broke it by beginning applause in which others joined in heartily. After shaking hands all around, we left the Chamber and returned to the Citadel."

Later in the afternoon, Mackenzie King drove with Churchill to Wolfe's Cove Station where he and his daughter Mary took the train for Niagara Falls. During their drives that afternoon, Churchill talked very freely to Mackenzie King who noticed "in Churchill's discussions he continually draws similes from family relationships and particularly . . . similes drawn from lives of wild animals, tame animals and the like, the cat and the mouse business; growling; and when one gets one's back up it is hard to get it down."

One of the subjects they discussed again during the afternoon was the recognition of the French National Committee. Mackenzie King said "it might be better for the recognition to be given in an identical statement, but separate by the President and himself, Canada making her own statement. I gave him a copy of what we proposed, to read over and to show to the President. Churchill said: 'I hope you won't become allergic to the Anglo-American expression.' He went on to say he wanted to tie the Americans down to the recognition and to hold them as closely as possible in everything. I pointed out that it was necessary to keep the Dominions in the picture and not to let it become too exclusively Britain and the U.S.

"I said to him when we were talking that I believed he was the one man that had saved the British Empire. He said 'No, if I had not been here someone else would have done it.' I said I did not believe that was so. I could not think of any other man who could have done what he did at the time. It was so necessary. He then said he had had very exceptional training, having been through a previous war and having had large experience in government. I said, 'Yes, it almost confirmed the old Presbyterian idea of pre-destination or pre-ordination; of his having been the man selected for this task.' I truly believe that but for his bold stand and vision Britain would never have been able to meet the situation as she has." For Mackenzie King, "the day altogether was a very happy one."

The following afternoon Mackenzie King had tea and a "very interesting conversation" with Mrs. Churchill who "spoke about how much Churchill relied upon me and spoke of how glad he was to be with me and to share days together." Mrs. Churchill told him "many things about Winston. One thing was that his being out of office for a number of years and writing the Life of Marlborough had had a real effect upon his character. He had discovered that Marlborough possessed great patience. That patience became the secret of his achievements. . . . That Winston would ask her whether she thought he would ever be back in government again. That she had told him he might not. She then told me that when Neville Chamberlain took over and succeeded Baldwin, and did not invite him into the Cabinet, she said then she did not think he would be in any future Government. She told me finally it was only four days before the war actually came on that Chamberlain told him he would like to have him in the Cabinet in the event of war, but she went on to say that if war had not come, he would not have been taken into the Cabinet."

Later that same afternoon, while walking in the Citadel grounds with one of his secretaries, Mackenzie King "saw the Canadian flag [red ensign] and the Union Jack flying side by side in the grounds. This I arranged yesterday. I had been put out when I saw the Union Jack and Canadian flags flying one beneath the other—the Canadian flag beneath the Union Jack, the day that Churchill arrived." He had subsequently spoken to Churchill about flying the three flags side by side and had then given directions that this should be done. "I can now say," he wrote, "that this was done with agreement between the Prime Minister of the United Kingdom and the Prime Minister of Canada." He added that both of them agreed that "the Canadian flag should come in the centre." He hoped "we might settle the whole flag business by getting the people accustomed to seeing our own flag flying in equality with the Union Jack. People will appreciate on Canadian soil at least having the Canadian flag appear when the U.K. and U.S. were represented." It did not prove so simple.

Churchill returned to Quebec from Niagara Falls and Hyde Park on Sunday, August 15. Almost the first word he said to Mackenzie King on his arrival "was that he was so glad to be back in his own Headquarters. He then spoke of what an ideal place Quebec was for a conference meeting." In outlining his talks with the President at Hyde Park, Churchill told Mackenzie King that the President had agreed to Howe being on the Combined Committee on Atomic Energy and said the agreement they had reached "contained references to not using this against each other, etc. It was important to get under way. He did not want the Russians in particular to get ahead with the process.

"He then spoke of the question of recognition of the French National Committee in Africa. Said the President and Mr. Hull were quite determined not to use the word 'recognition.' He, Churchill, had sought to persuade them if they were to do anything to do it generously. The President was to see Mr. Hull today. If they won't agree to recognition in the same terms that we wish to make it, then we will have to make our own statements separately, and we will go full length on our own."

When Churchill spoke about a meeting to be arranged with Stalin, Mackenzie King said he "thought a good plan would be for the President and himself to go out and see the developments of the Alaska Highway and to get the other gentleman to meet them out there. He [Churchill] said: 'I will have to be here about two months. I won't be on your back all the time. The President has invited Mrs. Churchill and myself and Mary to go down and spend a little time with them at Hyde Park after the Conference. We can then arrange for something else.' Referring to Stalin, he said: 'We will send the 'blighter' an invitation to try and have him meet us. If he does not accept it, we can't help it. We must try to arrange something now if we can.' " The meeting finally took place at Teheran, not in Alaska.

On the following day (August 16), Mackenzie King had luncheon alone with the Churchills and their daughter, Mary. Just before the luncheon Churchill gave Mackenzie King a memorandum about securing for British military canteens a "supply of whiskey from Canada. The memorandum said they could not get these supplies because the Prime Minister [of Canada] had threatened to stop the export of spirits, and that the Ministry of Supply [Munitions and Supply] was agreeable to having spirits exported. When I read over the memo, I said to Mr. Churchill that the representations were entirely false. There had been no restriction placed on export by the Government. That it was a matter of the distillers being obliged to make industrial alcohol instead of whiskey, and not wishing to cut into their own supplies. . . .

"This led to my speaking at the table of my course in regard to temperance as against prohibition, during which I said I had made up my mind at the beginning of the war that it would be much better to abstain altogether than to be making exceptions. That I felt I would be better in my own health and judgment by taking a rest instead of stimulants and that I had decided also to take nothing for the period of the war. Mrs. Churchill said that I looked remarkably well and I replied that it was due in large part to having given up stimulants. Churchill said that he had not, but he was feeling well. I said that, of course, everything depended on habits that a man had from youth. That were he to give up completely, it would probably kill him. I felt no embarrassment in the conversation."

The memorandum Churchill gave Mackenzie King that day was no doubt the sequel to a conversation Mackenzie King had had with Malcolm MacDonald on July 6, when "MacDonald came by appointment and handed me an aide-mémoire which was not signed. He said in a few words it was a request from the British Government to let more whiskey and gin be manufactured in Canada and shipped for the troops, etc. The aide-mémoire indicated the substance of what he said. I replied that I did not think the Government could consider allowing any increase. . . . That already it was clear there was a shortage of manpower, and that we had fought a battle on our policy and had resisted all the pressures, and that we certainly would not, at this time, agree to place ourselves in the position where it could be said that the liquor interests, in the end, had control. I also said I thought it was a terrible thing to have liquor purchased for the use of troops, particularly strong spirits. He asked me if it could not be done for the British Government. I told him I did not think it could. However, I would have the matter taken up. He said he had understood the Government had considered the matter and was prepared to modify its policy. I said I had not heard anything of the kind and did not know who could have given that impression. This is a pretty good instance that what one prevents is so much greater than what one is able to do."

Mackenzie King noted that "Churchill also told me before we sat down that he had some remarkable news today. Overtures for peace from Italy. That he would let me see the communications after luncheon. This he did." He added that "Churchill said he was not disposed to be too literal on the unconditional surrender. The thing was to get the Germans out of Italy and to get Italy out of the war or fighting with the Allies. The emissary from the Italian Government had stressed the importance of the Italians fighting against the Germans."

Churchill also spoke of the Canadian troops being "out of the fight for a time in order to be ready to invade Italy. . . . He then said that the question had been raised by McNaughton, I gathered, as to whether our men going to Italy was to be regarded as part of the one operation. He asked me if I could say that it was. I told him I had always understood that Sicily was simply a step to invading Italy, and to the invasion of Europe from the South. I would, however, like to confer with the Minister of Defence before giving a definite word. He said to me they may be landing there at any moment. They are probably already almost there. I said I would have the matter checked up, but I felt quite sure that the Government had always regarded the whole operation as one. Apparently McNaughton has questioned this." Later in the day Mackenzie checked with Ralston who was in Ottawa and who, after examining the record, was satisfied the Canadian troops had been committed for Italy and not just Sicily and said McNaughton was being advised.

At the table, Mackenzie King and Churchill got into discussion about the relationship of the nations of the Commonwealth. Mackenzie King spoke about "how the Dominions had come into this war. Churchill replied that all having done what they had on their own was one of the finest things that the world had ever seen. He agreed with me that if we had said that they had to go into war because of being part of the British Empire, there would have been resistance. He said: 'I am of the view that when the King is at war, we are all at war, but it is for each Dominion to decide for itself whether it will participate or not.' I remarked that it would be the enemy who would probably determine who was at war under the King.

"When Churchill spoke about the Conservatives holding to the idea of Empire, the Radicals pulling away, I said to him that in Canada I thought the Liberals were just as much for being a part of the British Empire or Commonwealth—whichever it was called—as the Conservatives, though the latter sought to monopolize the loyalty cry and to have it appear that the others took a different view."

Churchill talked at some length about the "unnecessary war" and how it might have been prevented. He asked Mackenzie King whether he remembered "the night [in London in 1936] when I told you war would be coming. I said I did, and he had said the German army would be in England four years from that time, unless conditions were changed. That was in 1936. That really came to the date of the collapse of France. Churchill said: 'You looked surprised.' I said to him I really felt no other man could have saved the day for Britain. He was quite quiet and reflective and said: 'It really looks as though I were reserved for that purpose. It was fortunate that I was out of office for ten years. It gave me time to study the situation.' I added: and it avoided his making enemies. . . . When he spoke of being reserved, I said that there was no doubt in my mind there were forces playing about our lives far beyond our ken, which were responsible for controlling and guiding in ways we did not know."

Mackenzie King noted that Churchill "could not have been kinder or really in a more gentle mood. He seemed to like to talk just quietly and reflectively. He then asked me to come and see the map room. We went together. As we went through the sun room, he said: 'I love this room; I love this country.'

"At luncheon, he had said the one place he would like to see was Churchill, and went on to tell how it had been named after the Duke of Marlborough. I told him I had many letters suggesting that he should visit Churchill. He thought that if they went to Winnipeg, there might be a chance. Mrs. Churchill asked where Winnipeg was. We explained: half way across the continent. He then spoke of it being a miracle that a country stretching 4,000 miles was held together as it was, with all its problems, and then asked about the Doukhobors. I gave him an account and told him the story of when Bennett, Gardiner, and myself were in the House and I was questioned by Esling." W. K. Esling, M.P. for Kootenay West, had asked Mackenzie King what the Prime Minister would do if three naked Doukhobor women appeared on his lawn and the reply was "I would send for the Leader of the Opposition [R. B. Bennett] and the Leader of the United Farmers [Robert Gardiner]."

The next day (August 17) the Governor-General and Princess Alice arrived at Quebec in time to receive President Roosevelt. Mackenzie King called on them at the station. He talked first with Princess Alice who "spoke of how much they had enjoyed their stay at Kingsmere." When they joined the Governor-General, he "spoke much in the same way that Princess Alice had spoken of their visit to Kingsmere."

Later in the day, Mackenzie King and Churchill drove in an open car to Wolfe's Cove to meet Roosevelt. On the way, Mackenzie King "spoke to Churchill about the memorandum re gin and whiskey and the memorandum I had sent to him. He said he did not care about the memorandum, as long as he got the whiskey. I then told him what the facts were and the kind of things that had been put into the memorandum were the sort of thing that was circulated by political opponents. He said he thought the memorandum was an impertinent one and that he would send a note to the Quartermaster-General telling him he thought so. I took advantage of this to show Churchill the little prayer pamphlet issued on 'Our Leaders,' and spoke of the billboard and of the detraction that had followed." [This was the pamphlet issued by Knox Church in Winnipeg.] Churchill told him "not to be concerned about that. He knew all about that sort of thing. He said, after all, what can you expect. You kept your opponents out of office for twenty years and you cannot expect any love from them or anything but bitterness just because you have defeated them. He then said to me: Did I not think it might be necessary to join with Conservatives to keep the C.C.F. from getting control of things? I said that the Conservative party was going down and down. They were at the bottom of everything. I could not see what strength they would bring to the Government, and I felt certain that were I to join with them, a very large part of my own party would leave me and join with the C.C.F. That I felt the Liberal party was the only one that could hold the country. That the way things were now, I felt it was better for our own party to proceed on lines as they had begun."

When Mackenzie King met Roosevelt "he spoke at once about the visit to Ottawa. Has now finally decided he will be there Wednesday of next week. I asked him if I might announce some days before that he would be there that day. He said the security men were always fearful about an announcement being made. He said to me at dinner tonight, go ahead and make it; never mind what they say. He, at first, had wished to be there on Monday. Churchill used what persuasion he could to have him remain over Tuesday. He, himself [Roosevelt], wanted to go back to Hyde Park from Ottawa; not to come back here which I think was sensible. He told me tonight he would spend the morning on the Hill; lunch with the Governor-General and would like to see [Princess] Juliana and his godchild. Would also like to go out to Kingsmere and would leave from Laurier House for his train to Hyde Park." The Governor-General and Princess Alice gave a dinner that evening in honour of the President and Churchill.

The following evening (August 18) Mackenzie King was host at a dinner for Roosevelt and Churchill. He noted that when they "spoke of the toasts, the President asked me if we might remain seated as we had done last night . . . as he had not his steel braces with him." When it came to the time of the toasts, Mackenzie King began by saying he wished "to take the earliest opportunity to extend to the President and to the Prime Minister a very hearty welcome on behalf of the Government and people of Canada, and to express to the President and Mr. Churchill, our appreciation of their having selected Canada as a place of meeting for the present Conference and Conference of their Staffs, and the City of Quebec in particular. In years gone by, the fate of nations had been decided here. The fate of the nations might again be decided for the future. The President, last night, had referred to anniversaries. I reminded him and those present that five years ago today, we had been together at Kingston at Queen's University, and referred to the President's assurance that the United States would not stand idly by if Canada were threatened by another power. I had said, in reply, that we had our own obligations and responsibilities, and would see as far as possible that enemy forces by water, air, or land would not cross our territory into the United States. We were realizing now how well those promises had been kept.

"I then spoke of today being the fifth anniversary of the opening of the bridge over the Thousand Islands, as a symbol of association of our two countries. Then spoke of three years ago, the meeting at Ogdensburg where the Permanent Joint Board of Defence had been established, and a beginning of the wider measure for defence between the Empire and the United States. Then referred also to the President having referred last night to a dream being realized in that he had spoken when he was here with Lord Tweedsmuir, of Quebec being an ideal place for an international conference. I said I, too, had had my dreams, and one that I had cherished through life was that the British Empire and the United States might be drawn closer together, and that, in some small way, immediate or remote, Canada might be an instrument toward that end and toward furthering the friendship between the two. . . . I felt that this gathering was helping toward that end. I then spoke of the personal pleasure it was to me to have the privilege of having, as a guest, Mr. Roosevelt, and of the length of time during which the President and I had known each other. I referred to our Harvard association and of how our friendships had become really intimate through the years. Of the many times I had enjoyed his hospitality at the White House, etc. I would leave them to imagine the delight it was to me to have the honour of representing my country, to receive him in my own homeland; to have the honour of entertaining him along with the Prime Minister of Britain. I then asked the guests to drink the President's health and extend to him the wish that he might be given the health and strength needed for the continuance of the mighty task in which he was engaged on behalf of freedom and the well-being of mankind. I spoke slowly and deliberately and I think freely and impressively. It seemed doubly impressive that we should have all remained seated while the toast was proposed and in drinking the President's health.

"The President, in replying, expressed appreciation of what I had said, and being in Canada. Particularly at Quebec. I thought he made clear that he, himself, had suggested Quebec as the place of meeting. Referred to his having had an association with Canada from the time that he was teething. Brought in about the family having had an island at Campobello and of his being brought there as an infant.

"Later when he came to speak of Harvard, he said he was working away as an undergraduate at the time I was getting high scholarship in the nature of a Ph.D. degree, and made some very pleasing reference to the friendship which we had shared over some forty years. He then spoke of the visit that the King and Queen had paid to Hyde Park. That he, himself, had arranged that I should accompany Their Majesties, and that, throughout their visit to the U.S., I was the Foreign Minister. From this, he went on to speak of how much they had enjoyed the visit of the King and Queen, and from that, he went on to propose the health of the King.

"After the King's health was drunk, after a few moments' pause, I spoke of the great pleasure it was to us all to have Mr. Churchill again in Canada. That he had paid Canada several visits over many years. It was now some twenty months since he had been in Canada. At that time, he came to us as one who had seen Britain through her dark days. That I wished to say I believed, and thought all present did, that he was the one man who had saved Britain at that time; but for him and his courage and leadership, the British Empire would not be in existence tonight, and he had really saved the British Empire. I felt this most strongly. That he now, along with the President, was helping to save the free world.

"I then spoke also of the personal friendship and association I had enjoyed with him, referring to having enjoyed his hospitality in London, in 1907. . . . We had had many meetings since and recently many communications, and how honoured I felt to enjoy his confidence and share with him the friendship which I had been privileged to share. I spoke of his bringing Mrs. Churchill with him to Canada, saying it . . . helped to give us even more feeling of all being part of a family community comprising the British Commonwealth. I said I hoped our guests would make their stay as long as they could in the Dominion. Concluded by proposing Mr. Churchill's health."

Churchill, in proposing Mackenzie King's health, "spoke about visits to Canada, very feelingly about the British Empire and Commonwealth, as he called it. Referred particularly to how magnificent Canada had been in her war effort. . . . He then went on to speak of the position of Canada in the U.S. and Britain, and how all-important it was for the future of the world that the British Empire and the U.S. should continue to work together in closest friendship and harmony for the future of the world. He then began to speak of myself as one person who had done so much to bring about that closer relationship. He then became quite personal in his references and said no one knew this country or the two countries better than I did. Spoke of my having rendered service alike to the Empire and the U.S. and Canada. He then spoke of myself as one who had brought together the forces at the right time, and had never failed to see that the right action was taken at the right moment. He presented a sort of picture of one who brings together the different elements of the nation and, when a critical situation arises, causes them to act as one and to strike with unanimity at the right time. It was a reference to my years of gaining the confidence of different elements and to the action of Parliament in coming into the war. He went so far as to say that my service was one which would be recognized as a service to civilization itself.

"I am sorry I cannot recall the exact words used but no words could have been uttered by anyone which could have gone further in the way of expressing service to the world than his words in reference to myself. He spoke very deliberately and toward the end, almost with some slight emotion, as he spoke of the part which I had taken in world affairs. When the President was speaking, he referred to the experience which he and Mr. Churchill and myself had of affairs, and said that added together, our careers in the way of public service would run beyond a century. Churchill said something about the three of us having had more experience in public life than any man of these times. Later when we were speaking informally, he agreed that no three men had had more mud thrown at them or had been more bitterly attacked by their opponents than each of us had in the course of our public careers. Several present expressed the wish that someone might have been present to record what had been said. I confess I wish very much that this might have been done. I would like to have had the exact phrases used by Churchill and the President."

Mackenzie King thought "all present felt that the dinner was a really memorable occasion and an impressive one. I confess the remembrance of the dinner left me with a feeling of something very sacred and beautiful. After the party had broken up at night and it was exactly midnight on my watch when I looked at it, the President, Churchill, and I sat together for quite a little time."

The next few days were filled for Mackenzie King with almost unending interviews with the visitors to Quebec. On August 21, for example, he had Brendan Bracken, the British Minister of Information, to lunch. Mackenzie King recorded that "they lunched together in a small dining room. Continued talking at the table after luncheon. Bracken was enjoying a drink of Scotch and soda and enjoying talking. He talked straight ahead all the time. . . . It was only when I was told that Mr. Hull had arrived, shortly after 4, that he rose to leave. I enjoyed the conversation exceedingly. . . . The main purpose of his call had been to have me, if possible, have a word with Hull to help to influence him toward having recognition of the French National Committee given by the U.S. He said: 'You know Mr. Hull very well and perhaps could help to persuade him of the wisdom of this.' "

They also talked about Mackenzie King visiting "England and I explained the difficulties of leaving Canada just now when there were so many fences to be mended to keep my party together. . . . Bracken said what I had said in London was sound. He agreed it was a mistake to bring Prime Ministers from their own Dominions unless some urgent matters demanded it. If a Conference or a meeting of Prime Ministers came, and nothing made of it, it would occasion disappointment. I pointed out that we should keep our eye on winning the war, each one of us in our own countries. Also that it might create a reaction in Canada itself if I went to England unless there was obvious reason for it, causing some people to say that I had become more interested in Churchill and Imperial politics than our own. He agreed entirely with my point of view. I said I hoped he might help to have Churchill see the wisdom of not trying to arrange for a meeting there."

Mackenzie King "quite enjoyed the talk with Bracken though he talks so much on every subject that one can really say nothing. I allowed him to sail out and I am sure that gave him the most satisfaction. The talk, I am sure, was quite worth while." He "took advantage of the opportunity to impress on Bracken the importance of not having different parts of the Empire appear, in the eyes of the Americans, to be ganging up against them on the air business. I pointed out how the American press might begin a tremendous pressure on the Government, and that there would be further pressure from the two Houses of Congress. . . .

To remember, too, the pressure to take out of the President's hand the making of executive agreements, and substituting therefor treaties which would tie his hands very much."

When Brendan Bracken left, Cordell Hull was waiting. Mackenzie King took him for a drive and on the way brought up the question of recognition of the French National Committee. He found Hull suspicious "that the British had been so close to de Gaulle that arrangements might come to a point where the French Government would be prepared later to give preferences in matters of trade to the British. He spoke of the amount of money that had been given to de Gaulle and what had been done for him by the U.S. He had used a good deal of it in attacking the Americans. He spoke of him as a man that could not be trusted. He was one thing to one, and another to another."

While the Quebec Conference was going on, the American-Canadian military expedition landed on Kiska in the Aleutian Islands. They had found no Japanese there. After several days it was decided to announce the landing on August 21. Mackenzie King was to broadcast the announcement. As early as August 12, the Americans had agreed to give seventy-five minutes' advance notice so there could be a simultaneous announcement in Canada. A broadcast had been prepared and approved at the time. A great deal of difficulty subsequently arose over the timing of the announcements and a situation like that over the Sicilian landing almost developed, with the Americans instead of the British as the villains. As the Japanese had already left Kiska and there had been no fighting, one of Mackenzie King's secretaries questioned the wisdom of any broadcast, but Mackenzie King "pointed out that if we let this opportunity go by, of giving a background of the planned expedition, with the chance it afforded of showing the extent to which Canadian forces had joined with the Americans in protecting the Alaskan and Aleutian areas, we would never have this chance again."

The previously prepared text of the broadcast had to be altered and Mackenzie King had great difficulty in making changes which satisfied him. "It was nearly 8," he noted, "when I got this draft completed for typing by Handy. Had then to get dinner. After that, had only time for a rest of less than an hour before starting off for the studio. Had only time to read the manuscript first. At the studio at the Chateau, there was too much confusion for a second reading, and I had to go on the air feeling very nervous and very tired. A noise started in part of the broadcast which was like a motor, and I nearly turned once or twice to have the noise stop. Feeling so worried, I almost felt I would have to give up and throw the manuscript away, but I pulled myself together, and by exercising all the control possible, got through, but not with the inflection or ease that I should like to have had in speaking."

After the broadcast, Mackenzie King went "back to the Citadel and on reaching there, about a quarter to 11, went in to join the President and Mr. Churchill who, earlier in the day, had invited me to dinner with them tonight quietly. I had to give up this opportunity, broadcast not having been sufficiently prepared in advance and also to get a chance for a little rest before speaking."

When he arrived he found Roosevelt and Churchill talking with Anthony Eden, "the President in an arm chair in a bright red quilted evening smoking jacket, and slippers: Churchill in his grey zipper suit and slippers with hand-worked initials on. Eden in easy jacket and slippers similar to Churchill's hand-worked initials." Mackenzie King "apologized for not having been at dinner and did not offer to sit down, but offered to excuse myself after a few words—but Churchill at once said, 'No, we want you here.' "

They had begun talking about the post-war organization of the world. Churchill was not in favour of making any public pronouncements, but Roosevelt felt some statement would be necessary in advance of statements by any other presidential aspirants in the 1944 elections. Mackenzie King observed that "the embarrassment of a fixed time for the election lay in part at the root of the discussion."

Roosevelt and Churchill could not agree about the place of China in a world organization. Churchill was not impressed by the power of the Chinese, while the President expressed the need to have them as a buffer state between Russia and America. Mackenzie King expressed the view that "the new generation of Chinese were quite different from the old. There was a new China, a youthful China that had to be reckoned with and must not be underestimated. I said regarding the 'Big Four' that I thought great care would have to be taken. I did not believe the other United Nations would like it, and I knew the Dominions would resent it. We would not agree to a government of the world by the four most powerful powers—it was contrary to conception for which this war was being fought. Churchill had thought there was much to be said for a transitional period and allowing matters to develop in that time. He was all for having . . . an Assembly in which all nations would be represented—they could talk all they liked and could agree on who should represent them on a Council which would be a link between all the nations thus represented and the Big Four. Eden said, and I thought exactly, that there was little that could be added to what had been thought out re the League of Nations. Churchill said the League had not failed—the nations had failed the League. Eden spoke of the Council being a necessary and effective body and favoured something like it being represented as the link—pending the working out of a final arrangement. I said I thought the other United Nations and the Dominions in particular would take much from Churchill and the President and I would suggest letting the evolution of the final 'order' follow naturally from control at the outset by the powers that did the conquering of the enemy . . . but not arrange anything too final in advance." In this discussion, Roosevelt indicated clearly that he wanted the United States to have a place in the world organization but doubted "if he could if all is to be centred again in Europe." Mackenzie King noted that "what was said was along lines the President had previously discussed with me.

"The next question discussed was that of recognition of French National Committee, an effort to have President take a generous attitude. . . . There was much general conversation during the night. . . . It was 2 o'clock when we broke up conversation. I walked beside the President's chair as far as the head of the stairs; on the way the President said: 'Isn't it fine we can all talk so freely, conceal nothing?' I said, as a parting word, to watch the Big Four idea, be careful to remember what the United Nations and the Dominions would feel. Better proceed from himself and Churchill gradually in the planning of the future, meeting situations as they arose, and having plan work out naturally, with power required to maintain positions kept in their hands, and added to and taken from by degrees as circumstances might require and warrant. It was nearly 3 when I got to bed, as I spent a little time after looking over letters, memos, etc. It had been a memorable day, and night."

On Monday, August 23, at noon, Churchill and Mackenzie King "drove together through the streets of Quebec. It was a triumphal procession from the time we reached the Garrison Club at the foot of the Citadel until the time of our return. There was a great demonstration in front of the City Hall. Churchill was visibly pleased. He remarked on the happy expression of the people. Indeed as we looked at the people from the car, it was like a vast throng hailing a deliverer. Churchill was dressed in a white linen suit. At times, he sat up at the back of the car. I had a grey suit and was careful to remain seated except for a moment at the City Hall."

Mackenzie King noted he "could see that Brendan Bracken had told him of my conversation about coming to England this autumn. I said to Churchill that he would see how great the necessity was for me to begin the mending of my fences, getting my party properly organized and seeing to it that I did not lose any members through the C.C.F. That Curtin's victory in Australia was certain to be of assistance to the C.C.F. . . . Churchill's reply was that Smuts would be coming to England for a short visit. That he would then be coming on to America, and that we would have him here. He recognized that I had a big problem and said: 'You may be sure that I will do all I can in return to help you.'

"He then told me he was preparing a speech to be delivered on Saturday night which would refer to Canada's war effort—addressed not to the people of Quebec but to the larger audience of the Dominion as a whole. Said he intended with Mrs. Churchill to spend the next couple of days, after the President left, at Lac des Neiges, where he would try to work on a really first class speech; also prepare something for Harvard University."

The following day (August 24), Mackenzie King wrote that at 12.30 he had "presided at a meeting between the President and Churchill and the press. We were gathered together on the deck at the Citadel. The President was seated to my right; Churchill, to my left. The press gathered around in a semi-circle. I made a few introductory remarks. Gave the photographers four minutes to take pictures, before calling on Churchill to speak first. The President had suggested I should do that, reversing the order of Casablanca. When I told Churchill of it, he said it was pretty short notice.

"He began feeling his way and before he had concluded he had delivered quite a speech. He had spoken of Britain, the U.S. and Russia, but had made no mention of China. I whispered to him to say a word on China. This he did in a very satisfactory way. . . . The omission of any mention of China in his address before Congress had raised a great deal of comment when he was last in the U.S. The President in speaking made a special reference to Canada and to our forces. Said to me afterward he had thought it well to do that as Churchill had omitted any reference to them. . . .

"When the President had concluded speaking, I said that I would like, before the Conference broke up, to say in the presence of the press, how pleased the Canadian people were and how honoured we felt when we learned that the President and Mr. Churchill had agreed on Canada as a place of meeting and particularly the old historic city of Quebec. I then thanked them for having thus honoured our country and said a word or two about the Conference itself. I tried to meet certain local feeling and comment about the non-appearance of Churchill and the President by saying that we all wished that we could have seen more of the President and Mr. Churchill in public, but it must be remembered that they were dealing with the greatest problem of our times, the most serious of all questions, and had not the opportunities to move about which they might have wished. That I had been behind the scenes and knew how fully occupied every hour of the time had been with the most important of public affairs.

"I then spoke to the press and said I should like, on behalf of the Government, to express to them our appreciation of the manner in which they had co-operated with the Government in giving to the world a picture of the background of the Conference; the atmosphere in which discussions were carried on, and what was possible to give out. I thanked them for what they had given of information to the public and for the manner of giving of it.

"This [press] conference," he added, "is the outcome of [Davidson] Dunton [General Manager of the Wartime Information Board] speaking of it yesterday, and my having a word with [Brendan] Bracken last night, and his urging on the President and Churchill the importance of something being said. He [Bracken] told me over the 'phone that these 'two boys' had been pretty rough in the matter of not answering any questions. I had the press understand it was not a question and answer affair, but phrased it as an exchange of greetings. As a matter of fact, the conference concluded without a single question being asked."

That afternoon (August 24), Mackenzie King left for Ottawa to be there to receive Roosevelt the following day. Roosevelt arrived in Ottawa on the morning of August 25 and spoke from a platform in front of the Peace Tower on Parliament Hill at noon. "Fortunately," Mackenzie King wrote, "the day opened favourably. It was a bit cloudy at times, in the early part of the morning, but cleared up in a wonderful way from 11 o'clock on till 3. Sunshine could not have been brighter, or weather pleasanter. Absence of wind; not too hot. Everything that one could have desired. There was an enormous crowd on Parliament Hill. Indeed I have never seen anything to compare with it. A beautiful looking crowd as people were wearing their bright colours. Having the stand immediately under the archway added tremendously to the effect of the whole appearance of the platform for address purposes. . . .

"When Princess Alice arrived, I brought her forward to the front of the platform and later took a seat where it was not too warm pending the arrival of the President and His Excellency the Governor-General on the Hill. It really was a wonderful sight to see the crowds, hear them cheering as the President drove in and stopped to review the guard of honour. The band played 'The Star Spangled Banner' and, when the President arrived, I greeted him beneath the arch of the Memorial Chamber. Gave him a warm welcome saying I was so glad that he was here at last. . . . He had arrived a minute or two ahead of time which necessitated our all waiting for a moment before the firing of the noon day gun. . . . After the firing . . . the Carillon played 'O Canada' overhead. The flags had been appropriately arranged. . . .

"I received a fine ovation from Members of Parliament and others on the Hill when I came forward to speak; also there was considerable applause at the appropriate places in the course of speaking. I found it quite easy to proceed and believe I got through without any slip. . . . The President stood throughout the ceremony. Quite an effort as one could see, and shaking a good deal. . . . I noticed that he had the speech in a ring binder so as to prevent the leaves slipping away. He followed what he was saying by running his little finger along the lines as he spoke. He was given a most attentive hearing and a fine ovation at the close. . . . All was carried out with great dignity."

Mackenzie King and the President drove out to Kingsmere after luncheon. Unfortunately they were late and it was raining, which disappointed Mackenzie King very much. They returned to Laurier House for tea and after tea Mackenzie King "took the President up to my Library. Showed him Mother's picture and also her hair and ring. Had him write in my guest book. Showed him later the proclamation on Grandfather's head and the Order-in-Council bringing Canada into the war. Gave him a glimpse of the sun room. I showed him the little book given me by friends. He had been under the impression, like others, that my residence was the Prime Minister's residence. I told him those circumstances as we were driving."

From Laurier House, they drove to the station and after the President's train left Mackenzie King then went back to Laurier House to telephone friends about the day. It was, for him, a great occasion.

The Members of the War Committee had to return to Quebec for a meeting with Churchill which was fixed for August 31. Mackenzie King and several of the Ministers travelled down together on August 30. When they arrived, they learned Mr. and Mrs. Churchill were still at the fishing camp where they had gone for a rest. On August 31, Churchill returned about 11. Mackenzie King noted that he "worked a little on his broadcast and rested until its delivery at one o'clock. He left one camp last night at midnight. Reached the other about a quarter to two. Received there his pouch with despatches, etc. Worked until 4. Naturally was very tired on reaching Quebec this morning."

At one o'clock the members of the War Committee, and a few others, assembled in the sun room of the Citadel to listen to Churchill's broadcast. Mackenzie King felt "it was well done. A well built structure, world scale with a fine moral appeal. He made a very generous reference to myself as an experienced statesman who had led Canada unitedly and unanimously into war at the moment needed. When the broadcast was over, I left the room to meet and congratulate him. He asked me if it was all right. I told him I thought he had touched on the subjects all were most interested hearing a word about and I did not think he had made any omissions of significance. . . . I thanked him for his personal references to myself. He said: 'I wanted to say what I did, and I wanted to say you are the only man who could have brought Canada into the war unitedly.' I said something about this being too much and he replied: 'Not at all, not at all. I don't know how we could have done without you. Your services have meant everything.'

"At the War Cabinet, this afternoon, he said in the presence of the Ministers and Chiefs of Staff, words something to the same effect, after speaking about Canada's war effort. Made it very personal that my leadership had meant everything in the war effort. Later when we were walking together on the Citadel deck, he spoke to me about coming to England again. At luncheon, he had said he thought the meeting in England would have to be in November. I said to him he would see for himself that there was a good deal of work to be done in Canada. I did not want to get my party undermined by the C.C.F. He said: 'Yes, in this great, broad country, there is much to be done,' but went on to say that he hoped I would come in November. . . .

"He was looking exceedingly well after his broadcast. Looked fresh and rested, and very relieved. After greeting the Ministers in the sun room, we went down to the dining-room. I was seated to his right. . . . I found myself excessively tired; almost impossible to keep up conversation. . . . However, Churchill and I worked into an interesting talk on a number of questions." One of these subjects was the proposed invasion of Italy of which Churchill said: "The whole business will have unfolded itself in two weeks' time. But say nothing about it meanwhile. He went on to say that he was not at all averse to another [Canadian] division going from Britain to Sicily and Italy for battle experience; not averse to Canada having an Army Corps in Italy, but he would have to bring back British divisions to London to keep faith with the Americans as to keeping a certain number of divisions in England. He spoke of Montgomery having been very tactful in the way he had spoken about the Canadians. He knew he was highly pleased with the quality of their fighting. They had proven themselves splendid soldiers."

Another subject Churchill talked about was "Basic English" in which he was much interested at that time. He told Mackenzie King he had spoken to the President about "some organization for dealing with basic words. He said: 'I will get you to be a member of it.' It has to do with finding words which would have the same meaning wherever they were heard. He thought that people with a mastery of about 800 basic words would be able to converse on almost any subject. It would be a great thing for the world if a knowledge of 800 words would enable men in all countries to discuss important questions.

"He then said something about the murder of Caesar by Brutus, saying that was a great affair. That really it was just the murder of a Prime Minister by his colleagues. That Brutus loved Caesar but felt he had to be killed. Julius Caesar was—not a scheming, but some word like that—politician. This grew out of my referring to what he had said in his broadcast of Ciano's remark that Mussolini had gone to war because there was not likely to be such a chance in another 5,000 years to be famous. He described the ambition of the man. I had said I thought there were too many busts of Caesar in Rome for the good of their public men."

Churchill met with the War Committee immediately after the luncheon. Mackenzie King opened the proceedings "by mentioning that I had had the advantage of knowing what had been going on behind the scenes and some of the conclusions reached. That perhaps he would give my colleagues such information as he felt could be disclosed." Churchill "then read the paper which was being distributed to the Dominions—very privately to the Prime Ministers of the Dominions—and handed me a copy to keep, but stressed its sense of secrecy, owing to the fact that the Prime Ministers of other Dominions had not yet received a copy.

"We took up the question of different countries of the Empire meeting to discuss air transport policy, civil aviation, etc. I made it clear that we would not be averse to having someone represent us in London. . . . Mr. Howe would probably be the one. We felt it important to keep the Americans in the know of what we were doing, though we agreed that we must be free, all parts of the Commonwealth, to confer together on any matter. He [Churchill] promised that he would talk the matter over with the President, telling him what we proposed to do and would let me know whether he had or had not any objection. He would, of course, not do anything that the President would take exception to. I pointed out that our concern was more with American public opinion as framed by the press and Congress, and had reference to many post-war issues.

"We discussed also a little the post-war order. He gave a desultory sort of account of the scheme that he, himself, had in mind, and what the President had talked of, but there was nothing very definite about it.

Nothing is to be published at present as coming out of the Conference. ... I pointed out the unwisdom of talking too much about the Big Four governing in the post-war world. That, unhappily, we could not count on having the President and himself at the head of affairs for all time. That any post-war order would have to take account of the persons who might take their places, and that each nation would want its say and that the Dominions would wish their individuality respected. He spoke of different nations and said something would have to be worked out. It was clear, however, from what Churchill said that nothing was too definite even in his own mind."

After some discussion, Mackenzie King "mentioned we did not wish to keep him too long. I wanted to say the pleasure it had been to us all to have him in Canada, in the city of Quebec, and particularly at the table at which we were then gathered. It had been a privilege to all Canada to have him there, and to feel that it had been possible for him to enjoy a little change and freedom here. I expressed the hope that he would return refreshed by the change. That the visit had served a useful purpose—the purpose of the Conference, etc. Churchill made a fitting acknowledgment of what I had said, speaking quite deeply of the hospitality extended by Canada, thanking us all very warmly.

"I felt so tired that I could hardly express any words, and did not do so felicitously. My whole brain feels as though it were completely exhausted. I think part is the pain of eyestrain, but certainly today I have hardly been able, at times, to tell my own age. ... I wish very much it had been possible to speak naturally but all day I have found it impossible to do this."

Churchill himself wrote later 'I attended a meeting of the Canadian Cabinet and told them all they did not already know about the Conference and the War. I had the honour of being sworn a Privy Counsellor [*sic*] of the Canadian Cabinet. [Actually Churchill had become a Canadian Privy Councillor in December 1941.] This compliment was paid me at the instance of my old friend of forty years' standing and trusted colleague, Mr. Mackenzie King.'[2]

After the meeting Mackenzie King went to bed for an hour's rest and then went to the station to say good-bye. As the train moved away, Mackenzie King proposed three cheers. "Churchill came to the end of the car window and said: 'God Bless You All.' He was clearly touched by the friendly feeling of those who were assembled to say good-bye. It was amusing to hear one little child call out 'Churchill' and draw his attention."

[2]W. S. Churchill, *The Second World War*, vol. V, p. 119.

CHAPTER TWENTY

The Political Watershed, 1943

IN THE LATTER HALF of 1943, Mackenzie King gave a good deal of attention to domestic politics and to the political effects of the Government's war policies.

One of the thorniest political problems the Government faced was the constitutional requirement to arrange for a redistribution of the membership of the House of Commons by provinces in accordance with the 1941 census. On the basis of population Saskatchewan would have lost several seats, and the Members from the Province naturally wanted to postpone the redistribution. On the other hand, the country generally was over-represented in relation to the Province of Quebec and the failure to redistribute could be represented as discrimination against Quebec. Whatever course was taken was bound to displease one or other of these traditionally Liberal provinces. The problem was further complicated because Mackenzie King had announced before the war that he favoured redistribution by an independent commission rather than by a parliamentary committee.

The Cabinet had first discussed redistribution on January 22. Power was in favour of having an independent commission. "Gardiner spoke about loss of seats in Saskatchewan. I said that might be all to the good if the C.C.F. were going to make inroads there. . . . I said quite frankly I would not agree to any repetition of what had taken place in a previous redistribution, of Members arranging themselves for political purposes. It must be understood the Cabinet had, some time ago, decided to have the matter referred to a commission. . . . The principle must be understood as agreed to by the Cabinet. I had Power's strong support in this. . . . I said I thought we might have to consider allowing soldiers overseas to elect their own Members of Parliament. That appealed to Power immediately who saw in it a means of meeting the most difficult part of the whole business, namely getting the soldiers' votes, etc., should the war still be on. There had been some suggestion we should not attempt redistribution because of the war. I pointed out . . . we could not ask the British Government to amend the British North America Act to postpone redistribution."

No action had been taken early in the session, but at the Cabinet meeting on May 14 Mackenzie King had "told Ministers I felt we should go through with redistribution this year. . . . By this time next year, Members will have become reconciled to the inevitable. I stated that I could not think of going to the country in an election without having had the application of the constitution as to redistribution every ten years fulfilled. . . . The reason for bringing the matter up today was that the morning paper stated it was likely redistribution would not be enacted this year. I said if we were to introduce the bill after I got back from Washington [the visit in May], it would be thought at once that was in consequence of my visit there, and of a decision to have an election this year. By mentioning the matter now, there could be no such interpretation. Council agreed. Power, who was absent, agreed when I told him at the House what we had planned before I made a statement."

After his statement, the chief Liberal whip had told Mackenzie King "that the whips of all the Provinces had met together and that all were agreed we should not have a redistribution this year. . . . I told them that I would much prefer having no redistribution to having one at this time. On the other hand, I did not see how, if we had no redistribution this year, we would escape bringing in the bill next year. . . . I did not see how I could have an election any time after a decennial census without having complied with the constitution. . . . I expressed myself as agreeing to a committee seeking to work out any plan which they could. . . . That, as Liberals, we must base our actions on the constitution. I said to them I did not think there would be an election this year—almost certainly next. If there was [an] Allied victory, there would be no question as to the party coming back, of the Government being supported again by the people. If there was an Allied defeat, nothing could save the party or any party associated with us. I said I thought I would know when the right time would come to act, but I must have the redistribution settled before that time came."

This was, however, far from the last word on the question of redistribution. At the Cabinet meeting on June 10, Mackenzie King had indicated that he had changed his mind and felt that "it would be preferable to have the B.N.A. Act amended so as to postpone the time at which redistribution would have to be made by the Commons." The proposed Amendment would postpone redistribution "until the session of Parliament which came immediately after the cessation of hostilities. That will permit of an election taking place on the constituencies as at present determined, at the same time requiring a redistribution by a new Parliament before another election could take place." The Cabinet agreed on this change, after Mackenzie King "stressed strongly the terrible position we would all be in if Parliament were acrimoniously debating the boundaries of constituencies while our men were being killed at the front."

On June 14, Mackenzie King had announced in the House of Commons the postponement of redistribution; the announcement was received "with general applause in different parts of the House. It is natural the Members should approve as it means each one retains his present constituency as it is. On the other hand, it is a very generous and patriotic gesture on the part of the Government which has the right to make a redistribution which would govern in the next election and might well be the basis of elections during the next ten years. We could, if we were like the Government of Sir John Macdonald in earlier days, gerrymander at least some of the constituencies to make more certain of winning them at the campaign." He added that "it took an immense load off my mind once this statement was made and so well accepted. It leaves me perfectly free to bring on an election at any time without the upsetting effects of a redistribution just prior to the election and, what is even worse, a redistribution at a time of war."

On July 5, the proposed Amendment to the B.N.A. Act was introduced by St. Laurent. Mackenzie King felt that, in his speech, St. Laurent "brought in much too much material on race and religion. I was partly to blame in not having said frankly to him, when he indicated the line he might take, that it might be better not to follow it. I realize he had a problem in his own province. What he should have done was to hold in reserve for reply much that he brought in at the beginning." The debate was completed in a single day and the Amendment was approved. On July 24, Mackenzie King observed that "St. Laurent made a good suggestion that, if returned, we should put through a redistribution measure which would give Ontario the present numbers of Members it has, and make it the province to have the stated representation; then base the representation of the other provinces on the Ontario unit. That would increase the representation in Quebec, also be helpful in Western provinces. I think the suggestion is an excellent one. It has been good strategy leaving the whole redistribution matter so near the end; taking the course we did take, and then arranging rapid progress through the British House. Except for the malcontents, the whole business has gone through with complete satisfaction all around."

This judgment was hardly correct. The postponement of redistribution became just one more grievance in Quebec to be exploited by the Government's political opponents. Mackenzie King learned on November 3 "how keenly Godbout and other of his colleagues had felt about postponement of redistribution. Evidently, the matter had not been fully explained to Godbout." He added that he had "come to the conclusion that it might, after all, have been wiser to have gone ahead with redistribution, regardless of what it would have involved in recrimination. . . . However, it was wholly in the interests of the war effort that the postponement was made. Unfortunately, it has given rise to the wider contention. There are no other constitutional issues which the minorities in Quebec—and Duplessis and Cardin in particular—could make more of."

In the summer of 1943 Mackenzie King's mind was turning increasingly in the direction of new social security legislation. Active interest in the subject had been stimulated by the publication of Sir William Beveridge's Report on Social Security in England and by his visit to Canada. Mackenzie King had heard Beveridge speak at the Ottawa Canadian Club on May 25 and was "inspired by the parallels in his life interests with my own. Arnold Toynbee was in part the inspiration of his life work. He was Assistant Warden of Toynbee Hall. I lived at Hull House and Passmore Edwards Settlement. He was Director for a time of the London School of Economics. I was there in the first year of its existence." Mackenzie King felt that in *Industry and Humanity* he had "anticipated very much the programme Sir William is putting forward today. . . . Our lives have been given over very largely to life-long study of social problems." Mackenzie King was asked to thank Beveridge at the Canadian Club and "was delighted to find that I was able to speak with exceptional fluency. Thoughts came rapidly to my mind and shaped themselves into utterances that in part were really of an inspirational character. I was given, if anything, a greater round of applause than Sir William himself."

Mackenzie King's interest in social legislation was further stimulated at this time when on June 8 he happened to find and re-read the addresses he had given in 1899 and 1900 at the Passmore Edwards Settlement in London. In these addresses he "could see the man I was in those days, the singleness and earnestness of purpose, and I realize—and have been realizing very deeply of late—what I might have done in the way of leadership, if my life's interests had never become as scattered as they have, or my spiritual power impaired by undercurrents which should never have been permitted to waste energy, strength, and purpose. However, I may still be able to redeem the time that has been lost. This feeling of wishing to get back to the early part of my life as an inspiration to the latter part is growing stronger than ever."

At the same time he began to feel he should go through another election. On Sunday, June 6, he wrote in his diary: "I have come to have a great desire to go on with my life work—to play a larger part with the people—Dr. Benes' visit has been an inspiration. [Dr. Benes, of Czechoslovakia, had just visited Ottawa and made a great impression on Mackenzie King.] His life and work has brought that of grandfather's very close to me—their lives were much alike in what they represented of 'turbulent' effort for the rights of free men—they were both true patriots. My life should have been more expressive of those forces within myself and its real purpose. I have felt a certain return of health and with it a willingness to try one more political campaign."

Despite the renewed interest in social legislation, Mackenzie King did not forget the immediate situation; at the Liberal caucus on June 9 he "lashed out very strongly on the importance of giving first place in everything to the man who was offering his life voluntarily for the service of his country while the rest were remaining at home. I said it was the glory of our country that service overseas had been voluntary, and the Government's policy was to see that the men lacked nothing that they should have in the way of equipment, supplies, reinforcements, etc. That we had a splendid record in our war effort. Could appeal to the people on that record as a Government that were capable of carrying on in post-war times. There was only one thing that could undo it, which was a failure at some point on the Government's part to have anticipated the needs of the soldier that had to be met.

"I said we had no right to be complaining about increasing old age pensions and all these local matters when these men were offering their lives. They were entitled to first consideration. I said Members did not understand human nature, if they believed people of the country generally, farmers, workmen and others, were to be swept off their feet by a lot of promises of this and that. They were going to judge instinctively, in a large way, the capacity of men who were administering the nation's affairs. I said if we won the war, we could sweep the country on our record, particularly as, in the Conservative ranks, they had a leader who was afraid—afraid to be elected; would never come into Parliament." After a reference to the other two parties, he added "that our business was to keep our forces united. Let them see there was really no alternative Government. That particularly the people should be asked what Government was best to participate in a peace conference."

He told the caucus "that results of the war would settle everything. I added a reference to the times that were ahead of us. That I thought our own losses and sacrifices would be so great that everything that had passed would pale before them in the minds of men. Remember there were very few families that had not men overseas. Doing all we could for these men was our supreme duty. Any failure there would mean deserved defeat. Caucus accepted all I was saying in a splendid way. Indeed they gave me a rousing reception at the end though I had gone into caucus without a line of preparation."

At the Liberal caucus on June 30, there were a good many Members who wanted to see an immediate increase in the indemnities paid to Members of Parliament. "Ilsley made a first-rate presentation of the reasons why this could not be done without occasioning similar requests all along the line from different classes of persons who have been having additional expenses when away from home, etc. He stressed the very serious effect politically which would follow Members doing for themselves what could not possibly be done for others, without great confusion through the country and feeling of injustice on the part of people." Mackenzie King himself "pointed out that some Members of the Government and party had already lost sons in the war. That numbers of people in the constituencies, the same. That all who had men at the front were incurring sacrifices which would not be measured in terms of money, and that if we were discussing a matter of the kind in Parliament while severe losses were coming in from the battlefields, the party would find itself in an appalling position. I said we had to remember this was at a time of war and that we could not escape sacrifices and must be prepared to make them. It is one of the few times I have had to oppose quite strongly the wishes of almost the entire party but I am sure I was helping every man in so doing."

There were, at this time, four vacancies in the House of Commons, one in Saskatchewan, one in Manitoba, and two in Quebec: August 9 was the date fixed for the by-elections. Although he was not optimistic about the results, it was not the Conservatives that Mackenzie King feared. Indeed, the Conservative leader, John Bracken, came to see him on June 30 and told him that "his party had decided not to place any candidates in the field in the four by-elections. I said to him there was no doubt that the C.C.F. was a common enemy. I said to him I had been expecting he, himself, might run in Selkirk. His reply to this was that he could hardly hope to win there, and he would be finished altogether if he were defeated. He asked me if there would be any opposition to his getting a seat if one of the Conservatives resigned so as to enable him to come into the House. I said to him that the Government would not offer any opposition. He then asked me if I could arrange to get accommodation for three, including himself, to go to England. I asked him at what time, and he said: early in August. I said I thought this could be arranged. I had said to him there would probably be heavy fighting before that time. He then asked me if it would be in the Mediterranean and if some of our men would be there. He said that he had learned this from other sources. I said that certainly there would be fighting in the Mediterranean and that some of our men would be there." On this occasion, Bracken pointed out that, in his speeches, "he had not been saying anything which would make matters difficult" for the Government.

It was just after this talk with Bracken that Robert Manion, the former Leader of the Conservative party, died on July 2. Mackenzie King was a pallbearer at his funeral on July 5. He noted there was "not a single representative of the Conservatives among the pallbearers. Bracken and Meighen and Drew . . . all stood together outside the entrance of the house. None of them came to the cemetery. Our Ministers were much more in evidence than members of the Conservative Party."

After paying a tribute to Manion in the House of Commons that day (July 5), Mackenzie King administered a blistering rebuke to Bracken for a speech he had just made in Toronto in which he was reported to have said that the war policy of the Government had been "in too many of its aspects prompted by political cowardice." Mackenzie King said to the House that "had Mr. Bracken, as leader of the Progressive Conservative party, been a member of this House of Commons, I should today at once have asked you, Mr. Speaker, to see that Mr. Bracken was obliged immediately to withdraw his charge of political cowardice. As one who himself has been a member of a legislative assembly, Mr. Bracken must know that these untrue and offensive words could not have been used in this House or in the legislature of any province without the House insisting upon their being withdrawn. As Mr. Bracken is not in the House, I suppose I must content myself by saying that a charge of 'political cowardice' comes with ill grace from a leader of a political party who, throughout the whole of a session of parliament, following his appointment as leader of his party, has avoided attempting its leadership on the floor of the House of Commons."

In his diary, he noted that "not a member of the Conservative party rose to say a word in the exception I took to Bracken's statement at last Friday night's meeting which I really imagine was prepared for him by Meighen. I think he will be a bit surprised when he sees he was taken to task in the particular terms in which I referred to him. I had in mind his having said to me [in their conversation on June 30] he had been going about, but had not been saying anything harmful to the Government."

Despite the obvious weakness of the Conservative party, Mackenzie King was, as he told the Cabinet on July 20, "very concerned" about all four by-elections. He "spoke out again about the shame it was there was no organization and no literature. Said . . . that once our party began to lose by-elections, it was doomed, and . . . if we lost the four by-elections we might as well regard any return of the Government in a general election as out of the question. I do not know that the words will do any good but, at any rate, I have helped to put myself on record and give the right directions to those who should handle those matters."

Power wrote Mackenzie King a letter on July 22 suggesting an election in the fall. "What surprised me most," Mackenzie King noted, "was his frank admission that we had gone too far in the size of our Army, in the air, in munitions, etc., and that contractions would have serious results. Also he felt results of Army in Sicily with what would probably happen by way of success on the Pacific, and the wish of the country not to swap horses in mid-stream, would probably mean the return of the Government. He foreshadowed the greater difficulties that would arise next year when fighting would be fierce." Mackenzie King reflected: "Were I looking at the matter purely from the point of view of winning an election, I would feel there might be much to be said for an appeal this year. On the other hand, I do not believe the Canadian people want an election any sooner than it is necessary to have one, and I would like to see the war over before it becomes necessary to make the appeal. As long as there is the prospect of the war ending by the autumn of 1944, I think I shall hold off for that length of time, be the consequences what they may. I can see more and more clearly, however, that the party feel it would be almost necessary for me to go through another campaign and that the party feel my position in relation to world affairs is stronger than that of any other man in the country."

Just before the Quebec Conference opened in August, the Liberal party suffered two severe shocks. The first came in the general election in Ontario, held on August 4: the Government of Harry Nixon was crushingly defeated, both the Conservatives and the C.C.F. electing many more Members than the Liberals, though no party had a clear majority. During the day Mackenzie King wrote: "I do not see how the Liberals could win a majority for the following reasons: first, a house divided against itself is sure to fall. Hepburn began to divide the house immediately after taking office. This division has been kept up throughout. Cleavages in the party extending continuously over four or five years. In the second place, the Liberals perpetuated themselves in office —two terms. This contrary to views of electorate and also always a sign of weakness. Should have had an election without any extension of term. Third, Hepburn's action transferring leadership to Conant—Conant hanging on, and later ousted by convention, and later appointed to office by Liberals. Delay on Nixon's part in bringing on election. Should have prepared for election the day after the Liberal convention. . . . No preparation for campaign in constituencies. No literature. Next, no platform for campaign. Greatest weakness of all running on the record of the Liberals which is really a thoroughly bad record. Nothing positive presented. Hepburn's nomination as Independent and supporter of Nixon. People bewildered as to the relationship. Speaker Clark's statement in Windsor. [Clark, the Speaker of the previous Legislature, had made a statement forecasting political union with the United States; see chapter Eighteen.] He should have been instantly repudiated. Not allowed to get the nomination. People have lost confidence in a Liberal administration at Queen's Park.

"Next reflection was that Conservatives would make a good showing, particularly Drew being a military man and soldiers' votes, etc., and old Conservative votes would return to him. . . . Expected the C.C.F. to make good runs in industrial areas, but not so good in rural areas. My feeling was that Nixon would get a good support in the rural constituencies. That might place him perhaps above Conservatives and C.C.F. but that none of the three would have a majority."

When the returns came in, Mackenzie King noted "that practically all Liberal Ministers excepting Nixon and Oliver had gone down. This showing pretty conclusively that men who had any association with Hepburn were doomed. The three men that stood by me against Hepburn were: Nixon, Oliver, and Laurier. Those three were returned. All others were defeated. . . . The C.C.F. have made a telling run in all industrial constituencies, particularly where there has been political unrest, making clear the combination of the industrial C.I.O. with the political C.C.F. Their campaign indicates they have been well financed. The Conservative results also show the effect of organization in campaigns, advertising, etc. . . . Results would seem to indicate that large bodies of Liberals had lost confidence in the Government. The Conservative-minded had thrown their support to the Conservatives and the radical-minded, their support to the C.C.F. I must confess that while I deeply deplore the breakup, the collapse of the Liberal party in Ontario, which may be the beginning of the end of the power of the Liberal party federally, it has seemed to me all along that the results which have now come to pass were inevitable, with Hepburn retained as a Liberal leader and allowed to play the fast-and-loose part he did.

In my inner nature I feel a sense of relief that a Cabinet that has been so unprincipled and devoid of character has been cleaned out of Queen's Park, and that a new Administration, be it what it may, will have to take over affairs for a time. Instead of injuring the federal party, excepting temporarily, it may help to save us in the end. It will show our men, above all, the need for unity and for organization."

Mackenzie King feared the results in Ontario would "ensure the election of C.C.F. candidates in [the federal by-elections in] Selkirk and Humboldt. I also fear the loss of Stanstead [Quebec]. As the months pass and a Conservative party tries to carry on at Queen's Park, the C.C.F. and Liberals opposing them, and an extreme opposition confronting them, people will see more clearly the wisdom of the course which I have taken in helping to maintain, as far as it was in my power, the unity of the party and unity in the country. It is significant that the C.C.F. were opposed to our participation in the war and have never given the war effort real support. . . . Their whole role has been contemptible from the point of view of true patriotism. . . . My hope is that Nixon and his following will not join with the Conservatives, but reserve an independent position. . . . The Liberals should not join in with Drew and the Conservatives to attempt anything in the nature of a national government. . . . After all Nixon is far from being in as bad a position as I was in when I took over the leadership of the party in 1919 and led the men who had been true to Laurier throughout."

The second shock came on the day of the by-elections, August 9. Mackenzie King wrote on that day that he "did not believe we would carry any one of the four federal by-elections. I felt this absolutely with regard to the two Western seats which I was sure the C.C.F. would sweep." He expected the Bloc Populaire, the newly formed and radically inclined anti-war party in Quebec, to carry Stanstead (as they did), but felt the C.C.F. was likely to win in Cartier (they did not). He was dining at the Citadel in Quebec [the Quebec Conference was about to open] when the news came that the election was going against the Liberals in Cartier and Stanstead. He felt the main cause "was the price ceiling policy and restrictions generally. Above all, no organization. Also bad handling of labour policies, National Selective Service policies in particular." He added that any Government holding office in wartime was "sure to suffer as a consequence of war policies. It is a pretty sad sort of business to have to meet Churchill and the President the moment after losing four by-elections and the party being defeated in a Provincial Election."

He hoped the C.C.F. gains of the two seats and the victory of Fred Rose, the Labour-Progressive (Communist) in Cartier, might cause "some of our people to realize that labour has to be dealt with in a considerate way. In my heart, I am not sorry to see the mass of the people coming a little more into their own, but I do regret that it is not a Liberal party that is winning that position for them. It should be, and it can still be that our people will learn their lesson in time. What I fear is we will begin to have defection from our own ranks in the House to the C.C.F."

He reflected that "there is only one thing that can save the situation for the Liberal party, and that is that out of the meeting at Quebec of Churchill and the President, Canada can be roused to the conviction that, as leader of the Liberal party, I hold a place which no other man in Canada holds in the way of a key position to help the peace and post-war policies, and that the war should end in time to appeal to the people for the party that is to represent them at the peace conference. I believe it is not too late for that, and that a really effective organization of men in Canada who wish to see a sound sensible administration, not one of experiment and foolish measures, should back the Administration. I confess I am, however, far from sure of this result." At the close of that day (August 9), Mackenzie King wrote, "I would like, however, to carry the Liberal party through another victory and then pass on the torch of freedom to some other man. One who is a true Liberal at heart. I wish Rogers had been spared in health and strength."

This threat to the Liberal party from the C.C.F. in the English-speaking provinces and from the Bloc Populaire—which was, in some ways, the counterpart of the C.C.F in Quebec—Mackenzie King attributed to the resentment of labour at the wage stabilization policy of the Government and even more to what he felt sure was the failure of some of his colleagues in the Government to show sympathy for the aspirations of organized labour for increased recognition. One of the focal points in this connection was the National War Labour Board. The Board, under the chairmanship of Mr. Justice McTague, had been entrusted, at the time the steel strike was settled early in 1943, with the task of considering and recommending modifications which might be needed in the Wage Stabilization Order and with the drafting of a Labour Relations Code. Mackenzie King had seen Judge McTague on May 28 and had been "re-assured" as to the progress of this undertaking. He noted that he liked McTague "exceedingly and his views and mine are very much the same on labour matters. He is doing well." While Mackenzie King was in Quebec in August, a sharp difference developed between McTague and Joseph Cohen, one of his colleagues on the Board who was a lawyer in Montreal with a considerable trade union practice, and they had prepared separate Reports to the Government. The Reports were, of course, not to be made public until the Government had had time to consider them. Mackenzie King discussed this labour problem with those of his colleagues who were with him on the train going to Quebec on August 30 for the final meeting of the War Committee with Churchill, and "stressed the need of our stating very definitely our labour policy and the party taking a truly Liberal position, as being neither reactionary nor extreme radical, but we must be Liberal."

The Trades and Labour Congress was holding its annual meeting in Quebec, and, on August 31, after Churchill's departure, Mackenzie King, despite his fatigue, paid a surprise visit to the Congress. Percy Bengough, the President of the Congress, spoke to him about McTague's and Cohen's Reports and expressed the fear they would be made public before the rival Canadian Congress of Labour had its annual meeting. Bengough felt this would be unfair to his Congress. Mackenzie King told Bengough "I would see to it that this was not done. Said it would take us at least a fortnight to consider the Reports. That I wanted them studied with care. There had been no chance, thus far."

The visit to the Congress, he noted, gave him "real sadness at heart to think that the labour movement which I had made so much my own, had been getting away from the Government of which I am the head simply because of the degree to which some of my colleagues have become surrounded by interests that are at least not sympathetic to labour. . . . My whole sympathies are with labour and I even feel I would rather be defeated as a Government, and have labour come into fuller rights, than to win and have labour deprived of greater freedom, if these were the necessary alternatives. I do not believe they are. I think, in the end, Labour can win the most by returning a Liberal Government, but I know much work will have to be done to effect that end." There is no question that, at this time, he felt that the loss of labour's support was the greatest threat to the chances of the Liberal party winning the next election.

As soon as Mackenzie King returned from Quebec, the Government had to deal with the open difference between McTague and Cohen; this difference had been aggravated by a speech Cohen had made to the Trades and Labour Congress in which he was critical of the Government. McTague saw Mackenzie King on September 3 and told him "he could no longer sit with Cohen, that he was a political intriguer, had changed his attitude on the night of the Ontario Election, when he saw how C.C.F. were turning out, mentioned his different moves as to announcing his decisions. Spoke of his treachery in going to Quebec and making the address he did, etc. He, McTague, is agreeable to continuing on with another colleague."

Despite his attacks on the Government, Cohen had made no move to resign from the National War Labour Board and the Government had to decide, at the Cabinet meeting on September 7, what to do about the situation. Meanwhile Bengough, the President of the Trades and Labour Congress; Mosher, the President of the Canadian Congress of Labour; and Ward of the Railway Brotherhoods had asked to see the Prime Minister together. Mitchell, the Minister of Labour, told Mackenzie King they intended to urge him to keep Cohen on the Board, but Mackenzie King stated emphatically that he "would not be a party to reinstatement of Cohen." When he saw the labour leaders after the Cabinet meeting they complained about the delay in the publication of the Reports by Cohen and McTague. Mackenzie King told Mosher of the assurance he had already given to Bengough at Quebec "that if they were made public before the Canadian Congress of Labour meeting, the A.F. of L. people would say we were favouring them. This they had to agree to." Mackenzie King assured them the Reports would be considered as quickly as possible. The labour leaders then told the Prime Minister they had "tried to prevail on Cohen to go back and sit on the Board; try out some cases, and asked if I would not urge him and assist in getting the Board to go on. That these cases could be heard and settled before the Reports were made public. If after the Reports were made public Cohen wished to discontinue as a member of the Board, that would be for him to decide then. They rather gave their hand away in this, but I made it clear to them definitely that I would not interfere at all. That I regarded the Board as a Court. . . . Bengough then handed me a letter which the three of them had signed. They had prepared it in advance. It was to the effect that they had agreed in asking Cohen to go back and continue on the Board. I felt perfectly sure when I looked at the letter that it had been prepared by Cohen himself."

The next day (September 8) when Mackenzie King reported to the Cabinet on this meeting, "Ilsley stated that he thought the Government was losing both honour and standing by not having dismissed Cohen. It was a sort of reflection that I should have acted sooner. I explained . . . that I could not proceed on newspaper reports. That I wanted something definite to go on. I mentioned that McTague had asked to come to see me, and that I thought he should be asked to write me of the situation on the Board. That I would suggest this to him, and if he did, I would be prepared to take action at once. That I thought we would make a mistake in dismissing Cohen simply because of what he might have said . . . in Quebec which was what Ilsley took exception to." Mackenzie King said he did not think the Government "should give labour and the public a chance to say he was being dismissed simply because we were sensitive." Mackenzie King felt that he should, instead, secure from McTague a formal letter of complaint about Cohen's conduct on the Board.

After the Cabinet meeting Mackenzie King saw McTague who "brought with him a letter Cohen had written him saying he was going to sit on the Board because requested by the labour men to do so. McTague said he would not sit with him. That he regarded him as an intriguer, working against the national interest and his purpose being to destroy the Government politically."

McTague then undertook to write a letter to Mackenzie King the following morning to ask the Government to dismiss Cohen, which Mackenzie King agreed would be done at once. Cohen was dismissed on September 9, and on September 10, Mackenzie King noted that Cohen was "trying to create prejudice against myself personally for his dismissal, putting it on my anti-labour attitude. This is all part of the political game of the C.C.F. They have not dared to attack me personally while seeking to have Cohen create prejudice."

Meanwhile, at the Cabinet meeting on September 1, Mackenzie King, while still feeling the fatigue resulting from the Quebec Conference, had taken up "the political situation" and had told his colleagues he "was beginning to wonder whether I should not ask that a younger man should take charge of the party. That a campaign of detraction had gone on against me for years. That I had received no support in off-setting it from members of the party. I had urged time and time again that an effective organization should be brought into being. Nothing had been done. No literature prepared; by-elections lost through indifference. Ontario allowed to go to pot through no action being taken against Hepburn and his continuous attacks on myself, etc.

"I said that while I was ready to do all I could to serve the party and the country, I would not think of going through another election unless evidence was shown in advance of the party's readiness to effect a strong organization. I then said that I was debating in my mind whether I should not bring on an election this year or, at latest, at the very beginning of a new session. That I did not propose, unless matters changed very much meanwhile, to go into the House of Commons to be attacked from within by different oppositions, from without by the press, and witness our own men desert, some of them to the C.C.F. and some of them to the Bloc Populaire, and finally be driven into a campaign to sustain defeat as Meighen had been after holding on the way he did after the last war. That I wanted them to realize that I was in earnest about that, and also that the right of advising the Governor re dissolutions, etc., was in my own hands. I proposed to exercise it in accordance with my own judgment, this in order to prevent the party itself being so divided as not to be able to regain its strength.

"I then said I had every confidence in being able to win at the right moment, if there was preparation in advance and an attitude taken toward myself as leader which would let the country realize that my leadership would mean something for the post-war period. They had heard what the President and Mr. Churchill had said. That surely my own party could afford to be as outspoken as they were in regard to services I was rendering the country and other nations at this time of war."

Mackenzie King said he "wanted a meeting of the party called at once. Suggested Members should be brought together in a couple of weeks. McLarty spoke of the National Federation being brought together. After a short discussion, it was decided on Members meeting first and that meeting was to be followed by one of the Federation. I then asked the Members who were not of the War Committee to arrange for these meetings at once, to take place within the next couple of weeks."

The following day (September 2) he reflected that the next election campaign could not "be won on any war record of the past. It will have to be won on the confidence which the great majority of people may have in one leader rather than another. I think labour, farmers and the general public still have more faith in myself than in Bracken, Coldwell or others, for the Government that will have to deal with international problems in the next few years. The unfortunate part is we have no man in the party who seems to be qualified in a large way as a manager of a political party. However, I have got the men stirred up and I have no doubt that now that they see what the situation is, they may find themselves equal to it eventually. They are far too timid about speaking out." What he meant by having someone who could speak out was illustrated by a wistful entry in his diary of August 29 about talking on the telephone to Grattan O'Leary, of the Ottawa *Journal*, of his son who was missing on active service. He described O'Leary as "a fine fellow" and added: "I wish I had him to be my champion in the press."

The caucus of Liberal Members of Parliament called on September 1 met on the morning of September 24. Mackenzie King found "an amazing note of defeatism about the whole gathering." He began his speech "by extending congratulations to Prince Edward Island as helping to save the day. [The Liberals had won a provincial election there on September 15.] I then began to speak of the purpose of the caucus which was to begin examining causes of the results and defeat in Ontario and four by-elections. I lost no time in telling the Members that I thought Hepburn and the Toronto *Globe* were responsible for the position in which the Liberal party had been brought over the past five years. Hepburn ... had done his utmost to destroy myself personally and the Liberal Government at Ottawa. He had played fast and loose with his own party in Ontario until he had not a friend left.... I then went on to say that I did not regard the Government as a Liberal Government and that, but for my friendship with Nixon personally, I would not have voted at the recent elections. I felt sure the Liberals would not bring themselves to vote for the kind of thing that had gone on previously and no new platform had been put forward.... That I had been silent prior to the elections so as not to embarrass anyone, but now was the time to speak out.

"I then went on to speak of our own party, and launched out strongly at the complete absence of organization. Told of how I had asked the Members, both in the Cabinet and in party caucus, time and time again, to see that work of organization was started and something effective done. I could not get any response. I pointed out we were wholly without organization at present. I then said I had begun to wonder if the fault might not lie in myself and to think it was in the party's interest for the party to choose another leader. I sometimes felt that my colleagues regarded me as good natured, well meaning, etc., but no longer having the authority which the leader of a party should have in directing its affairs. That I realized only too well I was not as young as I used to be, that I could not do the things that I could do as a younger man; the last five years had caused strain and separated me from personal contact, etc. I wondered whether the time had not come for the party to choose a younger man among the Members, or someone outside the House. I told them to be perfectly free to do so.

"I then spoke of the feeling I had that men had begun to hesitate even to speak of leadership in the federal arena. The worst thing that had ever happened had been the way in which, at the time of the Victory Loan, the party had permitted the placarding of bulletins with pictures of Churchill and Roosevelt as 'our Leaders,' and that that had given rise, through its extension and perpetuation, to the policy of sabotaging by the Tory party, the press, and the radio, with no reference to myself or to my utterances. I drew from my pocket the little leaflet which was issued by a Knox Church clergyman, and told the Members I had shown it to Churchill and the President, that they might understand the kind of campaign I was up against. What amazed me was the silence in which men of the party itself had ignored all this kind of thing. No one had suffered more in the way of detraction and insult than I had been subjected to in all the years of my leadership. . . .

"I then told them I had called the party together for plain speaking and hoped that they would speak out. I was setting them an example in that regard. I wished to make it now perfectly clear that I myself would not lead the party without organization, and that unless an organization could be effected, which would be effective, I would have to ask them to choose someone else. Apart from this, I said there were many reasons why a younger man should be chosen.

"I spoke about not accepting their view as to the lack of confidence in the Administration on the part of the people. I was not afraid of the people. It was unreasonable to believe that our war effort, being what it was, the people would ignore that. I said I had a duty as leader of the party, which was, if possible, to see that its existence was prolonged, the party itself not destroyed. I felt, if no organization could be immediately effected, the sooner the people were given a chance to say what party they wished to have take on the war effort the better. . . .

"I found my throat troubling me a good deal in speaking, and my head not too clear. Thought that I was perhaps getting off on a note I had not intended and carrying it a little too far, so did not continue to say much beyond, of course, acknowledging the individual and personal loyalty of the men toward myself over the years I had been leader, and referring to the importance of the war effort, and my desire to see the party really fight for Liberal principles.

"I should say that, in speaking about difficult situations, I said that I found within the party itself very different views as to how an Administration should carry on. That there were those who believed in the iron hand; that because we had a Government ruling in time of war everyone was to be expected to do everything the Government proposed. . . . I myself did not believe in that method of carrying on government; that there was such a thing as appeal to reason, and that the government could not be carried on in that way. It might be that the party would prefer someone with the iron hand point of view. In that event, I could not too quickly make way for another. I had had experience in leadership over a quarter of a century and had never attempted anything of the kind and would not attempt it.

"I spared no one's feelings in talking out. I told the Members I hoped they would do the same. . . . The caucus quickly caught the note, and Member after Member spoke out from the shoulder."

The caucus sat until 1.30 in the afternoon and again from 3 to 6, and in the evening from 8.15 until after eleven. It continued the next day (September 25). Mackenzie King noted that the "morning and afternoon were like the morning and afternoon yesterday but with perhaps even better speeches." Late the second afternoon the "Members kept demanding that I should speak. I did so for how long, I cannot say, but I imagine good part of an hour. . . . I reviewed the resolutions placing my interpretation upon them, and thanking the Members for their expression of confidence in the Government's war effort as being the one thing that mattered." One of the resolutions dealt with party organization and Mackenzie King "drew attention to the words 'the proper authorities' . . . and said I wanted a clear understanding as to what those words meant. If they meant I was the proper authority, I would have to tell caucus I could not do the work or undertake it. It was impossible for me to do it; that, moreover, unless somebody was found to do it, I would have to give up the leadership.

"I said I am making that plain in the presence of you all. I here and now say to my colleagues that I feel that is their duty, and it is the duty of Ministers of every province to be responsible first and foremost for the organization of their own province, and for all the federal organization collectively. That I did not end the responsibility there. That M.P.'s could help. I saw a number of Senators present. I would say there was not a Senator who did not owe his position for life as a Senator to the Liberal party. That I thought they owed it to the party to help in the work of organization. I thought, too, some of the Members were in a position to do a good deal themselves. I then went beyond and spoke of members of the party and the men and women from coast to coast who should be sought out and asked to help. I said I hoped it would not be a matter of the meeting being over and then going back in the Cabinet to find that nothing was done or would be done. That I knew there were some in the party who thought the main thing in a meeting was to get it over as soon as possible. For all Members to speak. Give them entertainment, and then say: the boys got away in a good mood. That was not what I wanted. I wanted the wishes of the Members carried out. If they were not carried out I intended to call another caucus before Parliament reassembled and would ask them to consider more seriously whether there was not really need for another leader. I said, too, that what was needed was an organization—something like what we had in every campaign which would reach institutions, churches and homes—an organization federally, also by provinces and constituencies."

He went on to speak "of the men who were dying at the front, fighting the battle of freedom abroad and sacrificing their lives at the front. I then turned on the caucus with all the moral indignation of which I was capable and said in very impressive words—words which I do not think any Members present will forget—that I wondered if they noticed that while we had spent five sessions discussing the all-important issues of the day, not a single word had been said about the men at the front. There had been no allusion whatever to them. The fact that they were fighting in order that we might be preserved in freedom which we, ourselves, had been enjoying; that while our minds had been filled with little inconveniences occasioned by restrictions in time of war, not having all the beer we wanted to drink, etc. not an expression had been given by any of those who had spoken or in any of the resolutions to these men who, as I said, were sacrificing their lives for their country.

"I told them that I had a resolution which I had drafted myself, while the caucus was on, which I would move as Prime Minister and which I hoped and knew would be accepted. I then read the resolution which I had drafted first in caucus this morning, after seeing the report that was brought in, and improved on during interval at lunch. This resolution [which expressed confidence in the Canadian armed forces and assured them of the utmost support of the caucus] took the caucus by storm. I could see that the whole lot of them were stunned. They were all for it. All wanted it. I told them that I knew that back of every man's heart, while he was not expressing it, in his own mind was the thought therein expressed and that I was giving expression to the thoughts and feelings that had not been uttered. I was saying what I was, not by way of reflection upon them but as something more significant. That I thought their minds were reflecting the mood of the people of Canada today. That they were all believing that the war would be won, the only thing from now on was to think how we could win elections. How we could make things easier for ourselves, but no thought or inadequate thought of what lay ahead.

"I then told caucus that while I prayed . . . that the war might be over by December . . . that I knew that neither Churchill nor Roosevelt held that view, and that they were not at all sure that the war would be over even a year from now. That is the war against Germany. There still remained the war with Japan. That we might be another one, two or three years at war. I said I agreed with what Mr. Churchill said that the bloodiest part was yet to come for Canada, America, and Britain.

That great losses were all ahead. That I was not usually mistaken in what I saw ahead of us. I could only see that Canada had yet her greatest ordeal through which to pass—her Gethsemane. That I felt until that was over, we had better not give all our time to questions which related to restriction, etc., asking the taxpayers to carry a still heavier burden to meet expenditures on social questions. That, by all means, to have everything in readiness for the moment the war was over, to improve conditions, but that we should not forget until that moment came that the supreme duty of the Government and everyone in the country was for the men at the front and the winning of the war. I then closed by referring again to my own feelings regarding the leadership of the party.

"I then took up the question of a general election. Told them that I did not share their views at all about not being able to win; that with a great issue, I felt sure we would win. That it was inconceivable that if an election were held tomorrow, the people of Canada would return the C.C.F. to carry on the war, or the Tories and not return this Government which had carried on that task so magnificently. I said, however, we had to consider the effect that an election would have on the men at the front. If I were thinking only of the party, I would lose no time in dissolution. . . . However, there were many considerations.

"I said one of them was to consider the effect of a last session of Parliament. That nothing could be worse for a party than to run to the last hour. Parties that had done it usually had been wiped out for years to come. It was the case with Bennett, also with the Government that succeeded Sir John Macdonald, staying until the stroke of the clock in 1896 and not coming back until 1911. That I greatly feared at another session we might be faced with a situation paralleling that at the time that Hepburn and his friends took the stand they did against the Government. That we would be battled from without and Heaven only knew what might arise within. That while I had great faith in human nature, great faith in men, I knew something of human nature. Politics was a very crude business, though a very fine one at times. I knew in the last session there would be many men who would wish to have their own price for their support. Some would want to know who were going to the Senate, or whether we would go so far in old age pensions, and the like. That unless each one was pleased in accordance with his wishes, we might expect defections from our own ranks. Above all, the Opposition would make our path as difficult as possible and would seek to block our legislation, etc. Moreover, what was most trying of all, we might have a situation arise in party government where only an appeal to the people would enable any Government to continue longer. That they must be prepared. Some issues could only be decided in that way. Consciously or unconsciously, we had thought of only four years of war. The air training scheme had at the outset been fixed for three. We might be in for several years of war still. Clearly, a dissolution might come at any moment. We must learn to be prepared.

"I then said, if we did have another session, I would have to ask them to organize for fighting in the House and to maintain a proper discipline. I then brought matters to a close by coming back to a reference to what I had said about leadership. That I did not wish them to misunderstand me. I did not want eulogies or praise or persuasions. I just had to realize that while there had been mention of 25 years of leadership, after my next birthday I would be in my 70th year and I could not do at 70 what I could do as a young man. That my strength was not what it was. I rose in the morning feeling that I could tackle anything, ready to talk with everyone; make contacts; be on time for Cabinet. When the time of evening came, I found myself unequal to the tasks of the day. When I thought of what might come in the future—attending Imperial Conferences across the sea, another session of Parliament, an election, etc., I just had to wonder whether my strength was equal to the task.

"It was only fair I should tell the party these things that they must be prepared at any moment to bring on someone else to lead them. That I still hoped for another fight. Would be glad to go through it if an organization could be effectively arranged, but after that I would hope that, if spared, I might then look forward to a little of the quiet of life to enjoy in retrospect, if not for long, in other ways some of the things in life that I valued most, and had not been able to enjoy in the years that I had given to public affairs. I told them that so long as I had the strength, I was ready to serve my country and the cause of Liberalism. That what my strength or days might be rested with a Higher Power in the Beyond.

"When I had finished, the Members gave a very warm reception to what I had said. . . . No one waited for further speeches from any of the Ministers. Indeed I was surprised to see it was nearly half past six. . . . Looking back, I feel that the two days have been the most profitable in the history of the party. I am not satisfied with the way I spoke. I was too tired, too pressed to do anything as I would like to have done it, but it was as plain as day that I have had guidance and help from Beyond and certainly for bringing in the resolution in regard to the men overseas. . . . One thing is certain, that the Members of the party, however they may disagree among themselves, are to a man with me as far as I could see. That confidence is very, very marked. . . . I believe if our own people had more faith and would work, we would find the same to be true from coast to coast, [though] not to the degree it was in the last general election."

Meanwhile, Mackenzie King had had Brooke Claxton, who was his Parliamentary Assistant, working with the Ministers, whips and other Members on the preparation of proposals for a post-war programme. Claxton and his assistants worked around the clock from Saturday until Monday.

All day Sunday (September 26) Mackenzie King worked on his speech for the Advisory Council of the National Liberal Federation, which was to meet the next day. He started to work immediately after breakfast and kept on writing until nearly six. He then took a short rest and, after dinner, went over what he had written. He noted that "most of the Laurier House staff were at work typing and we were able to get all this material out of the way shortly after midnight."

The next morning (September 27) he "was pretty tired having worked so hard yesterday, and pretty anxious, still having to complete my speech for tonight." While he was waiting at the Chateau Laurier for the meeting to be called to order, Angus Macdonald asked him "to come to one side as he had something to tell him. I sat on the sofa at the entrance to the ballroom, and he sat on a chair beside me. He said: 'I have bad news to give you; it relates to the attack upon our convoy, which was out last week. I am afraid your nephew [Dr. William Lyon Mackenzie King, one of the twin sons of the Prime Minister's only brother] is among the number missing. We do not know yet all particulars, but it would seem that he was on the destroyer 'Ste Croix.' She was torpedoed. It would seem that half of the men got off and were picked up by another British warship, the 'Itchen,' which also picked up some British sailors from another ship. Then the 'Itchen' was torpedoed and as far as we can learn all on board seem to be lost. I am awfully sorry to have to tell you this and wondering whether I should do so just at this moment as you are going in to speak.' I thanked Angus for telling me what he had in a kindly and thoughtful way. I said to him, at once, that I felt sure Lyon's life and influence would continue to be felt in this world; that I believed strongly in survival of human personality; that he left a boy who carried his name, and that I was sure this little lad would carry on his work, just as Lyon had sought to carry on his own father's work.

"I said that what I felt most deeply was the loss to the country at this time and in the years to come of one who, I believed, would have been one of the great surgeons and members of the medical profession. He had given some eleven years of his life to preparing wholly for the work of surgery, and never allowed himself to attempt any general practice, wanting to become highly skilled in his work. I spoke of his wife, his mother, and of Arthur [Lyon's twin brother] and felt very deeply for all of them."

Mackenzie King added that in opening the proceedings, he "naturally found it difficult to be at all light-hearted in meeting the members when I went in to speak and, in fact, felt no concern about anything other than to speak out quite definitely what might come into my mind. I made my remarks mostly in reference to the war and how serious the present situation was, and what terrible fighting there would still be. How much more our own men would be involved in it. . . . I told members above all else to keep uppermost in their minds the lot of the men and women who are giving their lives, as I said with real feeling, in order that we may continue to enjoy the freedom that we have here to be able to meet and discuss matters pertaining to the well-being of the people of our country. I ended my address by imploring the members to keep in mind, first and foremost, until the war was over, the men who were giving their lives at sea, on land and in the air and the homes and families from which they came, and to do all in their power to shorten the war by concentrated effort of all that would help to win the war.

"I had begun by speaking of the reasons for the calling of the meeting; the political situation as it had developed, Ontario election, by-elections, etc. . . . It being Ralston's birthday I mentioned this fact and extended warmest congratulations to him and then spoke to the meeting of what the country, the Empire and the free world owed to his conscientious and indefatigable labours. Wished him long continued service in health and strength. I then mentioned Ilsley as being, along with Ralston, the two Ministers who had, I thought, the heaviest burdens to carry at this time.

"I also referred to the necessity of reviving young people's clubs; how serious the situation was for the young people as they faced the future; of the need to have them given a full understanding of the problems and of enlisting their active sympathy in political affairs. Spoke of the necessity of preparing for the future. Begged them not to fall into the error of making all kinds of promises and attempting schemes impossible of achievement which would only bring disillusionment. Said even if the war ended sooner than was anticipated there would be years of revolution and great difficulties. I was surprised to find how easy it was for me to speak and how clear my vision was in regard to all that I wished to say. I suppose I was roused and stirred, which goes to show what the mind is like once it is free from the impediments of the body. I was given a splendid reception both before and after speaking. . . .

"When I was telephoning to Laurier House for the car, Chubby Power came and spoke to me about Lyon's loss. He was quite sympathetic in his way of speaking. He said Angus had told him about it. I was just walking opposite the Chateau, along Rideau Street, when Ralston followed me out to express a word of sympathy. We had just a word about the career that Lyon might have had. He was genuinely kindly in the way he spoke.

"It was about 12.30 when I got back to Laurier House. I felt I could not trust myself to telephone to Margery [Mrs. Lyon King] or Lyon's mother, or to speak to Arthur today, with the speech still to be written. Thought it best to go straight on with the speech." He did not conclude the preparation of his speech for the dinner until 6.30.

Mackenzie King described the Liberal Federation dinner as a "fine affair" and noted that he "spoke with the greatest possible ease and with a fine choice of words. Found it very easy and a delight to speak." After the preliminary courtesies at the opening of his speech, he "then delivered the speech I had written out. It was followed from beginning to close with the closest possible attention and with real appreciation of the different points as they were made. The references to the Ontario Government were loudly applauded and the words that Harry Nixon was not in any way responsible for the results. I must have spoken in all considerably over an hour. The applause at the close was strong and sustained. . . . It was like the old days, each one was saying that the last speech was the best of all. It seemed to have pleased the party very much that I had spoken out so strongly, and no one took exception to any point made; it gave me a tremendous satisfaction to say what I did about the conscription issue, the country being torn from end to end, and showing in no way, since the beginning of the war, had ships been available in sufficient numbers to take available men overseas."

In his diary later, Mackenzie King wrote: "At the dinner tonight the Committee had prepared a sort of souvenir symposium, containing quotations and figures of war leaders, reference to Canada's war effort and pictures of Churchill and Roosevelt and their references to myself, quotation or two of speeches of my own. It is well prepared and is the kind of literature that is very much needed. It will go very far in helping to win the day when a campaign comes.

"When I got back to Laurier House I sat quietly for a time thinking of what the day had brought and of tonight's meeting, and how it would rouse up the Conservatives, C.C.F., and others. It had marked the beginning of an offensive and a strong beginning at that. I feel we have moved on into the enemy's territory and must now go forward in a militant way to increasingly win the confidence of the people.

"Lyon and my brother were mostly in my thoughts. . . . I thought of the little lad who bears the same name [Lyon's son] and the possibility that some day he will either take a leading part in public affairs or in the profession in which his father and grandfather gave their time, thought and energy. At least for a century the name has stood for what is best in the ideals of the nation that may be borne further down the centuries in that association." The following morning Mackenzie King called Mrs. Lyon King and "told her I had learned she had received word from the Naval Department. Said to her I would keep her informed of any word that might come; to believe strongly that all was for the best. I did not encourage her to feel that, while the report was that Lyon was missing, there was any hope, but rather said the word that I trusted might help to cause her to feel that Lyon was still at her side."

Later that day (September 28) Mackenzie King examined the Resolutions of the Liberal Federation and impressed on Brooke Claxton that "care be taken not to issue it as a programme settled by the Liberal party, but merely as some suggestions from the Advisory Council to the Government." He was deeply gratified by the report in the Toronto *Saturday Night* of October 2, of the meeting of the Liberal Federation. An advertisement on the back cover "contained a picture of Mr. Churchill, the President, and myself seated side by side. On the front page was a recent picture of myself taken by Karsh. It was entitled: 'Latest picture of the Rt. Hon. W. L. Mackenzie King, who apparently will continue to be Canada's Prime Minister at least until war has ended, it was indicated this week.' The article begins: 'The complete and unquestioned acceptance of Mr. King's leadership by the Liberal party of Canada was reaffirmed this week at a general party convention, following a two-day caucus of the Ottawa members.' The article itself is an excellent one and wholly true. It continues: 'Outsiders find it difficult to understand the disparity between the violence (a little abated recently) of the personal attacks upon Mr. King and the lack of any indication of popular agreement upon any conceivable Government that could succeed his own.' "

On October 6, Power passed to Mackenzie King a suggestion made to him in Montreal looking to "a national Government as a means of ensuring defeat of the C.C.F. I told Power and he agreed that I would never form a national government with the Tory party. I would prefer to do so with the C.C.F. I said I did not intend to do either. I thought business men would find it to their interests to get behind the Liberal party if they wanted to be sure of one of the parties getting a majority. That was the doctrine they should be taught. Power seemed to think they felt pretty certain that Bracken was going to win. I told him that was all nonsense. He, Power, offered to organize the debating forces in the House at the next session. Seemed very keen on helping in every way he could. He was in good shape."

In his diary on October 8, Mackenzie King wrote: "I have been anxious to record a feeling which I have very strongly, namely that I have been able to find the best of reasons for continuing in office until the war is over. I have been able to get matters in such a position that obviously the country itself is demanding that the present Administration should remain in office until the war is over. If I am spared, that will enable me to at least complete my political life and having been the Prime Minister of Canada at the time of the world's greatest war; to have been longer at the head of the Administration in that period than I think any other Prime Minister in any part of the British Empire or any of the political leaders of the United Nations, and what is most important of all to have had the nation's war effort under the present Administration made so effective that it has been recognized, ere the war was over, that, having regard to Canada's size, population, etc., that effort has not been surpassed by any country in the world, and, on top of all, the country has remained united throughout the whole of that time, and that such service as there has been overseas has been on a voluntary basis. That is a great record, something which will loom larger and larger as Canada's part in the present war comes to be seen in the perspective of history.

"With the confidence expressed so completely by the Liberals' vote in and out of Parliament, and the demand of the country as expressed by opponents as well as friends of the Administration, I have now the best of reasons for continuing to remain in office, if my health permits, until the war is over. If when the war is over, it should happen that because of having remanied in office so long the party and myself encounter defeat, the inevitability of such a result will be pretty apparent and what will be sure to happen is that any Administration taking on post-war problems will, by contrast, find itself increasingly discounted, and the worth of the Liberal Administration correspondingly appreciated and emphasized by the people."

On October 9, Mackenzie King "received a cutting from the Toronto Daily *Star* of October the 7th giving an account by [W. A.] Fisher, the stoker who survived the Ste. Croix, and which contained the following mention of Lyon: 'Surgeon-Lt. Mackenzie King, nephew of Canada's Prime Minister, went down with the Itchen. He was on his way to the ship's sick bay when the first torpedo struck. Some men saw him later, but it is believed he fell into the water when that section containing the sick bay was hit by a second torpedo. He was a swell fellow and everybody liked him; he was really one of the men', Fisher said." On October 13, Arthur King brought Able Seaman Fisher to Kingsmere to see Mackenzie King. "Fisher told me," he wrote, "that he thought he was about the last one to see Lyon." Mackenzie King recorded in his diary the whole story as given to him. He "was greatly taken with Fisher, such a gentleman in his way of speaking—his table manners, his courtesy, thoughtfulness, and his fine open simple natural frank manner. These men are the salt of the earth. He likes the sea, it makes him feel healthy and strong—something in it appeals to him—is ready to go back —meanwhile is to have a few days with his wife in Edmonton. Married only this year, has one short leave before going to sea. I was very proud of him as a sample and symbol of young Canadian manhood. He and Arthur left together immediately after luncheon."

In mid-October Mackenzie King began sitting for the sculptor Avard Fairbanks who had been commissioned to do a bust of the Prime Minister by a group of Liberals headed by G. G. McGeer, the Liberal Member of Parliament for Vancouver-Burrard. While thrilled at the start, Mackenzie King became impatient as the number of sittings increased. On October 17 he wrote: "I felt too tired to say much and rather put out at the 'overstaying' of time so long, fearful of the servants, etc., but I must say no man could have worked harder, or more earnestly and steadily. He is a fine character, sound in heart and soul, but just lacking in 'understanding' of some things, but it has been an event in my life to have had him with me for an entire week and these records made. It was 7.30 when Fairbanks left, I confess I was relieved to see the little station car start off with its box at the back, flash a red light on as it reached the road gate."

On October 22, Mackenzie King "had a short interview with Flight Lieutenant [James] Sinclair [M.P. for Vancouver North], who has just returned from Italy. His squadron first to enter Sicily. Looks exceedingly well. Is going to remain now in civil life. Follow up Parliamentary duties. He told me the Air Force were strongly behind Power. . . . The officers of the Army practically all Tory, and men strongly C.C.F. though all admit present Government has been splendidly behind armed forces. . . . I confess I felt a little discouraged at the word he brought about the men in the Army. He thinks the Navy is Liberal. He came on one of the destroyers. Says what those men endure is greater than anything endured by either the Army or the Air Force."

On October 23, Mrs. Arthur King, his nephew's wife, telephoned to ask Mackenzie King how he was. He reflected that this was "one of the very few times that anyone related by marriage or any other way has made an inquiry concerning my health. It shows how completely isolated one has become in giving one's years as well as days in public affairs and allowing all elements of home and its associations to slip by unshared. I am becoming increasingly conscious of the loneliness which years can bring, though this perhaps can be kept off by continuous hard work and reading and writing."

A few weeks later, the biographer Emil Ludwig proposed to write a "portrait" of Mackenzie King. In a letter received on November 21, Ludwig wrote: "As a painter, I would ask you to sit for some hours and I hope you will kindly allow me some time." Mackenzie King was "filled with uncertainty as to the wisdom of anything appearing about myself until at least I am out of public office. However, I feel Ludwig has an understanding of character and our short acquaintance made me realize that we had no end of kindred sympathies and aims. I believe he can be trusted to do something that will be helpful. His name lends at least a note of authority and distinction to anything he may have to say." He accordingly decided to get in touch with Ludwig and have him come to Ottawa. "I pray that his thought and hand may be guided in what he writes. I have always felt I would rather write my own life before having anyone else attempt it, but this will be a mere portrait—as he says—a characterization, not a biography. He has a genius for portraiture and letters." Ludwig dined with Mackenzie King on November 23 and began his writing at once. The result could not be called his greatest book.

In the autumn of 1943, Mackenzie King had to deal with a good many irritating and difficult problems, some of them of the greatest importance. One irritating question of lesser importance was what to do about the Canada Medal. This Medal had been established some time before without any clear conception of its purpose. E. H. Coleman, the Under Secretary of State, had prepared a memorandum on the procedure for awards of the Medal which Mackenzie King went over with him on October 29. He was "exasperated at the whole business. It was simply a case of giving to him that hath, following a list of precedence from the G.G. down, including Princess Elizabeth of England. The Medal was to be one for fairly wide distribution to people who had rendered extra special service, something beneath the decorations. I told Coleman I would not take the responsibility of making any recommendations and thought we would be wise to withhold all awards of this Medal until after the war."

At the Cabinet meeting on November 3 his colleagues agreed the Canada Medal was intended to be awarded "because of extra-special service, not something to be given to all those who already have the highest positions." When it was suggested the Government might have to proceed to make awards because of steps already taken, Mackenzie King observed "this got under my skin at once and I said it was the strongest of reasons why we should not proceed any further; that I objected altogether to these matters being forced on the Cabinet; that nothing should be done." When it was decided not to proceed, Mackenzie King observed that "it would have been a scandal to permit this kind of thing to mar the face of the Government with the problems that are confronting it at this time. . . . Perhaps the country itself will have little comment on the decision we have made. On the other hand, had we continued with the granting of decorations when there is no time to consider them, we would have had a very bitter opposition aroused against us from coast to coast and in Parliament itself."

Mackenzie King decided at the end of October that the Canadian Legation in Washington should become an Embassy. He had discussed this proposal with Roosevelt and Churchill at Washington in May and he now arranged for the necessary submission to the King in order to "have this change effected in time to have an announcement made on Remembrance Day, November 11. I feel it important in view of further conferences in Britain, and conferences that have to do with settlement of war and post-war problems that Canada, having taken the part she has in two world wars, should not hold in the eyes of the world a subordinate place to that of other much less important countries; also to give to Canada a standing of her own at the side of the United Kingdom when it comes to signing the peace, etc. By associating this announcement with Remembrance Day, it should help to bring home to the peoples of the world what Canada's sacrifice has been in this World War, and what she is entitled to in the way of recognition. Creation of Embassies should now make complete in form as well as reality, and reality as well as form, the status of Canada as a nation in all its attributes and powers."

But the most difficult problem which faced the Government in the latter part of 1943 was what to do about the Report made by Mr. Justice McTague, the Chairman of the National War Labour Board, incorporating his recommendations for a wartime Labour Relations Code and modifications in the Wage Stabilization Order. The proposed Labour Relations Code dealt with union recognition, the right of collective bargaining and related matters; the modifications suggested for the Wage Order would have given the National and Regional War Labour Boards the power to authorize increases in sub-standard wages. The decision on the Labour Relations Code proved much easier than that on the amendment of the Wage Order. After the Cabinet meeting on September 16, Mackenzie King wrote that "the main achievement of the afternoon was having the Cabinet accept, in its entirety, the recommendations of the Advisory Economic Committee on the Labour Relations part of the McTague report." The Cabinet discussed the Committee's report paragraph by paragraph and W. A. Mackintosh, now Principal of Queen's University, who was then in the Department of Finance, made to the Cabinet what Mackenzie King called "an excellent presentation. The main gain so far as labour is concerned was acceptance by the Cabinet of compulsory collective bargaining in all war industries and labour-management committees in all war plants."

On September 30, W. C. Clark, the Deputy Minister of Finance, Arthur MacNamara, the Deputy Minister of Labour, and Mr. Justice McTague were all brought into the Cabinet meeting to discuss the proposed modifications of wage stabilization. Mackenzie King thought that McTague "made a good presentation" of his recommendations; that "there was really very little difference between Clark and McTague," and that the Ministers "had begun pretty well to see our way through the situation or its essential features." Actually he was far too optimistic, as the consideration of the problem and agreement on the new policy took until the end of November. The Cabinet "had another long session over labour policy" on October 1. "Judge McTague, Clark and MacNamara all present. I doubt if we would ever have got matters satisfactorily settled without having Judge McTague in Council. I am glad I insisted on that. He understands the psychological side of the labour problems. Recognizes he is dealing with human life rather than piles of wood and tons of iron."

Mackenzie King agreed with McTague's view that "gross injustices" in wage scales could be corrected without endangering over-all wage stabilization and price control. The Minister of Finance and the economic advisers of the Government feared that any wage adjustments would start an upward movement of wages which would make effective price control impossible. They had suggested instead the possibility of introducing family allowances to relieve the hardships caused by wage stabilization. Mackenzie King noted that "McTague was most emphatic about not allowing any discussion of family allowances to become a part of the labour policy as such. Rather they were to be considered in connection with a social security programme." Mackenzie King's own first reaction to the suggestion of family allowances was to point out that "to tell the country that everyone was to get a family allowance was sheer folly; it would occasion resentment everywhere. Great care has to be taken in any monies given out from the Treasury as distinguished from exempting portions of income already earned."

On October 5, the Cabinet spent the afternoon "largely in approving outlines on which an Order-in-Council is to be drafted, setting forth the policy on stabilization of wages. These directives have been prepared by the Departments of Labour and Finance jointly. At some points, they have swung back to what . . . Judge McTague has objected to, as I thought, on very reasonable grounds. I insisted that while an Order might be drafted on the lines proposed, it should not be considered as approved, even in principle, till we had heard the objections to it from McTague and considered the whole business in the light of his opinions. It is a very great problem indeed, and I am not at all sure that, in an effort to preserve the price ceiling policy, the Government may not, so far as labour is concerned, be making the last stage worse than the first. I pray myself for guidance in helping to have the matter so shaped and presented as to let labour see that we are really seeking its good in what we are doing."

The Cabinet on October 7 "discussed again the price and wage stabilization policy. I can see wherein, while it was apparent that we have reached a point where no one can be at all sure that we can hold the ceiling much longer, it is going to be difficult to continue what we are doing without antagonizing labour. It seems that it will be impossible to stabilize prices without stabilizing wages. . . The mistake that was made was not seeking to remove injustices at the outset. The Finance Department were responsible and they should never have frozen an increasing injustice. I feel the necessity of giving much of my time to this labour policy. I hope I can get time to do it."

Before the labour policy was finally settled a month elapsed and the Government was faced with a strike of the coal miners in Alberta and British Columbia. The Ministers directly concerned with economic policy were opposed on November 2 to conceding anything to the strikers, "otherwise might as well give up trying to preserve price ceiling. . . . I asked if they would like to take over the mines as was done in the U.S.; they did not seem to favour that. When there was some talk of conscripting the men to work or using force, I asked how coal could be mined in that way." This strike had occurred while a Royal Commission was investigating the grievances of the coal miners and Mackenzie King agreed that "the miners are wrong having gone out while the Commission is investigating their demands for higher wages. I also believe that the strike is linked up with the strike in the United States. Howe suggested we should wait and see what response came to the President's Order to the men to return to the mines. . . . I suggested that a carefully prepared statement should be given to the press so that the facts would be perfectly clear in any public discussion that might ensue. I am afraid that it is going to mean a very difficult situation: a coal strike calculated to occasion a fuel famine, with the approach of winter and at a time of war."

Meanwhile Ilsley had submitted to the Cabinet a proposed public statement on the importance to the public and to the war effort of maintaining the price ceiling. On November 3, when the Cabinet was discussing this statement, "all of a sudden, Ilsley launched out in very emphatic fashion about the mistake that had been made in the settlement with the steel workers." This was the wage increase arranged on Mackenzie King's initiative but with the concurrence of the Cabinet early in 1943. When Ilsley made this comment, Mackenzie King was annoyed and "immediately said that I was glad he had spoken out as he did. That I felt very keenly the indirect attacks which seemed to be directed at myself for having had to do with that settlement. That I much preferred to have direct statements made. That I wished to say that I did not agree at all with the statement Ilsley was making as to the action at that time having been unwise. I recalled the information we had before us at the time re the danger of the submarine menace and what a continued steel strike would have meant to the U.S. and Canada, and of the appalling situation which might have developed. I pointed out further that all the Members of the Cabinet had been a party to what was done and had agreed, step by step, to what was done. That my own belief was that no action since the beginning of the year in the Cabinet had meant more than the particular settlement of that dispute at that time. . . . Ilsley inquired as to why the public had not been told the reason. . . . I pointed out we were precluded from giving confidential information at the time.

"He and Howe then spoke of the need of some statement being given to the public just now in regard to the coal situation and the strike, and the demands of the miners, through taking advantage of existing conditions. I agreed that, at an appropriate time, such a statement might be made, and Howe stated he felt we should wait to see what action might be taken by the miners in the States. He seemed to have the opinion that the miners would go back without their demands being met. He said that, in time of war, it was necessary to be tough; that the armed forces ordered men at the front to fight, etc. I at once said that was true, because if they did not obey orders, they themselves stood to be shot, but I asked if he could run the nation on that basis, and if he thought that coal could be mined by having men driven into mines for fear of being shot from behind. I said the truth was we were dealing with human beings, who had to be dealt with as such.

"I then said I was becoming more convinced than ever that I was not the right person to lead the present Government; that all my training had been to use the art of conciliation to the limit in dealing with human relations, seeking to obtain by reason, rather than force, what was necessary. Apparently, however, there had come to be a belief in force on the part of the Members of the Government, which I could not accept, and it was entirely foreign to my nature." Mackenzie King added that he "honestly felt it would be better, if it was thought that the Government could only be run by coercion in regard to price ceilings, wage levels, etc., for me to leave it to those who had that belief." He indicated to his colleagues that he thought "they were quite mistaken in believing that just because the Government said a thing was to be done that it could be done; that there were some things a Government could not do, and they would find that out. Ilsley said he agreed, but said he thought the public should be so informed. I told him I was quite ready to do my part in that way, when the right moment came. I question very much if he will be able to hold to the price ceiling policy in a rigid way."

As Ilsley read his draft statement Mackenzie King "suggested modifications, which would make it clear that the Government would put forth its utmost effort to do certain things and that all should co-operate." When Ilsley said "he was fearful that might indicate we could not hold the situation," Mackenzie King "said I thought he ought to tell the country that and said it should realize it could not be held without the co-operation of all." Ilsley's draft statement which had occasioned this discussion was the basis of the broadcast on "The Fight against Inflation" which Mackenzie King finally delivered early in December.

The coal strike took up most of the time of the Cabinet on November 4. Mackenzie King "said very little but was interested in hearing some of the Members of Council talk about what we should do as a Government. That there could be no power greater than the Government." He did point out that "deep mining was not something that we could force any man to undertake against his will with any hope of result. I reminded Council again that there were some things that Government could not do, and it was as well to have this in mind in viewing this situation, but not to attempt a course that would result in failure and aggravate a situation, but find some alternative."

Just before this meeting on November 4, Mackenzie King had received a letter from Roosevelt in which the President referred to the coal strike in the United States and expressed the fear that the American price control could not be maintained. Mackenzie King noted that, "having Roosevelt's letter in mind, I reminded the Cabinet how we had taken the position that we should wait and see what happened in the States, the implication being we might find it well to follow a similar course. I said it was hardly probable that the Canadian Government would be able to do what a powerful country like the United States was not in a position to do in dealing with this situation. I favoured the idea Mitchell had put forward of allowing the Commission to go ahead and have the Government accept its findings, provided this was agreeable to the National War Labour Board, and also to the men who had returned to work while the inquiry was on. Not getting full agreement in Council on that, decided we should wait a little longer though I had pointed out that every moment was, in my opinion, important in dealing with a situation which resembled that of 1906." This strike of coal miners in Western Canada in 1906, which resulted in a serious coal famine on the Prairies, often came to Mackenzie King's mind at such times as this; he, as Deputy Minister of Labour, had settled that strike.

After the Cabinet meeting on November 4, Mackenzie King asked Ilsley, Macdonald, and St. Laurent to remain and "read them a couple of paragraphs from Roosevelt's letter which made clear that he had despaired of trying to avoid inflation, and that increases would have to be given. Also he had pointed out what was happening in the U.S. would have its effect on us. I thought it was well to let them have an inside view of how impossible it may be to attempt to hold a rigid wage stabilization line. They were, I think, a bit impressed by what I read them.

"Later, St. Laurent told me that last night he had thought of dropping into Laurier House to talk with me. . . . He wanted me to realize that while members of Council had spoken out strongly . . . it was not through any lack of confidence in me. That, as a matter of fact, they all marvelled how I had carried the Government through four years of war as we have done. He said that Ralston had never believed we would get on without conscription, and now was compelled to concede that I had done the right thing in taking the course I did. He said it might be conceded grudgingly but his attitude had changed entirely. He thought that was true of others."

There was another long Cabinet meeting on November 5 where there was discussion on "first the Labour Relations Code with Judge McTague present, and later the miners' strike in the West. It was distinctly helpful having McTague present as he and I see more or less eye to eye on these matters." Mackenzie King noted that he "allowed discussion to go as as far as possible, and then left two debatable matters in abeyance. Managed to cover the code. On the Western strike, I had to be as cautious as possible in steering between the Scylla of Mitchell's desire to get a speedy settlement along lines which he felt alone would be acceptable to men, and the Charybdis of the determination of other members to settle the strike by force. I had continually to bring the Cabinet back to the main consideration which was that unless coal were mined, we would have an appalling situation in Western Canada. I knew that Judge McTague felt strongly on the matter of this strike as threatening the usefulness of the National War Labour Board. I called on him first to give his views which he did very clearly. As Ministers were wholly in the dark and very vague about how long the fight could be kept up, I sent for the Coal Controller, Brunning, who came with his Assistant. I questioned him on the existing supply, etc. He pointed out that railways and coal companies had supplies enough to last half a year. However, in private homes, about half were supplied. Other half, practically at the margin. With regard to public utilities, power, lighting, etc., there were supplies in the average to last three or four weeks. In regard to private industries, many were very short of supplies and would have to close up in a couple of weeks. As to getting coal from the United States, the great difficulty was transportation, as locks will be closing in a fortnight; also doubtful if miners in the U.S. would work to supply extra coal to defeat strikers in Canada. I pointed out the U.S. settlement had given miners practically everything asked for in their demands. We had been told to wait for their decision. Having waited, it was now clear we had everything to lose letting the strike run on, and nothing to gain from it."

Mackenzie King then read to his colleagues part of the Report he had made in 1906 on the coal shortage on the prairies. He felt "this had a very sobering effect on everyone and helped to bring home the reality of the situation. Even McTague said that there was what was equivalent to an over-riding consideration to be taken account of, on what might follow a prolonged cessation of coal mining. . . . I pointed out that the weekend was a psychological time to get matters settled. Backed Mitchell up in advocating having the Commission given powers of Regional Board to continue inquiry, if men returned immediately to work. Labour leaders now in Ottawa have put that forward. . . .

"I did my best possible work with the Cabinet in keeping the distant objective constantly in view, and allowing discussion to the point where it became too irrelevant. I kept insisting on the condition we were facing, not one that we would like, or what might be right, etc., or what should be done, but rather on what was necessary to get work resumed, while it was obviously necessary at this time of war. I felt considerably relieved at the end of the meeting."

The next day (November 7) Mackenzie King arranged with Mitchell to have the Labour Department prepare a draft agreement that coal miners would return to work at once if the Royal Commission then investigating their grievances was given the powers of a Regional War Labour Board to adjust wages subject to review by the National Board. He told Mitchell "he and MacNamara better have an understanding with the men . . . that the miners would accept the proposal." Meanwhile the Cabinet had met and "just before luncheon MacNamara brought a letter from the men to Mitchell along lines I had indicated earlier in the morning. No one in Council was aware of this excepting Mitchell. Mitchell had prepared, in addition, his reply to the men undertaking to submit their proposals immediately after word received that men had returned to work. Yesterday's discussion had had a very sobering effect on all present. . . . Members all saw, from previous days' discussion, how close we were to a very difficult situation. Council accepted both communications as basis of settlement. McTague being present, I asked him whether this would affect him adversely. He replied that in the circumstances, he could offer no objection, or words to that effect."

Having thus found a way of dealing with the miners' strike for the moment, the Cabinet resumed consideration of the Wage Stabilization Order and finally decided to give the Regional and National War Labour Boards authority to adjust wages which were grossly unjust without tying the Boards to any specific formula.

The provincial Ministers of Labour had at this time been invited to a conference at Ottawa with Mitchell to discuss the wartime Labour Relations Code. Mackenzie King presided at a dinner for the provincial Ministers on November 8 and in speaking assured them the federal Government was not "seeking to infringe on jurisdiction of provinces, but necessity of federal Government assuming obligations of price ceiling and wage stabilization regardless of consequences. Made a final appeal for closest measure of co-operation between all."

The next day (November 9) Mackenzie King "phoned Mitchell about having his Department collect together statement of all the grievances labour has against the Government, to have them properly listed that they may be discussed in the Cabinet before we announce our labour policy, and suggested when this has been done, having a meeting with labour leaders; also a gathering such as last night's gathering. What I said seems to have been very greatly appreciated."

About half the coal miners had, by this time, returned to work and the Cabinet on November 10 decided to approve the draft agreement that would permit the Royal Commission to sit as a Regional Labour Board to settle wage rates in the industry subject to approval of the National War Labour Board. This decision overcame the coal crisis but it took most of the rest of November to put the general policy into final form.

Mackenzie King, on November 25, "spent the afternoon in Council, going over labour legislation. Had both Judge McTague and the Labour Relations Officer of the Department of Labour come into Council to discuss what we were proposing. That was quite a debate. It was apparent there was a certain jealousy and lack of sympathy and co-operation between McTague and Mitchell and his Labour Relations men, I think, partly, because each desires to have all features of the Act as much as possible under his own control. At the end of an hour's sitting, I suggested we should send to New York for Bryce Stewart [at that time an industrial relations counsellor, who had served as Deputy Minister of Labour earlier in the war] to come and view the different attitudes and advise the Government as to what it was best to do. Council were all agreed to this." The differences were subsequently ironed out and a satisfactory line drawn between the functions of the Department of Labour and the proposed Labour Relations Board.

The difficulties over wage stabilization were not the only threat to the economic stabilization policy. On October 19 the Cabinet had before it a question of subsidizing increased hog shipments to Britain involving additional scarcity at home. The discussion became very acrimonious and Mackenzie King expressed the fear that "conditions might become such in Parliament, and such throughout the country, with endeavour to keep price ceilings, etc., that in the face of attacks, members of the Government themselves might be glad to have a campaign (i.e. an election) as the only way of clearing the atmosphere. Ilsley said that is exactly how he felt. . . . I made it clear that I thought the time had come when we should consider the Canadian people themselves. Not necessarily meet every request that came from Britain in the light of all that we had done, specially anything that involved extra taxation and subsidies on top of rationing our own people." The discussion continued on October 20 and Mackenzie King "spoke of the need for Ilsley to show reduction in the Budget instead of increase at the session immediately before the election. Further taxation would mean we might as well hand over the Government in its entirety to the C.C.F." The Cabinet decided "to send less hogs to Britain, also remove restrictions; allow prices to be improved for farmers."

Mackenzie King referred once more, at the War Committee on October 21, to the need of improving the budgetary position, when he "spoke plainly before the Chiefs of Staff, as well as colleagues, of the necessity of the Minister of Finance bringing in a Budget this coming year which would reduce taxation and show reduced expenditures, pointing out that heavy taxation and outlays would raise such a feeling throughout the country that the Government would certainly meet with defeat, and [make it] equally certain that the C.C.F. would come in its place, which would immediately take steps to reduce all the services and would see that this was carried very far in the post-war years. I wanted the Chiefs of Staff to realize not only what the position of the Government was but their position as well, in meeting the developments of the future."

Throughout the autumn Mackenzie King was a good deal concerned about his promise to Churchill to visit England. When Churchill referred in the British Parliament on September 22 to a meeting of Commonwealth Prime Ministers in the spring, "this was an immense relief" to Mackenzie King's mind. But this announcement by Churchill did not finally dispose of the question of a visit. In late October and early November there was much discussion back and forth with Churchill. Mackenzie King was vastly relieved when the visit was definitely postponed until the spring of 1944 by a telegram from Churchill which he received on November 8. He felt "that was all to the good. We could adjourn Parliament if we thought it advisable; if not, I would be freed for a while of part of the strain, and the mission overseas would be attracting attention of the country and helping to give me greater prominence in international affairs before another appeal to the country which, politically, would be helpful."

The next morning (November 9), Mackenzie King "listened to Churchill speaking at the Mansion House. Many parts of the address were excellent, spendidly framed and most encouraging of all was his clear statement that we might reasonably expect 1944 to see the end of the war in Europe. However, this was coupled with the statement, most important of all, that the early part of the year would witness sacrifice of human life for the British and the Americans on a scale beyond comparison with either Waterloo or Gettysburg. In his speech, Churchill made fitting references to the Russian achievements, etc., but it had the fault of practically all of his utterances, all but ignoring the part played by the Dominions. I confess that the closing portion of his speech filled me with indignation and made me sick at heart. He talked of the war being brought to a victorious close by the British and Americans, and I thought of how our own Canadians had stood as the spearhead of that appalling possible sacrifice, what they were doing in Italy, to which there was again no allusion, of what the Canadian Air Force is doing over Europe, and what the Air Training Scheme has meant; also the part played by Australians and South Africans. Such praise as there was for South Africa was all directed to Smuts' leadership. No reference to the lives of the men. . . . He also had his usual reference to Britain standing alone at the beginning. This is not all mere chance or oversight, as the matter has been repeatedly brought to his attention, and it was clearly so brought at the Conference at Quebec. It is the John Bull and his Island attitude of self-sufficiency and unconscious superiority of certain of the British stock. They would drop us all in a moment tomorrow if it served their purpose to do so, forgetting wholly the contribution and sacrifice which Canada has made. All this causes me to be equally indignant with the subserviency of some of our own people."

On November 9, Mackenzie King also listened to Roosevelt's broadcast inaugurating the United Nations Relief and Rehabilitation Administration. He noted that "unlike Churchill, Roosevelt seeks on all occasions to think of all the countries concerned, and to give some expression to views which will cause them to realize their service and their needs are in his thought. In matters of the kind, my own position is quite difficult or could be made so, and very embarrassing if I chose to make difficult situations more difficult instead of seeking to have everything go as smoothly as possible."

As the year drew to a close, Mackenzie King began to feel the strain. On November 29, he referred in his diary to how completely run down nervously he had become. "I seemed good for nothing all morning, though I had expected today to be equal to any task. I can only touch the correspondence in a desultory sort of way. As my nerves seem to be completely on edge, almost anything makes me feel that I might break down." He decided he must get away for "some sort of a change." The next day (November 30) he "told the Cabinet that I had been much worried as to what it was best to do. That while I had been resting and looked well, I was, nevertheless, greatly fatigued and had found it next to impossible on Sunday and yesterday to do any work at all. That I must get away for a change. I could not face the possibiliy of meeting Parliament in the condition I was in or even preparing the sessional programme, let alone waiting to make a broadcast where the material was not available." The broadcast he referred to was the one he was to deliver on December 4 on "The Fight against Inflation."

He was also irritated because certain changes had not been made in the Liberal organization in Ontario and he told his colleagues he wished "with all my heart that they would arrange to have someone take over the leadership of the party and let me out of it altogether. That I was most sincere in saying that I thought the time had come when a change should be made and someone placed in control whose words would carry some weight."

He wrote afterwards that he "was very tired and very weary and spoke out even more strongly than I have indicated here. . . . I said that in the seventeen years I had been at the Council table I had never had occasion to speak out to colleagues as I had this afternoon. I then said I was sorry for what I had said, but that it was meant for what was most in the party's interests." The next day (December 1), he noted that he disliked "very much this way of being obliged to do things. I decided that I would go on quietly as long as I could and seek from now on to say nothing except with great reserve and self-control, if that were possible. To try and hold on until the war is over."

Despite the feeling of pressure and fatigue Mackenzie King succeeded in completing and delivering his broadcast on "The Fight against Inflation" on December 4. It was a momentous speech and for once he was pleased. "In preparing broadcast," he wrote afterwards, "I went a long way in stating Government policy without further consultation with the Cabinet. For example, came out squarely for the floor under farm prices as post-war policy. Also with what I had in mind from the beginning, post-war social security and human welfare policy—the idea of a national minimum for the whole people. Also got cost-of-living bonus as being imbedded in the basic wage rate, which means a permanent rise in the standard of labour for all time to come. Declared the compulsory collective bargaining policy, and announced the labour code, etc. It was really a far-reaching statement of Government policy. In the last three days, if not in the last two or one, I have succeeded in making declarations which will improve the lot of hundreds of thousands of farmers and working people from one end of Canada to the other. Dealt strong blow for the living standard of the masses of the people from coast to coast. I think I have cut out the ground in large part from under the C.C.F. and Tories alike and certainly have given the Liberal party a place of new beginning, if we will only follow up with effective organization."

Having delivered his broadcast, Mackenzie King left the next day for Washington to visit Cordell Hull with whom he dined on December 6. Hull gave him a long account of his recent visit to Moscow which Mackenzie King set down in detail in his diary. Hull felt the war in Europe might continue all through 1944 and that "they might be killing each other while the Presidential elections were on." Mackenzie King told Hull he "had sought to arrange matters so as to have the Government continue while the war was on. We had till late spring or early summer of 1945 to run if we so desired. He thought this very fortunate. I spoke to him about my remaining in the States for a few days so as to be here when the President arrived, to be among the number to greet him." The President was absent at this time for the meeting with Churchill and Stalin at Teheran.

The next day (December 7) Mackenzie King went on to Williamsburg for a rest. Two days later he "wakened completely discouraged this morning. Found it impossible to throw off depression throughout the day.... I feel, too, as if I had made a mistake in planning this trip at this time of war. The Canadian public will get the wrong impression which will be assiduously fostered by political enemies. I felt more convinced of this tonight when, on returning to the suite, I saw a long despatch from the Canadian Press indicating I had gone south with private car and had three members of the staff with me. Apart from that, however, I think I would have been wiser to have stayed and cleared up arrears before this year of my life is out."

He decided not to stay in the United States until Roosevelt returned, and on Saturday, December 11, went to New York City for the day. He wished to take a friend to the Metropolitan Opera and had the clerk at the Harvard Club, where he was staying, telephone for tickets. Seats were secured only through a direct application to Edward Johnson, the Canadian Manager. Mackenzie King was surprised, when he reached the Opera, to be shown into Johnson's own box and both surprised and a little embarrassed to find Johnson's daughter, Mrs. George Drew, whom he had not previously met, already seated in the box. When he expressed the hope his presence was not embarrassing,

Mrs. Drew was very pleasant and said they "were on neutral ground dealing with art and music." There was also some reference made to Mackenzie King's part in arranging for Drew's visit overseas with Bracken's party. Johnson told Mackenzie King that when the clerk had called about the tickets "he thought some one was pulling his leg." Mackenzie King was greatly delighted by the whole experience. The opera was *Tristan and Isolde*. He found "the singing and music very lovely and inspiring. It was a great event in itself. . . . I was delighted with Johnson himself. He is a charming man. Mrs. Drew, too, was exceedingly pleasant."

That evening he went to spend the night and the following day with Mr. and Mrs. John D. Rockefeller at their Park Avenue apartment. "When I arrived," he wrote, "they both gave me the warmest of welcomes. Nelson was there. Had remained to have a talk before going on to Washington at night. He is a fine, big, strong-looking fellow. We sat in front of a fire until almost on to midnight. Mr. Rockefeller came to my room with me, and it was rather amusing how we shook hands a couple of times in saying good night. Both he and Mrs. Rockefeller spoke of how natural it seemed for us all to be together as though there had not been an absence of a day or two since we last met."

He stayed with the Rockefellers until Monday morning when he returned to the Harvard Club. During their final talk on this visit Rockefeller said to Mackenzie King: "You have done more for me than anyone. Repeated what he had said before Mrs. Rockefeller last night, that he had found my judgment invariably sound and good. He had been amazed at how, at every step, I had known what course to take, and it was the right one. He repeated that this morning and said: 'You have meant everything to me at a time when I needed guidance in many matters and your whole outlook and attitude have helped me tremendously.' "

The next day (December 14) at the Harvard Club, Mackenzie King received from Rockefeller "as beautiful a letter as I have ever received in its expression of friendship and of what my life had meant to him." Mackenzie King recalled that their friendship had begun in a breakfast at the Harvard Club in 1914 and he felt it was "indeed significant that this expression of what the intervening years have meant to each of us should have come to me at the Harvard Club in this particular week and year."

On December 15, Mackenzie King called on Mrs. Andrew Carnegie and "had a delightful talk with her in front of the fireplace in the library, where I sat beside Mr. Carnegie years ago."

Despite his love of New York and the pleasure of meeting old friends, Mackenzie King wrote: "Thinking over the trip, I must confess I have had a bit more anxiety on it than I have had pleasure or rest. Have been haunted with a feeling that much may be made of the fact I have gone to the States at a time of war, private car, staff, etc. . . . This may be used by the Tories and the C.C.F. against me. The fact that I have not seen the President before returning makes the situation embarrassing. . . . Perhaps when we get back to Ottawa and I get into the regular routine of work again, I may be able to enter upon the new year of my life in a way that will make its beginning worthy of the purpose which I have most at heart."

Churchill was ill in Cairo after the meeting with Roosevelt and, on December 22, Mackenzie King received a message in which he said: "My wife and I have read with great pleasure of the moving telegram which you have addressed to the Deputy Prime Minister about my illness. I hope that we are through our principal difficulties, and I have at no time relinquished my part in the direction of affairs. I may, however, be advised to take a few weeks' rest as a half-timer at some sunny place up here before returning to the fogs and flu of London. This further manifestation by you of our long friendship gives me great pleasure. Give my best of wishes to all our colleagues. Very hard days lie ahead of all of us and I am glad to think that we shall meet in the spring." Mackenzie King noted: "It gave me much happiness to have this direct word from Churchill, first because of the assurance it brought of his recovery, and secondly, in what it expresses of genuine friendship. I confess the reference it contains to very hard times ahead is what I, myself, have all along been anticipating. The mention of it from him adds greatly to my concern."

On December 31, Mackenzie King wrote: "As the year draws to its close, I feel that it has been in many ways the best year of my life; that I have made more progress in the things of the mind and spirit than any other year, and had gained a measure of health and strength, physical, moral and spiritual, which is greater than I had a year ago. I feel that God has guided my path and that, by trusting to Him, I shall yet have time and strength to fulfil the purpose of my life. My heart is full of gratitude and thanks. My thoughts are mostly of the coming year, of our men fighting overseas, and of the bereavements in homes. May God grant that in the New Year and ere too many months have passed we will have peace."

CHAPTER TWENTY-ONE

General McNaughton's Retirement

ON NOVEMBER 30, 1943, the day of the outburst in the Cabinet mentioned in the previous chapter, Mackenzie King had told his colleagues that he "had many problems to contend with of which none of them knew and of which I could speak to none." Undoubtedly what was in his mind was the impending retirement of General McNaughton as Commander of the Canadian Army. This retirement had just been agreed to after very difficult exchanges by cable back and forth across the Atlantic with Ralston and McNaughton. As early as 1942 when McNaughton had been home in Canada on leave, Mackenzie King had recorded his concern as to whether McNaughton would have the health and strength to lead the Army in the field. But the definite probability of McNaughton's retirement first arose just after the Canadian troops landed in Sicily.

At that time General Stuart, the Chief of the General Staff, was in England and he sent Brigadier R. B. Gibson home to report. Gibson delivered this report to Mackenzie King and Ralston at the Prime Minister's Office on July 10, 1943. The report indicated that the invasion of France across the Channel would not begin before May 1, 1944, and that Stuart was concerned about the effect of the delay on the morale of the Canadian Army. Mackenzie King reported that Ralston felt this would mean the Canadian Army "would not have much fighting in the war and that Canada's voice in peace and post-war would not be so effective. I said that they would probably be the first to enter Germany and to bring Hitler to his knees . . . that what would be appreciated most was bringing war to its close and securing the unconditional surrender, and that this would require great strength, planning, etc. Ralston thought our Army might only become an army of occupation in Europe and that what counted from the Army point of view—the members of the forces—was the action at the outset, having men in action since beginning. . . . The question in these circumstances was, should another division be sent to Sicily or the south. I pointed out it had, I thought, been understood, after some battle experience, present division might be brought back. Another might be exchanged, but it was a good deal of risk sending divisions back and forth."

In his account of this meeting, Mackenzie King noted that Gibson had indicated that McNaughton naturally preferred to keep the Army intact "for the final blow" but was agreeable to a second division going to the Mediterranean. Mackenzie King also noted that Ralston would like to see a Canadian Corps established in Sicily under the command of General Crerar and that he wanted to go to England at once to join General Stuart and settle the question. Mackenzie King finally agreed that Stuart should remain in England and that Ralston should join him as soon as the session of Parliament ended. Ralston did, in fact, go to England at the end of July, but he was called back for the Quebec Conference before he was able to go on to Sicily as he had planned to do, and before the question of establishing a Corps there could be considered.

When Ralston reached Quebec on August 10, he had a long talk with Mackenzie King about his conversations in England with McNaughton, in which he reported that McNaughton seemed favourable at first to the idea of another division going to Sicily and possibly to the formation of an Army Corps, but that, later, he had objected to the breaking-up of the Canadian Army. He stated that, at one stage, McNaughton had suggested that Ralston did not care anything about the Canadian Army. When Ralston recalled his defence of the Army in Parliament and said he could not understand McNaughton's statement, McNaughton had referred to conversations Ralston had had with the Chief of the Imperial General Staff, Sir Alan Brooke, and other British officers about the disposition of Canadian troops.

Ralston also told Mackenzie King that Brooke had expressed surprise at the judgment McNaughton had shown in military exercises in Britain earlier in the year which were called by the code name "Spartan." Similar criticism from Brooke had, Mackenzie King recalled, been contained in the report General Stuart had sent back with Brigadier Gibson in July. Mackenzie King's diary gives no clear account of the way in which McNaughton's judgment was supposed to have been at fault in the "Spartan" exercise.

There is no doubt, however, that the possibility of McNaughton's retirement as Commander of the Canadian Army became an active possibility from this time on. Mackenzie King saw General Stuart in Quebec on August 14 and Stuart confirmed what Ralston had told him, and indicated that McNaughton had himself spoken of the possibility of resigning. Both Ralston and Stuart reported that McNaughton seemed much older and suffering a good deal from strain.

Stuart also indicated that Brooke and General Paget, who was Commander in Chief of the Home Forces in Britain, no longer felt confidence in McNaughton's capacity to command troops in actual combat. Mackenzie King was deeply concerned by this statement. Stuart reported that "both Paget and Brooke were particularly enthusiastic about Crerar. Felt he was an exceptionally good officer, and Crerar was very popular with the men. Stuart said that Montgomery would not allow McNaughton to cross over to Sicily or to have any part in the operations there. That apparently they had had some very sharp words and McNaughton had gone back to Britain very much annoyed at not having been permitted to cross from the mainland into Sicily."

Mackenzie King felt it was clear from his conversation with Stuart that "one of the most difficult problems to settle at this [Quebec] conference will be the command of our force, and what is to be arranged for McNaughton." He added: "I have come to the conclusion that, quite apart from any differences between Ralston and himself, and incompatibility between the temper of the two men, there may be a necessity for someone else having command of the operations on the Continent. It is really too bad as the Army is really due to McNaughton and he has lived in the hope of commanding it in action. I can understand, however, how four years of service with health not too good may have affected his judgment."

Later in the day (August 14), Mackenzie King had a talk with Sir Alan Brooke whom he "liked exceedingly." Brooke told Mackenzie King McNaughton "seemed to have become more suited for planning and research than for action in the field. He said he ought to be the head of a great research institute. I said: 'As you know, he was head of our Research department.' He replied: 'Yes, and excelled himself at that kind of work. Full of inventive genius, but interested in study.' His conversation rather confirmed what Stuart had said to me. When I mentioned Crerar, Brooke said he had the very highest opinion of Crerar. Could not have a better man. Would trust him in command anywhere, etc. I did not in any way ask for an opinion on either of the men. All was volunteered.

"After Brooke had spoken of McNaughton, I said what he had just said I had felt a little about myself. That I had been getting out of touch with the men in the party who were in the field, concentrating more on the work in hand, and that, as one got older, one became more interested in philosophical thought and the like. He said that was it exactly."

Mackenzie King had a talk with Ralston and Stuart together at Quebec on August 31 about the question of another division going to Sicily. He told them he "was quite agreeable to that and having a Canadian Corps formed there, if desired. They read me wires which indicated the possibility of Crerar receiving the appointment of Commander of the Corps there. I expressed myself as in agreement with that, if approved by McNaughton. They will let me see the wires to pass on shortly. The more of our men participate in the campaign in Italy, the fewer there are likely to be who will be involved in the crossing of the Channel which, as Churchill says, will be a very tough business. I believe the Canadian people would rather have our men in action in Italy than remain inactive in Britain throughout the winter. At most, it would be one more division, probably the third. The question of reinforcements is, of course, an important consideration. Battle experience means the saving of life in the end."

For Mackenzie King, the matter rested there until October 8. Ralston was in Camp Borden that day and Angus Macdonald, who was acting Minister of National Defence, and General Stuart saw Mackenzie King about a message from London indicating that "the Chiefs of Staff had reviewed the situation and were prepared to have another Canadian division proceed to Italy and a British division brought back to Britain; also a Canadian Headquarters to be established in Italy which would take the place of one of the British headquarters. . . . Stuart was much elated. Said it was a great compliment to Crerar. Spoke of what it would mean to have a Canadian Armoured Division in Italy. That they were as fine an armoured division as there was in the world—splendid looking Canadians. All young Canadians of the very best type and training. They might be expected to give a magnificent account of themselves.

"The telegram had been telephoned to Ralston who had made three suggestions for a wire to McNaughton—one was that he could count on our Government giving immediate approval. The second, he should proceed at once to get on with the movement. The despatch had indicated something about shipping. Thirdly—that if he wished to make any comments, they would be received. In referring to this third suggestion, Stuart said he was sure Ralston would be just as well pleased if that were left out altogether. There was no need to send it. I immediately said I thought what he was going to say was that the third statement should be made the first in the wire. That I felt that was McNaughton's due; that as long as we continued him as Chief of the Army, we should have confidence in him. Stuart said that he was not at all sure that McNaughton would like the course now suggested by Brooke and the Chiefs of Staff. That it would, of course, mean breaking-up of the Canadian Army in England.

"Stuart went on to say that at one stage in conversations between them in England, McNaughton had indicated that if the matter were so decided, he, himself, would have to cease to take the responsibility. In other words, would resign as Commander-in-Chief. I said I doubted very much if matters would so develop. That McNaughton himself knew that there was a very strong feeling in Canada that our men should be given an opportunity of participating in an active theatre of war. That they had had a very long wait, and he must also know that among the men in the Army themselves, they were feeling that way.

"I said he would further know that the fact that they were being kept so long in England at first, had been put down to the Government and particularly to myself. He now knew that the mistaken view had now been corrected and more or less wiped out, and that it was rather upon his own head that the criticism was being directed. That I would be surprised if he did not feel that, with the success which the First Division had had in Italy, there were strong reasons for having the Division become a Corps and extra battle experience secured in Italy itself.

"I went on to say that I thought the second suggestion, namely that he should prepare, which was equivalent to an order saying he should proceed with the movement, should not read as mandatory, but that he might proceed, the assumption being that this would necessarily carry with it his approval. The General was not sure that McNaughton would give his approval. He said he might say nothing at all. He went on to say that, after all, it was McNaughton's business to carry out the orders of the Government and to do the fighting, but not to decide the policy. I replied that, on the other hand, it was obviously our duty to receive from him comments that he might wish to make and give them the consideration they merited. He should be allowed to register his position in the light of the responsibilities he had and his duty to advise to the best of his judgment.

"I went on to say that I was not at all sure that McNaughton would not be ready to acquiesce in what was now about to be suggested by the Chief of Staff. That he, Stuart, would remember when McNaughton was here last, that he himself was deeply concerned as to whether or not his own judgment was right as to keeping the Army intact in Britain, and, in that connection, he had asked Brooke and others to be most frank in stating their views to him. That they were all of that view. . . .

"I then stressed the importance of the record being such as to make clear that McNaughton had not been 'ignored or walked over'—the exact expression I used—that he had had full opportunity to make his own position and views known. I said, if he registered objections and indicated that he would not continue to take command for the forces if the Army were broken up, it would then be for the Government to decide whether we should retain him as Commander or change him, because of the necessity of making a change. I myself do not feel, however, that matters would come to this point if we proceeded in the right way and right spirit. If we ignored him he might well resign, and there would be great feeling throughout the country that he had done the right thing. . . . As I spoke, Stuart took down in rough outline what I had indicated and read over to me the outline he had made. I agreed it was in accord with what I had said, but asked that I should see the final draft before it went off. Not that I do not feel sure it would be all right, but that there might be implications or shadings or words which I would not wish to be responsible for, something not expressed in the way I thought would be wholly satisfactory.

"While we were talking a further message came from Ralston which seemed to emphasize what had been said in a previous message. In the course of the interview, Angus Macdonald mentioned that he thought it was best, in Ralston's absence, to take this up direct with me, especially as it involved the important matter of McNaughton's position. I said the General knew I was aware of the situation that has been under discussion and consideration for some time past; that I understood what was involved and, for that reason, I was glad they had come to talk the matter over before any further communications were sent. I repeated that I was particularly anxious to avoid anything that could be construed as being unfair to McNaughton or which would give rise to recriminations later on. That I felt if we proceeded in the right way all would come through satisfactorily."

On October 12, Ralston telephoned Mackenzie King that there was a "message from McNaughton which, as I had expected, accepted the situation, with as little in the way of demurring as could have been expected, if he McNaughton were to do justice to his own position and view."

Meanwhile McNaughton had reported on conversations he had had with the British military authorities and particularly General Paget "concerning the changes in the position of our forces and additional changes in organization." Stuart in turn made a report for the War Committee which was considered on October 21. Mackenzie King "thought Stuart's report was well prepared, and I confess to having felt a considerable relief of mind at what is now proposed and likely to take place. Instead of having all our five divisions kept in England and used for the final attack on Germany, without any of them having had battle experience in advance, or what was originally in the minds of those who were planning the campaigns, there has since come about the sending of one division and brigade to Italy, and its participation there along with the British troops and Americans, and now the sending of a second division and a motorized division, and the establishment of a Canadian Army Corps in Italy.

"There will remain a Canadian Army Corps in Britain. Then, when the main assault comes, instead of our men bearing the brunt of this assault, it will be divided between the British, Americans, and ourselves. . . . This, I think, will mean a considerable saving of life of our own troops and it will also have the advantage of Canada sharing in such successes as there may be in the south as well as in the north. By the time spring comes around, Germany will have received such an additional amount of bombing that I think there is every chance of the assault, when it comes, coming speedily and bringing the war to a termination. . . .

"The serious personal part of this—and it is a political problem as well—is that it is almost certain to involve, if not the retirement of McNaughton, at all events his position as Commander being more nominal than real. It certainly rules out altogether the possibility of his commanding the Canadian forces in the final engagement in Europe. General Stuart was very frank in the way he spoke to the War Committee about the situation as it really is. . . . He knew that the [United Kingdom] Chiefs of Staff would not entrust him [McNaughton] with the command of the men in Europe. He felt that this should be made known to McNaughton and was prepared himself to go over and discuss the situation with him at first hand."

Mackenzie King took the view that McNaughton should first be asked for his own views on this proposal to divide the Canadian Army into two separate Army corps, one to operate in Italy, the other to remain in Britain, with its consequent effect on the Army headquarters. He reported that both Ralston and Stuart would have preferred to act without asking McNaughton to comment, but that all finally agreed to approve the proposal, subject to reconsideration if McNaughton commented unfavourably.

On October 28, Mackenzie King noted there had been a telegram from McNaughton which "would indicate that he more or less sees the situation as it has developed with respect to the Canadian Army." That same day Ralston told Mackenzie King he felt he must go overseas to deal with the Army situation. Mackenzie King noted that he himself was anxious to keep McNaughton "in control as long as possible as I know he will make no demand for conscription. If Crerar or others were at the head, they would not hesitate to do so, though I think the day has gone by when conscription, even if attempted, could be of any service, and this would be so recognized. It would only serve to destroy the finest aspect of the Canadian war effort, namely, its voluntary character."

Shortly afterwards Ralston and Stuart went to England to deal with the situation on the spot. The first word of the results of Ralston's visit which Mackenzie King received was a message from McNaughton on November 10 in which McNaughton submitted his resignation and indicated he could not continue to command the Army under any Government of which Ralston was a member. The reason for his taking this position was that he blamed Ralston and not the British Chiefs of Staff for first suggesting that he was no longer able to command troops in actual combat.

Mackenzie King was deeply concerned by this message and noted in his diary: "I turned over in my mind very carefully what it was best to do. I came to the conclusion that I should ask both Ralston and McNaughton to come to Canada so that the matter could be threshed out face to face here. I recognize, of course, that it is creating a very serious situation with regard to our Army. McNaughton has many more friends than Ralston in the Army and in the country. It may be that McNaughton is not physically equal to the task, but there can be no doubt that Ralston and General Stuart have been a little over-anxious to get a change made instead of allowing time to help bring this about. I have been afraid of this right along. I think they have been most anxious to get Crerar in McNaughton's place. One danger there is that Crerar may seek to bring about conscription. McNaughton would never admit it. However, I feel now the absence of any need of conscription can be made very apparent and will not be attempted at this stage."

Later that day, Mackenzie King talked the situation over with St. Laurent. He noted: "I have more confidence in his judgment than that of any other colleague. Told him what had happened; what I had in mind, and asked his opinion. His first remark was that Ralston might think I was seeking to discipline him by asking him to return. I pointed out it was quite the opposite. It was to get responsibility shared here with others, and not attempting to settle the matter at arm's length, which would be impossible. I did not know whether I was the right person to accept McNaughton's resignation. That I thought the Minister would have to deal with it. . . . St. Laurent suggested it might be well to get Ralston's comments first. McNaughton had mentioned he had given a copy of his telegram to Ralston. I said I liked, in a matter of the kind, to send as near as possible identical telegrams to both parties. St. Laurent thought I might, in asking Ralston for his comments, say it seemed to me I should ask both to come out, and if he, Ralston, approved, I would telegraph McNaughton to come. This seemed to me the best course to pursue. I pointed out to St. Laurent that I thought McNaughton's telegram should be answered at once, and suggested letting him know I had not heard from Ralston, asking him to await a further communication from me. To begin the telegram by saying I was greatly distressed at its word. St. Laurent thought that was all right. Suggested putting the words 'no further step' until I had received some word from Ralston. I could then communicate with him [McNaughton] again. I made notes of these points on a bit of paper which I read over to St. Laurent. . . . I then dictated the wires along the lines St. Laurent and I had agreed upon." The telegrams were not, however, despatched that night.

At the close of the diary entry for the day Mackenzie King wrote: "A somewhat ludicrous aspect of the whole affair is that Ralston has never yet withdrawn his resignation as Minister, but left it in abeyance, I having refused to accept it, so that literally I have, at the moment, both McNaughton's and Ralston's resignations in my possession."

The following day (November 11) Mackenzie King decided that, since Power was Acting Minister in Ralston's absence, he should let him know what was taking place. When Power arrived in his office, Mackenzie King showed him the message from McNaughton and read the draft telegrams to Ralston and McNaughton which he had been preparing. Power took the position that McNaughton's resignation should be accepted and Ralston given unqualified support. Mackenzie King "agreed at the outset that a wire to Ralston himself should be the first thing. Gave up thought of any identical wire. As we went along, Power seemed most anxious to have me take the position that Ralston was wholly right in everything, and regarded the question solely as one merely affecting the relations between the Minister of Defence and the Officer in Command of the Canadian forces. I told him that the real situation to be considered was much larger than this. That what had to be considered was not so much the position either of McNaughton or Ralston, but the supreme interest of the State at a time of war. . . .

"As Power kept pressing this line of argument, and emphasized it by saying if he had been in Ralston's place, he would have dismissed McNaughton instantly . . . I felt the time had come to speak out very plainly. I got up from the table, walked up and down, and said quite frankly that I felt the supreme issue was the one I had mentioned, and that I must shape my telegrams accordingly. He had previously agreed to inserting in the telegram word about the supreme interest of the State and danger of controversy, but kept urging that some word be sent to Ralston which would let him know that I and other members of the War Committee would back him up to the limit. I pointed out that if the message contained words that the War Committee had approved his action, etc., this was reducing action on the part of the War Committee to a cipher. Also I felt that before any final action was taken, I should talk with both Ralston and McNaughton. . . . I made it clear we could not ignore McNaughton's service over the four years, and that I felt the whole business had grown out of weariness on McNaughton's part which had led to exasperation in the end."

He finally decided to send a message to McNaughton asking him to give him an opportunity to communicate with Ralston and one to Ralston sending the exchange of messages with McNaughton and urging that no further steps be taken without consultation with Ottawa.

The next morning (November 12) Mackenzie King drafted a message to Ralston and "then . . . sent for Power and read the message over to him. He said at once that he thought Ralston ought to be told that we supported him and that he was right. What he seemed more anxious about than anything else was that the message should contain the specific statement that it was now decided that McNaughton could not command in the field. He thought if I sent that word to Ralston, he would be perfectly happy, or if I said that the War Committee were entirely in accord with the course he had adopted or was proposing. When he made the latter suggestion, I again rose from my seat, walked up and down a little and said that I could not honestly say that to Ralston. I was perfectly sure that it was now clear that McNaughton would not command in the field. It was inevitable in the light of statements that had been made and were committed to writing, including opinions of Brooke and Paget. . . . I did not think it would be wise to order him on leave immediately, thought it might become necessary, but that what at all costs must be averted, was the situation becoming known." Power then "said he was afraid he, Ralston, would not like the message. I said if he did not, he would be most unreasonable, as he knew perfectly well what I had said before he left, that I was prepared to back him up in the matter of having ascertained exactly from Brooke and Paget their views, and telling McNaughton of them. Power again spoke of having War Committee behind him, and I repeated that we had had no meeting of War Committee. Ralston would have to be here himself for that assurance. He then insisted very strongly that I should let Ralston know that I agreed with the decision that he [McNaughton] could not command in the field.

"I said that while I agreed it had become impossible, I was not the one to say that there had been any decision. That was a military matter which would have to be decided by military men. . . . When I continued to refuse to include any word about the decision, Power said he felt he could not be of much further use in helping the drafting of the message. I told him that he had been of use, but that I felt he would find the message would be understood all right by Ralston. In the course of conversation, I pointed out that McNaughton was highly regarded by the people of Canada and by the fighting men. Would become more so once it was known that he had become what might be termed 'a martyr.' . . . That I certainly did not wish to allow anyone to say this had been due to the callous and indifferent action of the Government in not recognizing his state of mind and his life service to our country as well as particularly his service through the trying period of the past four years."

Mackenzie King added he felt Power was wrong in saying the Government had "built up McNaughton, made a hero of him." He himself felt that McNaughton owed his reputation to his own efforts and really in spite of detraction. I positively declined to alter what I had written." The message actually sent to Ralston stressed the importance of avoiding controversy and reaching an understanding with McNaughton.

After dinner that evening, Mackenzie King "began drafting a message to McNaughton expressing some of the views which I had put forth in my last telegram to Ralston urging the necessity of the situation not becoming public." He noted in his diary that he had "felt from the beginning that there was a great danger in Ralston being the one to have to impart the information he did to McNaughton. Had he been a little less zealous of doing himself the thing he felt must be done, he might have succeeded in having either Brooke or Paget approach the matter themselves." In the telegram he sent to McNaughton, Mackenzie King "did bring into the last paragraph . . . a reference to his telegram to me having shown evidence of the great strain he had been under and was under. I did not go further than this, and I have taken no notice either in my telegrams to Ralston or McNaughton of what each has said about his resignation."

The next morning (November 13), Mackenzie King received "a telegram from Ralston sent yesterday containing a memorandum prepared by Stuart for him of the sequence of events and representations made regarding doubts as to McNaughton's capacity to command in the field. Its opening paragraph mentioned that it was obvious from McNaughton's cable to me that he believed that Ralston by suggestion and implications had initiated the chain of events which had culminated in the present situation. That brought instant relief to my mind. I immediately . . . drafted a telegram to Ralston saying that my recollection of the sequence of events and other representations in Stuart's memo was wholly in accord with what was there expressed. I also agreed with Stuart's view that McNaughton's wire to me was to be explained in the light of his belief that Ralston had initiated the conversation regarding McNaughton's fitness to command in the field. That we must view the situation in that light and I felt sure McNaughton's feelings would change once he came to realize what the sequence of events had really been. I concluded by telling Ralston that I fully appreciated what all this had meant to him and was deeply grateful for his forbearance. . . . Meanwhile we must seek to solve the situation in a way which will wholly protect the combined war effort."

Mackenzie King reflected that Ralston would "probably have felt that I was leaning more toward McNaughton's side than his, because of my not having expressed any opinion of McNaughton's message or given any word of intention to support him in his attitude. . . . I felt the time had now come to make clear to him not by any verbal assurance, but by agreeing with Stuart's memo, that I would be solidly behind him on the facts of the case. He, on his part, will, I think, come to see that my judgment as to how the matter should be dealt with is sounder than that which his wire to me with its recommendations of accepting McNaughton's resignation was." This is a reference to a message from Ralston which assumed that McNaughton's resignation would be accepted. Mackenzie King noted: "If it should prove that I have been able to get these difficulties bridged in a manner which will prevent their disclosure at least until after the war, I will have done the war effort a greater service than many armies could render, and Canada and the British Empire, a service beyond calculation."

On Sunday, November 14, Mackenzie King received messages from both Ralston and McNaughton and learned that "there had been a meeting between McNaughton, Brooke, Paget, Stuart, and Ralston at which Brooke and Paget had made clear the criticism etc. had originated with them, and McNaughton had fully accepted their word, had expressed his regret to Ralston, Ralston had accepted the amend, that

McNaughton wished me to accept his resignation, but would stay on in command of the Army till his successor was appointed, the telegram from him to me was now completely 'washed out,' Ralston had spoken of the relief to himself and the terrible ordeal the whole business had been for him etc. etc." Mackenzie King referred to Stuart's part in bringing about this understanding as "a noble part . . . a *very* difficult role, but one fearlessly and honestly and chivalrously taken. Robertson's own act of keeping at getting in touch with London cannot be too highly praised. He, like Skelton, is fidelity itself." This last reference was to the way in which Norman Robertson had worked day and night to make sure that communications were maintained between Ottawa and London during these delicate three-way negotiations.

That evening, Mackenzie King noted that "Robertson had 'phoned me latest telegram from Ralston, telling of the way in which everything had been settled, his two hours' conference with McNaughton, of the understanding on all sides, of his leaving for Italy tomorrow. I dictated over the 'phone a message to Ralston, which I later very slightly revised by one addition or two when it was sent out, and then drafted a message also to McNaughton expressing my great relief and thanking him and saying I would telegraph in the morning, and a message of appreciation to Stuart, without whose tact and judgment and integrity and known friendship with all concerned, I doubt if the day could have been saved. It was a great relief to have the circle completed."

After the Cabinet meeting on November 18, Mackenzie King "told Angus Macdonald of the week's correspondence with Ralston and McNaughton. I was surprised to see how little he seemed to realize what had been at stake. He seemed more concerned about how Ralston might feel. Spoke well of McNaughton's services in the past but showed no real appreciation of the situation. He, himself, looks pretty tired and worn. Says he is very soon going to Baltimore for a check-up. I was almost sorry that I mentioned the matter to him though I felt that being one of the Ministers of Defence to whom I had not spoken before Ralston's return, he, Macdonald, might have thought I was not prepared to share a confidence with him in a matter which related so immediately to the war."

On November 23 reports began to appear in the Canadian newspapers that McNaughton's retirement was imminent and General Stuart saw him to work out a statement to be issued after approval by Ralston and Mackenzie King. The statement attributed his retirement to the state of his health. McNaughton himself suggested that he first have a medical examination and have the report of the examination sent to the Prime

Minister. Mackenzie King received it on November 27. It indicated that McNaughton was suffering from fatigue and recommended a rest of three months. Ralston felt no statement should be made until his own return to England from Italy. Before he returned McNaughton had become more seriously ill and been obliged to take to his bed and when Ralston reached London on December 10, McNaughton sent him a message asking to be relieved from his command as soon as possible on the ground that he had not the strength left to look after the Army properly. After a good many communications back and forth to Ottawa it was decided to appoint Stuart as temporary Commander of the Canadian Army and to announce McNaughton's retirement on December 27. On December 26, Mackenzie King decided to send McNaughton "in the name of the Government and people of Canada, an expression of thanks for his services during the term of his command." He felt it was most important "to have the announcement come out with a word that the Prime Minister had, at the moment of McNaughton's giving up the command, expressed to him the thanks of the Government and the people of Canada for his services since the beginning of the war. . . . As McNaughton says in his telegram to me, we have ended Chapter I. So far as he and I are concerned, there has been implicit confidence and unbroken affection throughout. No word or undertaking between us has been broken in any particular. I have been true to him and he has been true to me, and both throughout have been true to the cause."

After McNaughton's retirement at the end of 1943, the subject was not referred to again in Mackenzie King's diary until February 1, 1944. Parliament had met on January 27 and it was clear that the question of McNaughton's retirement would be raised in debate. On February 1, Mackenzie King reported a talk with Ralston "going over what he intended to say in Parliament about McNaughton." Mackenzie King "counselled him strongly against making any mention of communications which would involve his tabling correspondence. Also to hold, as he had outlined to me he would, to matters related to McNaughton's illness, though he intends to refer to his interviews with Paget and Brooke. This may throw the fat into the fire, especially if it should arouse McNaughton's ire. He is expected, by the way, to arrive tomorrow. Yesterday Ralston said to me that McNaughton had resigned, and his resignation had been accepted before he was relieved of command. I told him I had declined at any time to accept his resignation. On looking through the records, he saw that I was right, though it was clear McNaughton had tendered his resignation, and he told him to hold on until a successor would be appointed. I could not help thinking of how different Ralston's attitude was today, grateful for my sympathy and understanding in the difficult situation he is now in, than what it was a year or two ago when sitting in the same chair, refusing to withdraw his resignation as I would not agree to conscription. I view with a little concern the debate on the Defence Department and, in particular, McNaughton's retirement. However, the situation can never be what it would have been, had it broken out when Ralston was in England."

On February 3, Mackenzie King noted that in the House of Commons "shortly after 3, Ralston leaned over and told me that McNaughton had arrived at the Seigniory Club. While at Montreal, he had been met by the press and had given an interview which was belligerent and stated he was perfectly fit and called on those who had talked about his health to explain the situation. Later I saw the press accounts which I think are most unfortunate. Ralston himself had thought he, McNaughton, would say this, but I did not believe he would. I did my best to keep Ralston quiet and have him pursue the course which he had originally proposed of making the statement which he had previously shown to me."

Both Mackenzie King and Ralston feared that after McNaughton's press interview had appeared, his retirement would become a partisan political issue. The Conservatives did try to exploit it at once. Mackenzie King noted in his diary for February 3: "At a meeting last night, Drew said that McNaughton had had a dirty deal so there seems little doubt that the Tories will seek to make great difficulty between us and him. The whole business is most unpleasant and trying, but I feel quite calm in my own mind as I know I have helped to save a much worse situation, and have kept within the narrowest possible bounds a situation that might have worked great injury to our war effort. Knowing what the correspondence reveals . . . what I think is most serious is that it was upon representation of the British War Office that he was really relieved of his command. That will put the Tories in a difficult position. It will make stronger the position I have taken about this country having its own policy on defence."

On February 4, the War Committee was discussing the best time to deal in Parliament with McNaughton's retirement "when word came from Graydon [Leader of the Opposition] at noon that he proposed to ask me to make a statement in the afternoon. It was decided wisely that a single statement on McNaughton's illness should be made, but that the whole question should be taken up when there was opportunity for a full discussion. I spoke accordingly in the House this afternoon. The Opposition tried to make the situation as embarrassing as possible, but did not, I think, make much impression. As a matter of fact, they are leading themselves into a ditch as they will find later on when the facts are disclosed, that it was really the British command that are responsible; that those in charge of operations in Europe are the ones who are really responsible for McNaughton's relinquishment of the command of the Canadian Army. The Tories will be in a difficult position in attacking the British High Command."

He added: "We need attack no one, simply let the facts speak for themselves. If Ralston is wise enough himself to not become provocative or show feeling against McNaughton, the issue will soon die down. Ralston's feelings, however, ran very high. He referred, for example, today to the Jekyll and Hyde attitude of McNaughton on some matters—one day having one position, and the next day another. I said quite openly to him I thought he was not right in using that expression. McNaughton's temperament was one of elation, one moment, and depression in another, which was evidence of the condition he was in. That I did not attach any importance to what he had said at the Seigniory Club, beyond that the two statements gave evidence of the difficulty in maintaining the mental poise he would wish to have."

Mackenzie King noted that in replying to Graydon's question in the House of Commons he "was quite firm in my stand. Had been considerably worried before speaking, knowing the mischief that would be wrought through the country in letting matters stand over, but felt quite sure it was the proper course to follow. Also, as Power said in War Committee, the Tory press will probably go sailing into the Government meanwhile, and will find to their surprise later on that the Government's position is the only one that could be taken. They will be very discomfited, when they find the real issue is between the British High Command and McNaughton rather than between our Government and him." The firm stand Mackenzie King took was that the House must await a comprehensive statement by the Minister of National Defence at a time when it could be debated fully.

Later that day (February 4) Mackenzie King telephoned to invite General and Mrs. McNaughton to lunch with him at Laurier House on the following Monday (February 7). During their telephone conversation, McNaughton "himself spoke of the trouble the press had made, saying that except for what the press had said, in not creating the correct impression as to what he had said, everything was well. I then said something about the press making no end of trouble, always desirous to be sensational and the like. He joined with me that the darndest difficulties were created in that way. He gave me to understand he had not intended to say anything that would be in any way embarrassing."

The next day (February 5) Mackenzie King read "anew the correspondence which took place with McNaughton, Ralston, etc., last November and December. . . . There is no doubt in my mind that what should now be done is for McNaughton himself to write me, deploring that the question of his health has led to discussion in Parliament which may provoke controversy, and make a clear statement himself; that the fundamental issue was the question of his having been given to understand by those in charge of operations that it was questionable if the strain he had undergone would make possible his command in the field when the time arrived. This, combined with the temporary breakdown which he had had in his health: influenza, etc., caused him to ask that he be relieved at once of the command of the Army and that a successor might be appointed, and express the hope that for the sake of the men this matter be not made one of political controversy; that, having made clear the position as to his health, etc., the matter might not be one of public discussion.

"Whether he will do this or not I cannot say, but I have come to the conclusion it is my duty, in the interests of the war, to advise him to take some steps of the kind, otherwise it is certain that the correspondence will have to be disclosed and, if it is, it will make perfectly clear that those in charge of operations felt that McNaughton was not able to command, that he was given definitely so to understand and, in the end, he will suffer more on that account." Mackenzie King later told Ralston he had arranged to see McNaughton and he let Ralston know "that the General had expressed his feeling that the press had not been fair to him in their statement." Towards the end of the day (February 5) he reflected in his diary: "It is now possible to see what a terrible situation would have arisen had the matter developed as a feud at the time between Ralston and McNaughton with dismissals, suspensions, resignations, and so on, before the question of his health had come to speak for itself as it now does."

On Monday morning, February 7, McNaughton came to Laurier House and talked to Mackenzie King in the morning from 11 o'clock to one. Mrs. McNaughton then joined them for lunch and after lunch they resumed their talk. Mackenzie King recorded the talks in detail. McNaughton "started in of his own accord without any remarks on my part to say that he wished to report to me direct and very fully on the situation that had developed." He first referred to a report made in 1935 in which "he had laid down the principle of complete autonomy of the Dominions, and this is the basis on which all defences should be worked out.

"At this stage, or I think perhaps a little earlier, he said to me: 'Let me say first of all that you are the rock to which I have held (or on which I have built) all the time that I have been abroad. But for knowing you and where you stood, that you had no interest other than that of the service of the State and knowing that you had views of Canada's position similar to my own, we thought alike on constitutional relations, I could not have gone on . . . but I knew I had your backing and approval in the line that I was taking in our constitutional relationships.' I said that when he was appointed, he would recall we had spoken of this, and were agreed on the point of view we shared.

"He then said: 'I was determined that our men should not be used uselessly or experimentally in war. That when it came to operational affairs, of course it was for those in charge of operations to determine plans, etc. If I were assured they were right, I would approve them.' . . . I said I recalled the last words we had had as he left my office, that, above all, he would be careful of human life, and that I had always felt a confidence in him in that regard."

After expressing the satisfaction he had felt in working with Norman Rogers, McNaughton went on to say he had "told Ralston several times that I thought his motives were the highest. That he was thoroughly sincere but, when it came to certain crises, our minds did not look at things in the same way. We could not see things in the same light, and that it would be very difficult for us to work together. He said that when he learned of Ralston's appointment, he became very doubtful as to whether they would be able to work together. He had thought of writing me confidentially and saying he doubted if they could work together. He did not, however, feel that it was for him to say who should be in authority and made up his mind it was his duty to do the best he could, which he had sincerely tried to do."

McNaughton gave a detailed account of his relations with Ralston as he saw them and Mackenzie King described what had taken place as he had observed the relationship. He noted that, during their conversation, McNaughton "admitted quite frankly that his health was impaired; that at one time he had felt it might be necessary for him to give up command in the field. He then spoke of the interviews with Stuart in London and of his feeling that he should have a medical examination before he relinquished the command of the Army."

At about this point they broke off for lunch and, when they returned to the library after lunch, McNaughton said: " 'I have wanted to report direct to you on the position of the Army; to make it very clear that as matters stand, there is a real danger of the Army "evaporating" unless we can hold the control that we should have over our own men; that there is this danger of it being used in pieces. What should be done is to try to get some of the men that are in Italy back to strengthen the formation in England.' "

McNaughton then spoke of the need of appointing a new Army Commander and Mackenzie King "said to him: 'What do you think of Crerar?' He said he thought Crerar would be all right. I said how do you feel about his views on these constitutional relations. He said: 'I think he will be all right. I think he understands that situation.' Earlier when we had been discussing the sending of the men to Italy, McNaughton said that the decision had been a political one; not a military one. I said to him that there were two main reasons, as I understood it. One was the importance of battle experience for the men so that our whole Army would not go onto the Continent with no prior battle experience. Secondly, the question of morale, and the misinterpretation that was being given to the existing situation. That it was questionable whether the morale of the Army could be kept through another winter. The *Globe and Mail* and some of the papers were saying that the Army was being kept there so that they would not fight—which was directed against me; that they were being kept there for McNaughton's sake, that he might lead them—that that was directed against him. That the British, Americans, Australians, New Zealanders, and soldiers from other parts had all been in the fighting, and there was a necessity for the active participation by Canada as well as necessity for battle training.

"He, McNaughton, nodded his head approvingly of that; said that when the decision was made, he had bowed to it and had done all possible to get things arranged as they should, and had succeeded well. Had even surprised others who said that some things could not be done. He said there had been an understanding that some of the men would be brought back after having had some experience. I said I understood there was that possibility. He said if Crerar was to command, he should be in England at once. I said: 'Would it be interfering with plans of strategy or operations if we took it into our own hands to have him come back [from Italy]?' He said: 'If I were acting, I would bring him back without asking anyone'—or words to that effect. That should be our business.

"He then said that brings me to another thing, which is that unfortunate mischievous business—or words to that effect—of the interview that appeared in the press. He was quite indignant about this, and said it was all misconstrued. First of all, he had been assured that he would be free of the press, suddenly he found himself surrounded by them and they were asking all kinds of questions, for example, whether he intended to go into politics. He said he had said: 'No, under no consideration.' They had left it as if it was an open question. He said that is the last thing, as you know, I would want—to go into politics. He then said that people had been spreading reports about his having tuberculosis, and he heard that in New York and elsewhere. That his answer to his health had reference to those things. There was nothing organically wrong with him, but that the last thing he had wanted to do or intended to do, was to have anything said which would raise any question at all at this time.

"He said: 'What I have now thought of doing is to issue a statement of my own, making clear what the position is.' He said the press have made their statement about what I have said. I now feel what I should do and would like to do, would be to issue a statement of my own. He then drew from his pocket a page of paper on which he had written in his own handwriting, and read to me what he had written. It was to this effect that there had been wrong interpretations put upon his statement about his health. That his health was impaired, and that he needed a rest. . . . The intimation he proposed for the press was more particularly confined to his going away for a rest, and he said he wanted matters to be left at that point. He hoped there would be no further questions on that matter. At the end of a long period of rest, he hoped he would be in a position to serve, and would be ready to do so. He then said to me: 'Did I recall the statement that he made in England when he relinquished the Army, when he said good-bye to the troops, etc.' He said he had made it plain to them he was relinquishing command because of his health, and he thought that statement covered all that it was necessary to say.

"The communication went a step further and said he had, since his return, reported fully to the Prime Minister the problems, as he saw them, which needed to be considered, and that he was sure that all these matters would be most carefully looked into. . . . I then said to him, in view of what the press had reported, the matter had now got into Parliament, and that I thought every effort should be made to control the situation in a way that would avoid controversy; that the first consideration we must have in mind was the war, and the effect of anything said or done upon the war. McNaughton said he agreed to that."

Mackenzie King went on to say that it might "be difficult to prevent further discussion. As he will have seen, the House is already demanding a statement in Parliament, and Ralston is ready to make the statement.

I said I cannot tell you what he will say. My understanding is he will refer to your illness as being the cause of the resignation. Also I think he will say that the whole matter had its origin in what had been said in reference to command in the field. To this, McNaughton instantly reacted and said that would put the whole thing back on me. If he does that, then there will be a real situation to face. That will be reflecting on my ability to command, etc. I said I did not think that that would necessarily be so. That it would undoubtedly involve a statement that those in charge of operations had raised this question as a possibility, and that that was the beginning of the whole matter. The General then said that it was the feeling that he had had, for a year or two, that he had always to be looking over his shoulder to see what others were doing behind his back which had given him such a strain and which was responsible for his breakdown when the time came. That if he had had the backing that he should have had, and not the feeling that both Ralston and Stuart were taking a different view of what the Army should do, etc., he would not have reached the point of breakdown he had reached.

"He then said that there was little use in trying to prevent an investigation. That so much had been said and talked about everywhere, he felt sure sooner or later some full inquiry would have to be held. I said I agreed with that, but I had to ask myself what would be the effect on the war effort at this time. . . . I said that I hoped some way could be found short of all this coming out at this time. He said he had thought that what he was proposing might meet that end; to simply have it stated that what was agreed to in England when he left was where matters stood now."

McNaughton told Mackenzie King that "he had no concern about the future. I said to him there was no question about the future. . . . There were many positions he could fill. . . . He said 'I think it would not be well of you to make any suggestion of anything to me; otherwise it might be said that a decision had been come to in view of what had been proposed to me.' I said I agreed entirely with that, and would make no proposal at all."

Mackenzie King noted that the press had photographers at the door as General and Mrs. McNaughton left Laurier House and added: "I am sure that having McNaughton come to Laurier House, and Mrs. McNaughton to lunch, etc., and the friendly expression on the faces of all, was only too evident as they left Laurier House. This will create a fine impression throughout the country and will do very much toward helping to silence further discussion as to McNaughton's relations with the Government."

In the evening Mackenzie King told Ralston of the interview. "When I came to what McNaughton had said at the end about issuing a statement of his own to the press, making clear his health had been impaired and that he needed a rest and wanted to be left alone, and that he had made a full report to me of situations which he felt sure would be carefully considered," Mackenzie King found that Ralston seemed to be relieved at the thought of McNaughton issuing a statement. Most of the next day was spent in an attempt to work out, through an intermediary, a statement that McNaughton would make which would satisfy Ralston and the public. It was finally decided a statement would not be helpful and McNaughton agreed not to issue any.

Mackenzie King had a long talk with Ralston that day (February 8) about tactics in Parliament. He was very insistent that Ralston should "deal with McNaughton's resignation on the basis of medical certificates. He admitted that there had been controversies before between them but that these had been adjusted, and that there was nothing to be gained by going into what had happened prior to the resignation. That all of that could be settled later on when it was over and would not alter existing situation." At the end of the talk Mackenzie King picked up his portfolio with all the correspondence inside it and said: "Knowing all that is in this and particularly the wire McNaughton had sent me, that if all that was held to the very end, and brought out only under compulsion, the whole situation would be viewed entirely differently by the public, and in its true light. They would then say that Ralston, instead of being precipitate and anxious to get McNaughton, had shown extraordinary restraint in the face of the greatest possible provocation, and it would be made clear from McNaughton's way of expressing himself, that he was not in a condition to command. I said to deliver all this at the start would be simply . . . handing to people that wished to make trouble, just what they would wish to have."

Ralston's proposed statement was considered at the War Committee on February 9. He had prepared a brief one along the lines Mackenzie King had suggested, "beginning by simply stating the fact as to McNaughton's illness as certified by physicians and admitting there were differences of view between them which could be discussed in dealing with relevant matters. He could go into matters as to the past, etc., but he hoped that might not be necessary at this time. The statement was well prepared and, I thought, calculated to be least likely to invite a bit of controversy at the outset and to get the true position before the public. Ralston himself said he favoured the longer statement which he had prepared earlier and which faced squarely the matter of command in the field." After some discussion, most of the members of the Committee agreed "it was best to proceed on lines which could not be construed as seeking to go after McNaughton at the time he was ill, but rather seeking to protect him in what was said. If forced to go further the onus would be on others who insisted on bringing on the controversy."

The next day (February 10) Mackenzie King had a further talk with Ralston, urging him to take out of his statement "everything provocative as far as possible. Ralston seemed to be realizing more than ever how serious the whole business was and to have come around to the point of view of my taking leaders of parties into confidence in advance. . . . I feel strongly my duty is to prevent anything that would help to destroy the morale of . . . our men in the Army." Ralston spoke in the House of Commons on February 11. Mackenzie King felt he "got on just at the right moment. He was able to describe his trip through Italy, came to the McNaughton matter in the course of his general speech" and thereby was able "to avoid answering questions as to the causes for McNaughton's resignation. He was quite subdued in speaking. One could see he had been under, and was under, great strain. The House was thin —Friday afternoon. Altogether it was very fortunate that things worked out in this way. Indeed it seemed to me if there was ever a case of Providence answering prayer, it has been in this matter—first, in getting the situation quieted when the break came in England, quieting it again after McNaughton's utterances at the Seigniory Club and getting time this week, and above all bringing matters to where it was possible to present particulars as to McNaughton relinquishing command wholly on the basis of certificates of ill health secured by himself. Certainly thus far a very serious situation has been prevented by persuading Ralston to, in no way, show any sign of bitterness and getting everything in a form which was devoid of provocation."

The next day (February 12) Mackenzie King considered the possibility of having a secret session of the House of Commons to place before the Members the correspondence which had led to McNaughton's resignation. He discussed the idea with Ralston who "said in regard to yesterday that it bore out what he feels about my judgment in the matter of timing. I told him it bore out my belief in prayer in dealing with these situations. I am sure there has been great guidance in bringing things to pass in the order in which they have in this week. My talk with McNaughton on Monday; seeing the whole situation from his point of view; taking the stand I did against the procedure proposed first by Ralston . . . and then the delays that have brought everything about in a manner which gives the public, over this week-end, to see what is fundamental in the situation at the moment."

In the Cabinet meeting on February 14, Mackenzie King found that Ralston, to justify his own position, wished to make a more elaborate statement about McNaughton's resignation in the House that afternoon. Mackenzie King, thereupon, outlined "what was the main point of difference, and read to the Cabinet for the first time the telegram which McNaughton had sent to me tendering his resignation, etc. on November the 10th. . . . When Ralston read over what he had in mind saying I again spoke out and said I thought he ought to confine himself to saying no useful purpose would be served by going further into the matter. That I was prepared to have the Government take a firm stand at that point, and not allow anything more to be said. Ralston felt that this would be a reflection on himself. . . . He thought unless the facts came out, people would think that he had something to hide. I took the position that the public now knew that McNaughton was a sick man and, if the controversy made him worse, it might lead to his collapse altogether. It would then be said that Ralston had not only persecuted him but killed him. I thought he should take the ground that public policy demanded no further discussion, and let us as a Government stand on that. . . . I suggested that we ought to consider either a secret session or showing the correspondence to the leaders. A secret session was strongly opposed as likely to give rise to all kinds of versions. No secrecy in the end, and there was a good deal of opposition to showing the correspondence to the leaders. Ralston, Power, and Macdonald all held out for Ralston making simply the statement that he had been advised that McNaughton was not fit to command in the field and had accepted the advice, etc. I knew this would bring a terrible explosion from McNaughton, so I kept on pressing that this should not be done. Finally I said that I thought if Graydon pressed the question, I should, myself, as Prime Minister, say that I thought there were reasons of public policy why the question should not be answered, and then extend an invitation to the leaders to meet me and give me a chance to put the correspondence before them. It was 10 to 3 before the Cabinet agreed to this."

During the afternoon, the debate on the War Appropriation Bill continued. Late in the afternoon, Mackenzie King noted, Ralston "came to the McNaughton matter, and [it was] almost six when Graydon began to press the question. I then rose and read what I had written out. Meanwhile I had mentioned to Ralston in his seat what I had written. He suggested words which left the situation a little more open, and I added words that I knew he was ready to answer the question immediately, which completely satisfied him with what I was intending to say. When I came on with the statement, I could see at once that the House felt the right line had been taken. The leaders agreed to see me. The whole matter closed just before six." He added: "I had a very difficult time in speaking to not say anything that could injure McNaughton or injure Ralston's feelings. I took advantage of an opening to get on record the telegram I had sent McNaughton thanking him for his service in the past. I wanted that to be on Hansard and felt it might help to ease the situation, though Ralston may have felt when I was reading this that I was unduly praising McNaughton."

The next morning (February 15) Mackenzie King "met Graydon, Grote Stirling, Coldwell, and Blackmore along with Ralston, Power, Macdonald, and Robertson. Read despatches, and had a short discussion. ... I think all who came were impressed with the unwisdom of having a public disclosure of what the despatches revealed, and the effect this would have upon the morale of the troops, and on the United Nations effort, comfort to the enemy, etc. ... The line of criticism was, and rightly so, that it did not appear that the Canadian Government itself had sufficient voice in planning and control over their own troops. There was, of course, full disclosure of the Brooke-Paget correspondence and relations. ... My own guess is that there will be little said about command in the field end of things, and that there will be discussion on Canada's control over her own Army, and differences with McNaughton over keeping the Army complete, and the Army being broken up by some troops going elsewhere."

That evening Mackenzie King felt "immensely relieved about the McNaughton matter, that whatever may blaze up from now on, will not create the appalling situation that would have happened had there been a real break in November or December, or if Ralston had taken the course he proposed after the outburst by McNaughton at the Seigniory Club. I can take credit to myself for having saved these situations. I have held to my ground against all the Defence Ministers in preventing a crisis. Now fortunately responsibility is so widely shared that I think, instead of attack upon us by the Opposition for political reasons, there will be sober thought on the part of their leaders as to their responsibilities in connection with Canada's war effort."

Before the House opened on February 16, Mackenzie King met Graydon and Ralston in his office. "Graydon said he intended to simply say on the Orders of the Day that he had seen the correspondence and that there were other things than merely McNaughton's health which entered into the resignation. The real point was that he would not take any responsibility one way or the other; the Government would have to take the responsibility of not disclosing them, etc. It was a typical position. Ralston was quite perturbed. Wanted me to say several things. During the noon hour he wrote out a page himself. However, I took the line that I thought was adequate, meeting his main wishes, as to making clear the Government had approved the statement which he had made. He has told me that it was a statement which McNaughton himself had approved and initialled. It contains a reference to command in the field but not in such a way that might imply that he had been ruled out. I made, I think, an effective reply, again refusing to allow the matter to be discussed further. Graydon's remarks [in the House] gave chance to Ralston to supplement matters from his own point of view. Both Coldwell and Blackmore said [in the House], from what they had seen, they felt it was not desirable to have the matter further discussed. It was really a complete triumph to have taken the three leaders and placed no obligation on them but their own consciences, and to have all three admit having seen the correspondence. They thought it was inadvisable to have matters discussed further. Surely my steps in this matter have been guided by Providence. I don't know what might have arisen out of the situation had it broken in a different way. Now while public interest has not abated in the matter, so much has been told and discussed that if it ever comes to be further discussed, the force behind it would be spent. It was a tremendous relief to my mind."

And so ended the first act of the Mackenzie King–Ralston–McNaughton drama.

CHAPTER TWENTY-TWO

Planning the Post-War Future

WHEN THE YEAR 1944 opened, no one in the free world doubted that the United Nations would eventually win the war. There was no longer any serious controversy over the nature or the scope of the Canadian war effort in Europe. Even the political opponents of the Government had stopped demanding a total war effort. Indeed the whole political emphasis had shifted to concern about the post-war period and the problems of demobilization, industrial reconversion, reconstruction, and other preparations for the end of the war. The war against Japan had never really caught the imagination of Canadians, and any plans for participating in the fighting in the Pacific had no political pressure behind them. When 1944 began, no one suspected that, before it ended, the greatest political crisis of the war would develop over the reinforcing of the Army in Europe—a crisis which would almost destroy the Government. Indeed Mackenzie King himself wrote in his diary on January 12 that "having reached 1944 without conscription . . . I don't think we will be troubled with that issue before the war is over."

It is interesting, if idle, to speculate on what might have happened if Mackenzie King had carried out the intention he had expressed in 1940 of recommending Ralston's appointment as Chief Justice of Canada. The term of Sir Lyman Duff as Chief Justice had twice been extended by statute beyond his seventy-fifth birthday and was coming to an end. The Government decided against asking Parliament for a third extension. On January 5, Mackenzie King told Ralston he felt Mr. Justice Thibaudeau Rinfret, as the Senior Judge, should be appointed. Ralston agreed "that Rinfret would fill the position very well." Mackenzie King, knowing Ralston's own ambition, was "very pleased." He also spoke to St. Laurent, and, when the appointment was approved on January 7, he wrote that St. Laurent "would, I believe, have been the best possible appointment." But he added that St. Laurent was "greatly needed in the Cabinet just now. Ralston, too, is needed there. Could not possibly be given that position at this time. Is needed with what may come up in regard to changes overseas." What Mackenzie King had in mind, of course, was McNaughton's retirement from the Army and the possible political repercussion in Parliament and the country.

The session of Parliament was to open on January 27, and Mackenzie King resolved to give his full attention to preparing for it. But there were certain inevitable distractions throughout the month. On January 9, he received word that J. W. Dafoe, the Editor of the Winnipeg *Free Press*, had died that afternoon. Mackenzie King considered "this is a great loss. In some ways, he was the source of greatest strength I have at the present time. Atkinson [of the Toronto *Star*] is another powerful ally. He, too, may pass away at any time. Dafoe was particularly valuable in dealing with all international affairs and also as being in a position to give an unbiased estimate of my own public service to others. More significant in that at one time—after 1917—he opposed me very strongly for having supported Laurier and being against conscription, and in fact I believe said I would never have a place in public life again. He has since written in his own hand assigning the place that he believes my name will hold in history."

Mackenzie King went to Toronto for Sir William Mulock's one hundredth birthday on January 19. The two of them had breakfast together, after being photographed for the press, and Mackenzie King spent the whole morning at Mulock's house. In the early afternoon, the "Men of the Trees" had a ceremony planting a walnut tree. Mulock and the Prime Minister "went downstairs with overcoats on where the 'Men of the Trees' and some of the guests were assembled. [Premier George] Drew was among the number. He was very pleasant. Spoke of the meeting with his wife at New York. Said he had been interested to learn of it and they had enjoyed it. I told him I had said to her I thought I had spoiled the day for her. He has a fine appearance and very pleasant manner. If he were not so bitter, and such poor judgment in some ways, he might easily have a real career."

Mackenzie King dined that evening with Joseph Atkinson, who spoke about the future of Liberalism and assured him "the *Star* would like to make a real fight. He would undertake a campaign along the lines that the *Star* had for the Aid-to-Russia Fund, were he to get the things to fight for. He thought Family Allowances was a very absolutely necessary and right measure. He would like to see the age for Old Age Pensions reduced at once. Felt the health policy was also good and should be followed up. . . . He doubted if we could hold labour as we had in the previous campaigns. . . . He agreed it would be well to avoid an election until the European war was over. He thought we should not wait until the end of the war with Japan. The words that he seemed to wish to impress upon me were: Not too little or too long, meaning not to do too little in the way of social reform, or to wait too long in what we had to do. He thought if we had a strong programme at this time announced in the Speech from the Throne, we would gain right along from now on."

On his way to the train, Mackenzie King called in to say good-night to Sir William whom he found "remarkably fresh and clear in his mind." He added: "All through the day I felt a great serenity and I recognized the same in Sir William. He did not seem to become ruffled or emotional at any time, smiling most of the time and looking really very happy. I would not like to have missed the day for anything."

Apart from occasional distractions, Mackenzie King worked hard all through January on preparations for the session and particularly on the post-war programme. He had first been concerned as early as November 14, 1943, with the problems likely to result from reducing the air training programme, "of finding places for the men and the women who will begin to be out of employment. It discloses the necessity of putting into operation a concrete programme which will look to the post-war situation and the construction of homes." During that day he had a talk with Power about a "Ministry of Reconstruction which he agrees is desirable and should be taken up immediately." He also talked with Howe who was "strongly for Ministry of Reconstruction. Thinks a business man should be at the head." At the Cabinet meeting Mackenzie King suggested a Department of Reconstruction "to enforce a positive policy of employment through construction." Though there were one or two dissenters, he thought most of his colleagues were favourable.

The subject came up again on December 5 in conversation with Power who thought Howe was the best man to be Minister of Reconstruction but felt "there is a strong prejudice against him on the score of association with big business and restrictions identified with the Munitions Department. I asked him what about himself. He said he thought he and Howe were the only two men in the Government who could handle a Reconstruction Department energetically but veered away from taking the job himself." It was many months before Mackenzie King finally made the choice between Howe and Power.

The serious discussion of the parliamentary programme began on January 6. Each of the Ministers had submitted suggestions, of which the most comprehensive had come from the Department of Finance. Mackenzie King read this submission to his colleagues to bring "home to the Ministers the many matters that have to be settled. As we proceeded Members began, I think, to appreciate . . . how exceedingly difficult the whole matter of reconstruction and post-war re-organization is going to be." Mackenzie King added that he feared "the possible repudiation of many obligations with capital levies under some Government returned as a result of promises impossible of fulfilment. I am determined to avoid bringing our party into that category." Mackenzie King observed that the meeting was "regarded as a preliminary canter" and that "one question on which there seems to be great diversity is Family Allowances."

The discussions continued for several days. On January 11 the Cabinet agreed on three new Departments: Reconstruction, Veterans Affairs, and National Health and Welfare, as they ultimately came to be called. It was also decided to proceed with the decennial revision of the Bank Act. But the most controversial issue was not decided until January 13, at a Cabinet meeting which Mackenzie King described as "one of the most impressive and significant of any I have attended. . . . I had let it be understood we would settle the Government's policy on Family Allowances which goes to the very root of social security in relation to the new order of things which places a responsibility on the state for conditions which the state itself is responsible for creating." Ilsley had asked to have W. C. Clark, the Deputy Minister of Finance, attend to present the case. Mackenzie King asked Clark "to explain the reasons why the Finance Department had come to hold the view it had on Family Allowances. He made a very fine presentation, stressing among other things how serious might be the solution of some other questions, e.g.: relief, housing and the like, unless Family Allowances measure were introduced. . . . He estimated the cost would run to two hundred million dollars which would be half the pre-war budget. . . . That was a pretty big item for Ministers to face, let alone swallow. However, Clark took up the different objections that he thought might be raised and gave answers to them. . . . At five o'clock, Ralston suggested that where we were having an intense sitting of the kind, a recess of five or ten minutes might be all to the good. This was arranged, and we resumed again shortly after five. I then went around the table asking Ministers individually whether they were prepared to support the principle of the measure." Mackenzie King noted that he "came around on the side that I thought would help to give most support in the first instance," and that "when all had concluded, I said I would give Council my own views and then spoke strongly along the lines that I have in *Industry and Humanity*, pointing out that my views were not those of the politics of today but what I had become convinced of with respect to social legislation when I wrote my book on industrial reconstruction at the end of the last war. I had previously read to Council the Speech from the Throne of the last session, my statement to the American Federation of Labor [in Toronto in October 1942], my statement at the time of speaking on inflation in relation to a national minimum [broadcast, December 1943], and reminded Members of Council this had been agreed to by them at different times, and no exception taken to what I had said publicly. . . . In speaking in conclusion I said quite frankly that I thought the Creator intended that all persons born should have equal opportunities. Equal opportunity started in days of infancy and the first thing, at least, was to see that the children got the essentials of life. I then spoke of modern society making impossible chances in life for multitudes of people."

When one of Mackenzie King's colleagues interrupted "to say that most men would come up who had this early struggle; to ease it for them was not to help eventually, I replied to him that we all knew the individual cases of this kind. . . . What was not known was the multitude of persons who were crushed at the beginning of life and never had a chance to start at all. I then spoke of having no greater friend than Mr. Rockefeller, Jr., but who could say that children of a multitude of men who had furnished the millions for his family began to have the same chances in life as his several splendid sons. That if we believe in equality at all it was not an equality of certain races or privileged classes. It was equality of opportunity for everyone. I then read to the Cabinet a brief statement on the arguments which Pickersgill had written out and gave them as my own convictions—as a summary of the convictions which I held. . . .

"I felt at the end of the day that I perhaps might have left the matter there and not gone over the field myself in the way I did, especially in reading of the arguments at the end. It was unnecessary, and may have seemed to some of my colleagues as though I were wishing to take too much to myself. However, I felt it was desirable I should speak my mind very strongly and let them see what I feel. . . . Tonight before going to sleep I rang up Clark and congratulated him on his presentation. I let him see how happy I felt about it. I said I thought I had made a mistake in adding anything at the end of the discussion. He was quite positive, however, in saying 'not at all.' That what I had said was what was needed to bring the whole matter to its proper proportion and would be appreciated by those present. He said he was glad Cabinet was so nearly unanimous and had been surprised that it was so. He added that he felt in dealing with this measure we had given real evidence of our zeal for social security and there could be no questioning of motives or sincerity of the Government in its endeavour to do something practical in this way."

On January 15, when Mackenzie King began to work on the Speech from the Throne, he "had just been reading words to the effect that Canada had become a world power and was debating how wise it was to insert them when I opened the first letter that came to me in the morning mail. It was from an insurance man in Simcoe named James H. Crabb. . . . To my surprise it contained these words: 'I know that history books will undoubtedly place you with Laurier and Macdonald. In fact, as the outstanding statesman for bringing Canada into her place as a world power.' " This was the first time Mackenzie King used this description of Canada to which he became greatly attached.

But it was not until a week later, after many interruptions, that he settled down seriously to the drafting of the Speech. On January 22 he "was far from satisfied with what we did throughout the day but feel we have . . . a programme of social legislation that really rounds out what I have worked for through my life, namely, gaining recognition of the fact that where the state, through organization of industry, etc., being what it is, gives great opportunities to a few, and robs the many of many opportunities, it should become the duty of the state to work out some scheme of social justice which will see that opportunities are widened for the many and that, at least, for all there shall be a minimum standard of life. The doctrine of national minimum standard of life which I have set forth in my *Industry and Humanity* in 1918 as part of the post-war policy, I have now worked into the words of the Representative of the King, to be spoken from the Throne as Government policy. That makes life worth while. . . . At least the great numbers of people . . . will see that I have been true to them from the beginning of my public life to its close."

He took up the draft of the Speech with the Cabinet on January 24, and reported "there was the closest possible attention as I read through from beginning to close. . . . When I concluded, I called for comments generally before taking up the speech anew clause by clause." One of the Ministers said "the impression it had left was that of being very leftist, and that there was need of something being inserted which would not cause a large section of the country to say: well, these men are seeking to outdo the C.C.F. We might as well join the Tories." Another spoke "of the necessity of leaving some encouragement to business that might wish to revive after the war, as having done something for them in the way of reducing taxation." One or two others objected to Family Allowances. When Mackenzie King "saw that they were liable to re-open the discussion" on Family Allowances, he "reminded them this had all been agreed upon." As for health insurance, the Cabinet had never made a definite decision and Mackenzie King pointed out at this meeting "that what we were doing was to try to get a national scheme of social security of which health was to be a part, but that the provinces would have to be prepared to do their part in allowing us to hold some of the revenue, if we would undertake to make grants from the federal Treasury to them. . . . I pointed out that nothing was to be gained by promising something that we could not implement without taxation the people would not agree to bear, and insisted on agreements being reached with the provinces first of all."

The Cabinet agreed that Mackenzie King should discuss the cost of health insurance further with Clark. The next morning (January 25) he told Clark "frankly I did not think the Treasury could stand it. That we had to hold consistently that whatever was done for health was a part of a nation-wide scheme. Something that would integrate both provincial and federal services along lines of social security. I pointed out that having secured Family Allowances, I did not think we could take on the other until the agreements had been reached in conference between the provinces and the Dominion on the various social service obligations and sources of revenue. Clark seemed relieved and said Ilsley would be, if that was the view."

The new post-war programme was threatened with eclipse and the whole character of the opening of the Parliamentary session seemed about to change as a consequence of a speech given by Lord Halifax, the British Ambassador to the United States, in Toronto. On January 24, when Mackenzie King came out of the Cabinet, one of his secretaries told him that "Halifax was making a perfectly terrible speech in Toronto."

Four passages from Halifax's speech were given particular emphasis by the press which interpreted them as a plea for a centralized Commonwealth, to become one of the four great powers of the post-war period. These passages were: 'In the field of defence, while there must be individual responsibility, there must also be a unity of policy. I suggest that in the years of peace it was a weakness, which we should try to cure, that the weight of decision on many problems of defence was not more widely shared. . . . I do not mean that we should attempt to retrace our steps along the path that led from the Durham Report to the Statute of Westminster. To do so would be to run counter to the whole course of development in the Commonwealth. But what is, I believe, both desirable and necessary is that in all the fields of interests, common to every part of the Commonwealth—in foreign policy, in defence, in economic affairs, in colonial questions and in communications—we should leave nothing undone to bring our people into closer unity of thought and action. . . . Today we begin to look beyond the war to the re-ordering of the world which must follow. We see three great powers, the United States, Russia and China, great in numbers, areas and natural resources. . . . If, in the future, Britain is to play her part without assuming burdens greater than she can support, she must have with her in peace the same strength that has sustained her in this war. Not Great Britain only, but the British Commonwealth and Empire must be the fourth power in that group upon which, under Providence, the peace of the world will henceforth depend.'[1]

The next morning (January 25), when he "read something of what Lord Halifax had said at Toronto last night," Mackenzie King "was simply dumbfounded. It seemed such a complete bolt out of the blue, like a conspiracy on the part of Imperialists to win their own victory in the middle of the war. I could not but feel that Halifax's work was all part of a plan which had been worked out with Churchill to take advantage of the war to try and bring about this development of centralization, of makings of policies in London, etc. As Englishmen, of course, they seek to recover for Britain and the United Kingdom and the Empire the prestige which they are losing as a nation. In a moment, I saw that again it has fallen to my lot to have to make the most difficult of all the fights. This perpetual struggle to save the Empire despite all that Tories' policies will do—by fighting the Tories, save the British Empire from its dismemberment through their own policies. There is nothing truer than that, from the days of Lord North to the present, English Tories have learned nothing." He felt that Halifax's speech "marks the beginning of the real political campaign of this year. I should not complain about what Halifax has done, for he has handed me, as someone said in Council this afternoon, an issue which ensures or should ensure the return of the Liberal party just as completely as Lord Byng, when he refused to grant a dissolution. I am perfectly sure that Canada will not tolerate any centralized Imperialism on foreign policy." As a precaution he telephoned Leighton McCarthy at the Canadian Embassy in Washington to find out if he had seen Halifax's speech and learned that "Halifax never mentioned a line of what he had in his mind or intended to say." He later told the Cabinet "I had never been more surprised. That it was what I had said many times would happen as soon as the war was over. I had not thought it would happen while it was on. I found all Members of Government thoroughly incensed. . . . I did not discuss the matter at length but said I would speak in Parliament on Monday. . . . There was mention that I would have to speak as Coldwell had taken a very strong stand [in the press], and it would not do to let him steal our whole position."

[1] From text in Montreal *Star*, January 25, 1944.

Later in the day Mackenzie King told the Governor-General that, "if it were not for the war, I would this evening be asking him for a dissolution of Parliament to appeal to the people on this issue. I then said I could not understand Halifax having never said a word to me about what he intended to say, and coming to Canada to make a speech which raised the most controversial issue we had, with the possible exception of conscription. . . . However I said I would have to speak in Parliament on Monday, but would be as careful as I could; to avoid anything that would prejudice a position of the kind. I said if Hitler himself wanted to divide the Empire—get one part against the other, he could not have chosen a more effective way, or a better instrument. I said that politically, as far as I was concerned, I had no doubt it would help to defeat the Tories. He could see how Coldwell had spoken, and also that Bracken did not wish to touch the question."

The next day (January 26) Mackenzie King felt "more relieved about Halifax's speech in that I had not had to make any pronouncement yesterday and had time to consider how it may best be dealt with in Parliament. Feel that Halifax has done the damage. I must seek to repair it so far as its effect on the war effort is concerned. Do what I can in what I say not to widen the division between different parts of the Empire which his provocative speech, made at this time, has already occasioned, but make a common statement that will make my own position clear and leave matters at that for the present." During the day, he saw Malcolm MacDonald who had just returned from Britain and told him he "had never had a blow like it in my life, and could not understand with all I had done to help in this war, how Halifax could have made the speech he did, without ever consulting me about it either directly or through our Ambassador at Washington. . . . I said to him the extraordinary thing was that the speech seems to have been circulated well in advance. Was in full in *The Times*. Had been sent to Conservative papers here last week, but that no copy had come to me nor to any Members of the Government or to our legation at Washington, or any officials in External Affairs." He noted that "Malcolm felt sure Halifax would not have done anything of the kind intentionally so far as I was concerned. That he had the highest regard for me; affection as well, and what he had said about me at Toronto in the beginning of his speech about what I had done for the war, my leadership, etc., was evidence of it. That he could not have had any desire to work an injury politically. I, of course, could not accuse him of that, but as I said to Malcolm, it looked to me as if the whole business was part of a Tory attitude of mind, feeling they must force their views regardless of consequences to others." Mackenzie King also "told Malcolm I was speaking only personally to him. I had thought of sending a cable to Churchill to say that Halifax's speech had been most embarrassing to the Government, but thought it well to just keep quiet and say nothing. That I was determined not to make any situation more difficult while the war was on, but that once again I had had to allow myself to be put in a false position in appearing either to let a great issue of the kind pass and go into the hands of Coldwell and others, to the discrimination of my own party, or be placed in the position of helping to divide the Empire, working up separation, etc., while the war was still on. It was all very trying, but I would seek above all else to keep the war in mind."

On January 27, Mackenzie King "was immensely relieved in seeing in the evening paper that Attlee today had said in the British House that the Government felt no useful purpose would be served by a debate on Empire policy at the present time. That is precisely the view I have taken all along with respect to Prime Ministers' Conferences, Imperial Conferences, and the like. Our foreign policy is the winning of the war. We had better leave all controversial questions to the side until the war is won." Mackenzie King added that was the line he had pretty well decided to take in the House on Monday, the 31st. On January 29, two days after Parliament opened, he received from Malcolm Macdonald "a communication from Halifax regretting that he should have been causing me embarrassment, and pointing out how unconscious he had been that his speech would cause any concern. Malcolm seemed most anxious to know how far I would be going on Monday. I told him I intended to try to avoid controversy. To say as little about the speech as possible beyond making it clear that I favoured consultation, co-operation and co-ordination of policies within the Empire for the same reason that I favoured it among nations, but not for the purpose of having the British Empire line up against the rest of the world. That I would dwell on the perspective in keeping till after the war for discussion, matters related to constitutional changes."

Halifax's speech was Mackenzie King's main concern when he spoke in Parliament on the Address in Reply to the Speech from the Throne on January 31. He had no text prepared and he was "conscious of leaving out parts of what I wished to say, and really suffered a good deal of mental confusion.... I was so disappointed with myself, I could not tell whether or not the Members were genuine in saying that I had made a good speech.... I felt genuinely depressed, knowing I had missed what could have been so easily done most effectively, had I but had a real rest beforehand." Later in the evening he wrote that he had "seldom felt more depressed or disgusted.... I went to bed feeling that, in a way, I had been forsaken."

In his speech, Mackenzie King had stated that "the question that has come very much to the fore in the last few days is whether there is to be a common policy for all parts of the Empire or Commonwealth on foreign relations, defence and other matters—a single or common policy as distinct from each nation of the British Commonwealth having its own policy on foreign affairs, on defence and on other matters." After stating his belief that there could not be "too close consultation and co-operation," he gave a fairly lengthy description of all the existing methods of consultation with their historical background. He next pointed out the difficulty of making decisions at an Imperial Conference in London where the Prime Ministers of the overseas members of the Commonwealth were necessarily separated from many of their colleagues and advisers, and the advantages of achieving co-operation between cabinets through existing means without attempting centralization of Imperial institutions. In reply to a question, Mackenzie King emphasized the fact that Halifax had spoken for himself and not for the Government of the United Kingdom. He concluded by reading a carefully worded statement which took direct issue with the conception of a world dominated by four great powers and urged that all peace-loving nations, great and small, should join together, after the war, to preserve the peace. He spoke throughout with great moderation and restraint.

Next morning (February 1) Mackenzie King read the papers in bed and "felt considerable relief as a consequence. Was really immensely surprised when I read opening paragraph of Bishop's 'Glimpses of Parliament'—The Prime Minister made a towering contribution yesterday to the opening debate of the session, and following on that line. [The writer of this column in the Ottawa *Citizen*, Charles Bishop, later appointed to the Senate, was a friend and confidant of Mackenzie King.] It is clear that the press appreciated my taking only two or three subjects and dealing with them and not speaking at too great length. I have made a great mistake in the way I have prepared speeches, instead of learning the subject and speaking extemporaneously." When Mackenzie King read the speech in Hansard he "was really surprised and pleased to see how well on the whole it read." Later in the day, he "was interested to see that Churchill had stated today in the House that Halifax's speech was without authority of the British Government. Malcolm MacDonald 'phoned to the office to say that he thought my speech of yesterday was 'a grand performance.' He was sure his people at home would be delighted at the statesmanship shown and that Lord Halifax would feel that I had treated him as a friend. He added that nothing could have been better than the way I had handled the whole business. That is a source of immense comfort and satisfaction to me.

There is an editorial in the [Montreal] *Gazette* today which is most appreciative of my attitude. Altogether the reactions on yesterday's speech have been more than I could have hoped for at all."

The next day (February 2) Mackenzie King concluded his diary entry with these words: "I begin . . . to see more clearly that Monday's speech may prove to be one of the most significant I have made in my life. It opens up the great broad division between centralized and decentralized organization, not only of Empire activities but the larger question of power politics by a few great nations leading inevitably to war against the conception of international world co-operation of nations great and small. In other words, a future world organization. Matter of preserving peace and preventing war. The largest subject that it is possible to deal with in politics."

On February 3, Mackenzie King "rang up Malcolm MacDonald today to ask him to thank Halifax for his message to me. To let him know I had been most concerned about his not conferring with me before delivering an address which stressed the need for closer co-operation but, above all, was concerned about the issue which I knew his speech would raise and which would be far-reaching and embarrassing all around. . . . He then said he thought I had made a magnificent statement. . . . I said to Malcolm I felt I had made a sort of mess of things. . . . I had really been quite sick at night. His reply was that instead of making a mess of things he thought I had cleaned up a terrible mess. He went on to refer to how fortunate the whole speech was."

On February 8, L. B. Pearson was in Ottawa on a visit from Washington and he reported to Mackenzie King that he had told Lord Halifax that if he had consulted the Embassy, by a change of a few paragraphs, the speech would have been made quite all right and that "Halifax had expressed himself as being very sorry that he had embarrassed me. Pearson thought he had not done so deliberately, but it was all part of the Tory centralized policy that was ingrained in him. . . . What Pearson told me was much the same as Malcolm MacDonald. He, I think, made very clear to Halifax what injury his speech was certain to work. . . . I told Pearson to tell him it was not a matter of annoyance with me but of dismay when I read what he had said. . . . I said, as a matter of fact, I thought he had done me a service in helping to avoid discussion on these matters being pursued at any great length at the meeting of Prime Ministers in Britain [in May 1944]."

Shortly after the session of Parliament got under way, the Government was obliged to make a decision about the role of the R.C.A.F. in the war against Japan. This subject had been engaging Mackenzie King's attention since November 16, 1943, when Power had spoken to him about the probable effects of a British decision to start winding up air training in Canada. Mackenzie King had seen Malcolm MacDonald that day to ask him "if the British Government had considered what the reaction might be in the U.S. to a reduction of air training in Canada. Whether it would not immediately occasion them to feel that Great Britain intended to pay little attention to defeat of Japan after the defeat of Germany."

A meeting with the representatives of the British Air Ministry had been fixed for early 1944. Power had told Mackenzie King, on January 5, that he would like "to have Canada agree to contributing 60 or 70 squadrons toward British and American effort over the Pacific, and bringing back all other Canadian airmen—those serving in British squadrons included. He wants to notify the British at once. The Navy is sure to wish to play a prominent part. Power and I agreed that there was really no place for sending any army over the Pacific. The Canadian people, excepting the Province of British Columbia, are not going to be enthusiastic about going on with the war against Japan. However, I feel we have an obligation to share with . . . the British, Americans, and Australians in this, but it will be reasonable to take into account our four years of war to the Americans two. Also we may be sure we will get little credit for anything we do, either on the part of the United States or Great Britain." In the Cabinet the next day, Mackenzie King had found little desire to reach any decision on this question.

A month later the decision could no longer be postponed and, on February 9, at the War Committee meeting, "Power presented the outline of what he proposed to submit to [Harold] Balfour [Parliamentary Under-Secretary of the Air Ministry] as Canada's policy, and proposed procedure with respect to the R.C.A.F., making it plain that our intention was to proceed on lines which would bring our own men into our own squadrons under our own direction, there being at the present time an average of one-third Canadians . . . in the R.A.F. It was plain from Balfour's remarks that the British wished to be free to determine what should be done by all in the war against Japan. . . . What Power set forth was that we would ourselves decide the extent of our contribution and whether our men would serve along with the Americans, we being a Pacific Coast nation, or with the British in India or in other ways. In principle the War Committee were unanimous on what was proposed."

The next day (February 10) Mackenzie King revised a statement "setting forth the Government policy with respect to getting Canadians back into Canadian squadrons, out of mixed squadrons and making clear that we intended to both plan and control our own Air Force in the transitional period and decide ourselves what contribution we would make toward the Japanese war. It was the strongest assertion made thus far of Canada's position as a nation, demanding an equal voice on matters which pertained to her own forces. The British have been casually assuming that they would make disposition of forces generally both as to numbers, composition, location, etc. In this document, we have made clear we may decide to have our forces co-operate mainly with the United States, as we are a Pacific power, instead of those of Britain."

While Mackenzie King threw himself vigorously enough into the consideration of problems related to the war when they arose, it is fair to say that, apart from the flurry occasioned by McNaughton's return to Canada, his main preoccupation in these early months of 1944 continued to be with what would happen after the war. On February 11, he spoke at a dinner given by the National Liberal Federation where he "took advantage of the occasion to speak on organization, partly in the country and partly in Parliament, and need for keeping in touch with the working classes and farmers. Danger of Liberal party being eliminated altogether in Canada if we did not organize and fight for our principles. Pointed out how C.C.F. were stealing our ground. . . . Generally spoke out very strongly about my own feeling that Liberalism related to the conditions of the people." He was given a great ovation at the close and felt "it was like an old-time Liberal gathering, but what I regret is how little representative gatherings of the kind really are, of the younger element."

He also continued to deplore the extent to which the Liberal party appeared to be losing the support of organized labour to the C.C.F. and sought to recover some of the lost ground by consultation with the Labour Congresses in the final stages of the preparation of the Labour Relations Code which the federal Government had been working out with the provincial Governments since November 1943. The Code was finally settled and announced on February 17 and Mackenzie King noted that night that "Bengough and Mosher both commented very favourably on the Code in what came over the radio. It relieved a tremendous weight from my mind and I felt we had at last done the right thing."

The next day (February 18) Mackenzie King had a talk with Bengough who had asked to see him about proposed verbal modifications of the wages control Order. "He told me labour was quite prepared to accept wage control and indeed practically everything that was in the Order, but was not prepared to accept its wording which was simply hopeless. He also told me he wanted to be helpful. Did not want to see the C.C.F. make any headway."

On February 25, the Cabinet received the annual delegation from the Trades and Labour Congress and Mackenzie King considered that "Bengough made the finest presentation thus far made to the Cabinet. Exceedingly helpful, constructive document; not hesitating to give credit where credit was due. A complete contrast to the presentation of the Canadian Congress of Labour. I made what others told me was a most effective reply to the one or two critical points raised. The first in regard to the Wages Order, but more particularly with regard to the Family Allowances. Spoke of their purpose and gave the arguments for, refuting the idea they were any substitute for low wages. At the end of the meeting, shook hands with the delegates, many of whom thought I was altogether right on the Family Allowances. I believe that gathering would have supported the Administration by 90 per cent as against the other parties. The Labour Code has brought a lot of kudos to the Government."

One of Mackenzie King's greatest worries was about the growth of the influence of the United States in Canada, and the possible domination of post-war Canada by the Americans. This fear was reflected in a discussion on February 17 at the War Committee on "The Canol Project," which had reference to the oil pipeline from Norman Wells, N.W.T. The pipeline had been constructed as a joint enterprise for military purposes, but Mackenzie King did not want the Americans to control the oil wells. He "held strongly with one or two others to the view that we ought to get the Americans out of the further development there, and keep complete control in our own hands. As discussion went on and it became apparent that that part of Canada may possess oil areas as vast as those countries like Roumania and California . . . the thought came to my mind that Canada might well become the occasion of another great war unless matters are handled with the greatest possible care. There is going to be a desire on the part of all nations for a sharing of resources that are needed to supply such wants as those of gasoline and the like on which the commercial world of the future would depend. Also with Canada holding a position geographically advantageous in air routes as well as in resources there will be a demand on this country to make very great concessions to other nations. With the United States so powerful and her investments becoming greater in Canada we will have a great difficulty to hold our own against pressure from the United States. Then, with Russia a near neighbour, and what Japan and China may come to demand as well, and with Britain probably looking to the Dominions primarily and seeking to hold exclusively as her own their resources, what may be the outcome of it all is a prospect that is hard for me to contemplate. . . . With the tiny population we have, relative to what we possess in the way of resources, this country [might] become a scene of battle and pass into other hands. I know of nothing which has grown out of the war which seems to me to require more careful consideration than all this side of things."

The subject of "Canol" came up again at the War Committee meeting on March 15, when Mackenzie King "stressed the necessity of seeing that whatever was done in the way of allowing the Imperial Oil to go on with development, there should always be the opportunity of having the whole business revert to the Government. Broadly the decision was to recognize the need for pursuing development of oil in that region, first because of the need of oil for defence purposes, and for the opening-up of new resources which might be all important in that region. Equally the necessity of going ahead because we had become dependent on the United States for oil from California to meet our needs, and that supply is becoming limited and Americans are urging that unless we help to develop our fields, we may be cut off from theirs. . . .

"I felt clear in my own mind it was necessary to have private enterprise make a beginning. Equally clear that there should be no parting over any length of time with resources; also that the areas should be kept restricted and that obligations should be placed on any private corporation to see that development was made in a way that would give Canada benefits from them, e.g., construction of pipelines."

Mackenzie King felt the same concern to keep control of civil aviation, both international and domestic, in public hands, in order to protect the national interests and identity of Canada. This attitude had already been taken in 1943 and asserted against the proposal for a Commonwealth policy on the occasion when Churchill attended the War Committee meeting in Quebec. In 1944 it brought a sharp difference with the Canadian Pacific Railway whose President, D. C. Coleman, came to see Mackenzie King on February 23. Coleman felt the C.P.R. should be allowed to develop transoceanic and transcontinental air transport and "said that the Company wanted to know exactly the Government's policy with regard to private enterprise developing air transport, and referred more particularly to companies which have begun to operate in the northwestern part of Canada. . . . He asked if the matter had been discussed recently. I replied that the statement which I had given to Parliament early last year set forth the Government's policy and that there had been no departure from it of which I was aware; that the matter had not been discussed recently, but I would see that it was brought before the Cabinet anew without delay."

Coleman's approach led to a thorough reconsideration of civil aviation policy over several weeks. The first discussion took place on March 2 and the Cabinet was "unanimous as to Trans-Canada Airways maintaining monopoly in international aviation" and in endorsing the statement made by the Prime Minister in April 1943 regarding both international and domestic policy. Mackenzie King found "a certain sympathy with the idea that for pioneering work in a new country charters should be given to privately owned companies and that as accidents, delays and the like were inevitable in those areas the reputation of the Trans-Canada Airways would be hurt and the Government embarrassed if this pioneering work should be taken on by the Government. . . . There was agreement as to . . . the desirability of creating a Canadian Civil Aeronautical Authority to have to do with planning and advising and also with judicial decisions as to rates, etc. . . .

"The more the matter was discussed," Mackenzie King continued, "the more convinced I became that the C.P.R is doing what Mackenzie and Mann did in the buying-up of pieces of road which necessitated an ultimate purchase by the Government and a competing transcontinental line [the Canadian Northern Railway]. I am sure that what is now proposed by the C.P.R. would give them the best for the future of the Canadian northwest and of what will be the most important air route around the world. I intend to use my influence more strongly than ever in the Cabinet to see that these areas do not fall to private monopoly which has been doing all it can to destroy the present Government and myself in particular and which is wholly indifferent to the trend of public demand."

At the Cabinet meeting on March 6, Mackenzie King "held out strongly for complete control of the air by the Government, opposing the C.P.R. effort to construct a second line. It is vital to the future that we do not allow private companies to begin to restrict the Government's freedom of developments within Canada and with other countries beyond. It is important, too, that we should preserve for our young pilots who have been overseas their chance to work out a future in pioneering areas." The next day (March 7) the Cabinet considered a draft of a letter to Coleman, which "first of all asserted the external and domestic policies as set out in my statement to Parliament last year. It was also agreed that we should appoint an Air Transport Board which would advise the Minister with respect to licensing of companies, planning for areas, for service, etc. Also that there should be no privately owned monopoly in any part of the country. That we should divorce air transport from railway transport." On this occasion, Mackenzie King "spoke particularly of the future, the need of the Government being free to decide all its policies in relation to international co-operation, etc., without any pressure from or interference on the part of private corporations."

At the Cabinet meeting on March 9, one of the Ministers "asked why we were rushing matters so" and Mackenzie King "pointed out that the reasons were that the President of the C.P.R. had . . . within the past fortnight or so, called on the Prime Minister to know where the C.P.R. were at so that they could make their plans definitely. . . . I promised that the matter would come up before Council at once and that I would give him an answer without delay." He observed that Howe would have to make a statement on civil aviation [to the House] in a few days and that civil aviation was on the agenda of the Commonwealth Prime Ministers' meeting [to be held in May]. "I wished to be able to say that in Canada we had complete Government control of the air. I told Council quite frankly that when I was seated at Downing Street I was really dealing with the C.P.R. there; that after all that was where the C.P.R. was owned, and that its policies were really directed from London and aimed at carrying out Imperial policy rather than leaving Canada free to carry out her own." Mackenzie King also referred to "the need of the Government having a perfectly free hand in the world organization of the air and in the decision upon routes, what was needed for defence, strategic reasons, etc. We should not link up with private interests where there were these vaster national considerations."

Mackenzie King felt that if the Government "did not declare our policy at once we would find that the C.C.F. would declare for out and out control. It would be supported by the Social Credit party and we would find that large numbers of our own men would join with them; that Hanson and some of the Tories would join with us, and we would have succeeded in completely handing over the control of Government for the next five years to the C.C.F. That would be giving them exactly what they wanted: the two old parties standing for private interests against the people's rights to control natural monopolies, etc. . . . When I had made this statement, which I did in a pretty clear and convincing fashion, there was a dead silence in Council, and from that time on little more was said of not definitely confirming the decision previously reached as to the Government controlling the policy respecting air transport and stating that policy frankly within the next few days. Howe promised to have his speech in shape by Monday along lines that Council had decided. I feel this is a tremendous achievement. There will be difficulties—there will be a great battle against the Government, tremendous lobbying, but to have settled and stated at once definitely what the policy is was a great triumph and will make all the difference between conflict all along the way or starting out in the wrong direction, having to change later, even if given a chance to change and winning the support of the people for what is obviously the right path to take."

On March 17, Howe made his statement in the House of Commons on domestic and international civil aviation. Mackenzie King thought "the policy outlined is as fine as anything the Government of Canada has done at any time. I cannot but regret that I did not make the statement regarding international aviation, leaving to Howe the statement regarding domestic aviation. I outlined both in relation to the Trans-Canada Airways in part last year, but should, as Minister for External Affairs, and Prime Minister, have outlined the international policy this time." Mackenzie King noted that "it was clear that the C.C.F. were 100 per cent behind us in the policies announced. The Tories looked very disconcerted. Howe tells me that the so-called Progressive-Conservatives have taken a view somewhat similar to ours but that members of the old party resented it very strongly."

The C.P.R. did not give up the struggle. On March 31, the members of the War Committee received a delegation headed by D. C. Coleman who read a "letter setting out their view re air transport policy. When Coleman had concluded, I said a word of explanation about the talk we had had together, of my interpretation of it along lines set out in my telegram to him; the necessity of making a statement of policy to Parliament first and of having read before the Cabinet several times his letter to me of last year, the representations of which were almost identical with those of the letter presented this morning. I pointed out that there were international reasons as well as domestic reasons for making the pronouncement of policy when we did. . . . I spoke out quite plainly about the Government having the feeling that the C.P.R. did not take in earnest its policy as announced a year ago in the House of Commons, but seemed to feel they should go ahead regardless of the statement of policy as made in the House. Also I said there had been much pressure and lobbying in regard to the branch services, the individual services in the West and mentioned Mr. Coleman having spoken of the Company's desire to have a line from Seattle to Alaska; having discussed with me the desirability of that, notwithstanding the Company knew that these cross-boundary services were to be kept in the Government's hands. I made clear what the policy was.

"When I had finished, Coleman took exception to the statement that they had gone ahead in defiance of the Government's policy and, in referring to the policy as having been settled, said they had received their death sentence. That apparently there was nothing that could come out of their representations. I replied to this by saying I had not spoken of defiance. I had only referred to what had been going on in an active way, as if the Government had not really meant what it said was and would continue to be its policy. As to the 'death sentence,' I said that I merely indicated the policy as it had been previously expressed, and it was necessary in the light of conditions. I pointed out that during this period of war, many changes had come quickly. That anyone who understood what was at the bottom of this great struggle would realize, where there were natural monopolies, governments and not private enterprise would have to control. Especially with regard to air transport, had this become increasingly clear for both national and international reasons. That had our Government not taken the position we did, we would simply have been leaving the way open for the C.C.F. to take it as their policy. . . . Certainly many from our own party have felt very strongly on the matter and that the result would only be to ensure the return, on a great issue of this kind, of the C.C.F."

He also told "the delegation I sometimes thought that Canada might become the scene of the next war. That vast resources which were disclosing themselves . . . could not be monopolized by a small population holding such vast areas. That with Russia and the United States as near to us as they were, we could not take too far-sighted a view of the inevitable developments of the future, and not allow any trends which were likely to prove inimical. . . . I concluded what I had to say by repeating to Coleman how appreciative I had been of his own attitude. I may have been a little more outspoken than I should have been, but it seemed to me, knowing how the C.P.R. has been lobbying against the Government, supplying funds for Conservative conventions, Bracken's campaigns, their men lobbying Prince Albert to bring pressure to bear on me [Canadian Pacific Air Lines served Prince Albert and Mackenzie King felt they were seeking to influence him as Member for that constituency], and also realizing that we are right in our policy and that they have been doing what they can to prevent its realization, it was just as well to speak out." That interview ended the agitation for the time being.

Towards the end of February 1944, Mackenzie King became greatly concerned about the health of the Minister of Finance. Although his personal relations with Ilsley were never close, and although he frequently deplored what he called Ilsley's rigidity, Mackenzie King realized how large a contribution he had made to the war effort, how great his prestige was in the country, and how much the Government would be weakened if Ilsley should be unable to carry on. At the

Cabinet meeting on February 24, Ilsley "finally spoke of the need to get away at once, and I could see he was almost on the point of breaking completely. I told him we would all be pleased if he would [get away], and went over different matters with a view of letting him get off immediately. After Council I stayed and talked with him. He began nearly to collapse, saying that the strain had become too great for him. . . . I felt very sorry for him. It was clear that another day might break him down completely." As Ilsley was sensitive about the wartime restrictions against holiday travel, Mackenzie King arranged to have him go to an UNRRA meeting at Atlantic City and then on a mission to Washington. He felt that if Ilsley would stay away for a month all would be well, but that "if he stays longer here we will lose his services altogether" and he noted that Ilsley was "absolutely indispensable, not only to Canada but to the war effort of the United Nations." Ilsley went on this mission, but on March 8 Mackenzie King was amazed to see him back in the Cabinet "and it was apparent to me, as soon as Council met, that he was just about where he was when he left." On March 10 both Mackenzie King and Ralston "had a serious talk" with Ilsley, "with a view to having him get away for a time, but he said that matters only piled up when he was away. He looked, however, very driven, and may at any time have a crash." Mackenzie King noted later that Ralston had been "helpful in getting this matter settled," and on March 16, Mackenzie King announced in the House of Commons that he "had persuaded Ilsley to take a much needed rest. Without this I am sure he would have a complete nervous breakdown which would have impaired his whole future." When he returned on April 14, Mackenzie King noted that he looked "quite well and strong again."

Mackenzie King himself was in exceptionally good health throughout the session and took a good deal of satisfaction out of participation in the debates. On February 22, for example, on the motion to set up the War Expenditures Committee, Graydon had announced that the Conservative party would not support the motion. Mackenzie King commented that this gave him "a splendid opportunity to register the real position of the Tory party toward the Government in meeting situations arising out of the war." He felt he "spoke in a very clear, emphatic, and direct way, and indeed, before concluding, lashed out at the Opposition. I think in a way it was the most effective speech I have made in Parliament at any time. Our men were highly pleased and it so discomfited the Tories that when the motion came to set up the Committee, they were still wondering where they were at and, though Graydon had stated they would be against the motion, no one opposed it and it carried unanimously." He reflected that he "could be more effective there than anywhere were I free to give all my time to the House. Also that public speaking is really my forte. It is a great comfort to realize that in that particular field I am coming back into my own by degrees."

One result of this new confidence was that, on March 4, he wrote a letter "agreeing to accept the nomination of the Liberals at Prince Albert." On March 28, Dr. J. K. Blair, the M.P. for North Wellington, Ontario, tried to persuade Mackenzie King to give him a post as political organizer and accept the nomination in North Wellington, saying he "had little chance in Prince Albert." Mackenzie King told him "that so far as I was concerned, I could not very well think of leaving a constituency that had stood by me for eighteen years without admitting defeat even before the fight had taken place. That I must stay by Prince Albert, win or lose. If the party felt I was so indispensable, they would find means of assisting to win seats but if they did not, I would be honourably discharged from further duties either to the party or to the country in Parliament. I am entitled to have, when I am seventy years, and on, a chance to do some of the things I have never had a chance to do in the course of my life." The subject was often referred to again before the final decision about a constituency was made a year later, but, in the end, he accepted the nomination in Prince Albert and was defeated there in 1945.

On March 10, Mackenzie King had told the Liberal caucus he was anxious to win the next election: "That I had taken the preservation of the trust that had come down to me from the past and also a trust for the present given by the party. I had carried it on . . . through twenty-five years of leadership . . . at the sacrifice of home, friends and the like and in some other particulars of many of the joys of life that I would have liked to have had. I would not like to see all this lost at the end, but also I felt deeply for the men who had been around me and whom I saw before me. I had their future at heart and would like to see them carry on the cause of Liberalism in future Parliaments. That no matter what came the next would be the last Parliament in which I would wish to serve or could be expected to serve. That I was really anxious to see others carrying on before the close of my life. I then stressed what was needed to ensure that end. Claxton and others came up and spoke to me about how very effective these remarks had been. I record them here because it was the strongest intimation I have thus far made to the party about my own close relationships with it. I think it let the men see just how I felt."

Mackenzie King was well aware that most of his colleagues and many supporters of the Liberal party regarded the wartime restrictions on the supply of beer as a serious political liability. On February 25, the Canadian and Catholic Confederation of Labour had, in the course of its presentation to the Government, objected to the beer restrictions. In replying to them Mackenzie King "said enough to indicate that we did not propose to keep up regulations on beer in any post-war period."

At about the same time, the Liquor Control Board of Ontario began posting notices in the beverage rooms in that province stating that the quantity of alcoholic beverages saleable was limited by reason of the Order-in-Council passed by the federal Government. This statement was not, in fact, correct as the restriction imposed within the province on the quantity of beer available to beverage rooms was far greater than that provided in the federal Order.

On March 8, Arthur Mathewson, the Provincial Treasurer of Quebec, saw Mackenzie King about "the problem which the restriction of beer was giving the Government there. He brought with him the advertisement of the Ontario Government blaming the federal Government for all difficulties arising out of the restriction; a letter from Godbout hoping we could find some solution of the problem which was becoming very embarrassing. As we discussed the matter, I told Mathewson I intended, when I got out of office, to strongly advocate complete government ownership and control of all breweries and distilleries. It is the only way of getting rid of the most corrupt and baneful factor in the life of the nation. I agreed, however, that Drew's effort to embarrass instead of co-operate with the federal Government in its restriction of the sale of beer as a necessary and desirable war measure, and also an announcement published today by the Treasurer of Alberta, Low, stating that the federal Government had shown favours to Quebec, made it desirable to take some immediate steps to expose the deceit of these particular provinces in claiming that it was the 10 per cent restriction on the beer which was causing all the embarrassment, whereas, in fact, there are economic reasons, such as shortage of materials, manpower, bottles, etc., that really explained the present situation."

Mackenzie King told Mathewson he "would think over carefully cancelling our restriction so far as beer is concerned and putting it up to the provinces to control that particular beverage. Mathewson saw no reason for altering the restriction on spirits and wine but he thought a step like this with regard to beer would make a vast difference. I think Drew has given just the opening needed." Accordingly Mackenzie King spent some time in the next few days working over a statement on the beer situation, making use of "some excellent material that was in the

Toronto *Star* editorials on the way the Liquor Control Commission and the Attorney-General had misrepresented the Dominion's action; changing the allotment in beverage rooms from 90 per cent to 75 per cent allotment and having it appear this was all due to the Dominion's restrictions. Finally, I tried to work out the real reason for discontinuing the restriction, namely, the friction that was developing between the Provincial and Dominion Governments." On March 13, he told the Cabinet he had "a statement here which I think will meet with the unanimous support of all present, and then read the statement through without any comment. I never saw a group of men more visibly pleased. Several of them expressed themselves as thoroughly delighted. Felt that what I had written out was a masterpiece. That I had taken just the right moment and said just the right thing. There was not a suggestion of the change of a line."

He had the necessary Order-in-Council ready and signed it at once. In the House that afternoon, "the beer statement was received with applause at different points. It was obvious that our men were pleased. The Tories looked thoroughly discomfited. . . . All our men saw at once just where Drew and the Ontario Government were. The position they had gotten themselves into in trying to throw onus on myself by their beer notices. I seldom have had more satisfaction out of showing up political motives of the Tories in Toronto, putting them in the box they are now in and where they will be left without any excuse of attacking the federal Government on this issue." He added that "the position respecting beer had become impossible and we would have been allowing ourselves to be simply trodden on had this action not been taken. I think it has been taken just at the right time."

On the following day (March 14) Mackenzie King wrote that "Drew has been very nasty and Hepburn joined with him" about the removal of the beer restriction. He noted that, on the previous evening, when he was opening some personal letters, "the first was from Drew. As soon as I saw it I was certain he would make some point concerning it, so kept the envelope which showed that the letter could not have been received until today. Sure enough he read the letter to the [Ontario] Legislature and said that it was typical of me to have said nothing of his having written and that what I had said he took to be my method of answering his letter. I might have gone after him very hard but decided I would simply place the true report on Hansard, which I did when the House opened, in a statement which makes the record clear, but which will probably provoke Drew and Hepburn still further. However, I have no doubt the people of the Province will see the truth for themselves and judge accordingly." The next day (March 15) Mackenzie King "drafted a little letter to Drew in reply to his communication. Gave it a different tone to his utterances. Completely ignored his imputations."

In 1944, a Parliamentary Committee had been making an investigation of the Canadian Broadcasting Corporation and the Cabinet discussed the C.B.C. on March 16. Mackenzie King reminded his colleagues that "our policy was government ownership and control, and members of the party must not begin to favour private interests in competition, but hold to the policy laid down by the Aird Commission. I then spoke of the necessity of getting a Chairman who would give all his time to the work of the Board. Referred to the importance of its utility in the national life of the country and of getting the best possible man. I said I wanted to bring up again the name of B. K. Sandwell [the Editor of Toronto *Saturday Night*] who I felt was the best person we could get in Canada for the position of Chairman. Mentioned his intellectual powers and interests. His knowledge of the press and method of dealing with the press. His . . . broad human liberal sympathies. His broad attitude toward the French Canadians, he having lived for years in Montreal. His appreciation of artistic matters." Mackenzie King was authorized to offer the position to Sandwell, which he did the same day.

When Sandwell expressed doubts about his own qualifications Mackenzie King "replied that what was needed in a Chairman was one with an understanding heart and knowledge of affairs and liberal mind, broad sympathies, etc., someone who could deal with prima donnas. Had high standards in matters of cultural education. Could make the necessary contacts and effectively carry out the relationship arising out of international affairs which the radio had today. Who had vision as to its future. A belief in public ownership and control. Understood the press and relationships with the press. Could act with a Board of Governors, etc. That I wanted someone who would be perfectly impartial as between political parties and who understood the educational value of the radio. One who could harmonize the relationship between private companies and the radio, etc. I said I thought he possessed all these qualities." Sandwell was obviously attracted by the offer, but in the end did not accept, much to Mackenzie King's disappointment.

At this time, Mackenzie King began again to think about settling the question of a national anthem and a flag. In his diary for March 20, he wrote: "Before waking, was dreaming of what to do about a national anthem for Canada. There came to me very strongly the idea that 'God Save the King' should be made the anthem of the British Commonwealth of Nations, and that 'O Canada' should be the national anthem for

Canada. It ['God Save the King'] could be sung in any part of the Commonwealth excepting Ireland. If they did not like it, they could go without. It would disclose the association of the different parts of the Empire and would leave each individual part free to have its distinct anthem. . . .

"I then thought of the Union Jack. Felt that it could be proclaimed the national flag of the United Kingdom; that the Dominions could have a Union Jack in the corner, to show historical evolution and present association with the United Kingdom, though with each having its own distinct flag as well. I believe those ideas would please the King and meet with universal acceptance. Similarly, the Union Jack could be seen either completely by itself or in the corner of the national flag in any part of the Commonwealth." At the caucus on March 28, Mackenzie King suggested a way to meet the anthem and flag questions was to have 'God Save the King' as the anthem of the nations of the British Commonwealth, and allow each country to have its own national anthem. 'O Canada' for Canada. Regarding a flag, have the Union Jack a part of each flag that belonged to the British Commonwealth of Nations thereby disclosing a common historical association with Britain. . . . Advised that Canada take the Canadian Ensign and accept it at once as her national flag. Not wait to design a special flag. Later a Committee could be appointed to consider new designs. As I dictate, I think more and more of the wisdom of having a resolution of Parliament to adopt these two things before the present session is over. I may take up this matter at the meeting of Prime Ministers." He did neither.

The day before (March 27) Mackenzie King had an interview with Gordon Edwards who had heard his house at 24 Sussex Street might be bought for a Prime Minister's Residence. Mackenzie King said he "had never even thought of the idea and doubted if I could be the one to put it forward at all. . . . I agreed that no more suitable place could be found, but told him it was not probable the Government would purchase it." But from that moment the idea was in Mackenzie King's mind and the property was ultimately acquired.

The development of the National Capital was also a subject of consideration. On March 28, Mackenzie King was shown the plans for a building for the National Film Board to be built in Hull. He felt the plans made it look like "an ordinary factory" and suggested the "type of architecture" of "the Research Building" and also urged having "land bought up between the bridge and where the new building could be placed." On April 20 Mackenzie King told the Cabinet "of my wish to speak on the Federal District as a real memorial to our men." He suggested a Parliamentary Committee to plan the development of the Capital and "also backed the proposal for constructing a public building for the Film Board on the Hull side of the Ottawa River, but stated I thought Public Works should not proceed with building until general plans for development of certain areas had been made, and expropriation of property between the bridge and the park, the main street and the river." In the House of Commons on April 21, he "put forward the idea of a larger Ottawa to be administered by a Commission and to include an area in the Province of Quebec, equal to that in Ontario, and the further idea of having, as a memorial to the service and sacrifice of men and women who have participated in the present war, a capital city which would be a model to other cities and other countries. As now we had the War Memorial symbolical of the last war, in the heart of the Capital, so succeeding generations would have, as the memorial of this war, the National Capital in the form of a greater Ottawa, with the Ottawa River running through the heart of the Capital instead of being a boundary on one side. It would be a great symbol of the elements that have gone to make the present Canada what it is, and the future of Canada what it will become."

Amid all these preparations for the future, the prosecution of the war was not forgotten. Towards the end of March, Ralston began to be concerned about meeting the manpower requirements of the Army and to feel the need of a stronger Adjutant-General. He approached Victor Sifton to return to the service. It was represented to Mackenzie King that Sifton's position in directing the Winnipeg *Free Press* was more important to the Government and that politically it would be a misfortune if Sifton came to Ottawa. He, however, assured Ralston that if Sifton was really needed, he felt the first duty was to the war. When Ralston told him on March 28 that "Sifton was needed to get the necessary men," he noted that "Ralston does not want to have any recourse to conscription and feels, if properly handled, there will be no need for it. He wants now to have the slogan of 'volunteer army' which is what I have been after from the start." Accordingly, Mackenzie King had a long talk on March 31 with Victor Sifton who "said he was most anxious to be of service, if he was needed and I believed he could do the thing I felt should be done. He said, however, he doubted very much if the latter were possible. He gave me his reasons in confidence, these being he doubted if Ralston would back up the changes that he thought would have to be made." Sifton said he had left the service earlier in the war because the "brass hats were determined not to have any civilian come in and be given a real place. He would be up against that very strongly if he returned. . . . He also said everything had been left to the eleventh hour. He had pointed out many of these things to the Minister when he was in the Department. Ralston somehow did not seem able to face up to them. He realized it was very difficult for him to do so. He thought Ralston had been wholly honourable in everything; in his treatment of McNaughton as well as in all else. That the organization was so powerful, he just could not prevent its getting its own way in many things, whether he wished the opposite or not. He told me, too, about how serious the position of the *Free Press* was at this time, but said he told his brother Clifford if it would make a difference of one life, they had no right to consider themselves, and he would be prepared to come.

"I said all he had told me made me feel more strongly than ever that he was needed, and should come, though personally, if I look at the political end, I would prefer to have him stay with the *Free Press* continuing to assist the Government as it had, but that I had always taken the position that if the war demanded any sacrifice, we should be prepared to incur it. I took that view now in relation to himself. I thought he was justified in getting from Ralston the assurance that he would be supported in what he felt would be essential.

"I was quite impressed with his earnestness and with clear way in which he viewed matters. I doubt very much, however, if he will accept. Indeed I should be amazed if he does. It would certainly be an evidence of real sacrifice if he consents. One can hardly blame him, all circumstances considered." Sifton did not accept.

Mackenzie King was, from the outset, interested in the development of atomic power and he noted on April 12 that the War Committee "decided to take a step in the way of further developing in Canada the secret process which has such appalling possibilities of enormous destruction. A committee on which England, the United States, and Canada are represented are anxious to have this development continued in our country because of the near proximity and of the resources we have. If perfected, as believed, the processes will not only have terrific destructive powers but may be used for many purposes for which electrical power is used. Howe mentioned that a fountain pen filled with the desired substance would propel a steamship across the Atlantic. It is a solemn business dealing with matters of this kind. Whatever will end this war before the enemy becomes possessed of like inventions is necessary in the interests of mankind."

There was less labour unrest in 1944 than in 1943. All through 1943, Mackenzie King had been filled with admiration for the way Mr. Justice McTague, as Chairman of the Labour Relations Board, had dealt with labour policy and more than once had seriously considered inviting him to join the Government as Minister of Labour. On February 11, 1944, for the first time, he expressed some doubt as to whether McTague's influence was "as helpful as it should have been." He added that "after all he has a Tory mentality"; that he was "doing a very useful work, but his attitude has been less liberal than I thought it would be." On February 23, McTague saw him to say he wanted to return to the Bench. "He says he is fed up, and indeed looks very tired. Speaks of the work on the Board at present as being very monotonous and within small compass. He has been serving in war work in one form or another for the last four years. I am surprised at his feeling he has done his part. It will be very difficult to replace him but there may be some advantage in so doing, as his standing with labour today is not what it was some time ago. I think too he is a little too legalistic." McTague's resignation was later received; it was accepted and announced on March 16, and McTague returned, for the time being, to his position on the Bench of Ontario.

On April 21, Mackenzie King "was somewhat disturbed today to learn that McTague might become a Conservative candidate in the next campaign. It shows the unwisdom of taking men from other parties for any position in which they can build up their own strength for party ends. I thought McTague, being on the Bench, would have maintained a strict neutrality for the remainder of his days." Two days later (April 23), Mackenzie King "was incensed tonight when I heard over the radio that McTague, who has resigned his judgeship, will become National Chairman of the Progressive Conservative party." Mackenzie King was indignant at a man who had been "taken into the confidence of an Administration; deserting the Administration at the time of its greatest need in prosecuting the war, and this, while the war is still raging, and the Government doing its best to help to end it. To come out and spend the remainder of his time trying to destroy the Administration, and do all in his power to maim its strength meanwhile. This kind of thing I do not believe will succeed, but it is typical of what we may expect from the Tory party, and what I have all along said will be pretty certain to happen once we were bound down to the obligation of carrying on the war when they were left free to fight."

On April 25, Mackenzie King spoke in Cabinet "about the significance of McTague's action in accepting the position he did on the Progressive Conservative National Committee. Also of Henry Borden becoming Secretary. Each of them issuing a statement declaring the present Government would be defeated, and McTague stating that he would be a candidate. Bracken had spoken of their action as 'noble actions of public servants.' In other words, men leaving public affairs in time of war to seek to destroy the Government that has given them positions of prominence they had enjoyed, and this, at the moment the Prime Minister is leaving for overseas [to attend the meeting of Commonwealth Prime Ministers]."

Before leaving for London, Mackenzie King had to decide who should be Acting Prime Minister in his absence. Since the death of Lapointe, Crerar, as Senior Privy Councillor, had invariably acted when he was in Ottawa, but, after a good deal of reflection, Mackenzie King decided to ask Ralston on this occasion. He told Crerar on April 20 he had "been in doubt as to whether he was equal to the strain of being Acting Prime Minister and Acting President of Council. That I had thought of having Ralston act in my absence. He was quite clearly disappointed. Said he felt I would be expecting him to act. I told him I had been concerned about his health of late and I did not want him to run any chances of breakdown. Also that I felt Members of the House would take advantage of him in ways that they would not of Ralston . . . that Ralston had been dealing with financial and defence questions which would be the main ones which the Acting Prime Minister would have to deal with in my absence. Also that I thought of speaking to him about his intention at the time of the general election. I said I had been holding a Senatorship for him in Manitoba, because of a request he made some time ago. He told me he did not want to run again but added, unless I wanted him to do so. . . . I said that was one of the reasons I thought it was better to have a young man take hold of some of these posts."

Mackenzie King himself felt "quite sure that colleagues generally in the Cabinet would prefer Ralston. Considering the part he has taken, excepting the tendering of his resignation which I still have in my possession, he certainly merits that mark of confidence. He is very thorough." The next day in the House of Commons Mackenzie King "made announcement about Ministers to act in my absence overseas. I had earlier 'phoned Crerar telling him of my final decision, and read him what I proposed saying. He said it was quite all right. . . . I am quite convinced I have made the only decision I could properly make in the interests of the House and party, in having Ralston act as Prime Minister but, at the same time, keeping Crerar as President of the Council and Chairman of the War Committee. The civil authority will be obviously, if not controlling, having a final word in any decision. I could see that the House accepted quite well the distribution of powers which I mentioned. St. Laurent is ideal for External Affairs and Ralston will be, I know, exceedingly conscientious. The only thing I fear is that there may be an effort to again force conscription to the fore when I am away, but I think it has lost its force. I am quite sure Ralston will not do anything in my absence which he knows I would not wish to have done. When I spoke to him over the 'phone and told him I wished him to act in my absence, he at once asked if I had spoken to Crerar. I told him what I had said. He then suggested that possibly Ilsley, who will be dealing with most of the questions, had better act. I told him I felt Ilsley had a heavy enough load as it was, and also I was a little fearful Ilsley might not be equal to the task which he now has. I am deeply concerned about this. I am afraid he let the strain get beyond him for too long a time. However, when he begins debating in the House on his measures, it may revive his spirits anew. Ralston thanked me for the confidence I reposed in him, and was exceedingly pleasant in his attitude generally. . . . I can, of course, fully understand Crerar's feeling. He has doubtless looked forward to acting in my absence as a sort of final recognition of his life work. However, my first duty has been to see that the affairs of government are carried on in the most effective way possible."

Mackenzie King had a special caucus on April 25, the day before he left for London. He spoke to the caucus "about McTague's action and Borden's. Stressed the need of organization to parallel what they were doing, and outlined aspects of the situation that I thought were bad. As I anticipated, the discussion afterwards for the most part took the form of criticism of the Government for having appointed Tories. Some of the Members were, I think, too outspoken in attacks they made on some of the Ministers. In fact, most of those who spoke attacked the Government quite strongly for having had any Tories fill the positions that they have. . . . I ended up the proceedings with a pretty effective reply pointing out that they would recall the efforts which had been made to have a National Government. It was essential our Government should make it clear we were not trying to win the war by making the war a preserve for Liberals only. That men within the sound of my voice wanted a National Government. If we had had a National Government the only difference would be that most of us would not be there. . . . It was a miracle that, toward the end of five years of war, we should find our party as united and so strong, carrying on the Government with the magnificent record which we had made. I gave them my belief that the country would not be taken in by the actions of these men. . . . Mentioned we were all the same men in Government as the day before

McTague and Borden had taken the action they did. It all went to show what the Tory party were prepared to do. I spoke of the money which they must have, and the great care with which everything was planned, just as army headquarters would plan a campaign. I spoke of the necessity of our getting good men as candidates—that candidates were three-quarters of the battle. I spoke of the Government having been applauded for appointing McTague, right up to the last moment. That as he was a Judge of the Supreme Court of Ontario, we could hardly have made a choice that was more impartial for the kind of position he held.

"Then I spoke of the Government's policies. Many of the men had complained they were not consulted enough before policies were announced. I asked them if, at any time, any party ever received more credit for policies than we did in those that were set out in the Speech from the Throne. They had not been discussed in caucus beforehand. I ended up by making mention of going overseas shortly and wished to have the occasion to speak to men of the armed forces in different parts, and wanted to be able to say that I carried to all of them a message of solid backing of our party. I stressed how they were giving their lives for the country. We should forget differences, and think of the necessity of the Liberal party being true to its great work in the Dominion. . . . That I believed the fate of Canada was bound up with the fate of the Liberal party. . . . Never once had I, since the war began, done other than seek to take those steps which would keep Canada united to tackle and carry on the war effort most effectively. I said that everything considered, it was marvellous what had been achieved in that way. I then, with a last word about the soldiers, ended my remarks. . . . I don't think those present realized I would not be in the House again before I left."

April 25 was Mackenzie King's last day in Ottawa before leaving for London to attend the meeting of Commonwealth Prime Ministers. The meeting had been arranged more than a month before. He recalled the agony he had suffered in 1941 in preparing his Mansion House speech and, in 1944, he was determined to complete before he left Canada the speech he knew he would be expected to make in London. On April 5, he "was most anxious to get on with the speech for England which should be the most important that I have ever made," and noted that "while at lunch, I thought of a sentence or two which enabled me to get the plough into the ground and begin a furrow. It gives me the lead I shall follow and which I think will make possible an interesting statement of some real value." These sentences read: "I should like to speak to you today of the spirit of Canada as it is exemplified in Canada's war effort, and of its meaning to us in the present world-wide fight for freedom. The qualities (or significance) of a nation's spirit are something to be revealed rather than to be defined. More or less, they defy definition. They are most readily ascertained as they manifest themselves in the collective acts of a people. This expression of a people's spirit (or the power of the spirit) is inevitably heightened at a time of war." Mackenzie King worked off and on at the speech for the rest of that week and on Sunday afternoon, April 8, began revising it with two of his secretaries. After dinner that evening, he "felt well pleased with it. Enough has been done to make sure that the speech for London will be complete in time. The introduction and the conclusion have still to be written. . . . It is perfectly amazing how long it takes to prepare one of these broadcasts. Already I have given all of half of a week of my time to what has been done thus far." The speech was, of course, not completed before he went to London. Indeed, the revision was still going on the evening before it was delivered.

Mackenzie King had, from the outset, hoped he might be invited to address the British Parliament. A message came on April 20 "from Mr. Churchill inviting me to address a gathering of both Houses of Parliament when in London and mentioning that if it was desired, he, himself, would preside. This is a very high honour. Were I up to date on my work and not so fatigued, I would be extremely happy at the thought of it. However, the mere thought of not being prepared and the fear of what I have prepared being not really suited to the occasion, made me feel very depressed through the afternoon." He told Malcolm MacDonald how honoured he felt but said to him "it was at times like these that one's thoughts naturally went back to one's father and mother, and, in my case, to my grandfather. The happiness that it would have given them; the reverence my father had for the Old Country, even on entering the door of Westminster."

On April 22 he was working on the speech again. "I was not satisfied with the last part which might occasion some controversy," he wrote, "the part which would seek to define the Commonwealth. Rather have I decided to seek to work out something on co-operation between all parts and extension of that idea to other nations. Also to further develop my thought of continuing conference of Cabinet Councils which might reach into consultation with Cabinets of other countries as is already the case between Canada and the United States."

Mackenzie King left Rockcliffe airport in a specially fitted-up United States Air Force Liberator bomber on April 26 and arrived at Bovington airport near London in the late afternoon of April 27.

CHAPTER TWENTY-THREE

The Meeting of Commonwealth Prime Ministers, 1944

MACKENZIE KING approached his second wartime visit to Britain in a very different spirit from the first. He now knew Churchill very well and, despite occasional differences, they had become quite congenial. He had no worries about his position at home and no uneasiness about his reception in London. His own prestige had grown with the growth of Canada's wartime achievements.

The morning after he arrived, April 28, his classmate and fellow-rebel from University of Toronto days, Viscount Greenwood, called on him. Greenwood told him that "Churchill had been immensely impressed at the intimacy of the friendship between the President and myself. Questioned him as to how we had become such friends. Said it had made a profound impression on him. . . . Said that Churchill, Duncan [Sir Andrew Duncan, a member of the British wartime Government who had been Chairman of the Duncan Commission in Canada in 1927] and one or two others he named were all strong boosters of mine and all converts, but that Bennett was not."

Mackenzie King had, however, not changed his attitude toward any move to centralize the Empire and expected to have a real struggle in resisting moves to establish central Commonwealth machinery in London. He lost no time in making his own position clear. He talked first to Lord Cranborne, the Dominions Secretary, on April 28, and "told him of my problem with general elections ahead, and the absolute necessity that I must not do anything which would look like making a commitment in advance of any decision by the Canadian Parliament on anything that might be vital. He said he saw my position clearly. I told him I thought it was a mistake to try to define things too closely or to institutionalize in any way. That, of course, we could seek agreement on policy in as many directions as possible but each part in its own province. I got him to tell me what was meant by Commonwealth and Empire. He said Winston had coined the phrase and they had all followed. The Commonwealth meant the five completely self-governing countries: Britain being one of the five. I said: 'the Balfour Declaration.' He said: 'Yes.' That Empire meant the Colonial Empire—Colonies and India. I asked him whether England did not necessarily become a part of the Empire as the seat of government was here. He said: 'Yes, that was true.' I said in this way, Britain did come in twice."

In the afternoon Mackenzie King called on Churchill at Downing Street. In the course of their talk Churchill told him that "this Conference was not to settle the future of the world, but that great decisions were to be taken. He went on to indicate two things that he thought might come out of it—one was there should be at least an annual Conference of Prime Ministers, in England for the most part, at other times in other parts, Australia, New Zealand, South Africa or Canada, mentioning Vancouver. He thought of London more frequently. The other thing was for meetings of the Committee of Defence, referring to the Chiefs of Staff meeting together for keeping in touch with the needs of defence; matters of strategy, etc. As to the first, I said that I hoped that nothing too definite as to time would be arranged. That it was very difficult for Prime Ministers to get away from their countries. Matters shaped up frequently in their absences. It broke into the continuity of their affairs. I thought that occasions would arise where obviously meetings should be held. I said nothing about the second, feeling that I would want to know more exactly what was desired.

"He then spoke to me of impending events and said, if I wished it, he would tell me about the plans. But would not wish me to tell any of my colleagues. That I could let them know that I knew, but he thought it would be better not to reveal more than that. He added: as your men in such numbers will be fighting, you should perhaps know, but I will leave that to you. I said to him that I thought I should know, and would be glad to know before I left; would be glad if he would give me the information." After a brief reference to the invasion across the Channel and northwards from Italy, "Churchill then went over to the map of Europe, looking at it from the North, and describing the contour around to Greece, he said that the enemy would be like a bear out in the snow. The heat, bit by bit, would be taken out of his body till he has nothing left but a little warmth in his heart. . . . I asked him the direct question: 'Is the war likely to be over this year?' He said immediately and positively no—not the fighting, unless something psychological should bring it about. That the Germans, realizing this cannot last, might bring things to an end. . . .

"I said to him that I thought one of the greatest things he had done, if not the greatest in connection with the war, was the way in which he had kept off the time of the invasion over the past couple of years. He said he felt that way himself and hoped that I would express that view. So many people all said that Churchill was impetuous; also others thought matters should come sooner but he said we would have been all slaughtered if it had. It would have been terrible."

After the talk, Mackenzie King recorded his feelings "about Churchill's health and appearance. As he talked, I became increasingly impressed with his great weariness. I have observed that he was quite stooped as he walked out to be photographed and looked a little older, but as he stood facing me, I became convinced that his real spring has gone. His face took on a quite flabby appearance. His eyes seemed to get quite weary and to continuously fill with water. I was surprised at the extent of this. His nose seems to have enlarged a bit; to have lost its shape in a way, to be a little more contracted toward the centre. His hand seems steady enough, but I felt I was talking to a man who would find it hard just to have to do anything for very long, and whose judgment, except for the great background, knowledge, and experience he has, would hardly serve him too well. In fact, the impression I got in talking with him was much like what I have had in talking lately with Sir William Mulock whose mind, at times, is keen enough, but who, one feels, is thinking of other things while one is talking.

"He asked me about the situation politically in Canada, saying: when we were out [at the Quebec Conference], there had been some by-elections and things were down a bit, but you have rallied your men. I then replied that the Opposition had begun to take very unfair advantage of the Government but that I had stated we would remain in office until the war with Germany was over. . . . That I had to face a difficult situation with an election before me. Churchill said: this is no time for an election; you have had yours. I said: yes, four years ago. He said: you cannot be having an election all the time. I said I had until the spring of next year to run on. He then made it quite clear that he did not think it would be wise to have any election this year. . . . He then said something about addressing the two Houses of Parliament. I thanked him warmly for the invitation. He said to me: You can put it all over him (referring to [John] Bracken) in that. He then said he hoped I would say something about the Old Country people, meaning that they needed all the cheering up they could get. Asked me if I took any exception to his speaking of the Mother Country; did I like Sister Nations. He said he did not care for that phrase. I said to him neither did I, but to remember that in Canada, for example, Britain was not the Mother

Country of the French Canadians, who were over one-third of the population. Nor did it mean much to the younger generation. That, for example, my father would speak of the Mother Country, because his parents had been born in Scotland. That my mother would have thought in a similar way, but that the next and third generation did not think of Britain or Scotland as the Mother Country. Much less did those who had been following on.

"I then asked him what he meant by the British Commonwealth and Empire. He took quite a different view than Cranborne had taken in the morning. He said he liked to talk about the British Empire. I said I had always spoken of both alternately. He said he did the same. He thought its use would depend upon who was speaking. . . . In recent times, the Conservatives were talking of the Empire, and the Liberals, of a Commonwealth. He said to me that the Conferences would be Conferences of the British Empire and Commonwealth. That we need not be afraid of being outvoted by the dependencies. I said I had not been thinking on those lines at all." Mackenzie King noted parenthetically that "Hamar Greenwood said this morning that there is one thing about Churchill. He does not understand the Dominions as separate nations." Mackenzie King added "the more I think of the talk I had with him [Churchill] and his appearance, the more I feel that a great strain at any time might suddenly carry him off. He is no longer the man he was at Quebec. I should indeed be surprised if he is spared to preside at a Peace Conference. Even to see the day of Armistice. It gives me a feeling of deep sadness, compassion, and concern."

The meeting of Commonwealth Prime Ministers opened in the Cabinet room at 10 Downing Street at noon on May 1. At the meeting, in addition to Churchill, Mackenzie King, Curtin of Australia, Fraser of New Zealand, and Smuts of South Africa, there were six British Ministers: Attlee, Sir John Anderson, Eden, Cranborne, A. V. Alexander of the Admiralty, Brendan Bracken—twelve in all with the Secretary of the British Cabinet. "When all were seated, Churchill extended a welcome and spoke of the Conference being necessary on account of the war situation being at the critical stage it is, but even more because of our allies to whom, among others, it was desirable to have the solidarity of the Commonwealth made apparent." When Churchill concluded, Mackenzie King was the first to speak. He "expressed thanks for the welcome. . . . Mentioned that I brought greetings from my colleagues. . . . That, in lesser ways, we had, through our responsibilities, come to realize how great theirs were. Said that all he had expressed found an echo in our hearts: after the successful way in which we had all co-operated during five years of war, I did not think there would be any difficulty in our continuing to work equally well together in the course of the present meeting. I ended up by saying that, at this moment, the Prime Minister would find us all closer than ever at his side."

After the preliminaries, "Churchill began by stating that the first business this afternoon would be review of the war situation which he would give at length. That the Dominion Prime Ministers would follow on matters on which they might wish to speak. It was thought that this might even run beyond today and would be continued tomorrow morning.... He spoke of the war being a long one, and indicated till the end of the year but said that, as far as the war with Japan was concerned, we would begin to assist in the Pacific the moment ports had been secured on the coasts of Europe which would free some ships. That Britain had promised to do all she could against Japan and that that pledge would be carried out. Japan had suffered a good deal already. He, himself, doubted if the war with Japan would last long after Hitler was defeated. That was his own feeling, though he had nothing in the way of facts to prove it by.

"Fraser had wanted to take up the war on the Pacific immediately after the European matter. Churchill had to agree to have the agenda recast. Sir John Anderson seemed anxious to have questions of monetary standards and economic questions brought forward this week. Curtin had been over the agenda and was quite emphatic about certain changes being made. He brought up the question at once about the afternoon meeting and whom he might bring with him. Said he would like to have Blamey, his military adviser, and Shedden, Secretary of the War Committee of Australia. That he wanted these men as ears to keep in mind questions that would be raised. Matters that would have to be considered. Keep him, so to speak, on the rails. He would give the orders when the locomotive was to move. Churchill spoke at once about not wanting to have too many present. That we must keep the circle as small as possible. He looked to me to express a view. I said it would depend on the nature of the remarks that he would be making. If they were to be very confidential only to the Prime Ministers, that would be one thing, but if they went beyond, that would be another. For military matters alone, the Chiefs of Staff might be sufficient, but that [Norman] Robertson ... knew inside of all situations much better than Stuart, and I would feel I should like to have him present as well. I suggested both should come. They could leave the room or be brought in as might be necessary. Fraser was very strong on having both his men present. Smuts took the position we could not have many present;

that matters were much too secret. Finally Churchill said there would have to be two meetings—one at which he would leave out part of what he would have to say of a very confidential nature. He was certainly not going to tell anyone but the Prime Ministers the date of the invasion. Curtin mentioned that he had wished to bring a Minister with him. That that had been ruled out. He was more dependent than ever on two officials he had at his side."

Mackenzie King noted "one could not but feel how unfair the position was with matters of foreign policy and the rest of it carefully studied, as Churchill said, by a special Committee selected in advance on which none of the Dominions had been represented. That we should be there without any advisers. That there should be six British Ministers to the four other self-governing parts, all of them with their colleagues and officials close at hand. Also British Ministers were prepared to lead off in discussions, knowing what they were to say, but expecting Premiers to deal with matters in reply. Personally I felt the hopelessness of the situation; so far as really being able to battle on matters that might require discussion, my attitude would be to make clear I am not the Cabinet and that decisions on matters of contribution to the war would have to depend on decisions of our War Committee."

Mackenzie King added that he had spoken in the morning to Cranborne "about Churchill's desire for annual Conferences. Told him I would not myself be able to support the proposal as I felt certain when next year came, I would not be able to carry it out, with general elections on hand. There was also the possibility of a new Government and I doubted if any Prime Minister would wish to take on an Imperial Conference first thing. Cranborne . . . loathes the word 'machinery.' I explained to him that behind the machinery there was always the assumption of commitments. I let Cranborne understand that I felt consideration should be shown for my attitude."

The afternoon session was taken up with a very confidential statement on the war by Churchill. The only other speech referred to by Mackenzie King was one by Smuts who, he wrote, "spoke in a penetrating way of the situation as he saw it and which he regarded as being anything but something to be sure of. He feels the might of Germany and the preparations they have made, the territories they hold, etc., will mean a very heavy struggle. I am deeply impressed with Smuts and his vision and have come to like him very much in the closer contact I am at present having with him. He is, I think, worthy of the high place which the British give him."

The following day (May 2) the Prime Ministers met only in the morning and reviews of the military situation were given by the British Chiefs of Staff. Cranborne then gave a small luncheon for Mackenzie King, and after the luncheon, made a short speech welcoming his guest. In replying Mackenzie King "took advantage of the occasion to let those present see the reasons why I thought it would be unwise to attempt any kind of new machinery. To leave well enough alone, not to create some facade that would only raise suspicion as to commitments and also quite emphatically urging not to attempt anything in the nature of commitments for annual meetings of Prime Ministers in London. I could see this is what all of them are set on more than anything else. I pointed out how difficult it would have been for me to get away at different times without running great risks to our war effort; also the suspicion that there was in the minds of Members of the House with regard to the things being done in London. We could get the purposes fully accomplished without raising any question as to commitments. I spoke of what we have now in the form of continuing conferences of the Cabinets of the Commonwealth and of the importance of getting decisions made in the presence of all Ministers." He "stressed the advantage of meeting for special occasions, but said I would not be able to support an annual conference, knowing that next year, I would have an election in which event I could not undertake to come over. That if I were defeated, as I might well be, I am sure my successor would not want to begin by attending a Conference of Prime Ministers in London. I said how much better it would be to take advantage of occasions such as meeting for peace negotiations and for other purposes, having meetings more frequently but not trying too much in the way of rigidity, not to kill reality for appearances. I mentioned to them that Menzies was the classical example of the folly of Prime Ministers spending their time in London when they should be in their own country. Sir John Simon spoke about the abdication, and said that was an evidence of how well all parts of the Empire had reached agreement in their several capitals without having any conference. It was much to the point."

The proceedings on May 3 were largely concerned with the war in the Pacific. Mackenzie King took very little part in the discussion. He noted that "Curtin did not spare anyone's feelings in the way in which he spoke out. I confess I admired his straightforward direct statement. I equally admire Churchill's restraint in listening to the presentation as Curtin made it. . . . He stated emphatically that he wanted Australia to be on the highest level, when it came to reaching decisions on the peace. For that reason, he intended to maintain a certain military force."

When they were coming out of the meeting, Churchill stepped behind to have a word with Mackenzie King who thought Churchill "has felt throughout my sympathetic attitude toward him as questions arise. I told him I was truly amazed and delighted at the vigour which he was showing. When I saw him on Friday last, I was really concerned. I thought he looked tired out and was really very anxious about his health. I confess, however, being with him through this week, I felt sure that he had all the vigour he formerly possessed. That really I was delighted. I could see that even these few words seemed to cheer him up considerably. After I left the room, he came to the door and calling out 'Mackenzie' begged of me to come back. He said to me, you are coming down at the weekend, are you not? I told him how much I was looking forward to it. He then said to me: I hope you will be able to stay till the big event. I then mentioned to him the date at which I thought I should return on account of Parliament being in session. When I did, he expressed anew the hope that I would wait over beyond that time saying something to the effect that it would be something to be here for. I gave him no encouragement. Told him frankly that I was concerned about leaving Parliament so long. That the Opposition had begun to play politics for all they were worth, and I did not want matters to get out of hand too much before my return. I must hold decidedly and finally to this. I am sure there would be general expression of discontent if I remained away more than a month. It would be thought that I was deliberately keeping away from Parliament.... Remaining a week after the Conference for getting in contact with the troops and airmen is, I feel quite sure, all the time I can reasonably afford."

The meeting on May 4 began with a survey of foreign affairs by Anthony Eden. Mackenzie King noted that "both Fraser and Curtin, while criticizing in many directions, each concluded what they had to say by expressing their view that the British foreign policy had been sound. I felt it would be a mistake to let the meeting break up without a word or two. I said that I was glad to hear Fraser speak as he did of the soundness of the British policy and also Curtin, but I felt in considering the two conflicts which had to be watched at one and the same time, the war between nations and the fight between classes in different countries, that the Government had handled things—knowing the considerations of which they had to take account with the Allies—on very sound lines and wanted to associate myself with both Curtin and Fraser. I told them that in thus expressing myself, I was speaking on the part of Canada. I had in mind that this foreign policy had been reached as a result of consultation with ourselves and the other Dominions and that it made clear a common policy could be reached without any centralization here in London. The Tory press are seeking to make it appear that I am opposing common policy. I thought it well to let all present see just how I viewed the entire situation. That my view was quite the opposite with respect to the purpose all had at heart, and to make it clear the purpose had best been fulfilled by the methods adopted right along.

"Churchill, at the close, spoke quite eloquently and somewhat emotionally of the real aim of the British foreign policy which is to see that the world never again gets involved in war. The formation of some kind of international organization with force behind it which will ensure a durable peace. He said that unless such could be accomplished, he did not know what would happen to the world."

In the course of the morning Curtin asked Mackenzie King "what I thought of having someone put in the Foreign Office here from each of the Dominions to get more information. I told him that everything over here was on the ratio of 8 to 1. He would see that from the table we were sitting at. I later said to him I thought he would get more information by appointing his own Ministers to the different capitals, where they could gather their own opinions. They are beginning to see pretty clearly the dangers of having matters settled in London. I should perhaps add that I, myself, do not, by any means, share the view that is so predominant in our External Affairs office of emphasizing too emphatically an isolationist or autonomous position in intra-Imperial relations. I feel that Canada will greatly need strength alike of the British Commonwealth as a whole and of the United States in protecting her position. Of all countries, we are really the most vulnerable because of our extensive territory, resources and the like. There is no doubt the British people have shown disposition to defend their liberties as no others. The one thing we must seek to avoid is . . . centralization and to strengthen all we can the goodwill between all the parts and extend that policy to other nations of the world.

"On leaving the Cabinet Council, Eden thanked me very warmly for what I had said. Churchill called me back to have a word, calling me 'Mackenzie' as he does when we are not formally meeting. Said to me that I had not said much about our position in the discussions on the military situation, and also this morning had not had a chance to say much, and he hoped I would feel free to take any part and to arrange for conferences with others. I told him I was quite satisfied; that if there was anything I wished specially to stress, I would do so. He had said in the morning referring to economic discussions, that he had a war to look after and when they got into those subjects, he was going to get under the table. Before leaving, I said to him that when it came to the economic discussions, I would get under the table with him.

"I have intended to record my feelings about the British Ministers. They all seem to be much quieter and more subdued than when I was here last. Very intent on the questions before them. Churchill has greatly surprised me in his vitality this week. Eden looked distinctly tired at the end of his remarks this morning. He undoubtedly has lost strength. He has just been away for three weeks. The rest has done him good but I can see he is quite worried and anxious. A fine character, I think; most upright. Archie Sinclair also looks very tired. Yesterday he seemed to be almost lifeless in appearance but I recall he has always had an almost sallow look. Amery looks very wizened and like a man who had been much crushed. He has lost much of his assertiveness. Sir John Anderson and Oliver Lyttelton look well and strong. Bevin looks pretty heavy and worn. Alexander, much the same. Altogether as a Ministry, they seem to me to be working better than they were two years ago. Beaverbrook looks like a gnome."

The discussion on foreign affairs continued on May 5. Churchill asked Mackenzie King to open the discussion. He was followed by Smuts. When Mackenzie King talked with Smuts at the end of the morning meeting, "and said how similar our views were on many things, he [Smuts] said he thought the Prime Minister would be on the back of both of us in talking of 'Imperial Unity and damn nonsense of the kind.'" Mackenzie King noted with amused approval how Curtin and Fraser "strike out against any Tory attitude. In fact, Curtin used the word 'Tories' today as meaning that no progress could be made anywhere as long as they were around. He was stressing the point, and Fraser, too, that the only offset to Communism was to give the people the knowledge that they were getting their share of the world's plenty." He added that "Churchill wound up the discussion giving his own views in regard to the future. . . . He was quite eloquent and spoke, this morning, as a real Liberal. Began with our own Commonwealth and Empire keeping together in friendly co-operation, fitting ourselves into the larger framework of free nations, and above all, having the fraternal association with the United States perpetuated at all costs, and finally a world order which would compel nations to maintain order. There would not be disarmament. Each country would have to make its contribution. He looked for a United States of Europe which would preserve the culture of separate nations and which could make its contribution to the world. He thought it might be made so complete and secure that it might itself become a bar to Russian encroachment. It is clear he feels that Russia has barbaric manners, but does not himself believe or cannot bring himself to believe, that they will attempt aggression further. He does not think anything of China as a military power. Feels, too, that she is very corrupt, and that there will be internal trouble there between Communism and the Government. His speech in every way was admirable."

That session concluded the first week of the Prime Ministers' meetings. During the week Mackenzie King had been twice to Buckingham Palace. There had been a dinner for all the Prime Ministers on May 1 at which Mackenzie King sat between the Queen and Princess Elizabeth who was attending her first official dinner and whom he found "very natural, not in the least shy. Looked very pretty and very happy and graceful." He had a long talk with the Queen in the course of which they talked of the Royal visit of 1939 and "went over incidents of the trip, visit to Ottawa, visit through the West and Hyde Park. . . . I spoke of the help that I thought the visit of herself and the King had been in unifying the country just at the right moment. The Queen referred to the visit as the happiest time in their lives. She said it had done a lot for them. Toward the end of the dinner, she turned to me and said: Mr. King, we all have great confidence in you—repeated this remark once or twice. I said, at once, that it was the people who were doing everything of their own accord, and spoke particularly of the whole effort being a voluntary effort; of all the men that had come abroad having come voluntarily. The Queen said that is magnificent; what a wonderful record Canada has. It was clear that she was familiar with it all, and felt that it could not have been better than it was. . . . The conversation throughout was, in every way, as natural as any conversation could be between persons who had shared like experiences, and very happy, and were glad to reminisce about them.

"After the ladies withdrew, the King called me to come over to his side of the table and asked me to be seated to his right. . . . I found the King looking older, inclined to be rather excitable in expressing himself with reference to certain matters as, for example, his references to the loss of his brother in the plane accident." It was almost midnight before the King and Queen withdrew. In saying goodnight to Mackenzie King, the King said it had been an historic evening.

On May 3, Mackenzie King had a buffet luncheon alone with the King and Queen. They had let the servants go and had a "sort of picnic luncheon so that we can talk freely. She asked me if I remembered the luncheon at Hyde Park, on the Sunday, with the hot dogs. I spoke of the picnic luncheon up at Balmoral [in 1941]. ... I found the luncheon very pleasant. The King was exceedingly nice and friendly. The Queen could not possibly have been more so. There were many references to Canada and to the trip both in Canada and the United States, but we managed also to get on to a number of matters relating to the Conference, and questions being discussed there. I was able to emphasize to the King the importance of my being able to say that all the decisions reached, as far as Canada was concerned with respect to this war, had been reached in Canada itself as a result of Cabinet discussion. That nothing was either the result of pressure from Britain or the result of the surroundings here. I pointed out how suspicious many of the people were of anything that emanated from London. They seemed to see design in it all.

"I spoke of the continuing conference of Cabinets of the Commonwealth. Spoke of the conference for exchange of views as helpful, but not for the purposes of decision. Both the King and Queen showed a keen appreciation of what I had said, and said something to the effect they did not assume there would be any effort to press decisions here. I explained to them the position I might be in next year, should I have a general election. ...

"In speaking of the Conference, the Queen seemed to feel that too many were not wise, and the King asked how many Ministers had been over. Said he was quite sure that he had seen a considerable number, and spoke of having seen Ralston two or three times, and of his arthritis. He agreed that conferences on special subjects would be preferable to too many general conferences. I spoke of using other occasions, for example the making of the peace, etc., to bring Prime Ministers together. The King asked me pointedly if it was necessary for a Prime Minister to come every time. I told him I did not think it was. I also said I preferred it should be special Ministers for special subjects. I think I succeeded in making clear the value of Cabinet decisions made in respect of matters which come under their own sovereignty."

On Saturday, May 6, Mackenzie King motored down to Chequers to spend the weekend with the Churchills. "Churchill was extremely interesting in his conversation throughout the evening," he wrote at the end of the day. "He spoke eloquently of the spectacle of the British Empire. All parts rising up during the war, and asked how this could be accounted for. I said it was the British freedom and the British sense of justice. Churchill instantly said: 'Say that in your speech.' He spoke of the occasion being a very great one. On the eve of very great events of the times, adding that it would be on the day on which fighting will begin in Italy. He suggested to me to read over Smuts' address [to the Houses of the British Parliament on an earlier visit during the war]. Spoke of . . . the speech being heard all over the world. He then said to me before Sir Alan Brooke: 'We all look to you as the link with America. That fraternal association must be kept up.' He then turned to me personally, and as we were going out of the door, said: 'You, alone, could have done it. We look to you above all else to keep the two together. Canada is the interpreter.' He told me not to hesitate to speak for an hour."

On Sunday (May 7) "at lunch today and at dinner tonight, Churchill talked very freely on many matters. At luncheon, he sat at the side of the table with myself to his right. He spoke of plans for post-war organization. Of a Council composed of the four Great Powers. China thrown in to please the United States. They would have authority to see that action was taken to preserve the peace, and that action taken by means of force to which these Great Powers would be responsible and to which other countries would contribute according to their means. There would be a World Court before which nations could be brought. Also Regional Councils in Europe, Asia and America. In Asia, the Regional Council would be composed of the nations opposed to Japan. [The Council of] Europe would have a representative of the United States. He hoped to see a United States of Europe which would help to restore the culture of the smaller nations and would be a means of keeping Russia at bay. Russia would, of course, join, and he hoped Germany would within a year or two after the war. On the Regional Council in the Americas, Britain would hope that Canada would represent Britain. There would be a General Assembly on which the different nations would be represented."

Mackenzie King questioned two points: "First: whether he would make it plain that the four Great Powers were only taking the position they were because there had to be a place of beginning but that this did not signify . . . control by the Great Powers. His answer to that was: it was only a control for the maintenance of peace; also there would be plenty of chances for other Powers to make regulations at the Assembly, etc. The other point I took exception to was Canada representing Britain. I doubted whether we should undertake that role. I might have said there were no differences so unfortunate as family differences. That I felt Canada would not wish to take on that responsibility. Churchill mentioned that Britain, of course, would have representatives. She had her possessions in the West Indies and, of course, as such, would perhaps be entitled to be represented on the Regional Council of

America. All this, of course, is what I had heard first from the President, and later from Roosevelt and Churchill together at Quebec, discussed in tentative outline, Eden being present during part of the discussions."

Churchill "also talked about Preferences, the sentimental aspect, as he said, more important in a way than the economic and which hung like a loose girdle around the person of the Empire, so to speak. He clings to that vision of Empire very strongly. . . . In talking at the table, and before Sir Alan Brooke, he spoke of what a wonderful part Canada had taken. . . . He was much stirred up over speaking of these different matters in the talk with Brooke and myself. He then used these words: 'I am not one to believe that the war will be over in October or November, 1944, nor perhaps in November, 1945. It may last a long time.' Then Sir Alan Brooke agreed with this. He said: 'No, he did not believe it would be over by October or November.' Churchill then added: 'Maybe it will.' . . . Both he and Churchill agree that the Air Force is not sufficient. There has to be fighting on land. . . .

"Before saying goodnight, the last words Churchill said to me just before he left the room were: Have you got through your 'magnum opus' meaning, of course, the speech for Thursday afternoon. He had been exceedingly nice about this speech. I can see he is most anxious that it should be worthy of the occasion in every way. He has indicated to me what he has in mind saying by way of introduction, referring to our years of friendship; Canada's war effort. My part as a link with the United States and of bringing Canada into the war. His suggestion that I should read over Smuts' speech was meant to be helpful, of the kind of thing that would be desired, etc. He has really a very kindly gentle, fraternal—almost paternal nature." After returning to London Mackenzie King spent most of May 8 and whatever time he could find in the next two days on his speech.

On May 9 Churchill gave a dinner for the Prime Ministers at Downing Street. He turned to Mackenzie King "just before starting the dinner and asked whether I thought grace should be said. I waited to see what he might say first himself and he said I think it should. Whereupon he stood himself and quite reverently used the little blessing: 'For what we are about to receive we thank God.' I was very pleased to see him do this. I am coming more and more to the conclusion that at heart he has a deep religious feeling. I am certain that he looks on the British Empire and all connected with it as a great mission. Indeed, he said to Smuts that he was right in viewing it as a mystery and a mission. He feels that the mission is to help to save the world from what may become world deception. It is a vision of Empire that appeals both to his religious and romantic instinct.

"Before speaking himself, he asked me if I had any objection to his mentioning that my grandfather had been a rebel. Also, he wanted to say a word about Smuts having captured himself [Churchill] in Africa and something about Curtin being of Irish descent. He made a very short speech in a very light mood. It was all unexpected." Mackenzie King replied to Churchill. He felt afterwards he "should have begun by thanking him for the invitation and speaking of what it meant, but began on a sideline wishing one might have his facility of expression for the occasion. Did not at any time express thanks for the hospitality extended, nor did I refer to the pleasure of meeting the high officials which I should like to have done. At the end I brought in a reference to my other grandfather in replying to what he had said about Mackenzie. This should have been brought in at the beginning. I did refer to the relations of Canada with the United States and pointed out that I thought the British connection was stronger than ever as a result of the Americans not being in the war for two years and the pride we felt at having been with the British in defending freedom in arms as we did.... I really missed a real opportunity and I might have spoken with real facility."

He added that "Curtin and Fraser made more or less ordinary speeches, using old dogmas, etc. Smuts availed himself of the opportunity to make a really inspiring speech. It followed much along the line of what he had said of the Empire as a mission in his address before Members of the Houses of Parliament. After dinner I had a little talk with him and invited him to Canada. He raised the question of this not being a good year for the President [1944 being a Presidential election year] and I agreed with him in the end. What interested me particularly was the way in which he said that all this business of Empire unity, etc., was a thing of the past. That it did not belong to this particular time."

Next day (May 10) Mackenzie King worked on his speech for Parliament until it was time to go to the Guildhall where Curtin and Fraser received the Freedom of the City. At the Guildhall, when he turned to take his seat, "the first person I saw was Bennett. I said to him: 'Well, Bennett, how are you?' and put out my hand to shake hands with him. He shook hands and said: 'Very well, how are you?' or some such expression. But that was all. Not the slightest look of even normal recognition. His face struck me as that of a man who must be suffering a great deal in his own mind. Had a sort of cut-to-pieces appearance, much as I have seen him look when he has been very much overwrought in Parliament. He looks considerably older." At Churchill's luncheon after this ceremony Mackenzie King "recalled that today was the fourth anniversary of the formation of his Government and told him I would make an exception to my rule and take a little liquor in a glass to extend congratulations to him on the four years of leadership and my best wishes. This seemed to please Churchill very much." That afternoon and evening were spent in completing the revision of the speech.

Mackenzie King did, however, attend two important meetings with the other Prime Ministers during this week. The first was on May 9 when "Eden spoke on post-war settlement and Churchill put forward a paper which he had drafted. We had a very important discussion. Churchill stressed very strongly the desirability of a United States of Europe and Regional Councils in Asia and America. Eden put more emphasis on central organization and other regional councils evolving from them. I spoke out emphatically about the danger of beginning with Regional Councils as in all probability leading—certainly in the case of America—to the continent taking more or less an isolationist position, being concerned with its own affairs. To keep the world as united as possible, the emphasis must be on a central organization. I also spoke of the need of giving small nations recognition in some way, and not merely to Great Powers, and hinted at the desirability of Britain being represented in her own right at the Central Council, but not as representing the entire Commonwealth and Empire. All of this ran, of course, counter to Churchill's own wishes. I had previously mentioned to him privately that I did not think Canada should represent Britain on any Council in North America. That she should have her own representation."

The other meeting was on the morning of the day (May 11) he addressed the British Parliament. This session was devoted to world organization which involved the "important issue of whether representative on World Organization was to be of British Empire and Commonwealth as Churchill was anxious to have it, or Britain alone. I had myself to assert that the United Kingdom should be represented—be entitled to representation on the World Council of itself. I used the parallel of what was going on in the war. We had accepted the leadership of Churchill and Roosevelt but had been in consultation, etc. We would wish to have our own right of representation, if not as one of the big three or four, at least as one of the medium powers that would be brought into the World Organization in some relation which would recognize that power and responsibility went together and recognize our individual position.

"When all were assembled in the Council Chamber," Mackenzie King wrote, "it looked for a while as if no one would wish to say anything. Churchill rather hesitated to begin discussion. Eden did not wish to open up particularly. There seemed to be some doubt as to just what was to be discussed. Finally both Curtin and Fraser spoke of having prepared some written statements which would set out their respective positions on the memorandum regarding world organization, whereupon I at once chipped in and said I also had a statement. As someone had indicated I should begin the discussion, I started in and read the statement through from beginning to close. At the end of it, Churchill asked me if he could have the statement to be printed. He stated there were parts of it which ran counter to his views. What he is most concerned about is establishing a United States of Europe as a Regional Council. He has evidently brought in the Council of Asia and America to help balance what he has in mind. He spoke very eloquently of the necessity of Europe saving itself and not being a perpetual chaos; of trying to get Russia in with the rest of Europe, saying quite frankly that he did not want the polar bear coming from the white snows of the steppes of Russia to the white cliffs of Dover. That he greatly feared this possibility and the total destruction of Europe, unless, in some way, Russia could be brought into a European United States. He saw great difficulties but he spoke very deeply and earnestly of the appalling dangers in the position which will follow the war. He mentioned, among other things, not only the power and military genius of Russia but also their inventive genius. Said they had gone as far as the British in their inventions. I know what he had in mind, and if any developments continued on those lines, there would be nothing left but the most terrible of wars within another generation. He is anxious to have Germany in such a United States; though it might be terrible to say it, he would like this within five years.

"Curtin and Fraser each made their contributions, but what pleased me most of all was that Smuts followed immediately after what I had said and backed up what I had said as to the necessity of each part of the Commonwealth maintaining its own identity and being represented in its own right, the danger of anyone speaking with a single voice for the Empire and Commonwealth.

"It was the hardest battle of the Conference thus far because it required very straight and direct talking to and differing from Churchill on the things he feels most deeply about. The truth is, as he speaks of Communism, etc., being a religion to some people, the British Empire and Commonwealth is a religion to him. . . . I think Eden was very pleased with what I said. I think all of those who are liberal-minded in matters of trade were equally so. Churchill himself and die-hard Tories and others like Amery will be unmoved and disappointed. However, while Curtin did say a few words about the need of there being something like an Empire policy, on the whole, he and Fraser were with me, Fraser particularly so."

Mackenzie King's speech to the two Houses of Parliament was delivered that afternoon. He was escorted to the Chamber where he was to speak by Churchill. On the way, he spoke to Churchill about a despatch he had received from Lord Halifax "about how closely the Americans were watching the Conference, and what the despatch said about not speaking of preferences. Churchill at once said he hoped that I might say something of preferences or that, if I did not, certainly not to say anything against them. I told him that I, of course, would not touch on any specific subject of the kind, but that I thought what I had to say would be helpful in America as well as here, certainly in the light of the despatch from Halifax. He spoke again about the Empire. Hoped I would have something to say of it." At the entrance to the Robing Chamber they were met by the Lord Chancellor, the Speaker of the House of Commons, Attlee, and Cranborne. "The large hall was filled to capacity. Churchill opened the proceedings with a few exceptionally well chosen and extremely kind remarks. He went all out in his references to myself and my part in the war, saying that no other man . . . could have brought Canada so unitedly in the war. Also spoke of my twenty-five years of leadership of the party and eighteen years as Prime Minister of Canada. Referred to the magnificence of Canada's war effort and to maintaining the fraternal association of the United States and British Commonwealth and Empire.

"I was given a fine reception when I stepped forward to speak. There were very bright lights trained on the platform, but I did not find them too inconvenient. I took a long chance, however, in wearing for the first time the bifocal glasses which I bought a couple of years ago, but hesitated to use for the giddy feeling they gave me each time I put them on. However, I found them wholly satisfactory so far as reading the manuscript and seeing the audience were concerned. I did not attempt to speak extempore, but followed the manuscript in a straightforward way. I experienced no nervousness in speaking and felt that the vast audience was quite receptive, as indeed they were. The entire audience rose to its feet when I came forward and before I began to speak and gave me a fine ovation in a very dignified way. The address itself was interpolated with applause throughout; so far as I can recall, I had to run back once or twice because of applause but made one slip—said United States for United Nations which, however, I caught in time. I felt that what I had to say about better conditions, more abundant life for the people, was well received. I was particularly pleased that I had included reference to Australia, New Zealand, and South Africa. When I was through speaking, the applause lasted for a considerable time.

"When Churchill concluded his introduction, I shook him by the hand before going forward to begin the address. When I had concluded, he shook me by the hand. He then went forward and called on Sir John Simon, the Lord Chancellor, to move a vote of thanks which he did extemporaneously in words that were well chosen. He then called on the Speaker of the House to second the motion which the Speaker did in a few sentences. When the motion was put, Churchill called for the ayes and nays, and the entire room responded with ayes. I felt it was necessary to make just an acknowledgement of the vote of thanks, and did so in a word first to the Lord Chancellor and then to the Speaker of the Commons. It was just a word, and then referred to what Churchill had said and remarked that it touched my heart very deeply and that I believed it would touch the heart of Canada also, and thanked the Members of the Lords and Commons for the courtesy they had shown in being present in such numbers and the way they had responded to the vote. I added that the ayes were very pleasing to the leader of a Government. I noticed that Eden caught and enjoyed that remark. These few words were spoken quite extemporaneously and, indeed, had not been so much as thought of except while I was on my feet.

"The proceedings having thus concluded, Churchill began to walk with me down the aisle. Mrs. Churchill joined us and I walked with her.... Mrs. Churchill, Churchill and I then walked to his office through the different corridors. On the way, he said to me that the speech was very good, very good indeed. I felt, however, that it must have been a disappointment to him that I did not make some colourful reference to the Empire. In introducing me, Churchill went so far as to say he was sure in speaking, I would have a reference to Empire, etc. In fact, he has kept me literally at his side right along, over the weekend at Chequers, dinner the night after, luncheon at Downing Street the day after, and today, presiding. It required a lot of courage, if I say it myself, to hold firmly to the line I felt would be right, and not be influenced by . . . hospitality. General Smuts came out with us. He and Churchill are very close together. It is natural it should be so. Churchill mentioned to me that most of his old friends had gone. That Smuts was one who had been through the last war, and he could talk with him of the old associations. I know what that feeling is, with the changes that have taken place in my own Cabinet. Smuts came into the Prime Minister's office with us. . . . We sat and talked for a few minutes.

"On the way returning, I thanked Churchill very deeply for what he had said of me and of Canada. I told him that I felt it was due very much to his personal friendship. That I could not begin to express the gratitude I felt to him. He always comes back that he is just stating what is the truth. I believe it is true that no other, even in my own land, has ever spoken so wholeheartedly and in downright fashion of what I have tried to do in my public life. Coming from Churchill at this time, these words should have a far-reaching effect. Indeed, the honour done me at Westminster in asking me to speak before both Houses and the reception given by the Members, and Churchill's references might well be the means of winning the party an election in Canada. It will do so if our people really go about matters in the right way. However, it is not of the elections I am thinking, but of the winning of the war. That task is far from over as yet."

In his speech Mackenzie King had used a paragraph from a speech made by Churchill in 1907 which defined the British Empire. Later in the day, he reflected that "most of what I said today really ran counter to what Churchill himself has come to feel. He told me that he had forgotten the speech that I had quoted from, and said to let him know where it was. The thought suddenly came to me that, being taken from the speech Churchill made against preferences, it might seem to him, should he come to see the context, that it was like going into a man's house, accepting his hospitality and, as it were, helping to destroy the things that were most precious to him. As a matter of fact, had I known at the time that the quotation came from the speech that related to preferences, or had known how strongly he felt on preferences, I might have hesitated to use it altogether. I have not seen the context myself, was given only the text as it was. This made me feel a bit sad. I hope that nothing of the kind will be thought of by anyone, for nothing could have been further from my mind. I have been aiming only at the truth and the quotation I made was one which should help him with the whole of the United Nations at this time."

The next afternoon (May 12) Mackenzie King and Smuts went with Churchill by train for a visit to army manoeuvres and a dinner with General Eisenhower. After they were seated in the railway car, Churchill asked Mackenzie King if he "had seen the *Manchester Guardian* which, he said, contained a very full account of my speech. . . . He said to me that I had done him exceedingly well in what I had said. Sitting on the platform, he had not been able to hear what was being said. He spoke quite highly of the speech." At 8 o'clock both Churchill's and Eisenhower's trains were at Ascot so Eisenhower could dine with the Prime Ministers. The conversation went on until midnight. Mackenzie King "was very favourably impressed by Eisenhower. He is a fine manly type. Has a strong powerful hand. Lines very deep." After going back to his compartment Mackenzie King "made a few notes of significant remarks which, while very confidential at present, it seems well to have of record." The notes of this conversation are, in fact, not very interesting. Mackenzie King evidently felt this, for he added: "All this is imperfectly recorded from a few notes made at the time, just sufficient to bring back to one's memory enough of the evening to recall some of its outstanding features. I would have given very much had I been sufficiently rested and free of restraint to have been able to remember all that took place. I should not have missed for anything meeting General Eisenhower. Meeting him has given me a degree of confidence greater than any I otherwise would have had. Churchill has indeed been right in his keeping off the invasion as long as possible. . . . The night's conversation left on my mind the impression that the war might well run on for a considerable time into next year. Both Eisenhower and Churchill felt that might be the case. Just as I recall Churchill and Sir Alan Brooke also thought that this might be so. I am afraid that the loss of life once the invasion begins will be staggering, without the help of Providence, favouring wind and tide, and initial success. The war even now might not be won, but the result a stalemate after five more years of war. Something, however, deep down in one's heart and being seems to cause me to feel that before the month of November is over, there may again be an armistice between Germany and the forces which have opposed her efforts at domination."

The following morning, the train took the party to Portsmouth and they went by boat from Portsmouth to Southampton to see the invasion fleet. During the course of their conversations, Mackenzie King told Churchill he "did not believe there would have been a war if the League of Nations had never existed. The nations would have prepared their alliance and not depended upon a mere facade with the United States out and all looking to England. He [Churchill] defended the League stoutly. He claimed that if action had been taken promptly when Hitler went to invade the Ruhr things would never have got any further. When Germany was permitted to renew conscription that was the evil moment. I also said to him that I thought if there had been no National Government [in Great Britain] before the war there would have been no war. It caused the parties to neutralize their efforts. They were neither hot nor cold. He said: 'I agree with you entirely on that' and went on to point out the mistakes that had been made."

The meeting of Commonwealth Prime Ministers was by this time over except for the preparation of the final communiqué. On Monday, May 15, Mackenzie King was shown "the draft of the proposed statement to be signed by the Prime Ministers today." The draft had been prepared by the Secretary to the British Cabinet, Sir Edward Bridges. Norman Robertson had already seen it on the previous Saturday and mentioned it then to Mackenzie King, who "at once asked if a single policy had been set out and Robertson replied that was the one point he, himself, had caught and said to Bridges: better change that to policies. I said that was the one thing we would have to stand firmly for. Bridges, he said, was making the change in the draft he was sending Churchill. In the communication received this morning, I suggested a change to make—'we' which referred to the Prime Ministers in the first instance, to be changed to 'our countries.' I also pointed out that there was no single clause which expressed our gratitude direct to our own fighting forces who were giving their lives to preserve our liberties, and I suggested a separate paragraph which would express our gratitude to them. . . . I also pointed out that the draft contained no specific mention of China though it referred to the United States and Russian forces. I suggested including the phrase 'long resistance of China.' Robertson subsequently 'phoned the suggested changes to Bridges who thought all of them were helpful. I also suggested we should have originals signed, so that each Prime Minister would be provided with a separate copy signed by the others."

In the afternoon at Downing Street, the meeting began at once to consider the draft communiqué. "Brendan Bracken opened up by saying that he thought the statement was altogether too lukewarm. That it needed to have some punch or something of the kind. That it was not positive enough. Altogether too general, vague. Immediately Fraser chimed in the same way. He said he thought it ought to have much more direct statement. Curtin, too, chimed in by saying it needed to tell the world more what we were doing. One of the other British Ministers spoke of Germany's effort to have it appear that we were divided and the necessity of putting into it some things, in an emphatic way, to make clear how much we meant business—not those words, but something to that effect. Attlee was presiding, having said that the Prime Minister was kept away on account of some urgent matters connected with operations. . . . Attlee had asked me what I thought of the statement and I had said that I was pleased with it. It was after this that Bracken began opening up as he did. . . . I then pointed out there were no references there to our own armed forces. No word of what we owed to them. Suggested a paragraph. Outlined the one I had suggested in the morning to Robertson expressing our gratitude for their preserving our liberties by their lives. . . . I also pointed out there was no mention of China. Curtin said he did not think China needed any mention. They were not doing much. Someone else made a somewhat slighting reference. I said that perhaps they would recall that the Prime Minister in one of his broadcasts had left out any reference to China and the American Press generally had raised considerable comment. I said I thought if they did not want to revive that feeling, they might bring in something about the long resistance of China. After all, China had been in this war for seven years. It was then, I think, pretty well agreed that reference would come in at a spot a little further down.

"The real discussion took place when we came to the line: 'We were all agreed on plans for the future of the war with Germany and Japan.' I suggested that the clause should be omitted. Curtin and some of the others took exception, and Bevin tried some alternatives. Bracken again spoke very strongly. When someone asked why it should be omitted, I said: 'Because it was not a fact.' Finally I said it had been stated at the table that the British Government itself had not worked out its plans in regard to Japan. That none of us had discussed the future plans. They were not settled at all. Curtin began to speak at length saying that he thought we had worked them out, and I asked him to give me the outline of what they were. In doing that, he used the expression after running over the preliminary matter, 'the British Government is to consider what it is going to do.' I took these words down in pencil and kept them so as to have that record. This was part of his argument that we were all agreed on plans.

When he had finished, I said to him he had spoken of what the British Government were to do, Australia and others but, in all that he had said, he had made no mention of Canada. I assumed they would wish Canada to take some part in the war against Japan, and certainly our plans were not settled at all. What our plans would be, would depend on how the war developed. I said I might as well give an instance at once, that we had yet to decide whether our Air Force would act in co-operation with the British Air Force, with some other parts of the Commonwealth, or whether it would act with some of the American squadrons. I said we were co-operating together on the sea in the Pacific. Our men had been fighting with the Americans in Alaska and along the Pacific Coast, and their airmen protecting parts of our coast. It might be thought wise in the strategy of war for us to continue in that way, when attacking Japan. I also said our armed forces had been co-operating with the Americans in the attack on Kiska. We had all combined together there. I assumed we had to consider this aspect in the war against Japan. Then the discussion touched on the point that we were perhaps attaching too much attention to war plans. I agreed to the suggestion that 'general plans' might be substituted, as being what we were agreed on, but insisted that the word 'all' before *plans* should be struck out.

"Even keener debate came up when the paragraph was reached which spoke of our different policies—of agreement on foreign policies. Eden himself sought to substitute the word 'policy' for 'policies.' I waited to see what would develop. Australia and New Zealand agreed. Attlee said 'we are all agreed.' I immediately said: 'No. This is rushing the pace a little too rapidly.' I would not agree to the use of the words 'one policy.' In our discussions, it was settled that our policies would converge. There was no agreement about there being one foreign policy. I took exception to that, saying that was not true. We were not agreed on all aspects. That foreign policy was inexorably linked with international trade policies, commercial policies. The Prime Minister had told us himself that the Members of the British Cabinet were divided on commercial policy. How could we say we were all agreed on all aspects of foreign policy; as a matter of fact, we were not agreed on that aspect of international relations. I spoke pretty emphatically and made it clear I was holding to my ground. The matter then was not pressed further. . . .

"Finally Fraser and Curtin thought the draft could be sent to the Prime Minister who would look at the suggestions that had been made and work out a real rousing declaration. Having received the original draft from the Prime Minister this morning, I took no exception to that. . . . It was well I was present and spoke out pretty plainly. Every effort was made, despite all that has been said thus far, and the Canadian attitude made so plain. Had I not spoken as I did, we would have been completely crowded out of our true position."

The meeting then turned to a discussion of Imperial defence cooperation after the war. Cranborne "read a long paper putting forth different suggestions as to policies and so forth, piling one on top of the other, and among other things, asking for . . . an Imperial Joint Board for Defence. Everything that they had been trying for years was jammed into this statement. When Cranborne had completed, Attlee asked me what I had to say. I replied that that statement would be an interesting one for the Cabinets of the different Governments to consider. That I would be pleased to see that the different suggestions made were considered. Frankly I would not undertake to express opinion on any one or give any undertaking respecting it. I went on to say that I thought we had better wait until the present war was over and we saw how it resulted before we started to discuss new methods of organization.

I ended up by saying that I did not think we should have been expected to discuss this matter at this time. It was plain from my attitude, and what I said, that it was a bit of underhand work. It really amounted to high pressure of the worst kind in trying to shove this kind of thing through, at the last moment . . . after we had come to an agreement on a statement which covered the whole proceedings. Curtin then presented a lengthy statement which we were supposed to discuss. I said I would be pleased to regard it in the same light as the statement in regard to world security, and would have to take it up with my colleagues. . . .

"I then spoke very plainly and said everyone should try to understand what my attitude was. That I did not regard myself as the entire Cabinet. I was but one member of the Cabinet, and I felt that my colleagues were entitled to have their views and opinions known and expressed in a matter that bound us all. That I could not say anything which would be worth anything without making a commitment, and a commitment which would involve expenditures of public money. That I could not begin to speak without approval of the Government, and I certainly would not bind my colleagues to anything that would involve commitments. I said that such success as I had had with Governments and with my Parliament, was the result of allowing all my colleagues their fair share of consideration of policy; also we had our own Chiefs of Staff and military advisers, and I felt their loyalty would be made stronger than it was, if that was possible, by letting it be known they were being consulted before any commitments were being made. I don't think there could be plainer speaking but I found that it was necessary and it had to be done.

"When I was through, I said to myself, I have fought my last battle at this Conference, meaning not perhaps the last battle of all, but the last of this particular Conference, and had held my ground throughout. I was happier than ever that I had been so emphatic when I spoke and that I did not hesitate to put in my speech at the Lords what I said about Cabinets deciding things in their own countries." After dinner, in dictating his record of the day's proceedings, Mackenzie King added: "The more I think of the high pressure methods that have been used, the more indignant I feel. It makes me tremble to think of what Canada might be let in for if a different type of person were in office. Where would we have been had Bennett been in office at this time? What annoys me is the social devices and other attentions paid with a view to getting some things done, to influence one's mind even against one's better judgment. I think I have gone through this battle without wavering."

A final plenary session of the Prime Ministers' meeting was held on May 16. Mackenzie King was thoroughly dissatisfied with what had been prepared by his staff for him to say on that occasion. He began to revise the statement late in the morning and noted that he had "to rush off at five to twelve without having had time to revise what had been finally dictated." Churchill presided at this meeting where "the first matter taken up was the draft declaration. It was subjected to discussion in which again I had to hold my ground. . . . Unless I did not catch something that was done in revision, the declaration is all right. . . . Churchill suggested that the declaration should be signed on behalf of the Governments of the different countries. I had to say before the others that I could not agree to that as the Governments had not received a copy and knew nothing of the contents. That I thought my colleagues would want to know what they would be responsible for. Churchill said something about 'these matters which keep cropping up'; but when he saw how the declaration had been printed and that it only called for signatures of Prime Ministers, he was quite satisfied. We had to wait a short time while the corrections were being made on the document which we all signed later. Before the signatures, there followed a number of speeches.

Churchill spoke feelingly, briefly and very well. Had I not been completely tired out and worried, I could have followed him in reply without reading. As it was, I found myself at the end of the first sentence unable to think of what he had said and what I naturally would have said in reply. So I resorted, at once, to what was dictated. . . . I felt, in what I was reading, I was not doing justice to the occasion which humbled me very much in the presence of others, so much so I almost lost my voice. Later when I was asked to sign one or two photographs for the Government I found in the first signature that I had to stop in the middle of my name and made a very shaky signature. Curtin followed me without any notes and made a really excellent speech and impression. Fraser read what he had to say which was better in substance than what I said, but not delivered as effectively. Smuts made, as usual, a very fine speech in conclusion. When the speeches had concluded all excepting the Prime Ministers withdrew, and we remained to sign the document. I heard Churchill congratulating Curtin very warmly on his speech."

Immediately after the meeting broke up Mackenzie King went to King's Cross Station to take Churchill's train, which had been lent to him, to Goldsborough to visit the Canadian Bomber Group. He was very depressed on the journey and noted in his diary that he "worried all afternoon, feeling that when the speeches are published, both in Canada and elsewhere, particularly in England, they will reveal that I have been less cordial and gracious than the others. What, up to yesterday, would have left the impression that I had perhaps contributed more than the other Prime Ministers to the shaping of the Conference proceedings, will now, in large part, be undone, and Government circles will be informed that Smuts and Curtin have been outstanding at this Conference in their presentation, contribution, and attitude. Fraser and I will be put down in that or the reverse order. While I care little, so far as I personally am concerned, I should like the last impression, both on my mind and on the mind of others, to have been a good one." In actual fact, no one paid any attention to these speeches.

The day was wet with heavy rain so no bombers were taking off that night, but Mackenzie King was interested in what he saw and particularly pleased by the quality of the officers and men. "I liked both [Air Vice Marshal C. M.] McEwen and [Air Commodore C. R.] Slemon very much," he wrote. "Both of them [the senior officers of the Canadian Bomber Group] are exceptional men. Indeed, all the officers strike me as being exceptionally fine types, a great many Saskatchewan men among them."

The following day Mackenzie King visited the Canadian Army and he was greatly impressed by what he saw during the afternoon of May 17. He "had interesting talks with Crerar during the day. Among other things he said to me that if he were killed he thought [General Guy] Simonds should succeed him. To keep this in mind confidentially. That Simonds was a very good soldier, though he might not be the best man for post-war planning. He, Crerar himself, thought it was important we should make known at an early date our post-war policy regarding the Army. He himself hopes we will keep compulsory training to keep men in proper shape as a national means of keeping to a standard of manhood. He does not think that the Army will be much needed against Japan. Indeed he seemed to attach little or no importance to sending any of the Army there unless it were simply as a token force. I spoke to him about conscription, pointing out how the country had been kept together. He told me that he thought our policy had worked out well. What alone was causing him anxiety was the men that would be required for the three French Canadian regiments in case there were great numbers lost; that they, at all costs, must be kept up to strength. . . . I gathered from what he said there would not be any likelihood of a call. They would get along without having to have reinforcements under compulsion."

During the day Mackenzie King was immensely pleased at the appearance of the Canadian flags [the red ensign with the Canadian coat-of-arms]. They looked very well and Crerar commented on it being the way to settle the flag problem. We had apparently sent them a lot of new flags, which was a suggestion I made. Crerar believes the war will be over this year. He told me quietly that he felt it was a pity that the Americans had forced so strongly the landing by the crossing of the Channel rather than by proceeding from the southern route north." During the day Mackenzie King "felt deeply moved on one or two occasions. Once when I thought of my grandparents, father and mother, as these troops were marching by and I was standing in the heart of Britain taking their salute, but particularly as I thought of these men about to enter on the greatest engagement in the world's history." He added that "during the day I asked both Crerar and Simonds if there was anything we could do that was not being done for the men. They could think of nothing. Crerar was quite strong in his statement. That much of the present plan was based on experience derived from Dieppe."

The following day (May 18) Mackenzie King drove to General Montgomery's headquarters for lunch. Montgomery, he wrote, "greeted me very cordially with a happy laugh. He asked me if I remembered our meeting at Dover, and then as we were about to go into his working room, he suddenly turned back and said: 'Our photographers here must have a picture of you and me. We will have to go and stand in front of them.' After a few pictures had been taken we then went on into his room which was a little larger than my sunroom at the farm at Kingsmere. His chair was near a window and I was between the window and an open fireplace. An armchair was near the fireplace in which he asked me to be seated. The light was coming so strongly through the window that I could not see his face. My eyes being very tired I put on my glasses. He asked me if I found the light too strong. I told him it was all right, but I could see this arrangement was evidently planned to give him an advantage in talking with others.

"He began by speaking of the Canadian Army. How proud he was of our men and what splendid men they were and how eager. He mentioned that in Italy (or Sicily) they had worn shorts. The Americans had worn long trousers. He said our men were terribly burned with the heat and nipped with the flies on their bare legs and at the end of two days were quite exhausted. They had gone at things so hard. He had to pull them out at the end of two days on this account. He seemed to infer that long trousers would have been better for warfare in that particular locality at that time.

"Montgomery spoke well of Crerar. He said it would have been better if he could have had a little more battle experience. That there were some things he had to keep advising him on. He then spoke of Simonds as being a first class officer, a little headstrong perhaps, but very quick and able. He said if it became necessary to have anyone succeed Crerar he would strongly recommend Simonds. Crerar had said the same thing the day before.

"Montgomery then said there are just two things that I keep before me and before the men at all times. That is to win battles and save lives. From that he went on to say that he hoped that so-called national considerations would not be allowed to override military considerations. In other words, that he should not be obliged to govern his actions because of political necessity where his judgment indicated that there were military reasons which made that inadvisable. He said, more or less directly, that Crerar had kept asserting there were national reasons why such and such a thing should be done. He had reference to keeping all the Canadian formations together in the fighting, and, at all times, having Canadians commanded by Canadian officers as against British officers. He said some of the officers had not had the experience that was needed for commanding, particularly in the initial assault. That it was dangerous to have lives of men entrusted to those who had not had the needed experience.

"I said to him that he must understand I was a civilian and knew nothing of military affairs and tactics and the like, but as the head of the Government, I had from the beginning of the war insisted that no political considerations of any kind should be permitted to override a military consideration. Other things being equal, I felt that so-called national considerations should, of course, be taken account of at all times, but should not be allowed to override military considerations where the latter were of real importance. That our men, naturally, would wish to fight together and might fight better together than under others. That they like their own officers, etc. Montgomery said there might, however, be occasions on the battlefield where it might be necessary to have the line formed of different groups, and emergency in the field might lead to separation and amalgamation, all of which had to be done very quickly. He said he felt the military rule must govern there. He said: 'I hope you will back me up there.' I said: ' I will give you the assurance that the Government of Canada will not put any pressure on you for political reasons, or ask that any such pressure be placed upon you where there are military considerations involved.' " . . . My own feeling is that Montgomery's view is the one which is sound in actual battle. I pointed out to Montgomery that, of course, Canada itself would hope that her own men could, as largely as possible, be brought together and kept together, and he said he quite understood this and would watch that end. Montgomery spoke of his liking for the Canadians. He said he had talked this all over with Colonel Ralston, for whom he had a real affection and very high regard. He wanted me to give his warmest remembrances to him. . . .

"He was very confident about the winning of the war. I asked him directly about what he felt about the actual landing of the troops, establishing a bridgehead and holding it. He said he had not the least doubt that this could be done and would be done successfully, but he said there would be a great slaughter the first couple of weeks. We must not look for anything decisive for a period of less than three weeks. By that time we shall have established ourselves and shall be pressing on. There will be need to get great masses of supplies and equipment onto the Continent before we try to make any onward progress. Then suddenly he stopped and said . . . I don't want anyone else around at that time. I don't want Mr. Churchill to be anywhere near, meaning that he did not want anyone to interfere with him. . . . Montgomery firmly believes that the war would be over by the month of November. I told him I had said on the last Armistice Day that I thought it would be another year from that date before the war would come to a close. He did not himself once indicate that the war would last longer than this year. He stressed how formidable the Germans were as fighters. Much tougher fighters than others believed. As he kept talking he was smiling all the time. He has a manner of a mystic who sees into the future quite clearly. He keeps smiling at what he sees as likely to take place and is sustained by a vision which is beyond the immediate perils and dangers. . . .

"After luncheon Montgomery took me back to his room and spoke to me about McNaughton. He said that he had noticed that his, Montgomery's, name had been brought into discussion in Canada. He spoke nicely of McNaughton, but said it was clear that while he was good as an engineer and for organizing purposes, he was not the man to command troops in the field. I said to Montgomery he must not pay any attention to what had been said in the press. There were always people seeking to make trouble, and it was unfortunate that the press got after McNaughton at the time of his arrival, that he was caught unawares. I told him of the difficulty I had had in preventing the correspondence being made public. . . . He seemed anxious that his own actions should not have been misunderstood. I told him I thought there had been some feeling about McNaughton not having been allowed to go to the front in Italy. He made no apology for that, saying that where the men were fighting there could be only one direction, or something of the kind.

"He showed me a little book in which different persons had written on three different occasions, each related to a significant part of the war. . . . He then asked me if I would write something. I inserted words to the effect that Canada was pleased that her men were entrusted to his care, and that the country had entire confidence in him. He then said he would like to come out to Canada when the war was over. I told him he must do so and he would receive a marvellous welcome but must plan to go from coast to coast." Mackenzie King added that "the impression left on my mind was a wholly satisfactory one. I found him very much a man after my own heart. A man in whom I would have complete confidence. I did not see about him any evidences of the showman of which I have heard so much from time to time. He seemed to me to have that almost boyish light-heartedness of manner which was evidence of a free and kind nature, and of one who is sure of himself and whose convictions are founded in a sound belief."

During this last week in London, Mackenzie King spent an evening (May 15) with his old friend, Violet Markham, who "expressed strongly the view that I would be wise not to continue in public life after the war but rather to become the elder statesman who would be called in for purposes of counsel. She spoke of new forces that were moving in the world, but more particularly of the ingratitude of peoples invariably shown after a war. If one were to remain in public life, all that one had done during the war would be forgotten, and one would be saddled with endless abuse. Her reading of history showed that it was invariably so. I told her I had no desire to remain in public life any longer. Indeed, if I could get out after my return to Canada, I would. She said, no—one should stay on until the war is over, if one could avoid an election and all that business. I said, even if I won an election, I would drop out immediately after. If I did not win, I would have an honourable exit." He added: "Violet Markham thought I should write my life. . . . We have been friends for forty years. She said she remembers distinctly Lord Grey bringing her across a small drawing-room to introduce me to her, saying on the way: I want to introduce you to a young man who some day will be Prime Minister of Canada."

When he returned from the visit to the Canadian Army on May 17, Mackenzie King went to Buckingham Palace to say good-bye to the King. He reported that they "sat facing each other at the side of the fireplace. The conversation began by references to the Conference which the King said he thought had gone well and said that Churchill was much pleased with it. From the way the King spoke I could see that Churchill had been telling him to hold out for preferences. Also that he was strongly for having mixed forces in the air. He said that he understood nothing had come of the 'Secretariat.' I spoke to him about the Conference of Cabinets as a better means of proceeding. He congratulated me on my speech to the Houses of Parliament. . . . He told me he had luncheon with Churchill once a week. Sometimes he met him along with the Chiefs of Staff. Other times with members of the War Committee of the Cabinet. I asked him if his presence caused the men to discuss matters less freely. He said not at all. They spoke quite frankly back and forth. He found it very helpful.

"He asked me how his uncle was getting along. I spoke of being exceedingly pleased with Lord Athlone. That he was so considerate, etc. He asked me how often I saw him. I said sometimes quite a little period went by. Sometimes, some weeks would go by—other times I would see him more frequently. It was then that he spoke about seeing Churchill once a week. I spoke of Princess Alice. He said she was always very lively and helpful. He asked me if I had anyone in mind for Governor-General. I told him I thought it would be best to have everything left until after the war." The King said "he thought if it were convenient to have the Athlones stay until after the war it would be helpful, as no one could get either home or servants in England at the present time.

"He spoke of the constant pressure of work that there was and, when I was leaving, I said something to the effect how greatly he was helping to keep all parts together. He said each of us had to do the best he could, and he was trying to do his best. Before I left he asked if I would sign a birthday book which he had given to Princess Elizabeth. He showed me where to sign, which was immediately below Churchill's name. It had been signed by Churchill today. He was quite like his father in his manner of talking at times. Still finds it a little difficult to use certain words but seems to overcome that difficulty amazingly. His manner changes considerably. At times he finds it difficult to speak. At other times he works himself up into a very happy mood. Referred to the strain there had been through bombing for a little while. Says that he and the Queen sleep in a shelter each night, partly because of the noise. He pointed out where the different corners of the Palace had been bombed. Extended good wishes. As I left I asked him to convey my greetings to the Queen and to say good-bye to her. I thanked him for all the kindness shown myself and the members of the party during our stay here."

On May 19 Mackenzie King went to Downing Street to say good-bye to Churchill. "When I went in," he wrote, "Churchill was seated alone with his back to the fire. He asked me to sit beside him. He mentioned that he would be leaving the city in the afternoon to see some of the troops and might not get a chance to see me again before I left. He began by saying he wished to thank me again for the help that I had given—the way I had helped things along. He thought the Conference had been quite successful." They had some talk of the date of the invasion and "Churchill said that none of us knew definitely. Everything depended on wind, tide and the like. No one, not even himself could say the time, which I said was quite correct. . . . I then said to him that I was not anxious to know any exact time, but that, with the numbers of men that we had and the part we were taking, I would be glad if he would let me know in a general way so that I might have matters in my mind. He then gave me enough to satisfy me, but he said he hoped I would not find it necessary even to tell Ralston. I said I would not. He then said 'I would be able to send you more particular word as we get along.' "

Churchill read Mackenzie King "a letter which had come to him from Eisenhower in which Eisenhower had asked Mr. Churchill to say to me he hoped it would not be necessary for an announcement to be made as to the time of the Canadians going into action. That it was very desirable the enemy should not find it out. That in our own interests and the interests of the campaign the enemy should have to find out for himself what forces were being used. . . . It was desirable, for the first part of the assault, to have reference made only to Allied forces. He suggested that I might take that position in answering any questions, or in explaining the situation, and say that we did not propose to let the enemy know anything about where our forces were, until the discovery was made by the enemy himself. In other words we would not be telling him where they were, whether they would come in one place or another. . . .

"He then spoke about the President saying that he and Roosevelt might wish to have another talk together, depending on whether the President's health would permit his moving about. Asked me if the Citadel would be available should they wish to use it. I said certainly, to count on that at any time. That anything we could do in any way we would be glad to arrange."

The rest of the day and Saturday morning were spent in farewells. On Saturday afternoon (May 20) Mackenzie King and his party left London and flew home by Prestwick, the Azores, and Newfoundland. It was ten o'clock on Sunday evening, May 21, when Mackenzie King caught sight of the lights of Ottawa. When the aircraft landed at Rockcliffe, Mackenzie King noted: "To my amazement I found the airport filled with people. Ralston had rounded up Members of the Government and Members of Parliament. The Mayor and others were also there. They gave me a great cheer as I came to the door of the 'plane. I shook hands first with Ralston and then with Crerar and then when I stepped down the little ladder I met the Members of the Government one after the other and the Members of Parliament. . . . In shaking hands one stood under a glare of light. Then came the unexpected obligation of making an address over the microphone. I felt very hesitant at first, but having had a few thoughts in my mind I was able to express them better than I had believed might be possible. At the end of the welcome Ralston and I drove back together."

At that moment Mackenzie King had reached the very peak of his career. The great problems of the war had been met; preparations for the post-war period were well in hand; and there seemed to be smooth sailing ahead.

Appendix

THE MACKENZIE KING MINISTRY
SEPTEMBER 1, 1939–MAY 31, 1944

SEPTEMBER 1, 1939

Prime Minister, President of the Privy Council and Secretary of State for External Affairs	W. L. Mackenzie King
Leader of the Government in the Senate	Raoul Dandurand
Minister of Mines and Resources	T. A. Crerar
Minister of Justice	Ernest Lapointe
Minister of Public Works	P. J. Arthur Cardin
Minister of Finance	Charles A. Dunning
Minister of Trade and Commerce	W. D. Euler
Minister of National Defence	Ian A. Mackenzie
Minister of Pensions and National Health	Charles G. Power
Minister of National Revenue	J. L. Ilsley
Minister of Fisheries	J. E. Michaud
Minister of Labour	Norman McL. Rogers
Minister of Transport	C. D. Howe
Minister of Agriculture	James G. Gardiner
Postmaster General	Norman A. McLarty
Secretary of State of Canada	Ernest Lapointe *Acting Minister*
Minister without Portfolio	James A. MacKinnon

CHANGES

Sept. 6, 1939	J. L. Ralston succeeded C. A. Dunning in *Finance*
Sept. 19, 1939	Norman McL. Rogers succeeded Ian A. Mackenzie in *National Defence*
	Ian A. Mackenzie succeeded C. G. Power in *Pensions and National Health*
	C. G. Power succeeded Norman A. McLarty as *Postmaster General*
	Norman A. McLarty succeeded Norman McL. Rogers in *Labour*

Appendix

April 9, 1940	C. D. Howe became Minister of *Munitions and Supply*, remaining also in *Transport* until July 8, 1940
May 9, 1940	James A. MacKinnon succeeded W. D. Euler in *Trade and Commerce*
May 10, 1940	Pierre F. Casgrain became *Secretary of State*
May 23, 1940	C. G. Power became Minister of *National Defence for Air*
June 10, 1940	Norman McL. Rogers was killed in an air crash; C. G. Power became Acting Minister of National Defence on June 11, 1940
July 5, 1940	J. L. Ralston became Minister of *National Defence*
July 8, 1940	J. L. Ilsley succeeded J. L. Ralston in *Finance*
	Colin Gibson succeeded J. L. Ilsley in *National Revenue*
	W. P. Mulock appointed *Postmaster General*
	P. J. A. Cardin succeeded C. D. Howe in *Transport*
July 12, 1940	C. G. Power became Associate Minister of *National Defence* in addition to being Minister for Air
	Angus L. Macdonald became Minister of *National Defence for Naval Services*
	James G. Gardiner became Minister of *National War Services* as well as of *Agriculture*
June 11, 1941	J. T. Thorson succeeded J. G. Gardiner in *National War Services*
Dec. 10, 1941	Louis S. St. Laurent became Minister of *Justice*, following the death of Ernest Lapointe
Dec. 15, 1941	Humphrey Mitchell succeeded Norman McLarty in *Labour*
	Norman McLarty succeeded Pierre Casgrain (who was appointed to the Bench) as *Secretary of State*
March 11, 1942	Raoul Dandurand died
May 12, 1942	Following the resignation of P. J. A. Cardin, C. D. Howe became Acting Minister of *Transport*
May 13, 1942	J. E. Michaud became Acting Minister of *Public Works*
May 26, 1942	J. H. King became Minister without Portfolio as *Government Leader in the Senate*
Oct. 6, 1942	Alphonse Fournier appointed Minister of *Public Works*
	J. E. Michaud appointed Minister of *Transport*
	Ernest Bertrand succeeded J. E. Michaud in *Fisheries*
	L. R. LaFlèche succeeded J. T. Thorson (who was appointed President of the Exchequer Court) in *National War Services*

Index

ABBOTT, Douglas C.: speech in House on finance (1940), 169; possible Cabinet post, 223, 452; on Plebiscite, 362
Abdication, Dominions and, 669
Aberhart, William, 160, 161
Advisory Economic Committee, and McTague Report, 590
Aid-to-Russia Fund, 631
Air Training Conference (May 1942), 410, 411–12
Air Transport Board, 646
Aird Commission (1929), 654
Alaska, defence of, 685
Alaska Highway, 436, 514, 543
Albany Club (Toronto), 329
Alberta: and Dominion-Provincial Conference (1941), 160–2; beer restrictions in, 652
alcoholic beverages, restrictions on, 460–4, 485–8, 543–4, 546–7, 652–4
Aldershot (Eng.), 257–9, 260
Aleutians, military action in, 379, 415, 494, 515–17, 552–3
Alexander, A. V., 666, 672
Algoma, steel mills in, 441, 470, 472–4
Alice, Princess, Countess of Athlone, 74–5, 111, 146, 530–1, 546, 556, 694
aliens: internment of, 97, 285, 354–5; and Arvida strike, 228, 230, 231, 233
Aluminum Company of Canada: mines in Greenland, 107, 112; strike at Arvida plant, 228–33
American Federation of Labor, 444
Amery, L. S., 672, 679
Anderson, Sir John: atomic research, 531–2, 536; aviation policy, 539, 540; Conference of Prime Ministers (1944), 666, 667, 672
Andrews, J. M., 219
anniversaries, WLMK and, 53–8, 105, 191, 288, 476, 548, 589, 677–8, 683, 692

Annuities Bill, 477
apple producers, subsidy to, 28
Army, Canadian: creation of Expeditionary Force (1939), 21, 28, 29, 30, 37–9; relation to other services, 40–1, 76, 220, 303–4, 313; departure of First Division, 37–9, 53, 59; discussion of Army Corps (1940–1), 76, 158; supplies for, 86, 131, 133, 154–5, 261, 263, 314; fall of France, 92, 126; possible action outside U.K., 156, 220–1, 239, 244, 261, 265, 358, 419, 423, 435, 437, 494–504, 519, 539; size of, 157, 158–9, 303–4, 312–13, 325, 326, 334, 357, 359–60, 438–9, 443, 464, 490, 500, 568; WLMK's visit to, in England (1941), 236, 257–61, 262–3; qualities of, 253, 535, 558, 607, 690; at Hong Kong, 298, 315–16, 325; Dieppe raid, 416–17, 436, 437, 496; Mediterranean campaign, 466, 494, 497–504, 520–6, 527, 537–8, 545, 558, 567, 568, 587, 599, 604–5, 606–10, 622; invasion across Channel, 495–504, 565–6, 579–80, 583, 604, 607, 610, 690–2, 695; attack on Aleutians, 515–17; political interests in, 587–8; reinforcements for (1944), 630, 689; in war against Japan, 642, 689; WLMK's visit to, in England (1944), 670, 689–90
Arvida, aluminum works in, 189, 196, 228–33, 268
Ashby Hall (Eng.), 264
Athlone, Earl of, 111, 136, 255; appointed Governor-General, 74–5, 99; relations with WLMK, 146, 694; Roosevelt's proposed visit to Ottawa (1941), 196–7; Air Training Conference (1942), 411–12; Quebec Conference (1943), 528, 530, 546; Roosevelt in Ottawa (1943), 547,

556; Lord Halifax's Toronto speech (1944), 638
Atkinson, Joseph: National Government, 176; post-war policy, 444–5, 493, 631–2; friendship with WLMK, 493, 631
Atlanta (Georgia), 106
Atlantic Conference (1941), 196–7, 201, 233–5, 237, 242, 244, 246, 247, 256, 412
atomic energy research, 413–14, 503, 532, 536, 657; Combined Committee on, 536, 543, 657
Attlee, Clement: in Ottawa (1942), 420–1; landing in Sicily, 537; Empire policy, 639; Conference of Prime Ministers (1944), 666, 680, 684, 686
Attu, 516
Australia: Air Training Plan, 40, 41, 42, 45–7, 48, 410; Roosevelt proposal re British fleet, 118, 120, 121; North African and Mediterranean campaigns, 156, 505, 622; as member of Commonwealth, 234, 241, 250, 409, 430, 529, 599, 678–9; war with Japan, 245, 411, 516, 642, 669, 685; Conference of Prime Ministers (1944), 664–73, 678–9, 684–9
aviation, post-war policy for, 519, 539–40, 551–2, 645–9
Aylesworth, Sir A., 475
Ayr (Scotland), 264
Azores, 135, 695

BADMINTON (Eng.), 254, 255
Baldwin, Earl, of Bewdley, 245, 542
Balfour, Harold, 41, 42, 45, 47, 48, 642
Balfour Declaration (1917), 664
Ballantyne, C. C., 92
Balmoral, WLMK's visit to, 254–7, 674
Bank Act, revision of (1944), 633
Bank of Canada, 161; French deposits in, 180–5, 194
Basic English, 558–9
Battle of Britain, 108, 142, 145
Beatty, Sir Edward, 99; and Bennett in Cabinet, 172–4, 489; death of, 488–9
Beaver Club (London), 253
Beaverbrook, Lord, 188–9, 247–9, 672
beef, price of, 441
Belgian Congo, uranium in, 413
Belgium, 117, 433
Bell, R. A., 455
Benes, E., 565
Bengough, Percy, 572–3, 643–4

Bennett, R. B.: as Conservative leader, 38, 276, 454, 458, 546, 687; suggested for Cabinet (1941), 172–4, 489; peerage, 213, 243; defeat as leader, 465, 478, 519, 580; in England, 663, 677
Berlin (Ont.). *See* Kitchener
Bermuda, 117, 130, 141, 196
Bertrand, Ernest: conscription, 378, 390; Minister of Fisheries (1942–   ), 442–4
Beveridge, Sir William, 433–4, 476, 564
Bevin, Ernest, 672, 685
"Big Four," in post-war, 553–4, 560, 637, 640, 641, 675, 678
Biggar, O. M., 138
Bill 80 (1942), 368–403, 406–7, 415, 416, 437, 443
"billion dollar gift," 333–4
Bishop, Charles, 462, 640
Blackmore, R. D., leader of Social Credit party, 84, 298, 328, 352, 355, 404, 628, 629
Blair, J. K., 651
Blamey, Mr. (adviser to Curtin), 667
Blanchette, Joseph, 16, 17
Bloc Populaire, 570, 571, 574
Bloom, Sol, 506
Bonneau, M. (representative of Free French), 535
Borden, Henry, 490, 659, 660
Borden, Sir Robert, 31, 376, 510
Bouchard, T. D., 292
Bowman, C. A., 440
Bowmanville (Ont.), 421
Bracken, Brendan, Minister of Information (U.K.), 239; Quebec Conference (1943), 551–2, 554, 556; Conference of Prime Ministers (1944), 666, 684
Bracken, John: Dominion-Provincial Conference, 160, 161; possible Conservative leader (1941), 276–7; conscription, 313; chosen Conservative leader (1942), 452, 454, 456–60, 464, 466, 476, 482; entry into House, 477, 478, 566–7; party leader, 479, 565, 575, 586, 659, 665; trip to U.K. (1943), 566–9, 602; Manion's funeral, 567; Toronto speech (July 1943), 567; Lord Halifax's Toronto speech (1944), 638
Brais, Philippe, 290, 362, 439
Brazil, and U.N., 529
Bridges, Sir Edward, 666, 684
British Columbia: Japanese Canadians, 149–50, 151, 299, 354; Dominion-

Index

Provincial Conference (1941), 160–2; and tax fields, 176; trade with Japan, 206; possible Japanese attacks, 379, 390, 415; war against Japan, 642
British Commonwealth, Canada's relation to, 11–22, 43, 44, 93, 117, 135, 143, 149, 193, 203, 208, 226, 234, 241, 242, 250–1, 297–9, 308, 317, 318, 328–9, 350, 409, 436, 505–7, 508–12, 517–19, 523, 529, 539–40, 541, 545, 636–41, 662, 663–74, 675, 677, 678
British Commonwealth Air Training Plan: importance in Canada's war effort, 29–30, 40–1, 45, 48, 59; creation of, 36, 40–5; signing of agreement, 39, 45–58; shortage of aircraft (1940), 115, 117; development of, 190, 599; expiration of, 410, 581, 632, 642
British North America Act, 561–3
Brockington, L. W., 31, 32, 33, 161
Brooke, Sir Alan: relations with McNaughton, 359, 605–7, 613–15, 617, 628; use of Canadian troops, 423, 495, 497; at Chequers (1944), 675, 676; ending of war, 683
Brooke-Popham, Sir Robert, 41, 49, 51–2, 53, 56–9
Brown, E. K., 475
Bruce, Herbert, 223, 487
Bruce, Stanley M., 215, 250
Brunning, E. J., 595
Buck, Tim, 470, 471
Buckingham Palace, WLMK at, 673–4, 693–4
business: leaders of, in Government, 81–2, 84, 85, 94, 176, 178, 632; in post-war, 635
butter, rationing of, 464
Byng, Lord, 637

CABINET (federal): composition of (1935), 34; (1939), 25–6; (1940), 77, 79, 81–2, 91, 94, 95, 98, 99–102, 172; (1941), 170, 172–4, 176, 223, 271, 284, 285, 287, 289–94, 309–12, 332; (1942), 442–4

WLMK's relations with, 7, 82–3, 214, 216, 274–5, 294, 331, 594–5, 600, 604, 634, 686–7, 688, 696; conscription issue, 28–9, 84–5, 281–2, 295, 305–9, 312–17, 335–6 (see also Plebiscite; Bill 80); Air Training Plan, 40–1, 45, 46, 47, 48; unemployment insurance, 61; election of 1940, 61, 63, 64, 65; St. Lawrence Waterway, 61–2, 77, 162; National Government, 81, 82–3, 101, 175; war production, 85–7, 154–5, 178; fall of France, 92; Houde's arrest, 104–5; Ogdensburg Agreement, 137; Dominion-Provincial Conference, 159–61; first Ilsley budget, 176–7; Arvida strike, 232; price and wage control, 268–71, 440–1, 466–75, 590–8, 644; Meighen as Conservative leader, 279, 281–2; war against Finland, Hungary, Roumania, 296–7; war with Japan, 297, 298–9; war programme for 1942, 302, 304–9, 312–17, 334–5; Plebiscite, 334–5, 336, 338–40, 341, 375; movement of Japanese Canadians, 354, 446; preparation and passage of Bill 80, 365, 366–70, 371–2, 378–9, 382–4, 385, 392–4; Air Training Conference (1942), 412; Dieppe raid, 416–17; relations with Vichy, 427; wartime information, 439; selective service, 446; restrictions on liquor traffic, 460–4, 485–8, 653; butter rationing, 464; National Capital, 464–5; post-war social programmes, 476, 632–6; Mutual Aid, 483; War Appropriation Bill (1943), 483–4; manpower allotment (1943), 490–1; Aleutian expedition, 516; recognition of Canada, 538; redistribution of constituencies, 561–3; general labour policy (1943), 572–4, 597; reorganization of Liberal party, 574–5, 576, 578, 600; Canada Medal, 589; coal strike (1943), 591–7; McNaughton's retirement, 627; Lord Halifax's Toronto speech (1944), 637; aviation policy, 646–8; policy on C.B.C., 654; McTague and Conservatives, 658–9

Cabinet (federal), War Committee of, 84, 213, 221, 506, 668; membership of, 6, 26, 100–1, 376, 659–60; election of 1940, 63; creation of Army Corps, 76, 158; war production, 85–6, 154–5, 158–9; Mobilization Act, 95; relations with post-surrender France, 98–9, 319, 320; despatch of destroyers to U.K. (1940), 116; Ogdensburg Agreement, 140; Japanese entry into war, 151–2; compulsory military training, 155–6, 158; action

702 Index

for Army outside U.K. (1940–1), 156, 221–2; war programme (1941), 158–9; Lend-Lease, 187, 189; relation of military commands, 203; conscription issue, 219–20, 303–4; public information about war, 222; WLMK's visit to Britain (1941), 264–5; war programme (1942), 302–4, 314, 376–7; troops for Hong Kong, 315–16, 325; Churchill in Ottawa (1941), 325–6, 328, 419; McNaughton reports to (1942), 358; Japanese activities in Aleutians, 379–80; Dieppe raid, 416; proposed McNaughton mission to Moscow, 419–20; shackling of prisoners, 421; Alaska Highway, 436; selective service, 445, 448–9, 450; steel strike (1943), 467; Mutual Aid, 483; War Appropriation Bill (1943), 484; manpower allotment (1943), 489–90; Mediterranean campaign, 494, 501–2, 520, 610; plans for invasion, 496–7; attack on Aleutians, 515–17; French-speaking naval recruits, 519–20; Quebec Conference (1943), 531, 533–4, 538–40, 557–60, 572, 645; post-war aviation policy, 559; future Budget concerns, 598; McNaughton's retirement, 613–14, 618, 619, 625–6; R.C.A.F. in war against Japan, 642–3; "Canol" project, 644–5; atomic research, 657
Caesar, Julius, 559
Cairo, 603
Calgary, WLMK in (1941), 224–6
California, oil in, 644, 645
Cameron Highlanders, 255
Campbell, George, 404–5
Campbell, Sir Gerald, High Commissioner for U.K.: Air Training Plan, 43, 44, 45–7, 49, 50, 53; British war purchasing, 127, 185–6; Atlantic bases for U.S.A., 128, 129, 130, 139, 142; appointment to Washington, 192
Campbell, Thane, 160
Campbell, Wallace, 27
Campobello (N.B.), 549
Canada Medal, 588–9
Canadian and Catholic Confederation of Labour, 652
Canadian Broadcasting Corporation, 33, 457, 654
Canadian Club, 265, 564
Canadian Congress of Labour, 269, 572, 643–4

Canadian Construction Company, 256
Canadian Information Office (N.Y.), proposed, 273
Canadian Legion, 274
Canadian Manufacturers' Association, 86–7, 99
Canadian National Railways, 135, 270
Canadian Northern Railway, 646
Canadian Pacific Railway, 278, 488; and aviation policy, 645–9
Canary Islands, military action in, 135, 494, 497, 500
"Canol" project, 644–5
Cardin, P. J. A., 85, 97, 163, 170; Quebec election of 1939, 35–6, 373; St. Lawrence Waterway, 77, 164; Minister of Public Works (–1942) and of Transport (1940–2), 101, 373, 444, 464; Houde's arrest, 104–5; conscription issue, 222, 307–8, 314, 316–17; illness of (1941), 271, 275, 284, 290, 342, 371, 373, 386; Cabinet reorganization (1941), 289–93, 310; relations with WLMK, 290, 342, 371, 373, 386–7; Plebiscite, 336–7, 338, 339, 341, 342, 362, 363, 365–70, 373, 391–2; leader for Quebec, 342, 361; resignation from Cabinet, 370–3, 374, 389, 442; as private Member, 370, 373, 381–2, 479–81; redistribution of House seats, 564
Carnegie, Mrs. Andrew, 602
Cartier (constituency), 570
Carton, Sidney, 505
Casablanca Conference, 494, 496, 555
Casgrain, Pierre, 311, 442
Chaloult, René, 97
Chamberlain, Neville: Munich agreement, 12, 179, 238–9; Air Training Plan, 40–2, 44, 45, 51, 52, 54, 55; resignation of, 77–8, 179; and relations with U.S.A., 114; proposal of Imperial Council, 212; relations with Churchill, 251, 328, 542
Chanak incident, 11
Charlottetown, 384
Charpentier, Alfred, 269–70
Chateau Frontenac (Quebec City), 529, 531, 539, 552
Chateau Laurier (Ottawa), 324, 361, 373, 477, 582
Chequers, 417; WLMK at (1941), 239, 242, 244–8, 249, 251, 254, 272, 505; Hanson at (1941), 273; WLMK at (1944), 674–6, 681

Cherwell, Lord, 503
Chester, Philip, 99
Chiang Kai-shek, 433
Chiang Kai-shek, Madame, 517
Chiefs of Staff (Canada): in Washington (1940), 124, 126, 127–8, 133, 138; war with Japan, 300; and voluntary enlistment, 304, 376–7; Atlantic command, 326; Allied strategy for 1942, 376–7; relations with Government, 501–2, 598, 687; Mediterranean campaign, 502; in Washington (1943), 503; Aleutian expedition, 515–17; French-speaking naval recruits, 519–20; Quebec Conference (1943), 529, 530
China: and Indian self-government, 408; pilots of, 410; post-war role, 431, 432, 553–4, 637, 644, 673, 675; war role, 479, 517, 555, 673, 684–5
Christie, Loring, Canadian Minister to U.S.A., 115, 116, 129; appointment, 31; defence of Greenland, 112; Hyde Park Conference, 128; destroyers for Britain, 129–30; illness of, 175
Church, T., 518–19
Churchill, Mary, 531, 534, 536, 543
Churchill, Winston, 294, 398, 401, 412, 430, 476, 570, 576, 577; speeches of, 32, 33, 87–8, 94, 121, 123, 142–3, 157, 224, 244, 245–6, 247, 248, 324, 327–8, 445, 505–6, 555, 557–8, 559, 599–600; recognition of Canadian troops, 39, 412, 505, 525–6, 527–8, 535, 537–8, 555, 558, 599, 676, 695; becomes Prime Minister, 78, 212; fall of France, 87–8, 91, 92, 94, 546; role of Canada as linch-pin, 106, 143, 317, 318, 508, 512, 550, 675, 676, 680; Roosevelt's proposal re British fleet (1940), 118–28; destroyer-bases deal, 132, 133, 136–7, 140–3; Ogdensburg Agreement, 137, 139–40, 143; relations with WLMK, 143, 188, 236–54, 272, 284, 321, 327, 330, 331, 419, 485, 499, 505–6, 509, 511, 529, 531, 537–8, 541, 542, 548–50, 554, 558, 560, 575, 584, 585, 603, 662, 663, 670, 676, 680–2; Howe's visit to England (1940), 153, 157; war purchasing in U.S.A., 183–4; Atlantic Conference, 196–7, 201, 233–5, 237, 242, 244, 246, 247, 256, 412; importance for Allied cause, 201, 245, 251, 325, 511, 542, 546, 549, 665, 666, 678; relations with Vichy and Free French, 212, 242, 318–24, 424, 535–6, 541, 543; peerage for Bennett, 213, 243; proposals for Imperial Cabinet/Conferences (1941–4), 213, 215, 216–17, 238, 240–1, 507–8, 666, 668; and British Cabinet, 214, 238, 672; conscription in Northern Ireland, 218–19; WLMK's trip to Britain (1941), 236–54, 266–7, 284, 321; conscription and National Government in Canada, 238, 244, 273, 279–80, 284, 325, 326–7, 328–31, 415; relations with Roosevelt, 242, 317–18, 326, 511, 535, 554; possible Japanese entry into war, 245–6, 296, 305; Hanson's visit to U.K., 272–3; in Washington (Dec. 1941), 317–18, 321–6, 429–30; in Ottawa (Dec. 1941), 317–18, 324, 325–31, 332, 333–4, 419, 485; member of Privy Council, Canada, 326, 560; "billion dollar gift," 333–4; in Washington (June 1942), 391–2, 393, 414–16; fall of Tobruk, 391; and India, 408, 505, 509; Allied cross-Channel invasion, 414–15, 495–504, 507, 519, 533, 535, 579, 599, 607, 665, 668, 683; McNaughton's proposed Moscow mission, 417–20; shackling of prisoners, 421–2; meeting with Stalin and Roosevelt, 432–3, 513–14, 537, 543, 601, 603; Quebec Conference (August 1943), 466, 527–60, 572, 665, 666, 676; and abstinence, 487, 544; in Washington (May 1943), 494, 502–14; Casablanca Conference (1943), 494, 495; Canadians and Mediterranean campaign, 494–504, 519, 525–6, 527–8, 537–8, 558; proposed meeting of Commonwealth Prime Ministers (1943), 504, 507–11, 538, 554–5, 598, 603; role of Commonwealth and Empire, 505–7, 508–9, 512–13, 637, 663–4, 666, 672, 673–4, 676, 679, 681–2; post-war international relations, 509–10, 512–13, 553–4, 559–60, 670, 672–3, 675, 678–9; Canadian Embassy in Washington, 512, 589; post-war aviation, 539–40, 559, 645; Lord Halifax's Toronto speech (1944), 637, 639, 640; Conference of Prime Ministers (1944), 662–96; on National Government (G.B.), 683; and Mont-

gomery, 692; second Quebec Conference proposed, 695
Churchill, Mrs. Winston S., 246, 247, 531, 534, 536, 542, 543, 544, 546, 549, 555, 557, 681
Churchill (Man.), 546
Ciano, G., 559
Citadel (Quebec City), 528, 529, 531, 533, 534, 538, 540, 553, 554, 555, 558, 570, 695
Citizen (Ottawa), 329, 363, 440, 462, 640
Civil Liberties League, 354–5
Civil Service Commission, 449
Clark, J. H., 517–18, 519, 569
Clark, W. C., Deputy Minister of Finance: WLMK's opinion of, 28, 177; financing war programme, 155; dollar shortage, 184–5; Lend-Lease and Hyde Park Agreement, 187, 189, 191–4; price and wage control, 268–9, 590; family allowances, 633–4, 636
Claxton, Brooke, 9, 651; possible Cabinet post, 223; Assistant to President of Council, 479, 519, 582; post-war Liberal programme, 582, 585
coal mining: labour for, 472, 489–91; strikes in (1906) 594, 595, (1943) 591–7
Coburn, John, 462, 487
Cohen, Joseph, 571–4
Coldwell, M. J., leader of C.C.F. party, 84, 90, 100, 328, 348, 355, 575; participation in war, 14–15, 298; French Minister's position, 209; relations with WLMK, 209; Hong Kong inquiry, 352, 404, 405; landing in Sicily, 524; McNaughton's retirement, 628, 629; Lord Halifax's Toronto speech (1944), 637, 638, 639
Coleman, D. C., 645–9
Coleman, E. H., 69, 70, 588–9
collective bargaining, 233, 268, 270, 355, 590, 600
command, military, problems of, 203, 221, 234, 263, 317, 324, 325–6, 412, 496–504, 515–17, 539, 620, 622, 628, 642–3, 664, 691–2
"Commonwealth and Empire," origin of phrase, 663–4, 666
Commonwealth Prime Ministers, Conference of: proposed (1943), 504, 507–11, 513, 514, 538, 551, 554–5, 558, 581, 598, 639; held (1944), 598, 603, 641, 647, 655, 659–89, 694–6; in future, 664, 669, 674
compulsory military training: term of, 155–6, 157, 158, 437, 489; for local and coast defence, 219, 307, 312, 314, 315, 331, 333, 340, 388, 399, 490, 515; and voluntary enlistment, 312, 331, 333, 349, 399; Cardin's amendment re (1943), 479–81; in post-war, 689. *See also* Conscription issue (1939–44); National Resources Mobilization Act
compulsory saving, 416
Conant, Gordon: becomes Premier of Ontario (1942), 453, 454–6; federal liquor restrictions, 485, 487–8; Ontario Liberal convention (1943), 491–2, 569
Conant, James B., 532
Coney Island, 515
Congress party (India), 408
Connally, Tom, 506
Conniffe, Miss Margaret, 5
conscription issue (1939–44): WLMK's pledge re, 21, 23, 29, 96, 219, 261–2, 275, 280, 333, 338, 341, 343, 344, 346, 360, 364, 374, 406; importance of issue, 22–3, 84, 222, 246, 303, 316–17, 333; and Cabinet, 28–9, 84–5, 281–2, 295, 305–9, 312–17, 335–6 (*see also* Plebiscite; Bill 80); and Air Training Plan, 40; and military events of 1940, 79–80, 84, 95, 96, 167; campaign for in 1941, 205, 218, 219–22, 225–7, 261–2, 273–4, 275–6, 277–84, 300–2, 325; WLMK's discussions of, with Churchill (1941), 238, 244, 273, 279–80, 284, 325, 326, 330–1; and war programme for 1942, 302–8, 312–17; leading up to Plebiscite, 333–51, 355–6, 357, 358, 360, 362–4, 365–8, 373, 374, 375, 376, 382, 384, 392, 405, 406, 408, 409; Bill 80, 368–403, 406–7, 415, 416, 437; in Sept.–Dec. 1942, 423, 437, 439, 442–3, 448, 450, 452, 456, 458, 462, 466; in 1943, 484, 495, 500, 584, 594–5, 611; in 1944, 630, 638, 660
Conservative party: and declaration of war, 14, 16; conventions of, 9, 14, 103, 173, 276–9, 407, 442, 449, 450, 452, 453–60, 481, 649; and French Canada, 14, 277, 278, 388–9; leadership of, 14, 78–9, 103, 276–9, 330; and conscription, 22–3, 225, 271, 273,

277-8, 280-4, 300-2, 312, 330, 371, 405; and National Government, 22-3, 82, 94-5, 101-2, 170, 174, 278, 280-4, 328, 329, 387, 444, 450, 452, 454, 585, 660-1; and British connection, 118, 217, 238, 244, 278, 329-30, 518-19, 523, 528, 545, 618-19, 637, 638, 671; reorganization of, 167; attacks on WLMK, 179, 188, 217, 234, 238, 244, 273, 329-30, 346, 395-6, 475, 576, 585, 603; Churchill's visit to Ottawa (1941), 328-30; Plebiscite and Bill 80, 337, 338, 339, 341, 350, 362, 387, 396, 403; by-elections (1942), 343-4, 347-9, 456; Hong Kong inquiry, 404-7; selective service, 449, 450, 452; Bracken chosen leader (1942), 452, 454-60, 465, 476, 477, 478, 565; change in name of, 457, 458, 459, 465, 466, 478; House leader for (1943), 478, 481; recognition of Canada, 524, 538; WLMK's view of fortunes of, 547, 567, 580, 584, 601; by-elections (1943), 566; Ontario election (1943), 568-70; adherents in Army, 587-8; McNaughton's retirement, 618-19; in post-war, 635; aviation policy, 647, 648; beer restrictions, 653; McTague as National Chairman, 658-9

C.C.F. party, 455, 466, 603; as national contender, 9, 382, 453, 466, 547, 554-5, 558, 566, 571, 575, 580, 584, 598, 635, 647; and declaration of war, 14-15, 570; by-elections (1942), 343-4, 347, 456; conscription of wealth, 350, 391; and Bill 80, 382; labour relations, 440, 569, 571, 574, 601, 643-4; redistribution of House seats, 561; by-elections (1943), 566, 570-1; Ontario election (1943), 568-70, 572; adherents in Army, 587-8; aviation policy, 647, 648, 649

cost-of-living bonus, 600
Crabb, James H., 635
Crabtree, Harold, 86, 99
Cranborne, Lord: WLMK's visit to England (1941), 244, 246; Menzies' defeat (1941), 250; Conference of Prime Ministers (1944), 663-4, 666, 668, 669, 680, 686
Crerar, H. D. G., General: as Chief of General Staff, 129, 357; Hong Kong inquiry, 352; relations with Army, 498, 606; Mediterranean campaign,

500, 605; Commander (1943), 606, 607, 611, 622; and conscription, 611, 689; WLMK's visit to Army (1944), 689-90; Montgomery and, 691
Crerar, T. A., 26, 77, 92, 170, 289; relations with WLMK, 8, 285, 696; Ogdensburg Agreement, 140; war with Japan, 150, 299; post-war aviation, 540; choice of Acting Prime Minister (1944), 659-60
Cromwell, James, 111
Cross (Arthur), 473
Curtin, John, Prime Minister of Australia, proposed meeting of Prime Ministers, 514; election win (1943), 555; conference of Prime Ministers (1944), 666-80, 683-9; war in Pacific, 669; and "Tory" attitude, 672
Czechoslovakia, 149, 564

DAFOE, John, 356; conscription and Bill 80, 227; and movement against French Canada, 388-9; death of, 631
Dakar, 147
Dandurand, Raoul, 266, 327; relations with WLMK, 8; and successor to Lapointe, 290, 291-2, 293; and Plebiscite, 314, 316; death of, 361-2, 372, 376, 442
Danforth (constituency), 395
Darlan, Admiral Jean, 319, 428-9, 535
Defence of Canada Regulations, 232, 354-5
Defence Purchasing Board, 27
demobilization, 630, 646
Denmark, conquest of, 77, 107
destroyers: sent to U.K. from Canada (1940), 116, 122; exchanged by U.S.A. for bases, 128-32, 137, 138, 140, 142, 145, 146-7
De Valera, E., 218-19
Dexter, Grant, 270
Diary, of WLMK, description of, 3, 228, 254
Diefenbaker, John, 348; Select Committee on War Expenditures, 171-2; Bill 80, 395-6, 398; Hong Kong inquiry, 405-6; Conservative convention (1942), 457, 458; possible House leader, 478
Digby (Eng.), 264
Dieppe, raid on, 416-17, 421, 436, 437, 496, 502, 533, 690
Dill, General Sir John G., 128; possible invasion of England, 129

disarmament, post-war, 430, 431, 433, 510, 672
dollars, shortage of, 146, 179, 180–6, 189–94
Dominion-Provincial Conference (1941), 145, 159–62, 163
Dorion, F., 456
Douglas, T. C., 209
Doukhobors, 546
Dover (Eng.), 253, 690
Drew, George, 567; Leader of Opposition (Ont.), 36, 69, 70–1; federal election (1940), 62, 69, 70–1, 72; Conservative leadership, 277, 278; Hong Kong inquiry, 403–6; Conservative convention (1942), 454, 456, 457, 458; Ontario election of 1943, 569–70; trip to U.K. (1943), 602; McNaughton's retirement, 618; at Mulock's 100th birthday, 631; beer restrictions, 652–4
Drew, Mrs. George, 601–2, 631
Duff, Sir L. P.: Chief Justice, 75, 630; Administrator (1940), 67, 83; as possible Governor-General, 74; Hong Kong inquiry, 352–4, 403–6
Duncan, Sir Andrew, 663
Duncan, J. S., 94, 96, 100
Dunkirk, retreat from, 87
Dunn, Sir James, 473
Dunning, Charles, 25
Dunton, A. Davidson, 440, 556
Duplessis, Maurice, 34, 291, 293; Quebec election of 1939, 35–6, 60, 62, 373; Mobilization Bill, 97; redistribution of federal House, 564
Dupuy, Pierre, 147–8, 191, 208–12, 216, 241–2, 322, 424
Durham, Lord, 364, 375, 636

EDEN, Anthony, Foreign Secretary of U.K.: relations with Vichy, 241; proposal for Imperial Conference, 250; use of Canadian troops, 500–1; post-war international relations, 553–4, 676, 678, 679; Conference of Prime Ministers (1944), 666, 670, 671, 681, 686; WLMK's view of, 672
Edmonton, 433, 587
Edwards, Gordon, 655
Eggleston, Wilfrid, 168
Egypt, 219, 221, 415
Eire, 218–19, 246, 655
Eisenhower, General D. D., landing in Sicily, 522, 525, 537–8; WLMK meets (1944), 682–3; news release on D-day, 695
Elections, federal: (1911), 212; (1917), 22–3, 308–9, 460, 631; (1921), 25; (1926), 34; (1935), 3, 8, 12, 13, 34, 60, 310; (1940), 8, 9, 24, 60–73, 108, 329, 482, 582, 665; (1942 by-elections), 309, 311, 316, 339, 340–1, 343–50, 444, 449, 456, 461; (1943 by-elections), 538, 566, 568, 576, 583, 665; (1943–5, proposed), 568, 574, 580–1, 601, 631, 651, 655, 669
Elections, provincial: Ontario, (1934) 34, (1943) 466, 568–70, 572, 576, 583, 584; Prince Edward Island, (1943) 576; Quebec, (1935) 34, (1936) 34, (1939) 35–6, 60, 62, 373
Elizabeth, Princess, 254, 256, 257, 588, 673, 694
Elizabeth, Queen, 197, 254–7, 289, 519, 549, 673–4, 694
Emile Bertin, 98–9
Empire Council (Cabinet). *See* Imperial Council
Empire Parliamentary Association, 518
Esling, W. K., 546
Essex East (constituency), 375
Estevan Point (B.C.), 390
Europe, proposed United States of, 672, 675, 678, 679
Evatt, Herbert, 409
excess profits tax, 416
Exchequer Court, 444, 477
External Affairs, Dept. of, and autonomy of Canada, 538, 671

FADDEN, A. W., 249–50
Fairbairn, J. V., 46, 47
Fairbanks, Avard, 587
family allowances, 590–1, 631, 633–6, 644
farm prices, floor for (post-war), 600
Ferguson, G. V., 226
Financial Post, 273
Finland, 30, 297
Firefighters, Canadian Corp of, 252–3, 265
First World War: Canada's entry into, 11; expeditionary force for, 30; status of Canadian command in, 49, 52, 240; conscription issue in, 73, 81, 281, 283, 307, 308–9, 314, 336, 376, 382, 443, 631
Fiset, Sir Eugene, 289, 534, 541

Fisher, W. A., 586-7
flag, of Canada: at Quebec Conference, 542-3; design for, 655; for Army, 690
Flanagan, J. W., 175
Four Freedoms, 431
Fournier, Alphonse, Minister of Public Works (1942-), 442-4, 464-5
France: approach to war, 12-13, 17, 18, 20; position of, in war, 30; fall of (1940), 78, 85, 87, 91, 92-3, 94, 95, 96, 99, 115, 117, 120, 123-4, 132, 546; money reserves of, 98-9, 180-7, 191, 194, 201; fleet after surrender, 125, 147, 212; post-surrender relations with Allies, 145, 147-8, 182, 191, 201, 208-12, 241-2, 318-24, 416, 422-9; Japanese attack on Indo-China, 207; Vichy and Germany, 208, 210, 211, 216, 319, 426, 427-8; raids on, 221, 415, 416-17. *See also* French Committee of National Liberation
Fraser, Peter, Prime Minister of New Zealand: proposed Prime Ministers' meeting, 214, 216, 238; Conference of Prime Ministers (1944), 666-80, 683-9; and "Tory" attitude, 672
Free Press (Winnipeg), 227, 270, 388-9, 438, 631, 656, 657
Freetown, 135
French Canada: and participation in war, 14, 22, 23, 308, 351, 360, 412; and Conservative party, 14, 277, 278, 388-9; attitude to conscription, 22-3, 73, 303, 307, 312, 345, 346, 351, 462-3, 479-81 (*see also* Plebiscite and Bill 80); and Liberal party, 73, 277, 307, 337, 351, 373, 382, 388-9, 393, 561; fall of France and Vichy, 99, 423; national registration, 104-5; Plebiscite and Bill 80, 316-17, 336-7, 339, 362-4, 366, 367, 369, 370-6, 377, 381-2, 384-5, 386, 390, 398, 403; and British connection, 508, 665-6; recruits for R.C.N., 519-20; regiments in Army, 689. *See also* Quebec, Province of
French Committee of National Liberation, 519; formation of, 517; recognition of, 535-6, 539, 541, 543, 551, 554

GANDER AIRPORT, 132, 140, 237, 695
Gardiner, J. G., 85, 316; relations with WLMK, 8, 84; defence of WLMK (1940), 83-4; redistribution of House seats, 561
Minister of National War Services (1940-1), 100, 103, 158, 222
Minister of Agriculture (1939-), 103, 312; price ceiling, 441-2; butter rationing, 464
Gardiner, Robert, 546
Garson, Stuart, 482
Gaspé, 375
Gaudrault, Father, 286
Gaulle, General Charles de, 423; and St. Pierre-Miquelon, 147, 321-2; French Committee of National Liberation, 517, 535-6, 552
Gazette (Montreal), 273, 302, 641
George VI, King, 78, 117, 298, 299, 300, 519; Air Training Plan, 54-6; appointment of Governor-General, 67, 74, 694; Table of Precedence, 92; WLMK at Balmoral (1941), 249, 254-7, 674; at Hyde Park (1939), 194, 549, 673; tour of Canada (1939), 197, 241, 289, 673, 674; WLMK at Buckingham Palace (1944), 673-4, 693-4; and Churchill, 694
Georgian Bay, 416, 514, 528
Germany, 499; approach to Second World War, 12-13, 15, 17-20, 33, 78, 133, 297, 431, 545-6, 683; possible peace offer (1940), 117, 120-1, 122-3; invasion of Britain, 129, 142, 148, 152, 157, 158, 179, 267; possible attacks on Atlantic coast, 139, 189, 196, 307, 312, 375; formation of Triple Axis, 150; relations with U.S.S.R. (pre-conflict), 151; and Vichy, 208, 210, 211, 216, 319, 426, 427-8; war with Russia, 224-5, 312, 410, 415, 517; war with United States, 298, 306, 312; campaign in North Africa, 219, 312 (*see also* North Africa); atomic research, 413, 532; shackling of prisoners, 421-2; surrender and post-war, 431, 432, 433, 436, 503, 534, 604, 675, 679; and Allied invasion, 535, 579, 604, 610, 642, 664, 667, 683; Italian surrender, 544-5
Gettysburg, 599
Gibson, Colin, Minister of National Revenue, 101, 350, 486
Gibson, James, 5-6

Gibson, Brigadier R. B., 604–5
Giraud, General H. H.: French Committee of National Liberation, 517, 535–6; in Ottawa (1943), 535–6
Gladstone, W. E., 356
Glasgow, 157
Glen, J. Allison, 327, 328
Globe and Mail (Toronto), 33, 91, 175, 273, 277, 446, 622
"God Save the King," 519, 654–5
Godbout, Adelard, 439; unemployment insurance, 61; St. Lawrence Waterway, 77, 162–4; Mobilization Bill (1940), 97; at Dominion-Provincial Conference, 160; Arvida strike, 229–30, 233; possible federal Minister, 233, 285, 287, 288, 290–4, 310; Plebiscite, 316, 361, 362; federal restrictions on liquor, 462, 485, 487, 652; Quebec Conference (1943), 534, 541; redistribution of federal House, 563–4
gold mines, closing of, 445, 446
Goldsborough (Eng.), 688
Gordon, Donald: Deputy Governor, Bank of Canada, 98, 269
     Chairman, Wartime Prices and Trade Board, 269, 271, 441–2; selective service, 445–6; butter rationing, 464
Gordon, King, 407
Government Printing Bureau, 465
Graham, George, 475
Grand Trunk Railway, 135
Gray, Thomas, 246–7
Graydon, Gordon, Conservative House leader (1943–   ), 478, 480, 482; McNaughton's retirement, 618, 619, 627–9; War Expenditures Committee, 650–1
Graydon, Mrs. Gordon, 482
Greece, campaign in, 145, 179, 193, 195, 219, 220, 664
Green, Howard: Special Committee on War Expenditures, 170–1; National Government, 174; trade with Japan, 206, 207; Conservative convention (1942), 457, 458; possible House leader, 478
Greenland, 246; and Atlantic defence, 107, 112, 114, 117, 125, 208, 498
Greenwood, Hamar, Viscount, 663, 666
Grey, Lord, 693
Grierson, John, 222–3
Guildhall, WLMK at (1944), 677–8

HACKETT, John, 455
Halifax, Lord, Ambassador to U.S.A., 157, 248–9, 251, 320, 325; and WLMK in Washington (1941), 192–3; speech in Toronto (Jan. 1944), 636–41; despatch to WLMK re preferences (1944), 680
Halifax, defence of, 121, 135, 196; transfer of destroyers (1940), 146–7; Churchill at (1943), 531, 532–3
Hallé, Maurice, 479
Hamilton East (constituency), 310, 311
Hamilton, H. S., 16, 17
Hammell, Jack, 175–6
Handy, J. E., 5, 264, 552
Hanson, R. B., 92, 142, 348, 455, 519; landing in Sicily, 524; aviation policy, 647
     Leader of Opposition (1940–3), 78, 79, 82, 88, 89, 90, 96, 100, 103, 104–5, 138, 171, 273, 328, 342–3; National Government, 94, 95, 97–8, 100, 101–2, 300–2, 328, 519; at session of Parliament Nov. 1940, 167–9; Special Committee on War Expenditures, 170–2; Hyde Park Declaration, 203–4; proposed Imperial Council, 204, 212; relations with Vichy, 209, 210, 211; trip to Britain (1941), 271–3, 302; withdrawal as Leader, 276–9, 352–3, 477–8; war with Japan, 297–8, 300, 302; conscription, Plebiscite, and Bill 80, 300–2, 305, 363, 372–3, 396, 402; Churchill in Ottawa, 328, 329; Hong Kong inquiry, 352–4, 404–6; secret session (Feb. 1942), 355; attacks on WLMK as leader (Feb. 1942), 356, 372–3, 396
Harper's Magazine, 475
Harris, Joseph, 395
Harris, Sir Percy, 519
Harris, Walter, 479, 520
Harvard Club (N.Y.), 193, 194, 601, 602
Harvard University, 330, 511, 532, 548, 549, 555
Hawaii, 297
health insurance, 631, 635–6
Hearne, John, 218–19
Heeney, Arnold, 6, 26, 69, 70, 116, 161, 166; Air Training Plan, 54, 55, 58; landing in Sicily, 523
Henry-Haye, Gaston: St. Pierre-Miquelon affair, 322, 323

Index

Hepburn, Mitchell, 34, 445; WLMK's opinion of, 23, 34, 62, 161, 345, 348–9; alliance with Duplessis, 34; St. Lawrence Waterway, 34, 36, 60, 110, 162; Ontario Resolution of 1940, 62, 69–72, 525, 580; opposition to federal Government, 80, 81, 159, 160, 449, 519, 574, 576; illness (1940), 93; Dominion-Provincial Conference, 159–62; Sirois Report, 175; Plebiscite, 337; federal by-elections (1942), 344, 347, 348–9, 478; resignation as Premier (1942), 453–5, 465, 478; Ontario Liberal convention (1943), 492–3; Ontario election of 1943, 568–70; beer restrictions, 653

Herridge, W. D., 38, 108

Hindmarsh, H. C., 445

Hitler, Adolf, 273, 305, 340, 342, 421, 436, 638; WLMK's opinion of, 12, 17–19, 21, 30, 224–5; activities of, before war, 12–13, 14, 431; possible peace offer (1940), 117, 126, 127; invasion of Britain, 157, 158; and Vichy, 319, 428

hogs, shipments to U.K., 597–8

Hong Kong: Canadians at, 298, 315–16, 325; loss of, 351–2; Royal Commission on, 352–4, 403–7

Hopkins, Harry, 157, 511; Roosevelt papers, 109; dollar shortage, 192; Hyde Park Conference (1941), 196–8, 200, 201, 202, 242; Churchill comments on, 326; Allied cross-Channel invasion, 409, 416; Munitions Assignment Board, 411, 416; relations between FDR and WLMK, 435; landing in Sicily, 521; WLMK in Washington (1942), 429, 430, 431

Houde, Camillien, 97; arrest of (1940), 104–5

housing, post-war, 632, 633

Howe, C. D., 34, 75, 235, 248, 316; relations with WLMK, 8, 153, 202, 230–3, 264, 274, 366, 388; National Government, 176; conscription, Plebiscite, and Bill 80, 316, 337, 366, 388; by-elections (1942), 347, 350; aviation policy, 559, 647–8; proposed Minister of Reconstruction, 632
Minister of Transport (1939–40), 26, 27, 77, 101; St. Lawrence Waterway, 36, 37, 77; Air Training Plan, 41, 51–2
Minister of Munitions and Supply (1940–), 77, 86, 91, 95, 96, 101, 117, 127, 141, 158, 159, 169, 170, 172, 191–2, 193, 197–8, 202, 233, 265, 312, 317, 355, 632; relations with labour, 91, 96, 228–33, 268, 271, 274, 310–11, 468–9, 471, 474, 475, 486, 593; visit to U.K. (1940), 145, 153–4, 157–8, 214; Arvida strike, 228–33; atomic research, 413–14, 536, 543, 657; visit to U.K. (1942), 423; manpower allotment (1943), 489–90; coal strike (1943), 592–3

Howe, Mrs. C. D., 154

Hull, Cordell, 30, 74, 108, 415, 429; defence of Greenland, 107, 112–13, 114; possible presidential candidate, 108–9, 113; St. Lawrence Waterway, 111; discussions with WLMK (April 1940), 111–14; American neutrality, 112–13, 190, 242, 246; Roosevelt proposal re British Navy, 116–28; passports for Canadians, 136; relations with WLMK, 188; discussions with Japan, 190, 320; discussions with WLMK (April 1941), 190; relations with Vichy and Free French, 318–24, 424–6, 543, 551, 552; discussions with WLMK (Dec. 1943), 601

Hull, Mrs. Cordell, 323

Hull, and National Capital, 464–5, 655–6

Hull House (London), 564

Humboldt (constituency), 570

Hungary, war against, 297

"Husky" operation, 502, 504

Hutchison, Bruce, 356

Hyde Park, 235, 547; museum at, 109, 194, 228; Conference at (April 1941), 193–204, 242, 332; Declaration, 198–204, 220; King and Queen at (1939), 256, 549, 673; WLMK at (Nov. 1941), 275; Churchill at (Aug. 1943), 531, 533, 543

hydro-electric power. *See* St. Lawrence Waterway

ICELAND, 196, 246, 432; and Atlantic defence, 125, 154, 208, 226, 227, 498; U.S. bases in, 125, 208

Ilsley, J. L.: relations with WLMK, 8, 101, 583, 649; acting Minister of Finance (1939), 25, 28; Minister of National Revenue (1939–40), 28, 101; Plebiscite and Bill 80, 347, 381,

393, 394; possible successor to WLMK, 445; crisis re Joseph Cohen, 573–4; possible Acting Prime Minister (1944), 660
   Minister of Finance (1940–), 91, 95, 101, 158, 162, 169, 173, 176–7, 205, 220, 312, 391, 416, 437; Dominion-Provincial Conference, 159; dollar shortage, 180; price and wage control, 268, 441–2, 468, 474, 590–1, 592, 593, 594, 597; selective service, 446; liquor restrictions, 461, 463, 486; butter rationing, 464; Mutual Aid, 483; War Appropriation Bill (1943), 483–4; Budget (1943), 484–5; indemnities to Members, 566; strain of post, 583, 649–50, 660; future Budget concerns (1943), 598; social security programmes, 632–6
Imperial Conferences, 412; (1911), 212; (1937), 12, 34; proposals for (1941–4), 216–17, 225–7, 233, 234, 238, 240–1, 507–11, 513, 639, 640, 666, 668. *See also* Imperial Council
Imperial Council (Cabinet), possibility of, 203, 204, 205, 212–16, 239–40, 247, 420, 519. *See also* Imperial Conferences
Imperial Oil, Ltd., 645
India: possible hostilities against, 149, 224, 408; self-government for, 408, 429; troops of, 505; in Commonwealth and Empire, 509, 664; Canadian troops in, 642
Indo-China, Japanese intervention in, 207
Industry: leaders of, in Government, 27, 84, 178; mobilization of, for war, 38, 39, 79–80, 84–5, 220; war production, 85–7, 154–5, 159, 220, 342; American war orders, 191–4, 197–8, 203–4
Industry and Humanity, 434, 476, 477, 564, 633, 635
International Exposition, Paris (1937), WLMK's speech at, 12
International Joint Commission, 433
Invasion, Allied, across Channel: discussion of, 157, 377, 409–10, 411, 414–15, 432, 435–6, 491, 494–504, 507, 533, 563, 565–6, 601, 604, 610, 664–5, 668, 676, 683, 690–2, 695
Ireland. *See* Eire; Northern Ireland
Italy: entry into war, 30, 88, 89, 90, 114–15, 120, 124, 187; Triple Axis, 150; war with U.S.A., 298, 306; invasion of, 501, 502, 504, 533, 535, 545, 607, 608, 610, 664, 675; surrender of, 544–5, 558
Itchen, 582, 587

JAMES, William, 532
Japan: approach to Pearl Harbor, 30, 112, 114, 121, 145, 149, 150–3, 158, 190, 206–8, 245–6, 266–7, 296, 305, 320; exports to, 177–8, 206–7; Allies freeze assets of, 207–8; declarations of war on, 297–300; war activities of, 306, 307, 314, 340, 354, 379, 390, 408, 415, 499, 515–16, 552; treatment of prisoners, 354; conclusion of war against, 433, 534, 579, 631, 641–3, 667, 685; in post-war, 644, 675
Japanese Canadians: military training of, 149–50, 151; registration of, 151; and Japan's entry into war, 299; transfer from coast, 354, 446
Jean, Joseph, 390
Johnson, Edward, 601–2
Johnston, H., 492
Journal (Ottawa), 279, 387, 458, 525, 575
Juliana, Princess, 547

KARSH, Yousuf, 328, 585
Keenleyside, Hugh: missions to Washington (May–June 1940), 115, 116–23; Permanent Joint Board of Defence, 138
Kent, Duke of, 673
King, Arthur, 583, 584, 587
King, Mrs. Arthur, 588
King, Isabel Grace (Mrs. John), 198–9, 531, 557, 662, 666, 690
King, John (grandfather of WLMK), 531, 677, 690
King, John (father of WLMK), 531, 662, 666, 690
King, Margery (Mrs. W. Lyon M.), 584, 585
King, W. Lyon M., 582–7
Kingsmere, 4, 93, 99, 102, 117, 146, 179, 218, 224, 230, 264, 297, 438, 531, 536, 587, 690; possible museum at, 228, 266; Athlones at, 530–1, 546; Roosevelt at, 547, 556
Kingston (constituency), 73, 101, 102
Kinnear, Helen, 311
Kiska, 415, 494, 515, 552, 685

Index   711

Kitchener (Ont.), 493
Knox, W. F., Secretary of Navy (U.S.A.), 110, 125, 242, 246, 328
Knowles, Stanley, 456
Knox Church (Winnipeg), pamphlet of, 528, 547, 577
Kootenay West (constituency), 546

LABOUR, Government policy re, 91–2, 178, 228–33, 268–71, 309–10, 312, 355, 452–3, 570–4, 575, 590, 591, 597, 600–1, 643–4; price and wage control, 268–71, 440–1, 466–75, 538, 571, 590–7, 643–4
Labour Progressive party, attitude to war, 14; government action against, 37; Russo-German conflict, 225; steel strike (1943), 470; by-election in Cartier (1943), 570–1
Labour Relations Board, 597, 657
Labour Relations Code (1944), 571–4, 590, 595, 596, 600, 643, 644
Labour Supply Board, 268, 270, 271
Labrador, and Atlantic defence, 189, 196, 378, 498
Lac des Neiges, 555
LaFlèche, L. R., Minister of National War Services (1942–   ), 442–4, 456, 461
LaGuardia, Fiorello: Chairman, Permanent Joint Board Board on Defence, 138–40
Lapointe, Ernest, 34, 77, 84, 92, 97, 158, 163, 169, 170, 223, 233, 265, 292, 348; relations with WLMK, 7, 8, 73, 74–5, 83, 264, 278, 279, 284–9, 342, 349, 356; participation in war, 21–2, 164, 169, 308, 373; conscription, 29, 95, 96, 220, 222, 261, 303; Quebec election of 1939, 35–6; election of 1940, 62, 63–4, 71, 73, 75, 76, 83; death of Lord Tweedsmuir, 67; appointment of Athlone, 74–5; illness of (1940), 103–4; Ogdensburg Agreement, 140; St. Pierre-Miquelon, 147; war with Japan, 150; Dominion-Provincial Conference, 161, 177; National Government, 174–5, 176; possible Imperial Conference, 217; illness and death (1941), 271, 274, 275, 278, 284–9, 290, 291, 342, 360, 361, 362, 372, 376, 659; compared with Cardin and St. Laurent, 290, 342, 382, 390
    Minister of Justice, 26, 37, 75, 285, 293; arrest of Houde, 104–5; Arvida strike, 229, 232, 233
Lapointe, Madame E., 285, 286, 288
Lapointe, Hugues, 257, 285, 286, 288, 520
Laurier, Robert, 344–5, 445, 455–6, 569
Laurier, Sir Wilfrid, 35, 228, 252, 289, 292, 293, 344, 348, 361, 390, 438, 635; Canada's relations with Britain, 12, 213; conscription and election of 1917, 23, 73, 281, 283, 308–9, 315, 336, 340, 341, 570; centenary (1941), 286, 288, 289; WLMK as Minister under, 481, 511
Laurier House, 4–6, 75, 179, 218, 246, 278, 291, 292, 300, 301, 309, 317, 328, 332, 358, 402, 420, 447, 482, 582, 584, 585, 619, 620, 624; future use of, 228, 285–6; Roosevelt in, 547, 557
Laval, Pierre, 416, 423–4
Layton, Sir Walter, 183
League of Nations: Canada's commitments to, 11; structure of, 553–4; WLMK's view of, 683
Lehman, Governor H. H., 436
Lend-Lease, 185–9, 190, 193, 197, 200, 483
Letson, General H. F. G., 446
Liberal party: national convention (1919), 10, 309, 475, 570; organization of, 9, 76, 466, 538, 554, 568, 570, 574–82, 583–5, 600–1, 643, 660–1; and declaration of war, 15; WLMK as leader of, 25, 75–6, 80–1, 82–3, 95, 105, 172–4, 176, 205, 209, 221–2, 228, 248, 274, 278, 281–4, 284–5, 300–1, 309, 330, 331–2, 344, 362, 363, 370–1, 374–5, 383–4, 385, 387, 392, 438, 444–5, 475–6, 482–3, 493, 511, 564–5, 568, 571, 574–82, 585–6, 600, 651, 693; and French Canada, 73, 277, 307, 337, 351, 373, 382, 388–9, 393, 462–3; post-war policy for, 466, 476–7, 482–3, 582, 585, 631–2, 635; convention in Ontario (1943), 491–3, 569; and Commonwealth connection, 545, 637, 638; in relation to C.C.F., 547, 554–5, 558, 571, 575, 585–6, 601, 635, 643; and redistribution, 562; by-elections (1943), 568, 574, 576, 583; Ontario election (1943), 568–70, 574, 576, 583; 584; P.E.I. election (1943), 576;

adherents in armed forces, 587-8; aviation policy, 645-9
Liberal party, Members of Parliament, caucus of, 215; WLMK's relations with, 9, 80-1, 407, 565-6, 574-82, 651, 660-1; National Government, 24, 65, 80-1, 101, 282-4, 660-1; election of 1940, 65-6; defeat of France (1940), 87-8, 96-7, 101; and wheat, 177-8, 437; conscription and Plebiscite, 275-6, 279-80, 282-4, 306, 338, 339, 340-2, 343-4, 350-1; by-elections (1942), 349-50; preparation and passage of Bill 80, 365, 366, 373-6, 377-9; Hong Kong inquiry, 407; wartime taxation, 437; post-war programme, 482-3; liquor restrictions, 488; indemnities for Members, 566; reorganization of party (1943-4), 575-82, 585-6, 651, 660-1; Canada's flag and anthem, 655
Libya, 415
Lincoln, Abraham, 65-6
liquor advertising, 461-3, 485-6
Liquor Control Board, Ontario, 652-3
Little, Elliott M., 445-52
Little Current (Ont.), 531
Lloyd George, D., 476, 511
London School of Economics, 564
Lothian, Lord: discussions with WLMK (1940), 114, 115; destroyer-bases deal, 128, 129, 135; dollar shortage, 184
Louise, Lake, 534
Low, Solon, 652
Lowell, James Russell, 17
Ludwig, Emil, 588
Lyttelton, Oliver, 672

Maclean's, 144, 273
Malay States, 149
Manila, 297
Manion, Robert: declaration of war, 14, 16, 17, 18; as Leader of Opposition, 23, 24, 78; election of 1940, 60, 61, 64-8, 72-3, 79, 108, 478; post-election post, 92; and Liberal party, 442, 457, 460, 465, 567; death of, 567
Manitoba: at Dominion-Provincial Conference (1941), 146, 161; resolution of Legislature re conscription (1941), 313-14
Manchester Guardian, 682
Manitoulin Island, 528, 529, 531, 533
Mann, Donald, 646

Mansion House, WLMK's speech at (1941), 244, 246-7, 251, 252, 253, 265, 272
Marden Park (Eng.), 259
Margaret Rose, Princess, 254, 256, 257
Markham, Violet, 693
Marlborough, Duke of, 419, 542, 546
Marler, Sir Herbert, 31
Marshall, General G. C., and attack on Continent, 409, 411
Martin, Paul, 375-6
Mary, Queen, 254, 255
Massey, Denton, 457
Massey, Vincent, High Commissioner in U.K., 86-7, 216, 240, 250, 300; WLMK's trip to Britain (1941), 237, 253; shackling of prisoners, 422; landing in Sicily, 520-1, 522, 537
Matthews, Albert, 36, 69-70
Mathewson, Arthur, 229-30, 652
Matsuoka, Yosuke, 206
Mediterranean, military activities in (1943-4), 435, 494, 497-504, 520-6, 537-8, 558, 567, 599, 604-5, 606-10, 664, 675, 690
Meighen, Arthur, 454, 481, 519, 567, 575; Leader of Opposition in Senate, 79, 82, 92, 309; possible Leader of Conservatives in Commons (1940), 79, 80, 82, 103; National Government (1940), 81; fall of France, 92; becomes leader of Conservative party (1941), 276-9, 280-4, 285, 286, 289, 301, 307, 314, 331; conscription and National Government (1941), 280-4, 300, 307, 313, 330, 336, 341; by-election (Feb. 1942), 309, 343-4, 344, 347-8, 478; Churchill in Ottawa (1941), 329-30; role after electoral defeat, 353, 407, 442, 449, 465; Conservative convention (1942), 450, 452, 454, 456-60, 476
Men of the Trees, 631
Menzies, Robert: visit to Ottawa (1941), 213-16, 238; proposal for Imperial Council, 213-16, 234-5, 250; resignation of (1941), 215, 244, 249-50, 252, 508, 669
Metropolitan Opera, 601-2
Mexico, 234
Michaud, J. E., 444
Millard, Charles, 440-1, 470, 472-4
Ministerial Association, 487
Miquelon, and Free French, 147, 318-24, 423

Index

Mitchell, Humphrey, Minister of Labour (1941–), 310–12, 336, 470; election to House, 340, 343, 344, 347–8, 350; steel strike (1942, 1943), 440–1, 467–74; selective service problems, 447–52; relations with labour, 452–3, 467, 470, 597; manpower allotment (1943), 489–90; crisis re Joseph Cohan, 573–4; coal strike (1943), 595, 596

Moffat, Pierrepont, Minister of U.S.A. to Canada, 111; WLMK's appeal to Reynaud, 124; meeting of Chiefs of Staffs, Washington (1940), 126, 127–8; Ogdensburg Conference, 131, 136, 139; St. Lawrence Waterway, 163, 164; WLMK's trip to U.K. (1941), 266–7; Washington Conference (Dec. 1941), 318; St. Pierre and Miquelon, 320

Molotov, V. M., 432

monetary standards, 667

Monroe doctrine, and Greenland, 113

Montague, Price, 258, 263

Montgomery, General B.: WLMK's visit to (1941), 253, 690; on Canadian troops, 253, 558, 690, 691; relations with McNaughton, 606, 692–3; WLMK's visit to (1944), 690–3

Montreal: airports at, 236, 264; liquor advertising and, 463; proposed visit by Churchill, 534

Montreal St. Mary's (constituency), 344, 347

Moore, Miss Florence, 5

Moore, Tom: possible Minister of Labour, 91, 94, 96, 99, 100, 172, 309–12, 470; and Government's labour policy, 178, 269–70, 310

moral embargo, favoured by WLMK, 108, 112, 115

Morgenthau, Henry, 435; British war purchases in U.S., 113–14, 142, 154, 183; war supplies for Canada, 133, 141, 142; visit to Canada (1940), 140–2, 183; Allies' dollar shortage, 180–7, 191–6, 197–9

Morley, Lord, 201

Morrison, Herbert, 252–3, 265

Mosher, A. R., 269–70, 468, 470, 573, 643

Mulock, W. P., 101

Mulock, Sir William, 71, 175, 438, 444, 475, 518, 631, 632, 665

Munich agreement, 12, 179, 238–9

Munitions and Supply, Dept. of: creation of, 27, 77; personnel, 153; and export of whiskey, 543

Munitions Assignment Board, 410–11, 412, 416

Murray, Philip, 468

Muselier, Admiral Emile, 318–24

Mussolini, B., 88, 114, 124, 187, 559

Mutual Aid, 483, 484

MacBrien, Sir James, 38

McCarthy, Leighton, Canadian Minister to U.S.A., 175, 273, 324, 416, 521; relations with Vichy, 425; Quebec Conference, 528–9; Lord Halifax's Toronto speech (1944), 637

McCullagh, George: series of broadcasts (1939), 32–3; relations with Hepburn, 23, 70–1, 175; WLMK's opinion of, 23, 175; WLMK's visits (1941), 175; Meighen as Conservative leader, 277

McConnell, J. W.: Quebec election (1939), 35; possible Cabinet Minister, 94, 99, 100, 172; St. Lawrence Waterway, 164

Macdonald, Angus: relations with WLMK, 8; St. Pierre-Miquelon, 147, 320; Select Committee on War Expenditures, 170–1; possible successor to WLMK, 221–2; Arvida strike, 229; by-elections (1942), 345, 350; shackling of prisoners, 421; steel strike (1943), 467; Quebec Conference (1943), 533; coal strike (1943), 594; McNaughton as Commander (1943), 607, 609, 616, 627, 628

Minister of National Defence for Naval Services, 100, 101, 102, 133, 153, 155, 168, 169, 226, 304, 355, 379, 453, 484, 490, 616; conscription, Plebiscite, and Bill 80, 222, 303, 307, 331, 332, 336, 345–6, 365–72 *passim*, 377–9, 383, 384, 390, 393, 398, 403; Washington Conference (Dec. 1941), 317–18, 320, 324; size of forces overseas, 334; "Husky," 502; death of Lyon King, 582–3, 584

Macdonald, Bruce, 209–10, 429

Macdonald, Sir John A., 289, 438, 475, 519, 563, 580, 635

MacDonald, Malcolm, U.K. High Commissioner, 178–9, 229, 240, 250, 317, 318, 320, 408–9, 419, 662; conscription in Northern Ireland, 218; At-

lantic Conference, 233, 234; WLMK and Hanson in U.K., 272-3; atomic research, 412-13, 503; shackling of prisoners, 422; landing in Sicily, 525; Quebec Conference (1943), 527-8; whiskey for British troops, 544; Lord Halifax's Toronto speech (1944), 638-41; air training in Canada, 642
MacDonald, Ramsay, 178
MacDonald, Mrs. Ramsay, 178
Macdonnell, J. M.: possible Cabinet post, 100, 172; Civil Liberties League, 354
McEwen, Air Vice Marshal C. M., 689
McGeer, G. G., 587
McGill University, 415
Mackenzie, C. J., 413
Mackenzie, Ian, 7, 25, 26, 475-6
MacKenzie, N. A. M., 440
Mackenzie, William, 646
Mackenzie, William Lyon, 198; as inspiration to WLMK, 9, 71, 74, 141, 405, 408, 531, 565, 662, 690; memorial to (Queen's Park), 85; and Churchill, 331, 677; and Roosevelt, 557
McKinnon, Hector, 268-9
MacKinnon, J. A., 8
Mackintosh, W. A., 590
MacLachlan, Grant, 88, 89
McLarty, Norman: Postmaster General (1939), 26; Minister of Labour (1939-41), 26, 27, 268, 271, 310; Secretary of State (1941-), 310, 312; and National Liberal Federation, 575
Macmillan, A. S., 160
Macmillan, Harold, 239
Macmillan Company of Canada, 228, 239
McNair, J. B., 160
MacNamara, Arthur: National Selective Service, 448-50, 452; steel strike, 474; coal mining issues, 489, 490, 596; wage control, 590
McNaughton, General A. G. L.: appointment as Commander, expeditionary force (1939), 37-8; relations with WLMK, 38-9, 357, 360, 621; departure for England (1939), 37-9, 86, 154; creation of Army Corps, 76; possible Minister of National Defence (1940), 91; relations with British command, 253, 359, 417-20, 497, 499, 605-6, 608, 610; WLMK's visit to Army (1941), 257-64; and Dept. of National Defence, 258, 262, 265, 357-9, 379, 499, 500, 605, 606, 611, 615, 620-1, 624; views on conscription, 261-2, 357, 358, 360, 611; in Ottawa (1942), 356-60, 604; composition of Army overseas, 357-8, 359-60, 605, 608-9, 610-11, 621-2, 628; strain of command, 357, 359, 360, 498, 606, 617, 620, 621, 623-4; possible return to Canada (1942), 359; plans for offensive against Continent, 410, 418, 435-6, 494, 496-7, 502, 610; proposed mission to Moscow, 417-20; Mediterranean campaign, 494, 499-501, 502, 545, 604-5, 606-10, 622, 657; retirement from Army, 604-29, 631, 643, 657, 692-3
McNaughton, Mrs. A. G. L., 620, 624
MacPherson, M. A., 277, 407, 454, 456-9
McTague, C. P.: Chairman, National War Labour Board, 471, 472, 474-5, 571-4, 589-97, 657; return to Bench, 658; National Chairman, Progressive Conservative party, 658-9, 660-1

NAPOLEON, I, 224
National Defence, Dept. of: relations with Government, 220-1, 232, 312, 316, 331, 352, 368, 392, 483-4, 499, 501-2, 656-7; relations with military command, 258, 262, 263, 265, 276, 331, 357-9, 379, 439, 499, 501-2, 515, 656-7, 691; deputy ministership, 438-9
National Film Board, 222-3, 655-6
National Government: a central issue, 22-3; WLMK's view of, 23-4, 65, 79, 81, 95, 97-8, 102, 110, 174, 326-7, 340, 660-1, 683; agitation for, Sept. 1939, 23-4; and election of 1940, 61, 63, 65, 66, 68-9, 72; in May-June 1940, 79-80, 81, 82, 91, 94-5, 97-8, 100, 101, 167; in Feb. 1941, 170-4, 176; in Nov.-Dec. 1941, 278, 281-4, 300-2, 304, 325, 326-7, 336; and selective service (1942), 450, 452; and Conservative convention, 454, 456
National Health and Welfare, Dept. of, creation of, 633
National Liberal Federation, 575, 582-5, 586, 643

National Patriotic Fund (First World War), 84, 85
national registration, 104–5, 135
National Research Council, 37, 655
National Resources Mobilization Act, 96–8, 100, 104, 135, 155–6, 219, 276, 282, 302, 315, 339, 340, 479, 515; amendment of, by Bill 80, 365, 366–7, 368, 369–70, 373, 382, 391
National Security and Defence Committee, proposed by WLMK, 84–5
National Selective Service, 305, 345, 437, 443, 444–52, 456, 490, 570
National War Labour Board, 270, 310, 467–9, 471, 472, 474–5, 485, 571–4, 589–90, 594–6
National War Services, Dept. of, 100, 223, 439, 443, 460–1
Nehru, J., 408
Netherlands: invasion of, 117; pilots of, 410
Neutrality Act (U.S.A.), 30–1, 90, 112, 115
New Brunswick, at Dominion-Provincial Conference (1941), 160
New York: WLMK in (April 1941), 193; (May 1943), 514–5; (Dec. 1943), 601–3, 631
New Zealand: and Air Training Plan, 40, 41, 42, 45–7, 58, 410; Roosevelt proposal re British fleet, 118, 121; North African and Mediterranean campaigns, 156, 505, 622; as member of Commonwealth, 234, 678–9; Pacific war, 411; Conference of Prime Ministers (1944), 664–73, 678–9, 684–9
Newfoundland: defence of, 29, 107, 132, 134, 135, 137, 138, 196, 202; U.S. bases in, 125, 128, 129, 130, 132, 137, 139, 141, 196; Canadian forces in, 140, 330, 340, 378; Atlantic Conference, 196, 233, 246; and Confederation, 202, 430; and St. Pierre-Miquelon, 318, 321; military command in area of, 326
Niagara Falls: possible attack on, 189; Churchill in, 531, 533, 541, 543
Nixon, Harry: resignation from Ontario Cabinet (1940), 69, 71–2, 347; federal by-election (1942), 347; change of Ont. premiership (1942), 455–6; chosen Ont. leader, 491–3; Ont. election of 1943, 568–70, 576, 584

Nixon, Mrs. Harry, 72
Noble, Admiral Sir Percy, 496
Nome (Alaska), 433, 514
Nomura, Kichisaburo, 246, 249
Norman Wells (N.W.T.), 644
North, Lord, 637
North Africa, campaigns in, 156, 157, 195, 219, 312, 423, 424, 428–9, 429, 432, 435, 491, 498–9, 502, 505, 535
North Wellington (constituency), 651
Northern Ireland, 218–19
Norway: conquest of, 77, 107; pilots of, 410; atomic developments, 532
Norway, Crown Princess of, 429
Noseworthy, Joseph, 344, 347
Nova Scotia, at Dominion-Conference (1941), 160

"O Canada," 518–19, 654–5
Ogdensburg: Conference at (1940), 130–6, 548; Agreement, 137–40, 141, 142, 167
old age pensions, 565, 580, 631
O'Leary, Grattan, 63, 144, 458, 525, 575
Oliver, F. R., 569
Ontario: resolution of Legislature re war effort (1940), 62, 65, 69–71, 314; and tax fields, 176; war expenditures in, 178; liquor traffic in, 463, 488, 652–4; election of 1943, 466, 568–70; seats in federal House, 563
Ontario Resources Act, 36
Orange Order, 303
Oslo, 532
Ottawa, as National Capital, 464–5, 655–6
Ouimet, Odette, 288
Ouimet, Roger, 285, 288
Outremont (constituency), 442, 443, 444, 456, 461

Pacific coast of North America: defence of, 101, 108, 112, 138, 305, 307, 314, 326, 340, 345, 354, 355, 379–80, 415, 517
Pacific Ocean, war in, 121, 207–8, 215, 305, 411, 516, 568, 630, 641–3, 667, 669, 685
Pacific War Council, 409, 414–15, 502, 510
Paget, General Sir Bernard, 606, 609, 613–15, 617, 628
Panama Canal, 135

Papineau, Louis-Joseph, 141
Parliament Hill (Ottawa), Roosevelt on, 556–7
Passchendaele, battle of, 52
Passmore Edwards Setlement (London), 564
"Pat," 228, 323
Patterson, W. J., 160
Pattullo, T. D.: and Japanese Canadians, 149–50; at Dominion-Provincial Conference (1941), 160, 161
peace conference, plans for, 476, 565, 589, 669, 674
Pearkes, General G. R., 259–61, 516
Pearl Harbor, 145, 294, 296, 305, 320
Pearson, L. B.: relations with WLMK, 216; landing in Sicily, 521; Lord Halifax's Toronto speech (1944), 641
Permanent Joint Board on Defence, 197; establishment of, 131–4, 137–9, 548; initial meeting (1940), 139–40; Aleutian expedition, 515
Pétain, Marshal Henri, 93, 208, 211, 319, 423, 428
Phillips, Sir Frederick, 180–3, 184–5, 191
Pickersgill, J. W., 6–7, 161, 270
Pitt, William, 287
Plebiscite, on conscription, 275, 306, 308, 313–17, 331, 333, 334–51, 355–6, 360, 362–4, 365–8, 373, 375, 376, 382, 384, 392, 408, 409, 432. *See also* Bill 80
Poland, invasion of (1939), 13, 15, 18, 20, 30, 40, 117, 149, 297
Pope, General Maurice, 501
Pouliot, J. F., 480
Pound, Admiral Sir Dudley, 265, 411
Powell, R. E., 229–30
Power, C. G., 61, 89, 97, 170, 223, 271, 280; relations with WLMK, 8, 361–2; Minister of Pensions and National Health (1939–40), 26; Postmaster General (1939–40), 26, 101; and organization of government for war, 26, 27; Quebec election of 1939, 35–6; Air Training Plan, 49, 115; election of 1940, 61; Acting Minister of National Defence (1940), 91; relations with France, 147; choice of St. Laurent as Minister, 290, 292, 350; possible Minister of Labour, 452–3; redistribution of House Seats, 561–2; proposed election (1943), 568; death of Lyon King, 584; reorganization of Liberal party (1943), 585–6; proposed Minister of Reconstruction, 632
  Minister of National Defence for Air and Associate Minister of National Defence (1940–), 75, 79, 93–4, 95, 102, 132, 134, 138, 169, 305, 355, 379, 412, 484, 490, 587; war with Japan, 150; Canadians for North Africa, 156, 220; conscription and Plebiscite, 307, 312, 314, 316, 330–1, 339, 362, 377; troops for Hong Kong, 316, 352, 354; Washington Conference (Dec. 1941), 318, 320, 324; shackling of prisoners, 421; "Husky," 502; McNaughton's retirement, 612–14, 619, 627, 628; R.C.A.F. in war against Japan, 641–2
Precedence, Table of, 92–3
Preferences, Imperial, 676, 680, 682, 694
Press conferences, WLMK and, 202–3, 239–40, 555–6
Prestwick, 264, 695
price and wage control, 268–71, 437, 440–2, 466–75, 538, 566, 570, 571–4, 590–8, 643–4
Prime Minister, residence for, 655
Prince Albert, 69, 226–7, 649, 651
Prince Edward Island: Dominion-Provincial Conference (1941), 160; election in (1943), 576
Prince Rupert, 528
Prince County (P.E.I.), constituency of, 25
Prince of Wales, 247
production, of war materials, by Canada, 85–7, 154–5, 159, 191, 197–8, 203–4, 231, 273, 334, 342, 360, 388, 410–11, 416, 437, 568
Progressive Conservative party. *See* Conservative party
Progressive party, 47
Public Information, Bureau of, 31–3, 439
Public information, re war effort, 31–3, 179, 200, 203, 205, 216, 222–4, 439–40
Purvis, Arthur, 113, 127, 128, 141, 183–4, 186–7, 235

QUEBEC, Province of: election of 1939, 35–6, 60, 62, 373; representation in federal Cabinet, 35–6, 284, 288,

289–94, 303, 310–11, 342, 360–2, 372, 442–4; and tax fields, 176; war expenditures in, 178; restrictions on alcoholic beverages, 462–3, 652; Churchill visits Cabinet of, 541; scats in federal House, 561, 563–4. *See also* French Canada
Quebec City: WLMK visits (Oct. 1940), 147; Lapointe's funeral, 289; Conference at (1943), 466, 510, 527–60, 568; Joseph Cohen's speech in (1943), 572–4
Quebec Conference (1943), 466, 510, 527–60, 568, 570, 574, 599, 606, 676
Quebec East (constituency), 292, 293, 316, 339, 341, 343, 347–8
Queen's University, 548

RAILWAY BROTHERHOODS, 573
Ralston, J. L., 25, 77, 79, 99, 101, 170, 223, 290, 316, 352, 376, 633, 650; relations with WLMK, 8, 25–6, 28, 153, 312, 385–6, 395, 400, 583, 659–60; possible successor to WLMK, 25, 75–6, 82–3, 221–2, 300, 316, 385; appointment of McNaughton, 38; 1940 election, 63, 64; possible Chief Justice, 75, 630; death of Rogers, 88, 89; and labour policy, 178, 229, 232, 467; birthday of (1943), 583; death of Lyon King, 584; Acting Prime Minister (1944), 659–60; reception for WLMK, Rockcliffe (1944), 696
    Minister of Finance (1939–40), 25, 27, 28, 36, 76, 81, 84, 86, 95, 98–9, 154; Air Training Plan, 41, 50, 51–4, 57, 59, 115; unemployment insurance, 61; St. Lawrence Waterway, 61–2, 77, 110
    Minister of National Defence (1940–), 91, 93–4, 112, 131, 133, 156–9, 169, 172, 290, 292, 302, 303–5, 306–7, 309, 312–13, 314, 334–5, 379, 438–9, 452–3, 483, 484; Ogdensburg Agreement, 137, 140; visit to U.K. (1940), 145, 153, 154, 156–7, 214; St. Pierre-Miquelon, 147, 320; expansion of forces overseas, 157, 158–9, 303–4, 312–13, 325, 326, 334, 343, 400, 498, 500; war with Japan, 150, 299; conscription, 219–22, 303–4, 306–7, 309, 312–13, 314, 331, 332, 336, 349, 350, 594, 618, 656; use of Canadian Army (1941), 220–1, 265; relations with McNaughton, 262, 263, 265, 357–9, 379, 500, 605, 606, 614, 615–16, 618, 619, 624–6; visit to U.K. (1941), 262, 265, 274, 275, 276; at Washington Conference (Dec. 1941), 316–17, 320, 324; Plebiscite and Bill 80, 338–9, 343, 345–6, 349, 365–403; Hong Kong Expedition, 352–4, 403–7; secret session of Parliament (Feb. 1942), 355; proposed resignation (1942), 384–402, 612, 618; proposed McNaughton mission to Moscow (1942), 417–20; visit to U.K. (1942), 420, 421, 423; shackling of prisoners, 421; manpower allotment (1943), 489–91; Mediterranean campaign, 494, 497–9, 501–2, 503, 519, 520–4, 533, 545, 604–5, 607–10; plans for invasion, 496, 497–9, 503, 519, 533, 604, 610–11, 695; Aleutian expedition, 516; Quebec Conference (1943), 529, 539, 605; General McNaughton's retirement, 605–29, 631, 657; trip to Italy (1943), 616, 617, 626; proposal to V. Sifton (1944), 656–7; and George VI, 674; and Montgomery, 692
Ralston, Mrs. J. L., 401
Rebellion of 1837–38, 364
reconstruction, 630; Ministry of, 632, 633; and Dept. of Finance, 632–3
reconversion, of industry, 630
recruiting. *See* Voluntary enlistment
Redfern, Sir Shuldham, 54, 55, 56
redistribution, of constituencies, 561–4
Referendum. *See* Plebiscite
relief, in post-war, 633
Reynaud, Paul, 93; WLMK's appeal to, 92, 123–4
Rideau Club (Ottawa), 173
Rimouski, Que., 197
Rinfret, Thibaudeau, 630
Ristelhueber, Denise, 209–10, 429
Ristelhueber, René, 147, 191, 208–12, 241, 319, 321, 322, 423–9, 535
Ristelhueber, Mrs. R., 429
Riverdale, Lord, 41–5, 47, 48–59
Rivière du Loup, 290
Robertson, Norman: relations with WLMK, 6, 167; price ceiling, 268
    Under Secretary of State for External Affairs, 216; relations with Vichy, 211–12, 319, 320, 424–8; trip

to Britain (1941), 236; war with Japan, 297, 298; Washington Conference (Dec. 1941), 320, 323; landing in Sicily, 521; Quebec Conference (1943), 527; McNaughton's retirement, 616, 628; Conference of Prime Ministers (1944), 667, 684

Rockcliffe airport, 662, 696
Rockefeller, John D., Jr., 111, 602, 634
Rockefeller, Mrs. John D., Jr., 602
Rockefeller, Nelson, 436, 602
Rockefeller Foundation, 330
Roebuck, Arthur, 491
Rogers, Norman, 34; relations with WLMK, 7, 8, 89–90, 166–7, 571, death of, 88–91, 92, 93, 166
  Minister of National Defence (1939–40), 26, 37–8, 75–6, 79, 86, 90, 107, 114, 117, 621; Air Training Plan, 41, 48–51, 58, 59, 115; election of 1940, 62, 71, 72, 73
Rogers, Mrs. Norman, 89
Roosevelt, Eleanor (Mrs. F. D.), 198, 275, 434–5, 505
Roosevelt, F. D., 442, 445, 469, 516, 570, 576, 577; American neutrality, 30–1, 90, 106–7, 115, 129, 141, 165, 187, 195, 196, 227, 242, 249, 266–7, 548; importance for Allied cause, 74, 77, 148, 163, 242, 325, 511, 549, 679; St. Lawrence Waterway, 77, 110–11, 162, 164–5; relations with WLMK, 106, 108, 111, 165, 168, 187, 188, 200, 242, 279, 318, 321, 330, 411, 435, 436, 499, 511, 523, 548–50, 554, 575, 584, 585, 663; with WLMK at Warm Springs (1940), 106–11, 128, 162; defence of Greenland (1940), 107, 117; interest in Canadian affairs, 108, 549; presidential election (1940), 108–9, 110, 113, 128, 145, 148–9; and post-war service, 109, 433–4; national government (U.S.), 110, 131; Italy in the war, 114–15, 187; proposal re British fleet (1940), 116–28, 129, 130; Atlantic bases–destroyer deal, 128, 130, 132, 136–42; Ogdensburg Conference, 130–6, 168, 548; Lend-Lease, 185, 186, 187, 189, 197; with WLMK at Washington and Hyde Park (April 1941), 189–90, 193, 194–204, 242, 275, 332; Atlantic Conference, 196–7, 201, 233–4, 235, 242, 244, 256, 412; attitude to cities, 198; relations with Churchill, 242, 317, 326, 511, 535, 554; possible Japanese entry into war, 246, 249, 296; with WLMK at Hyde Park (Nov. 1941), 275; war with Japan, 297; with Churchill and WLMK in Washington (Dec. 1941), 317–18, 320–5, 332, 429–30; relations with Vichy and Free French, 320–4, 425–7, 535–6, 541, 543, 554; with WLMK, Washington (April 1942), 409–10; and cross-Channel invasion, 409–10, 579; with Churchill and WLMK, Washington (June 1942), 414–16; McNaughton mission to Moscow, 420; with WLMK, Washington (Dec. 1942), 429–36; post-war international relations, 430, 431–3, 436, 510–11, 512–13, 553–4, 676; meeting with Stalin and Churchill, 432–3, 513–14, 528, 537, 543, 601; Quebec Conference (Aug. 1943), 466, 527–60, 676; with Churchill and WLMK, Washington (May 1943), 494, 502–14; Casablanca Conference (1943), 494; Canadian Embassy in Washington, 512; proposed visit to Ottawa (1943), 514, 528, 529, 530, 533; landing in Sicily, 521–6, 537–8; visit to Ottawa (Aug. 1943), 547, 556–7; post-war aviation, 559; coal strike (1943), 592–4; inauguration of UNRRA, 599; presidential election (1944), 677; second Quebec Conference proposed, 695

Rose, Fred, 570
Roumania: war against, 297; oil wells in, 644
Rowan, Mr. (Churchill's secretary), 505
Rowe, Earl, 82, 83
Rowell-Sirois Report. *See* Royal Commission on Dominion-Provincial Relations
Roy, J. S., 169, 480
Royal Air Force, 140, 145, 253, 412, 642
Royal Canadian Air Force, 316, 342, 583; Air Training Plan, 40, 45, 48–57; role of, 76, 220, 304, 412, 505, 517, 599; supplies for, 86, 189; WLMK visits in England (1941), 264; home defence, 379–80; and Power as Minister, 587; in war against Japan, 641–3; WLMK's visit

Index

in England (1944), 670, 688. *See also* Compulsory military training; Conscription issue (1939-44); Voluntary enlistment
Royal Canadian Mounted Police, 104, 232
Royal Canadian Navy, 316, 342, 583, 588; role of, 76, 220, 304, 517; provision of destroyers to Britain, 116, 122; exchange of U.S. destroyers (1940), 136, 137; home defence, 379-80; French-speaking recruits, 519-20; political interests in, 588; in war against Japan, 642, 685. *See also* Compulsory military training; Conscription issue (1939-44); Voluntary enlistment
Royal Commission on Dominion-Provincial Relations, report of, 145, 159, 160, 175, 177
Royal Rifles of Canada, 316
Royal Roads, 255, 257
Rush-Bagot Agreement, 433

SAGUENAY (constituency), 456
St. Catharines, steel workers in, 469-70
Ste. Croix, 582, 587
St. Laurent, Louis: relations with WLMK, 8, 349-50, 377, 389-90, 594-5, 611; appointment to Cabinet (1941), 290-4, 306; conscription, Plebiscite, and Bill 80, 294, 314, 336, 341, 362, 365-6, 368, 387, 389-90; election to House, 339, 341, 343, 344, 347-50, 372, 389; joins War Committee, 376-7; Ralston's proposed resignation (1942), 397; possible successor to WLMK, 445; steel strike (1943), 474; Giraud dinner, 535-6; coal strike (1943), 594; McNaughton's retirement, 611-12; possible Chief Justice (1944), 630; Acting Secretary of State for External Affairs (1944), 660
Minister of Justice (1941-), 294-5; Hong Kong inquiry, 404; redistribution of House seats, 563
St. Lawrence Waterway, 34, 36, 37, 60, 61-2, 77, 110-11, 113, 146, 162-5, 177, 187
St. Lin (Que.), 286-9
St. Pierre, and Free French, 147, 318-24, 423
Sandwell, B. K., 354, 654
San Francisco, 314

Sardinia, attack on, 494, 497, 502
Saskatchewan: Dominion-Provincial Conference (1941), 160; seats in federal House, 561; and R.C.A.F., 689
Saturday Night, 354, 585, 654
Sault Ste. Marie, steel mills in, 468
Savoy, luncheon for WLMK at (1941), 240-4
Scapa Flow, 157
Scotland, 246, 264, 666
Scotland, Church of, Moderator of General Assembly, 255, 256
Scott, Gordon, 153, 154
Second World War: Canada's entry into, 11-22, 33, 43, 44, 238-9, 243, 296-300, 545, 557; nature of Canada's participation in, 28-30, 38, 39, 40-1, 45, 77, 85-6, 154-5, 156, 188, 220, 304, 324-5, 408-9, 508, 517, 568, 630; military developments in, 30, 77, 79, 82, 85-90, 92-3, 96-7, 99, 107, 115, 116, 120, 147-8, 179, 193, 219, 296-7, 305, 312, 315-16, 330, 375, 379, 390, 391, 415, 416-17, 423, 466, 469, 494, 515, 516, 520, 544-5
secret session, of House of Commons (Feb. 1942), 355
Seeley, Sir J. R., 430
Seigniory Club, 141, 618, 619, 626, 628
Selkirk (constituency), 477, 566, 570
shackling of prisoners, 421-3
Shedden, Mr., Secretary, Australian War Committee, 667
Shelburne (N.S.), 196
Shields, T. T., 480-1
Sicily, Allied attack on, 494, 502, 504, 517, 520-6, 527, 533, 535, 537, 545, 552, 558, 568, 604-5, 606, 607, 690
Sifton, Clifford, 176, 657
Sifton, Victor, 438-9, 656-7
Simcoe (Ont.), 635
Simon, Sir John, 669, 680, 681
Simonds, General Guy, 689, 690, 691
Simonstown, 121
Sinclair, Sir Archibald, 672
Sinclair, James, 587-8
Singapore, 120, 121
Sirois Report. *See* Royal Commission on Dominion-Provincial Relations
Skelton, O. D., 31, 62; relations with WLMK, 6, 7, 146, 166-7, 170, 616; Air Training Plan, 43, 44, 53, 58; French gold reserves, 98; defence of

Greenland, 112; Roosevelt proposal re British navy, 116–23; Ogdensburg Agreement, 137; death of, 146, 165–7, 170; position of St. Pierre-Miquelon, 147; war with Japan, 150; St. Lawrence Waterway, 163, 165
Skelton, Mrs. O. D., 166
Slaght, Arthur, 23–4, 168
Slemon, Air Commodore C. R., 689
Smith, Sidney, 457, 458
Smuts, General J. C., 599; possible Imperial Conference, 214, 217, 238, 247; post-war role, 510–11; proposed meeting of Commonwealth Prime Ministers (1943), 514, 538, 555; actual meeting (1944), 666–89; WLMK's opinion of, 668, 677; address to British Parliament, 675, 676, 677; friendship with Churchill, 681
Social Credit party, 100, 108; declaration of war, 14; Bill 80, 382; aviation policy, 647
social security, in post-war, 215–16, 433–4, 444–5, 476–7, 482–3, 564–5, 580, 591, 600–1, 631–6
South Africa: Roosevelt proposal re British fleet, 118, 120; North African campaign, 156, 505; British gold reserves in, 186, 191; as member of Commonwealth, 234, 599; Conference of Prime Ministers (1944), 664–73, 678–9, 684–9
"Spartan" exercises, 605
Speeches, WLMK's preparation of, 4–5, 8–9, 31–3, 66, 79, 224, 225, 337, 480
  Broadcasts: Sept. 3 (1939), 16; Oct. 25 (1939), 32–3; Oct. 31 (1939), 32–3; Dec. 17 (1939), 59; Feb. 7 (1940), 66–7; Feb. 21 (1940), 68; Feb. 23 (1940), 68–9; March 21 (1940), 72; March 23 (1940), 72; Oct. 18 (1941), 271, 441; Dec. 8 (1941), 300; April 7 (1942), 362, 368, 370, 387; April 24 (1942), 362–3; April 25 (1942), 363; Dec. 16 (1942), 464; Aug. 21 (1943), 552–3; Dec. 4 (1943), 593, 600–1, 634
  Parliament (Canada): Sept. 8 (1939), 13, 17–21; Sept. 12 (1939), 24; May 20 (1940), 79; June 18 (1940), 96; June 20 (1940), 97–8; Nov. 12 (1940), 168; Dec. 3 (1940), 169; Feb. 17 (1941), 170; March 12 (1941), 187–9; April 28 (1941), 205; Nov. 12 (1941), 279–81; Jan. 26 (1942), 335, 338, 342–3; Feb. 25 (1942), 355–6; May 11 (1942), 372–3; June 10 (1942), 380–1, 385–6; July 7 (1942), 394; July 23 (1942), 402–3; Feb. 19 (1943), 480; April (1943), 645, 646, 648; July 1 (1943), 518–19; July 14 (1943), 524; July 15 (1943), 524–5; Jan. 31 (1944), 639–41; Feb. 4 (1944), 618, 619; Feb. 14 (1944), 627–8; Feb. 22 (1944), 650–1
  Public addresses: International Exposition (1937), 12; Toronto (Mar. 14, 1940), 71–2; Dominion-Provincial Conference (Jan. 14, 1941), 161; possible address to Congress, 200; Princeton University (1941), 224; Canadian Society, N.Y. (1941), 224; on Western trip (1941), 224–7; Mansion House (1941), 244, 246–7, 251, 252, 253, 265, 272, 661; visit to troops in England (1941), 258–61; Canadian Clubs, Ottawa (1941), 265–6; American Federation of Labor, Toronto (Oct. 1942), 444, 634; Victory Loan, Montreal (1942), 445; Empire Parliamentary Association, Ottawa (June 1943), 518; dinner for British M.P.'s, American Congressmen, Ottawa (June 1943), 518; Giraud dinner (July 15, 1943), 535; Canadian Club, Ottawa (May 25, 1943), 564; National Liberal Federation (Sept. 27, 1943) 582–4, (Feb. 11, 1944) 643; British Parliament (May 11, 1944), 661–2, 665, 674, 676, 677, 678, 680–2, 687, 694
Spinney, G. W., 99, 100, 172
Stalin, Joseph: pact with Hitler, 14, 30, 224; Allied relations with, 418, 430, 431, 432, 503, 537; meeting with Churchill and Roosevelt, 432–3, 513–14, 528, 537, 543
Stanstead (constituency), 570
Star (Montreal), 35, 104, 164, 227, 637
Star (Toronto), 176, 344, 444–5, 493, 586–7, 631, 653
Statute of Westminster, 114, 250, 251, 636
steel, strike of workers, 440–2, 466–75, 571, 592
Steel Commission: formed (Sept. 1942), 441; report of (1943), 466–7, 469
Steelworkers Organizing Committee, 440–1, 468

Index

Stevens, H., 457, 458
Stewart, Bryce, 269, 448, 449, 450, 597
Stimson, Henry, Secretary of War (U.S.A.), 126, 242, 246, 328, 516; at Ogdensburg Conference, 131, 132, 133-6
Stirling, Grote, 105; possible member of Cabinet (1940), 81, 82, 84, 95, 100-1, 102; National Government, 94; Ogdensburg Agreement, 138; Special Committee on War Expenditures, 170-2; secret session (Feb. 1942), 355; McNaughton's retirement, 628
Stuart, General K., Chief of General Staff, 357, 446; 1942 war programme, 304, 334, 376-7; Pacific Coast defence, 379; relations with Ralston, 379; Dieppe raid, 416-17; McNaughton's proposed mission to Moscow, 418; Mediterranean campaign, 494, 497-9, 504, 605, 607-10; plans for invasion, 498-9, 604, 610; size of Army, 500; attack on Aleutians, 515-17; General McNaughton's retirement, 605-17, 621, 624; temporary Army Commander, 617; Conference of Prime Ministers (1944), 667
Suez, 156
survival after death, WLMK's belief in, 4, 287-8, 289, 356, 582
Switzerland, 422
Sydney (N.S.), steel mills in, 467, 468, 470, 472-3

TAGGART, Gordon, 464
Taylor, E. P., 153, 193
Teheran Conference, 543, 601
Tennyson, Alfred, Lord, 246, 331
Thailand, 246
Thompson, Walter, 33
Thorson, J. T.: Committee on War Expenditures, 223; Minister of National War Services, 223; President, Exchequer Court, 444, 447
Thousand Islands, bridge over, 548
Time, 421
Times, The, 239-40, 638
Times Herald (Washington), 253
Tobruk, 391
Tomii, Baron, 149, 151, 152-3
Toronto: butter supplies in, 464; proposed visit by Churchill, 534; Bracken's speech in (1943), 567; Lord Halifax's speech in (1944), 636-41
Toronto, University of, 663

Toronto Broadview (constituency), 518
Towers, Graham, 45, 46, 48, 180, 268-9
Toynbee, Arnold, 564
Toynbee Hall (London), 421, 564
Trades and Labour Congress, 91-2, 178, 269-70, 309, 572-3, 643-4
Trans-Canada Air Lines, 646, 648
travel restrictions, war-time, 650
Tristan and Isolde, 602
"tube alloys," 536
Turnbull, Walter, 6
Tweedsmuir, Lord, 548; Air Training Plan, 44, 54-8; election of 1940, 61, 64; death of, 67, 166

U-BOATS, losses from (1943), 469, 471, 491, 495, 496-9, 592
unemployment insurance, 60-1, 450
Union Government (1917-21), and French Canada, 22-3, 376
Union Jack, and Canada, 542-3, 655
Union Nationale, 373; formation of, 34; and military service, 97, 316
U.S.S.R.: non-aggression pact with Germany (1939), 14, 15; attacks on Poland, Finland (1939), 30; relations with Axis, 149; interception of ships of (1941), 151-2; war with Germany, 224-5, 266, 312, 410, 415, 499; relations with Japan, 415, 433; proposed McNaughton mission to, 417-20; post-war role, 431-3, 539, 553-4, 637, 644, 649, 673, 675, 679; relations with Allies, 479, 503, 517, 555, 599, 684; atomic research, 532, 543, 679
union recognition, 590
United Church of Canada, 460, 462
United Farmers, 546
United Kingdom: Canada's entry into war, 11-22, 243, 297; course of war for, 30, 78, 79-80, 87-8, 92-3, 97, 99, 116, 117, 120, 129, 142-3, 147, 148, 154-7, 194, 248-9, 267, 330, 665; Air Training Plan, 40-59, 114; relations with Canada, 87, 93, 108, 111, 117, 125, 132, 143, 187, 188, 202, 234-5, 237, 240, 243, 266-7, 317-18, 325, 326, 351, 408-9, 416, 420, 512, 520-6, 527-8, 531, 540, 548, 675-6, 678; French monetary reserves, 98-9, 180-2, 184-5, 187, 201; war supplies for, from U.S.A., 113-14, 127, 136-7, 142, 180-7,

226–7, 266, 412; relations with U.S.A., 113–14, 117, 120–8, 184–8, 226–7, 242, 248–9, 266–7, 317–18, 412, 413, 508, 532; Roosevelt's proposal for fleet (1940), 116–28, 130; Atlantic bases–destroyer deal, 128–42, 188; post-surrender France, 145, 147–8, 208, 212, 241–2, 318–24, 424–9; possible Japanese entry into war, 150–3, 206–8, 245–6, 266, 296; shortage of American dollars, 180–7, 191; Lend-Lease, 185–7, 197, 204; WLMK's visit to (1941), 226, 231, 233, 235, 236–67, 332; War Cabinet of, 214, 238, 248–52; war with Japan, 297–300; "billion dollar gift" to, 333–4; and India, 408; atomic research, 413–14, 503; shackling of prisoners, 421–2; post-war role, 431–3, 553–4, 560, 637, 644, 672, 675; liquor restrictions, 461; post-war aviation, 539–40, 551–2, 559; French National Committee, 535, 541, 552

United Nations, 628, 630; landing in North Africa, 425, 426, 427; name of, 429–30; and Mutual Aid, 484; in post-war, 510, 553–4, 640–1, 672, 675, 678–9; and Quebec Conference, 529, 539; UNRRA, 599, 650

UNRRA, 599, 650

United States Air Force, shipping for, 495–7

United States of America: importance of its support to Allies, 30, 74, 77, 88, 90, 97, 107, 120–1, 127, 188, 242, 248–9, 294; St. Lawrence Waterway, 62, 77, 162–5; relations with Canada, 87, 93, 97, 98–9, 101, 108, 111, 117, 124, 132, 135–6, 143, 149, 165, 168, 188, 190–1, 200, 202, 203, 215, 234, 237, 279, 308, 317–18, 323–4, 326, 351, 408–9, 412, 416, 436, 508, 517–19, 520–6, 527–8, 548, 642–3, 671, 677, 680; gradual involvement in hostilities (1939–41), 107, 112, 115, 120–6, 132, 149, 152, 186, 189, 190, 192, 195–6, 208, 215, 226–7, 242, 248–9, 266–7; relations with U.K., 113–14, 117, 120–8, 184–8, 226–7, 242, 248–9, 266–7, 317–18, 412, 413, 508, 532; citizens of, in Allied forces, 114, 115–16; Atlantic defence (1940–1), 128–42, 188, 195–6, 226–7, 256, 326; passports for Canadians, 134–5, 139; war supplies from, for Canada, 133, 141; possible Japanese entry into war, 150–3, 207–8, 245–6, 249, 266, 296; British and Canadian dollar shortage, 180–6, 190–4, 198–8; Lend-Lease, 186–9, 190, 193, 197, 204; Pearl Harbor and active hostilities, 294, 295, 296–300, 304, 305, 312, 315, 340; compulsory military service in, 294, 302, 312, 375; relations with Vichy and Free French, 318–24, 424–9; atomic research, 413–14, 503; post-war role, 431–3, 553–4, 560, 637, 649, 672, 675; price and wage stabilization, 437, 594; Aleutian expedition, 515–17, 552–3; post-war aviation, 539–40, 551–2, 559; coal strike (1943), 592–4; economic interests in Canada, 644–5

United Steelworkers (U.S.A.), 468, 473, 474

Uplands airport, 328

uranium, 412–13, 532

VANCOUVER: relations with Japan, 151; Japanese and Russian contraband, 152; recruiting in, 222; WLMK in (1941), 226; as site of Prime Ministers' Conference, 664

Vancouver-Burrard (constituency), 587

Vancouver North (constituency), 587

Vanier, George, WLMK's trip to Britain (1941), 236, 237, 264

Versailles, 323

Veterans Affairs, Dept. of, creation of, 633

Vichy. See France

Victoria, Queen, 74, 531

Victory Loans, 445, 486, 528, 576

Vien, Thomas, 442, 443, 444

Villeneuve, Cardinal J. M. R., 287, 291, 293

Vining, Charles, 439, 440

Virginia Beach, 106, 189, 193, 194

Virginia, University of, Roosevelt at (1940), 124

voluntary enlistment, 219–21, 261, 316, 333, 334, 343, 345, 349, 350–1, 357, 370, 375, 376–7, 380, 399, 412, 437, 565, 611, 656. *See also* Compulsory military training

WAGE CONTROL. *See* Price and wage control

War Appropriation Bill: (1943), 483–4; (1944), 627

Index

War Committee. *See* Cabinet, federal, War Committee of
War Expenditures, Committee on, 170–2, 223, 650
War Measures Act, 15, 20, 35, 66, 75, 94, 330, 487
War Memorial (Ottawa), 656
War Supply Board, 27, 41
Ward, Mr. (Railway Brotherhoods), 573
Ward, J. B., 269–70
Warm Springs (Georgia), 106, 110, 111, 128, 162, 189
Warsaw, 40
Wartime Elections Act (1917), 80
Wartime Information Board, 439–40, 556
Wartime Prices and Trade Board, 28, 268–71, 441–2, 445, 464
Wartime tax agreements, 146, 159–62, 176–7, 205
Washington: WLMK in, (April 1940) 111–15, 116, 117, (April 1941) 189–93, 332, (Aug. 1941—proposed) 235, 242, (April 1942) 409–10, (June 1942) 414–16, 424, (Dec. 1942) 429–26, 452, (Dec. 1943) 601; Churchill and WLMK in, (Dec. 1941) 317–18, 332, (May 1943) 494, 502–14; Embassy for Canada in, 512, 589
Waterloo, battle of, 599
wealth, conscription of, 350–1, 391, 416, 437, 485
Welland (constituency), 311, 340, 343, 345, 347–8, 350
Welles, Sumner, 111, 416, 424, 429
West Indies, 146, 675; U.S. bases in, 125, 128, 129, 130, 132, 135
Westerham (Eng.), 534
Western Canada, WLMK's tour of (1941), 205, 216, 217, 224, 225–8, 246, 252, 332
wheat: surplus of, 177–8; price ceiling for, 437
Williamsburg (Virginia), 111, 601
Willkie, Wendell, 131, 328, 418, 442
Wilson, Morris, 81–2
Windsor (Ont.), 569
Windsor, Duchess of, 505
Windsor, Duke of, 505, 506
Winnipeg: WLMK at (1941), 227; Conservative convention (1942), 449, 450, 452, 453, 455; proposed visit of Churchill, 546
Winnipeg North Centre (constituency), 456, 461
Wolfe, James, 534
Woodsworth, J. S.: and participation in war, 14–15, 19; death of, 362
Woodward, W. C., 153
"world power," Canada as, 635
world tour, of WLMK (1908), 350, 408
Wright, W. H., 446

York South (constituency), 343–4, 347–8
Yoshizawa, Seijiro, 206–8, 229, 412–13
Young, E. C., 168
Yugoslavia, attack on, 145, 179, 194, 195

Zavitske, Miss L. F., 5